ENVIRONMENTAL ECONOMICS

AN INTRODUCTION

THIRD EDITION

Barry C. Field
Department of Resource Economics
University of Massachusetts–Amherst

Martha K. Field
Department of Business and Information Technology
Greenfield Community College

Boston   Burr Ridge, IL   Dubuque, IA   Madison, WI   New York
San Francisco   St. Louis   Bangkok   Bogotá   Caracas   Kuala Lumpur
Lisbon   London   Madrid   Mexico City   Milan   Montreal   New Delhi
Santiago   Seoul   Singapore   Sydney   Taipei   Toronto

Mcgraw-Hill Higher Education

A Division of The McGraw-Hill Companies

ENVIRONMENTAL ECONOMICS: AN INTRODUCTION
Published by McGraw-Hill/Irwin, an imprint of The McGraw-Hill Companies, Inc. 1221
Avenue of the Americas, New York, NY, 10020. Copyright © 2002, 1997, 1994 by The
McGraw-Hill Companies, Inc. All rights reserved. No part of this publication may be
reproduced or distributed in any form or by any means, or stored in a data base or
retrieval system, without the prior written consent of The McGraw-Hill Companies, Inc.,
including, but not limited to, in any network or other electronic storage or transmission,
or broadcast for distance learning.
Some ancillaries, including electronic and print components, may not be available to
cutomers outside the United States.

This book is printed on acid-free paper.

1 2 3 4 5 6 7 8 9 0   FGR/FGR   0 9 8 7 6 5 4 3 2 1

ISBN 0-07-242921-6

Publisher: *Gary Burke*
Executive sponsoring editor: *Lucille Sutton*
Developmental editor: *Aric Bright*
Marketing manager: *Martin D. Quinn*
Associate project manager: *Destiny Rynne*
Production supervisor: *Carol A. Bielski*
Media producer: *Craig Atkins*
Senior designer: *Jennifer McQueen*
Cover design: *JoAnne Schopler*
Cover image: *©Kennan Ward/CORBIS*
Supplement coordinator: *Erin Sauder*
Printer: *Quebecor World Fairfield, Inc.*
Typeface: *10/12 Palatino*
Compositor: *Precision Graphics, Inc.*

Library of Congress Cataloging-in-Publication Data
Field, Barry C.
    Environmental economics: an introduction/Barry C. Field, Martha K. Field.--3rd ed.
    p. cm.
    Includes bibliographical references and indexes.
    ISBN 0-07-242921-6 (alk. paper)
    1. Environmental economics. 2. Economic development--Environmental aspects. I.
Field, Martha K. II. Title.
HC79.E5 F47 2002
333.7--dc21

2001030662

www.mhhe.com

ABOUT THE AUTHORS

BARRY C. FIELD is Professor of Resource Economics at the University of Massachusetts in Amherst. Previously he taught at the University of Miami and The George Washington University. He received his B.S. and M.S. degrees from Cornell University and his Ph.D. from the University of California at Berkeley.

At the University of Massachusetts he has devoted many years to teaching environmental economics to students at all levels and has worked to develop an undergraduate major in environmental and resource economics.

MARTHA K. FIELD is Professor of Economics at Greenfield Community College in Massachusetts. She has taught classes at the University of Massachusetts, Mount Holyoke College, Westfield State College, Holyoke Community College, and the Consumer Cooperative Institute in Gomel, Belarus. She holds a Ph.D. from the University of Connecticut. Her research areas include international and environmental economics, economic impacts of education, and distance learning assessment.

To Tory, Sidney, and Leslie

CONTENTS

PREFACE

When our descendants look back at the last part of the 20th century, we want them to be able to say: "That's when they began to take the degradation of the natural environment, with its threats to human life and the life of the planet, seriously." Furthermore, we would like them to be able to see that around this time we took serious steps to halt and reverse this process. This book is an introduction to environmental economics, one way of approaching the steps that need to be taken. It's about the way human decisions affect the quality of the environment, how human values and institutions shape our demands for improvement in the quality of that environment, and, most especially, about how to design effective public policies to bring about these improvements.

Problems of environmental quality are not something new; in fact, history is filled with bleak examples of environmental degradation, from deforestation by ancient peoples to mountains of horse manure in urban areas in the days before automobiles. But today's world is different. For one thing, many people in economically developed countries, having reached high levels of material well-being, are beginning to ask questions: What good is great material wealth if it comes at the cost of large-scale disruptions of the ecosystem by which we are nourished? More fundamental, perhaps, is the fact that with contemporary economic, demographic, and technological developments around the world, the associated environmental repercussions are becoming much more widespread and lethal. What once were localized environmental impacts, easily rectified, have now become widespread effects that may very well turn out to be irreversible. Indeed some of our most worrisome concerns today are about global environmental impacts.

It is no wonder, then, that the quality of the natural environment has become a major focus of public concern. As we would expect, people have responded in many ways. Environmental interest groups and advocates have become vocal at every political level, especially in those countries with open political systems. Politicians have taken environmental issues into their agendas; some have sought to become environmental statespersons. Environmental law has burgeoned, becoming a specialty in many law schools. Thousands of environmental agencies have appeared in the public sector, from local conservation commissions to environmental agencies at the United Nations. At the scientific level environmental problems have become a focus for chemists, biologists, engineers, and many others. And within economics a new focus of study has appeared: *environmental economics,* the subject of this book.

Environmental economics focuses on all the different facets of the connection between environmental quality and the economic behavior of individuals and groups of people. There is the fundamental question of how the economic system shapes economic incentives in ways that lead to environmental degradation as well as improvement. There are major problems in measuring the benefits and costs of environmental quality changes, especially intangible ones. There is a set of complicated macroeconomic questions; for example, the connection between economic growth and environmental impacts and the feedback effects of environmental laws on growth. And there are the critical issues of designing environmental policies that are both effective and equitable.

The strength of environmental economics lies in the fact that it is analytical and deals with concepts such as efficiency, trade-offs, costs, and benefits. Many believe strongly that the times call for more direct political action, more consciousness-raising, more political organizing, and, especially, more representation and influence of environmental interests on the political scene. Nobody can doubt this. We live in a complicated world, however, where human problems abound; domestically we have health care, drugs, education, violence, and other critical issues, all competing for attention and public resources. Throughout the world, vast numbers of people struggle to alter their political and economic institutions, develop their economies, and raise their material standards of living.

In these settings, just raising the political heat for environmental issues is necessary but not sufficient. We have to get hard scientific results on how people value environmental quality and how they are hurt when this quality is degraded. We also have to put together environmental policy initiatives that get the maximum impact for the economic and political resources spent. This is where environmental economics comes in. It is a way of examining the difficult trade-off types of questions that all environmental issues entail; it is also a valuable means of inquiring why people behave as they do toward the natural environment, and how we might restructure the current system to rectify harmful practices.

In fact, the subject is important enough to deserve to be widely available to the nonspecialist. Economics is a discipline that has developed a sophisticated body of theory and applied knowledge. Courses in economics now follow a hierarchy of introductory- and intermediate-level principles that are designed to lead students along and prepare them for the more advanced applications courses. But these run the risk of closing off the subject, making it inaccessible to those who do not want to become specialists. This book is intended, instead, for people who have not necessarily had any economics courses, at least not yet. It was written on the assumption that it's possible to present the major principles of economics in a fairly commonsensical, although rigorous, way and then apply them to questions of environmental quality.

This book is an introduction to the basic principles of environmental economics as they have been developed in the past and as they continue to evolve. The real world, certainly the real world of environmental policy, is much more complicated than these principles would often seem to imply. The examples discussed represent only a sample of the full range of issues that actually exists. If and when you confront that real world of environmental politics and policy, you will find it necessary to adapt these principles to all the details and nuances of reality. Unfortunately, there is not enough space in one book to look at all the ways that environmental economists have found to make the basic concepts and models more specific and relevant to concrete environmental issues. So we stick to the basic ideas and hope they excite your interest enough to make you want to pursue the refinements and adaptations of these ideas as they relate to a subject of growing relevance and importance.

When the first edition was published, there was no way of knowing how many others might be teaching a course similar to the one from which the book sprang: a course in environmental economics for people who have not necessarily had a course in economics. The reception that the first two editions have had, therefore, is gratifying. The comments received, sometimes directly and sometimes via the grapevine, have in general been quite positive. We hope the third edition will be as well received.

The basic structure, and sequence of chapters, are unchanged. The first section of the book is an introduction, beginning with a chapter on what environmental economics is about, followed by one on the basic relationships between the economy and the environment. The next section is devoted to studying the "tools" of analysis, the principles of demand and cost, and the elements of economic efficiency both in market and nonmarket activities. These chapters are not meant to be completely thorough treatments of these theoretical topics; however, given the objective of the book, the introductory chapters are essential. Even those who have had a course in microeconomic principles might find them valuable for purposes of review. Section Two also contains a chapter in which these economic principles are applied to a simple model of environmental pollution control. In these chapters, as well as the others, we have tried to leaven the presentation with examples taken from current sources, such as newspapers.

Section Three is on environmental analysis. Here we look closely at some of the techniques that have been developed by environmental economists to answer some of the fundamental value questions that underlie environmental decision making. We focus especially on the principles of benefit-cost analysis. After this we move to Section Four, on the principles of environmental policy design. It begins with a short chapter dealing with the criteria we might use to evaluate policies, then moves on to chapters on the main approaches to environmental quality management.

Sections Five and Six contain policy chapters, where we examine current developments in environmental policy with the analytical tools developed earlier. Section Five is devoted to environmental policy in the United States, covering federal policy on water, air, and toxic materials. It also contains a chapter on environmental issues at the state and local levels. Finally, the last section looks at international issues, such as environmental policy developments in other countries, global environmental issues, and the economics of international environmental agreements.

The third edition contains much new material. The basic concept chapters are of course unchanged, but these now have new exhibit and example material, and new discussion questions. Some new discussion topics in these chapters include voluntary pollution control, the incentive effects of standards, and the revenue aspects of emission charges. In the policy chapters there is much new material, including exhibits, discussion questions, and new coverage on global warming, the Kyoto agreement, brown fields, social justice, the TMDL approach to water pollution control, and NO_x trading programs. In addition we have brought up to date as much as possible all data tables.

At the end of each chapter we have indicated several websites on which relevant material may be found. Additional sources can be found on the website that is associated with this book: www.mhhe.com/economics/field3.

The website also contains other material that students and instructors will find useful.

ACKNOWLEDGMENTS

This text is the result of teaching the subject for many years in the classroom, so I must first thank all those students through the years who have listened, asked questions, and provided the feedback that shaped the book. Special thanks go to Stephen Fazio for his assistance in tracking down tons of material in the library, to Bill Thompson and the staff of the government documents section of the library at the University of Massachusetts, and to the reference librarians and interlibrary loan staff who helped me locate background material. Sincere thanks also to the following economists who reviewed earlier editions: Roger Bolton, Williams College; James F. Booker, Alfred University; John Braden, University of Illinois; Richard Bryant, University of Missouri-Rolla; Dallas Burtraw, Resources for the Future; Donald J. Epp, Pennsylvania State University; Rick Freeman, Bowdoin College; C. N. Gomersall, Luther College; Keith C. Knapp, University of California-Riverside; Henry McCarl, University of Alabama-Birmingham; Jon P. Nelson, Penn State University; Lars Olson, University of Maryland at College Park; Robert W. Reinke, University of South Dakota; J. Barkley Rosser, James Madison University; Kristin Skrabis, Dickinson College; and John Stranlund, University of Massachusetts-Amherst. On the third edition, special thanks go to Anne E. Bresnock, California State Polytechnic University-Pomona; Richard F. Kosobud, University of Illinois; Jeffrey Krautkraemer, Washington State University; Peter J. Parks, Rutgers University; and Duane J. Rosa, West Texas A&M University. On the third edition, special thanks also go to Brian Henninger, U.S. Environmental Protection Agency, and our students, who were not shy in pointing out places where the treatment could be improved.

As always, special thanks to Darleen Slysz and Eileen Keegan for their fine work on this edition, and to Lucille Sutton and the other folks at McGraw-Hill who continue to represent the book so strongly.

Barry C. Field

Martha K. Field

INTRODUCTION

This first section contains two introductory chapters. The first is a brief, non-technical review of some of the main topics and ideas within environmental economics. The second contains a general discussion of the interactions that exist between the economy and the environment, and introduces some fundamental concepts and definitions that are used throughout the book.

WHAT IS ENVIRONMENTAL ECONOMICS?

Economics is the study of how and why individuals and groups make decisions about the use and distribution of valuable human and nonhuman resources. It is not solely the study of profit-making businesses making decisions in a capitalist economy. It is much broader than this; it provides a set of analytical tools that can be used to study any situation in which the scarcity of means requires the balancing of competing objectives. It includes, for example, important questions in the behavior of nonprofit organizations, government agencies, and consumers.

Environmental economics is the application of the principles of economics to the study of how environmental resources are managed. Economics is divided into **microeconomics,** the study of the behavior of individuals and small groups, and **macroeconomics,** the study of the economic performance of economies as a whole. Environmental economics draws from both sides, although more from microeconomics than from macroeconomics. It focuses primarily on how and why people make decisions that have consequences for the natural environment. It is concerned also with how economic institutions and policies can be changed to bring these environmental impacts more into balance with human desires and the needs of the ecosystem itself.

One of our first jobs, therefore, is to become acquainted with some of the basic ideas and analytical tools of microeconomics. To do this at the very beginning, however, would risk giving the impression that the tools are more important than their uses. The tools of analysis are not interesting in themselves but for the understanding they can give us about why the natural environment becomes degraded, what the consequences of this are, and what can be done effectively to reduce this degradation. For this reason, the first chapter is devoted to sketching out, in common-sense terms, the kinds of questions environmental economists ask and the kinds of answers they seek. After a brief discussion of some general issues, we look at a series of examples of some of the problems addressed in environmental economics.

ECONOMIC ANALYSIS

To study economics is to study the way an economy and its institutions are set up, and how individuals and groups make decisions about transforming and managing scarce resources to increase human wealth, in its broadest sense. Environmental economics focuses on a society's natural and environmental resources, and examines the way people make decisions that lead to environmental destruction and environmental improvements.

Environmental economics is an **analytical subject.** We want not only to describe the state of the environment and changes in it, but also to understand why these conditions exist and how we might bring about improvements in environmental quality. This means we will have to introduce a specialized set of concepts and vocabulary. We also will have to use specialized means of expressing connections between important factors that are involved in the environmental quality issues we explore. To do this economists use what are called **analytical models.** A model is a simplified representation of reality, in the sense that it isolates and focuses on the most important elements of a situation and neglects the others. The models we will use are graphical in nature, and they will be quite simple.[1]

It is important to distinguish between **positive economics** and **normative economics.** Positive economics is the study of what is; normative economics is the study of what ought to be. Positive economics seeks to understand how an economic system actually operates by looking at the way people make decisions in different types of circumstances. A study to show how the housing market reacts to changes in interest rates is an exercise in positive economics. A study to estimate how electric utilities would respond to a new tax on sulfur emissions is also an example of positive economics. However, a study to determine what kind of regulation we ought to adopt for a particular environmental problem is a case of normative economics because it involves more than just knowing how things work; it also involves value judgments. We make use of this distinction repeatedly throughout the book.

The economic approach to environmental issues is to be contrasted with what might be called the **moral approach.** According to the latter, environmental degradation is the result of human behavior that is unethical or immoral. Thus, for example, the reason people pollute is because they lack the moral and ethical strength to refrain from the type of behavior that causes environmental degradation. If this is true, then the way to get people to stop polluting is somehow to increase the general level of environmental morality in the society. In fact, the environmental movement has led a great many people to focus on

---

[1] The web page associated with the book contains a section on working with graphs. See **www.mhhe.com/economics/field3.**

questions of environmental ethics, exploring the moral dimensions of human impacts on the natural environment. These moral questions are obviously of fundamental concern to any civilized society. Certainly one of the main reasons environmental issues have been put on the front burner of social concern is the sense of moral responsibility that has led people to take their concerns into the political arena.

But there are problems with relying on moral reawakening as the main approach to combatting pollution. People don't necessarily have readily available moral buttons to push, and environmental problems are too important to wait for a long process of moral rebuilding. Nor does a sense of moral outrage, by itself, help us make decisions about all the other social goals that also have ethical dimensions: housing, health care, education, crime, and so on. In a world of competing objectives we have to worry about very practical questions: Are we targeting the right environmental objectives, can we really enforce certain policies, are we getting the most impact for the money, and so on. But the biggest problem with basing our approach to pollution control strictly on the moral argument is the basic assumption that people pollute because they are somehow morally underdeveloped. It is not moral underdevelopment that leads to environmental destruction; rather, it is the way the economic system, within which people make decisions about how to conduct their lives, has been arranged.

THE IMPORTANCE OF INCENTIVES

People pollute because it is the cheapest way they have of solving a certain, very practical problem. That problem is the disposal of the waste products remaining after consumers have finished using something, or after business firms have finished producing something. People make these decisions on production, consumption, and disposal within a certain set of economic and social institutions;[2] these institutions structure the **incentives** that lead people to make decisions in one direction rather than another. What needs to be studied is how this incentive process works and, especially, how it may be restructured so that people will be led to make decisions and develop life styles that have more benign environmental implications.

One simplistic incentive-type statement that one often hears is that pollution is a result of the **profit motive.** According to this view, in private enterprise economies such as the Western industrialized nations people are rewarded for maximizing profits, the difference between the value of what is produced and the value of what is used up in the production process. Furthermore, the thinking goes, the profits that entrepreneurs try to maximize are strictly monetary profits. In this headlong pursuit of monetary profits, entrepreneurs give no thought to the environmental impacts of their actions because it "does not pay." Thus, in this uncontrolled striving for monetary profits, the only way to reduce environmental pollution is to weaken the strength of the profit motive.

---

[2]By "institutions" we mean the fundamental set of public and private organizations, laws, and practices that a society uses to structure its economic activity. Markets are an economic institution, for example, as are corporations, a body of commercial law, public agencies, and so on.

But this proposition does not stand up to analysis. It is not only "profit-motivated" corporations that cause pollution; individual consumers are also guilty when they do things like pour paint thinner down the drain or let their cars get seriously out of tune. Because individuals don't keep profit-and-loss statements, it can't be profits per se that lead people to pollute. The same can be said of government agencies, which have sometimes been serious polluters even though they are not profit motivated. But the most persuasive argument against the view that the search for profits causes pollution comes from looking at the recent history of Eastern Europe and the former USSR. With the collapse of these ex-Communist regimes, we have become aware of the enormous environmental destruction that has occurred in some of these regions—heavily polluted air and water resources in many areas, which have a major impact on human health and ecological systems. Many of these problems exceed some of the worst cases of environmental pollution experienced in market-driven countries. But they happened in an economic system where the profit motive was entirely lacking, which means, quite simply, that the profit motive, in itself, is not the main cause of environmental destruction.

In the sections and chapters that follow, we will place great stress on the importance of incentives in the functioning of an economic system. *Any* system will produce destructive environmental impacts if the incentives within the system are not structured to avoid them. We have to look more deeply into any economic system to understand how its incentive systems work and how they may be changed so that we can have a reasonably progressive economy without disastrous environmental effects.

INCENTIVES: A HOUSEHOLD EXAMPLE

An **incentive** is something that attracts or repels people and leads them to modify their behavior in some way. An "economic incentive" is something in the economic world that leads people to channel their efforts at economic production and consumption in certain directions. We often think of economic incentives as consisting of payoffs in terms of material wealth; people have an incentive to behave in ways that provide them with increased wealth. But there are also nonmaterial incentives that lead people to modify their economic behavior; for example, self-esteem, the desire to preserve a beautiful visual environment, or the desire to set a good example for others.

For a simple first look at the importance of changing incentives to get improvements in environmental quality, consider the story shown in Exhibit 1-1. It is about new ways of paying for trash disposal, focusing on the experience of a New Hampshire town. Before the program, people in the town paid a flat annual fee to have their trash collected. This is common practice in most communities. The problem with this approach is that there is simply no incentive for any individual family to limit its trash production, because they will pay the same annual trash-collection fee no matter how much, or little, they produce. This might not be a problem if there were ample landfill space and if there was no danger that the landfill would contaminate the surrounding

EXHIBIT 1-1

PAY-AS-YOU-THROW, DOVER, NEW HAMPSHIRE

Getting Started: Why Pay-As-You-Throw?
The City of Dover is a community of approximately 26,000 people on New Hampshire's seacoast. Our municipal landfill was closed in 1979, and at that time the city entered into a relationship with a private hauler for collection and disposal at a privately owned and operated landfill. The city collected approximately 24,000 tons of trash each year, of which approximately 11,000 tons were residential refuse.

Before 1989, Dover had no recycling program. Any and all trash residents wished to discard was left at the curb, and $3^1/_2$ truck routes were needed to collect the refuse daily. The cost of refuse collection and disposal was escalating rapidly. Responding to citizen pressure, the Dover city council created an ad hoc committee on recycling in the fall of 1989.

The committee urged the immediate establishment of a drop-off recycling center designed to collect a wide range of materials. The recycling center opened in May 1990. It quickly became very popular and a source of civic pride.

The recycling center was run initially as an all-volunteer effort. After a few months, the city hired a solid waste coordinator, who began working in conjunction with the ad hoc committee and several city councilors to urge the establishment of curbside recycling and the bag and tag program, which was then unknown in northern New England.

Overcoming Public Dissent
The three public meetings we held were filled with heated vocal dissent. However, we soon convinced the public to accept these programs with a couple of basic premises. The first premise was that recyclable materials are a commodity, and anything that is disposed of in the landfill is waste. We argued that the costs for producing wastes should be borne by the user and that the costs of recycling, because of its social and environmental benefits, should be borne by the city.

In September 1991, the city began curbside collection of recyclables, and a month later the bag and tag program was implemented.

Since the program was initiated we have had annual public meetings and have raised the price once. We have not had any significant public dissent at any meetings since the program's inception.

How Does It Work?
The city no longer provides for the collection and disposal of private dumpsters. Commercial generators pay the fees associated with the collection and disposal. For the residents, payment of the collection and disposal of wastes is accomplished through the purchase of bags and/or adhesive tags.

A special revenue fund was established to pay for the collection, disposal, and administrative costs associated with our residential solid waste. The fees generated by the sale of the bags and tags go into this fund as revenue. The goal is to maintain a neutral fund balance that can sustain the program, but not to build a large balance.

Success: Saving Money and Reducing Waste
As mentioned earlier, Dover used to produce approximately 11,000 tons per year of residential solid waste. Last year, we produced approximately 3,900 tons. In 1990 our budget for solid waste was approximately $1.2 million. Next year's budget (including trash and recycling) is approximately $878,000. Our current recycling rate is well over 50 percent for our residential waste stream—despite it being strictly voluntary.

Source: From the U.S. EPA Office of Solid Waste, Pay-As-You-Throw website, www.epa.gov/epaoswer/non-hw/payt/tools/ssdover.htm.

environment, such as a nearby groundwater system. But for most communities these conditions don't hold any more, if they ever did. The community in the story was confronted by rapidly escalating trash-collection costs. It faced the problem of how to get a significant reduction in the quantity of solid waste handled by the town.

The response in this case was to introduce a system that gives people an incentive to search for ways to reduce the amount of solid waste they produce. This was done by charging people for each bag of trash they put on the curb. What this does is to give families the incentive to reduce the number of bags of trash they set out. They can do this by recycling, by switching to products that have less waste, by putting food scraps in a compost pile, and so on. These have led, according to the story, to a large increase in the amount of trash recycled and a reduction in the total amount of trash. There are many other communities around the country where this system has been adopted. Of course, no system is perfect. Increases in illegal dumping and difficulties with applying the plan to apartment houses are problems. Nevertheless, the new approach does illustrate in a very clear way the effects of a shift from a system where there were no incentives for people to reduce their solid waste to one where there are such incentives.[3]

INCENTIVES IN INDUSTRY

Incentives are also critically important in reducing **industrial pollution.** All industrial firms work within a given set of incentives: In market economies this is normally to increase their net income. Firms have an incentive to take advantage of whatever factors are available to better their performance in terms of these criteria. One way they have been able to do this historically is to use the services of the environment for waste disposal. The motivation for this is that these services have essentially been free, and by using free inputs as much as possible a firm obviously can increase profits. It's this state of affairs that has contributed to the excessive levels of pollution we have today.

One policy approach is to pass and then try to enforce laws making pollution illegal. A more effective technique frequently will be to design a system that takes advantage of firms' normal monetary incentives in such a way as to lead them to pollute less. A way of doing this would be to charge firms for the pollution-causing material they emit into the environment. A charge of so much per pound, or per ton, would be put on the emissions, and the firms would be sent a bill at the end of each month or year, based on the total quantity of their emissions during that period. With environmental emissions now costly, firms would have the incentive to search for ways of reducing their emissions, perhaps by changing the production process, or by switching to a new fuel input, or adding certain treatment facilities. Emission charges of this type are the main subject of Chapter 12.

---

[3]The technical name for this approach is "unit pricing." See U.S. Environmental Protection Agency, *Unit Pricing* (EPA/530-SW-91-005), Washington, DC, February 1991.

A good recent example of this type of economic **incentive-based approach** is the use of **CO_2 taxes** by some European countries. Worldwide emissions of CO_2 are contributing to global warming, with potentially massive worldwide impacts for people and the ecosystem. The charge placed on CO_2 emissions will provide an incentive for firms in these countries to look diligently for ways of producing their output with smaller quantities of fuel inputs, or to switch to fuel types that produce smaller quantities of CO_2. It also will tend to increase the price of goods that require a lot of energy to produce more than those that use relatively less energy; thus, consumers will alter their consumption patterns accordingly.

THE DESIGN OF ENVIRONMENTAL POLICY

Environmental economics has a major role to play in the design of **public policies** for environmental quality improvement. There are an enormous range and variety of public programs and policies devoted to environmental matters, at all levels of government: local, state, regional, federal, and international. They vary greatly in their efficiency and effectiveness. Some have been well designed and will no doubt have beneficial impacts. Others, perhaps the majority, are not well designed. Not being cost effective, they will end up costing lots of money and having much smaller impacts on environmental quality than they might have had with better design.

The problem of designing efficient environmental policies is often not given the emphasis it deserves. It is easy to fall into the trap of thinking that any programs or policies that flow out of the rough and tumble of the environmental political process are likely to be of some help, or that they certainly will be better than nothing. But history is full of cases where policymakers and public administrators have pursued policies that don't work; the public is frequently led to believe a policy will be effective even when any reasonable analysis could predict that it will not. All of which means that it is critically important to study how to design environmental policies that are effective and efficient.

The Environmental Protection Agency (EPA) estimated that in 1990 the United States devoted about 2 percent of the total cost of goods and services in the country to pollution control and environmental cleanup. They expected this percentage to rise to around 2.8 percent by the end of the 1990s. These are very large sums of money, even though the percentage probably should be higher. But it is important not to get totally fixated on the percentage, whether it is high or low, whether it compares favorably with other countries, and so on. Of equal or greater importance is whether we are getting the most improvement possible in environmental quality for the money spent. Former EPA Director William Reilly is quoted as saying: ". . . at this level of expenditure, there's a very large obligation to get it right." By "getting it right" he means having programs that get the maximum improvement in environmental quality for the resources spent. Everybody has an interest in this: environmentalists, for obvious reasons; public regulators, because they are tapping a limited supply of taxpayer resources and consumer tolerance; and the regulated polluters themselves, because matters of efficiency are critical to business success.

To see what "getting it right" might entail, consider the 1990 Clean Air Act. It contains hundreds of provisions aimed primarily at three air pollution problems: urban smog, emissions of sulfur dioxide from power plants, and toxic chemical emissions. The law includes all kinds of things: tailpipe standards, new technology for gasoline nozzles, production of a variety of super-clean cars, new standards for toxic emissions, emission trading among power plants in the South and Midwest, and so on. Furthermore, it goes into enormous detail; for example, it required that fleet cars (taxis and the like) meet stricter tailpipe standards by 1998, but it exempted fleet cars that were parked at private homes at night! On a quick reading this looks like a serious law, that it will have an impact across a broad range of air-quality problems. But how can we be reasonably sure this great collection of bits and pieces represents anything like a cost-effective way of attacking these problems? How can we be sure that we have the right mix of techniques, that we don't have just a grab bag of items that have been pushed by a variety of interest groups on one side or another of this issue?

A major problem in environmental policy is that of **perverse incentives;** that is, incentives created by a policy that actually work against the overall objectives of that policy. Environmental policies have been notoriously subject to perverse incentives, because environmental policymakers have too often tried to legislate results directly, rather than establish the types of regulations that cause people to alter their behavior in desirable ways (see Exhibit 1-2).

Issues related to the design of environmental policy are a major part of environmental economics. It is important to know how alternative policy approaches measure up in terms of cost effectiveness, getting the most pollution reduction for the money spent, and, in terms of efficiency, appropriately balancing the benefits and costs of environmental improvements.

MACROECONOMIC QUESTIONS: ENVIRONMENT AND GROWTH

The incentive issues discussed in the previous section are microeconomic problems; they deal with the behavior of individuals or small groups of consumers, polluting firms, and firms in the pollution-control industry. The macroeconomy, on the other hand, refers to the economic structure and performance of an entire country taken as a single unit. When we study topics such as changes in gross domestic product (GDP), rates of inflation, and the unemployment rate, we are focusing on the performance of the country as a whole, that is to say, we are doing macroeconomics.

There are a number of important questions about the relationship between environmental issues and the behavior of the macroeconomy. One is the relationship between environmental pollution-control measures and the rate of unemployment and economic growth: Will stricter policies tend to retard growth and increase unemployment and, if so, how much? What impact will environmental regulations have, if any, on the rate of inflation? Example 1-1 puts some perspective on this issue. It discusses the role of environmental control costs in comparison to the total amount of economic activity in the country, in relation to expenditures on other types of goods and in comparison to other countries.

EXHIBIT 1-2

TOUGH MEXICAN CLEAN-AIR LAW MAKES POLLUTION MUCH WORSE

By Mark Fineman

It looked simple enough on paper six years ago, when Mexico City's lawmakers imposed their toughest scheme ever to clean up some of the worst air on the planet: Every workday, between 5 A. M. and 10 P. M., certain cars were banished from the city's streets, based on rotation of their license numbers.

A new study by Mexico City's Metropolitan Commission for Pollution Control and Prevention has confirmed what most of the city's estimated 20 million residents have suspected for years: The law doesn't work, and it hasn't since soon after it came into force.

The commission recommended that the law be either radically modified or altogether repealed.

The commission found that the federal district that includes the capital now consumes nearly 2 million more liters—or about 500,000 more gallons—of gasoline each day than it did when the law took effect.

The reason: About 2 million cars were on the streets on any given day in December, 1989; today, there are nearly 3 million.

Fueled by government policies that encouraged credit-financing—and by the Today Don't Drive law itself—most families simply bought a second, third or fourth car to get around the restriction, the study concluded.

The law bans cars one day a week according to the last digit of each license plate. If a plate ends with a 1 or 2, for example, the car may not be driven on Monday; a 3 or 4 bans the car every Tuesday, and so on through 9 and 0 on Friday. By buying additional cars, drivers could acquire a selection of plates that let them drive every day, undermining the system.

The study recommended that, instead of restrictions, the government should create greater incentives for drivers who install pollution-reducing catalytic converters—still a rarity in this city.

And experts stressed that the government also must go after businesses that are the worst polluters—a difficult task amid a deep economic crisis that already has hurt Mexican industry and cost more than 1 million jobs.

Yet to be incorporated in the debate is another study by the University of California, Irvine's atmospheric chemist F. Sherwood Rowland and senior research associate Donald Blake. Published in August, their findings indicate that the largest single source of smog in Mexico City is not vehicles but liquid petroleum gas leaking from millions of household cooking and heating tanks.

Source: Springfield (MA) *Union News,* November 26, 1995. Copyright © by the *Los Angeles Times.* Reprinted by permission.

One important macroeconomic question is the connection between environmental regulations, in total, and rates of economic growth. Virtually every country around the world, whether rich, poor, or in between, is struggling to increase or maintain economic growth rates. Some people hold the view that environmental regulations reduce growth rates, because environmental expenditures displace other types of productive investments. There are actually two parts to this issue: what is the relationship between environmental protection and growth, and if there are costs in terms of decreases in measured GDP, are they worth it? The last question is actually a benefit–cost type of question; the first has to do with understanding the macroeconomic implications of environmental policy. Exhibit 1-3 presents information on this issue from a recent EPA report.

EXAMPLE 1-1

POLLUTION CONTROL IN THE U.S. ECONOMY

In 1992, the U.S. gross domestic product (GDP) was $6,020,200,000,000. Since the estimated population of the country in that year was 253,615,000, the GDP per capita was about $23,740. The U.S. Environmental Protection Agency (EPA) has estimated that, in 1992, total expenditures on pollution control in the United States were $87,594,000,000. This amounts to 1.5 percent of GDP, about $345 per capita. This cost includes all the private costs of complying with pollution control laws, that is, all the costs of purchasing, installing, operating, and maintaining pollution-control technology that firms need to be in compliance with these laws.

Is the price high or low? It is impossible to answer that in an absolute sense, but we might be able to give it more meaning by making some comparisons. The following tabulation shows costs of certain categories of expenditures made by U.S. citizens in 1987 as a proportion of GDP in that year.

Clothing and shoes	4.2
Medical care	7.0
Food	11.7
National defense	6.9
Housing	9.3
Pollution control	1.7

Pollution control falls below medical care and housing and well below public expenditures such as national defense. Although pollution-control costs are expected to take a bigger share of GDP in future years, they will probably never get as large as the expenditures in basic consumer categories such as clothing, housing, and food.

Another interesting comparison is between the United States and other industrialized countries. The following tabulation shows pollution-control costs as a percentage of GDP in several countries for 1985:

United States	1.67
Finland	1.32
France	1.10
West Germany	1.52
Netherlands	1.26
Norway	0.82
United Kingdom	1.25

These proportions range from 0.82 to 1.67 percent, with the United States comparing quite favorably because it has the highest expenditure share of this group of countries. We cannot infer directly that people in the United States are enjoying a cleaner environment—less air pollution, cleaner water, and so on. Nothing is said here about the effectiveness with which pollution-control resources are being made in the different countries. It might be, for example, that although Norway spends less as a percentage of GDP on pollution control, it spends it more effectively than the resources spent in other countries. Another factor that is not taken into account in simple comparisons is the severity of the pollution problems in different countries. Because of differences in industrial structure and differences in environmental resources (e.g., meteorological patterns), it may cost more to reduce pollution to acceptable levels in one country than in another. The numbers are nevertheless interesting; it may be slightly surprising that most of these percentages are between 1.0 and 1.5.

EXHIBIT 1-3

ENVIRONMENTAL PROTECTION: IS IT BAD FOR THE ECONOMY?

Does Environmental Protection Cause Unemployment and Plant Closures, and Reduce International Competitiveness?

Another commonly held belief is that environmental regulations cause widespread layoffs and plant closures, and reduce the competitiveness of U.S. industries in the global marketplace. The star witness for this view is the unemployment caused by logging restrictions in the Pacific Northwest to protect habitat for the spotted owl, which indeed put a significant number of unfortunate people in the local timber industry out of work. But looking at the entire nation, it turns out that in reality few layoffs and plant closures occur as a result of environmental regulations. And, for several important reasons, environmental protection is unlikely to impair international competitiveness in any significant way.

Once reason why this popular perception is not accurate is that environmental regulatory costs for most industries are actually quite small. In fact, according to Census Bureau data, total 1991 pollution control expenditures as a percentage of value added—a good measure of the economic size of businesses—in manufacturing industries amounted to only 1.72 percent. Costs of this size are simply not large enough in most cases to cause layoffs and shut down plants. Of course, a few industries face somewhat larger environmental protection costs, but these are highly capital-intensive industrial sectors where competitors face similar regulatory costs and whose plants are large, expensive, and unlikely to be closed because of these costs.

Employment data back this claim. According to the Department of Labor, mass layoffs during the period 1987–90 that are attributable to environmental and safety regulations (a far larger universe of rules than EPA's regulations alone) were responsible for only a fraction of 1 percent of the total. In fact, of 2,546 layoff events during that period, only 4 were traced to environmental and safety regulations. Workers were about 500 times more likely to be laid off as a result of seasonal and other work slowdowns and contract completions than because of environmental and safety rules. Model changes alone account for 50 times the layoffs caused by environmental and safety regulations.

In addition, the pollution control sector itself is relatively labor-intensive compared with the rest of the economy, according to studies of the labor intensity of different industrial sectors in the U.S. economy. Thus, increased demand for environmental protection, if anything, tends to increase the demand for labor in the long run. As a result, contrary to the conventional wisdom, and excepting the misfortune of the few who are temporarily dislocated, environmental regulation is probably labor's friend, not its enemy.

Finally, environmental protection costs appear not to affect the competitiveness of U.S. industries in the global marketplace. Strong support for this conclusion is provided in a recent *Journal of Economic Literature* article surveying numerous academic studies of the possible effects of environmental regulation using various measures of those impacts. The authors conclude that there is no evidence at all that the stringency of environmental protection in the United States significantly affects our competitiveness relative to other nations either positively or negatively.

At 1.72 percent of value added, these costs are not very large in the scheme of things. Moreover, many of the major trading partners of the United States have similar environmental protection regulations and practices, so their industries face comparable pollution-control costs.

Source: Frank Arnold, "Environmental Protection: Is It Bad for the Economy?" a Nontechnical Summary of the Literature, U.S. EPA, Office of Economy and Environment, www.epa.gov/economics, 1999.

Another macroeconomic question concerns the impacts of economic growth on environmental quality. Do higher rates of growth, that is, increases in our traditional measures such as GDP, imply greater environmental degradation or might the opposite be true? Two economists who studied this problem recently concluded: "some pollution increases during the early stages of a country's development and then begins to diminish as countries gain adequate resources to tackle pollution problems." This happens because at low incomes people tend to value development over environmental quality, but as they achieve greater wealth they are willing to devote greater resources to environmental quality improvements. This is clearly a matter of great importance for developing countries, and we come back to it in Chapter 19. In developed countries also, macroeconomic problems—growth, recession, inflation, unemployment—are constant topics of national concern. So it's important to pursue studies of the relationships between these phenomena and questions of environmental quality.

BENEFIT–COST ANALYSIS

Effective decision making requires that there be adequate information about the **consequences** of the decisions. This is as important in the **public sector,** where the issue is effective **public policy,** as it is in the **private sector,** where the main concern is with the bottom line of the profit and loss statement. The primary type of public sector analysis in environmental policy questions is **benefit–cost analysis.** Policies or projects are studied in terms of the environmental benefits they would produce, and these are compared with the costs that are entailed. It was first used in this country early in the 20th century to evaluate water development projects undertaken by federal agencies.[4] Today it is used by many government agencies to help make rational policy decisions.

Benefit–cost analysis is such an important and widely used approach that we devote several chapters to it later in the book (Chapters 6, 7, and 8). In this type of analysis, as the name implies, the benefits of some proposed action are estimated and compared with the total costs that society would bear if that action were undertaken. If it is a proposal for a public park, for example, the benefits in terms of recreational experiences provided by the park are compared with the expected costs of building the park and of using the land in this way rather than some other way. Or a proposal to build a solid-waste incinerator would compare the costs of building and operating the incinerator, including the costs of disposing of the remaining ash and the costs of possible airborne emissions, with benefits, such as reducing the use of landfills for the solid waste. Exhibit 1-4 shows some results of a benefit–cost study undertaken not by a public agency but by an environmental interest group: the **Environmental Defense Fund.**[5] The subject is

---

[4]These were the U.S. Army Corps of Engineers in the Defense Department, the Bureau of Reclamation in the Department of Interior, and the Soil Conservation Service (now called the Natural Resource Conservation Service) in the Department of Agriculture.

[5] This group was formed in 1967 and is especially noted for its work in applying environ mental economics in its advocacy activity. It has recently changed its name to Environmental Defense.

EXHIBIT 1-4

THE BENEFITS AND COSTS OF CURBSIDE RECYCLING

By transforming waste materials into useable resources, recycling provides a way to manage solid waste while reducing pollution, conserving energy, creating jobs, and building more competitive manufacturing industries. Like burying trash in landfills or burning it in incinerators, recycling also costs money. Assessing society's interest in recycling requires a full appraisal of the environmental and economic benefits and costs of recycling, in comparison with the one-way consumption of resources and disposal of used products and packaging in landfills and incinerators. When all of these factors are taken into account, the overwhelming advantages of recycling are apparent.

Benefits

- Recycling cuts pollution and conserves natural resources. Studies show that, for 10 major categories of air pollutants and 8 major categories of water pollutants, curbside recycling results in a net reduction in pollution, relative to a system based on the use of virgin materials.
- Recycling conserves energy. By recycling a ton of materials in a typical curbside recycling program, at least $187 worth of electricity, petroleum, natural gas, and coal are conserved, even after accounting for the energy used to collect and transport the materials.
- Recycling avoids the costs of disposing of waste in landfills or solid waste incinerators. The costs of recycling are partially offset by avoided disposal fees and by revenues earned through the sales of materials. Disposal fees vary greatly between different regions, and markets for recycled materials are now booming. Disposal fees vary from $70 to $100 a ton

in the northeastern U.S., to $15 to $25 a ton in the west.

- Recycling creates jobs and makes manufacturing industries more competitive. For example, one recent study found that in 10 northeastern states alone, recycling adds $7.2 billion in value to recovered materials through processing and manufacturing activities. Approximately 103,000 people were employed in recycling processing and manufacturing jobs in this region in 1991, 2.7 percent of the region's total employment.

Cost

Trash collection costs vary enormously over the country. A recent study showed that recycling collection costs (exclusive of landfill costs or sales of materials) averaged $282 per ton for curbside programs that diverted less than 10 percent of wastes, $102 per ton for cities that diverted between 10 percent and 20 percent, and $93 per ton for cities that diverted more than 20 percent of their wastes through curbside recycling (not including yard waste composting). In other words, the cities with relatively high recycling rates had costs almost three times less on average than those with low recycling rates.

Thus for programs in which more than 10 percent of wastes are diverted to recycling, the benefits of curbside recycling outweigh the costs. Furthermore, future cost reductions can be expected as cities and private firms increase the efficiency of their operation.

Source: Excerpted from John F. Ruston and Richard A. Denison, "Advantage Recycling, Assessing the Full Costs and Benefits of Curbside Recycling," Environmental Defense Fund, New York.

---

recycling, and the analysis has the aim of determining whether the benefits of recycling outweigh its costs.

The benefit–cost approach implies that we need to consider both the benefits and the costs of environmental programs and policies. This often puts benefit–cost studies squarely in the middle of political controversy on many environmental issues. In the political struggles that characterize many environmental problems, groups on one side consist of people whose major concern is with the benefits, whereas groups on the other side are primarily concerned with costs. Environmental groups typically stress the benefits; business groups usually focus on the costs.

VALUING THE ENVIRONMENT

To complete successfully a benefit–cost analysis of an environmental program or regulation, it's necessary to estimate both the benefits and the costs of the actions. One factor that complicates this type of analysis is that the benefits of environmental improvements are usually **nonmarket** in nature. If we were trying to assess the benefits to society of a program to support potato farmers, we could get a good idea of the value of potatoes by looking at how much people are willing to pay for them when they buy them at the supermarket. But suppose we have a program of air pollution reduction that will, among other things, lower the risk that people in a certain region will have of contracting chronic bronchitis. How might we estimate the social value of this result? It cannot be done by looking directly at market behavior, as in the case of potatoes, because there is no market where people buy and sell directly the changes in health risk produced by the environmental program. Environmental economists have developed a series of **nonmarket valuation techniques** that are used to estimate these types of environmental out comes. We will discuss some of these techniques in Chapter 7.

SUBURBAN SPRAWL

One of the most important changes over the last century that has affected the lives of virtually everybody is the **suburbanization** of society. Essentially this means the spreading out of urban areas and lower-density living for a substantial fraction (not all) of the population. In the last few years the issue of suburbanization has again moved to the front burner of public attention, this time under the heading of **sprawl.** Sprawl is normally used in a negative sense, as something that is undesirable. The visual manifestation of sprawl is the proliferation of relatively low-density suburban developments on the fringe; "leapfrogging," in which new development leaves a temporary gap that gets filled in over time; and "edge cities," which are secondary centers of high density commercial development some distance from the center of a large, parent, urban district.

Sprawl is clearly a land-use, quality-of-life problem. Sprawl uses up large amounts of fringe area, with lost agricultural and ecological benefits. It has produced a massive growth in road congestion and the lost time this implies. Sprawl has important visual impacts. It also has important environmental effects. Urban air pollution is closely related to the tremendous amount of automobile commuting that goes with sprawl.

From the standpoint of economics, sprawl has many dimensions. There are essentially two tasks: to understand the factors that lead to inefficient levels of sprawl and then to come up with efficient and equitable policy prescriptions for changing it if that is what is called for. A major element in producing sprawl is the cost of transportation. The lower the costs of transport, other things equal, the more feasible it is for people to live farther away from their workplaces and commute. An important factor affecting travel costs is the way roads are managed. In effect many of them are treated as free goods; road access is open to anybody at any time. A scarce item, road capacity, is being used at zero price. There have been a few experiments around the world with changing drivers' congestion prices, but the idea is catching on only slowly in most places. Exhibit 1-5 discusses a recent effort by a team of environmental economists to survey peoples' attitudes (in California) toward using road congestion fees, and what steps might be taken to make this approach more acceptable to drivers.

INTERNATIONAL ISSUES

Many environmental problems are local or regional, in the sense that the causal factors and resulting damages lie within the same country. But many others are international in scope. Some are **international** simply because there is a national border between the pollution source and the resulting impacts. Airborne emissions that are carried from one country upwind to another downwind is a case in point, as is water pollution of a river that traverses several countries. There is another class of problems that are **global** in nature because they impact the global environment. One of these is the destruction of the earth's protective layer of **stratospheric ozone** by chemicals devised by humans for a number of industrial purposes. Another is the problem of **global warming,** the possible rise in surface temperatures of the earth stemming from the accumulation of carbon dioxide in the atmosphere. The 1997 Kyoto conference featured an attempt by developed countries to agree on future cutbacks of CO_2 emissions. Cost-effective CO_2 emission reductions and the design of equitable international agreements are two topics among many on which environmental economists have worked.

ECONOMIC GLOBALIZATION AND THE ENVIRONMENT

There is another sense in which global environmental problems have recently taken on greater urgency. These are the environmental implications of globalization. **Globalization** is a term used to refer to the perceived changes that are taking place in the world economy, including the rapid growth of **trade** among nations, **privatization** of economic institutions, massive international flows of **financial capital,** and growth in the numbers and sizes of **multinational firms.** Advocates of a more integrated world economy point to its potential for stimulating economic growth and increasing wealth in the developing world. But many people also have pointed to the potential downside of globalization, one part of which may be the degradation of natural environments in developing countries.

Globalization has become a politically charged concept; it is sometimes hard to cut through the rhetoric and identify the substantive issues that are involved.

EXHIBIT 1-5

PAYING TO DRIVE FREELY

By Winston Harrington

In grappling over the last 20 years to meet clean air goals, transportation analysts have come up with a number of workable schemes to reduce the number of cars on the road at any given time. These solutions include congestion pricing policies, whereby drivers pay to use freeways and major arteries during periods of peak demand.

As analysts and government officials have come to recognize, however, if and how traffic congestion is eased depends very much on those in the drivers' seats. Without public support, no plan to reduce congestion will work. For now, more drivers seem willing to sit in traffic than to pay to alter driving habits. But given time and more traffic, that attitude may change.

Meanwhile, interest in approaches like congestion pricing already is high among transportation planners, in large part because the old ways of dealing with traffic do not seem to be working any more. Building new roads to ease congestion, for instance, is no longer the obvious solution it once was. Public budgets are tighter and the environmental and quality-of-life repercussions of sprawl-induced travel are more in evidence.

From an economic point of view, collecting user fees to drive busy roads during peak demand is by far the most attractive way to curb traffic. If we add up all the costs, including the inconvenience associated with restricted travel and/or having to find alternative routes or modes of conveyance, we find that no other rationing method provides a given level of road service at lower total cost. Other approaches to rationing roadway use, most notably "high-occupancy-vehicle" (HOV) lanes restricted to cars carrying two, three, or four occupants, are less efficient. Yet it is HOV lanes that have been implemented in many places, while time-of-day user fees are rare. In North America such fees are collected in only two places: SR91 in Southern California, a private road built on public land (in the median of an existing freeway), and Route 407 in Toronto, Canada, designed from the ground up for electronic fee collection.

Last year, RFF Senior Fellow Alan Krupnick and I, along with Anna Alberini of the University of Colorado, worked with REACH to develop a telephone survey, which the California survey research firm Godbe Research and Analysis then administered to a sample of Southern Californians. Essentially, we asked respondents if they would be willing—with and without several different incentives—to pay a "user fee" to drive on freeways during rush hour. This article presents the results of that survey.

Of the motorists surveyed, 38 percent reported that they would support the base plan, with 56 percent opposed and 6 percent undecided. Thus the results suggest that nearly two out of five commuting motorists in Southern California will support congestion fees on the region's freeways even without being told with any specificity how the revenues are to be used. If we consider the intensity of preferences, however, we see that a much higher fraction of the opposition was "definite," suggesting that a congestion fee presented without rebate or other inducement will enjoy soft support and face hard opposition.

The results of our survey suggest that congestion tolls and vehicle emissions fees can attract majority support from the public in Southern California, at least in a hypothetical referendum and under some circumstances. The survey also revealed that providing a rebate of some portion of the fees to individuals can increase support, although in our case not by enough to win a majority. Moreover, support for all congestion fee plans was weak in this sense: Many more supporters said that they would "probably" rather than "definitely" support a fee plan, while opponents said the reverse was true. A referendum or similar proposal to adopt a congestion fee plan might be vulnerable to such qualitative distinctions—to the ferocity, say, of the opposition's sound bites during a related political campaign.

Source: Excerpted from "Paying to Drive Freely, RFF Surveys Public Attitudes to Congestion Fees," by Winston Harrington, *Resources,* Vol. 129, Fall 1997, pp. 9–12, Resources for the Future, Washington, DC, 1997.

One part of globalization is the substantial increase that has occurred in the volume of trade among nations. This has led to a concern about the implications of this on environmental impacts in both developed and developing countries. International trade in goods and services has been touted as an engine of growth for the countries involved. Some people take the view that the long-run environmental implications of this are positive. Many others feel that unrestricted trade will have severe environmental consequences. These opinions are discussed in Exhibit 1-6. We will take up this topic at greater length in Chapter 21.

Another aspect of globalization is the growth of multinational firms and the relocation of industrial firms from developed to developing countries. Environmental regulations are often less stringent in the latter than in the former. The fear is that some developing countries could become **pollution havens,** places to which firms move in order to have to spend less on pollution control measures. We will look more closely at this phenomenon in Chapter 20.

ECONOMICS AND POLITICS

Finally, we need to discuss briefly the question of how to achieve effective environmental policy in a highly **political policy environment.** Environmental policies not only affect the natural environment, they also affect people. This means that environmental policy decisions come out of the political process, a process where, at least in democratic systems, people and groups come together and contend for influence and control, where interests collide, coalitions shift, and biases intrude. Policies that come out of a process like this may bear little relationship to what we might think of as efficient approaches to particular environmental problems. Many people have questioned the very idea that a democratic political process could or should strive to produce policies that are efficient in some technical economic sense.

So where does that leave the environmental economist? Why spend so much time and energy on questions of efficiency and cost-effectiveness when the political process most likely is going to override these considerations and go its own way? Why worry about economic incentives and economic efficiency when "everything is political," as the saying goes? The answer is that although we know that the real world is one of compromise and power, the best way for scientists and economists to serve that process is to produce studies that are as clear and as objective as possible. It is the politician's job to compromise or seek advantage; it is the scientist's job to provide the best information he or she can. For economists, in fact, this means studies in which economic efficiency is a central role, but it means more than this. Because the policy process is one where "who gets what" is a dominant theme, environmental economics also must deal with the distribution question, on how environmental problems and policies affect different groups within society. It is also the role of scientists and economists to provide information to policymakers on alternative courses of action. Although we will focus in later chapters on what appear to be "the" most efficient policies or "the" least-cost courses of

EXHIBIT 1-6

WHEN GREEN VALUES MEET WORLD COMMERCE

By Ron Scherer

A year ago, Home Depot sent a message to its wood suppliers: Start sending us Douglas fir, plywood, and mahogany that meet international "green" standards. Since Home Depot is the largest home-improvement business in the world, the message reverberated like the sound of an ax in the forest. Hundreds of vendors started searching for wood companies that respect the rights of indigenous people, avoid clear-cut logging, allow their workers to organize unions, and don't pollute. But is Home Depot's new preference for green two-by-fours and molding an impediment to trade? Or is the giant retailer's move something all consuming nations should start to require? The issue of green standards promises to be one of the most contentious debates facing the World Trade Organization (WTO), as it begins negotiating a trade agenda for the next millennium. The spur, say environmentalists, came when environmental standards were left out of the debate over the North American Free Trade Agreement. To make this point, thousands have converged on this environmentally aware community, where they are arguing that increased trade and economic activity is [sic] bad for the environ-

ment. At the very least, they want a moratorium on a new trade pact until an environmental-impact study can be completed. Business groups have set up newsrooms to offer sound bites that they, too, care about the environment—but also want to make money and provide jobs.

Both sides are adept at using statistics to bolster their case. Businessmen point to a 1996 World Bank study that found open (nontariffed) economies grow twice as fast as closed ones. "There is strong correlation between environmental performance and the national income of the citizens," says Scott Miller of U.S. Trade in Washington. "Rich countries protect the environment more than poor ones." Not so, say environmentalists, who argue that transnationals from rich countries are exploiting poor countries. Logging is one of the most contentious issues. The U.S. will present to the WTO a plan to remove all tariffs on forest products, initially in the developed world, later for developing countries. "Our concern is that it would lead to increased logging in some of the most sensitive and biological forests in places like Malaysia, Chile, and Indonesia," says Antonia Juhasz, head of international

---

action, it has to be recognized that in the give-and-take of the political world in which policy is actually made, choosing among alternatives is always the order of the day.

But economists have no right these days to bemoan their fate in the environmental policy process. If anything these are the days of the rising influence of economists. Benefit–cost procedures and results have become more widely accepted, in public policy arenas and in law courts hearing environmental cases. New pollution-control initiatives incorporating economic incentive principles are being adopted at both federal and state levels in the United States. All the more reason, then, to study and understand the basic economics of environmental analysis and policy.

trade and forest products for the American Lands Alliance. Forest-products organizations, however, counter that a Clinton administration environmental-impact study concluded that removing tariffs on logging would increase consumption only 2 percent by 2010 and would increase logging activity by only 0.5 percent. "Environmentalists are incensed they did not get the answer they wanted," says Michael Klien of American Forest and Paper Association, a Washington lobbying group.

Environmentalists are also concerned that the forestry industry will try to block the certification arrangements that companies such as Home Depot are turning toward. "The Home Depot campaign has terrified the forest industry," says Ms. Juhasz, adding that the companies fear such programs will be implemented nationwide. "The companies will get certification outlawed as a nontariff barrier." She cites a Minnesota decision to increase the recycled content of paper it buys for state business. But Canadian companies complained they would be ineligible under the new requirement. They threatened to take the issue to the WTO, says Juhasz, if Minnesota did not change its standards. Environmentalists blame the WTO for other decisions they say hurt the environment. For example, the U.S. required all imported shrimp be caught using special nets that allow sea turtles to escape. "The sea turtle is the best example of the conflict between trade and the environment," says a press release from the Sea Turtle Restoration Project based in San Francisco. But business groups say the U.S. sea-turtle law was flawed. The issue went to the WTO, which ruled the U.S. law was a nontariff barrier to trade. Mr. Esty says there's a middle ground to this trade and environment debate. For example, he argues that eliminating tariffs on agricultural products and phasing out trade-distorting subsidies would benefit the environment since it would make land use more efficient. And he would like to see the WTO eliminate all tariffs on goods and services that protect the environment. "The old school greens said world growth stresses the environment, but the new paradigm says growth can be beneficial if it is done in ways that are good for the environment." That's one of Home Depot's goals. But meeting that goal is not easy. A year after asking more than 5,000 suppliers to buy green-certified wood products, there is only one such item available in all Home Depots—a special order mahogany door. "It's something we hope to work with our suppliers over time," says Kim Woodbury, manager of environmental systems for the Atlanta-based company.

Source: Christian Science Monitor, November 30, 1999. Reprinted with permission of the *Christian Science Monitor,* © 1999, The Christian Science Publishing Society. All rights reserved.

SUMMARY

The purpose of this brief chapter was to whet your appetite for the subject of environmental economics by indicating some of the main topics that the field encompasses, showing very briefly the approach that economists take in studying them. It's also to give you something to remember. When we get involved in some of the conceptual and theoretical issues that underlie the topic, it is easy to lose sight of what we are trying to accomplish. We are trying to develop these principles so that we can actually use them to address real-world problems such as those discussed in this chapter. Although the principles may appear abstract and odd at first, remember the objective: to achieve a cleaner, healthier, and more beautiful natural environment.

SELECTED READINGS

Davies, J. Clarence, and Jan Mazurek: *Pollution Control in the United States, Evaluating the System*, Resources for the Future, Washington, DC, 1998.

Miller, Alan S.: *Gaia Connections: An Introduction to Ecology, Ecoethics, and Economics*, Rowman and Allenheld, Lanham, MD, 1991.

Portney, Paul R., and Robert N. Stavins (eds.): *Public Policies for Environmental Protection*, 2nd ed., Resources for the Future, Washington, DC, 2000.

Rosenbaum, Walter A.: *Environmental Politics and Policy*, 4th ed., Congressional Quarterly Press, Washington, DC, 1998.

Stavins, Robert N. (ed.): *Economics of the Environment Selected Readings*, 4th ed., W. W. Norton, New York, 1999.

Vig, Norman J., and Michael E. Kraft (eds.): *Environmental Policy: New Directions for the Twenty-First Century*, Fourth Edition, Congressional Quarterly Press, Washington, DC, 1999.

THE ECONOMY AND THE ENVIRONMENT

The **economy** is a collection of technological, legal, and social arrangements through which individuals in society seek to increase their material and spiritual well-being. The two elementary economic functions pursued by society are **production** and **consumption.** Production refers to all those activities that determine the quantities of goods and services that are produced and the technological and managerial means by which this production is carried out. Consumption refers to the way in which goods and services are divided up, or distributed, among the individuals and groups that make up society.

Any economic system exists within, and is encompassed by, the natural world. Its processes and changes are of course governed by the **laws of nature.** In addition, economies make use directly of natural assets of all types. One role the natural world plays is that of provider of raw materials and energy inputs, without which production and consumption would be impossible. Thus, one type of impact that an economic system has on nature is by drawing upon raw materials to keep the system functioning. Production and consumption activities also produce leftover waste products, called "residuals," and sooner or later these must find their way back into the natural world. Depending on how they are handled, these residuals may lead to pollution or the degradation of the natural environment. We can illustrate these fundamental relationships with a simple schematic:

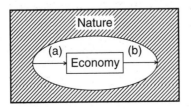

The link marked (a) represents raw materials flowing into production and consumption. The study of nature in its role as provider of raw materials is called **natural resource economics**. The link labeled (b) shows the impact of economic activity on the quality of the natural environment. The study of this residuals flow and its resultant impacts in the natural world comes under the heading of **environmental economics**. Although pollution control is the major topic within environmental economics, it is not the only one. Human beings have an impact on the environment in many ways that are not related to pollution in the traditional sense. Habitat disruption from housing developments and scenic degradation from any number of human activities are examples of environmental impacts that are not related to the discharge of specific pollutants.

The topic of this book is environmental economics. We will study the management of waste flows and the impacts of human activity on the quality of environmental assets. But in a real sense many of these problems originate in the earlier, raw material phase of the nature-economy interaction. So before proceeding we consider briefly the major dimensions of natural resource economics.

NATURAL RESOURCE ECONOMICS

In modern industrial/urban societies it is sometimes easy to overlook the fact that a large part of total economic activity still relies on the extraction and utilization of natural resources. **Natural resource economics** is the application of economic principles to the study of these activities. To get a general impression of what this discipline includes, the following is a list of its major subdivisions and examples of questions pursued in each one.[1]

Mineral economics: What is the appropriate rate at which to extract ore from a mine? How do exploration and the addition to reserves respond to mineral prices?

Forest economics: What is the appropriate rate to harvest timber? How do government policies affect the harvest rates pursued by timber companies?

Marine economics: What kinds of rules need to be established for managing fisheries? How do different harvest rates affect the stocks of fish?

Land economics: How do people in the private sector (builders, home purchasers) make decisions about the use of land? How do the laws of property rights and public land use regulations affect the way space is devoted to different uses?

Energy economics: What are the appropriate rates for extracting underground petroleum deposits? How sensitive is energy use to changes in energy prices?

Water economics: How do different water laws affect the way water is utilized by different people? What kinds of regulations should govern the reallocation of water from, for example, agriculture to urban users?

---

[1]Natural resource economics is the subject of a companion book written by one of the authors. See *Natural Resource Economics, An Introduction,* by Barry C. Field, McGraw-Hill, 2000.

Agricultural economics: How do farmers make decisions about using conservation practices in cultivating their land? How do government programs affect the choices farmers make regarding what crops to produce and how to produce them?

A fundamental distinction in natural resource economics is that of **renewable** and **nonrenewable** resources. The living resources, such as fisheries and timber, are renewable; they grow in time according to biological processes. Some nonliving resources are also renewable—the classic example being the sun's energy that reaches the earth. Nonrenewable resources are those for which there are no processes of replenishment—once used they are gone forever. Classic examples are petroleum reservoirs and nonenergy mineral deposits. Certain resources, such as many groundwater aquifers, have replenishment rates that are so low that they are in effect nonrenewable.

It is easy to see that the use of nonrenewable resources is a problem with a strong **intertemporal** dimension; it involves trade-offs between the present and the future. If more oil is pumped out of an underground deposit this year, less will be available to extract in future years. Establishing today's correct pumping rate, therefore, requires a comparison of the value of oil now with the anticipated value of oil in the future.

But complicated intertemporal trade-offs also exist with renewable resources. What should today's codfish harvesting rate be, considering that the size of the remaining stock will affect its future growth and availability? Should this timber be cut today or does its expected rate of growth warrant holding off harvesting until some time in the future? Biological and ecological processes create connections between the rates of resource use in the present and the quantity and quality of resources available to future generations. It is these connections that are the focus of what has come to be called **sustainability.**

A resource use rate that is "sustainable" is one that can be maintained over the long run without impairing the fundamental ability of the natural resource base to support future generations. Sustainability does not mean that resources must remain untouched; rather, it means that their rates of use be chosen so as not to jeopardize future generations. In the case of nonrenewable resources, this implies using the extracted resource in such a way that it contributes to the long-run economic and social health of the population. For renewable resources, it means establishing rates of use that are coordinated with the natural productivity rates affecting the way the resources grow and decline.

Many environmental problems also have strong intertemporal dimensions; that is, important trade-offs between today and the future. For example, many pollutants tend to accumulate in the environment rather than dissipate and disappear. Heavy metals, for example, can accumulate in water and soil. Carbon dioxide emissions over many decades have accumulated in the earth's atmosphere. What is in fact being depleted here is the earth's **assimilative capacity,** the ability of the natural system to accept certain pollutants and render them benign or inoffensive. Some of the theoretical ideas about the depletion of natural resources are also useful in understanding environmental pollution. In this sense "assimilative capacity" is a natural resource akin to traditional resources such as oil deposits and forests.

A resource that has only recently impressed itself upon us is one that resides not in any one substance but in a collection of elements: **biological diversity.** Biologists estimate that there may be as many as 30 million different species of living organisms in the world today. These represent a vast and important source of genetic information that is useful for the development of medicines, natural pesticides, resistant varieties of plants and animals, and so on. Human activities have substantially increased the rate of species extinctions, so habitat conservation and species preservation have become important contemporary resource problems.

One feature of the modern world is that the dividing line between natural resources and environmental resources is blurring in many cases. Many resource extraction processes, such as timber cutting and strip mining, have direct repercussions on environmental quality. In addition, there are many instances where environmental pollution or disruption has an impact on resource extraction processes. Estuarine water pollution that interferes with the replenishment of fish stocks is an example, as is air pollution that reduces agricultural yields. Furthermore, certain things, such as wildlife, may be considered both natural resources and attributes of the environment. In recent years there has been a substantial shift in public concern away from natural resource use in the traditional sense and toward **natural resource preservation.** This can be regarded both as a natural resource and an environmental decision.

Despite the very close connections, however, the distinction that economists have made between these two services of the natural world—as raw materials and as environment—is sufficiently strong and well developed that it makes sense for us to proceed with a book that focuses primarily on the latter. We begin by considering a somewhat more complicated version of the simple diagram depicted at the beginning of the chapter.

THE FUNDAMENTAL BALANCE

In this book you will find a lot of simple analytical "models" of situations that in reality are somewhat complex. A model is a way of trying to show the essential structure and relationships in something, without going into all of its details, much as a caricature of a person accentuates distinguishing features at the cost of all the details.

Figure 2-1 is a more complex rendering of the relationships shown at the beginning of the chapter. The elements within the circle are parts of the economic system, the whole of which is basically encapsulated within the natural environment. The economy has been divided into two broad segments, **producers** and **consumers.**

- The "producers" category includes all private firms that take inputs and convert them to outputs; it also includes units such as public agencies; nonprofit organizations; and firms producing services, such as transporta-

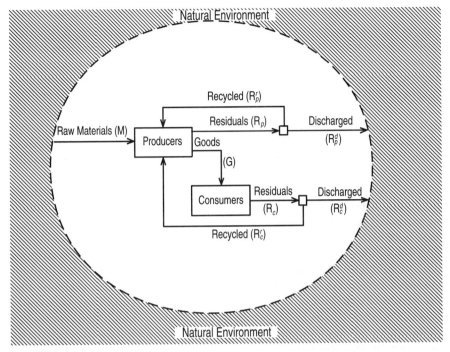

FIGURE 2-1
The Environment and the Economy.

tion. The primary inputs from the natural environment to the producing sector are materials, in the form of fuels, nonfuel minerals, and wood; fluids (e.g., water and petroleum); and gases of various types (e.g., natural gas and oxygen). All goods and services are derived from materials with the application of energy inputs.

- The "consumers" category includes all of the private households to whom the vast collection of final goods and services are distributed. One could argue that consumers sometimes use inputs directly from nature, like producers; many households, for example, get their water supplies directly from groundwater aquifers rather than water distribution companies. In the interest of keeping the model simple, however, we have not drawn this type of relationship.

It needs to be kept in mind that "producers" and "consumers" actually consist of the same people in different capacities. The "us vs. them" quality that characterizes many environmental disputes is really an internal disagreement within a single group. Society as a whole is essentially in the same position as a single household that pumps water from its own well and discharges wastes into its own septic system, which happens to be near the well.

Production and consumption create **residuals,** which is another way of saying leftovers. It includes all types of material residuals that may be emitted into the air or water or disposed of on land. The list is incredibly long: sulfur dioxide, volatile organic compounds, toxic solvents, animal manure, pesticides, particulate matter of all types, waste building materials, heavy metals, and so on. Waste energy in the form of heat and noise, and radioactivity, which has characteristics of both material and energy, are also important production residuals. Consumers are also responsible for enormous quantities of residuals, chief among which are domestic sewage and automobile emissions. All materials in consumer goods must eventually end up as leftovers, even though they may be recycled along the way. These are the source of large quantities of solid waste as well as hazardous materials such as toxic chemicals and used oil.

Let us first consider the question of production and consumption residuals from a strictly physical standpoint. Figure 2-1 shows raw materials and energy being extracted from the natural environment (M) and residuals being discharged back into the environment.

In the early days of environmental concern, the main focus was on the end flows of discharged residuals by producers (R_p^d) and by consumers (R_c^d). By treating these residuals and otherwise changing the time and place of discharge, their impacts on humans and the environment could be substantially changed. While this is still an important locus of activity, recent years have seen a broadening of perspective to what is called **environmental management.**

To appreciate this broadening of focus, let us consider the flows of Figure 2-1 in greater detail. From physics, the law of the conservation of matter assures us that, in the long run, these two flows must be equal. In terms of the symbols of Figure 2-1:[2]

$$M = R_p^d + R_c^d$$

We must say "in the long run" for several reasons. If the system is growing, it can retain some proportion of the natural inputs, which go toward increasing the size of the system through a growing population, the accumulation of capital equipment, and so on. These would be disposed of if and when the system ceases to grow. Also, recycling can obviously delay the disposal of residuals. But recycling can never be perfect; each cycle must lose some proportion of the recycled material. Thus, the fundamental **materials/energy balance** equation must hold in the long run. This shows us something very fundamental: To reduce the mass of residuals disposed of in the natural environment, it is necessary to reduce the quantity of raw materials taken into the system.[3] To look more closely at the various options for doing this, substitute for M. According to the flow diagram,

$$R_p^d + R_c^d = M = G + R_p - R_p^r - R_c^r$$

---

[2]To make these direct comparisons all flows must be expressed in terms of mass.
[3]Note that $G = R_c$, that is, everything that flows to the consumption sector eventually ends up as a residual from that sector.

which says that the quantity of raw materials (M) is equal to output of goods and services (G) plus production residuals (R_p), minus the amounts that are recycled from producers (R_p^r) and consumers (R_c^r). There are essentially three ways of reducing M and, therefore, residuals discharged into the natural environment.

Reduce G   Assuming the other flows stay the same, we can reduce residuals discharged by reducing the quantity of goods and services produced in the economy. Some people have fastened on this as the best long-run answer to environmental degradation; reducing output, or at least stopping its rate of growth, would allow a similar change in the quantity of residuals discharged. Some have sought to reach this goal by advocating "zero population growth" (ZPG).[4] A slowly growing or stationary population can make it easier to control environmental impacts, but for two reasons it does not in any way ensure this control. First, a stationary population can grow economically, thus increasing its demand for raw materials. Second, environmental impacts can be long run and cumulative, so that even a stationary population can gradually degrade the environment in which it finds itself. It is certainly true, however, that population growth will often exacerbate the environmental impacts of a particular economy. In the U.S. economy, for example, although the emissions of pollutants per car have dramatically decreased over the last few decades through better emissions-control technology, the sheer growth in the number of cars on the highways has led to an increase in the total quantity of automobile emissions in many regions.

Reduce R_p   Another way of reducing M, and therefore residuals discharged, is to reduce R_p. Assuming the other flows are held constant, this means essentially changing the amounts of production residuals produced for a given quantity of output produced. There are basically only two ways of doing this.

- Reduce the **residuals intensity of production** in all sectors of the economy by inventing and adopting new production technologies and practices that leave smaller amounts of residuals per unit of output produced. For example, in later discussions of CO_2 emissions and atmospheric warming, we will see that there is much that can be done to reduce the CO_2 output per unit of output produced, especially by shifting to different fuels, but also by reducing (actually by continuing to reduce) the quantities of energy required to produce a unit of final output. This approach has come to be called **pollution prevention, or source reduction.**
- Shift the composition of final output; that is, reduce those sectors that have relatively high residuals per unit of output and expand those sectors that produce relatively few residuals per unit of output. Output G actually consists of

---

[4]For example, see Herman E. Daly, *Steady State Economics, Second Edition with New Essays,* Island Press, Washington, DC, 1991.

a large number of different goods and services, with great differences among them in terms of the residuals left after they are produced. So another way to reduce the total quantity of residuals is to shift the composition of G away from high-residuals items and toward low-residuals items, while leaving the total intact. The shift from primarily a manufacturing economy toward services is a step in this direction. This is called a **sectoral shift,** because it changes the relative shares of the different economic sectors in the aggregate economy. The rise of the so-called information sectors is another example. It is not that these new sectors produce no significant residuals; indeed, some of them may produce harsher leftovers than we have known before. The computer industry, for example, uses a variety of chemical solvents for cleaning purposes. But on the whole these sectors probably have a smaller waste disposal problem than the traditional industries they have replaced.

Increase ($R_p^r + R_c^r$) The third possibility is to increase recycling. Instead of discharging production and consumption residuals into the environment, they can be recycled back into the production process. What this shows is that the central role of recycling is to replace a portion of the original flow of virgin materials (M). By substituting recycled materials for virgin materials, the quantity of residuals discharged can be reduced while maintaining the rate of output of goods and services (G). In modern economies recycling offers great opportunities to reduce waste flows. But we have to remember that recycling can never be perfect, even if enormous resources were devoted to the task. Production processes usually transform the physical structure of materials inputs, making them difficult to use again. The process of energy conversion changes the chemical structure of energy materials so thoroughly that recycling is impossible. In addition, recycling processes themselves can create residuals. But materials research will continue to progress and discover new ways of recycling. For a long time, automobile tires could not be recycled because the original production process changed the physical structure of the rubber. But recently new technological means have been found so that vast quantities of used tires, instead of blighting the landscape, can be incorporated into park benches, roads, and other products.

These fundamental relationships are very important. We must remember, however, that our ultimate goal is to reduce the damages caused by the discharge of production and consumption residuals. Reducing the total quantity of these residuals is one major way of doing this, and the relationships discussed indicate the basic ways this may be done. But damages also can be reduced by working directly on the stream of residuals, a fact that must be kept in mind in our later discussions.

THE ENVIRONMENT AS AN ECONOMIC AND SOCIAL ASSET

Inputs of natural resources have always been recognized as important in economic production. Environmental quality also may be thought of as a **productive asset** for a society. The productivity of the natural environment lies in its

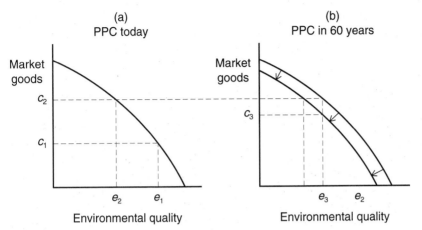

FIGURE 2-2
Production Possibility Curves for Current and Future Generations.

ability to support and enrich human life, as well as, in some cases, its ability to assimilate and render less harmful the waste products of the economic system. The quality of the environmental asset is directly affected by the quantities and types of residuals discharged from the economy.

One way of thinking about this is in terms of a **trade-off** between conventional economic output (conventional goods and services such as cars, loaves of bread, insurance policies, etc.) and environmental quality. A trade-off of this type is depicted in Figure 2-2. Consider first panel (a). This shows a **production possibility curve** (PPC), which is simply a curve showing the different combinations of two things a society may produce at any time, given its resources and technological capabilities. The vertical axis has an index of the aggregate output of an economy; that is, the total market value of conventional economic goods traded in the economy in a year. The horizontal axis has an index of environmental quality, derived from data on different dimensions of the ambient environment; for example, airborne SO_2 concentrations, urban noise levels, and water quality data. The curved relationship shows the different combinations of these two outcomes—marketed output and environmental quality—that are available to a group of people who have a fixed endowment of resources and technology with which to work.[5]

The exact shape and location of the production possibility curve are determined by the **technical capacities** in the economy, together with the ecological facts—meteorology, hydrology, and so on—of the natural system in which the society is situated. It says, for example, that if the current level of economic output is c_1, an increase to c_2 can be obtained only at the cost of a decrease in environmental quality from e_1 to e_2. One major objective of any society, of course, is

---

[5]The extremes of the PPC are drawn with dashed lines. It's not clear what an outcome would be with "zero" environmental quality, nor with "zero" economic output. Thus, these extreme points are essentially undefined, and we focus on points in the interior of the diagram.

to change the production possibility curve so that the underlying trade-off is more favorable; in other words, so that a given economic output is consistent with higher levels of environmental quality.

Although the PPC itself is a technical constraint, where a society chooses to locate itself on its PPC is a matter of **social choice.** This depends on the values that people in that society place on conventional economic output as opposed to environmental quality. Where values come from is an open question, but it is clear that values differ from one person to another and even for the same person at different points in time. The study of the values that people place on environmental factors is a major part of environmental economics and will be discussed in more detail in Chapters 7 and 8.

Another matter of concern is that current measures of **aggregate economic output** typically contain only measures of quantities of market goods. This is because the prices of these goods and services are provided by the markets in which they are traded, so their aggregate values can be assessed quite easily. Environmental quality, on the other hand, is generally a **nonmarket** type of outcome, in the sense that elements of environmental quality do not trade directly on markets where prices could be evaluated. If a society puts too much stress on increasing its measured output, it may end up at a point like (c_2, e_2) in Figure 2-2 (panel a), even though true social welfare may be higher at a point like (c_1, e_1).

Production possibility curves also can be used to elucidate other aspects of social choice about the environment. One of the fundamental distinctions that can be made in environmental analysis and the development of environmental policy is that between the **short run** and the **long run.** Short-run decisions are those made on the basis of consequences that happen in the near term or of impacts as they are felt by the present generation. Long-run decisions are those in which attention is paid to consequences that occur well into the future or to future generations. There is a widespread feeling that economic decisions today are being made primarily through short-run considerations, where environmental policy needs to be made with long-run considerations in mind. A good way of thinking about this is through the use of production possibility curves, introduced earlier in this chapter.

Consider again Figure 2-2. The two panels actually show production possibility curves for two time periods. Panel (a) shows the trade-offs facing the current generation. Panel (b) shows the production possibility curves for people in, say 60 to 80 years, the generation consisting of your great grandchildren. According to panel (a), the present generation could choose combinations (c_1, e_1), (c_2, e_2), or any others on the curve. But the future is not independent of the choice made today. It is conceivable, for example, that degrading the environment too much today will affect future possibilities—by depleting certain important resources, by pollution that is so high it causes irreversible damage, or simply by a pollutant that is very long-lived and affects future generations. In effect this could shift the future PPC back from where it otherwise would be. This is depicted in panel (b) of the diagram. Your grandchildren will be confronted with a reduced set of possibilities as compared to the choices we face today. The future generation, finding itself on the inner production possibilities curve, can still have the same level of marketed output we have today (c_2), but only at a lower level of environmental quality (e_3) than we have today. Alternatively, it could enjoy the same level of environmental quality, but only with a reduced level of marketed output (c_3).

It needs to be recognized, of course, that the influence of today's decisions on future production possibilities is much more complicated than this discussion might suggest. It's not only environmental degradation that affects future conditions, but also technical developments and changes in human capacities. Thus, today's decisions could shift the future PPC either in or out, depending on many dynamic factors that are hard to predict. But we need to be particularly alert to avoid decisions today that would have the effect of shifting the future PPC to the left. This is the essence of recent discussions about **sustainability.** Sustainability means that future production possibility curves are not adversely affected by what is done today. It does not mean that we must maximize environmental quality today, because that implies zero output of goods and services. It means simply that environmental impacts need to be reduced enough today to avoid shifting future production possibility curves back in comparison to today's production possibilities. We will meet the idea of sustainability at several points throughout this book.

TERMINOLOGY

Throughout the chapters that follow we use the following terms:

- **Ambient quality:** "Ambient" refers to the surrounding environment, so ambient quality refers to the quantity of pollutants in the environment; for example, the concentration of SO_2 in the air over a city or the concentration of a particular chemical in the waters of a lake.
- **Environmental quality:** A term used to refer broadly to the state of the natural environment. This includes the notion of ambient quality and such things as the visual and aesthetic quality of the environment.
- **Residuals:** Material that is left over after something has been produced. A plant, for example, takes in a variety of raw materials and converts these into some product. Materials and energy left after the product has been produced are *production residuals. Consumption residuals* are what is left over after consumers have finished using the products that contained or otherwise used these materials.
- **Emissions:** The portion of production or consumption residuals that are placed in the environment, sometimes directly, sometimes after treatment.
- **Recycling:** The process of returning some or all of the production or consumption residuals to be used again in production or consumption.
- **Pollutant:** A substance, energy form, or action that, when introduced into the natural environment, results in a lowering of the ambient quality level. We want to think of this as including not only the traditional things, such as oil spilled into oceans or chemicals placed in the air, but

also activities, such as certain building developments, that result in "visual pollution."

- **Effluent:** Sometimes "effluent" is used to talk about water pollutants, and emissions to refer to air pollutants, but in this book these two words are used interchangeably.
- **Pollution:** Pollution is actually a tricky word to define. Some people might say that pollution results when any amount, no matter how small, of a residual has been introduced into the environment. Others hold that pollution is something that happens only when the ambient quality of the environment has been degraded enough to cause some damage.
- **Damages:** The negative impacts produced by environmental pollution on people in the form of health effects, visual degradation, and so on, and on elements of the ecosystem through disruption of ecological linkages, species extinctions, and so forth.
- **Environmental medium:** Broad dimensions of the natural world that collectively constitute the environment, usually classified as land, water, and air.
- **Source:** The location at which emissions occur, such as a factory, an automobile, or a leaking landfill.

EMISSIONS, AMBIENT QUALITY, AND DAMAGES

Let us now focus on what happens at the end of those two discharge arrows at the right side of Figure 2-1. Very simply, **emissions** produce changes in ambient levels of environmental quality, which in turn cause damages to humans and nonhumans. Figure 2-3 shows one way of sketching out this relationship. It shows n sources of emissions;[6] they might be private firms, government agencies, or consumers. Sources take in various inputs and use different types of technologies in production and consumption. In the process they produce residuals. How these residuals are handled then has a critical effect on subsequent stages. Some may be recovered and recycled back into production or consumption. Many can be put through treatment processes (residuals handling) that can render them more benign when emitted. Some of these processes are strictly physical (mufflers on cars and trucks, settling ponds at wastewater treatment plants, catalytic converters); others involve chemical transformations of various types (advanced treatment of domestic wastewater).

All emissions must necessarily go into one or more of the different **environmental media,** and there is an important relationship among them. There is a natural tendency in policy deliberations to keep these different media in separate compartments, dealing with air pollution separately from water pollution, and so on. But they are obviously interconnected; once residuals are produced, all that are not recycled must end up being discharged into one or more of the

---

[6]In economic writing, the letter n is often used to designate an unspecified number of items, the exact value of which will vary from one situation to another.

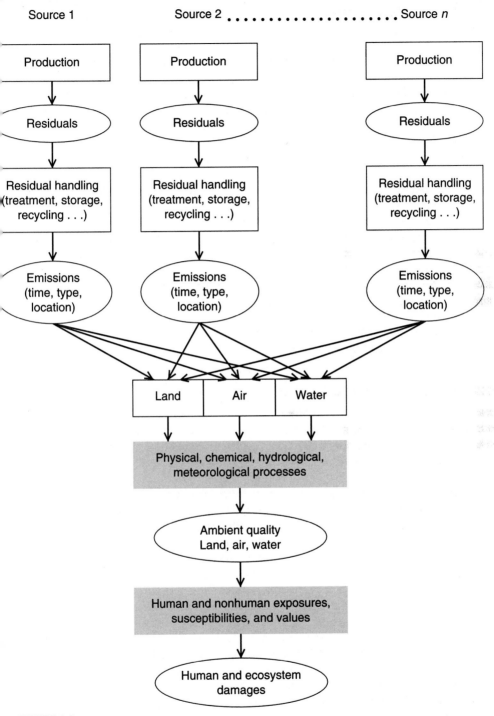

FIGURE 2-3
Emissions, Ambient Quality, and Damages. *(Inspired by John B. Braden and Kathleen Segerson, "Information Problems in the Design of Non-point Source Pollution Policy," in Association of Environmental and Resource Economics (AERE) Workshop Papers,* The Management of Non-point Source Pollution, *Lexington. June 6–7, 1991.)*

different media. Thus, for a given quantity of total residuals, if the amounts going into one medium are reduced, the amounts going into the others must necessarily increase. When sulfur dioxide (SO_2) is removed from the stack gases of power plants, for example, the sulfur compounds have not been destroyed. Instead, we end up with a sulfurous sludge that must be disposed of some other way, perhaps by land burial. If this material is incinerated, airborne emissions result, but there will still be certain quantities of solid residuals that must be disposed of elsewhere.

The streams of emissions come from the many different sources, but once emitted they merge into a single flow. In the real world this mixing may be complete; for example, the effluent from two pulp mills located at the same point on a river may mix so thoroughly that a few miles downstream it is impossible to differentiate one source's effluent from the other's. When there are a million or so cars moving about an urban area, the emissions from all become uniformly mixed together. In other cases the mixing is less than complete. If one power plant is just outside the city and another is 20 miles upwind, the closer plant will normally bear a greater responsibility for deteriorating air quality in the city than the other.

This mixing of emissions is a more significant problem than might first appear. With just a single source, the line of responsibility is clear, and to get an improvement in ambient quality we know exactly whose emissions have to be controlled. But with multiple sources, responsibilities become less clear. We may know how much we want to cut back total emissions, but the problem of distributing this total reduction among the different sources still exists. Each source then has an incentive to get the others to bear a larger share of the burden of reducing emissions. With every source thinking along the same lines, pollution control programs face a real problem of design and enforcement. We will run into this problem many times in the chapters to come.

Once a given quantity and quality of residuals have been introduced into a particular environmental medium, it is the physical, chemical, biological, meteorological, and so on, processes of the natural system that determine how the residuals translate into particular **ambient quality levels.** For example, wind and temperature conditions will affect whether and how residuals emitted into the air affect nearby neighborhoods, as well as people living farther downwind. In addition, because these meteorological conditions vary from day to day, the same level of emissions can produce different ambient quality levels at different times. Acid rain is produced through chemical processes acting primarily on sulfur dioxide emissions emitted far upwind; smog is also the result of complex chemical reactions involving sunlight and quantities of various pollutants. Underground hydrological processes affect the transportation of materials disposed of in landfills. And so on. Thus, to know how particular emissions will affect ambient quality levels, we must have a good understanding of the physical and chemical workings of the environment itself. This is where the natural and physical sciences come in—to study the full range of environmental phenomena, from small, localized models of groundwater flow in a particular aquifer, to complex models of large lakes and river basins, to studies of interregional wind patterns, to global climate models. The fundamental goal is to determine how particular patterns of emissions are translated into corresponding patterns of ambient quality levels.

Finally, there are **damages.** A given set of ambient conditions translates into particular exposure patterns for living and nonliving systems. Of course, these exposures are a function not only of the physical processes involved, but also of the human choices that are made about where and how to live, and of the susceptibilities of living and nonliving systems to varying environmental conditions. Lastly, damages are related to human values. Human beings do not have amorphous preferences over all possible outcomes of the economic/environmental interaction; they prefer some outcomes over others. A major part of environmental economics is trying to determine the relative values that people place on these different environmental outcomes, a subject to which we will turn in later chapters on benefit–cost analysis.

TYPES OF POLLUTANTS

Physically, the residuals identified in Figure 2-3 consist of a vast assortment of materials and energy flowing into the three environmental media. It is helpful to distinguish among broad types of emissions according to factors that critically affect their economic characteristics.

Cumulative vs. Noncumulative Pollutants

One simple and important dimension of environmental pollutants is whether they accumulate over time or tend to dissipate soon after being emitted. The classic case of a **noncumulative pollutant** is noise; as long as the source operates, noise is emitted into the surrounding air, but as soon as the source is shut down, the noise stops. At the other end of the spectrum there are pollutants that cumulate in the environment in nearly the same amounts as they are emitted. Radioactive waste, for example, decays over time but at such a slow rate in relation to human life spans that for all intents and purposes it will be with us permanently; it is a strictly cumulative type of pollutant. Another **cumulative pollutant** is plastics. The search for a degradable plastic has been going on for decades, but so far plastic is a substance that decays very slowly by human standards; thus, what we dispose of will be in the environment permanently. Many chemicals are cumulative pollutants; once emitted they are basically with us forever.

Between these two ends of the spectrum there are many types of effluent that are to some extent, but not completely, cumulative. The classic case is organic matter emitted into water bodies; for example, the wastes, treated or not, emitted from municipal waste treatment plants. Once emitted the wastes are subject to natural chemical processes that tend to break down the organic materials into their constituent elements, thus rendering them much more benign. The water, in other words, has a natural assimilative capacity that allows it to accept organic substances and render them less harmful. As long as this assimilative capacity has not been exceeded in any particular case, the effluent source can be shut off, and in a few days, weeks, or months the water quality will return to normal. Once emissions exceed this assimilative capacity, however, the process becomes cumulative.

Whether a pollutant is cumulative or noncumulative, the basic problem is essentially the same: trying to figure out the environmental damages and relating these back to the costs of reducing emissions. But this job is much more difficult for cumulative than for noncumulative pollutants. With noncumulative emissions, ambient concentrations are strictly a function of current emissions—reducing these emissions to zero would lead to zero ambient concentrations. But with cumulative pollutants the relationship is more complex. The fact that a pollutant cumulates over time in the environment has the effect of breaking the direct connection between current emissions and current damages. This has a number of implications. For one thing it makes the science more difficult. The cause-and-effect relationships become harder to isolate when there is a lot of time intervening between them. It also may make it more difficult to get people to focus on damages from today's emissions, again because there may only be a weak connection between today's emissions and today's ambient quality levels. Furthermore, cumulative pollutants by definition lead to future damages, and human beings have shown a depressing readiness to discount future events and avoid coming to grips with them in the present.

Local vs. Regional and Global Pollutants

Some emissions have an impact only in restricted, localized regions, whereas others have an impact over wider regions, perhaps on the global environment. Noise pollution and the degradation of the visual environment are local in their impacts; the damages from any particular source are usually limited to relatively small groups of people in a circumscribed region. Note that this is a statement about how widespread the effects are from any particular pollution source, not about how important the overall problem is throughout a country or the world. Many pollutants, on the other hand, have widespread impacts, over a large region or perhaps over the global environment. Acid rain is a regional problem; emissions in one region of the United States (and of Europe) affect people in other parts of the country or region. The ozone-depleting effects of chlorofluorocarbon emissions from various countries work through chemical changes in the earth's stratosphere, which means that the impacts are truly global.

Other things being equal, local environmental problems ought to be easier to deal with than regional or national problems, which in turn ought to be easier to manage than global problems. If I smoke out my neighbor with my wood stove, we may be able to arrange a solution among ourselves, or we can call on local political institutions to do it. But if my behavior causes more distant pollution, solutions may be more difficult. If we are within the same political system, we can call on these institutions to arrange solutions. In recent years, however, we have been encountering a growing number of international and global environmental issues. Here we are far from having effective means of responding, both because the exact nature of the physical impacts is difficult to describe and because the requisite international political institutions are only beginning to appear.

Point-Source vs. Nonpoint-Source Pollutants

Pollution sources differ in terms of the ease with which actual points of discharge may be identified. The points at which sulfur dioxide emissions leave a large power plant are easy to identify; they come out the end of the smokestacks associated with each plant. Municipal waste treatment plants normally have a single outfall from which all of the wastewater is discharged. These are called **point-source pollutants.** There are many pollutants for which there are no well-defined points of discharge. Agricultural chemicals, for example, usually run off the land in a dispersed or defused pattern, and even though they may pollute specific streams or underground aquifers, there is no single pipe or stack from which these chemicals are emitted. This is a **nonpoint-source** type of pollutant. Urban storm water runoff is also an important nonpoint-source problem.

As one would expect, point-source pollutants are likely to be easier to come to grips with than nonpoint-source pollutants. They will probably be easier to measure and monitor and easier to study in terms of the connections between emissions and impacts. This means that it will ordinarily be easier to develop and administer control policies for point-source pollutants. As we will see, not all pollutants fit neatly into one or another of these categories.

Continuous vs. Episodic Emissions

Emissions from electric power plants or municipal waste treatment plants are more or less continuous. The plants are designed to be in operation continuously, although the operating rate may vary somewhat over the day, week, or season. Thus, the emissions from these operations are more or less continuous, and the policy problem is to manage the rate of these discharges. Immediate comparisons can be made between control programs and rates of emissions. The fact that emissions are continuous does not mean that damages are also continuous, however. Meteorological and hydrological events can turn continuous emissions into uncertain damages. But control programs are often easier to carry out when emissions are not subject to large-scale fluctuations.

Many pollutants are emitted on an episodic basis, however. The classic example is accidental oil or chemical spills. The policy problem here is to design and manage a system so that the probability of accidental discharges is reduced. Yet, with an episodic effluent there may be nothing to measure, at least in the short run. Even though there have been no large-scale radiation releases from U.S. nuclear power plants, for example, there is still a "pollution" problem if they are being managed in such a way as to increase the **probability** of an accidental release in the future. To measure the probabilities of episodic emissions, it is necessary to have data on actual occurrences over a long time period or to estimate them from engineering data and similar information. We then have to determine how much insurance we wish to have against these episodic events.

Environmental Damages Not Related to Emissions

So far the discussion has focused on the characteristics of different types of environmental pollutants as they relate to the discharge of residual materials or energy, but there are many important instances of deteriorating environmental quality that are not traceable to residuals discharges. The conversion of land to housing and commercial areas destroys the environmental value of that land, whether it be its ecosystem value, such as habitat or wetland, or its scenic value. Other land uses, such as logging or strip mining, also can have important impacts. In cases such as these, the policy problem is still to understand the incentives of people whose decisions create these impacts and to change these incentives when appropriate. Although there are no physical emissions to monitor and control, there are nevertheless outcomes that can be described, evaluated, and managed with appropriate policies.

SUMMARY

The purpose of this chapter was to explore some basic linkages between the economy and the environment. We differentiated between the role of the natural system as a supplier of raw material inputs for the economy and as a receptor for production and consumption residuals. The first of these is normally called natural resource economics and the second environmental economics. After a very brief review of natural resource economics, we introduced the fundamental balance phenomenon, which says that in the long run all materials taken by human beings out of the natural system must eventually end up back in that system. This means that to reduce residuals flows into the environment we must reduce materials taken from the ecosystem, and we discussed the three fundamental ways that this can be done. This led into a discussion of the inherent trade-off that exists between conventional economic goods and environmental quality and between current and future generations.

We then focused more directly on the flow of residuals back into the environment, making a distinction among emissions, ambient environmental quality, and damages. The environmental damages from a given quantity of emissions can be very substantially altered by handling these emissions in different ways. Our next step was to provide a brief catalogue of the different types of emissions and pollutants, as well as nonpollution types of environmental impacts such as aesthetic effects.

QUESTIONS FOR FURTHER DISCUSSION

1 Economies grow by investing in new sources of productivity, new plants and equipment, infrastructure such as roads, and so on. How does this type of investment affect the flows depicted in Figure 2-1?

2 What is the difference between a "residual" and a "pollutant"? Illustrate this in the context of a common airborne emission such as sulfur dioxide (SO_2); with noise; with junked automobiles; with an unsightly building.

3 Why are long-lived, cumulative pollutants so much harder to manage than short-lived, noncumulative pollutants?

4 What is the relationship between "damages" from environmental pollutants and human values?

5 What considerations come into play when considering whether the United States or any other political entity is spending the "right" amount for environmental quality improvements?

WEBSITES

For an introduction to issues in environmental economics, see the website of Resources for the Future, **www.rff.org;** for another good source of material of this type see the reports of the Congressional Research Service, **www.cnie.org/nle/crs_main.html.**

SELECTED READINGS

Ayres, Robert U.: *Resources, Environment and Economics, Applications of the Materials/ Energy Balance Principle,* John Wiley and Sons, New York, 1978.

Ayres, Robert U., and Udo E. Simonis: *Industrial Metabolism: Restructuring for Sustainable Development,* United Nations University Press, New York, 1994.

Baumol, William, and Wallace Oates: *Economics, Environmental Policy and the Quality of Life,* Prentice Hall, Englewood Cliffs, NJ, 1979.

Enthoven, Alain C., and A. Myrick Freeman III (eds.): *Pollution, Resources and the Environment,* Norton, New York, 1973.

Kneese, Allen V.: *Economics of the Environment,* Penguin Books, New York, 1977.

Kneese, Allen V., and Blair T. Bower: *Environmental Quality and Residuals Management,* Johns Hopkins Press for Resources for the Future, Baltimore, MD, 1979.

Krutilla, John V.: "Conservation Reconsidered," *American Economic Review,* 57(4), September 1967, pp. 777–786.

Pearce, David, Anil Markandya, and Edward B. Barbier: *Blueprint for a Green Economy,* Earthscan Publications, London, 1989.

ANALYTICAL TOOLS

Scientific analysis consists of giving coherent explanations of relevant events and of showing how other outcomes might have occurred if conditions had been different. It is to show connections among variables and to detail the ways in which they are interrelated. To do this, a science must develop a specialized vocabulary and conceptual structure with which to focus on its chosen subject matter. In this section we cover some of the basic ideas of economics and of their application to environmental problems. Those of you who have already been introduced to microeconomics can treat the next few chapters as a review. For those who are seeing this material for the first time, remember that the purpose is to develop a set of "analytical tools" that can then be used to focus on issues of environmental quality.

BENEFITS AND COSTS, SUPPLY AND DEMAND

This and the next chapter contain discussions of certain basic tools of **micro-economics.** The objective is to provide enough of an understanding of fundamental concepts that they can be used later in analyzing environmental impacts and policies. The current chapter is about benefits and costs. The juxtaposition of these two words indicates that we are going to approach things in a **trade-off,** or **balancing,** mode. Economic actions, including environmental actions, have two sides: On the one side they create value and on the other side they encounter costs. Thus, we must have basic concepts that deal with these two parts of the problem. We look first at the question of value, later at costs.

It needs to be mentioned at the very outset that microeconomic theory is **abstract.** This means that it normally proceeds with simplified models that try to capture the essence of a problem without all the details that one observes in the real world. The reason for this is that we want to reveal basic connections and relationships among the important elements of a problem, relationships that are difficult to see if we just observe the surface richness of the real world. There are dangers in this, of course; one can inadvertently overlook details that do have an important impact in reality. For example, in the past many environmental models have been developed without considering the costs of actually enforcing environmental laws. But in the real world, **enforcement costs** are more than a detail; they can have a great impact on the outcomes of environmental regulations. Thus, we need to be careful that our abstractions truly serve to reveal basic connections and do not cover up important dimensions of problems we are trying to understand.

WILLINGNESS TO PAY

The value side of the analysis is based on the fundamental notion that individuals have **preferences** for goods and services; given a choice, they can express preferences for one good over another or one bundle of goods over another bundle. How to make visible this abstract notion of preference? We need to simplify the discussion; in a modern economy there are thousands of different goods and services available, so let us focus on just one of them. We now can present the following fundamental concept: The value of this good to a person is what the person is willing and able to sacrifice for it. Sacrifice what? It could be anything, but it makes most sense to talk about sacrificing generalized purchasing power. Thus, the fundamental idea of value is tied to **willingness to pay;** the value of a good to somebody is what that person is **willing to pay** for it.[1]

What determines how much a person is willing to pay to obtain some good or service or some environmental asset? It's partly a question of **individual values.** Some people are willing to sacrifice a lot to visit the Grand Canyon; others are not. Some people are willing to pay a lot for a quiet living environment; others are not. Some people place a high value on trying to preserve the habitat of unique animal and plant species; others do not. It is obvious also that a person's **wealth** affects the willingness to sacrifice; the wealthier a person is, the better that person can afford to pay for various goods and services. Willingness to pay, in other words, also reflects **ability to pay.**

Let's consider the willingness to pay of a person for a particular good. We want to build a graphic picture of willingness to pay for various amounts of this good. Assume that the person has none of the good to begin with. We ask her, or perhaps deduce from watching her spend her money, how much she would be willing to pay for a single unit of a good rather than go without. Suppose this is some number, such as $38 pictured in the top of Figure 3-1. We then ask, assuming she already has one unit of this good, how much she would be willing to pay for a second unit. According to Figure 3-1 her answer is $26. In similar fashion, her willingness to pay for each additional unit is shown by the height of the rectangle above that unit: $17 for unit 3, $12 for unit 4, and so on. These numbers depict a fundamental relationship of economics: the notion of diminishing willingness to pay. As the number of units consumed increases, the willingness to pay for additional units of that good normally goes down.

It is not very convenient to work with diagrams that are step-shaped as in the top of Figure 3-1. So we now change things a bit by assuming that people can consume fractions of items in addition to integer values (e.g., as in the number of pounds of bananas consumed per week). What this does is produce a smoothly shaped willingness-to-pay curve, such as the one pictured in the bottom of Figure 3-1. In effect the steps in the willingness-to-pay curve have become too small to see, yielding a smooth curve to work with. On this smooth

---

[1]It may sound as though we are limiting the analysis only to physical goods and services, but this is not true. The concept of willingness to pay is quite general, and in Chapter 5 we will apply it to differing levels of environmental quality.

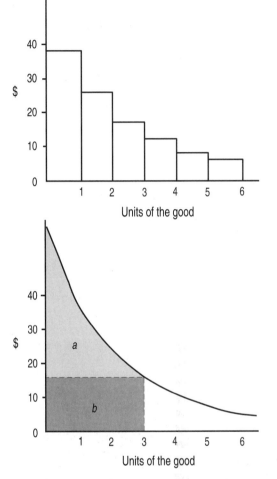

FIGURE 3-1
The Concept of Willingness to Pay.

function we have singled out one quantity for illustrative purposes. It shows that the willingness to pay for the third unit is $17.

The next step is to distinguish between total and marginal willingness to pay. Suppose a person is already consuming two units of this good; according to the willingness-to-pay curve, that person would be willing to pay $17 for a third unit. This is the **marginal willingness to pay**—in this case, for the third unit. Marginal is thus a word that describes the *additional* willingness to pay of a person for one more unit. So the height of the rectangles in the top of Figure 3-1 and the height of the curve in the bottom graph show the marginal willingness to pay for this good.

The **total willingness to pay** for a given consumption level refers to the total amount a person would be willing to pay to attain that consumption level rather than go without the good entirely. Suppose the person is consuming at a level of three units; her total willingness to pay for consuming this quantity is

$81, which is in fact the sum of the heights of the demand rectangles between the origin and the consumption level in question ($38 for the first plus $26 for the second plus $17 for the third). This corresponds, in the smooth version of the willingness-to-pay function, to the whole area under the willingness-to-pay curve from the origin up to the quantity in question. For three units of consumption, the total willingness to pay is equal to an amount represented by the combined areas *a* and *b*.

Demand

There is another way of looking at these marginal willingness-to-pay relationships. They are more familiarly known as **demand curves.** An individual demand curve shows the quantity of a good or service that the individual in question would demand (i.e., purchase and consume) at any particular price. For example, suppose a person whose marginal willingness-to-pay/demand curve is shown in the bottom part of Figure 3-1 is able to purchase this item at a unit price of $17. The quantity he would demand at this price is three units. The reason is that his marginal willingness to pay for each of the first three units exceeds the purchase price. He would not push his consumption higher than this because his marginal willingness to pay for additional quantities would be less than the purchase price.

An individual's demand/marginal willingness-to-pay curve for a good or service is a way of summarizing his personal consumption attitudes and capabilities for that good. Thus, we would normally expect these relationships to differ somewhat among individuals, because individual tastes and preferences vary. Some people are willing to pay more for a given item than other people. Figure 3-2 displays several different demand curves. Panel (a) shows two demand curves, one steeper than the other. The steeper one shows a situation in which marginal willingness to pay drops off fairly rapidly as the quantity consumed increases; while the flatter one shows marginal willingness to pay which, although lower to begin with, goes down less rapidly as quantity increases. These two demand curves could represent the case of one consumer

FIGURE 3-2
Typical Demand/Marginal Willingness-to-Pay Curves.

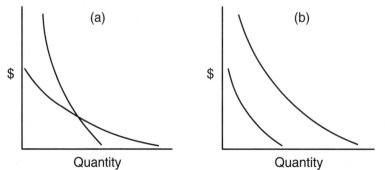

and two different goods or services; or the case of two different consumers and the same good or service.

Panel (b) of Figure 3-2 also has two demand curves; they have the same general shape, but one is situated well to the right of the other. The demand curve lying above and to the right shows a good for which the marginal willingness to pay is substantially higher than it is for the same quantity of the other good. What could account for the difference? They might represent the demand curves of two different people for the same good. But there are other possibilities. How much a person is willing to pay for something obviously depends on how much money she has; more than likely the higher her income, the more she is willing to pay. So the two demand curves in panel (b) could apply to the same individual and the same good, but at two different points in time, the one to the right being her willingness to pay after she has had a substantial increase in her income. The relationship between demand and income is an important one. When the demand for a good or service increases as income increases, we call it a **normal good.** Environmental quality is very much a normal good, as their incomes increase, people generally desire higher levels of environmental quality.

There is another way of looking at the two demand curves of panel (b), one that may be very important for the application of these ideas to environmental assets. People's tastes depend on a lot of factors of a psychological and historical kind that are hard to pin down and describe but are nevertheless real. They will depend in part on the experiences that people have and the information they gather over time about the qualities of different goods and how they feel about them. So, for example, the demand curve to the right could be the same consumer's demand curve for a good for which his appreciation has increased over time. For example, these might be his demand curves for outdoor wilderness experiences, the one to the left applying before he knows much about this type of activity and the one to the right applying after he has had some wilderness experiences and learned to like them. Other factors are information and psychology; the demand curve on the right might be a person's demand for a food item before an announcement of the presence of pesticide residues in it, with the curve on the left being the demand curve after the announcement.

Note that the demand curves are in fact curvilinear, rather than straight lines. A straight-line demand relationship would imply a uniform change in the quantity demanded as its price changes. For most goods, however, this is unlikely to be true. At low prices and high rates of consumption, studies have shown that relatively small increases in price will lead to substantial reductions in quantity demanded. At high prices and low quantity demanded, however, price increases have a much smaller effect: they produce much smaller reductions in quantity demanded. This gives us a demand relationship that is convex to the origin (i.e., relatively flat at low prices and steep at higher prices). (See Example 3-1.)

Economics is sometimes misunderstood as assuming that people are driven only by thoughts of their own welfare, that they are complete egoists. Because these are individual demand curves, they do indeed summarize the attitudes of single individuals, but this does not imply that individuals make decisions with only themselves in mind. Some people may indeed act this way, but for

EXAMPLE 3-1

THE DEMAND FOR WATER

Researchers have investigated the demand for water by households. Many might think that the amount of water a household uses would be related only to such things as the size of the family rather than the price of the water. This is not the case, however. In general, as the price people pay for water increases, the amount of water they use declines.

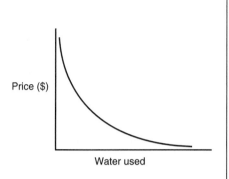

This demand is somewhat complicated. Water is used for a number of household purposes; for example, inside the house for sanitation and food preparation and outside the house for car washing, lawn sprinkling, and so forth. At higher prices, consumers will curtail unessential water uses substantially, but their water use for essential purposes will not decline as much in relative terms.

This means that the demand curve for water is shaped as in the diagram.

At low and moderate prices, increased prices will lead to a substantial drop in household water use as people cut back on unessential uses. Thus, the demand curve is relatively flat in this range. But, at higher prices where most of the water is going to essential purposes, further price increases will lead to relatively smaller drops in consumption, hence a steeper demand curve.

most there are many other powerful motives that affect their demands for different goods, including altruism toward friends and relatives, feelings of civic virtue toward their communities, a sense of social responsibility toward fellow citizens, and so on. Individual tastes and preferences spring from these factors as well as from more narrow considerations of personal likes and dislikes.

AGGREGATE DEMAND/WILLINGNESS TO PAY

In examining real-world issues of environmental quality and pollution-control policy, we normally focus our attention on the behavior of groups of people rather than single individuals. Our interest is in the total, or aggregate, demand/marginal willingness to pay of defined groups of people.

An **aggregate demand curve** is the summation of a number of individual demand curves. What individuals are involved depends on which particular aggregation we want to look at: the demand of people living in the city

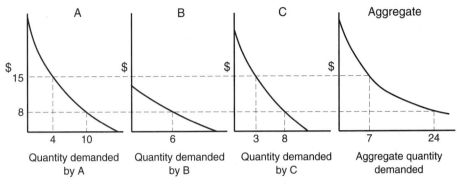

FIGURE 3-3
Aggregate Demand/Marginal Willingness-to-Pay Curves.

of New York for brussels sprouts; the demand of people living in New Orleans for clean water in the Mississippi; the demand of people living in the entire country for public parks; and so on. An aggregate demand curve is simply the summation of the demand curves of all the people in the group of interest.

Figure 3-3 depicts a very simple aggregate demand curve, one in which the "group" consists of only three people. At a price of $8, Person A demands 10 units of this good, whereas at the same price Person B demands 6 units and Person C demands 8 units of the good. Thus, the aggregate demand curve, pictured to the far right, shows an aggregate demand of 24 units for the price of $8. Note that we are summing these individual demand curves horizontally. Looked at in the other direction we note that when Person A is consuming 10 units his marginal willingness to pay is $8, whereas when Persons B and C consume, respectively, at 6 units and 8 units, their marginal willingness to pay is also $8. Therefore, on the aggregate level, the marginal willingness to pay is $8. If one more unit is made available to this aggregate, it must be distributed to Person A, Person B, or Person C, each of whom has a marginal willingness to pay of $8; thus, the aggregate marginal willingness to pay is also $8.

BENEFITS

We now come to the idea of **benefits.** Benefit is one of those ordinary words to which economists have given a technical meaning. When the environment is cleaned up, people obtain benefits; when the environment is allowed to deteriorate in quality, benefits are taken away from them—they are, in fact, being damaged. We need some way of conceptualizing and measuring this notion of benefits.

The word "benefits" clearly implies being made better off. If someone is benefited by something, her position is improved—she is better off. Conversely, if she is worse off, it must be because benefits were somehow taken away from

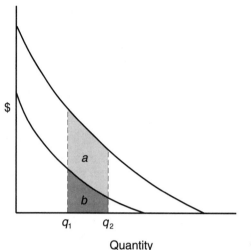

FIGURE 3-4
Quantity
Willingness to Pay and Benefits.

her. How do we confer benefits on somebody? We do this by giving him something he values. How do we know that he values something? We know by the fact that he is willing to sacrifice, or willing to pay, for it. According to this logic, then, the benefits that people get from something are equal to the amount they are willing to pay for it.

The logic behind this definition of "benefits" is quite strong. It means we can use ordinary demand curves to determine the benefits of making various things available to people. For example, Figure 3-4 shows two demand curves, and on the horizontal axis two quantity levels are indicated. Suppose we wish to estimate the total benefits of increasing the availability of this item from quantity q_1 to quantity q_2. According to our previous thinking, benefits are measured by willingness to pay, and we know that total willingness to pay is measured by areas under the demand curve, in this case the area under the demand curves between quantity q_1 and quantity q_2. So for the lower demand curve the benefits of such an increase in availability are equal to an amount shown by area b, whereas benefits in the case of the higher demand curve are equal to the total area $a + b$.

The logic of this seems reasonable. The people with the higher demand curve must place a greater value on this item; whatever it is, they are willing to pay more for it than the people whose demand curve is the lower function. This is in agreement with common sense. The more people value something, the more they are benefited by having more of that something made available, or, to say the same thing, you can't damage people by taking away from them something that they don't value.

This is the fundamental logic underlying much of environmental economics. It underlies, for example, questions of measuring the damage done to people when the natural environment surrounding them is degraded. It underlies the question of evaluating the impacts of environmental programs and policies undertaken by local, state, and federal governments. This is the strength of the economic approach, the fact that it is based on a clear notion of the value that people place on different things.

But the idea also has shortcomings. For one thing, demand and, therefore, benefits are often very hard to measure when it concerns environmental questions, as we will see in later chapters. For another, we have to remember that demand curves are critically affected by the ability to pay for something as well as preferences. In Figure 3-4, for example, the lower demand curve could represent a group of people with lower incomes than those with the higher demand curve. The logic of the argument would lead to the conclusion that the increase in quantity of $q_2 - q_1$ would produce fewer benefits among lower-income people than among higher-income people. This may not be a very equitable conclusion, depending on the circumstances. Thus, although the logic of the concept is clear, we have to be careful in using it, especially when we are dealing with groups of people with diverse income levels. The main step in doing this is to find out as clearly as possible how the various environmental policies and programs, present or proposed, affect people at different income levels. We discuss this at greater length in later chapters.

One other possible problem exists in using conventional demand curves to measure benefits. An individual's demand for something is clearly affected by how much she knows about it; a person would not be willing to pay for a good if, for example, she was ignorant of its very existence. In Figure 3-4, the higher demand curve might be the demand for a good before it is found out that it contains a carcinogenic substance, and the lower demand curve shows demand after this fact becomes known. There is nothing especially surprising about this; people after all do become more knowledgeable about things over time as a matter of course. But in today's world this could be a complication, especially with regard to the environment. We don't fully understand many of the effects of environmental degradation; furthermore, people's views about the importance of many of these effects are blown back and forth almost from day to day, by the media, by the scientific press, and so on. Care must be exercised in taking people's demand curves of the moment, influenced as they are by all kinds of real and imagined factors, as true expressions of the benefits of environmental actions. It is not that they are irrelevant; it is only that they have to be taken with a certain amount of caution.

COST

We now switch to the other side of the picture and consider costs. Although some things in life are free—an idea, for example—it is generally true that goods and services cannot be produced out of thin air; they require the expenditure of productive resources, or inputs, in the process. The more of something that is desired, the more resources we will have to devote to its production. What is needed is a way of describing and talking about the costs of producing useful things, whether these are normal consumer goods, such as cars or hot-water bottles, or services, such as transportation or insurance, or environmental quality through the treatment of waste residuals, recycling, or land-use controls.

Imagine a simple production process. Suppose, for example, we are producing a certain line of cardboard boxes. To produce boxes, many types of productive inputs are required: labor, machinery of various descriptions, energy, raw materials, waste-handling equipment, and so on. The first thing needed is a way of valuing these productive resources. If we are a private firm operating in a market economy, we would have little problem: We would value them according to what they cost to procure in the markets. Our profit-and-loss statement at the end of the year would reflect the monetary "out-of-pocket" costs of the inputs used in the production operation. But our concept of cost will be broader than this. From this wider perspective the costs of these cardboard boxes are what could have been produced with these productive inputs had they not been used in box production. The name for this is **opportunity cost.**

Opportunity Cost

The **opportunity cost** of producing something consists of the maximum value of other outputs we could and would have produced had we not used the resources to produce the item in question. The word "maximum" is used for a reason. The productive inputs used to produce the cardboard boxes could have been used to produce a variety of other things, perhaps automobiles, books, or pollution-control equipment. The opportunity cost of the boxes consists of the maximum value of the alternative output that could have been obtained had we used these resources differently.

Opportunity costs include out-of-pocket costs but are wider than this. Some inputs that are actually used in production may not get registered as cash costs. For example, the spouse of the cardboard box plant operator works as an unpaid assistant in the front office. This may not register as an out-of-pocket cost, but he certainly has an opportunity cost because he could have been working somewhere else if he was not working here. Even more importantly for our purposes, the cardboard box manufacturing process may produce waste products that are pumped into a nearby stream. Downstream these production residuals produce environmental damage, which are real opportunity costs of producing cardboard boxes, even though they do not show up as costs in the plant's profit-and-loss statement.

The opportunity cost idea is relevant in any situation in which a decision must be made about using productive resources for one purpose rather than another. For a public agency with a given budget, the opportunity costs of a particular policy are the value of alternative policies it might have pursued. For a consumer, the opportunity cost of spending time searching for a particular item is the value of the next most valuable thing to which the consumer could have devoted time.

How is opportunity cost measured? It is not very useful to measure it in terms of the number of other physical items that could have been produced. Nor is there enough information in most cases to be able to measure the value of the next best output that was forgone. In practice, therefore, opportunity costs are measured by the market value of inputs used up in production. For this to work, we have to take care that the inputs have been correctly valued. The office labor must be valued at the going rate even though it is not paid in practice. The effects on downstream water quality must be evaluated and included. Once all inputs have been accounted for, their total value may be taken as the true opportunity costs of production.

Private and Social Costs

Another important distinction is that between **private costs** and **social costs.** The private costs of an action are the costs experienced by the party making the decisions leading to that action. The social costs of an action are *all* of the costs of the action, no matter who experiences them. Social costs include private costs, but also may include much more in certain situations.

Consider the action of driving a car. The private costs of this include the fuel and oil, maintenance, depreciation, and even the driving time experienced by the operator of the car. The social costs include all these private costs and also the costs experienced by people other than the operator who are exposed to the congestion and air pollution resulting from use of the car. This distinction between private and social costs will be very important in later sections where we begin to analyze environmental problems with these tools.

Cost Curves

To summarize cost information, we use cost curves, which are geometric representations of the costs of producing something. And, just as in the case of willingness to pay, we differentiate between **marginal costs** and **total costs.** Consider the cost curves in Figure 3-5. They are meant to apply to a single producing organization, a firm, or perhaps a public agency that is producing some good or service. The graph is laid out, the same as in previous graphs, with quantity on the horizontal axis and a monetary index on the vertical axis. The quantity relates to some period of time, such as a year. The top panel shows marginal costs in terms of a step-shaped relationship. It shows that it costs $5 to produce the first unit of output. If the firm wants to increase output to two units, it must spend an added $7. The addition of a third unit would add $10 to total costs, and so on. Marginal cost is a symmetrical measure; it is the added costs, the amount by which total costs increase, when output is increased by one unit. It is also the cost savings if production were to decrease by one unit. Thus, the reduction in output from four to three units would reduce total costs by $15, the marginal cost of the fourth unit.

It is inconvenient to work with step-shaped curves, so we make the assumption that the firm can produce intermediate quantities as well as integer values. This gives a smooth marginal cost curve, as shown in the bottom panel of Figure 3-5. This curve now shows the marginal cost—the added cost of one more unit of output—for any level of output. For example, at an output level of 4.5 units, marginal cost is $19.

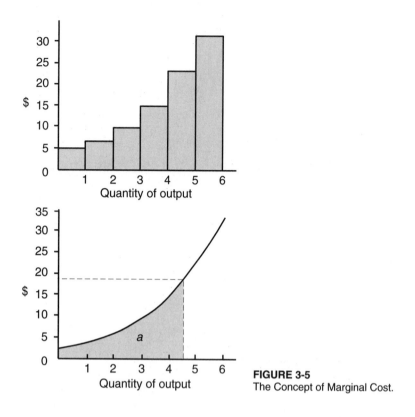

FIGURE 3-5
The Concept of Marginal Cost.

Marginal cost curves can be used to determine **total production costs.** On the stepped marginal cost curve of Figure 3-5, suppose we want to know the total cost of producing five units of this item. This is equal to the cost of the first unit ($5), plus that of the second ($7), plus that of the third ($10), and so on. This total is $60; geometrically this is equal to the total area of the rectangles above the first five units of output. Analogously, in the smoothly shaped marginal cost function in the bottom of the diagram, the total cost of producing a given quantity is the dollar amount equal to the area under the marginal cost curve between the origin and the quantity in question. The total cost of producing 4.5 units of output is thus given by the area marked *a* in the figure.

The Shapes of Cost Curves

The height and shape of the marginal cost curve for any production process will differ from one situation to another, based on several underlying factors. A key determining factor is the technology utilized in production, and we discuss this concept later. The price of inputs is also an important factor influencing the heights of marginal cost curves. In general, if input prices increase to a firm or group of firms, their marginal cost curves will shift upward. Another important

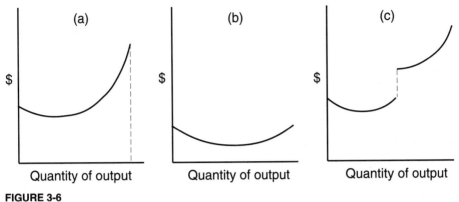

FIGURE 3-6
Typical Marginal Cost Curves.

element is *time,* specifically the amount of time that a firm has to adjust to changes in its rate of output. These factors may be better understood by looking at some actual marginal cost curves.

Figure 3-6 shows several marginal cost curves. Panel (a) shows a very typical marginal cost curve; initially it declines as output increases but then it increases as output gets larger. The initial decline comes about because of basic efficiencies achievable with larger quantities at this level. Suppose our "output" refers to the quantity of wastewater handled in a municipal treatment plant. At very low levels of output, the plant is not being fully utilized; thus, output increases in this range are accompanied by less than proportionate increases in production cost, giving marginal costs that diminish. But as output increases, the capacity of the plant is approached. Machinery must be worked longer, additional people must be hired, and so on. Thus, marginal cost begins to increase. As the capacity of the operation is neared, these problems become more acute. To continue to increase output, more extraordinary measures are required, which can only be done at a high cost; thus, marginal cost increases even more. A point may come at which it becomes almost impossible to increase output further, which is the same as saying that the marginal costs of production at this point increase without limit. This limit is indicated by the vertical dashed line in panel (a) of Figure 3-6.

This marginal cost curve depicts an important generic characteristic of all marginal cost curves, namely, that although they may initially decline, they will always increase, eventually, as output becomes large enough. These increases are related to certain underlying factors, such as increased plant utilization, the need to reach farther away for raw materials, and the inevitable higher management costs that accompany larger operations. Virtually all economic studies of particular operations and industries demonstrate increasing marginal production costs, and this fact will be an important shaping element in our later discussions specifically related to environmental quality management. (See Example 3-2.)

EXAMPLE 3-2

THE MARGINAL COSTS OF PRODUCING PIZZAS

Suppose a local pizza delivery operation has a baking facility and a fleet of three cars and plans to devote their entire operation to making and delivering pizzas. Let us consider the marginal cost of pizza production and delivery. The marginal cost of the first pizza may be fairly high because to begin production at all requires a certain minimum set of inputs. At slightly higher, but still low, rates of production, added output might be obtainable with relatively modest increases in cost because the oven is not being used intensively and a little added flour, sauce, spices, and gas for the cars may be all that is needed. In other words, at low levels of production, we might expect the marginal cost of pizza production to be relatively low or even declining. But at somewhat higher levels of production, marginal cost can be expected to increase. Once the oven is used intensively, larger amounts of other inputs (ingredients, more preparation space, added labor, more car repair, etc.) would be necessary to push production higher. At even greater levels of output, we would expect marginal costs to increase sharply as the overall limits of the facility in terms of pizza production and delivery are reached. All these considerations might be expected to give us a marginal pizza production cost function something like the one in this example.

All the reasoning of the preceding paragraph was based on the assumption that the owner had one oven and three cars. This is what economists call a **short-run** situation, because one or more of the essential production inputs is fixed in amount. In the longer run, the owner, of course, could obtain more ovens and cars and therefore be able to obtain increases in output at marginal costs lower than those pictured in the diagram. Yet even with increases in facilities we would expect marginal costs eventually to increase because it will become more costly to bid additional equipment away from other uses and because it will become more difficult to coordinate and carry out decisions over an ever-increasing size of operation. Thus, even in the **long run,** when all production inputs are freely variable in quantity, we would expect marginal costs to increase. Eventually, increasing marginal production costs characterize not just pizza production but the production of most goods and services, with appropriate differences of course in the technologies with which production is pursued in different circumstances.

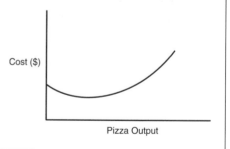

Cost ($)

Pizza Output

Panel (b) of Figure 3-6 shows a marginal cost curve similar in general shape to the one in panel (a), but with less pronounced curvature. In particular, although this marginal cost curve eventually increases, it does so less steeply than the first one. This is more typical of a long-run marginal cost curve; that is, one where enough time is given for operators of firms to adapt fully to an increase in the rate of output. In the short run, our wastewater treatment plant had a certain capacity that was basically fixed; but in the long run, there is time to build a larger treatment plant with higher capacities. For larger outputs, the marginal costs of this larger plant will be lower than those of the smaller plant. Yet, even in these long-run situations marginal costs will eventually increase, as is depicted in panel (b). *In our subsequent discussions we will assume that we are working with long-run marginal cost curves, unless specified otherwise.*

Panel (c) of Figure 3-6 represents a more complicated case where there is a discontinuity in the marginal cost curve. After a short downward section, the marginal costs generally trend upward, and at one point they jump upward by some amount. This might represent a "lumpy" investment in new types of technology at a certain point as output increases.

TECHNOLOGY

The most important factor affecting the shapes of marginal cost functions is the **technology** of the production process. By technology we mean the inherent productive capabilities of the methods and machines being employed. Any modern production requires capital goods (machinery and equipment) of various types and capacities, labor inputs, operating procedures, raw materials, and so on. The quantity of output a firm can get from a given set of inputs depends on the technical and human capabilities inherent in these inputs. The marginal cost curves pictured in Figure 3-6 could relate to different industries because the marginal cost curves are so different. But even within the same industry marginal cost curves can differ among firms. Some firms will be older than others; they may be working with older equipment that has different cost characteristics. Even firms of the same age may have different production techniques; past managerial decisions may have put them in different positions in terms of the marginal production costs they experience today.

This concept of technology is vitally important in environmental economics because **technological change** can provide ways to produce goods and services with fewer environmental side effects and also better ways of handling the quantities of production residuals that remain. In our simple cost model, technical advancement has the effect of shifting marginal cost curves downward. Technological progress makes it possible to produce a given increase in output at a lower marginal cost. It also reduces total production cost. Consider Figure 3-7. MC_1 is the firm's marginal cost curve before a technical improvement; MC_2 is the marginal cost curve after some technical improvement has been put into effect. The technical change, in other words, shifts the marginal cost curve downward. We also can determine how much total production costs are reduced as a result of the technological change. Consider output level q^*. With MC_1 the total annual cost of producing output q^* is represented by the

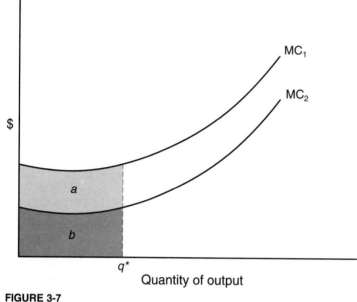

FIGURE 3-7
Technological Improvement.

area $a + b$, whereas after the reduction in the marginal cost curve to MC_2 the total annual cost of producing q^* is equal to area b. Thus, the reduction in total cost made possible by the technological change is equal to area a.

Technological change does not normally happen without effort; it normally requires research and development (R&D). R&D in environmental industries is obviously an important activity to promote, and one of the criteria we will want to use to evaluate environmental policies is whether the policies create incentives for individuals, firms, and industries to engage in vigorous R&D programs. In very simple terms, the incentive to engage in R&D is the cost savings that result from the new techniques, materials, procedures, and so on that are discovered in the effort. The cost savings shown in Figure 3-7 (area a) shows part of this incentive. This is the cost savings that would result each year, and the accumulation of these annual cost savings represents the full R&D incentive.

THE EQUIMARGINAL PRINCIPLE

We come now to the discussion of a simple but important economic principle, one that is used repeatedly in chapters to come. It is called the **equimarginal principle**. To understand it, take the case of a firm producing a certain product and assume that the firm's operation is divided between two different plants. For example, suppose there is a single power company that owns two different generating plants. Each plant produces the same item, so that the total output of the firm is the sum of what it produces in the two plants. Assume that the plants were built at different times and make use of different technology. The old one,

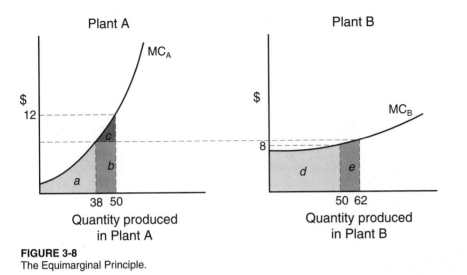

FIGURE 3-8
The Equimarginal Principle.

Plant A in Figure 3-8, has older technology; it has a marginal cost curve that starts relatively low but rises steeply as production increases. The new plant, Plant B in Figure 3-8, uses newer technology; it has a higher marginal cost at low output levels, but marginal costs do not rise as steeply as production increases.

Consider now a situation in which this two-plant firm wants to produce a total output of, say, 100 units. How many units should it produce in each plant in order to produce the 100 units at the *least total cost*? Would it be best to produce 50 units in each plant? This is depicted in Figure 3-8; at an output of 50, Plant A has a marginal cost of $12 whereas Plant B has a marginal cost of $8. Total production costs are the sum of total costs at each plant, or $(a + b + c) + d$. Here is the important point: The total cost of the 100 units can be lowered by reallocating production. Reduce production in Plant A by one unit and costs will fall by $12. Then increase the production in Plant B by one unit and costs there will rise by $8. Total output is still 100 units, but there has been a cost saving of $12 – $8 = $4. Thus, total cost, the sum of the costs in the two plants, has gone down.

As long as the marginal costs in the two plants differ from one another, we can continue to reallocate production—away from the high marginal cost plant and toward the low marginal cost plant—and get a reduction in total cost. In fact, the total costs of producing the 100 units in the two plants will be at a minimum only when the marginal costs of the two plants are equal, hence the "equimarginal principle." In the figure, this happens when the output in Plant A is 38 units and the output in Plant B is 62 units. Total costs in geometric terms are now $a + (d + e)$.

The equimarginal principle, therefore, says the following: If you have multiple sources to produce a given product or achieve a given goal, and you want to minimize the total cost of producing a given quantity of that output, distribute production in such a way as to equalize the marginal costs between the production sources. There is another way of saying it that may look different but actually is not: If you have a given amount of resources and you want to maximize the total amount produced, distribute total production among the sources in such a way as to equalize marginal costs. This principle will be very valuable when we take up the issue of getting maximum emissions reductions from given amounts of resources.

MARGINAL COST AND SUPPLY

A critical question in the analysis of any economic system is whether private profit-seeking firms (as well as public, politically minded agencies) will produce the correct quantities of output from the standpoint of society as a whole, not only for conventional items such as cardboard boxes, but also for less conventional items such as the amounts of environmental quality. To address this question one must understand how firms normally determine the quantities they will produce. The marginal cost of production is a key factor in determining the **supply** behavior of firms in competitive circumstances. In fact, the marginal cost curve of a firm acts essentially as a **supply curve,** showing the quantity of the good the firm would supply at different prices. Consider Figure 3-9. Assume that the firm with the indicated marginal cost curve is able to sell its output at a price of p^*. The firm will maximize its profits by producing that quantity of output where marginal cost is equal to p^*; that level is designated q^*. At any output level less than this, MC $< p^*$, so a firm could increase its profits by increasing output. At any output level above this, $p^* <$ MC, so a firm is actually

FIGURE 3-9
Marginal Cost and Supply.

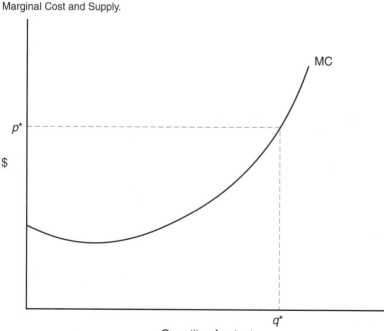

Quantity of output

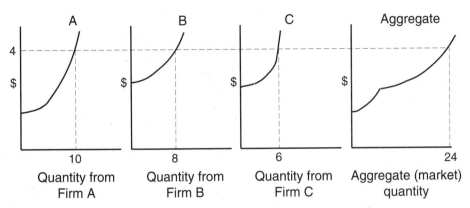

FIGURE 3-10
Derivation of Aggregate (Market) Supply from Individual Firm Supply Curves.

producing items for which the marginal cost is higher than price; in this case, the firm should reduce output if it wishes to maximize its profits.

We are often interested in the supply performance of industries composed of many firms rather than that of individual firms. An **aggregate supply** curve shows the amounts supplied by a collection of firms all producing the same output. The idea is analogous to the concept of aggregate demand we had in the previous section. The aggregate supply curve of a group of firms is the sum of the individual supply curves of all the firms in the group. This is depicted in Figure 3-10. There are three firms, A, B, and C, with marginal cost curves as depicted in the first three panels of the figure. At a common price, say $4, Firm A supplies 10 units, Firm B supplies 8 units, and Firm C supplies 6 units. Thus, the aggregate supply at that price is 24 units, as depicted in the far right panel of Figure 3-10.

SUMMARY

In this chapter we covered briefly some of the basic tools of microeconomics. Later chapters will rely heavily on these ideas, especially on the equimarginal principle and on graphs, where we will want to jump back and forth between marginal and total measures. When we begin to look at real-world problems of environmental analysis and policy design, it is easy to get pulled so far into the countless details that basic economic ideas get lost. It is the fundamental economic building blocks, such as those in this chapter, that allow us to identify the primary economic characteristics of these problems and proceed to develop solutions to them.

QUESTIONS FOR FURTHER DISCUSSION

1 Use the logic of willingness to pay to interpret the statement "I like clean air more than you do."

2 Below are the marginal willingness to pay functions (the demand functions) for three individuals. Determine the aggregate marginal willingness to pay (demand) function.

Quantities Demanded

Price ($)	A	B	C
10	4	1	0
9	6	2	0
8	8	3	0
7	10	4	1
6	12	5	2
5	14	7	3
4	17	10	4
3	20	15	5
2	24	25	6
1	30	50	7

3 What are the advantages and disadvantages of using willingness to pay as a measure of value? What are some alternatives?

4 Figure 3-10 illustrates the derivation of an industry supply curve under competitive conditions where each firm receives the same price for its output. What is the relationship of this procedure to the equimarginal principle discussed earlier in the chapter?

5 Consider the marginal cost curve associated with cleaning your dorm room. Label the vertical axis with "time" and the horizontal axis with "percent clean." What would this marginal cost curve look like?

6 Somebody invents a new small machine that electrostatically is able to remove dust from rooms very quickly. What does this do to the marginal cost curve depicted in question 5?

WEBSITES

There are several websites that feature instructional material in basic economics, for example the one put together by Roger McCain, at **william-king.www. drexel.edu/top/prin/txt/EcoToC.html,** and the one developed by Robert Schenk, at **ingrimayne.saintjoe.edu/econ/TOC.html.** See also the website associated with the text, at **www.mhhe.com/economics/field3.**

SELECTED READINGS

The subjects treated in this chapter—demand, supply, willingness to pay, costs, and so on—are treated in most introductory microeconomic texts. The best way to proceed, in order to get a somewhat deeper explanation of these concepts or a slightly different perspective, is to consult the appropriate chapters of one of these books. Some of the more popular texts are the following:

Baumol, William J., and Alan S. Blinder: *Microeconomics, Principles and Policy,* 8th ed., Harcourt College Publishers, Dallas, TX, 2000, Chapters 5, 6, 8.

Boyes, William, and Michael Melvin: *Microeconomics,* 4th ed., Houghton Mifflin, Boston, MA, 1999, Chapters 2, 3.

Case, Karl E., and Ray C. Fair: *Principles of Microeconomics,* 5th ed., Prentice Hall, Upper Saddle River, NJ, 1999, Chapters 4, 6, 7.

Frank, Robert H., and Ben Bernanke: *Principles of Economics,* Irwin McGraw-Hill, New York, 2000, Chapters 4, 5, 6, 7.

Lipsey, Richard G., Paul N. Courant, and Christopher T. S. Ragan: *Microeconomics,* 12th ed., Addison Wesley Longman, Reading, MA, 1999, Chapters 7, 8, 9.

McConnell, Campbell R., and Stanley L. Brue: *Economics,* 14th ed., Irwin McGraw-Hill, New York, 1998, Chapters 20, 21, 22.

Parkin, Michael: *Economics,* 5th ed., Addison Wesley Longman, Reading, MA, 2000, Chapters 4, 6.

Samuelson, Paul A., and William D. Nordhaus: *Economics,* 17th ed., Irwin McGraw-Hill, New York, 2001, Chapters 6, 8.

Schiller, Bradley R.: *The Microeconomy Today,* 8th ed., Irwin McGraw-Hill, New York, 2000, Chapter 2.

CHAPTER 4

ECONOMIC EFFICIENCY
AND MARKETS

This chapter has several objectives. First is to develop the notion of **economic efficiency** as an index for examining how an economy functions and as a criterion for judging whether it is performing as well as it might. Economic efficiency is a simple idea but one that has much to recommend it as a criterion for evaluating the performance of an economic system or a part of that system, but it has to be used with care. A single firm or group of firms may be judged very efficient in their own limited way as long as they are keeping costs low and making a profit. Yet, to evaluate the *social* performance of these firms, we must use the idea of economic efficiency in a wider sense. In this case it must include all the social values and consequences of economic decisions, in particular environmental consequences. It is important also to discuss the relationship between economic efficiency and **economic equity.**

The second task is to address the question of whether a **market system,** left to itself, can produce results that are socially efficient. We will see that there are cases in which a system of private markets will not normally be able to bring about results that are efficient in this wider sense. This leads into the next chapter, where we will examine the policy question; that is, if the economy is not operating the way we want it to, especially in matters of environmental quality, what kind of public policy might be used to correct the situation?

Economic efficiency is a criterion that can be applied at several levels: to input usage and to the determination of output levels. We are going to concentrate in this chapter on the second of these because ultimately we want to apply the concept to the "output" of environmental quality. There are two questions of interest: (1) What quantity ought to be produced and (2) what quantity is produced in fact? The first question deals with the notion of efficiency, the second with the way markets normally function.

ECONOMIC EFFICIENCY

In the preceding chapter we introduced two relationships, that between the quantity of output and willingness to pay, and that between output and marginal production costs. Neither of these two relationships, by itself, can tell us what the most desirable level of output is from society's standpoint. To identify this output level, it is necessary to bring these two elements together. The central idea of **economic efficiency** is that there should be a balance between the value of what is produced and the value of what is used up to produce it. In our terminology, there should be a balance between willingness to pay and the marginal costs of production.

Efficiency is a notion that has to have a reference point. It is critical to ask: efficient from the standpoint of whom? What is "efficient" for one person, in the sense of balancing costs and benefits, may not be "efficient" for somebody else. We want to have a concept of efficiency that is applicable to the economy as a whole. This means that when referring to marginal costs, *all* the costs of producing the particular item in question must be included, no matter to whom they accrue. When dealing with marginal willingness to pay, we must insist that this represents accurately *all* of the value that people in the society place on the item. This does not necessarily mean that all people will place the same value on all goods; it means only that there are no missing sources of value.

How do we identify the rate of output that is socially efficient? Suppose we focus on a particular type of output; in practice it could be refrigerators, automobiles, college educations, or a certain type of pollution-control equipment. Suppose that our item is currently being produced at a particular rate, and we wish to know whether it would benefit society to have this output level increased by a small amount. To answer this requires comparing the marginal willingness to pay for that extra output with the marginal opportunity costs of the output. If the former exceeds the latter, we would presumably want the extra output to be produced; otherwise we would not.

This can be analyzed graphically by bringing together the two relationships discussed in the last chapter. Figure 4-1 shows the aggregate marginal willingness-to-pay curve (labeled MWTP) and the aggregate marginal cost curve (MC) for the good in question. The efficient level of production for this item is the quantity identified by the intersection of the two curves, labeled q^e in the figure. At this output level the costs of producing one more unit of this good are just exactly equal to the marginal value of it, as expressed by the marginal willingness-to-pay curve. This common value is p^e.

The equality of marginal willingness to pay and marginal production cost is the test for determining if output is at the socially efficient level. There is another way of looking at this notion of efficiency. When a rate of output is at the socially efficient level, the net value, defined as **total willingness to pay** minus **total costs,** is as large as possible. In fact, we can measure this net value on the diagram. At q^e we know that the total willingness to pay is equal to an amount corresponding to the area under the marginal willingness-to-pay curve from the origin up to q^e; this area consists of the sum of the three

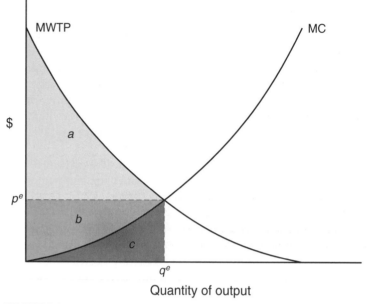

Quantity of output

FIGURE 4-1
The Socially Efficient Rate of Output.

subareas: $a + b + c$. Total cost, however, consists of the area under the marginal cost curve, or area c. Thus, the surplus is $(a + b + c) - c = a + b$, which is the triangular area enclosed by the marginal willingness-to-pay curve and the marginal cost curve. At any other quantity the corresponding value of total willingness to pay minus total production costs will be less than this area $a + b$.

Let's be clear on what this graph is saying. We noted previously that the marginal willingness-to-pay curve is assumed to represent accurately all the benefits that people in our economy actually experience when the good becomes available. The marginal production cost curve is assumed to contain all the true opportunity costs that are required to produce this good—no hidden or overlooked costs have been left out. Thus, the quantity q^e is **efficient** because it produces a balance between the two sides—between the marginal worth of a good, as indicated by consumers' willingness to pay for it, and what it costs society to produce it, as measured by marginal costs.

EFFICIENCY AND EQUITY

From the standpoint of society at large, production is at an efficient level when marginal benefits equal marginal production costs; that is, when net benefits are maximized *no matter to whom those net benefits accrue*. Efficiency doesn't distinguish among people. A dollar of net benefits to one person is considered to be worth a dollar to anybody else. One hundred dollars of benefits to one person is considered to be worth the same as one dollar of benefits to each of one hundred people. In the real world, an outcome that benefits very rich people at the expense of poor people would be regarded by most people as inequitable. This is simply another way of saying that an outcome that is efficient in this sense need not necessarily be equitable.

Equity is tied closely to the distribution of wealth in a society. If this distribution is regarded as essentially fair, then judgments about alternative output levels may justifiably be made using only the efficiency criterion. But if wealth is distributed unfairly, the efficiency criterion by itself may be too narrow. Having said this, however, we have to recognize that in judging economic outcomes the relative emphasis to be put on efficiency and equity is a matter of controversy. It is controversial in the political arena; it is controversial among economists themselves.

We will have much to say about distributional issues and equity throughout this book. Chapter 6 contains terminology for describing the distributional impacts of environmental policies. Chapter 9 contains a discussion of the role of economic equity as a criterion for evaluating environmental policies.

MARKETS

Having specified what economic efficiency means, the next question to ask is whether a market system, a system in which the major economic decisions about how much to produce are made by the more or less unhindered interaction of buyers and sellers, gives results that are socially efficient. In other words, if we rely entirely on the market to determine how much of this item gets produced, will it settle on q^e?

Why worry about this question? Why not simply jump to the question of public policy? Doesn't this question imply that, at bottom, we are committed to the market system, and isn't this the system that, from an environmental point of view, has gotten us into trouble in the first place? If the market doesn't do the job, maybe we should just ignore whatever the market does and proceed through political/administrative means to bring about the desired rate of output.

The short answer to this is that as a nation we are in fact committed to a market-based economy. For all its faults, a market system will normally produce better economic results overall than any other system. Those who doubt this need only look at the environmental horror stories uncovered in the countries of Eastern Europe following the Communist era. Of course, it needs to be remembered that although our system is "market based," we do not necessarily have to accept whatever results it yields. The results are acceptable only if they are reasonably efficient and equitable. We will find that in the case of environmental quality, market institutions are not likely to give us results that are socially efficient.

The slightly longer answer to the question is that the market system contains within it certain incentive structures that in many cases can be harnessed toward the objective of improved environmental quality. One of these is the cost-minimizing incentive that stems from the competitive process. Another is the incentive provided through the rewards that may be reaped through initiative in finding better, that is, less expensive, technical and organizational means of production. It will be far more effective in many cases to take advantage of these incentives than to try to do away with them. By altering them so that they take environmental values into account, the market system will yield more effective results than if we tried to jettison the whole system and adopt a different set of institutions.

A **market** is an institution in which buyers and sellers of consumer goods, factors of production, and so on carry out mutually agreed-upon exchanges. When they buy or sell on a market, people naturally look for the best terms they can get. Presumably buyers would like to pay a low price whereas sellers would prefer high prices. What brings all these conflicting objectives into balance is the adjustment of prices on the market.

Figure 4-2 shows a simple market model. Buyers' desires are represented by the **demand curve** labeled D; it shows the quantity of the good that buyers would buy at different prices. It has the typical downward slope; the higher the price, the lower the quantity demanded, and vice versa. Underlying the demand curve are such factors as consumer tastes and preferences, the number of potential consumers in the market, and consumer income levels.

The curve labeled S is the **supply curve,** which shows the quantity of the good that suppliers would willingly make available at different prices. It is upward sloping; higher prices represent greater incentives for suppliers, and, therefore, larger quantities are supplied, and vice versa. The main factors affecting the height and shape of the supply curve are production costs. These, in

FIGURE 4-2
The Market Model.

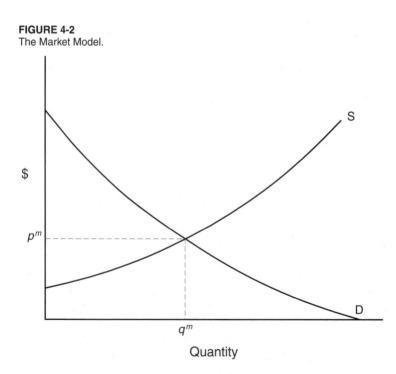

turn, are related to the prices of inputs used in the production of this item and the level of technology inherent in the production process.

It is important to keep in mind that the demand and supply curves represent possibilities, or alternatives. During any particular time, only one quantity of a good can change hands, and sellers and buyers can be on only one point of their supply and demand curves, respectively. It is easy to see that there is only one price at which the quantity demanded by buyers is consistent with the quantity that sellers will make available. That is the price where the two curves intersect, marked p^m. Similarly, the total quantity that buyers and sellers will exchange at this price is labeled q^m.

For the market to work effectively, there must be competition among sellers and among buyers. None can be large enough that their own performance affects market prices or powerful enough that they can control how the market performs. Price must be allowed to adjust freely so that it can "discover" the quantities that bring buyers and sellers into balance. At prices higher than p^m, sellers will attempt to supply more than buyers want. In a surplus situation such as this, competition among sellers forces prices downward. If prices are temporarily lower than p^m, a shortage develops and competition among buyers will force the price to adjust upward. At the equilibrium, quantity demanded equals quantity supplied.

It is important to look at it also from the other direction. At the quantity q^m there is an equality between the marginal willingness to pay by consumers for an additional unit of the item and the marginal costs of producing the item. These are equal at the value of p^m. If price and quantity are allowed to adjust freely and competition does in fact exist, an equality will arise through the normal interaction of buyers and sellers, between the marginal valuation that consumers have for a good (their marginal willingness to pay) and the cost of making available another unit of the good (the marginal cost of production).

MARKETS AND SOCIAL EFFICIENCY

The next question is whether markets ordinarily produce results that are efficient from the standpoint of society. Compare Figures 4-1 and 4-2. They look the same, but there is actually a big difference. The first shows a socially efficient rate of output for a particular item; the second shows the rate of output and price that would prevail on a competitive market for that item. Are these two rates of output, labeled q^e and q^m, likely to be the same in the real world? The answer is yes *if*, and it is a big *if*, the market demand and supply curves, as pictured in Figure 4-2, are the same as the marginal cost and willingness-to-pay curves shown in Figure 4-1. Here is the nub of the problem: When environmental values are concerned, there are likely to be very substantial differences between market values and social values. This is called **market failure,** and it will often call for public intervention, either to override the markets directly or to rearrange things so that they will work more effectively.

In the rest of this chapter we will discuss the performance of markets when matters of environmental quality are involved. There are two phenomena to account for, one on the supply side and the other on the demand side. Environmental effects can drive a wedge between normal market supply curves and true marginal social cost curves. On the other side of the market, environmental effects can create a difference between market demands and true social marginal willingness to pay. On the supply side the problem is "external costs," whereas on the demand side the problem is "external benefits."

EXTERNAL COSTS

When entrepreneurs in a market economy make decisions about what and how much to produce, they normally take into account the price of what they will produce and the cost of items for which they will have to pay: labor, raw materials, machinery, energy, and so on. We call these the **private costs** of the firm; they are the costs that show up in the profit-and-loss statement at the end of the year. Any firm, assuming it has the objective of maximizing its profits, will try to keep its production costs as low as possible. This is a worthwhile outcome for both the firm and society because inputs always have opportunity costs; they could have been used to produce something else. Furthermore, firms will be alert to ways of reducing costs when the relative prices of inputs change. For example, we know that during the U.S. energy "crisis" of the 1970s, when energy inputs became much more expensive, firms found ways of reducing energy inputs by using more energy-efficient machinery, changing operating procedures, and so on.

In many production operations, however, there is another type of cost that, while representing a true cost to society, does not show up in the firm's profit-and-loss statement. These are called **external costs.** They are "external" because, although they are real costs to some members of society, firms do not normally take them into account when they go about making their decisions about output rates. Another way of saying this is that these are costs that are external to firms but internal to society as a whole.[1]

One of the major types of external cost is the cost inflicted on people through environmental degradation. An example is the easiest way to see this. Suppose a paper mill is located somewhere on the upstream reaches of a river and that, in the course of its operation, it discharges a large amount of wastewater into the river. The wastewater is full of organic matter that arises from the process of converting wood to paper. This waste material gradually is converted to more benign materials by the natural assimilative capacity of the river water, but, before that happens, a number of people downstream are affected by the lower quality of water in the river. Perhaps the waterborne residuals reduce the number of fish in the river, affecting downstream fishers. The river also may be less attractive to look at, affecting people who would like to swim or sail on it. Worse, the river water perhaps is used downstream as a source of water for a

---

[1]External costs are sometimes called "third-party" costs. The first two parties are, respectively, the producer and the consumer. So a third-party cost is one that is inflicted on people who are not directly involved in the economic transactions between buyers and sellers. It is also sometimes called a "spillover" effect.

public water supply system, and the degraded water quality means that the town has to engage in more costly treatment processes before the water can be sent through the water mains. All of these downstream costs are real costs associated with producing paper, just as much as the raw materials, labor, energy, and so on, used internally by the plant. But from the mill's standpoint, these downstream costs are **external costs.** They are costs that are borne by someone other than the people who make decisions about operating the paper mill. At the end of the year the profit-and-loss statement of the paper mill will contain no reference to these real downstream external costs.

If rates of output are to be socially efficient, decisions about resource use must take into account both types of costs: the private costs of producing paper plus whatever external costs arise from adverse environmental impacts. In terms of full social cost accounting:

Social costs = Private costs + External (environmental) costs

This is pictured in Figure 4-3. The top panel shows the relationship between the rate of paper production and the occurrence of these downstream external costs. It shows that the marginal external costs increase as paper production increases. The bottom panel shows several things. It shows the demand curve for paper and the marginal private costs of producing paper. The intersection of these occurs at a price of p^m and a quantity of q^m. This is the price and quantity that would arise in a competitive market where producers pay no attention to external costs. But marginal social costs are in fact higher, as shown, because they contain both the marginal private costs and the marginal external costs. Thus, the full socially efficient rate of output is q^* and the associated price is p^*.

Compare the two rates of output and the two prices. The market output is too high compared to the socially efficient rate of output. In addition, the market price is too low compared to the socially efficient price. It's not hard to understand the reason for this. In considering just its private costs, the firm is essentially using a productive input it is not paying for. What is this unpaid input? The services of the river, which provides the firm with a cheap way to dispose of its production residuals. Although it may be cheap for the firm to do this, it may not be cheap to society; in fact, in this case we have costs being inflicted on downstream users that are being overlooked by the paper mill. So the private market system in this case produces too much paper at too low a price compared to socially efficient results.

Most of the cases of environmental destruction are related to external costs of one type or another. As a real-world example of external costs, consider the data shown in Example 4-1. It shows some results from a study of the environmental externalities stemming from electricity production. The external effects of a power plant differ according to the technology it uses (nuclear, coal, etc.) and its location relative to centers of population. The numbers in the example show estimates of external costs for a pulverized coal steam plant assumed to be located in the middle of New York City.

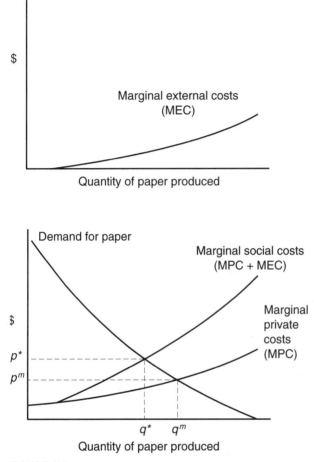

FIGURE 4-3
External Costs and Market Outcomes.

Note that external costs arising from air pollution account for about 98 percent of the total; that is, costs in terms of water and land pollution are relatively small. In addition, among the various airborne emissions, particulate matter is by far the most serious external cost of generating electricity in this situation.

There are many other types of external costs. Users of chemicals emit toxic fumes that affect people living in the vicinity; developers build on land without taking into account the degradation of the visual environment of local inhabitants; and so on. Nor are businesses the only ones responsible for external environmental costs. When individuals drive their automobiles, exhaust gases add to air pollution, and when they dispose of solid waste materials (e.g., old paint cans), they may affect the quality of the local environment.

EXAMPLE 4-1

**SUMMARY OF ESTIMATED EXTERNAL COSTS, BY TYPE,
FOR A 300-MEGAWATT PULVERIZED COAL STEAM POWER PLANT
ASSUMED TO BE LOCATED IN NEW YORK CITY**

Externality group Source group	$/Average residential customer[1]
Air	
Lead	$2.27
Mercury	0.0
Nitrogen oxides	0.38
Particulates (PM_{10})	16.22
Radioactivity	0.0
Sulfur oxides	2.93
Toxics	0.03
Air subtotal	21.83
Water	
Chemicals	0.06
Consumption	0.0
Toxics in ash	0.01
Water subtotal	0.08
Land/waste	
Land use/noise/terrestrial	0.25
Volume/land use	0.03
Land/waste subtotal	0.27
Total external costs	22.18

Source: Based on A. Myrick Freeman III: *The Environmental Cost of Electricity: An Exercise in Pricing the Environment,* Bowdoin College, Economics Department Working Paper 95–116, May 1995.
[1]Based on 4,303 kilowatt hours per year for the average residental customer of Consolidated Edison, as reported in Facts, 1999," at www.coned.com. Numbers may not add to totals because of rounding.

Most, but not all, environmental externalities are expressed through physical linkages among parties involved; that is, polluter and people damaged. The simplest is where there are just two parties involved: one polluter and one person suffering damages. An upstream pulp mill and a downstream firm that uses the river water in its production operations are an example. There are cases of single polluters and multiple damaged parties, such as a power plant that emits SO_2 affecting a group of community residents living downwind. Other cases involve multiple polluters but only one damaged party; for example, the runoff from many farms that affects a local water supply system. Finally, there are many cases where both polluters and parties damaged are many in number. An example of this is urban air pollution stemming from automobile emissions: Each driver is both a producer and a recipient of the externality. The same is true of global phenomena, such as the greenhouse effect.

Some externalities do not involve physical linkages. Degradation of the scenic environment through thoughtless land development is an example. In addition, some externalities involve neither physical linkages nor close proximity. People in one part of a country, for example, may feel loss when those in another region cause damage to an important environmental resource; for example, a unique species of animal or plant.

This brings up a problem that we will state but not solve. What is the limit, if any, to be placed on external damage that people may legitimately claim? I suffer damages when someone in my vicinity plays her stereo too loudly, but can I legitimately claim that I suffer damages if, for example, she adopts a life style with which I don't agree? If people in Boston pollute the waters of Boston harbor, may residents in California claim that they have been damaged? If residents of New Jersey thin out the suburban deer population in order to save their flower gardens, may people in Chicago justifiably claim that they have been damaged?

The answer to these questions hinges on the notion of willingness to pay. In this approach, whether someone has or has not been affected by another action hinges on their willingness to pay to have that action changed. If people in New York are willing to pay to preserve clean air in Tokyo, then this is evidence that air quality in Tokyo affects the welfare of people in New York. If people in Chicago are not willing to pay anything to clean up the Ohio River, we conclude that the water quality of that river has no effect on the welfare of people in Chicago. The presence or absence of willingness to pay, in other words, is the economic index of whether an action may be said to affect somebody.

Open-Access Resources

One source of external costs has been widely studied by environmental economists (as well as natural resource economists): open-access resources. An **open-access resource** is a resource or facility that is open to uncontrolled access by individuals who wish to use the resource. A classic example is an ocean fishery in which anyone willing to buy a boat and take up fishing is free to do so. Other examples are a pasture that is open to anyone to graze animals, a forest where anyone may go and cut wood, or a public park open to free access.

In these situations we have, in effect, problems in property rights—their definition, distribution, and/or enforcement. If someone owns a pasture or a forest, he or she will presumably keep out encroachers, or perhaps charge them for use of the resource or otherwise control their rate of access. But when a resource or facility is open to unrestricted access, there is no way of ensuring that its rate of use is kept to the level that will maximize its overall value.[2]

---

[2]This is what is involved in the "tragedy of the commons," as it was popularly termed by Garrett Hardin in "Tragedy of the Commons," *Science,* Vol. 162, December 13, 1968, pp. 1243–1248. His example was an open-access pasture on which all farmers had the right to pasture their sheep.

To understand this, consider the following example. Suppose there are four similar firms situated on a lake. The firms use the water of the lake in producing their output and discharge emissions back into the lake. Because of the emissions, each firm must treat the water taken from the lake before it uses the water in production. The treatment costs of each firm depend on the ambient quality of the lake, which of course depends on the total emissions of the four firms. Suppose that the cost of intake water treatment is currently $40,000 per year for each firm. A new firm is contemplating starting operations on the lake. If it adds its untreated emissions to those of the current four, it will make ambient water quality worse and drive the cost of water treatment for each firm up to $60,000 per year. When the fifth firm makes its location and production decisions, it will take into account its various operating costs, which will include the $60,000 per year of water treatment costs. But the total social water-related costs of the firm's decisions are higher. There are also external costs inflicted on the other four firms, amounting to $20,000 each of added water treatment costs if the fifth firm locates on the lake. The social marginal costs of water supply when the new firm locates on the lake are $140,000, consisting of $60,000 of internal costs of the new firm plus $80,000 ($20,000 × 4) of external costs inflicted on firms already on the lake. These are often called open-access externalities because they result from the fact that the firms have uncontrolled access to the lake.

We have focused on the externalities flowing from the fifth firm's decisions, but everything is symmetrical in the sense that we could say exactly the same thing about each of the other firms. Each firm will make its decisions without regard to the external costs inflicted on other firms. It is this reciprocal nature of these externalities that distinguishes them from the type we talked about before (e.g., the pulp mill upstream inflicting external costs on people downstream), but the effect is the same: Externalities that lead to rates of output that are too high compared to socially efficient rates.

As another example of an open-access problem, consider a road that is open to access by anyone desiring to use it. A road is not a natural resource but a person-made facility. But the essence of the uncontrolled access problem is identical, and perhaps it is easier to understand with this particular example. It uses very simplifying assumptions in order to highlight the basic issues. There is a road connecting two points—Point A and Point B. The figures in Table 4-1 show the average travel time it takes to get from Point A to Point B along this road, as a function of the number of motorists using the road. Thus, for example, if there are just 10 travelers on the road, it takes 10 minutes to get from A to B (we assume a speed limit that is enforced). Likewise, when there are either 20 or 30 motorists on the road the average travel time is still 10 minutes, but when the traffic increases to 40 travelers, the average travel time increases to 11 minutes. This is because of congestion; cars begin to get in each other's way and average speeds drop. As the number of motorists continues to increase, the congestion increases, thus driving up travel times even more.

Now suppose you are considering using this road to go from A to B and that there are already 50 cars using it. Suppose, furthermore, that you have an

TABLE 4-1
TRAVEL TIMES RELATED TO THE NUMBER OF CARS ON THE ROAD

Number of cars	Average travel time between A and B
10	10
20	10
30	10
40	11
50	12
60	14
70	18
80	24

alternative route that will take you 18 minutes. Assume that you know the state of the traffic and the resulting travel times. Because taking the given road will save you 4 minutes over the alternative, your individual decision would be to use the road. But from the standpoint of "society," in this case consisting of you plus all the other motorists on the road, this is not efficient. When you enter the highway on which there are already 50 cars, the added congestion causes an increase in average travel times of 2 minutes to the people already using the road. Thus, your 4-minute individual savings is offset by added travel costs of 100 minutes (50 cars times 2 minutes per car) on the part of the other motorists, meaning that if all minutes are treated as equally valuable, there is a net social loss of 96 minutes when you decide to use the road.

The problem arises because there is uncontrolled access to the road, and in using it people may inflict external costs on others in the form of added congestion and higher travel times. The same kind of effect holds when a fisher enters a fishery; in catching a portion of the stock, he leaves fewer to be caught by other fishers. When one farmer puts animals on a common pasture, he or she reduces the forage available to other herds on that pasture. When one person cuts wood from a communal forest, she leaves fewer trees for other users and makes it more difficult for them to supply themselves with wood. We can see that this is related to the notion of external costs. The added costs that one user of a common-property resource inflicts on other users of that resource are in fact costs that are external to that user but internal to the whole group of users. When a single individual is making a decision about whether and how much to utilize a common-property resource, she takes into account the costs and benefits that impinge directly on her. Some people might also altruistically take into account the common-property externalities they inflict on others, but most will not. The result will be, as it was with the road example, a rate of use that is higher than what is called for on grounds of social efficiency.

Thus, when external costs are present, private markets will not normally produce quantities of output that are socially efficient. This market failure may justify public policy to help move the economy toward efficiency. This may be done sometimes by changing rules, such as property rights rules, so that the market will function efficiently. Other cases may call for more direct public intervention. We will take up these matters again in Section Four. We must now move to the demand side of the market and consider another important source of market failure, that of external benefits.

EXTERNAL BENEFITS

An **external benefit** is a benefit that accrues to somebody who is outside, or external, to the decision about consuming or using the good or resource that causes the externality. When the use of an item leads to an external benefit, the market willingness to pay for that item will understate the social willingness to pay. Suppose a quieter lawn mower would provide $50 a year of extra benefits to me if I were to buy it. This is therefore the maximum that I would be willing to pay for this machine. But suppose my use of the new lawn mower would create $20 of added benefits to my neighbor because of reduced noise levels in the course of the year. These $20 of benefits to the neighbor are external benefits for me. I make my purchasing decision on the basis of benefits accruing only to me. Thus, my marginal willingness to pay for a quieter lawn mower is $50, whereas the social marginal benefits (where "society" in this case includes just me and my neighbor) is $70 (my $50 and her $20).

As another example of an external benefit, consider a farmer whose land is on the outskirts of an urban area. The farmer cultivates the land and sells his produce to people in the city. Of course, the farmer's main concern is the income he can derive from the operation, and he makes decisions about inputs and outputs according to their effect on that income. But the land kept in agriculture produces several other benefits, including a habitat for birds and other small animals and scenic values for passers-by. These benefits, although internal from the standpoint of society, are external from the standpoint of the farmer. They don't appear anywhere in his profit-and-loss position; they are external benefits of his farming decisions. In this case the agricultural value of the land to the farmer understates the social willingness to pay to have the land in agriculture.

Many goods do not involve external benefits. Indeed, when economists discuss the rudiments of supply and demand, the examples used are normally simple goods that do not create this complication. Farmers produce and supply so many thousand cantaloupes; individual and market demand curves for cantaloupes are easy to comprehend. If we want to know the total number of cantaloupes bought, we can simply add up the number bought by each person in the market. Each person's consumption affects no one else. In this case the market demand curve will represent accurately the aggregate marginal willingness to pay of consumers for cantaloupes. But in cases involving external benefits, this no longer holds. We can perhaps best see this by considering a type of good that inherently involves large-scale external benefits, what economists have come to call "public goods."

Public Goods

Consider a lighthouse. This is a service provided to mariners at sea so that they can locate themselves and avoid running aground at night. But the lighthouse has an interesting technical characteristic: If its services are made available to one mariner at sea, they immediately become available to all others in the vicinity. Once the services are made available to one person, others cannot be excluded from making use of the same services. This is the distinguishing characteristic of a **public good.** It is a good that, if made available to one person, automatically becomes available to others.

Another example of a public good is a radio signal. Once a radio station broadcasts a signal, it is available to anybody who has a receiver. Each individual can listen to the broadcast without diminishing its availability to all other people within range of the station. Note carefully that it is not the ownership of the supplying organization that makes a public good public. Lighthouses are usually publicly owned, but radio stations, at least in the United States, are typically privately owned. A public good is distinguished by the technical nature of the good, not by the type of organization making it available.

We are interested in public goods because environmental quality is essentially a public good. If the air is cleaned up for one person in an urban area, it is automatically cleaned up for everybody else in that community. The benefits, in other words, accrue to everyone in the community. Private markets are likely to undersupply public goods, relative to efficient levels. To see why, let's take another very simple example: a small freshwater lake, the shores of which have three occupied homes. The people living in the houses use the lake for recreational purposes, but, unfortunately, the water quality of the lake has been contaminated by an old industrial plant that has since closed. The contaminant is measured in parts per million (ppm). At present the lake contains 5 ppm of this contaminant. It is possible to clean the water by using a fairly expensive treatment process. Each of the surrounding homeowners is willing to pay a certain amount to have the water quality improved. Table 4-2 shows these individual marginal willingnesses to pay for integer values of water quality. It also shows the total marginal willingness to pay, which is the sum of the individual values.

TABLE 4-2
INDIVIDUAL AND AGGREGATE DEMAND FOR LOWERING LAKE POLLUTION

Level of contaminant (ppm)	Marginal willingness to pay ($ per year)				Marginal cost of cleanup
	Homeowner A	Homeowner B	Homeowner C	Total	
4	110	60	30	200	50
3	85	35	20	140	65
2	70	10	15	95	95
1	55	0	10	65	150
0	45	0	5	50	240

The table also shows the marginal cost of cleaning up the lake, again just for integer values of water quality. Note that marginal cost is increasing; as the lake becomes cleaner, the marginal cost of continued improvement increases. Marginal cost and aggregate marginal willingness to pay are equal at a water quality of 2 ppm. At levels less than this (higher ppm), aggregate marginal willingness to pay for a cleaner lake exceeds the marginal cost of achieving it. Hence, from the standpoint of these three homeowners together, improved water quality is desirable, but at quality levels better than 2 ppm total willingness to pay falls below marginal costs. Thus, 2 ppm is the socially efficient level of water quality in the lake.

This is depicted graphically in Figure 4-4. The top three panels show the marginal willingness to pay by each of the three homeowners. When summing individual demand curves for private goods, we could add together the individual quantities demanded at each price to get the aggregate quantity demanded. But with a public good people are, in effect, consuming the same units, so we must add together the individual marginal willingness to pay at each quantity to get the aggregate demand function, as shown in Figure 4-4. At a water-quality level of 3 ppm, for example, the marginal willingnesses to pay are, respectively, $85, $35, and $20 for individuals A, B, and C. Thus, the total marginal willingness to pay at this level of water quality is $140. The bottom panel of the graph shows the aggregate marginal willingness-to-pay/demand function labeled D, the marginal cost function (MC), and the efficient level of water quality.

Having identified the efficient level of water quality, could we rely on a competitive market system, where entrepreneurs are on the alert for new profit opportunities, to get the contaminant in the lake reduced to that level? Suppose a private firm attempts to sell its services to the three homeowners. The firm goes to person A and tries to collect an amount equal to that person's true willingness to pay. But that person will presumably realize that once the lake is cleaned up, it is cleaned up for everybody no matter how much each homeowner actually contributed. So A may have the incentive to underpay, relative to his true willingness to pay, in the hopes that the other homeowners will contribute enough to cover the costs of the cleanup. Of course, the others may react in the same way. When a public good is involved, each person may have an incentive to **free ride** on the efforts of others. A free rider is a person who pays less for a good than her or his true marginal willingness to pay; that is, a person who underpays relative to the benefits he receives.

Free riding is a ubiquitous phenomenon in the world of public goods, or in fact any good the consumption of which produces external benefits. Because of the free-riding impulse, private, profit-motivated firms will have difficulty covering their costs if they go into the business of supplying public goods.[3] Because of these reduced revenues, private firms will normally *undersupply* goods and services of this type. Environmental quality improvements are

---

[3]This sentence emphasizes the point made earlier: It is the technical nature of the good that makes it a public or private good, not whether the organization providing it is public or private. A lighthouse (a public good) might be built and operated by a private firm; insurance (a private good) might be provided by a public agency.

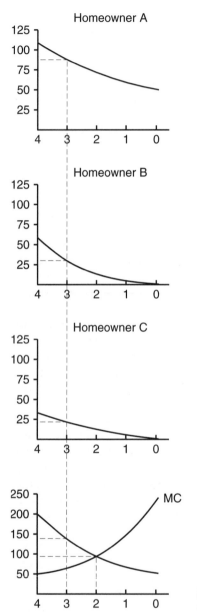

FIGURE 4-4
Aggregate Willingness to Pay for a Public Good.

essentially public goods. Because we cannot rely on the market system to provide efficient quantities of "goods" of this type, we must fall back on some type of nonmarket institution involving collective action of one type or another. In the lake example, the homeowners may be able to act together **privately,** perhaps through a homeowners' association, to secure contributions for cleaning up the lake. Of course, the free-rider problem will still exist even for the homeowners' association, but if there are not too many of them personal acquaintance and the operation of moral pressure may be strong enough to overcome the problem. When there are many more people involved (thousands, or perhaps millions, as there are in many large urban areas), the free-rider problem can be addressed effectively only with more direct governmental action. This opens up the huge topic of **public policy** for environmental quality, a topic we will spend much more time discussing throughout the rest of the book.

SUMMARY

The main goal in this chapter was to discuss the operation of private markets and then apply the market model to situations in which environmental quality is an issue. Markets are places where buyers and sellers interact over the quantities and prices of particular goods or services. Buyers' desires are represented by the aggregate demand curve, which shows the quantities demanded at alternative prices. Sellers' supply capabilities are represented by supply curves, which ultimately are based on underlying production costs and show quantities that would be made available at alternative prices. The intersection of supply and demand curves shows the unique quantity and price that can simultaneously satisfy both buyers and sellers. For many types of goods and services, market outcomes (output and price levels) also may be the outcomes that are socially efficient. Outcomes that are socially efficient are those in which aggregate marginal willingness to pay in society is equal to aggregate marginal social costs of production. When market results are not socially efficient, we speak of market failures.

We then discussed two main situations where market failures may result. The primary reason, on a conceptual level, is the existence of external costs and external benefits. In matters of the environment, external costs are the damages that people experience from environmental impacts that are not taken into account by the firms, public agencies, or consumers whose decisions produce them. A classic case is water pollution from an upstream pulp mill that damages people using the water downstream. Another important case is the external costs that users of an open-access resource inflict upon one another through uncontrolled use of the resource. External benefits are benefits accruing to people other than the direct buyers or recipients of a good. The classic case of external benefits is what are called public goods; these are goods or services that, when they are made available to one person, automatically become available to others.

Faced with external costs and benefits, public goods, and common-property resources, markets cannot be relied upon to supply efficient levels of environmental quality. Some type of nonmarket actions by private or public groups may be called upon to rectify these situations.

QUESTIONS FOR FURTHER DISCUSSION

1 Go back to question 2 of the last chapter. Suppose the marginal cost of producing this item is constant at $5 per item. What is the socially efficient rate of output?

2 Below are portions of the demand curves of three individuals for the water quality in a small pond. The water quality is expressed in terms of the parts per million (ppm) of dissolved oxygen (DO). Water quality improves at higher DO levels. The demand curves show the desired water quality of each individual in relation to the marginal costs of water quality improvements (the marginal cost of raising the DO level in the lake)

  (a) Find the aggregate marginal willingness-to-pay curve for these three people.

  (b) If the actual marginal cost of increasing DO is $12, what is the socially efficient level of DO in the lake, assuming these three people are the only ones involved?

Marginal cost of raising DO level (dollars per ppm)	Desired DO level (ppm)		
	A	B	C
10	0	0	1
8	0	1	2
6	1	2	3
4	2	3	4
2	3	4	5
0	4	5	6

3 Suppose, in question 1, that the demand curves related to the number of cantaloupes consumed per week, and the marginal cost referred to the market price of cantaloupes. Construct the aggregate demand curve for cantaloupes.

4 Considering the definition of public goods introduced in the chapter, is a bus a public good? A public telephone? A public park?

5 Consider the example of the three homeowners around the lake. Suppose the lake was cleaned up to the efficient level and that the total costs of the cleanup were shared equally among the homeowners (stick to integer values here). Will all three homeowners be better off? What problems does this bring up about sharing the costs of public goods?

WEBSITES

See the web pages listed for Chapter 3.

SELECTED READINGS

The same comment is relevant here as appeared in the bibliography of the last chapter: Consult the appropriate chapters of one of the popular microeconomics texts. In the present case you want to look specifically for "efficiency" and market failures in the face of externalities, public goods, and common-property resources. The best-known texts are:

Baumol, William J., and Alan S. Blinder: *Microeconomics, Principles and Policy*, 8th ed., Harcourt College Publishers, Dallas, TX, 2000, Chapters 5, 6, 8.

Boyes, William, and Michael Melvin: *Microeconomics*, 4th ed., Houghton Mifflin, Boston,

MA, 1999, Chapters 2, 3.

Case, Karl E., and Ray C. Fair: *Principles of Microeconomics,* 5th ed., Prentice Hall, Upper Saddle River, NJ, 1999, Chapters 4, 6, 7.

Frank, Robert H., and Ben Bernanke: *Principles of Economics,* Irwin McGraw-Hill, New York, 2000, Chapters 4, 5, 6, 7.

Lipsey, Richard G., Paul N. Courant, and Christopher T. S. Ragan: *Microeconomics,* 12th ed., Addison Wesley Longman, Reading, MA, 1999, Chapters 7, 8, 9.

McConnell, Campbell R., and Stanley L. Brue: *Economics,* 14th ed., Irwin McGraw-Hill, New York, 1998, Chapters, 20, 21, 22.

Parkin, Michael: *Economics,* 5th ed., Addison Wesley Longman, Reading, MA, 2000, Chapters 4, 6.

Samuelson, Paul A., and William D. Nordhaus: *Economics,* 17th ed., Irwin McGraw-Hill, New York, 2001, Chapters 6, 8.

Schiller, Bradley R.: *The Microeconomy Today,* 8th ed., Irwin McGraw-Hill, New York, 2000, Chapter 2.

5

THE ECONOMICS OF ENVIRONMENTAL QUALITY

In the preceding chapter we concluded that the market system, left to itself, is likely to malfunction when matters of environmental pollution are involved. That is to say, it will not normally produce results that are socially efficient. This brings us to the **policy question:** If we do not like the way things are currently turning out, what steps should be undertaken to change the situation?[1]

The policy problem includes a number of closely related issues. One of the first is that of identifying the most appropriate level of environmental quality we ought to try to achieve. Another is how to divide up the task of meeting environmental quality goals. If we have many polluters, how should we seek to allocate among them an overall reduction in emissions? Another issue is the question of how the benefits and costs of environmental programs are distributed across society and whether this distribution is appropriate. In this chapter we take up these issues on a conceptual basis; in subsequent chapters we will look at specific policy alternatives.

Before developing a simple policy model, it needs to be stressed again that effective public policy depends on good information on how economic and environmental systems actually work. This might be called the scientific basis of environmental policy; that is, the study of how firms and consumers normally make decisions in the market economy, how residuals are emitted into the natural environment, and the ways in which these residuals behave in that environment to produce human and nonhuman damages. Thousands of scientists have worked and continue to work on these issues to clarify these diverse linkages. Great effort will continue to be needed to expand the scientific base on which to develop environmental policy.

---

[1]This goes back to the distinction made earlier between positive and normative economics (see p. 4). Explaining why there is a certain amount of SO_2 in the air at any particular time is a question of positive economics; deciding what best to do about it is a case of normative economics.

POLLUTION CONTROL—A GENERAL MODEL

Diverse types of environmental pollutants obviously call for diverse types of public policy, but in order to build up the required policy analyses it is better to start with one very simple model that lays out the fundamentals of the policy situation. The essence of the model consists of a simple **trade-off** situation that characterizes all pollution-control activities. On the one hand, reducing emissions reduces the damages that people suffer from environmental pollution; on the other hand, reducing emissions takes resources that could have been used in some other way.

To depict this trade-off consider a simple situation where a firm (e.g., a pulp mill) is emitting production residuals into a river. As these residuals are carried downstream, they tend to be transformed into less damaging chemical constituents, but before that process is completed the river passes by a large metropolitan area. The people of the area use the waters of the river for various purposes, including recreation (boating, fishing) and as a source for the municipal water supply system. When the river becomes polluted with industrial waste, the people downstream are damaged by the disruption of these and other services provided by the river. One side of the trade-off, then, is the **damages** that people experience when the environment is degraded.

Upstream, the offending pulp mill could reduce the amount of effluent put in the river by treating its wastes before discharge, as well as by recycling certain materials that currently just run out of the discharge pipe. This act of reducing, or abating, some portion of its wastes will require resources of some amount, the costs of which will affect the price of the paper it produces.[2] These **abatement costs** are the other side of the basic pollution-control trade-off.

POLLUTION DAMAGES

By **damages** we mean all the negative impacts that users of the environment experience as a result of the degradation of that environment. These negative impacts are of many types and, of course, will vary from one environmental asset to another. In the river pollution example, damages were to recreators, who could no longer use the river or who suffered a higher chance of picking up waterborne diseases, and to all the city dwellers who had to pay more to treat the water before they could put it into the public water mains.

Air pollution produces damage through its impacts on human health. Excess deaths from diseases such as lung cancer, chronic bronchitis, and emphysema are related to elevated levels of various pollutants, such as particulate matter, asbestos fibers, and radon emissions. Air pollution can cause damages through the degradation of materials (all of the important outdoor sculpture from Renaissance Florence has had to be put inside to protect it from air pollution)

---

[2]The word "resources" has a double meaning in economics. On the one hand it is a shorthand way of referring to "natural resources." On the other hand, it is more generally used to refer to the inputs that are utilized to produce outputs.

TABLE 5-1
ESTIMATED BENEFITS (REDUCED DAMAGES) IN 2010 FROM CLEAN AIR ACT
REDUCTIONS OF CRITERIA POLLUTANTS

	$ millions (1990 dollars*)
Mortality[†]	100,000
Chronic illness	
Chronic bronchitis	5,600
Chronic asthma	180
Hospitalization	
All respiratory	130
Total cardiovascular	390
Asthma-related ER visits	1
Minor illness	
Acute bronchitis	2.1
Upper respiratory symptoms	19
Lower respiratory symptoms	6.2
Respiratory illness	6.3
Moderate/worse asthma	13
Asthma attacks	55
Chest tightness, shortness of breath	11
Work-loss days	340
MRAD/any of 19[‡]	1,200
Welfare	
Decreased worker productivity	710
Visibility-recreational	2,900
Agriculture	550
Acidification	50
Commercial timber	600
Aggregate	110,000

*This means that the estimates for 2010 were done in terms of 1990 dollars, that is, they were corrected for anticipated inflation between 1990 and 2010.
[†]This is the estimated value associated with the reduction in premature mortality.
[‡]Minor restricted activity days stemming from any of 19 different respiratory symptoms.
Source: U.S. EPA, "The Benefits and Costs of the Clean Air Act of 1990 to 2010," *EPA Report to Congress, EPA-410-R-99-001,* Washington, DC, November 1999, p. 102.

and the deterioration of the visual environment. Table 5-1 shows the range of impacts produced by the major air pollutants in the United States. It is in terms of the **damages reduced** (i.e., benefits) by the Clean Air Act.

Besides damage to human beings, environmental destruction can have important impacts on various elements of the nonhuman ecosystem. Some of these, such as the destruction of genetic information in plant and animal species driven to extinction, will ultimately have important implications for humans. Estimating environmental damages is one of the primary tasks facing environmental scientists and economists, and we will devote Chapter 7 to a discussion of this problem.

Damage Functions

In general, the greater the pollution, the greater the damages it produces. To describe the relationship between pollution and damage, we will use the idea of a **damage function**. A damage function shows the relationship between the quantity of a residual and the damage that residual causes. There are two types of damage functions.

- **Emission damage functions:** These show the connection between the quantity of a residual emitted from a source or group of sources and the resulting damage.
- **Ambient damage functions:** These show the relationship between concentration of particular pollutants in the ambient environment and the resulting damages.

Damage functions can be expressed in a variety of ways, but our primary model will make use of **marginal damage functions.** A marginal damage function shows the **change** in damages stemming from a unit change in emissions or ambient concentration. When necessary, we also can use these relationships to discuss total damages because we know that, graphically, the areas under marginal damage functions correspond to total damages.

The height and shape of a damage function depends on the pollutant and circumstances involved. Several marginal damage functions are depicted in Figure 5-1. The top two are marginal emission damage functions; the horizontal axes measure the quantity of an effluent emitted into the environment during some specified period of time. The exact units (pounds, tons, etc.) in any particular case depend on the specific pollutant involved. The vertical axes measure environmental damages. In physical terms, environmental damage can include many types of impacts: miles of coastline polluted, numbers of people contracting lung disease, numbers of animals wiped out, quantities of water contaminated, and so on. Every case of environmental pollution normally involves multiple types of impacts, the nature of which will depend on the pollutant involved and the time and place it is emitted. To consider these impacts comprehensively we need to be able to aggregate them into a single dimension. For this purpose we use a monetary scale. It is sometimes easy to express damage in monetary units; for example, the "defensive" expenditures that people make to protect themselves against pollution (e.g., heavier insulation to protect against noise). Usually, however, it is very difficult, as we will see.

The marginal emission damage function in panel (a) of Figure 5-1 shows marginal damages increasing only modestly at the beginning but more rapidly as emissions get larger and larger. Work by environmental scientists and economists seems to suggest that this is a typical shape for many types of pollutants, although probably not for all of them. At low levels of emissions, marginal damages may be comparatively small; ambient concentrations are so modest that only the most sensitive people in the population are affected. But when emission levels go higher, damages mount, and at still higher levels of emissions, marginal damages become very elevated as environmental impacts become widespread and intense.

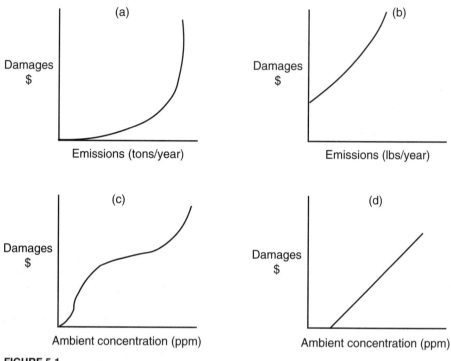

FIGURE 5-1
Representative Marginal Damage Functions.

Panel (b) shows a marginal (emission) damage function that has the same general shape as panel (a) (i.e., it shows increasing marginal damage), but it begins much higher on the vertical axis and rises more sharply. It might represent a toxic substance that has a deadly effect even at very low levels of emission.

The two bottom relationships in Figure 5-1 are marginal ambient damage functions. Whereas the vertical axes have a monetary index of damages, the horizontal axes have an index of ambient concentration, such as parts per million (ppm). Panel (c) shows a complicated function that increases at low concentrations, then tends to level off until much higher concentrations are reached, after which damages increase rapidly. This might apply, for example, to an air pollutant that causes marked damages among particularly sensitive members of society at relatively low concentrations, and among all people at very high concentrations, while in the middle ranges marginal damages do not increase rapidly. Panel (d) demonstrates an ambient marginal damage function that begins to the right of the origin and then increases linearly with ambient concentration.

Panels (a) and (d) illustrate a characteristic that is in fact quite controversial. They have **thresholds;** that is, values of emissions or ambient concentrations below which marginal damages are zero. Thus, the pollutant can increase to these threshold levels without causing any increase in damages. As will be seen in chapters to come, the assumed existence or nonexistence of a threshold in the damage functions for particular pollutants has had important impacts on real-world environmental control policies. There have been long, vigorous arguments about whether the damage functions of certain types of pollutants do or do not have thresholds.

Damage Functions: A Closer Look

We need to look more deeply into the concept of the damage function because it will be used later to express and analyze a variety of different types of pollution problems and public policy approaches. Accordingly, Figure 5-2 shows two marginal emissions damage functions. It is important to remember that, like the demand and supply curves discussed earlier, these are time specific; they show the emissions and the marginal damages for a particular period of time. There are a couple of ways of thinking about this. One is to assume, for purposes of simplicity, that the graph refers to a strictly noncumulative pollutant. Thus, all damages occur in the same period as emissions. A somewhat more complicated assumption is that for a pollutant that cumulates over time, the damage function shows the total value that people place on current and future damages. In Chapter 6 we will discuss this concept more fully.

Consider first just one of the marginal damage functions; for example, the lower one labeled MD_1. In previous chapters we discussed the relationship between marginal and total quantities; for example, the relationship between marginal and total costs. We have the same relationship here. The height of the marginal damage curve shows how much total damages would change with a small change in the quantity of emissions. When the effluent level is at the point marked e_1, for example, marginal damages are $12. That is to say, if emissions were to increase by one ton from point e_1, the damages experienced by people exposed to those emissions would increase by $12. By the same token, if emissions decreased by a small amount at point e_1, total damages would be reduced by $12. Because the height of the curve, as measured on the y-axis, shows marginal damages, the area under the curve between the point where it is zero and some other point, like the one labeled e_1, shows the total damages associated with that level of emissions. In the case of marginal damage function MD_1 and point e_1, total damages are equal to the monetary amount expressed by the triangular area bounded by the x-axis, the curve MD_1, and the effluent quantity e_1. That is area b in Figure 5-2.

What factors might account for the difference between MD_1 and MD_2 in Figure 5-2? Let us assume that they apply to the same pollutant. For any given level of emissions, marginal damages are higher for MD_2 than for MD_1. At emission level e_1, for example, a small increase in effluent would increase damages by $12 if the marginal damage function were MD_1, but it would increase damages by $28 if it were MD_2. Remember that any damage function shows the impacts of emitting a particular effluent in a particular time and place, so one possible explanation might be that MD_2 refers to a situation in which many people are affected by a pollutant, such as a large urban area, whereas MD_1 refers to a more sparsely populated rural area—fewer people, smaller damage.

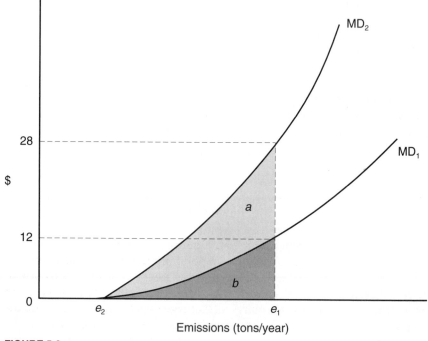

FIGURE 5-2
Anatomy of a Marginal Damage Function.

One major factor that moves damage functions upward, in other words, is an increase in the number of people exposed to a particular pollutant.

Another possibility that might offer an explanation of why one marginal damage function lies above another is that although they apply to the same group of people, they refer to different time periods. Damage results from ambient pollution, whereas what we have on the horizontal axis is quantity of emissions. The functioning of the environment is what connects these two factors. Suppose the pollutant in question is some sort of material emitted into the air by industrial firms located near an urban area and that the damage functions refer to impacts felt by people living in that area. Marginal damage function MD_2 might occur when there is a temperature inversion that traps the pollutant over the city and produces relatively high ambient concentrations. MD_1 would be the damage function, however, when normal wind patterns prevail so that most of the effluent is blown downwind and out of the area. Thus, the same emission levels at two different times could yield substantially different damage levels due to the workings of the natural environment.

Because MD_2 is above MD_1, it corresponds not only to higher marginal damages but also to higher total damages. At emission level e_1, total damages are equal to area b when the damage function is MD_1, but to area $(a + b)$ when the damage function is MD_2.

Having considered the concept of damages, it is now necessary to look at the other side of the trade-off relationship mentioned previously. It is tempting not to do this, to conclude instead that the damage functions themselves give us all the information needed to make decisions about pollution control. One might be tempted to say, for example, that society ought to strive for emission levels around point e_2 where marginal damages are zero, or perhaps even the origin, corresponding to a point at which emissions are zero. There may be certain pollutants and situations where the efficient level of emissions is indeed zero. But to determine this we have to look at the other side of the problem: abatement costs.

ABATEMENT COSTS

Abatement costs are the costs of reducing the quantity of residuals being emitted into the environment, or of lowering ambient concentrations. Think of the pulp mill located upstream. In its normal course of operation it produces a large quantity of organic wastes. On the assumption that it has free access to the river, the cheapest way to get rid of these wastes is simply to pump them into the river, but the firm normally has technological and managerial means to reduce these emissions. The costs of engaging in these activities are called "abatement costs" because they are the costs of abating, or reducing, the quantity of residuals put into the river. By spending resources on this activity, the pulp mill can abate its emissions; in general, the greater the abatement, the greater the cost.

Abatement costs normally will differ from one source to another, depending on a variety of factors. The costs of reducing emissions of SO_2 from electric power plants obviously will be different from the costs of reducing, say, toxic fumes from chemical plants. Even for sources producing the same type of effluent the costs of abatement are likely to be different because of differences in the technological features of the operation. One source may be relatively new, using modern production technology, whereas another may be an old one using more highly polluting technology. In the discussion that follows keep in mind that "abatement" is used with the widest possible connotation and includes all the many ways there are of reducing emissions: changes in production technology, input switching, residuals recycling, treatment, abandonment of a site, and so forth.

Abatement Cost Functions

We represent this idea graphically using the concept of the **marginal abatement cost** function. The units on the axes are the same as before: quantities of pollutants on the horizontal axis and monetary value on the vertical axis. Marginal emission abatement costs show the added costs of achieving a one-unit decrease in emission level, or alternatively the costs saved if emissions are increased by a unit. On the horizontal axis, marginal abatement cost curves originate at the uncontrolled emission levels; that is, emission levels prior to undertaking any abatement activities. From this origin point, marginal abatement costs show the marginal costs of producing reductions in emissions. Thus, these marginal cost curves rise from right to left, depicting rising marginal costs of reducing emissions.[3] Exhibit 5-1 shows data pertaining to the abatement cost function for cleaning up the water of Boston Harbor.

Figure 5-3 shows three alternative marginal abatement cost functions. The one in panel (a) depicts marginal abatement costs rising very modestly as emissions are first reduced, but then rising very rapidly as emissions become

---

EXHIBIT 5-1

THE ABATEMENT COST FUNCTION FOR CLEANING UP BOSTON HARBOR[1]

Cost/ household/ year	What you get	Effects on the community and the environment	Legality
$0.00	No running water; no sewage pipes to remove sewage from houses.	City life impossible; unsafe drinking water leads to disease; local ponds and rivers drained for water; water shortages; sewage in streets causes epidemics; local ponds and rivers destroyed by sewage; major changes in animal life and urban ecology.	($0) Illegal: Federal CWA and others violated.
$125.00	Running water in your house; clean, safe drinking water; no sewage removed from your house.	City life miserable due to raw sewage in the streets; epidemics caused by raw sewage; rivers, lakes, and harbor polluted with bacteria; destruction of local ponds and rivers by sewage; major changes in animal life and urban ecology; no safe swimming; coastal seafood contaminated.	($125) Illegal: Federal CWA and others violated.
$175.00	Running water in your house; clean, safe drinking water; sewage piped to harbor—no treatment.	Harbor unswimmable and smelly; health risk presented by raw sewage; harbor polluted by sewage and excess nutrients; shellfish contaminated; no safe ocean swimming; rats feed on fish killed by low oxygen levels.	($175) Illegal: Federal CWA and others violated.

(Continued)

---

[3]In Chapter 3, we showed marginal cost curves sloping upward to the right. The graph goes in the opposite direction because here we are producing *reductions* in emissions.

Cost/ household/ year	What you get	Effects on the community and the environment	Legality
$225.00	Running water in your house; clean, safe drinking water; sewage removed from house; primary treatment under typical conditions; frequent releases of raw sewage through combined sewer outfalls.	Boston Harbor polluted with bacteria and toxins; health risk presented by raw sewage in harbor; fish growth limited by low oxygen in the summer; all harbor seafood (except lobster) contaminated; beaches closed frequently in summer.	($225) Illegal: Federal CWA and others violated.
$725.00	Running water in your house; clean, safe drinking water; sewage removed from house; primary treatment under typical conditions; secondary treatment under typical conditions; many releases of raw sewage through CSOs per year.	Improvement in harbor from present; bacterial pollution and low oxygen levels caused by combined sewer outfall (CSO) releases; all harbor seafood (except lobster) contaminated; beaches closed frequently in summer.	($725) Legal: Under typical conditions. ($725) Illegal: Federal CWA violated during heavy rain storms.
$800.00	Running water in your house; clean, safe drinking water; sewage removed from house; primary treatment; secondary treatment and sludge recycling; long outfall; storage for CSO water; infrequent releases of raw sewage through CSOs.	Improvement in harbor from present; seafood caught in harbor is edible; few or no beaches closed during summer; harbor swimmable under good conditions.	($800) Legal: Federal CWA requirements met.
$1,200.00	Running water in your house; clean, safe drinking water; sewage removed from house; primary treatment; secondary treatment and sludge recycling; tertiary treatment; long outfall; containment of CSO water.	Sewage has no effect on harbor; healthy marine environment in harbor; harbor swimmable.	($1,200) Legal: Federal CWA requirements exceeded.

[1]These abatement costs are in terms of dollars per household per year. They are not, strictly speaking, marginal abatement costs, but you can determine what these are by looking at the differences in costs between the various levels.

Source: Exhibit material displayed at the New England Aquarium, Boston, MA, Spring 2000. Thanks to Stephen Costa for finding this material.

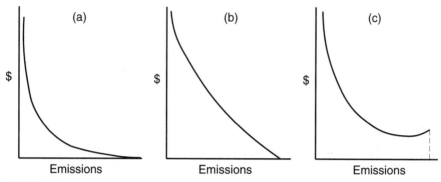

FIGURE 5-3
Representative Marginal Abatement Cost Functions.

relatively small. Panel (b) shows marginal abatement costs that rise rapidly from the beginning. Panel (c) shows a marginal abatement cost curve that has an initial declining phase, followed by increasing values; this might characterize a situation in which small reductions can be handled only by technical means that require a substantial initial investment. For somewhat larger reductions, the marginal costs actually may decline as it becomes possible to utilize these techniques more fully. Ultimately, however, marginal abatement costs increase. We have to keep in mind that in dealing with abatement costs we are dealing with a cost concept similar to that discussed in Chapter 3. The level of costs encountered when carrying out any particular task depends on the technology available to do the task and also on the managerial skills that are applied to the job. It is quite possible to suffer extremely high abatement costs if the wrong technology is used or if what is available is used incorrectly. In other words, the marginal abatement cost functions pictured are to be understood as the **minimum** costs of achieving reductions in emissions.

Abatement Cost Functions: A Closer Look

To investigate more deeply the concept of marginal abatement cost, consider Figure 5-4, which shows two marginal abatement cost curves. For the moment we focus on the higher one, labeled MAC_2. It begins at an effluent level marked $\bar{e}$, the uncontrolled emission level. From there it slopes upward to the left. Beginning at the uncontrolled level, the first units of emission reduction can be achieved with a relatively low marginal cost. Think again of the pulp mill. This first small decrease might be obtained with the addition of a modest settling pond, but as emission levels are reduced further the marginal cost of achieving additional reductions increases. For example, to get a 30–40 percent reduction, the pulp mill may have to invest in new technology that is more efficient in terms of water use. A 60–70 percent reduction in effluent might require substantial new treatment technology in addition to all the steps taken previously, whereas a 90–95 percent reduction might take very costly equipment for recy-

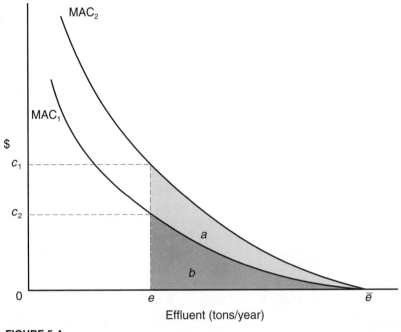

FIGURE 5-4
Anatomy of a Marginal Abatement Cost Curve.

cling virtually all of the production residuals produced in the plant. Thus, the larger the reduction in emissions, the greater the marginal costs of producing further reductions. This yields a marginal abatement cost function that gets steeper in slope as emissions are reduced.

Of course, there is an upper limit on these abatement costs. The extreme option for a single plant or pollution source is to cease operations, thereby achieving a zero level of emissions. The costs of doing this depend on circumstances. If the source is just one small plant within a large industry consisting of many such plants, the costs of closing it down may not be that great. In fact it may have very little impact on, say, the price to consumers of whatever is being produced (e.g., paper in the pulp mill), although the local impact on jobs and community welfare may be substantial. But if we are talking about the marginal abatement costs for an entire industry—electric power production in the midwestern United States, for example—the "shutdown" option, as a way of achieving zero emissions, would have enormous costs.

The marginal abatement cost function can express **actual** marginal costs of a source or group of sources or the **lowest possible** marginal abatement costs. Actual costs, of course, are determined by the technologies and procedures that firms have adopted in the past to reduce emissions. These could have been affected by a variety of factors, including managerial shortsightedness or public pollution control regulations. To use the model for studying questions of social efficiency and cost effectiveness, however, we don't want actual costs but the lowest possible abatement costs. In this case, we have to assume that sources have adopted whatever technological and managerial means are available to achieve emission reductions at the lowest possible costs. We have to assume, in other words, that sources are acting in a **cost-effective** manner.

As with any marginal graph, we can depict not only marginal but also total values. If emissions are currently at e tons per year, the value on the vertical axis shows the marginal cost of achieving one more unit of emission reduction. The area under the marginal abatement cost curve, between its origin at point $\bar{e}$ and any particular emission level, is equal to the **total costs** of abating emissions to that level. For example, with the curve labeled MAC_2, the total abatement cost of achieving an emission level of e tons per year is equal to the area under the curve between e and $\bar{e}$, the area $(a + b)$; remember we are reading the graph from right to left.

Consider now the other marginal abatement cost curve shown in Figure 5-4, labeled MAC_1. Its main feature is that it lies below MAC_2, meaning that it corresponds to a situation where the marginal abatement costs for any level of emissions are lower than those of MAC_2. At e tons per year of emissions, for example, the marginal costs of abating an extra ton are only c_2 in the case of MAC_1, which are substantially lower than the marginal abatement costs of MAC_2 at this point. What could account for the difference? Let us assume that we are dealing with the same pollutant in each case. One possibility is that these apply to different sources; for example, a plant that was built many years ago and another that was built more recently and uses different production technology. The newer plant lends itself to less costly emissions reduction.

Another possibility is that MAC_1 and MAC_2 relate to the same pollutant and the same source, but at different times. The lower one represents the situation after a new pollution-control technology has been developed, whereas the upper one applies before the change. Technological change, in other words, results in a lowering of the marginal abatement cost curve for a given pollutant. It is possible to represent graphically the annual cost that this source would save assuming the emission rate is e before and after the change. Before the firm adopted the new technology, its total abatement cost of achieving effluent level e was equal to $(a + b)$ per year, whereas after the change the total abatement costs are b per year. The annual cost savings from the technological change are thus a. This type of analysis will be important when we examine different types of pollution-control policies because one of the criteria we will want to use to evaluate these policies is how much cost-saving incentive they offer to firms to engage in research and development to produce new pollution-control technologies.

Aggregate Marginal Abatement Costs

The discussion of the last few pages has treated the marginal abatement cost function as something applying to a single firm; for example, a single pulp mill on a river. Suppose, however, we want to talk about the marginal abatement cost of a group of firms, perhaps a group of firms in the same industry or a group of firms all located in the same region. Most environmental policies, especially at state or federal levels, are aimed at controlling emissions from groups of pollution sources, not just single polluters. Suppose, furthermore, that the individual marginal abatement cost functions differ among the various firms. To control organic pollutants in Boston Harbor or San Francisco Bay, for example, would require controlling emissions from a large variety of different sources in different industries with different production technologies, and therefore with very different individual marginal abatement cost functions. In this case we would have to construct the overall or **aggregate marginal abatement cost function** for the collection of firms by adding together the individual marginal abatement cost curves.

Although this sounds simple, and it basically is, it nevertheless leads into one of the more important concepts underlying the design of effective environmental policy. It is critical to keep in mind the central idea of the abatement cost function. It is a function that shows the *least costly* way of achieving reductions in emissions for an individual firm if we are looking at an individual marginal abatement cost function, or for a group of polluting sources if we are considering the aggregate marginal abatement cost function.

Figure 5-5 shows, on the left, two individual marginal abatement cost functions, labeled Source A and Source B. Note that they are not the same (although remember that the scales are the same; that is, we are dealing with the same pollutant). MAC_A starts at 20 tons/week and rises rather rapidly as emissions are reduced. MAC_B also begins at the uncontrolled discharge level of 20 tons/week, but rises much less rapidly. Why the difference? Perhaps Source B is a newer plant with more flexible technological alternatives for pollution control. Or perhaps the two sources, although producing the same type of effluent, are manufacturing different consumer goods and using different production techniques. For whatever reason, they have different marginal abatement cost curves.

FIGURE 5-5
Aggregate Abatement Costs.

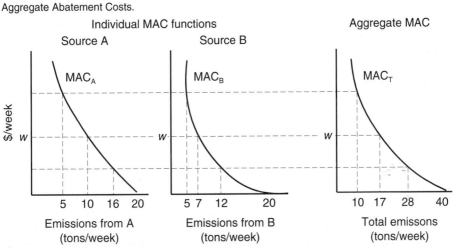

The aggregate marginal abatement cost curve is a summation, or aggregation, of these two individual relationships. But since the individual curves are different, it makes a great deal of difference how they are added together. The problem is that when there are two (or any other number greater than one) sources with different abatement costs, the total cost will depend on how the total emissions are allocated among the different sources. The principle to follow is to add together the two individual functions in such a way as to yield the lowest possible aggregate marginal abatement costs. The way to do this is to add them horizontally. Select a particular level of marginal abatement cost—for example, the one marked w in Figure 5-5. This level of marginal abatement cost is associated with an effluent level of 10 tons/week from Source A and an effluent level of about 7 tons/week from Source B. On the aggregate curve, thus, a marginal abatement cost of w would be associated with an effluent level of 10 tons + 7 tons = 17 tons/week. All the other points on the aggregate marginal abatement cost curve are found the same way, by summing across horizontally on the individual marginal abatement cost curves.

In effect what we have done here is to invoke the important **equimarginal principle,** an idea that was introduced earlier in Chapter 4. To get the minimum aggregate marginal abatement cost curve, the aggregate level of emissions must be distributed among the different sources in such a way that they all have the same marginal abatement costs. Start at the 10 tons/week point on the aggregate curve. Obviously, this 10-ton total could be distributed among the two sources in any number of ways: 5 tons from each source, 8 tons from one and 2 from the other, and so on. Only one allocation, however, will give the lowest aggregate marginal abatement costs; this is the allocation that leads the different sources to the point at which they have exactly the same marginal abatement costs. At the end of this chapter we will come back to this equimarginal principle, illustrating it with a simple numerical example.

THE SOCIALLY EFFICIENT LEVEL OF EMISSIONS

Having considered separately the marginal damage function and the marginal abatement cost function related to a particular pollutant being released at a particular place and time, it is now time to bring these two relationships together. This we do in Figure 5-6, which depicts a set of conventionally shaped marginal damage and marginal abatement cost curves labeled, respectively, MD and MAC. Marginal damages have a threshold at emission level $\hat{e}$, whereas the uncontrolled emission level is e'.

The "efficient" level of emissions is defined as that level at which marginal damages are equal to marginal abatement costs. What is the justification for this? Note the trade-off that is inherent in the pollution phenomenon: higher emissions expose society, or some part of it, to greater costs stemming from environmental damages. Lower emissions involve society in greater costs in the form of resources devoted to abatement activities. The efficient level of emissions is thus the level at which these two types of costs exactly offset one another; that is, where **marginal abatement costs equal marginal damage costs.**

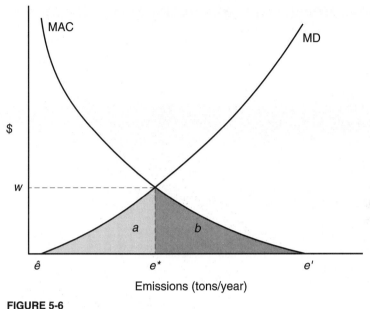

FIGURE 5-6
The Efficient Level of Emissions.

This is emission level e^* in Figure 5-6. Marginal damages and marginal abatement costs are equal to each other and to the value w at this level of emissions.

We also can look at this outcome in terms of total values because we know that the totals are the areas under the marginal curves. Thus, the triangular area marked a (bounded by points $\hat{e}$ and e^* and the marginal damage function) depicts the total damages existing when emissions are at level e^*, whereas the triangular area b shows the total abatement costs at this level of emissions. The sum of these two areas ($a + b$) is a measure of the total social costs from e^* tons per year of this particular pollutant. The point e^* is the unique point at which this sum is minimized. Note that the size of area a need not equal the size of area b.

You might get the impression, on the basis of where point e^* is located on the x-axis, that this analysis has led us to the conclusion that the "efficient" level of emissions is always one that involves a relatively large quantity of emissions and substantial environmental damages. This is not the case. What we are developing, rather, is a conceptual way of looking at a trade-off. In the real world every pollution problem is different. This analysis gives us a generalized way of framing the problem that obviously has to be adapted to the specifics of any particular case of environmental pollution. Figure 5-7, for example, depicts three different situations that might characterize particular environmental pollutants. In each case e^* depicts the efficient level of emissions and w shows marginal damages and marginal abatement costs at that quantity of emissions. Panel (a) shows a pollutant for which e^* is well to the right of zero (of course, since the horizontal axis has no units, it's not clear exactly what "well to the right" actually means here). Marginal damages at this point are quite small; so are total damages and

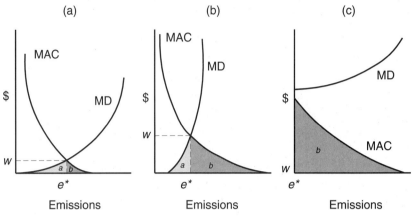

FIGURE 5-7
Efficient Emission Levels for Different Pollutants.

abatement costs, as shown by the small size of the triangles corresponding to these values. The reason is that this is a pollutant where both marginal abatement costs and marginal damages increase at first only very slowly.

Panel (b) shows a situation where the marginal abatement function rises moderately, then rapidly, whereas the marginal damage function rises very rapidly from the beginning. In this case e^* is well to the right of zero, and w lies well above what it was in the first diagram (assuming the vertical axes of these diagrams all have the same scale). Note, however, that at e^* total abatement costs are substantially higher than total damages, as is indicated by the relative sizes of the triangles that measure these total values (a and b). What this emphasizes is that it is not the equality of total abatement costs and total damages that defines the efficient level of effluent, but the equality of the **marginal abatement costs** and **marginal damages.**

In panel (c) of Figure 5-7 the efficient level of emissions is zero. There is no point of intersection of the two functions in the graph; area a does not even appear on the graph. The only way we could conceivably get them to intersect is if we could somehow extend them to the left of the vertical axis, but this would imply that emissions could actually be negative, which is an oddity that we will avoid. What makes $e^* = 0$ is that the marginal damage function doesn't begin at zero, but rather well up on the y-axis, implying that even the first small amount of this pollutant placed in the environment causes great damage (perhaps this diagram applies to some extremely toxic material). Relative to this the marginal costs of abatement are low, giving an efficient emission level of zero.

Changes in the Efficient Level of Emissions

The real world is a dynamic place, and this is especially true of environmental pollution control. For our purposes this implies, for example, that the level of emissions that was efficient last year, or last decade, is not necessarily the level that is efficient today or that is likely to be in the future. When any of the factors

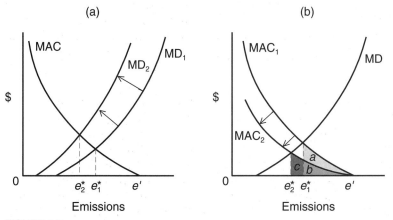

FIGURE 5-8
Changes in e^*, the Efficient Level of Emissions.

that lie behind the marginal damage and marginal abatement cost functions change, the functions themselves will shift and e^*, the efficient level of emissions, also will change.

Before taking a look at this we need to remind ourselves of what we are doing. Remember the distinction made earlier between positive and normative economics, between the **economics of** *what is* and the **economics of** *what ought to be.* The idea of the efficient level of emissions comes firmly under normative economics, under the idea of what ought to be. We are presenting emission level e^*, the level that balances abatement costs and damage costs, as a desirable target for public policy. Do not get this confused with the actual level of emissions. If the world worked so that the actual level of emissions was always equal to, or close to, the efficient level, we presumably would have no need to worry about intervening with environmental policy of one type or another. Of course it does not, which is why we must turn to public policy.

Figure 5-8 shows several ways in which e^* might change when underlying factors change. Panel (a) shows the results of a shift upward in the marginal damage function, from MD_1 to MD_2. One of the ways this could happen is through population growth. MD_1 might apply to a municipality in 1980 and MD_2 to the same municipality in 2000 after its population has grown. More people means that a given amount of effluent will cause more damage.[4] This leads to a conclusion that is intuitively straightforward: The efficient level of emissions drops from e^*_1 to e^*_2. With a higher marginal damage function, the logic of the efficiency trade-off would lead us to devote more resources to pollution control.

Panel (b) of Figure 5-8 shows the case of a shift in the marginal abatement cost function, from MAC_1 to MAC_2. What could have caused this? The most obvious,

[4]This diagram also could apply, of course, to a different situation. MD_1 could be the damage function pertaining to a relatively sparsely settled rural region; MD_2 could be the marginal damage function pertaining to a more populous urban area. Everything we say about the relationship between e_1 and e_2 applies also to cases like this where we are comparing two different places at the same time, in addition to the above comparison of the same place at two different times.

perhaps, is a change in the technology of pollution control. As stressed earlier, abatement costs depend critically on the technology available for reducing effluent streams: treatment technology, recycling technology, alternative fuel technology, and so forth. New techniques normally arise because resources, talents, and energy have been devoted to research and development. So the shift downward in marginal abatement costs depicted in Figure 5-8 might be the result of the development of new treatment or recycling technologies that make it less costly to reduce the effluent stream of this particular pollutant. It should not be too surprising that this leads to a reduction in the efficient level of emissions, as indicated by the change from e^*_1 to e^*_2. We might note that this could lead to either an increase or a decrease in the total cost of abating emissions. Before the change, total abatement costs were an amount equal to the area $(a + b)$; that is, the area under MAC_1 between the uncontrolled level e' and the amount e^*_1. After the change, total abatement costs are equal to area $(b + c)$, and the question of whether total abatement costs at the efficient level of emissions have increased or decreased hinges on the relative sizes of the two areas a and c. This in turn depends on the shapes of the curves and the extent to which the marginal abatement cost curve has shifted; the more it has shifted, the more likely it is that the efficient level of total abatement costs after the change will exceed the costs before the change.[5]

ENFORCEMENT COSTS

So far the analysis has considered only the private costs of reducing emissions, but emission reductions do not happen unless resources are devoted to enforcement. To include all sources of cost we need to add **enforcement costs** to the analysis. Some of these are private, such as added recordkeeping by polluters, but the bulk are public costs related to various regulatory aspects of the enforcement process.

Figure 5-9 shows a simple model of pollution control with enforcement costs added. To the normal marginal abatement cost function has been added the marginal costs of enforcement, giving a total marginal cost function labeled MAC + E. The vertical distance between the two marginal cost curves equals marginal enforcement costs. The assumption drawn into the graph is that marginal enforcement costs, the added costs of enforcement that it takes to get emissions reduced by a unit, increase as emissions decrease. In other words, the more polluters cut back emissions, the more costly it is to enforce further cutbacks. We will have more to say about enforcement and its costs in later parts of the book.

In effect, the addition of enforcement costs moves the efficient level of emissions to the right of where it would be if they were zero. This shows the vital importance of having good enforcement technology because lower marginal

---

[5]These diagrams also can be used to examine some of the implications of making mistakes. For example, suppose the public control authorities think that the real marginal abatement cost was MAC_1, but that, in fact, because there is a cheaper way of reducing this effluent that they do not know about, marginal abatement costs are actually MAC_2. Then we would conclude that the efficient level of effluent is e^*_1, whereas it is actually e^*_2. We might be shooting at a target that involves excessive emissions.

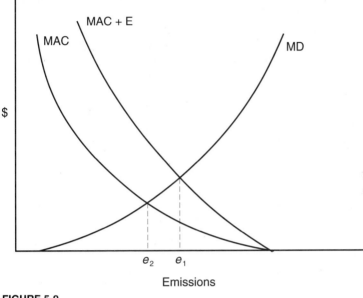

FIGURE 5-9
Enforcement Costs.

enforcement costs would move MAC + E closer to MAC, decreasing the efficient emission level. In fact, **technical change in enforcement** has exactly the
same effect on the efficient level of emissions as technical change in emissions
abatement.

THE EQUIMARGINAL PRINCIPLE APPLIED
TO EMISSION REDUCTIONS

Before going on we will take a last, very explicit look at the equimarginal principle. In the present context, the application of the equimarginal principle says
the following: If there are **multiple sources** of a particular type of pollutant
with **differing marginal abatement costs,** and if it is desired to reduce aggregate emissions at the **least possible cost** (or alternatively, get the greatest reduction in emissions for a given cost), then emissions from the various sources
must be reduced in accordance with the **equimarginal principle.**

To illustrate this, look at the numbers in Table 5-2. This shows explicitly the
marginal abatement costs of each of two firms emitting a particular residual
into the environment. If neither source makes any effort to control emissions,
they will each emit 12 tons/week. If Plant A reduces its emissions by 1 ton, to 11
tons/week, it will cost $1,000/week; if it reduces effluent further to 10
tons/week, its abatement costs will increase by $2,000/week, and so on. Note
that the marginal abatement cost relationships of the two sources are different:
that of Source B increases faster than that of Source A.

TABLE 5-2
THE EQUIMARGINAL PRINCIPLE

Emissions (tons/week)	Marginal abatement costs ($1,000/week)	
	Source A	Source B
12	0	0
11	1	2
10	2	4
9	3	6
8	4	10
7	5	14
6	6	20
5	8	25
4	10	31
3	14	38
2	24	58
1	38	94
0	70	160

Suppose that initially each plant is emitting at the uncontrolled level; total emissions would then be 24 tons/week. Now assume that we want to reduce overall emissions to half the present level, or a total of 12 tons/week. One way to do this would be to have **equiproportionate** cutbacks. Because we want a total reduction of 50 percent, each source is required to reduce by 50 percent. If Source A were cut 50 percent to 6 tons/week, its marginal abatement costs at this level would be $6,000/week, whereas at this level of emissions the marginal abatement costs of Source B would be $20,000/week. Total abatement costs of the 12-ton total can be found by adding up the marginal abatement costs; these are $21,000/week for Source A ($1,000 + $2,000 + $3,000 + $4,000 + $5,000 + $6,000) and $56,000/week for Source B ($2,000 + $4,000 + $6,000 + $10,000 + $14,000 + $20,000), or a grand total of $77,000/week.

The overall reduction to 12 tons/week, however, can be achieved with a substantially lower total cost. We know this because the equiproportionate reduction violates the equimarginal principle; marginal abatement costs are not equalized when each source reduces its effluent to 6 tons/week. What is required is different emission rates for the two sources, where, simultaneously, they will emit no more than 12 tons of effluent and have the same marginal abatement costs. This condition is satisfied if Source A emits 4 tons and Source B emits 8 tons. These rates add up to 12 tons total and give each source a marginal abatement cost of $10,000/week. Calculating total abatement costs at these emission levels gives $39,000/week for Source A ($1,000 + $2,000 +$3,000 + $4,000 + $5,000 + $6,000 +

$8,000 + $10,000) plus $22,000/week for Source B ($2,000 + $4,000 + $6,000 + $10,000), or a grand total of $61,000/week. By following the equimarginal principle, the desired reduction in total emissions has been obtained, but with a savings of $16,000/week over the case of an equiproportionate reduction.

Thus, we see that an emission reduction plan that follows the equimarginal rule gives emission reduction at minimum cost. Another way of saying this is that for any particular amount of money devoted to effluent reduction, the maximum quantitative reduction in total effluent can only be obtained by following the equimarginal principle. The importance of this principle cannot be overstated. When defining the efficient level of emissions, we were going on the assumption that we were working with the lowest possible marginal abatement cost function. The only way of achieving this is by controlling individual sources in accordance with the equimarginal rule. If we are designing public policy under the rule of equiproportionate reductions at the various sources, the marginal abatement cost function will be higher than it should be. One of the results of this is that the "efficient" emission level will be higher than it should be, or, to say the same thing, we will seek smaller reductions in emissions than are socially efficient.

LONG-RUN SUSTAINABILITY

The model discussed in this chapter hinges on the idea of efficiency, where decisions are made by comparing costs and benefits, in the case of pollution control comparing marginal abatement costs and marginal damages. A question arises over whether this approach is consistent with the notion of **long-run sustainability,** as discussed in Chapter 2. In comparing costs and benefits like this, are we not giving undue primacy to the people who are in the better position to have their values counted, namely, present generations? Are we perhaps not giving enough consideration to future generations? They are not here to be heard from directly, so the only way they can be factored in is through the bequest motive of present generations, which may not be strong enough.

This would not be a problem if all environmental resources were renewable and all pollutants noncumulative, but these conditions don't hold. Species extinctions are forever, and certain long-lasting pollutants can accumulate to become legacies from the present generation to those of the future. In the history of the human race, very long-run negative environmental impacts have often eventually undermined the productivity of a society's resource base.[6] Most of these have been regional or local in scope; for example, the salting of soils in the Tigris-Euphrates lowlands (1900–1600 B.C.).[7] Today these local and regional situations continue, but we also are concerned about long-run global sustainability.

The easy answer is to say that the marginal abatement cost and (especially) the marginal damage functions of the basic model must be interpreted as con-

[6]Eric P. Eckholm, *Losing Ground: Environmental Stress and World Food Prospects,* W. W. Norton, New York, 1976.
[7]B. L. Turner II, ed., *The Earth as Transformed by Human Action,* Cambridge University Press, Cambridge, England, 1990, pp. 27–30.

taining all impacts, both short and long run, insofar as we can predict them. Conceptually this is correct, but in practice it may be difficult to do. It is much easier to estimate short-run costs and damages than costs and damages occurring well off in the future. The great uncertainty about future impacts often means that more weight is put on the better-known short-run impacts. The other problem is how to compare present and future effects. Should we treat a dollar's worth of damage that will occur 100 years from now as equivalent to a dollar's worth of damages incurred today?

Some have suggested that it might be possible to identify an upper limit on damages strictly on physical grounds. Whatever the short-run trade-off to achieve efficiency, we may be able to identify emission levels that, if exceeded, would diminish significantly the long-run physical status of particular environmental resources. For certain renewable resources, such as animal and plant species, we could perhaps identify this point with some level below which extinction would result. But for most environmental resources, a physical limit is not definable. All decisions, even when long-run impacts are involved, must incorporate human judgments to some extent, and where judgments are involved, trade-offs automatically become relevant.

SUMMARY

In this chapter we have looked at a simple model of pollution control. It is based on the notion of a trade-off between environmental damages and pollution abatement costs. We introduced the notion of a **marginal damage function,** showing the marginal social damages resulting from varying levels of residual emissions or ambient pollutant levels. Then we looked at **marginal abatement cost** relationships, first for an individual pollution source and then for a group of such sources. By bringing together these two types of relationships we then defined an **efficient level of emissions:** that level at which marginal damages and marginal abatement costs are equal. At this level of emissions total social costs, the total of abatement costs and damages, are minimized.

The efficient level of emissions is subject to change as underlying factors shift. Population growth and the results of scientific studies can shift marginal damage functions; technological changes can cause marginal abatement cost functions to shift. We illustrated one case in which the efficient level of a particular pollutant is zero. Finally, we reviewed the equimarginal principle as it applies to pollution control. That principle states that when multiple sources have different marginal abatement costs, equalizing these costs will be the least-cost way of achieving a reduction in total emissions.

A word of caution is appropriate. The model presented in this chapter is very general and risks giving an overly simplistic impression of pollution problems in the real world. In fact, there are very few actual instances of environmental pollution where the marginal damage and marginal abatement functions are known with certainty. The natural world is too complex, and human and nonhuman responses are too difficult to identify with complete clarity. Furthermore, polluters come in all types and sizes and economic circumstances, and it takes enormous resources to learn even simple things about the costs of pollution abatement in concrete instances. Pollution control technology is changing rapidly, so what is efficient today will not necessarily be so tomorrow. Nevertheless, the simple model is useful for thinking about the basic problem of pollution control, and it will be useful in our later chapters on the various approaches to environmental policy.

QUESTIONS FOR FURTHER DISCUSSION

1 Prove (graphically) that the point labeled e^* in Figure 5-6 is indeed the point that minimizes total social costs, the sum of abatement and damage costs. (Do this by showing that at any other point this total cost will be higher.)

2 Suppose there is a river on which is located several paper mills, each of which discharges pollutants into the water. Suppose somebody invents a new technology for treating this waste stream that, if adopted by the pulp mills, could substantially diminish emissions. What are the impacts of this invention on (a) the actual level of emissions and (b) the efficient level of emissions?

3 Suppose there is a suburban community where domestic septic tanks are responsible for contaminating a local lake. What is the effect on actual and efficient levels of water quality in the lake of an increase in the number of homes in the community?

4 Below are the marginal abatement costs of three firms, related to the quantity of emissions. Each firm is now emitting 10 tons/week, so total emissions are 30 tons/week. Suppose we wish to reduce total emissions by 50 percent, to 15 tons per week. Compare the total costs of doing this: (a) with an equiproportionate decrease in emissions and (b) with a decrease that meets the equimarginal principle.

Emissions (tons/week)	Marginal abatement costs ($/ton)		
	Firm 1	Firm 2	Firm 3
10	0	0	0
9	4	1	1
8	8	2	2
7	12	4	3
6	16	6	4
5	20	8	5
4	24	12	6
3	28	20	7
2	36	24	8
1	46	28	9
0	58	36	10

5 Suppose a new law is put into effect requiring oil tankers to use certain types of navigation rules in coastal waters of the United States. Suppose that the very next year there is a large tanker accident and oil spill in these waters. Does this mean that the law has had no effect?

WEBSITES

For a glossary of terms used in environmental economics, see **www. damagevaluation.com/glossary.htm.** The EPA has a program in environmental economics with much useful information: **www.epa.gov/economics.** See other links listed on the web page associated with this book, **www.mhhe.com/ economics/field3.**

SELECTED READINGS

Freeman, A. Myrick, III, Robert H. Haveman, and Allen V. Kneese: *The Economics of Environmental Policy,* John Wiley, New York, 1973.

Hite, James C., et al.: *The Economics of Environmental Quality,* American Enterprise Institute, Washington, DC, 1972.

Kneese, Allen V., and Charles L. Schultze: *Pollution, Prices, and Public Policy,* The Brookings Institution, Washington, DC, 1975.

Magat, Wesley A.: *Reform of Environmental Regulation,* Ballinger Publishing Company, Cambridge, MA, 1982.

Mills, Edwin S., and Philip E. Graves: *The Economics of Environmental Quality,* 2nd ed., Norton, New York, 1986.

Pearce, David W., and R. Kerry Turner: *Economics of Natural Resources and the Environment,* Johns Hopkins Press, Baltimore, MD, 1990.

THREE

ENVIRONMENTAL
ANALYSIS

In the last few chapters we have used the concepts of "abatement costs" and "damages" without worrying too much about how the actual magnitudes of these factors might be measured in particular situations. In the next three chapters this is rectified. Several types of analysis have been developed over the years to provide environmental, economic, and social information to the policy process. In the next chapter we deal with these at the framework level. From the standpoint of economics, benefit–cost analysis is the primary analytical tool, so much of the chapter will be devoted to a discussion of its major elements. Then in the following two chapters we look more closely at the methods available for estimating benefits and costs relevant to environmental policy decisions.

FRAMEWORKS
OF ANALYSIS

Policy decisions require information and, although the availability of good information doesn't automatically mean that decisions also will be good, its *un*availability will almost always contribute to bad decisions. There are a variety of alternative frameworks for generating and presenting information useful to policymakers, calling for different skills and research procedures. We briefly review the most important of these, before focusing on benefit–cost analysis.

IMPACT ANALYSIS

"Impact" is a very general word, meaning the effects of any actual or proposed policy. Since there are many types of effects, there are many different types of impact analysis.

Environmental Impact Analysis

An Environmental Impact Analysis (EIA) is essentially an identification and study of all significant environmental repercussions stemming from a course of action. For the most part these focus on impacts that are expected to flow from a proposed decision, although retrospective EIAs are of great value also, especially when they are done to see if earlier predictions were accurate. EIAs can be carried out for any social action, public or private, industrial or domestic, local or national. They are largely the work of natural scientists, who focus on tracing out and describing the physical impacts of projects or programs, following through the complex linkages that spread these impacts through the ecosystem. They do not address directly the issue of placing social values on these impacts.

Many countries have laws requiring environmental impact studies when substantial public programs and projects are under consideration, as well as private projects in some cases. The one in the United States stems from the **National Environmental Policy Act of 1970** (NEPA). This law requires that agencies of the federal government conduct environmental impact assessments of proposed legislation and "other major federal actions significantly affecting the quality of the human environment." Over the years this has been extended to include any actions funded in part or regulated by the federal government, even though they are carried out by private parties.[1] The result of the assessment is an **Environmental Impact Statement** (EIS). NEPA also created the Council on Environmental Quality, an executive agency whose job is to manage the EIS process and publish an annual report on the state of the environment.

Although EISs are primarily the work of natural scientists, economics also has a distinct role to play. It is not only ecological linkages through which environmental impacts spread; they also spread through economic linkages. Suppose, for example, it is proposed to build a dam that will flood a certain river valley while providing new flat-water recreation possibilities. A substantial part of the environmental impact will stem from the inundation itself and the resulting losses in animals and plants, wild-river recreation, farmland, and so on. But much also could come from changes in patterns of behavior among people affected by the project. Recreators traveling into and out of the region could affect air pollution and traffic congestion. New housing or commercial development spurred by the recreation opportunities could have negative environmental effects. Thus, to study the full range of environmental impacts from the dam, it is necessary to include not just the physical effects of the dam and its water impoundment, but also the ways people will react and adapt to this new facility.

Economic Impact Analysis

When interest centers on how some action—a new law, a new technological breakthrough, a new source of imports, and so forth—will affect an economic system, in whole or in terms of its various parts, we can speak of **economic impact analysis.** In most countries, especially developing ones, there is usually wide interest in the impact of environmental regulations on economic growth rates. Sometimes the focus will be on tracing out the ramifications of a public program for certain economic variables that are considered particularly important. One might be especially interested, for example, in the impact of an environmental regulation on employment, the impact of import restrictions on the rate of technological change in an industry, the effects of an environmental law on the growth of the pollution-control industry, the response of the food industry to new packaging regulations, and so on.

---

[1]Many of the individual states also have laws requiring environmental impact statements for state-funded actions.

Economic impact analyses can be focused at any level. Local environmental groups might be interested in the impact of a wetlands law on the rate of population growth and tax base in their community. Regional groups might be interested in the impacts of a national regulation on their particular economic circumstances. At the global level, an important question is how efforts to control CO_2 emissions might impact the relative growth rates of rich and poor countries. Whatever the level, economic impact analysis requires a basic understanding of how economies function and how their various parts fit together.

The U.S. Environmental Protection Agency (EPA) has developed procedures for doing economic impact analyses of proposed environmental regulations. Over the years these have gone under different names, such as regulatory impact analyses, economic impact statements, and regulatory flexibility analyses. At bottom, however, they are all analyses of the benefits and costs of alternative regulatory approaches.

COST-EFFECTIVENESS ANALYSIS

Suppose a community determined that its current water supply was contaminated with some chemical and that it had to switch to some alternative supply. Suppose it had several possibilities: It could drill new wells into an uncontaminated aquifer, it could build a connector to the water supply system of a neighboring town, or it could build its own surface reservoir. A **cost-effectiveness analysis** would estimate the costs of these different alternatives with the aim of showing how they compared in terms of, say, the costs per million gallons of delivered water into the town system. Cost-effectiveness analysis, in other words, takes the objective as given, then costs out various alternative ways of attaining that objective.

Table 6-1 shows some of the results of a cost-effectiveness analysis done by the U.S. Office of Technology Assessment. The study looked at different ways of reducing mobile-source emissions of volatile organic compounds (VOCs), which produce smog. The results show the estimated reduction in tons of VOC emissions per $1,000 of cost for each of the different technological approaches listed. These cost-effectiveness coefficients range from 0.03 to 1.96. Thus, it would appear, for example, that $1 million put into making gas less volatile will reduce VOC emissions about 75 times more than the same amount put into the development of alternative fuels. These cost coefficients must be interpreted with care, however. Although the fuel volatility option has the highest tons of VOC reduced per dollar, we can't conclude from this that the best way to clean up smog in this region is to concentrate solely on this one approach. Each of the technologies has limits as to the total amount of VOC it is capable of reducing; therefore, depending on what the desired total reduction is, different combinations of these techniques will have to be utilized.

The equimarginal principle is clearly important in cost-effectiveness studies. In putting together an effective control program, authorities would want to choose techniques that have the lowest marginal abatement costs and combine

TABLE 6-1
COST-EFFECTIVENESS OF DIFFERENT MEASURES FOR THE CONTROL
OF VOLATILE ORGANIC COMPOUNDS (VOCS) IN NONATTAINMENT CITIES

Strategy	Tons of VOC reduced per $1,000
RACT	0.20
New CTGs	0.16
Federal controls	0.59
On-board controls	0.83
Stage II	1.00
Stage II and on-board controls	0.83
Enhanced I&M*	0.26
Fuel volatility[†]	1.96
New highway vehicle standards*	0.42
Methanol fuels	0.03

*Estimates reflect costs associated with VOC control only. Enhanced I&M controls also apply to NO_x and carbon monoxide emissions; new highway vehicle standards also apply to NO_x emissions.
[†]Estimates reflect cost-effectiveness during the five-month summertime period when controls are required.
Strategy Descriptions
RACT is the reasonable available control technology on all existing stationary sources that emit more than 25 tons per year of VOC; new CTGs are new control technique guidelines for existing stationary sources that emit more than 25 tons per year of VOC; federal controls are on selected small stationary sources of VOC (consumer and commercial solvents, and architectural surface coatings); on-board controls are on motor vehicles to capture gasoline vapor during refueling; stage II control devices are on gas pumps to capture gasoline vapor during motor vehicle refueling; enhanced inspection and maintenance (I&M) programs are for cars and light-duty trucks; fuel volatility controls limit the rate of gasoline evaporation; new highway vehicle emission standards are for passenger cars and light-duty gasoline trucks; methanol fuels are a substitute for gasoline as a motor vehicle fuel.
Source: Adapted from Office of Technology Assessment, *Urban Ozone and the Clean Air Act*, Washington, DC, 1988, p. 108.

them in a way that satisfies the equimarginal principle. Of course, this leaves out the important prior question. In this example, how much VOC reduction is efficient, in the light of damages done by these emissions? It can be seen that the efficiency question is intertwined with the issue of cost-effectiveness. The efficiency question cannot be answered until emission reduction costs are known, but these costs depend on the cost-effectiveness of the particular techniques chosen to reduce emissions.

It may make good sense to do a cost-effectiveness analysis even before there is a strong public commitment to the objective being pursued. In many cases people may not know exactly how much they value a given objective. Once a cost-effectiveness analysis is done, they may be able to tell, at least in relative terms, whether any of the different alternatives would be desirable. They may be able to say something like: "We don't know exactly how much benefits are in monetary terms, but we feel that they are more than the costs of several of the alternatives that have been costed out, so we will go ahead with one or both of them."

DAMAGE ASSESSMENT

In 1980, the Comprehensive Environmental Response, Compensation and Liability Act was enacted.[2] This law allows federal, state, and local governments to act as trustees for publicly owned natural resources and to sue people who are responsible for the release of harmful materials that damage these resources. This has led to a type of study called **damage assessment,** the objective of which is to estimate the value of the damages to an injured resource so that these amounts can be recovered from those held liable by the courts. The U.S. Department of Interior (DOI) was assigned the job of determining how "damages" are to be measured in these cases.

The conclusions of the DOI were that damages should be equal to the lesser of (1) the **lost value of the resource** or (2) the **value of restoring the resource** to its former state. Consider the following figures, which represent resource values and restoration values for several cases.

	A	B
Lost resource value	$1.2 million	$1.6 million
Restoration cost	0.6 million	3.8 million

For case A, the resource value lost from an oil or hazardous waste release is $1.2 million, but the cost of restoring the resource to its former state is only $0.6 million, so the latter is taken as the true measure of damages. In case B, the lost resource value at $1.6 million is substantially less than restoration costs; therefore, the former would be used to assess damages.

The lost economic values associated with a reduction in the quality of a natural resource can stem from many sources; for example, on-site recreation such as camping, hiking, or driving for pleasure; extractive uses of natural resources, such as energy production and mining; uses of stream flows for irrigation, municipal, and industrial water supplies; and transportation services. The task of measuring these values is very similar to the steps undertaken in standard benefit–cost studies of natural and environmental resource use, which we discuss next.

In recent years, as a result of challenges in court, the emphasis has shifted toward restoration costs as the preferred measure of damages. Restoration costs are defined to include restoration, rehabilitation, replacement, and/or the acquisition of equivalent resources. On the surface it might seem easier to measure restoration costs than lost resource value for damaged environmental

[2]This law will be studied in more detail in Chapter 16.

resources. Restoration appears to involve primarily engineering actions based on knowledge from physical and biological sciences, but "restoration" is in fact a rather complicated idea. In some cases restoration may be technically impossible; for example, when there is some element of uniqueness in the destroyed resource. Restoration of the physical values of a resource (e.g., soil pH, water temperature, amount of tree cover) may not restore all of its ecological characteristics. Experience with this law and its legal clarification is still developing.[3] As it does, it will be necessary to come to grips with the fact that it is impossible to discuss restoration in physical terms without considering its monetary costs. There are many thorny problems in evaluating the restoration costs of a damaged natural resource. For example:

- The determination of what the original or baseline resource quality actually was.
- The choice among alternative ways of restoring a resource in a cost-effective way.
- The determination of what is meant by a natural or environmental resource of equivalent value to a resource that was lost.

BENEFIT–COST ANALYSIS

Benefit–cost analysis is for the public sector what a profit-and-loss analysis is for a business firm. If an automobile company was contemplating introducing a new car, it would want to get some idea of how its profitability would be affected. On the one hand, it would estimate costs of production and distribution: labor, raw materials, energy, emission control equipment, transportation, and so forth.[4] On the other hand, it would estimate revenues through market analysis. Then it would compare expected revenues with anticipated costs. Benefit–cost analysis is an analogous exercise for programs in the public sector. This means there are two critical differences between benefit–cost analysis and the car example: It is a tool for helping to make **public decisions,** done from the standpoint of society in general rather than from that of a single profit-making firm, and it usually is done for policies and programs that have **unmarketed types of outputs,** such as improvements in environmental quality.

Benefit–cost analysis has led two intertwined lives. The first is among its practitioners: economists inside and outside public agencies who have developed the techniques, tried to produce better data, and extended the scope of the analysis. The second is among the politicians and administrators who have set the rules and procedures governing the use of benefit–cost analysis for public

---

[3]See, for example, Ellen Louderbough, "The Role of Science in Valuing Natural Resources after *State of Ohio vs. Department of Interior,* 880 F. 2nd 432 (DC Cir. 1989)," *Natural Resources Journal,* 32(1), Winter 1992, pp. 137–148.

[4]Of course, it probably would not factor in the costs of air pollution damage inflicted on people breathing the emissions of the new cars; if everyone did this without being required to, we probably wouldn't be here studying this topic.

decision making. In the United States, benefit–cost analysis was first used in conjunction with the United States Flood Control Act of 1936. That act specified that federal participation in projects to control flooding on major rivers of the country would be justifiable *". . . if the benefits to whomever they accrue are in excess of the estimated costs. . . ."* In order to determine if this criterion was satisfied for any proposed flood-control dam or large levee project, procedures had to be developed to measure these benefits and costs.

These procedures have been altered from time to time as benefit–cost analysis has evolved and matured. The status and role of benefit–cost analysis in public natural resource and environmental decision making have been the subject of continuing discussions as well as political and administrative conflicts. Public agencies often have been taken to task by outsiders for trying to use benefit–cost analysis in ways that would help them justify ever-larger budgets. Some observers have taken the position that benefit-cost analysis is really an attempt to short-circuit the processes of political discussion and decision that should take place around prospective public projects and programs.

In 1981 President Reagan issued an executive order requiring that benefit-cost analysis be done for all major government regulations. Within the U.S. Environmental Protection Agency these became known as **regulatory impact analyses.** In the 1990s, President Clinton renewed this requirement, in slightly revised form, and they are now being called simply **economic analyses.** Congress also has recently enacted laws requiring benefit-cost analysis of government regulations. Supporters of these laws argue that it is a way to ensure that costs are given appropriate weight in public regulation. Opponents say that, because many benefits are hard to measure, such a requirement will make it more difficult to pursue socially beneficial public regulation.

Despite these controversies, benefit–cost analysis has become the primary analytical method for evaluating public programs. This is not to say that actual government decisions are now being based on these analyses. The politics of public policy are vigorous and shifting, and it is unlikely that policy decisions ever will, or should, be based solely on benefit–cost criteria. But some success has been encountered recently in making benefit–cost analysis more relevant to environmental policy decision making. A number of programs have been evaluated from a benefit–cost perspective; for example, the plan for phasing out leaded gasoline, disposing of sludge from wastewater treatment plants, and establishing rules for municipal solid waste landfills.[5] In addition, the EPA as well as other federal agencies has sought to develop better methods for estimating the benefits and costs of environmental programs. Benefit–cost analyses of environmental programs will undoubtedly become much more common in the future.

---

[5]For a discussion of these and other examples of the use of benefit–cost analysis in environmental policy making, see Richard D. Morgenstern (ed.), *Economic Analysis at EPA, Assessing Regulatory Impact,* Resources for the Future, Washington, DC, 1997.

The Basic Framework

As the name implies, a benefit–cost analysis involves measuring, adding up, and comparing all the benefits and all the costs of a particular public project or program. There are essentially four steps in a benefit–cost analysis:

1 Specify clearly the project or program.
2 Describe quantitatively the inputs and outputs of the program.
3 Estimate the social costs and benefits of these inputs and outputs.
4 Compare these benefits and costs.

Each of these steps incorporates a number of component steps. In doing a benefit–cost analysis, the very first step is to decide on the **perspective** from which the study is to be done. Benefit-cost analysis is a tool of public analysis, but there are actually many publics. If we were doing a benefit–cost study for a national agency, the "public" typically would be all the people living in the particular country. But if we were employed by a city or regional planning agency to do a benefit–cost analysis of a local environmental program, we would undoubtedly focus on benefits and costs accruing to people living in those areas. At the other extreme, the rise of global environmental issues has forced us to undertake some benefit–cost analyses from a world-wide perspective.

Step 1 also includes a **complete specification of the main elements of the project or program:** location, timing, groups involved, connections with other programs, and so on. There are two primary types of public environmental programs for which benefit–cost analyses are done:

1 *Physical projects* that involve direct public production: public waste treatment plants, beach restoration projects, hazardous-waste incinerators, habitat improvement projects, land purchase for preservation, and so on.
2 *Regulatory programs* that are aimed at enforcing environmental laws and regulations, such as pollution-control standards, technological choices, waste disposal practices, restrictions on land development, and so on.

After specifying the basic project or program the next step is to **determine the relevant flows of inputs and outputs.** For some projects this is reasonably easy. In planning a wastewater treatment facility, the engineering staff will be able to provide a full physical specification of the plant, together with the inputs required to build it and keep it running. For other types of programs it is much harder. A restriction on development in a particular region, for example, can be expected to deflect development elsewhere into surrounding areas, the exact extent of which may be very hard to predict. It is in this step that we first have to recognize the great importance of time. Environmentally related projects or programs do not usually last for a single year, but are spread out over long periods of time. So the job of specifying inputs and outputs involves predictions of future events, often quite remote in time. This puts a premium on having a good understanding of issues such as future growth patterns, future rates of technological change, and possible changes in consumers' preferences.

The next step is to put **values on input and output flows;** that is, to measure costs and benefits. We could do this in any units we wish, but typically this implies measuring benefits and costs in monetary terms. This does not mean in market-value terms because in many cases we will be dealing with effects, especially on the benefit side, that are not directly registered on markets. Nor does it imply that only monetary values count in some fundamental manner. It means that we need a single metric into which to translate all of the impacts of a project or program in order to make them comparable among themselves as well as with other types of public activities. Ultimately, certain environmental impacts of a program may be irreducible to monetary terms because we cannot find a way of measuring how much people value these impacts. In this case it is important to supplement the monetary results of the benefit–cost analysis with estimates of these intangible impacts.

Finally, we must **compare benefits and costs.** To understand what is involved in very general terms consider the numbers in Example 6-1. These show the primary benefits and costs that were estimated in connection with the plan to phase out the production and use of leaded gas for motor vehicles. The costs of the phase-out are the added refining costs of $503 million for the one year of 1988. The benefits come from four sources: lowered vehicle maintenance costs; reduced damage from other pollutants because catalytic converters are not damaged through misfueling with leaded gas; and two types of medical benefits: avoided medical costs and avoided costs of remedial education. Total estimated benefits for 1988 were $1,289 million.

Benefits and costs can be compared in several ways: **net benefits** are simply total benefits minus cost. In the example they are $1,289 million − $503 million = $786 million. Another criterion sometimes used is the **benefit–cost ratio,** which is simply the ratio of benefits to costs, or the amount of benefits produced per dollar of costs. In the example this ratio is $1,289 ÷ $503 = 2.56.

Scope of the Program

One important problem in benefit–cost analysis is deciding on the **scope** of the project or program. A benefit–cost analysis must be specified completely in terms of its size or scope. In reality, however, it is always possible to make a project or program larger or smaller by some amount. How can we be sure that the program we are evaluating is of the appropriate scope?

To explore this issue, consider Figure 6-1. It shows the standard emission control model as developed in the last chapter, with marginal damage (MD) and marginal abatement cost (MAC) functions. Assume that the current level of emissions is e_1; that is, emissions are essentially uncontrolled. A control program is proposed that would lower emissions to e_2. For this program, total benefits (total damages reduced) are equal to $(a + b)$, whereas total abatement costs are equal to b. Net benefits are therefore equal to area a.

EXAMPLE 6-1

BENEFIT–COST ANALYSIS (REGULATORY IMPACT ANALYSIS) OF ACCERATED PHASE-OUT OF LEADED GAS

In the 1920s petroleum refineries began to add lead to automobile gasoline in order to enhance its octane, or anti-knock, rating. By 1970, about 200,000 tons of lead were being added to gasoline each year. In the 1970 Clean Air Act, Congress mandated the reduction of automobile tailpipe emissions of hydrocarbons (HC), nitrogen oxides (NO_x), and carbon monoxide. To accomplish this, car makers developed the catalytic converter. But the catalytic converter was a device that was essentially poisoned by the lead in gas. As a result, EPA proposed in 1972 to phase out the production of leaded gas. It promulgated a phase-out schedule lasting from 1975 to 1979, with small refiners being given until 1982 to meet the requirements. A further phase-out for lead in leaded gas was set to be achieved by 1982. The assumption was that, as older cars not having catalytic converters became a smaller and smaller portion of the car fleet, the use of leaded gas would eventually stop.

In the 1970s, a great deal of evidence was being discovered about the negative health effects of lead in the environment. Thus, EPA conducted a study to estimate the benefits and costs of achieving a faster, or accelerated, phase-out of leaded gas beyond 1982. They decided to study the benefits and costs for a year that was far enough in the future to give refineries enough time to adjust. The results for that year, 1988, were as follows:

Costs of the proposed accelerated phase-out:	
Increased refining costs	$503 million
Benefits of the phase-out:	
Reduced vehicle maintenance[1]	$660 million
Reduced damage from HC, NO_x, and CO emissions[2]	404 million
Reduced health effects:	
Avoided medical costs	41 million
Avoided remedial education costs	184 million
Total benefits	$1,289 million
Net benefits: $1,289 – $503	$786 million

[1]Lead in gas caused damage to spark plugs, exhaust systems, oil, and so on, leading to higher maintenance costs when leaded gas was used.

[2]Many people put leaded gas in cars with catalytic converters, which destroyed the effectiveness of the converters in reducing emissions of HC, NO_x, and CO. By switching to very-low-lead fuel, this misfueling would cease to be a problem.

There were other anticipated benefits, and a few costs, that the phase-out would produce, but these were not included in the study because of difficulties in measuring them. The fact that the proposed accelerated phase-out had such positive net benefits was one reason that the EPA did in fact opt for these regulations in 1988.

For further details, see Albert L. Nichols, "Lead in Gasoline," in Richard D. Morgenstern, (ed.), *Economic Analysis at EPA, Assessing Regulatory Impact*, Resources for the Future, Washington, DC, 1997, pp. 49–96.

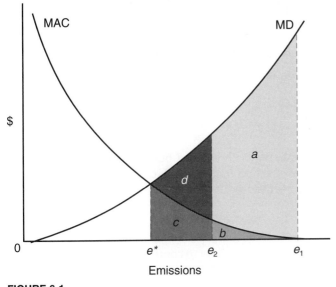

FIGURE 6-1
Establishing the Size of a Public Program.

For an emission reduction program to give maximum net benefits, however, it would have to reduce emissions to e^*, the level at which MD = MAC. Here, net benefits would equal $(d + a)$. The problem is when we do a benefit–cost analysis of a specific proposal, how can we be sure that we are dealing with one such as e^* in the figure and not one such as e_2?

The general procedure here is to carry out **sensitivity analyses** on these results. This means recalculating benefits and costs for programs somewhat larger and somewhat smaller than the one shown in the example. We would analyze a program that has somewhat more restrictive emission reductions, with appropriate enforcement resources, and one that is somewhat less restrictive. If the chosen program is indeed appropriately scaled, each of the variations will produce lower net benefits.

The benefit–cost ratio is often used in public debates in describing environmental projects or programs, but the efficient program size is not the one that gives the maximum benefit–cost ratio. At emission level e^* the benefit–cost ratio is equal to $(a + b + c + d) \div (b + c)$. At emission level e_2, the benefit–cost ratio is $(a + b) \div b$, which is higher than that at e^*. The benefit–cost ratio may be used to make sure that, at the very least, benefits exceed cost, but beyond this it is a misleading indicator in planning the appropriate scope of public programs.

Under some circumstances, there may be grounds for sizing programs at less than that which maximizes net benefits. Suppose there is a regional public agency in charge of enforcing air-pollution laws in two medium-sized urban areas. Suppose further that it has a fixed and predetermined budget of $1 million to spend. There are two possibilities: (1) Put it all in one enforcement program in one of the cities or (2) divide it between two programs, one in each city. Suppose the numbers are as follows:

	Costs	Benefits	Net benefits	Benefit–cost ratio
One-city program	$1,000,000	$2,000,000	$1,000,000	2.0
Two-city program				
City A	500,000	1,200,000	700,000	2.4
City B	500,000	1,200,000	700,000	2.4

In this case the agency can do better with its fixed budget by putting it into two half-sized programs rather than just one. In this case the correct approach is to allocate resources so that the net benefits produced by the total budget are maximized.

Discounting

We turn now to the important problem of how to compare costs and benefits that occur at very different points in time. In a pollution–control program, for example, how do we compare the high initial-year capital costs of abatement equipment with the long-run costs of maintaining it? In the global warming problem, how do we compare the very high costs today of controlling CO_2 emissions with the benefits that won't really start accruing for several decades? Suppose there are two programs, one with relatively high net benefits that materialize well into the future and another with smaller net benefits that occur in the near future. How do we compare these two options? The standard way to address problems such as these is through **discounting**, a technique employed to add and compare costs and benefits that occur at different points in time. Discounting has two facets: first, the mechanics of doing it; then, the reasoning behind the choice of discount rates to be used in specific cases. We take these up in turn.

A cost that will occur 10 years from now does not have the same significance as a cost that occurs today. Suppose, for example, that I have incurred a bill of $1,000 that I must pay today. To do that I must have $1,000 in the bank, or my pocket, with which to pay the obligation. Suppose, however, that I have a $1,000 bill to pay, not today, but 10 years from now. If the rate of interest I can get in a bank is 5 percent, and I expect it to stay at that level, I can deposit $613.90 in the bank today and it will compound up to $1,000 in 10 years, exactly when I need it. The formula for compounding this sum is

$$\$613.90(1 + .05)^{10} = \$1,000$$

Now turn this around and ask: What is the **present value** to me of this $1,000 obligation 10 years from now? Its present value is what I would have to put in the bank today to have exactly what I need in 10 years, and we get this by rearranging the above expression:

$$\text{Present value} = \frac{\$1,000}{(1 + .05)^{10}} = \$613.90$$

The present value is found by discounting the future cost back over the 10-year period at the interest rate, now called the discount rate, of 5 percent.[6] If it were higher—say, 8 percent—the present value would be lower—$463.20. The higher the discount rate, the lower the present value of any future dollar amount.

The same goes for a benefit. Suppose you expect someone to give you a gift of $100, but only at the end of six years. This would not have the same value to you today (i.e., the same present value) as $100 given to you today. If the applicable discount rate is 4 percent, the present value of that future gift would be

$$\frac{\$100}{(1 + .04)^6} = \$79.03$$

Discounting is used extensively in benefit–cost analyses. Its main role is to help in aggregating a series of costs or benefits that are strung out over the life of a project or program. Consider the following illustrative numbers, showing benefits for two different programs over their short lives:

	Benefits ($) in year:			
	1	2	3	4
Project A	20	20	20	20
Project B	50	10	10	10

If we simply add these benefits across the four years for each project, they have the same total: $80. But Project A has a series of equal annual benefits, whereas B has substantial benefits in the first period and lower annual benefits thereafter. To compare the total benefits of the two projects, we must calculate the **present value** of total benefits for each program. For illustrative purposes we use a discount rate of 6 percent.

$$PV_A = \$20 + \frac{\$20}{1 + .06} + \frac{\$20}{(1 + .06)^2} + \frac{\$20}{(1 + .06)^3} = \$73.45$$

$$PV_B = \$50 + \frac{\$10}{1 + .06} + \frac{\$10}{(1 + .06)^2} + \frac{\$10}{(1 + .06)^3} = \$76.73$$

Note first that both present values are less than the undiscounted sums of benefits. This will always be true when a portion of a program's benefits accrues in future years. Note also that the present value of benefits for B exceeds that of A, because more of B's benefits are concentrated early in the life of the program. That is to say, the time profile of B's benefits is more heavily concentrated in earlier years than the time profile of A's benefits.

Similar calculations are made for costs in order to find the present value of the stream of annual costs of a program. And the same reasoning applies;

[6]In general, the discount formula is $PV = m/(1 + r)^t$, where m is the future value, r is the discount rate, and t is the number of years involved.

discounting reduces the present value of a dollar of cost more the farther in the future that cost will be incurred. The present value of the stream of benefits minus the present value of costs gives the present value of net benefits. Alternatively, we could calculate for each year of the life of a project its *net benefits,* then calculate the present value of this stream of net benefits in the same way, by summing their discounted values.

Choice of Discount Rate

Because discounting is a way of aggregating a series of future net benefits into an estimate of present value, the outcome depends importantly on which particular discount rate is used. A low rate implies that a dollar in one year is very similar in value to a dollar in any other year. A high rate implies that a dollar in the near term is much more valuable than one later on. Thus, the higher the discount rate, the more we would be encouraged to put our resources into programs that have relatively high payoffs (i.e., high benefits and/or low costs) in the short run. The lower the discount rate, on the contrary, the more we would be led to select programs that have high net benefits in the more distant future.

The choice of a discount rate has been a controversial topic through the years, and we can only summarize some of the arguments here. First, it is important to keep in mind the difference between **real** and **nominal** interest rates. Nominal rates are the rates one actually sees on the market. If you take a nominal rate and adjust it for inflation, you get a real interest rate. Suppose you deposit $100 in a bank at an interest rate of 8 percent. In 10 years your deposit would have grown to $216, but this is in monetary terms. Suppose over that 10-year period prices increase 3 percent per year on average. Then the real value of your accumulated deposit would be less; in fact, the real interest rate at which your deposit would accumulate would only be 5 percent (8 percent – 3 percent), so in real terms your deposit would be worth only $161 after the 10 years.[7] So we have to be careful about the interest rate we use for discounting. If the cost estimates are expected real costs, that is, adjusted for expected inflation, we want to use a real interest rate for discounting purposes. If our cost estimates are nominal figures, then we use a nominal interest rate in the discounting analysis.

The discount rate reflects the current generation's views about the relative weight to be given to benefits and costs occurring in different years. Even a brief look, though, will show that there are dozens of different interest rates in use at any one time: rates on normal savings accounts, certificates of deposit, bank loans, government bonds, and so forth. Which rate should be used? There are essentially two schools of thought on this question: the **time preference approach** and the **marginal productivity approach.**

According to the time preference approach, the discount rate should reflect the way people themselves think about time. Any person normally will prefer a dollar today to a dollar in 10 years; in the language of economics, they have a

---

[7]These are slight approximations. The deposit would actually be worth $160.64, and the real rate of accumulation would be 4.89 percent.

positive rate of **time preference**. We see people making savings decisions by putting money in bank accounts that pay certain rates of interest. These savings account rates show what interest the banks have to offer in order to get people to forgo current consumption. We might, therefore, take the average bank savings account rate as reflecting the average person's rate of time preference.

The problem with this is that there are other ways of determining people's rates of time preference, and they don't necessarily give the same answer. Economists at Resources for the Future[8] completed a large survey in which they asked individuals to choose between receiving $10,000 today and larger amounts in 5 or 10 years. The responses yielded implied rates of discount of 20 percent for a 5-year time horizon and 10 percent for a 10-year horizon. These were substantially higher than bank savings rates at the time of the survey.

The second approach to determining the "correct" rate of discount is based on the notion of the marginal productivity of investment. When investments are made in productive enterprises, people anticipate that the value of future returns will offset today's investment costs; otherwise, these investments would not be made. The thinking here is that when resources are used in the public sector for natural resource and environmental programs, they ought to yield, on average, rates of return to society equivalent to what they could have earned in the private sector. Private-sector productivity is reflected in the rates of interest banks charge their business borrowers. Thus, by this reasoning, we should use as our discount rate a rate reflecting the interest rates that private firms pay when they borrow money for investment purposes. These are typically higher than savings account interest rates.

With the multiplicity of interest rates the real world offers, and these different arguments for choosing a discount rate, it is no wonder that practices differ among agencies in the public sector. In 1990, for example, the Office of Management and Budget, the major executive branch spending oversight agency, used a discount of 10 percent. The Congressional Budget Office, an oversight agency for the U.S. Congress, used a rate of 2 percent. The U.S. Environmental Protection Agency uses several discount rates for evaluating environmental programs. Some agencies also require sensitivity analysis, showing how program net benefits are affected when calculated with slightly higher or lower discount rates. We can conclude that although discounting is widely accepted, the rate controversy is far from being resolved.

Discounting and Future Generations

The logic of a discount rate, even a very small one, is inexorable (see the numbers in Example 6-2). A billion dollars, discounted back over a century at 5 percent, has a present value of only slightly over $7.6 million. The present generation, considering the length of its own expected life, may not be interested in programs having very high but long-run payoffs such as this.

---

[8]Resources for the Future (RFF) is a well-known Washington organization that specializes in natural resource and environmental economics research. It publishes a quarterly newsletter discussing its work. This information comes from RFF, *Resources*, No. 108, Summer 1992, p. 3.

EXAMPLE 6-2

THE EFFECTS OF DISCOUNTING

Discounting is a process that expresses the value to people today of benefits and costs that will materialize at some future time. As the time increases between today and the point where these benefits or costs actually occur, their present value diminishes. The following figure shows how much the present value of $100 of benefits, discounted at 3 percent, diminishes as the time when it will be received recedes into the future.

Similarly, for a given time period, the present value will diminish as the discount rate increases. The following figure shows how the present value of a $100 benefit, to be received 100 years from now, diminishes as the discount rate increases.

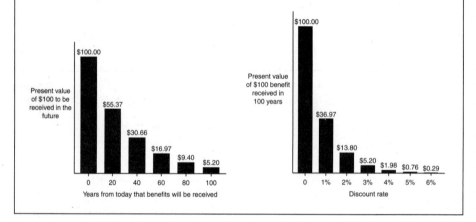

The logic is even more compelling if we consider a future cost. One of the reasons that environmentalists have looked askance at discounting is that it can have the effect of downgrading future damages that result from today's economic activity. Suppose today's generation is considering a course of action that has certain short-run benefits of $10,000 per year for 50 years, but which, starting 50 years from now, will cost $1 million a year *forever*. This may not be too unlike the choice faced by current generations on nuclear power or on global warming. To people alive today the present value of that perpetual stream of future cost discounted at 10 percent is only $85,000. These costs may not weigh particularly heavily on decisions made by the current generation. The present value of the benefits ($10,000 a year for 50 years at 10 percent, or $99,148) exceeds the present value of the future costs. From the standpoint of today, therefore, this might look like a good choice, despite the perpetual cost burden placed on all future generations.

The problems associated with using positive discount rates for environmental programs with long-run impacts are difficult to resolve. Many take the view that for long-run environmental projects the appropriate discount rate is zero. But we have to be very careful here. A great deal of harm has been done to natural and environmental resources by using very low discount rates to evaluate development projects. With low discount rates, it is often possible to justify very disruptive public infrastructure projects because enough distant and uncertain benefits can be accumulated to outweigh the tremendous near–term costs.

One factor that comes into play, and that is hard to pin down, is the extent to which the current generation is sensitive to the needs of future generations as it makes its decisions. Most people have a desire to leave something to descendents, and this acts to make present generations sensitive to the welfare of future generations to some extent. Most people also have some degree of social conscience that leads them to care about the distant future. Yet, are these motives strong enough to be sure that future generations are adequately represented today?

Given these uncertainties about discounting when looking at very long-run environmental impacts, we may want to fall back on additional criteria to help in making current decisions. One of these might be the concept of **sustainability,** an idea that has become very popular in recent years. Sustainability connotes the idea that courses of action should be avoided that reduce the long-run productive capabilities of the natural and environmental resource base. In practice the concept is very difficult to define exactly, and we will have much more to say about it in a later chapter on environment and economic development.

Distributional Issues

The relation of total benefits and total costs is a question of economic efficiency. Distribution is a matter of who gets the benefits and who pays the costs. In public sector programs, distributional matters must be considered along with efficiency issues, which implies that benefit–cost analyses must incorporate studies of how net benefits are distributed among different groups in society.

The distribution of benefits and costs is primarily a matter of equity, or fairness. There are two main types of equity: horizontal and vertical. **Horizontal equity** is a case of treating similarly situated people the same way. An environmental program that has the same impact on an urban dweller with $20,000 of income as on a rural dweller with the same income is horizontally equitable. Consider the following numbers, which illustrate in a simple way the annual values of a particular program accruing to three different individuals who, we assume, all have the same income. Abatement costs show the costs of the program to each individual; these may be higher prices on some products, more time spent on recycling matters, higher taxes, or other factors. The reduced damages are measures of the value of the improvements in environmental quality accruing to each person.

	Person A	Person B	Person C
Reduced environmental damages ($/year)	60	80	120
Abatement costs ($/year)	40	60	80
Difference	20	20	40

Costs and reduced damages are different for individuals A and B, but the difference between them ($20/year) is the same; hence the difference as a proportion of their income is the same. With respect to these two people, therefore, the program is horizontally equitable. It is not, however, for individual C, because this person experiences a net difference of $40/year. Because Person C is assumed to have the same income as the other two people, they are clearly better off as a result of this program; horizontal equity in this case has not been achieved.

Vertical equity refers to how a policy impinges on people who are in different circumstances, in particular on people who have different income levels. Consider the numbers in Table 6-2. These show the impacts, expressed in monetary values, of three different environmental quality programs on three people with, respectively, a low income, a medium income, and a high income. In parentheses next to each number is shown the percentage that number is of the person's income level. Note, for example, the "difference" row of Program 1; it shows the difference between how much the person benefits from the program (in terms of reduced environmental damages impinging on him) and how much it will cost him (in terms of the extent to which he will bear a part of the abatement costs of the program). Note that this net difference represents 1 percent of the income of each person. This is a *proportional impact*; that is, it affects the people of each income level in the same proportion.

Program 2, on the other hand, is *regressive*; it provides higher proportional net benefits to high-income people than to low-income people. Program 3 has a *progressive* impact because net benefits represent a higher proportion of the low-income person's income than it does of the wealthy person's income. Thus, an environmental program (or any program for that matter) is proportional, progressive, or regressive, according to whether the net effect of that policy has

TABLE 6-2
VERTICAL EQUITY*

	Person A		Person B		Person C	
Income	5,000		20,000		50,000	
Program 1						
Reduced damages	150	(3.0)	300	(1.5)	600	(1.2)
Abatement costs	100	(2.0)	100	(0.5)	100	(0.2)
Difference	50	(1.0)	200	(1.0)	500	(1.0)
Program 2						
Reduced damages	150	(3.0)	1,400	(7.0)	5,500	(11.0)
Abatement costs	100	(2.0)	800	(4.0)	3,000	(6.0)
Difference	50	(1.0)	600	(3.0)	2,500	(5.0)
Program 3						
Reduced damages	700	(14.0)	2,200	(11.0)	3,000	(6.0)
Abatement costs	200	(4.0)	1,000	(5.0)	1,500	(3.0)
Difference	500	(10.0)	1,200	(6.0)	1,500	(3.0)

*Figures in this table show annual monetary values. Numbers in parentheses show the percentage of income these numbers represent.

proportionally the same, greater, or less effect on low-income people as on high-income people.

It is to be noted that although the net effects of a program may be distributed in one way, the individual components need not be distributed in the same way. For example, although the overall effects of Program 2 are regressive, the abatement costs of that program are in fact distributed progressively (i.e., the cost burden is proportionately greater for high-income people). In this case damage reduction is distributed so regressively that the overall program is regressive. This is the same in Program 3; although the overall program is progressive, abatement costs are distributed regressively.

These definitions of distributional impacts can be misleading. A program that is technically regressive could actually distribute the bulk of its net benefits to low-income people. Suppose a policy raised the net income of one rich person by 10 percent, but raised each of the net incomes of 1,000 low-income people by 5 percent. This policy is technically regressive, although more than likely the majority of its aggregate net benefits go to low-income people.

It is hard to estimate the distributional impacts of environmental programs, individually or in total. To do so requires very specific data showing impacts by income groups, race, or other factors. In recent years, epidemiologists have collected much better environmental and health data broken down by income, race, and other socioeconomic variables. We still lack good estimates of how program costs are distributed among these groups because these depend on complex factors related to tax collections, consumption patterns, the availability of alternatives, and so on. Despite the difficulties, however, benefit–cost analyses should try to look as closely as possible at the way in which the aggregates are distributed through the population. We will meet up with distributional issues throughout the later chapters of the book.

RISK ANALYSIS

The future can never be known with certainty. Uncertainty about future benefits and costs can arise from many sources. It is difficult to predict exactly the preferences of future generations, who may feel differently than we do about matters of environmental quality. The complexities of world meteorological systems makes predicting future global environmental factors very uncertain. Uncertain advancements in pollution-control technologies could markedly shift future abatement costs. New chemicals, and even many that have been around for years, can have damage effects that are very uncertain.

Because of the high levels of uncertainty in environmental factors, policy analysts have sought to develop modes of analysis specifically directed at the risk factor in environmental decisions. **Risk analysis** involves essentially three steps:

- **Risk assessment:** The study of where risk comes from and how people normally respond to it.
- **Risk valuation:** The study of what values, in terms of concepts such as willingness to pay, people place on risk reduction.

- **Risk management:** The study of how different policies affect levels of environmental risk to which people are exposed.

Risk Assessment

Suppose there is a landfill into which a hazardous chemical has been dumped for a number of years. Suppose also that the residents of a nearby community rely on a local groundwater aquifer for their water supply. Risk assessment in this case means estimating the extent of the risk that the dump site poses for the community. It consists of several steps:

1 **Exposure analysis:** Engineers, hydrologists, and others must determine the likelihood that the chemical will migrate to the aquifer, and how much the citizens of the community will be exposed to it if it does. It could be that other pathways of exposure also might have to be considered.
2 **Dose-response analysis:** Scientists must determine the relationship between exposure levels to the chemical and impacts such as incidences of cancer. Relationships like this are sought by laboratory scientists and by epidemiologists.
3 **Risk characterization:** By combining steps (1) and (2) it is then possible to estimate the specific risks faced by members of the community in terms, for example, of the number of premature deaths they could expect.

Risk Valuation

While the work of risk assessment is the province of physical and health scientists, **risk valuation** falls primarily to economists. If the dump site is cleaned up, thereby leading to a reduced level of health risk to the nearby people, how much is this actually worth to them?

In order to answer questions like this, special concepts are needed with which they may be described. One of these is **expected value.** When future events are probabilistic, we may be able to estimate the "most likely" or "expected" values of their occurrence. Consider the problem of predicting the number of excess cancer deaths caused by the hazardous waste dump site. Suppose we are told by scientists that the probabilities in any year of getting cancer deaths from this source are as shown in Table 6-3. These show a **probability distribution** of excess cancer deaths. For example, the probability of having no deaths is 0.80, of one death is 0.14, of two deaths is 0.05, and so on.[9] The probability of getting four or more deaths is so low that we can treat it as zero. The expected value of cancer deaths is found by essentially taking a weighted average, where each number of deaths in the distribution is weighted by its probability of occurrence. According to this calculation, the expected number of deaths per year is 0.18.

[9]These are illustrative numbers only.

TABLE 6-3
CALCULATING THE ANNUAL EXPECTED VALUE OF CANCER
DEATHS FROM HAZARDOUS CHEMICAL AT LANDFILL

Number of deaths	Probability	Expected value of deaths
0	.80	$0 \times .80 = 0$
1	.14	$1 \times .14 = 0.14$
2	.05	$2 \times .05 = 0.10$
3	.01	$3 \times .01 = 0.03$
4	.00	$4 \times .00 = 0.00$
		Expected value: 0.18

We now can deal with the **valuation** question. Suppose it's estimated that cleaning up the hazardous waste site will lower the expected number of premature deaths from 0.18 to 0.04. How much is this worth to the people of the community? Experience has shown that the scientific results of relative risks stemming from different sources may not agree very well with how people actually feel about different types of risk. For example, people may be willing to pay substantial sums to have a chemical taken out of their water supply even though the health risk is relatively low, whereas they may not be willing to pay much for improved seat belts, which would reduce their overall risk by a great deal.

One way of looking at how people value risky situations is to look at how they react to cases that have similar expected values but quite different profiles of risk.

Consider the following numbers:

Program A		Program B	
Net benefits	Probability	Net benefits	Probability
$500,000	.475	$500,000	.99
$300,000	.525	−$10,000,000	.01
Expected value:	$395,000	Expected value:	$395,000

These two programs have exactly the same expected value. Suppose we have only a one-time choice between the two, which perhaps relates to the choice of a nuclear vs. a conventional power plant to generate electricity. With Program A the net benefits are uncertain, but the outcomes are not extremely different and the probabilities are similar—it is very nearly a 50–50 proposition. Program B, however, has a very different profile. The probability is very high that the net benefits will be $500,000, but there is a small probability of a disaster in which there would be large negative net benefits. If we were making decisions strictly on the basis of expected values, we would treat these projects as the same; we could flip a coin to decide which one to choose. If we did this, we would be displaying **risk-neutral** behavior—making decisions strictly on the basis of expected values. But if this is a one-shot decision, we might decide that the low probability of a large loss in the case of project B represents a risk to which we do not wish to expose ourselves. In this case, we might be **risk averse,** preferring Project A over B.

There are many cases in environmental pollution control where risk aversion is undoubtedly the best policy. The rise of planetary-scale atmospheric change opens up the possibility of catastrophic human dislocations in the future. The potential scale of these impacts argues for a conservative, risk-averse approach to current decisions. Risk–averse decisions also are called for in the case of species extinction; a series of incremental and seemingly small decisions today may bring about a catastrophic decline in genetic resources in the future, with poten-tially drastic impacts on human welfare. Global issues are not the only ones for which it may be prudent to avoid low risks of outcomes that would have large negative net benefits. The contamination of an important groundwater aquifer is a possibility faced by many local communities. In addition, in any activity in which risk to human life is involved, the average person is likely to be risk averse.

Risk Management

Once policymakers know how people value risk and the degree of risk inherent in situations of environmental damages, they are in the position to consider policies and regulations designed to manage those risks. This may incorporate **risk–benefit** analysis.

Suppose an administrative agency, such as the EPA, is considering whether a particular pesticide should be allowed on the market. It might do a study com-paring the benefits farmers and consumers would gain, in the form of produc-tion cost savings, when the pesticide is used, as well as of the increased health risks to farm workers, who must handle it, and possibly to consumers if there are pesticide residues on the market crop. In essence this is a benefit–cost analy-sis in which the cost side is treated more explicitly in terms of risk.

Another type of analysis is **comparative-risk** analysis, which focuses on looking at different policy options and the levels of risk they entail. For exam-ple, in the landfill example the authorities may look at the different ways of managing the landfill and water supply system (capping the landfills, looking for an alternative water supply) in terms of the levels of risk to which each alternative exposes people in the affected communities.

SUMMARY

In previous chapters we put the issue of environmental improvement in a trade-off type of format with willingness to pay (benefits) on one side and abatement costs on the other. In this chapter we started to focus on the problem of measuring these benefits and costs. To do this researchers have to use some underlying analytical framework to account for these benefits and costs. We considered several types of frameworks (impact analysis and cost-effectiveness analysis), then settled on the primary approach used in resource and environ-mental economics: benefit–cost analysis. The rest of the chapter was devoted to a discussion of the main conceptual issues involved in benefit–cost analysis. These are

- The basic analytical steps involved.
- Determining the appropriate size of a project or program.
- The difference between net benefits and the benefit–cost ratio as a decision criterion.
- Discounting.
- Distributional issues.
- Risk analysis.

Having discussed the basic structure of benefit–cost analysis, the next two chapters discuss the problems of actually measuring the benefits and costs of specific environmental programs.

QUESTIONS FOR FURTHER DISCUSSION

1 Suppose air pollution control authorities in Southern California propose to control mobile-source emissions by requiring that 10 percent of all new cars sold in the region be electric. Contrast the different perspectives that would be involved in analyzing this proposal with (a) economic impact analysis, (b) cost-effectiveness analysis, and (c) benefit–cost analysis.

2 Suppose we are comparing two ways of protecting ourselves against mobile-source air pollution: putting additional controls on the internal combustion engine or developing an entirely different type of engine that is cleaner. How would changes in the discount rate be likely to affect the comparison among these two options?

3 Below are some illustrative numbers for benefits and costs arising from a program to restrict emissions of a pollutant. Current emissions are 10 tons per month. Identify the emission level at which net benefits would be maximized. Show that this is not the same as the emission level that gives the highest benefit–cost ratio. Explain the discrepancy.

Emissions (tons/month)	Benefits ($ mil)	Costs ($ mil)
10	0	0
9	4	2
8	8	4
7	18	6
6	32	9
5	44	14
4	54	21
3	62	36
2	68	48
1	72	64
0	74	86

4 Suppose the costs of an environmental pollution-control program are expected to be equal to $80 per year, and that benefits will be $50 per year for 50 years, then $150 per year thereafter. At a discount rate of 4 percent, what are the net benefits of this program? What would the net benefits be at a discount rate of 2 percent? Comment on the difference.

5 When setting public policy on environmental risks, should we base it on the levels of risk to which people think they are exposed or on the risk levels as scientists have determined them to be in fact?

WEBSITES

For a private sector initiative in environmental benefit–cost analysis, see **www. damagevaluation.com.** The Office of Management and Budget has tried to develop guidelines for doing benefit–cost analyses: **www.whitehouse.gov/ OMB/inforeg/riaguide.html;** see also the links listed on the website of this book, **www.mhhe.com/economics/field3.**

SELECTED READINGS

Arrow, K. J., et al: *Benefit–Cost Analysis in Environmental, Health and Safety Regulation,* AEI Press, Washington, DC, 1996.

Boardman, Anthony E., David H. Greenberg, Aiden R. Vining, and David L. Weimer: *Cost–Benefit Analysis: Concepts and Practice,* Prentice Hall, Upper Saddle River, NJ, 1996.

Coker, Annabel, and Cathy Richards: *Valuing the Environment, Economic Approaches to Environmental Evaluation,* Belhaven Press, London and Boca Raton, FL, 1992.

Freeman, A. Myrick, III: *Air and Water Pollution Control: A Benefit–Cost Assessment,* John Wiley, New York, 1982.

Graham, John D., and Jennifer Kassalow Hartwell (eds.): *The Greening of Industry, A Risk-Management Approach,* Harvard University Press, Cambridge, MA, 1997.

Hahn, R. W. (ed.): *Risks, Costs and Lives Saved. Getting Better Results from Regulation,* Oxford University Press, Oxford, England, and AEI Press, Washington, DC, 1996.

Hammond, P. Brett, and Bob Coppock (eds.): *Valuing Health Risks, Costs and Benefits for Environmental Decision Making,* National Academy Press, Washington, DC, 1990.

Hanley, Nick, and Clive L. Spash: *Cost–Benefit Analysis and the Environment,* Edward Elgar, Aldershot, England, 1993.

Mogenstern, Robert D. (ed.): *Economic Analysis at EPA, Assessing Regulatory Impact,* Resources for the Future, Washington, DC, 1997.

Russell, Clifford S., and V. Kerry Smith: "Demands for Data and Analysis Induced by Environmental Policy," in Ernst R. Berndt and Jack E. Triplett (eds.), *Fifty Years of Economic Measurement,* National Bureau of Economic Research, Studies in Income and Wealth, University of Chicago Press, Chicago, 1990, pp. 299–340.

Ward, Kevin M., and John W. Duffield: *Natural Resource Damages: Law and Economics,* Wiley Law Publications, John Wiley, New York, 1992.

CHAPTER 7

BENEFIT–COST ANALYSIS: BENEFITS

We already have made the connection between benefits and willingness to pay. The benefits of something are equal to what people are willing to pay for it, remembering the provisos about the distribution of income and the availability of information. The question is: how is willingness to pay to be estimated in specific cases? For goods and services sold on markets it may be relatively easy to estimate willingness to pay. To estimate people's willingness to pay for potatoes, for example, we can observe them buying potatoes—so many potatoes at certain prices—and develop a good idea of the value people place on this item. This will not work, however, when valuing changes in environmental quality. There are no markets where people buy and sell units of environmental quality. Instead, we have to fall back on indirect means. As one environmental economist put it: ". . . benefit estimation often involves a kind of detective work for piecing together the clues about the values individuals place on [environmental services] as they respond to other economic signals."[1]

The measurement of benefits is an activity pursued on many levels. For an analyst working in an environmental agency, it can turn into a plug-in-the-numbers exercise. So many acres of clam bed destroyed (information provided by a marine biologist) times the going price of clams (provided by a quick trip to the local fish market) equals damages of water pollution in the "X" estuary. At the other extreme, for an environmental economist whose interest is in extending the technique, it can be an excursion into sophisticated means of squeezing subtle information from new sets of data. Our path in this chapter lies between these extremes. We review the main techniques environmental

---

[1] A. Myrick Freeman III, "Benefits of Pollution Control," in U.S. Environmental Protection Agency, *Critical Review of Estimating Benefits of Air and Water Pollution Control*, Washington, DC, EPA 600/5-78-014, 1978, p. II–16.

economists have developed to measure the benefits of improvements in environmental quality. The objective is to understand the economic logic behind these techniques, without getting bogged down in the theoretical and statistical details.[2]

THE DAMAGE FUNCTION: PHYSICAL ASPECTS

When environmental degradation occurs, it produces damages; the emissions control model of Chapter 5 is based in part on the relationship between emissions and marginal damages. Thus, the **benefits** of environmental quality improvements stem from the reduced damages this would produce. To measure an emissions damage function, it's necessary to go through the following steps:

1 Measure **emissions.**
2 Determine the resulting levels of ambient quality through the use of **diffusion models.**
3 Estimate the resulting **human exposure** that these ambient levels would produce.
4 Estimate the **physical impacts** of these exposure levels.
5 Determine the **values** associated with these physical impacts.

The primary work of environmental economists is in step 5, and we will devote most of the chapter to this activity. Let us begin, however, with some brief comments on the first four steps.

Some of the most important damages caused by environmental pollution are those related to human health. Air pollution, especially, has long been thought to increase mortality and morbidity[3] among people exposed to it, certainly in the episodic releases of toxic pollutants, but also from long-run exposure to such pollutants as SO_2 and particulate matter. Diseases such as bronchitis, emphysema, lung cancer, and asthma are thought to be traceable in part to polluted air. Water pollution also produces health damages, primarily through contaminated drinking water supplies. So the measurement of the human health damages of environmental pollution is a critical task for environmental economists.

Many factors affect human health—life styles, diet, genetic factors, age, and so on—besides ambient pollution levels. To separate the effects of pollution, one has to account for all the other factors or else run the risk of attributing effects to pollution that are actually caused by something else (e.g., smoking). This calls for large amounts of accurate data on health factors, as well as the numerous suspected causal factors. The major work here is that of **epidemiologists,** who derive statistical results from large data sets to derive relationships

---

[2]There are a number of books reviewing the current state of environmental benefits measurement. These are listed in the bibliography at the end of the chapter.

[3]Morbidity refers to the incidence of ill health and can be expressed in many ways; for example, days missed from work, days spent in the hospital, and the duration of particular symptoms.

between ambient pollution exposure and adverse health effects. One of the first such studies of air pollution and human health in the United States was done by Lave and Seskin in the 1970s.[4] The data were for 1969 and refer to published information on standard metropolitan statistical areas (SMSAs). They concluded that, in general, a 1 percent reduction in air pollution produces a 0.12 percent reduction in death rates. In the last few decades, literally thousands of additional studies have been done to investigate the linkage between pollution and human health, in terms of both premature mortality and morbidity. For example, a recent study by Pope et al. included 295,000 people spread throughout 50 U.S. metropolitan areas. They found a clear relationship between exposure to **particulate matter** and premature death.[5] Work by Schwartz shows clear linkages between air pollution and respiratory symptoms of various types.[6] These studies are gradually increasing our knowledge about how environmental pollutants affect the health and welfare of human beings as well as the health of the many nonhuman aspects of the natural world.

MEASURING DAMAGES DIRECTLY

Having assessed the physical relationship between pollution and physical damages, such as impaired human and ecological health, the next step is to place values on these outcomes. This is the arena where environmental economics is particularly helpful. Initially one might think of measuring damages directly, in terms, say, of the monetary expenditures the damages produce. A way of assessing health damages, for example, is to estimate the increased medical and other costs associated with particular pollution-related diseases. Table 7-1 shows data from a recent study of this type on asthma, a disease that has increased rapidly in recent years and that researchers believe may be related to air pollution. The estimates are divided into direct and indirect costs. Direct costs are the costs of medical visits to hospitals or doctors' offices, together with the costs of medications used to fight asthma. Indirect costs are related to the opportunity costs of lost work time for people who become ill, lost school days, and lost economic productivity of people who die prematurely from asthma.

The Effects of Pollution on Production Costs

Air pollution can reduce yields of exposed crops; it also can reduce the growth rates of commercially valuable timber. Water pollution can adversely affect firms and municipalities that use the water for production purposes or for

---

[4]Lester B. Lave and Eugene P. Seskin, *Air Pollution and Human Health,* Johns Hopkins Press, Baltimore, MD, 1977.

[5]C. A. Pope III, M. J. Thun, M. M. Namboodri, D. W. Dockery, J. S. Evans, F. E. Speizer, and C. W. Heath, Jr., "Particulate Air Pollution as a Predictor of Mortality in a Prospective Study of U.S. Adults," *American Journal of Respiratory and Critical Care Medicine,* Vol. 151, 1995, pp. 669–674.

[6]J. Schwartz, "Short Term Fluctuations in Air Pollution and Hospital Admissions of the Elderly for Respiratory Disease," *Thorax,* 50(5), 1995, pp. 531–538.

TABLE 7-1
ESTIMATED COSTS OF ASTHMA IN THE UNITED STATES, 1990

Cost item	Costs, $ millions
Direct medical expenditures:	
Hospital care	
Inpatient	1,559.6
Emergency room	295.0
Outpatient	190.3
Physician's services:	
Inpatient	146.0
Outpatient	347.0
Medications	1,099.7
Subtotal	3,637.6
Indirect costs:	
School days lost	899.7
Loss of work:	
Outside employment:	
Men	134.8
Women	211.5
Housekeeping	503.0
Mortality:	
Men	390.2
Women	429.1
Subtotal	2,568.4
Total costs	6,206.0

Source: K. B. Weiss, P. J. Gergen, and T. A. Hodgson, "An Economic Evaluation of Asthma in the United States," *The New England Journal of Medicine,* 326(13), March 26, 1992, pp. 862–866.

domestic use. Diminished water quality also can have a negative impact on commercial fishing industries. Soil contamination can have serious impacts on agricultural production. Pollution in the workplace can reduce the effectiveness of workers and often can increase the rate at which machinery and buildings deteriorate. In these cases the effects of pollution are felt on the production of goods and services. The damage caused by the pollution comes about because it interferes in some way with these production processes, in effect making it more costly to produce these outputs than it would be in a less polluted world.

How we actually measure production-related benefits of reducing pollution depends on circumstances. Suppose we are looking at a small group of agricultural producers living in a certain region who will be affected by reduced airborne emissions coming from an upwind factory. Pollutants from the factory have depressed yields, so reducing emissions will cause yields to increase. The crop being produced is sold in a national market, and its price will be unaffected by the output changes in this one region. This situation is depicted in Figure 7-1. In this diagram, S_1 is the supply curve for this group of farms before the improved air quality; S_2 is the supply curve after the improvement.[7] Price of

---

[7]See Chapters 3 and 4 for a discussion of supply curves.

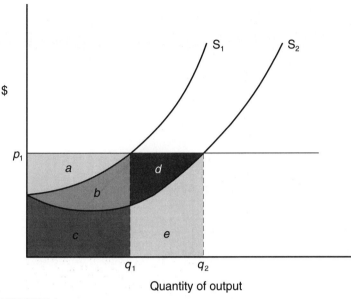

Quantity of output

FIGURE 7-1
Benefits from Reduced Production Costs.

the output is p_1. Before the change, these farmers produce at an output level of q_1, whereas after the improvement their output increases to q_2.

One way of approximating the benefits of this environmental improvement is to measure the value of increased output produced by this group of farms. This is the increased output, $q_2 - q_1$, multiplied by the price of the crop. This gives an estimate corresponding to the area $(d + e)$ in Figure 7-1.

A number of studies have been done along these lines.[8] Moskowitz et al.[9] studied the effects of air pollution on alfalfa in the United States. They measured the quantity of production lost because of air pollution and valued this loss at the going price of alfalfa. They found that air pollution was responsible for a loss in 1974 of between $24 million and $210 million. The difference between these figures comes about because of uncertainties over the actual pollution dose the alfalfa received in that year. Another study was done by Page et al.[10] to measure crop-related air pollution losses in a six-state area. They estimated annual losses in the production of soybeans, wheat, and corn and then

---

[8]These are reviewed in Gardner M. Brown Jr. and Mark L. Plummer, "Market Measures of User Benefits," in *Acid Deposition: State of Science and Technology*, Report 27, Methods for Valuing Acidic Deposition and Air Pollution Effects, National Acid Precipitation Assessment Program, Washington, DC, U.S. Superintendent of Documents, 1990, pp. 27–35 to 27–73.

[9]P. D. Moskowitz, E. A. Coveney, W. H. Medeiros, and S. C. Morris, "Oxidant Air Pollution: A Model for Estimating Effects on U.S. Vegetation," *Journal of Air Pollution Control Association*, 32(2), February 1982, pp. 155–160.

[10]W. P. Page, G. Abogast, R. Fabian, and J. Ciecka, "Estimation of Economic Losses to the Agricultural Sector from Airborne Residuals in the Ohio River Basin," *Journal of Air Pollution Control Association*, 32(2), February 1982, pp. 151–154.

aggregated these to see what the present value of total losses would be during the period 1976–2000. They came up with an estimate of about $7 billion.

A more refined approach to this problem is possible. The problem with taking just the value of the increased output is that production costs also may have changed. When air pollution diminishes, farmers actually may increase their use of certain inputs and farm this land more intensively. How do we account for this possibility? We can analyze the full change by using net incomes of the farmers (total value of output minus total production costs).

The situation before the change:

$$\text{Total value of output: } a + b + c$$
$$\text{Total costs: } b + c$$
$$\text{Net income: } a$$

The situation after the change:

$$\text{Total value of output: } a + b + c + d + e$$
$$\text{Total costs: } c + e$$
$$\text{Net income: } a + b + d$$

Thus, the improvement in net incomes is $(a + b + d) - a$, or an amount equal to area $b + d$ in Figure 7-1.

How we measure this amount depends on how much information we are able to get. If we have studied these farms and know their supply curves before and after the change, we can measure the increased net income directly. If the supply curves are not known, we might look at the increased values of agricultural land in the area. In many cases, added net incomes of this type will get capitalized into land values, and we can use the **increased land values** to estimate the benefits of the environmental improvements.

Materials Damage

Air pollutants cause damage to exposed surfaces, metal surfaces of machinery, stone surfaces of buildings and statuary, and painted surfaces of all types of items. The most heavily implicated pollutants are the sulfur compounds, particulate matter, oxidants, and nitrogen oxides. For the most part, the damage is from increased deterioration that must be offset by increased maintenance and earlier replacement. In the case of outdoor sculpture, the damage is to the aesthetic qualities of the objects.

In this case the dose–response relationship shows the extent of deterioration associated with exposure to varying amounts of air pollutants. The basic physical relationships may be investigated in the laboratory, but in application to any particular area one must have data on the various amounts of exposed materials that actually exist in the study region. Then it is possible to estimate the total amount of materials deterioration that would occur in an average year of exposure to the air of the region with its "normal" loading of various pollutants. One must then put a value on this deterioration. Taking a strict damage-function approach, we could estimate the increased cost of maintenance (labor, paint, etc.) made necessary by this deterioration,[11] but this would be an underestimate of the true damages from a willingness-to-pay perspective. Part of the damages would be aesthetic—the reduced visual values of less sightly buildings and painted surfaces. We might arrive at these values through contingent valuation methods, discussed later. In addition, the maintenance cost approach would not be complete if pollution causes builders to switch to other materials to reduce damages.

Problems with Direct Damage Approaches

The basic problem with direct damage estimates is that they are almost always seriously incomplete. Consider the case of measuring health damages by lost productivity and medical expenditures. We note, first, that these tend to be market measures. They measure the value of marketed goods and services a person might, on average, produce. So the many nonmarket contributions people make, both inside and outside the home, sometimes don't get counted. This method also would assign a zero value to a person with disabilities unable to work, or a retiree. There are also numerous monetary, as well as psychic, benefits received by others—friends and relatives, for example—that the productivity measure does not account for. Nor does it account for the pain and suffering of illness. Similar conclusions may be drawn about using medical expenditures to estimate damages from reduced environmental quality. Suppose we estimate the damages to you of getting a head cold. We come up with an estimate of $1.27, the cost of the aspirin you consume to reduce the discomfort. This probably would be a serious understatement of the true damages of the cold. If you were asked how much you would be willing to pay to avoid the cold, the answer is likely to be substantially more than the cost of the aspirin. This is perhaps an unfair example because major medical expenditures for a person suffering from air pollution–induced lung cancer are much more significant than a bottle of aspirin. But the principle is valid.

Another major problem with attempts to measure damage functions directly is that people and markets normally will change and adjust to environmental pollution, and a full accounting of the damages of pollution must take these adjustments into account. Farmers raising crops affected by pollution may shift to other crops, while the prices of the damaged crops may change, affecting consumers. People often will change their behavior when faced with polluted air or water, engaging in what is called **averting behavior,** or making major changes in life style. These effects are difficult to measure when using a direct approach to damage measurement. For this reason, we must turn back to our fundamental concept for determining value: willingness to pay.

[11]This approach is taken from R. L. Horst, E. H. Manuel Jr., R. M. Black III, J. K. Tapiero, K. M. Brennan, and M. C. Duff, "A Damage Function Assessment of Building Materials: The Impact of Acid Deposition," Washington, DC, U.S. Environmental Protection Agency, 1986.

WILLINGNESS TO PAY

There are essentially three ways of trying to find out how much people are willing to pay for improvements in environmental quality. We can illustrate them by considering a case of noise pollution. One feature of the modern world is high-speed roadways (expressways, freeways, and turnpikes), and a major characteristic of these roads is that the traffic on them creates noise. Thus, the people who live nearby suffer damages from this traffic noise. Suppose our job is to estimate the willingness to pay of people living near expressways to reduce traffic noise. How might we do this?

1   The homeowners themselves may have made expenditures to reduce the noise levels inside their homes. For example, they may have installed additional insulation in the walls of their homes or put double-thick glass in the windows. When people make expenditures such as these, they reveal something about their willingness to pay for a quieter environment. In general, then, if we can find cases where market goods are purchased in order to affect a consumer's exposure to the ambient environment, we may be able to analyze these purchases for what they say about the value people place on changes in that ambient environment.

2   The noise in the vicinity of the road may have affected the prices that nearby residents may have paid for their houses. If two houses have exactly the same characteristics in all respects except the level of exterior noise, we would expect the one in the noisier environment to be less valuable to prospective buyers than the one in the quieter environment. If the housing market is competitive, the price of the noisier house would be lower than the other one. Thus, by looking at the difference in house prices we can estimate the value people place on reduced noise pollution. In general, therefore, any time the price of some good or service varies in accordance with its environmental characteristics, we may be able to analyze these price variations to determine people's willingness to pay for these characteristics.

3   Both of the foregoing techniques are **indirect** in the sense that they look for ways of analyzing market data to find out what they imply about the willingness to pay of people for closely associated environmental characteristics. The third way is deceptively **direct.** It is to conduct a survey among homeowners and ask them how much they would be willing to pay for reductions in noise levels around and inside their homes. This direct survey approach has received a lot of attention from environmental economists in recent years, primarily because of its flexibility. Virtually any feature of the natural environment that can be described accurately to people can be studied by this method.

In the remainder of the chapter we will examine some of the ways these approaches have been applied to estimate the benefits of improvements in environmental quality.

WILLINGNESS TO PAY: INDIRECT METHODS

The thought behind these indirect approaches is that when people make market choices among certain items that have different characteristics related to the environment, they reveal the value they place on these environmental factors. Perhaps the most important is what they reveal about the values of health and human life.

Using willingness to pay to measure health benefits has the virtue of being consistent with other types of economic demand studies, and it recognizes that even with something as important as health care, it is people's evaluations of its worth that should count. But the concept must be used with care. In any real-world situation, willingness to pay implies ability to pay; one cannot express a willingness to pay for something if one lacks the necessary income or wealth. So we must be sensitive to the income levels of people whose demand we are trying to measure. If the analysis includes a substantial number of people with low incomes, the measured willingness to pay may be lower than justified. We may not want to lower the estimated health benefits of an environmental program simply because the target population has lower-than-average incomes.

Another feature about health care as a normal economic good is that people may be willing to pay for the health of others. I do not care if my daughter eats meat; her own willingness to pay is a good expression of her demand for meat. I do care about her health, however, and, to her own willingness to pay for good health, I would be willing to add a substantial sum of my own. Thus, strictly individualistic measures of willingness to pay for health improvements may underestimate the true benefits of programs that increase health.

The Value of Human Health as Expressed in "Averting" Costs

Air and water pollution can produce a variety of adverse health conditions, ranging from slight chest discomfort or headaches all the way to acute episodes requiring hospital care. People often make expenditures to try to avoid, or avert, these conditions, and these averting costs are an expression of their willingness to pay to avoid them. A number of studies have been done in which these averting expenditures have been analyzed for what they tell about willingness to pay.[12] One study was done of a sample of people in the Los Angeles area in 1986 looking at expenditures they made to avoid a variety of respiratory symptoms. Expenditures included such things as cooking with electricity rather than gas, operating a home air conditioner, and driving an air-conditioned car. Their estimates of the willingness to pay to avoid various respiratory symptoms ranged from $0.97 for shortness of breath to $23.87 for chest tightness.

---

[12]These are reviewed in Maureen L. Cropper and A. Myrick Freeman III, "Environmental Health Effects," in John B. Braden and Charles D. Kolstad (eds.), *Measuring the Demand for Environmental Quality*, North-Holland, Amsterdam, 1991, pp. 200–202.

The Value of Human Life as Expressed in Wage Rates

Diminished air quality and contaminated water can lead to deteriorated health and death. How are these impacts to be valued? It is tempting to say "human life is beyond measure," but that is not the way people behave in the real world. We can see by casual observation that individuals do not, in fact, behave as if prolonged life, or the warding off of disease, is in some sense an ultimate end to which all their resources must be devoted. We see people engaging in risky activity; in some sense trading off risk for the benefits received. Almost everybody drives a car, some people smoke, some rock climb, many strive to get tans, and so on. We also see people allocating portions of their income to reducing risk: buying locks, installing smoke alarms, staying away from dark places at night. In addition, we observe people making differential judgments of their own worth: parents with children buying more life insurance than single people, and so on. All of this suggests that people treat the risk of death in a reasonably rational manner, and that we could use willingness to pay as a way of evaluating the benefits of reducing the risk of death or illness.

But we must be clear on exactly what is involved. There is a joke about the stingy millionaire, walking down a street, who gets held up. The robber points a gun at her and says, "Your money or your life," and the victim replies: "Ah, let me think about that." Estimating the willingness-to-pay value of a human life does not involve this kind of situation. People are not asked for their willingness to pay to save their own lives. Under some circumstances a person presumably will be willing to give everything he owns, but these are not the kinds of situations people normally face. When I express a willingness to pay for reducing air pollution, the relevant concept is the value of the **statistical life,** not the life of some particular individual. This does not imply that people are assumed to care only about the average, or random, person and not specific people. People obviously feel closer to their relatives, friends, and neighbors than to strangers. What is involved is the value people place on rearranging the living conditions of a large group of people by, for example, reducing their exposure to environmental pollutants in order to lower the probability that some **randomly determined individual** from the group will suffer illness or premature death. Suppose, for example, that the average person in a group of 100,000 people would be willing to pay $5 to lower the probability of a random death among members of that group from 7 in 100,000 to 6 in 100,000. Then the total willingness to pay is $5(100,000) = $500,000, which is the value of a statistical life based on willingness to pay.

The most fully developed approach to measuring the willingness to pay for reducing risk to life is through **industrial wage rate studies.** Suppose there are two jobs similar in all respects except that in one, because of the type of machinery used, the risk of death is somewhat higher than in the other. Suppose that initially the wage rates in the two industries were the same. In this case it would obviously be preferable to work in the safer industry—same wage, lower risk. Workers would then seek to move from the dangerous to the safer industry. This would tend to drive down the wage in the safer industry and increase the wage in the other, as firms sought to keep workers from leaving that industry. Thus, a wage differential would evolve between the two industries; the amount of that differential would show how workers valued the differences between them in terms of risk of death. The wage differential, in other words, represents an implicit valuation of a statistical life. By analyzing wage differences such as this, we can get a measure of the benefits people would get from reducing pollution-related premature deaths.

Table 7-2 summarizes some of the recent results of wage-rate studies aimed at estimating the value of a statistical life in the United States. Note that the estimates range from $600,000 to over $10 million. What accounts for these differences? Different data and statistical techniques probably account for most of them. These studies are difficult because there are many other factors that have to be taken into account and because it is hard to get exactly the right data. For example, most worker accident and wage data apply to industry groupings, and within these groups there may be substantial variation among individual firms, not only because of technological differences among them but also because some firms may have done a lot more than others to make the workplace safer.

TABLE 7-2
IMPLIED VALUE OF STATISTICAL LIFE AS ESTIMATED IN LABOR MARKET
STUDIES IN UNITED STATES

Study	Value of statistical life 1990
Kniesner and Leeth (1991)	$0.6 million
Dillingham (1985)	0.9 million
Moore and Viscusi (1988)	2.5 million
Cousineau, Lacroix, and Girard (1988)	3.6 million
Olson (1981)	5.2 million
Viscusi (1981)	6.5 million
Herzog and Schlottmann (1990)	9.1 million
Leigh (1987)	10.4 million

Sources: Thomas J. Kniesner and John D. Leeth, "Compensating Wage Differentials for Fatal Injury Risk in Australia, Japan, and the United States," *Journal of Risk and Uncertainty,* 4(1), 1991, pp. 75–90; Alan Dillingham, "The Influence of Risk Variable Definition on Value-of-Life Estimates," *Economic Inquiry,* 23(2), 1985, pp. 277–294; Michael J. Moore and W. Kip Viscusi, "The Quantity-Adjusted Value of Life," *Economic Inquiry,* 26(3), 1988, pp. 369–388; Jean-Michel Cousineau, Robert Lacroix, and Anne-Marie Girard, "Occupational Hazard and Wage Compensating Differentials," University of Montreal Working Paper, 1988; Craig A. Olson, "An Analysis of Wage Differentials Received by Workers on Dangerous Jobs," *Journal of Human Resources,* 16(2), 1981, pp. 167–185; W. Kip Viscusi, "Occupational Safety and Health Regulation: Its Impact and Policy Alternatives," in J. Crecine (ed.), *Research in Public Policy Analysis and Management,* vol. 2. Greenwich, CT: JAI Press, 1981, pp. 281–299; Henry W. Herzog Jr. and Alan M. Schlottmann, "Valuing Risk in the Workplace: Market Price, Willingness to Pay, and the Optimal Provision of Safety," *Review of Economics and Statistics,* 72(3), 1990, pp. 463–470; J. Paul Leigh, "Gender, Firm Size, Industry and Estimates of the Value-of-Life," *Journal of Health Economics,* 6(3), 1987, pp. 255–273; For additional information see W. Kip Viscusi, *Rational Risk Policy, The 1996 Arne Ryde Memorial Lectures,* Oxford University Press, 1998, pp. 54–57.

It is also the case that wage-rate studies such as these are predicated on the reasonably efficient working of the labor market, and this may not be the case in
some industries. Union agreements, collusion among firm managers, and lack of
information can upset the competitive wage-making process in some industries.
These problems do not mean that these studies are not useful, only that we have
not yet reached a point where they are giving us a consistent story.

The Value of Environmental Quality
as Expressed in House Prices

The wage-rate studies we just looked at estimate the willingness to pay to be
exposed to a lower risk of death, which is a specific consequence of being
exposed to lower levels of environmental pollution. But there are wider benefits to a cleaner environment than simply health benefits. A more inclusive
approach is to examine people's willingness to pay to live in a less polluted
environment. This would include the health effects but also other dimensions
such as aesthetic impacts.

Suppose you had two houses that were exactly the same in terms of all their
physical characteristics—number of rooms, floor area, age, and so on—as well
as in locational factors—distance to neighbors, distance to shopping facilities,
and so forth. Assume, however, that one house is located in an area of substantial air pollution, whereas the other is located in an area with relatively clean
air. We would expect the market prices of these two houses to differ because of
the air quality difference. This conclusion generalizes to a large housing market
involving many properties. The surrounding air quality is essentially a feature
of the location of a house so, as houses are bought and sold in the house market,
these air quality differences would tend to get "capitalized" into the market
prices of the houses.[13] Of course, homes differ in many respects, not just in
terms of air quality. So it is necessary to collect large amounts of data on many
properties then use statistical techniques to identify the role played by air pollution, as well as other factors.[14]

Assuming we had collected enough data and conducted the appropriate statistical analyses, we might end up with a relationship such as that shown in
Figure 7-2. This shows that as the particulate content of the surrounding air
increases, house prices decrease, everything else held equal. Information of this
type can then be used to estimate homeowners' marginal willingness to pay
(benefits) for small decreases in particulate exposure. Smith and Huang
recently reviewed a number of studies of this type. They found that, in general,
the marginal willingness to pay for a one-unit decrease in exposure to total
suspended particulate matter (TSP) was in the range of $100 to $300 for most

---

[13]"Capitalized" means that house prices adjust to reflect the present value of the stream of
future damages to which homeowners would be exposed if they lived in the various houses.
[14]The technical name for this type of approach is "hedonic" analysis. When the price of something is related to the many characteristics it possesses, we can study patterns of price differences to
deduce the value people place on one of those characteristics.

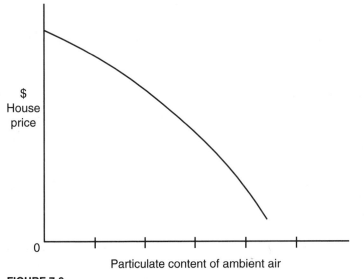

Particulate content of ambient air

FIGURE 7-2
Relationship of Ambient SO_2 Concentration and House Prices.

studies.[15] Another recent study of house prices by Chattopadhyay estimated that people are willing to pay on average about $310 for a one-unit decrease in exposure to PM_{10}.[16]

The same kind of approach might be used with some cases of water pollution. In Chapter 4 we used lake pollution to introduce the concept of a public good. Suppose a lake is surrounded by a number of residences. The market price of these homes will be affected by many things: their age, size, condition, and so on. They also will be affected by the water quality of the lake. If this water quality degrades over time, we would expect the market values of the surrounding properties to go down. The deteriorating water quality means that homeowners will obtain less utility from living in that vicinity, other things remaining equal, and this will get capitalized into the values of the houses. One approach to measuring the benefits of cleaning up the lake is to estimate the overall increase in property values among the homes in the vicinity of the lake. We have to remember, however, that this is likely to be only a partial estimate of total benefits. If nonresidents have access to the lake or park, they also would be gaining benefits, but these would not show up in property value changes. Property value changes to measure benefits from pollution reduction also can

[15]TSP is expressed in terms of micrograms per cubic meter. See V. Kerry Smith and Ju-Chin Huang, "Can Markets Value Air Quality? A Meta Analysis of Hedonic Property Value Models," *Journal of Political Economy*, 103(1), 1995, pp. 209–227.
[16]PM_{10} refers to the concentration of particulate matter composed of particles less than 10 microns in diameter. See S. Chattopadhyay, "Estimating the Demand for Air Quality: New Evidence Based on the Chicago Housing Market," *Land Economics*, 75(1), February 1999, pp. 22–38.

be used in other situations; for example, in valuing the damage from noise around airports and major highways and in measuring the benefits flowing from urban parks.

The Value of Environmental Quality and Intercity Wage Differentials

We talked about using wage rate differences among jobs to measure the value of reducing health risks from pollution. Wage rate studies also have been used to estimate the value of living in a cleaner environment. Suppose there were two cities, alike in every respect, but one has higher air pollution than the other. Suppose that initially wage rates in the two cities were equal. Since everything else is exactly the same, it would be more desirable to work in the less polluted city—same wages but less air pollution. Workers would, therefore, migrate to the cleaner city. To keep a labor force in the dirty city, one of two things must happen: The air must be cleaned up or a higher wage must be offered to offset the damages of living in more polluted air. So we could study wage rate differentials among cities with different degrees of air pollution to measure the value that people place on cleaner air. This would give us a way of estimating the benefits of cleaning up the air in the more polluted cities.

The Value of Environmental Amenities as Expressed in Travel Costs

One of the first approaches that environmental economists ever used to estimate the demand for environmental amenities is a method that takes travel costs as a proxy for price. Although we don't observe people buying units of environmental quality directly, we do observe them traveling to enjoy, for example, recreational experiences in national and state parks, swimming and fishing experiences in lakes and streams, and so on. Travel is costly; it takes time as well as out-of-pocket travel expenses. By treating these travel costs as a price that people must pay to experience the environmental amenity, we can estimate, under some circumstances, a demand function for those amenities.

By getting travel cost data for a large number of people, we can build up estimates of the aggregate willingness to pay for particular environmental amenities. Of course, information must be obtained on more than just their travel costs. Families will differ in terms of many factors, not just in terms of their travel costs to this park. They will have different income levels, they will differ in terms of the presence of alternative parks and other recreational experiences available to them, and so on. So surveys have to collect large amounts of data on many visitors to be able statistically to sort out all these various influences on park visitation rates.

This approach may be used to estimate the benefits of improving the quality of the environment at the visitation site; for example, by improving the water quality at a recreation lake so that fishing is better. To do this we must collect information not only on the travel costs of recreators to a single recreation site but on the travel costs to many different sites with differing natural characteristics. Then we can parse out the effects on visitation of various qualitative aspects of different sites. From this we can then determine their willingness to pay for improvements in these qualitative changes.

WILLINGNESS TO PAY: DIRECT METHODS

We come now to the direct approach to estimating willingness to pay, called the **contingent valuation** method. Contingent valuation (CV) is based on the simple idea that if you would like to know the willingness to pay of people for some characteristic of their environment, you can simply ask them. The word "simply" is a little extreme because it turns out not to be so simple, even though the basic idea seems straightforward. The method is called "contingent" valuation because it tries to get people to say how they would act if they were placed in certain contingent situations. If we were interested in measuring people's willingness to pay for something like potatoes, we could station ourselves at stores and see them choosing in real situations. But when there are no real markets for something, such as an environmental quality characteristic, we can only ask them to tell us how they would choose *if* they were faced with a market for these characteristics.

Contingent value studies have been done to date for a long list of environmental factors: air quality, the value of view-related amenities, the recreational quality of beaches, preservation of wildlife species, congestion in wilderness areas, hunting and fishing experiences, toxic waste disposal, preservation of wild rivers, and others.[17] In fact, CV methods have spread into nonenvironmental areas; for example, the value of programs for reducing the risks of heart attacks, the value of supermarket price information, and the value of a seniors companion program. Over time the method has been developed and refined to give what many regard as reasonably reliable measures of the benefits of a variety of public goods, especially environmental quality.

The steps in a CV analysis are the following:

1 Identification and description of the environmental quality characteristic to be evaluated.
2 Identification of respondents to be approached, including sampling procedures used to select respondents.
3 Design and application of a survey questionnaire through personal, phone, or mail interviews (in recent years, focus groups sometimes have been used).
4 Analysis of results and aggregation of individual responses to estimate values for the group affected by the environmental change.

---

[17]For a review of many of these studies and of the general problems of CV analysis, see Paul Cameron Mitchell and Richard T. Carson, *Using Surveys to Value Public Goods: The Contingent Valuation Method,* Washington, DC, Resources for the Future, 1989, and Ronald G. Cummings, David S. Brookshire, and William D. Schulze, *Valuing Environmental Goods: An Assessment of the Contingent Valuation Method,* Rowland and Allanheld Publishers, Totowa, NJ, 1986.

The nature of CV analysis can best be understood by looking more closely at the questionnaire design phase.

The Questionnaire

The questionnaire is designed to get people to think about and reveal their maximum willingness to pay for some feature of the environment. It has three essential components:

1 A clear statement of exactly what the environmental feature or amenity is that people are being asked to evaluate.
2 A set of questions that will describe the respondent in economically relevant ways, for example, income, residential location, age, and use of related goods.
3 A question, or set of questions, designed to elicit willingness-to-pay responses from the respondent.

The central purpose of the questionnaire is to elicit from respondents their estimate of what the environmental feature is worth to them. In economic terms this means getting them to reveal the maximum amount they would be willing to pay rather than go without the amenity in question. A number of techniques have been used to get at this response. The most obvious is to ask people outright to provide the number with no prompting or probing on the part of the interviewer. Other approaches include using a bidding game, where the interviewer starts with a bid at a low level and progressively increases the value until the user indicates that the limit has been reached. Alternatively, the interviewer could start with a high figure and lower it to find where the respondent's threshold value is located. Another method is to give the respondents printed response cards with a range of values, and then ask the respondents to check off their maximum willingness to pay. Exhibit 7-1 presents some examples of questions used in several contingent valuation studies.

Some Results

One great advantage of contingent valuation is that it is flexible and applicable to a wide range of environmental amenities, not just those that can somehow be measured in conjunction with some marketable good. Virtually anything that can be made comprehensible to respondents can be studied with this technique.

CV was first used in 1963 by Bob Davis to estimate the benefits of outdoor recreation opportunities in the Maine backwoods. He found that the modal willingness to pay per family for the use of a wilderness recreation area was between $1.00 and $2.00 per day.[18]

---

[18]Robert K. Davis, "The Value of Big Game Hunting in a Private Forest," in *Transactions of the Twenty-ninth North American Wildlife Conference,* Wildlife Management Institute, Washington, DC, 1964.

EXHIBIT 7-1

SAMPLE OF QUESTIONS USED IN SEVERAL CONTINGENT VALUATION STUDIES

Study to estimate benefits of national freshwater quality improvements

1 How many people in this household are under 18 years of age?
2 During the last 12 months, did you or any member of your household boat, fish, swim, wade, or water-ski in a freshwater river, lake, pond, or stream?

Here are the national water pollution goals:
Goal C—99 percent of freshwater is at least boatable,
Goal B—99 percent of freshwater is at least fishable,
Goal A—99 percent of freshwater is at least swimmable.

3 What is the highest amount you would be willing to pay each year:
a. To achieve Goal C?
b. To achieve Goal B?
c. To achieve Goal A?
4 Considering the income classes listed in the accompanying card, what category best describes the total income that you and all the members of the household earned in 20__?

Study to estimate the value of salmon restoration

Suppose that because of budget cuts, all state and federal funding to continue the restoration effort to restore Atlantic salmon to the Connecticut River is stopped. Without this funding, Atlantic salmon would soon be extinct in the Connecticut River. Now suppose that a private foundation is formed to continue the salmon restoration effort. This foundation would be funded by private donations. Please assume that next week a representative will ask for your donation.

The basic category would cost $_____. At this level of funding Atlantic salmon would continue to exist in the southern section of the Connecticut River, but in such small numbers that few people would see them and salmon fishing would not be allowed. Keeping in mind your budget and other financial commitments, would you pay this amount?

1 YES. In fact I would pay as much as $_____. (Please write in the MAXIMUM amount that you would pay.)
2 NO. The amount is too much. I would pay $_____. (Please write in the MAXIMUM amount that you would pay.)

Sources: Water quality: Robert Cameron Mitchell and Richard T. Carson, *Using Surveys to Value Public Goods: The Contingent Valuation Method,* Resources for the Future, Washington, DC, 1989. Salmon restoration: Tom Stevens, Martha K. Field, Thomas A. More, and Ronald J. Glass, "Contingent Valuation of Rare and Endangered Species: An Assessment," in *Benefit and Cost Transfers in Resource Planning,* 7th Interim Report, W-133, 1994.

A contingent valuation study of bird hunting in Delaware found that the average willingness to pay for a bagged duck was $82.17; this value was influenced by, among other things, the amount of congestion in the hunting area.[19]

A number of researchers have used the approach to estimate willingness to pay to avoid ill health. For example, Chestnut et al. asked respondents how much they would be willing to pay to reduce by half the number of bad asthma days experienced each year.[20] The mean response per asthma day was $10.

[19]John MacKenzie, "A Comparison of Contingent Preference Models," *American Journal of Agricultural Economics,* Vol. 75, August 1993, pp. 593–603.
[20]Lauraine G. Chestnut, Steven D. Colome, Robin L. Keller, William E. Lambert, Bart Ostreo, Robert D. Rowe, and Sandra L. Wojciechowski, *Heart Disease Patient's Averting Behavior, Cost of Illness and Willingness to Pay to Avoid Angina Episodes,* U.S. Environmental Protection Agency, EPA/230/10-88/042, Washington, DC, 1988.

Several CV studies have been done to measure the willingness to pay for increased visibility of the air in urban areas of the United States. The results that researchers have obtained vary a lot; for a 10 percent increase in visual range, estimates of the annual willingness to pay per household (in the early to mid-1980s) vary from $7 to $101, although most of the results are in the $20 to $40 range.[21] Brookshire and Schulze report on a CV study done to investigate how much people would be willing to pay for an increase in air visibility in the Grand Canyon. The average willingness to pay among their respondents was $9.20 for an iterative bidding approach and $5.69 for a payment card approach.[22]

Desvouges, Smith, and McGivney used CV to estimate the value of water quality improvements for water-based recreational purposes. They found that users of the recreation sites they sampled would, on average, be willing to pay $12.30 per person to increase the water quality from "boatable" to "fishable" and $29.60 per person to go from "boatable" to "swimmable" water.[23] Brookshire et al. used CV to measure the benefits of improving air quality. For the people in their study they found a mean willingness to pay of $14.50 per month to go from "poor" to "fair" quality air and $20.30 per month to go from "fair" to "good" quality air.[24]

Boyle and Bishop used CV methods to investigate the benefits of undertaking steps to preserve the bald eagle. Their results varied from $11.84 to $75.31 per person, depending on whether they had ever traveled to view bald eagles and whether they had ever contributed to Wisconsin's Endangered Resources Donation program.[25]

Crutchfield used CV methods to estimate household willingness to pay to protect themselves against nitrate pollution in the water supply. He estimated the average household willingness to pay at $128.[26]

Brookshire and Coursey did a CV study to determine people's willingness to pay for a change in tree density in an urban park from 200 to 250 trees per acre. The median willingness to pay among their respondents was $9.30. In eliciting these responses researchers showed respondents pictures of the park with different tree densities.[27]

---

[21]Gardner M. Brown Jr., and J. M. Callaway, *Acid Deposition: State of the Science and Technology,* National Acid Precipitation Assessment Program, Report 27, Washington, DC, U.S. Government Printing Office, 1990, pp. 27–164.

[22]David S. Brookshire and William D. Schulze, "The Economic Benefits of Preserving Visibility in the National Parks of the Southwest," *Natural Resources Journal,* 23(1), January 1983, pp. 149–173.

[23]William H. Desvouges, V. Kerry Smith, and Matthew P. McGivney, "A Comparison of Alternative Approaches for Estimating Recreation and Related Benefits of Water Quality Improvements," Environmental Protection Agency, EPA/230/05-83/001, Washington, DC, 1983.

[24]David Brookshire, Mark A. Thayer, William D. Schulze, and Ralph C. D'Arge, "Valuing Public Goods: A Comparison of Survey and Hedonic Approaches," *American Economic Review,* 72(1), March 1982, pp. 165–171.

[25]21 Kevin J. Boyle and Richard C. Bishop, "Valuing Wildlife in Benefit–CostAnalysis: A Case Study Involving Endangered Species," *Water Resources Research,* 23(5), May 1987, pp. 943–950.

[26]Stephen R. Crutchfield, "Benefits of Safer Drinking Water: The Value of Nitrate Reduction," U.S. Department of Agriculture, Economic Research Service, 1997.

[27]David S. Brookshire and Don L. Coursey, "Measuring the Value of Public Goods: An Empirical Comparison of Elicitation Procedures," *American Economic Review,* 77(4), September 1987, pp. 554–566.

Willingness to Pay vs. Willingness to Accept

An alternative way of approaching the problem of valuing environmental improvements is to ask people how much they would be **willing to accept** to give up some environmental amenity. To value better air quality we could ask either how much people would be willing to pay for a small improvement or how much they would have to receive to compensate them for a small reduction in air quality. Suppose public authorities are contemplating locating a hazardous waste incinerator in a particular community. As a measure of the damages suffered by the community, we could take the amount of money required to get the community willingly to accept the incinerator (rather than, in other words, the amount they would be willing to pay to keep it out).

Clearly, willingness to accept is not constrained by one's income, as is willingness to pay. So it may be no surprise that when people are asked willingness-to-accept questions, their answers are usually higher than their willingness-to-pay responses for the same item. To some extent it may depend on what they are asked. For a small change we would expect the two measures to be close. Suppose what is involved is a single cantaloupe. If I am willing to pay $1.99 for one more cantaloupe, that is also probably close to what it would take to compensate for my loss of a single cantaloupe, but for large changes (what are called "nonmarginal" changes) this may not be the case. If we are talking, for example, of large changes in air pollution in my neighborhood that will substantially change my welfare, the two measures may be quite different.

Economists have taken several approaches to resolving this problem. One is to look closely at the questionnaire and the way questions are asked of respondents. Experience has shown that responses will differ according to how questions are phrased; therefore, one possibility is that the differences between willingness to pay and willingness to accept are traceable primarily to the way questions are being framed. The other approach is to replace the standard economic principles, which imply that there should be no difference between these two measures, with new concepts that can explain the difference.

Nonuse Values

When people buy potatoes, we assume that they do so because they expect to eat them; the value of potatoes to people lies in their *use* value. This reasoning extends also to environmental assets, but in this case there may be more. When people voluntarily donate money for the preservation of unique environmental assets that they may never even see, except perhaps in photographs, something other than use value must be involved. People's willingness to pay for these environmental characteristics also must involve certain **nonuse values.** One possibility is that although perhaps not currently in a position to experience directly a particular environmental asset, people often want to preserve the option to do so in the future. **Option value** is the amount a person would be willing to pay to preserve the option of being able to experience a particular environmental amenity in the future. People may even be willing to pay to preserve something they in all likelihood will never see—African wildlife, for example. In this case, what is involved is **existence value,** a willingness to pay simply to help preserve the existence of some environmental amenity. Such altruistic values may be focused to some extent on future generations, in which case they might be called **bequest values.** Lastly, we might add a **stewardship value;** that is, a value not related necessarily to human use of the environment, but rather to maintaining the health of the environment for the continued use of all living organisms. One of the reasons contingent valuation studies have become more common is that questions can be phrased so as to get at these nonuse values.

SUMMARY

Benefit measurement is a major focus of study within environmental economics. New techniques are being developed to uncover values that previously were hidden from view. From legislatures and courts a brisk demand has arisen for benefits information on which to base laws and legal settlements. Public environmental agencies have devoted considerable time and effort to generating benefits estimates in order to justify their policy rulings. After reviewing briefly what we mean by "benefits," we discussed some of the main techniques environmental economists use to measure these benefits. Health impacts, previously assessed by direct damage estimation, are now more frequently pursued through willingness-to-pay procedures, especially wage rate studies showing how people value risks to health. We also covered house-price studies, production cost studies, and travel cost studies. Finally, we reviewed the technique of contingent valuation. This technique allows benefits to be measured over a much wider range of environmental phenomena than other techniques permit. Indeed, contingent valuation techniques allow analysts to push beyond traditional "use values" and explore some of the less tangible, but no less real, sources of environmental benefits, such as "option value," "existence value," and "stewardship value."

QUESTIONS FOR FURTHER DISCUSSION

1 Suppose you were hired by the homeowners located around a lake to determine the benefits of improving the water quality in the lake. How might you go about doing it?

2 One of the main studies used in evaluating the EPA's decision to ban leaded gasoline estimated that the avoided medical costs and avoided remedial education costs of such a ban would be about $225 million. What are the advantages and disadvantages of using this number as a measure of the health-related benefits of the ban? (For more on this, see Albert L. Nichols, "Lead in Gasoline," in Richard D. Morgenstern (ed.), *Economic Analysis at EPA, Assessing Regulatory Impact,* Resources for the Future, Washington, DC, 1997, pp. 49–86.)

3 Suppose you want to determine the aggregate willingness to pay among students at your school for reducing litter on the school grounds. How might you do this?

4 What is the usual meaning that economists give to the expression "the value of a human life"? What are the different ways of estimating this value?

5 Design some contingent valuation–type questions for evaluating the value to people of improving the air quality in the Grand Canyon.

6 Survey 10 other students, asking them how much they would be willing to pay for one visit to their favorite beach. What qualifying questions did your respondents ask you before they could assign a dollar value? What are some factors influencing people's willingness-to-pay value?

WEBSITES

The Environmental Protection Agency has a program called the National Center for Environmental Economics, which has a number of links to sites with benefit–cost information: **www.epa.gov/economics;** the World Bank has a site on environmental economics and indicators: **www-esd.worldbank.org/ eei/;** see also the links listed in the website of this book: **www.mhhe.com/ economics/field3.**

SELECTED READINGS

Bateman, Ian J., and Ken G. Willis: *Valuing Environmental Preferences,* Oxford University Press, Oxford, England, 1999.

Desaiques, Brigitte, and Patrick Point: *Economie du Patrimoine Naturel, La Valorisation des Bénéfices de Protection de L'environnement,* Economica, Paris, 1993.

Dixon, John A., and Paul B. Sherman: *Economics of Protected Areas, A New Look at Benefits and Costs,* Island Press, Washington, DC, 1990.

Freeman, A. Myrick, III: *The Benefits of Environmental Improvement: Theory and Practice,* Johns Hopkins Press for Resources for the Future, Baltimore, MD, 1979.

Garrod, Guy, and Kenneth G. Willis: *Economic Valuation of the Environment,* Edward Elgar, Cheltenham, England, 1999.

Hahn, Robert W. (ed.): *Risks, Costs, and Lives Saved: Getting Better Results from Regulation,* Oxford University Press, New York, 1996.

Kneese, Allen V.: *Measuring the Benefits of Clean Air and Water,* Resources for the Future, Washington, DC, 1984.

Krutilla, John V., and Anthony C. Fisher: *The Economics of Natural Environments,* Johns Hopkins Press for Resources for the Future, Baltimore, MD, 1975.

Mitchell, Robert Cameron, and Richard T. Carson: *Using Surveys to Value Public Goods: The Contingent Valuation Method, Resources for the Future,* Washington, DC, 1989.

U.S. Environmental Protection Agency: *The Economics of Improved Estuarine Water Quality: An NEP Manual for Measuring Benefits,* Washington, DC, EPA 503/5-90-001, September 1990.

CHAPTER 8

BENEFIT–COST ANALYSIS: COSTS

In this chapter we look at the cost side of benefit–cost analysis. The importance of accurate cost measurement often has been underestimated. The results of a benefit–cost analysis can be affected as easily by overestimating costs as by underestimating benefits. In developing countries, where people place a high priority on economic growth, it is critically important to know how environmental programs will affect that growth rate and how costs are distributed among different social groups. In industrialized countries, opposition to environmental policies frequently centers on their estimated costs, which means that those doing benefit–cost analyses of these programs are well advised to get the cost estimates right. In this chapter we will first take up some general considerations about costs, then look at some specific issues and examples of cost estimation.

THE COST PERSPECTIVE: GENERAL ISSUES

Cost analysis can be done on many levels. At its simplest, it focuses on the costs to a single community or firm of an environmental program or of a single environmental project, such as a wastewater treatment plant, incinerator, or beach restoration project. The reason for calling these the simplest is that they usually proceed by costing out a definite engineering specification that has clear boundaries and for which the "rest of the world" can rightly assume to be constant.

At the next level we have costs to an industry, or perhaps to a region, of meeting environmental regulations or of adopting certain technologies. Here it is no longer possible to rely on simple engineering assumptions; we must do things such as predict with reasonable accuracy how groups of polluting firms will respond to changes in laws on emissions or how they will respond to changes in recycling regulations. Problems will arise because not all firms will be alike—some small, some large, some old, some new, and so on—and each of them will usually have multiple possibilities for reacting to regulations.

At a still higher level, our concern may be with the costs to an entire economy of achieving stated environmental goals. Estimating costs at the national level calls for an entirely different approach. Here everything is connected to everything else; when pollution-control regulations are imposed, adjustments will reverberate throughout the economy. Tracing them out requires **macroeconomic data** and usually fairly sophisticated aggregate models. After taking a look at several general issues in cost estimation, we will deal with the subject at these different levels.

The With/Without Principle

There is an important principle that has to be kept in mind in this work. In doing a benefit–cost analysis of how firms will respond to new laws, we want to use the **with/without** principle and not the **before/after** principle. We want to estimate the differences in costs that polluters would have with the new law, *compared to what their costs would have been in the absence of the law.* This is not the same as the difference between their new costs and what their costs used to be before the law. Consider the following illustrative numbers that apply to a manufacturing firm for which a pollution-control regulation has been proposed:

Estimated production costs:

Before the regulation: $100
In the future without the regulation: $120
In the future with the regulation: $150

It would be a mistake to conclude that the added costs of the pollution-control regulation will be $50 (future costs with the regulation minus costs before the law). This is an application of the before/after principle and does not accurately reflect the true costs of the law. This is so because in the absence of any new law, production costs are expected to increase (e.g., because of increased fuel costs unrelated to environmental regulations). Thus, the true cost of the regulation is found by applying the with/without principle. Here, these costs are $30 (costs in the future with the regulation minus future costs without the regulation). Of course this makes the whole job of cost estimation harder because we want to know not historical costs of a firm or an industry but what its future costs would be if it were to continue operating without the new environmental laws. This is a problem of **baseline analysis.** The baseline is the level of costs that is expected to prevail in the absence of the regulation; this will be used to estimate the cost changes resulting from that regulation.

No-Cost Improvements in Environmental Quality

Sometimes environmental improvements can be obtained at zero social cost, except the political cost of making the required changes in public laws or regulations. In virtually any type of political system, usually some laws and administrative practices are instituted primarily to benefit certain groups within society for political reasons rather than to move toward economically efficient resource use or achieve deserving income redistributions. These regulations, besides transferring income to the favored groups, often have negative environmental effects.

Consider, for example, **coastal zone flood insurance** in the United States. Commercial insurance for property constructed in the coastal zone would normally have such high premiums, because of the expected losses from floods, that few coastal homeowners could afford it. The U.S. government, therefore, subsidizes coastal zone insurance so that people building in these areas can get insurance at substantially less than commercial rates. The effects of this have been to reduce the private monetary costs of building and maintaining houses in the coastal zone; so substantial development has occurred there, with attendant environmental impacts. A reduction in these public subsidies to coastal homeowners not only would work to reduce these environmental impacts but also would lead to an increase in national income. Of course, coastal homeowners would suffer losses.

There are many other examples such as this. **Agricultural subsidies** in many developed countries have provided the incentive to develop intensive, chemical-based production methods, which have resulted both in increased agricultural output and in the nonpoint-source water and air pollution to which these methods lead. Reducing these agricultural subsidies would increase national income and reduce the environmental impacts, though of course some farmers would be worse off.

The Distribution of Costs

The overall social costs of environmental regulations are important in assessing their cost effectiveness. Beyond this, however, a major factor behind many policy controversies is how these total costs are **distributed** among different groups in society. Environmental regulations initially may lead to increased production costs in the industry to which the regulation applies, as firms undertake the pollution-control steps required by the regulations. But changes will not be confined to this one industry. As firms alter production technology, input mixes, and other aspects of their operations, their **prices** are likely to change, for both outputs and inputs. So some, or perhaps all, of the consequences of the regulation will be shifted to consumers and input-supplying firms. Employees of the regulated firms will be impacted when production rates increase or decrease in the affected industries. Very often there will be important **regional** differences in these impacts, because often industries are more concentrated in certain regions than in others. It is important, then, to be concerned not only with total costs, but also with how these costs are distributed.

CONCEPTS OF COST
Opportunity Costs

In economics the most fundamental concept of costs is **opportunity costs.** The opportunity cost of using resources[1] in a certain way is the highest valued alternative use to which those resources might have been put and that society has to forgo when the resources are used in the specified fashion. Note the word "society." Costs are incurred by all types of firms, agencies, industries, groups, and so on. Each has its own perspective, which will focus on those costs that impinge directly on it, but the concept of **social opportunity costs** includes all costs, no matter to whom they accrue.

Sometimes items that a private group might consider a cost (e.g., a tax) is not a cost from the standpoint of society. Sometimes items that particular decision makers do not consider as costs really do have social costs. Suppose a community is contemplating building a bicycle path to relieve congestion and air pollution downtown. Its primary concern is what the town will have to pay to build the path. Suppose it will take $1 million to build it, but 50 percent of this will come from the state or federal government. From the town's perspective the cost of the bike path will be a half million dollars, but from the standpoint of society the full opportunity costs of the path are $1 million.

When most people think of cost they usually think of money expenditure. Often the monetary cost of something is a good measure of its opportunity costs, but frequently it is not. Suppose the bike path is going to be put on an old railroad right-of-way that has absolutely no alternative use, and suppose the town must pay the railroad $100,000 for this right-of-way. This money is definitely an expenditure the town must make, but it is not truly a part of the opportunity costs of building the path because society gives up nothing in devoting the old right-of-way to the new use.

Environmental Costs

It may seem paradoxical to think that environmental protection control programs might have environmental costs, but this is in fact the case. Most specific emissions-reduction programs are media based; that is, they are aimed at reducing emissions into one particular environmental medium such as air or water. So when emissions into one medium are reduced, they may increase into another. Reducing untreated domestic waste outflow into rivers or coastal oceans leaves quantities of solid waste that must then be disposed of, perhaps through land spreading or incineration. Reducing airborne SO_2 emissions from power plants by stack-gas scrubbing also leaves a highly concentrated sludge that must be disposed of in some way. Incinerating domestic solid waste creates airborne emissions.

---

[1]Remember that "resources" is a word that can have two meanings: It can be a short way of saying "natural resources" or a general reference analogous to the word "inputs." Here we are using it in the second sense.

Media switches are not the only source of environmental impacts stemming from environmental improvement programs. There can be direct effects; for example, sediment runoff from construction sites for new treatment plants or sewer lines. There also can be unforeseen impacts when firms or consumers adjust to new programs. Gasoline producers reduced the amounts of lead in their product, but because consumers still insisted on high-powered perform-ance they added other compounds, which ended up having environmental impacts in their own right. With the beginning of community programs to charge consumers for solid waste disposal, some have been faced with substan-tial increases in "midnight dumping", that is, illegal dumping along the sides of roads or in remote areas.

Some of the potential environmental impacts from these public projects or programs can be **mitigated;** that is, steps can be taken to reduce or avoid them. More enforcement resources can help control midnight dumping, extra steps can be taken to reduce construction-site impacts, special techniques may be available to reduce incinerator residuals, and so on. These mitigation costs must be included as part of the total costs of any project or program. Beyond this, any remaining environmental costs must be set against the overall reduc-tion in environmental damages to which the program is primarily aimed.

Enforcement Costs

Environmental regulations are not self-enforcing. Resources must be devoted to monitoring the behavior of firms, agencies, and individuals subject to the regulations and to sanctioning violators. Public environmental facilities, such as wastewater treatment plants and incinerators, must be monitored to be sure they are being operated correctly.

There is an important application of the opportunity idea in the enforcement phenomenon. Many environmental laws are enforced by agencies whose enforcement budgets are not strictly tailored to the enforcement responsibilities they are given. Thus, budgets can be stable, or even declining, at the same time that new environmental laws are passed. Enforcing the new laws may require shifting agency resources away from the enforcement of other laws. In this case the opportunity costs of new enforcement must include the lower levels of compliance in areas that now are subject to less enforcement.

COSTS OF SINGLE FACILITIES

Perhaps the easiest type of cost analysis to visualize is that for a single, engi-neered project of some type. There are many types of environmental quality programs that involve publicly supported construction of physical facilities (although the analysis would be the same whatever the ownership), such as public wastewater treatment plants, of which hundreds of millions of dollars' worth have been built over the last few decades. Other examples include flood control projects, solid-waste handling facilities, hazardous-waste incinerators, beach-restoration projects, public parks, wildlife refuges, and so on.

Facility-type projects such as these are individualized and substantially unique, although of course they have objectives and use technology that is similar to that used for many other projects. To estimate their costs, primary reliance is placed on engineering and technical specifications, developed largely through experience with similar types of facilities. Consider the simple example shown in Table 8-1. It gives the estimated costs of a new wastewater treatment plant for a small community. The plant is expected to use standard technology, as specified in the engineering plans for the treatment plant, collector lines, and other essential parts of the system. It will be built by a private firm but owned and operated by the town.

There are three types of **construction costs:** the treatment plant proper, conveyances, and sludge-disposal works. The latter refers to disposal of the solid waste produced at the plant. The waste materials extracted from the wastewater stream don't just disappear; these heavily treated substances must be disposed of in some fashion. There are various ways of doing this (composting, land spreading, incineration). In the case of land spreading, the costs involve

TABLE 8-1
PROJECTED COSTS OF A SMALL WASTEWATER TREATMENT PLANT ($1,000)

	Construction costs			
	Initial cost	Life (years)	Replacement costs	Salvage value
Treatment plant	3,000	60	25	544
Conveyances	1,639	95	245	651
Sludge-disposal works (land spreading)	24	40	—	—
Mitigation of construction-related environmental costs	24	40	—	—

Annual costs			
Operation and maintenance (O&M)		Environmental costs	
Pumping station	21	Mitigation costs	8
Treatment plant	131	Unmitigated environmental costs	46
Sludge disposal	4		
Total	156		

Present values		
Cost item	Total	Present value (@8%)
Construction	5,645	5,645
Replacement	370	107
Salvage values	−1,290	−320
Annual O&M	156	1,860
Annual environmental	54	644
Total		7,936

Source: Adapted from U.S. Environmental Protection Agency and Wisconsin Department of Natural Resources, *Environmental Impact Statement, Wastewater Treatment Facilities at Genwa Lake Area, Walworth County, Wisconsin,* Washington, DC, June 1984.

buying a large area of land on which the sludge will be spread and allowed to decompose and mix with the soil. The assumed life of the plant is 40 years. Some portions of the plant, for example, certain pieces of equipment, will wear out and have to be replaced during this period. The costs of this are listed under "replacement costs." In addition, certain parts of the plant and conveyance system are expected to have a salvage value at the end of the 40 years; these are shown in the last column. Note that allowances have been made for engineering work and construction contingencies. An estimate also has been included of the initial costs of some environmental mitigation activities.

Annual costs are divided into operation and maintenance (O&M) of the treatment plant, O&M of the pumping station, sludge-disposal operation, and environmental costs. The latter includes certain mitigation costs, together with some remaining, or unmitigated, environmental costs. The latter might refer, for example, to odor problems at the plant and on the sludge disposal lands. These are, in fact, environmental damages, which might be estimated, for example, with contingent valuation techniques.

The last section of Table 8-1 includes the **present values** of the costs, evaluated with a discount rate of 8 percent. Replacement costs are discounted to the present from the year in which they are expected to be required. Salvage values are discounted back from the end of the project's life, in this case 40 years. These appear with negative signs because they act to lower the total cost of the project. The present value of annual environmental costs is also included.

With the exception of unmitigated environmental costs, these items are all expenditure figures, and only close inspection can tell if they represent true social opportunity costs. Suppose, for example, that in the construction phase a number of local unemployed people are hired. Although the construction costs include their wages, their opportunity costs would be zero because society had to give up nothing when they went to work on the plant. It might be that the land on which the plant is to be placed is town land that is to be donated. In this case there will be no specific cost entry for land, but there will be an opportunity cost related to the value the land could have had in its next best use. Suppose that the construction firm, because it is working on a public project, is able to get subsidized loans from local banks (i.e., borrow money at lower than market rates). Then the true opportunity costs of construction will be higher than the monetary costs indicated. There are no specific rules for making these adjustments; only a knowledge of the specific situations can reveal when it is important enough to make them and where sufficient data are available to do the job.

COSTS OF A LOCAL REGULATION

Environmental regulations are frequently enacted at the local level and have an impact on local firms. In fact, in the political economy of pollution control, it is often the fear of these local impacts that deters communities from enacting the regulations. Fears of lost payrolls and the secondary losses to other firms from shrinking local markets loom large at the local level; from a national perspective the opportunity costs are less severe.

Suppose in a particular small town there is a large apple orchard that provides substantial local employment. Suppose further that presently the orchard managers use relatively large applications of chemicals to control apple pests and diseases, and that the chemical runoff from this activity threatens local water supplies. Assume the community enacts an ordinance requiring the orchard to practice **integrated pest management** (IPM), a lower level of chemical use coupled with other means to compensate for this reduction. Assume further, for purposes of illustration, that the IPM practices increase the costs of raising apples in this orchard.[2] What are the social costs of this regulation?

If the orchard raises and sells the same number of apples it previously did, the true social opportunity costs of the regulation are the increased production costs. If local consumers are willing to pay somewhat higher prices for locally grown apples, some of this cost gets passed on to these consumers. Suppose, however, that competitive conditions make it impossible for the orchard to sell its apples for any higher price than pertained before. In this case the higher production costs must be reflected in lower incomes of either the apple orchard owners themselves, or perhaps orchard workers, if they will accept lower wages.

Suppose the orchard was just breaking even before the local IPM ordinance, and that the statute leads to such cost increases that production is substantially curtailed; in fact, assume for purposes of argument that the orchard goes out of business. Clearly there will be local costs: lost payrolls of orchard workers, lost income to the local orchard owners, lost income to local merchants because their markets shrink. But these lost incomes are not likely to be social opportunity costs in their entirety, unless the workers become permanently unemployed. Assuming they transfer to other job opportunities (this requires, obviously, that the economy be operating at full employment), their new incomes will offset, at least partly, the lost incomes they were earning previously. There may be certain valid opportunity costs in the form of adjustment costs, as workers and owners have to move to new places of employment.

What about the value of the apples no longer produced in this orchard? If we assume that there are many other orchards in neighboring towns and other regions to take up the slack with essentially no cost increases, then this lost production is offset by others, consumer prices are stable, and the social opportunity costs of this marginal rearrangement of apple production are basically nil.

To summarize, when we are dealing with a single local ordinance affecting one firm and the economy is at or near full employment, ensuing resource adjustments ensure that social opportunity costs are small, limited to the costs of actually carrying out the adjustments. From the standpoint of the affected community, of course, costs will seem high, because of lost local incomes brought about by the increased apple production costs.

---

[2]In fact, various authorities and scientific studies suggest that some IPM practices can actually lower costs relative to chemical-intensive growing techniques.

COSTS OF REGULATING AN INDUSTRY

These conclusions do not follow when we impose an environmental regulation on an entire industry. Higher production costs for the industry are true social opportunity costs because they require added resources that could have been used elsewhere. But in dealing with whole industries, we cannot make the assumption, as we did with the one apple orchard, that its production could easily be picked up by the others.

Consider first the standard approach to estimating increased industry production costs, which is to measure the **added expenditures** that an industry would have to make to come into compliance with an environmental regulation. Cost estimation in this case requires the analyst to predict how polluters will respond to environmental regulations and then to estimate the costs of this response. If the regulation is very specific, requiring, for example, that manufacturing firms install a certain piece of pollution-control equipment or that farmers adopt certain cultivation practices to avoid soil runoff, the cost estimation may be fairly straightforward. But if the regulation leaves the polluters considerable latitude in making their response, it may be hard to predict exactly what they will do and, therefore, what their costs will be.

Suppose, for example, a group of pulp mills are required to reduce their emissions by some percentage, and that we (a public agency) wish to estimate the impact of this on the production costs of the firms in the industry. In effect, we want to estimate the aggregate marginal abatement cost function for this group of firms. To do this with reasonable accuracy requires enough knowledge about the pulp business to be able to predict how the firms will respond, what treatment techniques they will use, how they might change their internal production processes, and so on. Or suppose we wanted to estimate the costs among farmers of a ban on a certain type of pest control chemical. In this case the analysis would want to identify the alternatives that farmers had available to replace this chemical, what impacts this would have on yields, how much additional labor and other inputs they would use, and so on.

An Example

The metal finishing industry provides services to major industries such as aircraft, automotive, jewelry, and hardware. Products from these industries are provided with metal surfaces that enhance their durability, corrosion resistance, conductivity, and appearance. In the early 1970s the EPA was charged with estimating the costs to firms in the metal finishing industry of meeting proposed emission-reduction goals. As is true of most studies of regulatory impacts, there were too many firms in the industry to do a technical study of each one. A common way of addressing this problem is to estimate costs for the "average," "representative," or "model" plant, one that corresponds to typical operating conditions in the industry but not to any particular plant. But in this case, as in most cases, the size and technical heterogeneity of plants in the industry made it necessary to specify a number of representative plants, each of

TABLE 8-2
ESTIMATED COSTS ($1,000) OF COMPLYING WITH ENVIRONMENTAL REGULATIONS,
METAL FINISHING INDUSTRY (ANODIZING PROCESS)

	Size of plant (number of employees)			
	1–9	10–19	20–49	50+
Number of plants in size class	137	65	70	26
Investment costs:				
Equipment	46	57	72	264
Building and land	11	17	22	47
Equipment installation	9	12	14	53
Total	66	86	108	364
Annual costs:				
Capital costs*	3.3	4.3	5.4	18.2
Depreciation[†]	6.6	8.6	10.8	36.4
Labor	12.2	24.1	32.9	105.1
Energy	3.1	5.2	7.4	14.1
Other costs	8.7	12.3	19.8	28.3
Total	33.9	54.5	76.3	202.1

*10% of *average* investment costs. Annual investment each year of the project is equal to original investment minus depreciation. Average investment is the mean of these annual investments. Because depreciation is 10-year straight-line, average investment is actually equal to one-half of the original investment.
[†]Straight-line depreciation—10-year life.
Source: Adapted from U.S. Environmental Protection Agency, *Economic Analysis of Effluent Guidelines, The Metal Finishing Industry,* EPA 230/1-74/032, Washington, DC, September 1974.

which corresponded to one portion of the firms in the industry. Abatement costs are shown in Table 8-2 for four different plant sizes, where "size" is given by the number of employees working in the plant. The first row shows the estimated number of plants in each size class. Note that most of these plants are quite small; in fact, the metal finishing industry in the United States consists of a large number of relatively small firms.

The first section in the table shows **investment costs** needed to install the new equipment that will allow the firms to reduce their emissions flows. These are the "up-front" investment costs of new buildings, equipment, and the land to put them on. The second part of the table shows **annualized costs.** These include the conventional items such as energy, labor, and so on, and also the annualized investment costs. In the waste-treatment plant example provided earlier, we aggregated discounted annual operating costs and added these to initial investment costs to get the present value of total costs. The other way of adding initial investment costs and annual operating costs is to "annualize" the investment costs; that is, spread them out over the years of life that the investments are assumed to have. This is done in Table 8-2. Annualized investment costs consist of two parts: the opportunity costs of the capital and depreciation. The former is the forgone return that one could earn if the investment were made in some other industry. Depreciation is the cost associated with the progressive using up of the equipment and buildings over their useful life.

Total annual costs are shown for each of the representative plants. To estimate the total costs of meeting the emission standard for the entire industry, a weighted total can be calculated:

Size of firm (no. of employees)	Costs ($1,000)	No. of firms	Total costs ($1,000)
1–9	33.9	137	4,644.3
10–19	54.5	65	3,542.5
20–49	76.3	70	534.1
50+	202.1	26	5,254.6
Total			13,975.5

Thus, the anticipated total annual cost of this industry to meet the emission reduction standards is $13,975,500. Note that these costs are incomplete in at least one sense. In regulatory programs of any type, public enforcement resources are required in order to get large-scale compliance by the regulated firms. Table 8-2 contains nothing about these costs, but in a full social benefit–cost analysis, they obviously would have to be included.

Sources of Cost Data

Where does one get the cost data necessary to construct these representative firms? Many of the basic data are generated through **cost surveys** of existing firms. In effect, questionnaires are sent out to these firms asking them to supply information on number of employees, processes used, costs of energy and materials, and so on. With a sufficiently detailed questionnaire and a reasonably high response rate by firms, researchers hope to get a good idea of basic cost conditions in the industry and how they might be affected by environmental regulations.

One problem with cost surveys is that they are usually better at getting information on past cost data than on future costs under new regulations. Firms can probably report past cost data with more reliability than they can estimate future costs of meeting environmental constraints. Historical data may not be a good guide to the future, especially because environmental regulations almost by definition confront firms with novel situations. In these cases it is common to supplement survey data with technical engineering data that can be better adapted to costing out the new techniques and procedures that firms may adopt.

The "representative firm" approach, although dictated by the large number of firms in an industry, has its own problems, especially when those firms are substantially heterogeneous among themselves. In following this procedure, for example, the EPA runs into the problem of whether costs of the real plants in the industry, each of which is to some degree unique, can be accurately represented by a composite cost estimate. In this case "accurately" means close enough that individual firms will not be inclined to take the agency to court on grounds that their own unique cost situations are misrepresented by the figures for the "representative" firm. Many court battles have been fought over this issue.

Misrepresentation of Costs

Because the regulated firms themselves are the source of much cost data used to develop the regulations, there is clearly a question whether these firms will supply accurate data. By overstating the costs of reaching certain reductions in emissions, firms may hope to convince agencies to promulgate weaker regulations than they would if the agencies had an accurate idea of costs. It is a very common sight in public hearings on establishing emission control regulations to see firms making vigorous claims that the regulations will be unduly costly for them to meet. There is evidence that many of these claims have been exaggerated in the past. This issue will come up numerous times when we examine the incentives surrounding different types of environmental policies.

Actual vs. Minimum Pollution Control Costs

The costs shown in Table 8-2 show the estimated costs of the metal finishing industry meeting the environmental standards imposed by law. There is an important question of whether these costs are the *least* costs necessary to achieve the emission reductions sought in the law. This is an important point because, as we saw in Chapter 5, the efficient level of emissions or ambient quality is defined by the trade-off of emission abatement costs and environmental damages. If abatement costs used to define the efficient level are higher than they need to be, the point so defined will be only a **pseudo-efficient** outcome.

When there is a single facility involved, we must rely on engineering judgment to ensure that the technical proposal represents the least costly way of achieving the objectives. When what is involved is an entire industry, both technical and economic factors come into play. As discussed earlier, in order for the overall costs of a given emission reduction to be achieved at minimum cost, the equimarginal principle has to be fulfilled. Frequently, environmental regulations work against this by dictating that different sources adopt essentially the same levels of emission reductions or install the same general types of pollution-control technology. As will be seen in later chapters, many environmental laws are based on administratively specified operating decisions that firms are required to make. These decisions may not lead, or allow, firms to achieve emission abatement at least cost. Thus, industry costs such as those depicted in Table 8-2 may not represent minimum abatement costs.

There is no easy way out of this dilemma. If one is called on to do a benefit–cost analysis of a particular environmental regulation, one presumably is committed to evaluating the regulation as given. In cases such as this it would no doubt be good policy for the analyst to point out that there are less costly ways of achieving the benefits.

The Effect of Output Adjustments on Costs

The increase in abatement expenditures may not be an accurate measure of opportunity costs when an entire industry is involved. This is because **market adjustments** are likely to alter the role and performance of the industry in the wider economy. For example, when the costs of a competitive industry increase, the price of its output increases, normally causing a reduction in quantity demanded. This is pictured in Figure 8-1, which shows supply and demand curves for two industries. For convenience the supply curves have been drawn horizontally, representing marginal production costs that do not vary with output. Consider first panel (a). The initial supply function is C_1, so the initial quantity produced is q_1. The pollution-control law causes production costs to rise, represented by a shift upward in supply from curve C_1 to C_2. Suppose we calculate the increased cost of producing the initial rate of output. This would be an amount equal to the area $(a + b + c)$. The comparable cost in panel (b) is $(d + e + f)$. This approach to measuring costs, however, will overstate the true

FIGURE 8-1
Output Adjustments in Industries Subject to Pollution-Control
Regulations.

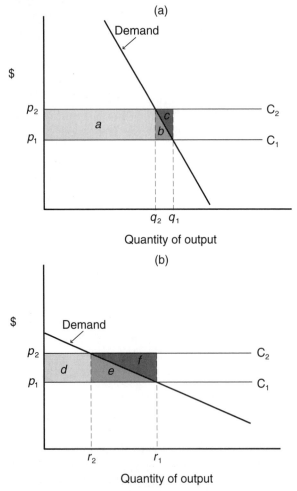

cost increase because when costs and prices go up, quantity demanded and output will decline.

How much output declines is a matter of the steepness of the demand curve. In panel (a), output declines only from q_1 to q_2, but in panel (b), with the flatter demand curve, output will decline from r_1 to r_2, a much larger amount. The correct measure of the cost to society is $(a + b)$ in panel (a) and $(d + e)$ in panel (b). Note that the original approach to cost estimation, calculating the increased cost of current output, is a much better approximation to the true burden on society in panel (a) than in panel (b). This is because the output adjustment is much larger in the latter. The lesson here is that if increased expenditures are to be taken as true opportunity costs, they must be calculated taking into account price and output adjustments that occur in the industries affected by the environmental regulations.

Figure 8-1 also can illustrate something about the distribution of pollution-control costs. Firms in the affected industries bear these costs in the beginning, but the final burden depends on how the cost increase is passed forward to consumers or backward to workers and stockholders. Note that in both panels (a) and (b) the market prices of the goods increased by the amount of the cost increase, but the response is quite different. In panel (a) consumers continue buying close to what they did before; little adjustment is called for in terms of output shrinkage in the industry. Thus, workers and shareholders in this industry will be little affected, in relative terms. In panel (b) the same price increase leads to a large drop in output. Consumers have good substitutes to which they can switch when the price of this output goes up; in effect, they can escape the full burden of the price increase. The industry adjustment, however, is large. Resources, particularly workers, will have to flow out of the industry and try to find employment elsewhere. If they can, the costs may be only temporary adjustment costs; if not, the costs will be much longer run.

Long-Run Technical Change and Pollution-Control Costs

In the short run firms must make whatever adjustments they can within the constraints of available technology and operating procedures. In the long run, however, costs can change because these technologies and procedures can be altered. Scientific and engineering **research and development** yield new and better (less costly) ways of controlling emissions. Some are straightforward, such as a new way of handling and treating residuals; some are more profound, such as a change in the basic technology of production so that fewer residuals are produced in the first place. When firms are subject to emission reduction requirements, they have an incentive to engage in research and development (R&D) to find better emissions abatement technology. There is some evidence that in reality this may draw resources away from output-increasing R&D efforts, thereby affecting the firm's ability to reduce costs in the long run. There is also evidence, however, that environmental regulations have led to unanticipated, marketable products or processes stemming from their research. Some studies have even shown that after investing in pollution-control R&D some firms have reduced their long-run production costs. In cases such as this, the short-run cost increases arising from pollution-control regulations are not accurate estimates of the long-run opportunity costs of these regulations.

Critical to the success of any effort to innovate in pollution-control technology is the economic health of the **envirotech industry.** This is the industry consisting of firms producing goods and services that are used by other firms to reduce their emissions and environmental impacts. It also contains firms that engage themselves in environmental clean-up, such as the clean-up of past hazardous waste dump sites. A healthy envirotech industry is one that produces a brisk supply of new pollution-control technology and practices. The growth of this industry over time will have a lot to do with how fast marginal abatement costs come down in the future (see Exhibit 8-1).

COSTS AT THE NATIONAL LEVEL

We finally come to the most aggregative level for which cost studies are normally pursued, the level of the **national economy.** The usual question of interest is the extent of the macroeconomic cost burden of the environmental regulations a country imposes, or might be planning to impose, in a given period of time. Sometimes interest centers on the totality of the regulations put in place. Sometimes the focus is on specific regulations that will nevertheless have a broad impact on a national economy, such as a program of CO_2 emissions reduction.

Table 8-3 shows a breakdown of total U.S. pollution-control costs among the different environmental programs, and how the EPA projected these costs to increase over the decade of the 1990s. It shows that total costs were expected to be about 500 percent higher in 2000 than they were in 1972. The rate of increase in the late 1990s was lower: The change from $26.5 billion in 1972 to $58 billion in 1980 was a 120 percent increase, whereas total costs increased about 60 percent in the 1990s. The effort accounting for the greatest share of control costs is

TABLE 8-3
TOTAL CONTROL COSTS,* ASSUMING FULL IMPLEMENTATION OF CURRENT POLICY (MILLIONS OF 1986 DOLLARS)

	1972	1980	1990	2000
Total costs	26,481	57,969	100,167	160,416
Percentage of GNP	0.88	1.58	2.14	2.83
Percentage of total costs:				
Air and radiation	30.1	30.7	28.0	28.0
Water	37.4	42.7	42.3	40.0
Land	31.8	23.5	26.5	28.8
Chemicals	0.3	1.6	1.6	1.8
Multimedia	0.4	1.5	1.6	1.4

*Includes compliance costs plus regulatory costs.
Source: U.S. Environmental Protection Agency, *Environmental Investments: The Costs of a Clean Environment,* EPA-230-12-90-084, Washington, DC, 1990, pp. 2-2–2-3.

EXHIBIT 8-1

THE ENVIRONMENTAL INDUSTRY

The U.S. environmental industry had total revenues over $190 billion in 1998 and employed more than 1.3 million people. These are very substantially higher than the comparable numbers of 1980, as the data below indicate. More than half of the industry actually comprises services, while the rest are technology and equipment based. The early growth of the industry was based on cleaning up the sins of the past, or controlling emissions from outdated facilities. Growth in the future will depend more on developments in pollution prevention.

ENVIRONMENTAL INDUSTRY—REVENUES AND EMPLOYMENT,
BY INDUSTRY SEGMENT: 1980 TO 1998
[59.0 represents $59,000,000,000. Covers approximately 59,000 private and public companies engaged in environmental activities.]

Industry segment	Revenue (bil. dol.)			Employment (1,000)		
	1980	1990	1998	1980	1990	1998
Industry total	59.0	150.3	191.5	462.5	1,174.3	(NA)
Analytical services[1]	0.4	1.5	1.1	6.0	20.2	(NA)
Wastewater treatment works[2]	10.9	20.4	25.3	53.9	95.0	(NA)
Solid waste management[3]	11.2	26.1	35.9	83.2	209.5	(NA)
Hazardous waste management[4]	0.6	6.3	5.7	6.8	56.9	(NA)
Remediation/industrial services	2.4	11.1	11.4	6.9	107.2	(NA)
Consulting and engineering	1.7	12.5	15.2	20.5	144.2	(NA)
Water equipment and chemicals	6.9	13.5	19.1	62.4	97.9	(NA)
Instrument manufacturing	0.2	2.0	3.4	2.5	18.8	(NA)
Air pollution control equipment[5]	3.3	13.1	16.2	28.3	82.7	(NA)
Waste management equipment[6]	3.5	8.7	10.0	41.9	88.8	(NA)
Process and prevention technology	0.1	0.4	1.0	2.1	8.9	(NA)
Water utilities[7]	11.9	19.8	28.5	76.9	104.7	(NA)
Resource recovery[8]	4.4	13.1	15.9	48.7	118.4	(NA)
Environmental energy sources[9]	1.5	1.8	2.9	22.4	21.1	(NA)

NA—Not available
[1]Covers environmental laboratory testing and services.
[2]Mostly revenues collected by municipal entities.
[3]Covers such activities as collection, transportation, transfer stations, disposal, landfill ownership, and management for solid waste.
[4]Transportation and disposal of hazardous, medical, and nuclear waste.
[5]Includes stationary and mobile sources.
[6]Includes vehicles, containers, liners, processing, and remediation equipment.
[7]Revenues generated from the sale of water.
[8]Revenues generated from the sale of recovered metals, paper, plastic, and so on.
[9]Includes solar, wind, geothermal, and conservation devices.
Source:Environmental Business International, Inc., San Diego, CA, *Environmental Business Journal,* monthly (copyright) (as published in *Statistical Abstract of the United States: 1999,* p. 251).

water pollution control, approximately 42 percent of the total in 1990. Air pollution control and land programs, chiefly solid waste disposal, are of similar magnitude, around 26 to 28 percent of total costs. Special programs to control chemical pollution accounted for less than 2 percent of total control costs in 1990, but these were projected to increase in the 1990s.

What impact did these expenditures have on the nation's economy? Considered as a single aggregate, an economy at any point in time has available to it a certain number of inputs—labor, capital, equipment, energy, materials, and so on—that it converts to marketed output. Suppose the firms in the economy are subject to a variety of environmental regulations requiring them, or inducing them, to devote a portion of the total inputs to reductions in emissions. Marketed output must go down (assuming full employment) because of the input diversion. By how much will it drop? There are two answers to this, one applicable to the short run and the other to the long run.

In the **short run,** marketed output must drop because a portion of total resources is devoted to pollution control rather than to the production of marketed output; however, if we simply add up the pollution-control expenditures made by all the industries subject to environmental controls, this may not give an accurate picture of how these controls are affecting the national economy. Expenditures for plant, equipment, labor, and other inputs for reducing emissions can affect other economic sectors not directly covered by environmental regulations, and macroeconomic interactions of this type need to be accounted for to get the complete picture. An industry subject to environmental controls, and trying to lower its emissions, puts increasing demand on the pollution-control industry, which expands output and puts increasing demands on other sectors, for example, the construction sector, which respond by increasing output.

Another economywide adjustment is through prices. Increased pollution-control expenditures lead to increased prices for some items, which leads to reductions in quantity demanded, which leads to lower outputs in these sectors and thus to lower production costs. Total employment also will be affected by pollution-control expenditures. On the one hand, diverting production to pollution control will lower employment needs in the sector producing marketed output. On the other hand, it will increase employment in the pollution-control industry. So the net result cannot be predicted in the absence of relatively sophisticated macroeconomic modeling.

In the **long run,** more complicated macroeconomic interactions are at work. Long-run economic change—growth or decline—is a matter of the accumulation of capital: human capital and inanimate capital. It also depends on technical change, getting larger amounts of output from a given quantity of inputs. So an important question is how environmental laws will affect the accumulation of capital and the rate of technical innovation. Diverting inputs from conventional sectors to pollution-control activities may lower the rate of capital accumulation in those conventional sectors. This can be expected to reduce the rate of growth of productivity (output per unit of input) in the production of conventional output and thus slow overall growth rates. The impacts on the rate of technical innovation in the economy are perhaps more ambiguous, as mentioned previously. If attempts to innovate in pollution control reduce the efforts to do so in other sectors, the impact on future growth could be negative; however, efforts to reduce emissions might have a positive impact on the overall rate of technical innovation, which would have a positive impact. More research is needed on this question.

The standard way to proceed in working out these relationships is through **macroeconomic modeling.** The basic question is whether, and how much, pollution-control expenditures have resulted in a lowering of national economic performance. To explore this, mathematical models are constructed using the various macroeconomic variables of interest, such as total output, perhaps broken down into several economic subsectors, employment, capital investment, prices, pollution-control costs, and so on. The models are first run using historical data, which show how various underlying factors have contributed to the overall rate of growth in the economy. Then they are rerun under the assumption that the pollution-control expenditures were in fact not made. This comes out with new results in terms of aggregate output growth, employment, and so on, which can be compared with the first run. The differences are attributed to the pollution-control expenditures.

Table 8-4 shows a few results of a review study done by the Organization for Economic Cooperation and Development (OECD) pertaining to the macroeconomic costs of environmental expenditures in a number of developed countries. They show the percentage difference in **gross domestic product** (GDP) with environmental regulations compared to what it would have been without the regulations. Two things stand out. One is that in several countries GDP was actually higher in the year indicated under environmental controls than it would have been without them. This is attributed to the fact that these years were relatively early in the life of the environmental programs, when the stimulating effect of pollution-control expenditures was still somewhat dominant. The other conclusion is that for countries whose GDP was lower as a result of the environmental programs, the effect was quite small. These results confirm what others have found—that environmental regulations have lowered the growth rates of the countries applying them, but only by small amounts.

TABLE 8-4
EFFECT OF ENVIRONMENTAL REGULATIONS ON GROSS
DOMESTIC PRODUCT, SELECTED OECD COUNTRIES

	Percentage difference of GDP with environmental regulations compared to without
Austria (1985)	0.2
Finland (1982)	0.6
France (1974)	0.1
Netherlands (1985)	0.6
United States (1987)	0.7

Source: Organization for Economic Cooperation and Development, *The Macro-Economic Impact of Environmental Expenditures,* Paris, 1985, p. 27.

SUMMARY

In this chapter we reviewed some of the ways that costs are estimated in benefit–cost studies. We began with a discussion of the fundamental concept of opportunity costs, differentiating this from the notion of cost as expenditure. We then looked at cost estimation as it applied to different levels of economic activity. The first was a cost analysis of a single facility, as represented by the estimated costs of a wastewater treatment facility. We then considered the costs of an environmental regulation undertaken by a single community, distinguishing between costs to the community and opportunity costs to the whole society.

We then shifted focus to cost estimation for an entire industry, giving special attention to the difference between short-run and long-run costs and the problem of achieving minimum costs. We finally expanded our perspective to the national economy as a whole, where cost means the loss in value of marketed output resulting from environmental regulations.

QUESTIONS FOR FURTHER DISCUSSION

1 Over the last two years, emission abatement costs in industry X have been about $1 million per year. A new regulation will lead to abatement costs of $1.8 million per year. Does this mean that the regulation will cause increased abatement costs of $800,000 per year? Explain.

2 In order to protect the quality of its nearby water resources, a community places a restriction on any housing development closer than 100 feet to a wetland. How might you estimate the social costs of this regulation?

3 "The costs of achieving emission reductions in the future will depend importantly on the types of policies used to reduce emissions today." Explain.

4 A tax on gasoline is proposed in order to raise money for pollution control activity of several public agencies. The tax will be 10¢ per gallon, and last year 10.3 million gallons of gasoline were used by motorists (this is strictly an illustrative number). Does this mean that we can anticipate $1,030,000 in revenues from this tax? Explain.

5 Most industries are composed of firms which, though perhaps producing roughly the same thing, are very different; some are large and some small; some are profitable and others not; some are located in one part of the country and some in others; some perhaps have undertaken a certain amount of voluntary emissions reductions and some have not; and so on. How does this complicate the job of estimating the total social costs of pollution control regulations?

WEBSITES

Resources for the Future, **www.rff.org,** has numerous reports available in which benefit-cost techniques are applied to environmental problems. Check under "Methods, Tools and Techniques." Costs are importantly affected by pollution-control technologies available, and there are a number of sites featuring information on this; for example, Green Pages—The Global Directory for Environmental Technology, **www.eco-web.com;** and Environmental Yellow Pages, **www.enviroyellowpages.com.** See also the links listed on the web page of this book: **www.mhhe.com/economics/field3.**

SELECTED READINGS

Babcock, Lyndon R.: "Costs of Pollution Abatement," in George S. Tolley, Philip E. Graves, and Glenn C. Blomquist (eds.), *Environmental Policy,* Vol. I, Ballinger, Cambridge, MA, 1981, pp. 75–91.

Boyle, A.E. (ed.): *Environmental Regulation and Economic Growth,* Clarendon Press, Oxford, 1994.

Christiansen, G. B., and T. H. Tietenberg: "Distributional and Macroeconomic Aspects of Environmental Policy," in Allen V. Kneese and James L. Sweeney (eds.), *Handbook of Natural Resource and Energy Economics,* Vol. 1, North-Holland, Amsterdam, 1985, pp. 345–393.

Kneese, Allen V.: "Costs of Water Quality Improvement, Transfer Functions and Public Policy," in Henry M. Peskin and Eugene P. Seskin (eds.), *Cost Benefit Analysis and Water Pollution Policy,* The Urban Institute, Washington, DC, 1975, pp. 175–206.

Organization for Economic Cooperation and Development: *Improving the Environment through Reducing Subsidies,* Parts I and II, OECD, Paris, 1998.

Palmer, Karen L., and Alan J. Krupnick: "Environmental Costing and Electric Utilities' Planning and Investment," *Resources,* 105, Resources for the Future, Washington, DC, Fall 1991.

U.S. Environmental Protection Agency, Office of Air Quality Planning and Standards: OAQPS Economic Analysis Resource Document, Washington, DC, EPA, April 1998 (see especially section 5; this document is available at **www.epa.gov/ttnecas1/ whatsnew.html**).

FOUR

ENVIRONMENTAL
POLICY ANALYSIS

The public policy problem arises when there is a discrepancy between the actual level of environmental quality and the preferred level. How can this state of affairs be changed? Something has to be done to change the way people behave on both the production and consumption sides of the system. The available public policy approaches for doing this are as follows:

Decentralized policies
Liability laws
Changes in property rights
Voluntary action
Command-and-control policies
Standards
Incentive-based policies
Taxes and subsidies
Transferable discharge permits

In the chapters of this section we discuss each of these policy approaches, but before that we must address briefly a prior question: What criteria are appropriate to evaluate alternative policies and identify the one best suited to any particular environmental problem? We consider a number of these criteria in the next chapter, then analyze in depth the specific policy approaches listed above.

CRITERIA FOR EVALUATING ENVIRONMENTAL POLICIES

There are many different types of environmental policies. Each type anticipates that administrators and polluters will respond in particular ways. Each type has specific characteristics that make it more likely to succeed in some circumstances and not in others. In evaluating the effectiveness and appropriateness of a policy for addressing a given problem in environmental pollution control, it is important to have clearly in mind a set of **policy evaluation criteria.** The criteria to be used in later chapters to discuss specific environmental policies are the following:

- Their ability to achieve efficient and cost-effective reductions in pollution.
- Their fairness.
- The incentives they offer to people to search for better solutions.
- Their enforceability.
- The extent to which they agree with certain moral precepts.

EFFICIENCY

By **"efficiency"** we mean the balance between abatement costs and damages. An efficient policy is one that moves us to, or near, the point (either of emissions or of ambient quality) where marginal abatement costs and marginal damages are equal.

One way of thinking about environmental policies is along a continuum from **centralized** to **decentralized.** A centralized policy requires that some control administrative agency be responsible for determining what is to be done.

183

To achieve efficiency in a centralized policy, the regulatory agency in charge must have knowledge of the relevant marginal abatement cost and marginal damage functions, then take steps to move the situation to the point where they are equal.

A decentralized policy gets results from the interaction of many individual decision makers, each of whom is essentially making her own assessment of the situation. In a decentralized approach, the interactions of the individuals involved serve to reveal the relevant information about marginal abatement costs and marginal damages and to adjust the situation toward the point where they are equal.

It is often the case that environmental damages cannot be measured accurately. This sometimes makes it useful to employ **cost-effectiveness** as a primary policy criterion. A policy is cost-effective if it produces the maximum environmental improvement possible for the resources being expended or, equivalently, it achieves a given amount of environmental improvement at the least possible cost. For a policy to be efficient it must be cost-effective, but not necessarily vice versa. A policy might be cost-effective even if it were aimed at the wrong target. Suppose the objective is to clean up New York harbor, regardless of what the benefits are. We would still be interested in finding policies that did the job cost-effectively; however, for a policy to be socially efficient, it must not only be cost-effective, it must also balance costs with benefits. To be efficient, the harbor-cleaning project must balance marginal benefits with marginal cleanup costs.

The capability of a policy to achieve cost-effective emission reductions (i.e., yield the maximum improvement for the resources spent) is also important for another reason. If programs are not cost-effective, the policymakers and administrators will be making decisions using an aggregate abatement cost function that is higher than it needs to be, leading them to set less restrictive targets in terms of desired amounts of emission reductions. This is shown in Figure 9-1, for a case of SO_2 emissions. With a cost-*ineffective* policy, the perceived marginal abatement cost is the higher one, labeled MAC_1; whereas with a cost-effective approach, marginal abatement costs would be MAC_2. Thus, with the MD function as shown, the emissions level a_1 appears to be the efficient level of pollution, whereas with a cost-effective program the efficient level would be a_2. The real problem with having costs higher than they need to be is that society will be inclined to set its objectives too low in terms of the amount of emission reduction sought.

Efficiency and cost-effectiveness are important because, although preserving environmental resources is critically important, it is only one of the many desirable things that people seek. Advocates are usually convinced that their objectives are automatically worth the cost, but success depends on persuading large numbers of other people that environmental policies are efficiently designed. Thus, the resources devoted to environmental quality improvement ought to be spent in ways that will have the greatest impact. This is especially important in less-developed economies, where people have fewer resources to put in environmental programs and can ill-afford policies that are not cost-effective and efficient. Cost-effectiveness also becomes an important issue in industrialized countries during times of recession or economic stagnation.

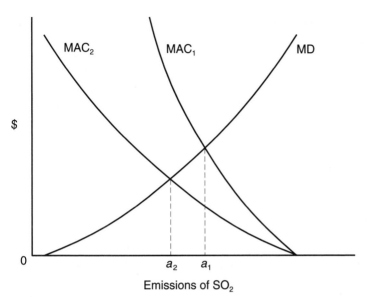

FIGURE 9-1
Mistaking the Efficient Emissions Level When Abatement Technologies Are
Not Cost-Effective.

FAIRNESS

Fairness, or **equity,** is another important criterion for evaluating environmental policy (or any policy, for that matter). Equity is, first and foremost, a matter of morality and the concerns about how the benefits and costs of environmental improvements ought to be distributed among members of society. Fairness is also important from the standpoint of policy effectiveness, because policies may not be supported as enthusiastically in the political arena if they are thought to be inequitable. Having said this, however, it has to be recognized that there is no agreement on how much weight should be put on the two objectives: efficiency and distribution. Consider the following hypothetical numbers, which might relate, for example, to the costs and benefits of several alternative approaches to air pollution control in a given region.

				Distribution of net benefits	
Program	Total costs	Total benefits	Net benefits	Group X	Group Y
A	50	100	50	25	25
B	50	100	50	30	20
C	50	140	90	20	70
D	50	140	90	40	50

The first three columns show total costs, total benefits, and net benefits, respectively. Suppose Group X and Group Y refer to a low-income group and a high-income group, respectively. Programs A and B have the same net benefits, but these are distributed more progressively in B than in A. We might agree that B is preferable to A because it has the same net benefits and "better" distributional effects. But compare Programs B and C. The net benefits of Program C are much higher than in B. Unfortunately, they are not distributed as progressively as those of B; in fact, they are distributed more toward high-income people. How should we choose between B and C? Some might argue that B is best, for distributional reasons; others might argue for C on overall efficiency grounds. Or compare Programs B and D. In this case, D has the advantage in overall efficiency, although, as in the case of C, more of the net benefits go to high-income people. Here we also see that low-income people would be better off in absolute terms, although not relatively, with D than with B. On these grounds, D might be preferred.

Suppose, on the other hand, that Group X and Group Y refer to people in two different regions of the country. Now we see that there is an issue of **interregional equity.** If we knew, for example, that the Group Y region was where the problem originated that is being addressed by these possible programs, C and D might definitely be regarded as inequitable, because most of the net benefits go to this region.

Equity considerations also loom large in the making of international environmental policy. As we will discuss later in chapters on global and international environmental problems, countries at different stages of development have different views on how the burdens of international pollution-control programs should be distributed. These views are driven by considerations of what seems fair in the light of the wide economic disparities around the globe.

Environmental Justice

Equity considerations are behind what has recently become known as the movement for **environmental justice.** The concern is that racial minorities and low-income people are disproportionately exposed to environmental contaminants, both those outside the home such as air and water pollution and those within the home and workplace such as lead. The primary concern has been largely about exposure to the pollutants coming from hazardous waste sites. The question is whether hazardous waste sites are disproportionately located in areas where there are relatively large populations of low-income people and people of color and, if that is so, what to do about it from a policy perspective. We will take up these matters at greater length in Chapter 16.

The relative scarcity of information on the distributional impacts of environmental policies argues for putting more effort into finding out what they are. Recently the U.S. Environmental Protection Agency has moved in this direction, although it has not yet become part of official policy. To the normal benefit–cost analyses of environmental regulations, it has suggested adding a "population distribution analysis" where appropriate.[1] This means an analysis that shows how the total benefits and costs of a regulation are distributed among various income, ethnic, and racial groups within society. If this effort is pursued with vigor, it should lead over time to better overall information about efficiency—equity trade-offs in environmental policies.

---

[1]U.S. Environmental Protection Agency, *Environmental Equity, Reducing Risk for All Communities,* EPA 230-R-92-008, Washington, DC, June 1992, p. 28.

INCENTIVES FOR LONG-RUN IMPROVEMENTS

In studying environmental policy, much of the focus normally gets put on the performance of public officials because they appear to be the source of that policy. What needs to be kept clearly in mind, however, is that it is private parties, firms, and consumers whose decisions actually determine the range and extent of environmental impacts,[2] and the incentives facing these private parties determine how and where these impacts will be reduced. Thus, a critically important criterion that must be used to evaluate any environmental policy is whether that policy provides a strong **incentive** for individuals and groups to find **new, innovative ways of reducing their impacts** on the ambient environment. Does the policy place all the initiative and burden on public agencies, or does it provide incentives for private parties to devote their energies and creativities to finding new ways of reducing environmental impacts?

It is easy to miss the importance of this sometimes by concentrating on particular abatement cost and damage functions in the standard analysis. These show the efficient level of emissions according to the current functions, but over the longer run it is important that we try to shift the functions. It is especially important to try to shift downward the marginal abatement cost function, to make it cheaper to secure reductions in emissions, because this will justify higher levels of environmental quality. Technological change, flowing from programs of research and development (R&D), shifts the marginal abatement cost function downward. So do education and training, which allow people to work and solve problems more efficiently. So ultimately we want to know whether, and how much, a particular environmental policy contains incentives for polluters to seek better ways of reducing pollution. The greater these incentives, the better the policy, at least by this one criterion.

Long-run technical change is hard to predict with accuracy. There are, of course, more factors involved in bringing about change than just the static financial impacts as depicted in our simple model. Another important element, for example, is the relative stability of the policy process as perceived by regulated firms. A regulatory environment that is easy to change, with requirements that are frequently adjusted and altered, will create uncertainties that reduce the incentives for long-run investments. Regulations that are expected to be in place over time will create stronger incentives, other things of course being equal.

Another factor that is important, although it cannot be shown in our simple model, is the status of competition within the **envirotech industry.** The envirotech industry consists of firms who develop and market better technologies and procedures for pollution control, selling them to firms that are subject to environmental regulations. Without the environmental regulations there would be little demand for these improved technologies and procedures, thus little incentive for activity in the envirotech industry. Exhibit 9-1 illustrates the interplay of environmental regulations and technology development, in this case for the reduction of emissions from diesel trucks.

---

[2]We must keep in mind, however, that many serious cases of environmental destruction have been caused by public agencies.

EXHIBIT 9-1

MAJOR STRIDES MADE IN TECHNOLOGY TO CURB DIESEL EMISSIONS, WORKSHOP TOLD

SAN DIEGO, Calif.—Diesel engine emission control technologies have advanced tremendously over the last 10 years, but innovations are needed to permanently disassociate the word "dirty" from diesel, according to industry and regulatory specialists speaking at an Aug. 20–24 workshop.

Sponsored by the U.S. Department of Energy and the California Energy Commission, the five-day meeting offered an expansive overview of dozens of research projects and demonstration programs competing to develop more environmentally friendly diesel engines.

Speakers at the Aug. 20 opening session agreed that while there are emerging technologies such as fuel cells that one day might power heavy-duty vehicles, diesel engines will be around for at least the next 20–30 years.

"Right now, there is no substitute for the diesel engine in terms of energy efficiency and work capability," Pat Flynn, vice president of Cummins Engine Co., told the workshop. "The diesel engine is still key to the transportation economy, and there's nothing anyone is going to do in the short run to change that."

Significant challenges remain for emission-control technology and fuels for diesel engines, Thomas J. Gross, deputy assistant secretary for transportation technologies at the Department of Energy, told attendees. Engines must become more fuel-efficient and less-polluting, but this must be accomplished without sacrificing safety and performance, he said.

One of the challenges will be compliance with the EPA's new proposed standards requiring 2010 model year diesel engines to emit 90 percent fewer pollutants, Gross said. Another challenge is to respond to a federal initiative to create more energy-efficient vehicles to reduce the nation's dependence on foreign oil and to reduce greenhouse gas emissions, he said.

Tougher emission standards, in Europe as well as in the United States, are driving research in diesel technologies, research that could possibly lead to even cleaner gasoline-powered cars, according to James J. Eberhardt, director of DOE's Office of Heavy Vehicle Technologies.

Sulfur traps and other after-treatment controls being developed for diesel engines may further reduce tailpipe emissions from passenger cars, he said.

Speakers also concurred on the need for low- and ultra-low sulfur diesel fuels to reduce nitrogen oxide (NO_x) emissions from diesel engines because sulfur damages catalytic systems.

"Two-thirds of all NO_x emissions in California come from on- and off-road diesel engines," California Air Resources Board Chief Deputy Executive Officer Tom Cackette told the workshop. "California wants these vehicles to be near zero-emitting."

Diesel exhaust is unhealthy, he said, explaining that CARB declared diesel soot a toxic air pollutant in August 1998. A study completed in November 1999 by the South Coast Air Quality Management District revealed that 70 percent of the cancer risk from air pollution in the Los Angeles area stems from the tiny particles of diesel soot.

Chung Liu, a deputy executive officer with SCAQMD in the Los Angeles area, provided an overview of regulations and technology advancement programs in place at the agency that are spurring development of diesel emission controls.

The air district recently adopted several measures aimed at public and private vehicle fleets, all with the goal of moving these fleets toward alternative-fueled, heavy-duty vehicles and ultra-low emitting light and medium cars and trucks, he said.

State funds, available through CARB and the SCAQMD, are available to help the regulated community buy the less-polluting vehicles, he said.

William Keese, chairman of the California Energy Commission, said the state is striving to "strike a balance between energy efficiency and air emissions." Strict state and federal regulations have made cars in California 90 percent cleaner, he said. It's time to sharpen the focus on diesel.

Source: BNA, Inc., *Environmental Reporter,* 31(34), August 25, 2000, pp. 1757–1758.

ENFORCEABILITY

There perhaps is a natural tendency among people to think that enacting a law automatically leads to the rectification of the problem to which it is addressed. Among the environmental community this tendency is depressingly strong. It occurs even among environmental economists, who sometimes implicitly assume that polluters will more or less automatically comply with whatever laws are enacted. A moment's reflection should convince us that this isn't so, even in countries that have relatively strong legal traditions and institutions. **Enforcement** requires energy and resources, just like any other activity, and there will always be other calls on these resources. Furthermore, there will always be people whose interests lie in not having environmental policies enforced. Thus, enforcement is unlikely to happen automatically.

It is difficult to get good information on enforcement and compliance behavior. The few studies that have been done show that there is cause for concern. The General Accounting Office (GAO) once surveyed a large number of major wastewater dischargers in the country to determine if they were complying with existing laws. They found that a substantial fraction (more than one-third) of the sources were not in compliance.[3]

Environmental economists at Resources for the Future (RFF) surveyed a large number of state enforcement agencies to determine common practices and costs associated with enforcing pollution-control regulations.[4] A very widespread practice is for agencies to require **self-reporting** of emissions by firms, with the public authorities carrying out periodic audits of these records and perhaps also periodic testing of emissions. The number of sources for which enforcing agencies were responsible varied enormously, with an average of 4,550 for air pollution sources and 1,770 for sources of water pollution. The costs per audit visit depended on whether the visit included the measurement of emissions along with the investigation of the firm's own records. When there was no emissions monitoring, the costs per visit averaged $155 for air and $301 for water sources. These jumped to $1,725 for air and $955 for water sources when emission measurement also was carried out. There was an enormous variation in these costs among agencies, however.

These results show that **enforcement costs** are an important segment of environmental quality programs. Public agencies virtually everywhere face budget stringencies, but also responsibilities that are large and continually growing. Thus, the costs of enforcement, although perhaps not as large as overall compliance costs in most cases, are critical to the success of environmental quality programs and ought to be treated explicitly in evaluating the overall social costs of these programs.

---

[3]U.S. General Accounting Office, *Wastewater Discharges Are Not Complying with EPA Pollution Control Permits*, Washington, DC, 1983.

[4]Clifford Russell, Winston Harrington, and William J. Vaughn, *Enforcing Pollution Control Laws*, Resources for the Future, Washington, DC, 1986.

The reason for pursuing this is that policies differ in terms of how easy it is to enforce them. Some may require sophisticated technical measures to get reasonable enforcement; others may be enforceable at much lower cost. There is no sense in attempting a dazzling new policy approach if it is essentially impossible, or very costly, to enforce. It may be better to settle for a less perfect policy that is more easily enforceable.

There are two main steps in enforcement: **monitoring** and **sanctioning.** Monitoring refers to measuring the performance of polluters in comparison to whatever requirements are set out in the relevant law. The objective of enforcement is to get people to comply with an applicable law. Thus, some amount of monitoring is normally essential; the only policy for which this does not hold is that of moral suasion. Monitoring polluting behavior is far more complicated than, say, keeping track of the temperature. Nature doesn't really care, and so it won't willfully try to outwit and confound the monitoring process. Polluters, however, who are intelligent human beings and who may stand to lose money if environmental laws are vigorously enforced, can usually find many ways of frustrating the monitoring process. The more sophisticated and complicated that process, the easier it may be for polluters to find ways of evading it. In recent years great strides have been made in developing monitoring technology, particularly for large sources of airborne and waterborne pollutants.

Sanctioning refers to the task of bringing to justice those whom monitoring has shown to be in violation of the law. This may sound like a simple step; if violators are found, we simply take them to court and levy the penalties specified in the relevant law, but things are much more complicated than this. Court cases take time and energy and resources. With many laws and many more violators, the burden on the legal system of trying to bring all violators to justice may be overwhelming. Violators are also reluctant participants; they may devote many resources to fighting the sanctions, turning the procedure into long, drawn-out, costly court battles. In many cases the data underlying the sanctions will be imperfect, leading to challenges and costly conflicts. To create a demonstration effect it may be desirable for authorities to sanction only a few of the most egregious violations, but this opens up the problem of trying to determine just which violators to single out. It is perhaps no wonder that in the real world many violators, especially first-time violators, are not sanctioned with the full penalties allowed by the law. Very often authorities try to achieve voluntary compliance and encourage violators to remedy the situation without penalty.

There is a paradox built into the sanctioning process. One might think that the greater the potential sanctions—higher fines, long jail terms for violators, and so on—the more the law would deter violators. But the other side of the coin is that the higher the penalties, the more reluctant courts may be to apply them. The threat to close down violators, or even to levy stiff financial penalties, can in turn threaten the economic livelihoods of large numbers of people. Courts are usually reluctant to throw a large number of people out of work, and so may opt for less drastic penalties than allowed by the law. So the sanctioning process can become much more complicated than the simple model implies.

MORAL CONSIDERATIONS

We earlier discussed questions of income distribution and the impacts of different environmental policies on people with different levels of wealth. These are ethical issues on which different people will have varied opinions, but they are important to discuss when deciding on alternative public policies. But moral considerations extend beyond these distributional questions. The innate feelings that people have about what is right and wrong undoubtedly affect the way they look at different environmental policies. These have to be weighed in the balance along with the more technical criteria discussed previously.

Take, for example, the question of choosing between effluent taxes and effluent subsidies. Both are economic incentive-type policies, and both might have roughly the same effect in given cases of pollution control. From the standpoint of effectiveness, one might argue that subsidies would be better. Polluters might very well respond quicker and with greater willingness to a subsidy program than to one that is likely to cost them a lot of money. Strictly from the standpoint of getting the environment cleaned up as soon as possible, subsidies might be the most effective; however, this may run counter to the ethical notion that people who are causing a problem ought not to be "rewarded" for stopping, which is how subsidies are sometimes viewed.

Some people would take this idea further, arguing that because we should regard polluting behavior as essentially immoral to begin with, we should adopt policies that tend to recognize it as such.[5] By this criterion, policies that declare outright that certain types of polluting behavior are illegal are to be preferred to policies that do not. Another idea grounded in morality is that those who cause a problem ought to bear the major burden of alleviating it. We see this, for example, in discussions of global environmental issues. The industrial nations, especially the most economically developed among them, are largely responsible for the atmospheric buildup of CO_2 and the deterioration of the protective ozone layer. Many people take the view that these countries ought to bear the major burden in rectifying the situation.

GOVERNMENT FAILURE

In Chapter 4, we discussed the idea of "market failure," a situation where, because of externalities of one type or another, unregulated markets may not yield efficient and equitable results. This is especially true in the case of pollution, because of the public good nature of environmental quality. This leads, in turn, to the conclusion that public policy is called for to rectify the situation.

It is important to recognize another type of failure, however, that makes the outcome of public policy somewhat problematic. This is called **government failure,** and its presence means that it cannot simply be assumed that each and every attempt at public environmental policy will make the situation better.

---

[5]Steven Kelman, *What Price Incentives? Economists and the Environment,* Auburn House, Boston, 1981.

Government failure refers to systematic tendencies and incentives within legislatures and regulating agencies that work against the attainment of efficient and equitable public policy.

There is sometimes the tendency to think of the public policy process as one where rational, socially minded people attempt to solve problems in an effective manner, but this is far from the case. In the United States, the policy process is an ongoing political struggle where ambitious politicians attempting to accumulate power, lobbying groups representing particular interests, administrative agencies with their own agendas, and others all come together in a process of conflict and strife. What comes out of this process may not resemble anything like informed, rational public policy that advances the welfare of society. What comes out of the process could make the situation worse in some circumstances.

SUMMARY

The purpose of this chapter is to review a number of criteria that may be useful in evaluating environmental policies in different circumstances. These criteria are

- Efficiency and cost-effectiveness
- Equity
- Incentives for long-run innovations
- Enforceability
- Agreement with moral precepts

With these criteria at hand, it is now time to launch into discussions of the various types of environmental policies. We will begin with several traditional decentralized approaches, following this with a look at the use of standards, a centralized approach that has been the most frequently used historically. Finally, we will look at what are called incentive-based types of policies.

QUESTIONS FOR FURTHER DISCUSSION

1 "Efficiency implies cost-effectiveness, but cost-effectiveness does not imply efficiency." Explain this statement.

2 Environmental policy is sometimes criticized for being a white, middle-class preoccupation. How might you interpret this position, using the concepts presented in this chapter?

3 Do you think that the impacts of the program to control automobile pollution are progressively or regressively distributed? How about the program to ensure the quality of public water supply systems?

4 Is there ever a justification for adopting an environmental regulation that cannot be, or will not be, enforced?

5 Suppose we adopt a regulation requiring that all new cars have catalytic converters installed to reduce tailpipe emissions. Explain how this could have a beneficial impact in the short run but a less beneficial impact in the long run.

WEBSITES

The OECD, **www.oecd.org/env/,** publishes many studies that look at the effectiveness of different types of environmental policies in various countries; see also the papers of the World Bank environmental group; **www.worldbank.org/ environment,** and the links listed on the website of this book, **www.mhhe.com/ economics/field3.**

SELECTED READINGS

Bernstein, Janis: "Alternative Approaches to Pollution Control and Waste Management: Regulatory and Economic Instruments," World Bank, Infrastructure and Urban Development Department, Washington, DC, Discussion Paper INU 79, May 1991.

Bohm, Peter, and Clifford S. Russell: "Comparative Analysis of Alternative Policy Instruments," in Allen V. Kneese and James L. Sweeney (eds.), *Handbook of Natural Resources and Energy Economics,* Vol. 1, North-Holland, Amsterdam, 1985, pp. 395-460.

Dewees, Donald N.: "Instrument Choice in Environmental Policy," *Economic Inquiry,* 21(1), January 1983, pp. 53–71.

Eskeland, Gunnar, and Emanuel Jimenez: "Choosing Among Policy Instruments in Pollution Control: A Review," World Bank, Country Economics Department, June 20, 1990.

Hird, John A., and Michael Reese: "The Distribution of Environmental Quality: An Empirical Analysis," *Social Science Quarterly,* 79(4), December 1998, pp. 693–716.

Organization for Economic Cooperation and Development: *Environmental Policies for Cities in the 1990s,* Paris, 1990.

Portney, Paul R.: "EPA and the Evolution of Federal Regulation," in Paul R. Portney and Robert N. Stavins (eds.), *Public Policies for Environmental Protection,* Resources for the Future, Washington, DC, 2000, pp. 11–30.

CHAPTER 10

DECENTRALIZED POLICIES: LIABILITY LAWS, PROPERTY RIGHTS, VOLUNTARY ACTION

By **"decentralized"** policies we mean policies that essentially allow the individuals involved in a case of environmental pollution to work it out themselves. Think back to the previous example of water quality in a lake. Suppose there are several industrial plants around the lake. One is a food processing plant, and the water of the lake is an important input in its operation. The other is an industrial operation that uses the lake for waste disposal. How is it possible to balance the pollution damage suffered by the first firm with the abatement costs of the second? A decentralized approach to finding the efficient level of ambient water quality in the lake is simply to let the two plants work it out between themselves. They might do this either through informal negotiations or through more formal interaction in a local court of law. Decentralized approaches can have several real advantages over other types of public policy:

- Because the parties involved are the ones producing and suffering the environmental externalities, they have strong incentives to seek out solutions to the environmental problems.
- The people involved may be the ones with the best knowledge of damages and abatement costs; therefore, they may be best able to find the right balance among them, that is, to find efficient solutions.

LIABILITY LAWS

Almost everybody has an intuitive notion of **liability** and **compensation.** To be liable for some behavior is to be held responsible for whatever untoward consequences result from that behavior. Compensation requires that those causing the damage compensate those damaged in amounts appropriate to the extent of the injury.

One approach to environmental issues, therefore, is to rely on liability laws. This would work simply by making polluters liable for the damages they cause. The purpose of this is not simply to compensate people after they have been injured, though that is important. The real purpose is to get would-be polluters to make careful decisions. Knowing that they will be held liable for environmental damages in effect **internalizes** what would otherwise be ignored **external effects.**

The Principle

Consider Figure 10-1. It's the familiar model of environmental pollution showing marginal abatement costs and marginal damages, both related to the rate at which some production residual is emitted. Suppose that the actual emission rate is initially at e_1, substantially above the efficient rate e^*. Suppose further that there now is put into place a liability law requiring polluters to compensate those damaged in an amount equal to the damages caused. The effect of the law is to internalize the environmental damages that were external before the law. They now become costs that polluters will have to pay and therefore will want to take into account when deciding on their emission rate. At e_1, the total

FIGURE 10-1
Policy Options: Liability and Property Rights Approaches.

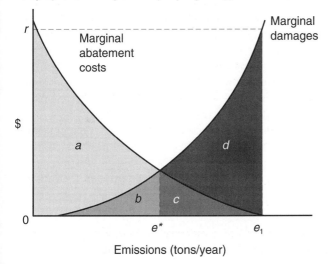

damages, and hence the amount of the compensation payment, would be a monetary amount equal to the area ($b + c + d$).

This polluter could reduce its compensation payments by reducing emissions. As it does that, of course, its marginal abatement costs increase. But as long as the marginal abatement costs are less than marginal damages, it would have an incentive to move to the left; that is, to reduce its rate of emissions. In theory, then, a liability system could automatically lead this polluter to emission level e^*. We say "automatically" because it would not require any centralized control authorities to intervene and mandate emission reductions. It requires rather a system of liability laws that would permit those damaged by pollution to be compensated for damages suffered.

Theoretically, this approach appears to address the incentive question—getting people to take into account the environmental damages they may cause—as well as the question of compensating those who are damaged. It may appear to solve the problem of determining just where e^* is along the emission axis. But whether this is actually true or not depends on the legal process through which the amount of liability and compensation is established. In the United States and other countries with similar legal traditions, this might be established through common-law processes. Alternatively, it might be the result of statutory enactments by legislators.

Common Law

Common-law systems rely on court proceedings in which plaintiffs and defendants meet to make claims and counterclaims, and in which juries often are called on to decide questions of fact and amounts of compensation. Judgments normally are based on precedent established from similar cases in the past.

A variety of legal doctrines related to nuisance and liability have developed over time. In the United States, the law now recognizes the difference between *strict liability*, which holds people responsible for damages regardless of circumstances, and *negligence*, which holds them responsible only if they did not take appropriate steps to avoid damage. A firm disposing of hazardous materials might be held strictly liable for damages done by these wastes. Thus, any damages that resulted, regardless of how careful the firm had been in disposing of the waste, would require compensation. On the other hand, negligence would hold it responsible only if it failed to take appropriate steps to ensure that the materials did not escape into the surrounding environment.

The question is whether common-law procedures can identify something approaching e^*, the efficient levels of emissions. In theory, and perhaps in practice, e^* may be discovered by the court by sifting through the claims and counterclaims made by polluters and parties suffering the damages. But many complexities can affect outcomes.

The critical factors in a liability system are where the **burden of proof** lies and what **standards have to be met in order to establish that proof**. In the United States, those who believe they may have been injured by pollution must file an action within a specified time period, typically two or three years, and then in court must establish a direct causal link between the pollution and the damage. This involves two major steps: first to show that the polluting material was a direct cause of their damage, and then that the material did in fact come from the specific defendant that appears in court. Both steps are difficult because the standards of proof required by the courts may be more than current science can supply. Most chemicals, for example, are implicated in increased disease only on a **probabilistic basis;** that is, exposure to the substance involves an increased probability of disease, not certainty. Even though we "know" that smoking "causes" lung cancer, for example, this causal link remains probabilistic; an increased number of people will get lung cancer if they smoke, but we can't tell exactly which ones. In Woburn, Massachusetts, contamination of well water was estimated by some epidemiologists to have probably caused 6 of the 12 excess cases of leukemia in the town. But under traditional standards of proof, a plaintiff could not conclusively prove that a *specific* cancer was caused by the water contamination. In other words, without being able to show explicitly how the polluting material operated in a particular body to produce cancer, the plaintiff cannot meet the standard of proof historically required in U.S. courts.[1]

The other link in the causal chain is to show that the material to which one was exposed came from a particular source. This won't be difficult in some cases; the oil on the Alaskan shoreline definitely came from the Exxon *Valdez* tanker wreck, the hazy atmosphere over the Grand Canyon definitely comes from the power plant, and so on. But in many cases this direct linkage is unknown. For an urban dweller in New York or Los Angeles, which specific industrial plant produced the SO_2 molecules that a particular person may have breathed? For the people living in towns of the Connecticut Valley, which specific tobacco farms were responsible for the chemicals that showed up in their water supply? Without being able to trace a polluting substance to specific defendants, those who have been damaged by it may be unable to obtain compensation.

Another major point to make about liability systems can best be understood by introducing the concept of **transactions costs.** In general terms, transactions costs are the costs of reaching and enforcing agreements. The concept was first introduced in economics to apply to the costs that buyers and sellers encounter in making a successful transaction: costs of searching out information, costs of bargaining over terms, and costs of making sure an agreement is actually carried out. But the transactions costs also apply to liability systems where plaintiffs and defendants are competing in a court of law to determine the question of liability and the appropriate amounts of compensation. In this case transactions costs are all the legal costs associated with gathering evidence, presenting a case, challenging opponents, awarding and collecting damages, and so on.

---

[1]In some cases the law is beginning to change to recognize the special characteristics of pollution-caused damage. For example, statutes of limitation are being changed to count from the time the disease first becomes apparent, in recognition of the fact that many pollution-caused diseases may not show up for many years after exposure. Some courts also are beginning to allow statistical cause-and-effect linkages.

If the case is relatively simple, with one party on each side and a reasonably clear case of damage, the liability system may function, with a minimum of transactions costs, to give something approaching the efficient level of emissions. In the case of the two small factories on a small lake, the two can go to court and argue about the economic values to each of them of using the lake for their purposes. Because these values are comparable, it presumably would not be too difficult for a judge to determine the extent of the damages that the one firm is inflicting on the other. But transactions costs in many cases are likely to be very high. Complicated scientific questions often are involved, and judges and juries may find it virtually impossible to sort them out clearly (see Exhibit 10-1). And there may be many, many more than two parties involved, making it very difficult to agree on comprehensive solutions. In the case of the Exxon *Valdez* oil spill, for example, probably tens of thousands of people regarded themselves as having been directly damaged, hundreds of lawyers represent all the different sides, and numerous environmental groups, government organizations, and business groups were involved.

EXHIBIT 10-1

COMMON-LAW COURTS AND QUESTIONS OF SCIENCE

The discussion moved on to the questions the jury would have to answer in reaching its verdict. Juries are usually asked simply whether they find for the plaintiff or for the defendant. But Judge Skinner pointed out that the date TCE and the other solvents arrived at the wells would be critically important in the second phase, the medical phase, of trial, presuming the case got that far. "Simply to say that the chemicals got there sometime before May 1979 is not going to do the trick," the judge told the lawyers.

He asked the lawyers to prepare a draft of the questions they thought the jury should answer. Schlichtmann would have liked one simple question for each defendant—Were Beatrice and Grace responsible for contaminating the wells before May 1979?—but nothing in this case had been that simple. Both Facher and Keating submitted long lists of complicated questions, all of which the jurors would have to answer in the affirmative to proceed to the next phase.

The lawyers and the judge argued for two days about the questions, endless arguments about phrases, words, prepositions, and commas, like rabbinical scholars arguing fine points of the Talmud. Schlichtmann kept trying to simplify, Facher and Keating kept trying to put elements back in. The judge seemed to recognize the need for simplicity. "My God," he said at one point. "To ask them a question like that! You're talking to plain folks, you know. You've got to cast these in some form of language that is not hedged around with reservations and clauses and subclauses and commas and all that."

"That's right!" agreed Schlichtmann. "It's the most ridiculous thing in the world."

In the end, however, the questions were the work of a committee whose members had already demonstrated their inability to agree on just about anything. The judge finally decided on four questions for each defendant, all of which contained plenty of clauses, subclauses, and commas. First: Had the plaintiffs established by a preponderance of the evidence that any of the following chemicals—TCE, perc, and 1,2 transdichloroethylene—were disposed on

We may rely on private liability arrangements through common law to identify efficient pollution levels when relatively few people are involved, causal linkages are clear, and damages are easy to measure. These conditions may be met in some localized cases of pollution, but for most cases of environmental externalities they are not, and so we must consider other means of arranging relationships between polluters and the people they affect.

Statutory Law

Another way to structure a liability system is to rely on statutory laws. Here a legislature enacts a law requiring the payment of compensation when a polluter causes damage.

A number of countries, individually and in international agreements, have sought to use liability laws to address the problem of maritime oil spills. Several international conventions have been devoted to specifying the liability requirements of companies whose tankers release, accidentally or not, large

---

EXHIBIT 10-1 (CONTINUED)

COMMON-LAW COURTS AND QUESTIONS OF SCIENCE

the Beatrice land after August 27, 1968 (in the case of W. R. Grace, after October 1, 1964, the date Well B had opened), and had these chemicals substantially contributed to the contamination of the wells before May 22, 1979? If the answer should be yes for one or more of the chemicals, then the second question: What, according to a preponderance of the evidence, was the earliest date—both the month and year—at which each of these chemicals had substantially contributed to the contamination of the wells? And then: Had this happened because of the defendants' failure to fulfill any duty of care due to the plaintiffs?

Finally, if the jurors answered yes to that question, then this puzzler: What, according to a preponderance of the evidence, was the earliest time (again, both the month and year) at which the substantial contribution referred to in question 3 was caused by the negligent conduct of this defendant. . . .?

All in all, the questions had the quality of a text that had been translated from English into Japanese and back again. The judge himself seemed to realize this. "I'm sure it

can be improved upon," he muttered at the end of his labors. "But with the shortness of life, it requires us to bring this to an end."

In truth, these questions were all but impossible to understand. An expert in semantics would have had a hard time finding his way through the thicket of words. But even worse, they asked for answers that were essentially unknowable. Science could not determine the moment when those chemicals had arrived at the wells with the sort of precision Judge Skinner was demanding of the jurors. The judge was, in effect, asking the jurors to create a fiction that would in the end stand for the truth. Or, if they found themselves unable to do that, to end the case by saying they couldn't answer the questions based on the evidence. If these questions really were necessary to a just resolution of this case, then perhaps the case was one that the judicial system was not equipped to handle. Perhaps it should never have been brought to trial in the first place.

Source: Jonathan Harr, *A Civil Action,* New York, Random House Vintage, 1996, pp. 368–369.

quantities of oil into the sea, and many countries have enacted laws specifying liability of their oil companies for damages from spills in coastal waters.[2] One particularity of oil tanker spills is that it is very difficult to monitor the behavior of the polluters in this case. It is an episodic emission, so there is no continuous flow to measure, and spill probabilities depend on many practices (navigation, tanker maintenance, etc.) that are difficult for public authorities to monitor continuously. When polluter behavior is extremely difficult to monitor, we nevertheless would like to know that the polluters have undertaken all appropriate steps to reduce the probability of accidents. Liability laws may be of great usefulness in these cases.

Other types of compensation laws also have been adopted. In Japan the compensation statute enacted in 1973 is called **The Law for the Compensation of Pollution-Related Health Injury.** The law establishes an administrative structure and a health certification procedure, whereby victims living in designated parts of the country can be compensated for medical expenses and lost earnings from specific, officially designated, pollution-related diseases. These diseases are minamata (mercury poisoning), itai-itai (cadmium poisoning), chronic arsenic poisoning, emphysema, chronic bronchitis, asthma, and asthmatic bronchitis. The effect of this law is to replace what in many countries would be a piecemeal process of individual court cases with an overall, centrally directed system for compensating those damaged by pollution. Although it is probably much less expensive than a case-by-case court approach, it still has many of the same problems; for example, determining whether health cases are in fact pollution related, establishing fair compensation levels, and so on.

The incentive effects of this approach may also be questioned. In a system where victims are free to sue particular companies for compensation of pollution-related disease, there is presumably a direct incentive for polluters to take steps to reduce their potential liability. But this incentive may be quite weak if a firm is just one among many that contribute to a particular case of pollution, because here the public-good nature of pollution works against individual responsibility. In the Japanese system the direct link between the behavior of individual firms and its compensation payments is broken. The fund from which victims are compensated is derived from taxes on polluters, especially on SO_2 emissions. The tax is established as a revenue source to get sufficient funds to cover compensation payments. Theoretically, this would be a reasonably efficient tax if compensation covered all damages, but the law specifies that only medical costs and lost wages may be compensated, which probably understates total damages by a substantial margin. The part of the law dealing with compensation for air pollution damages was terminated in 1988 as a result of pressure from industry and finance interests. Their view was that because ambient standards were then being met, there was no further need for compensation.[3]

---

[2]In 1990, the U.S. Congress enacted the Oil Pollution Prevention, Response, Liability and Compensation Act, which substantially increased the liability of ship owners for oil spills around the U.S. coastline.

[3]Ken'ichi Miyamoto, "Japan," in *European Environmental Yearbook,* 4th ed., Doc Ter, Institute for Environmental Studies, Milan, 1990.

A law of compensation for pollution damage also exists in the Netherlands. The compensation is paid from a special fund at whose expense ". . . any person suffering damage which is due to air pollution occurring above the territory of the Netherlands, and which for reasons of equity shall not be borne by that person, may be granted, on application, compensation."[4]

How well these types of statutory liability laws work in providing the correct incentive for polluters depends heavily on the formulas specified for determining the exact amount of the liability. The laws can provide the correct incentives only if the compensation approaches the actual amounts of damage.

PROPERTY RIGHTS

In the previous section we discussed the case of a small lake that one firm used for waste disposal and another for a water supply. On deeper thought we are led to a more fundamental question: Which one of the firms is really causing damage and which firm is the one suffering damages? This may sound counterintuitive because you might naturally think that the waste-disposing firm is of course the one causing the damage. But we might argue just as well that the presence of the foodprocessing firm inflicts damages on the waste-disposing firm because its presence makes it necessary for the latter to take special efforts to control its emissions. (Assume for purposes of argument that there are no other people, such as homeowners or recreators, using the lake.) The problem may come about simply because it is not clear who has the initial right to use the services of the lake; that is, who effectively owns the **property rights** to the lake. When a resource has no owner, nobody has a very strong incentive to see to it that it is not over exploited or degraded in quality.

Private property rights are, of course, the dominant institutional arrangement in most developed economies of the West. Developing countries also are moving in that direction, as are even the ex-Socialist countries. So we are familiar with the operation of that institutional system when it comes to person-made assets such as machines, buildings, and consumer goods. Private property in land is also a familiar arrangement. If somebody owns a piece of land, he has an incentive to see to it that the land is managed in ways that maximize its value. If somebody comes along and threatens to dump something onto the land, the owner may call upon the law to prevent it if he wants to. By this diagnosis, the problem of the misuse of many environmental assets comes about because of imperfectly specified property rights in those assets.

[4]Alfred Rest, "Responsibility and Liability for Transboundary Air Pollution Damage," in Cees Flinterman, Barbara Kwiatkowska, and Johan G. Lammers (eds.), *Transboundary Air Pollution, International Legal Aspects of the Co-operation of States*, Martinus Nijhoff Publishers, Dordrecht, Holland, 1986, p. 324.

The Principle

Consider again the case of the lake and the two firms. Apparently there are two choices for vesting ownership of the lake. It could be owned either by the polluting firm or by the firm using it for a water supply. How does this choice affect the level of pollution in the lake? Would it not lead to zero emissions if owned by the one firm and uncontrolled emissions if owned by the other? Not necessarily, if owners and nonowners are allowed to negotiate. Of course, this is the very essence of a property rights system. The owner decides how the asset is to be used and may stop any unauthorized use, but also may negotiate with anybody else who wants access to that asset.

Look again at Figure 10-1. Suppose the marginal damage function refers to all the damages suffered by the brewery—call this Firm A. Assume the marginal abatement cost curve applies to the firm emitting effluent into the lake—call this one Firm B. We have to make some assumption about who owns the lake, Firm A or Firm B. We will see that, *theoretically*, the same quantity of emissions will result in either case, provided that the two firms can come together and strike a bargain about how the lake is to be used.

In the first case, suppose that Firm B owns the lake. For the moment we need not worry about how this came about, only that this is the way it is. Firm B may use the lake any way it wishes. Suppose that emissions initially are at e_1. Firm B is initially devoting no resources at all to emissions abatement. But is this where matters will remain? At this point marginal damages are r, whereas marginal abatement costs are nil. The straightforward thing for Firm A to do is to offer Firm B some amount of money to reduce its effluent stream; for the first ton any amount agreed on between 0 and r would make both parties better off. In fact, they could continue to bargain over the marginal unit as long as marginal damages exceeded marginal abatement costs. Firm B would be better off by reducing its emissions for any payment in excess of its marginal abatement costs, whereas any payment less than the marginal damages would make Firm A better off. In this way, bargaining between the owners of the lake (here Firm B) and the people who are damaged by pollution would result in a reduction in effluent to e^*, the point at which marginal abatement costs and marginal damages are equal.

Suppose, on the other hand, that ownership of the lake is vested in Firm A, the firm that is damaged by pollution. In this case we might assume that the owners would allow no infringement of their property, that is, that the emission level would be zero or close to it. Is this where it would remain? Not if, again, owners and others may negotiate. In this case Firm B would have to buy permission from Firm A to place its wastes in the lake. Any price for this lower than marginal abatement costs but higher than marginal damages would make both parties better off. And so, by a similar process of bargaining with, of course, payments now going in the opposite direction, the emissions level into the lake would be adjusted from the low level where it started toward the efficient level e^*. At this point any further adjustment would stop because marginal abatement costs, the maximum the polluters would pay for the right to emit one more ton of effluent, are equal to marginal damages, the minimum Firm A would take in order to allow Firm B to emit this added ton.

So, as we have seen in this little example, if property rights over the environmental asset are clearly defined, and bargaining among owners and prospective users is allowed, the efficient level of effluent will result irrespective of who was initially given the property right. In fact, this is a famous theorem, called the "Coase theorem," after the economist who invented it.[5] The wider implication is that by defining private property rights (not necessarily individual property rights because private *groups* of people could have these rights), we can establish the conditions under which decentralized bargaining can produce efficient levels of environmental quality. This has some appeal. The good part of it is that the people doing the bargaining may know more about the relative values involved—abatement costs and damages—than anybody else, so there is some hope that the true efficiency point will be arrived at. Also, because it would be a decentralized system, we would not need to have some central bureaucratic organization making decisions that are based mostly on political considerations instead of the true economic values involved. Ideas like this have led some people to recommend widespread conversion of natural and environmental resources to private ownership as a means of achieving their efficient use.

Rules and Conditions

How well is this property rights approach likely to work in practice? In order for a property rights approach to work right—that is, to give us something approaching the efficient level of environmental pollution—essentially three main conditions have to be met:

1 Property rights must be well defined, enforceable, and transferable.
2 There must be a reasonably efficient and competitive system for interested parties to come together and negotiate about how these environmental property rights will be used.
3 There must be a complete set of markets so that private owners may capture all social values associated with the use of an environmental asset.

If Firm A cannot keep Firm B from doing whatever the latter wishes, of course a property rights approach will not work. In other words, owners must be physically and legally able to stop others from encroaching on their property. Owners must be able to sell their property to any would-be buyer. This is especially important in environmental assets. If owners cannot sell the property, this will weaken their incentives to preserve its long-run productivity. This is because any use that does draw down its long-run environmental productivity cannot be punished through the reduced market value of the asset. Many economists have argued that this is a particularly strong problem in developing

[5]See the references at the end of the chapter.

countries; because ownership rights in these settings are often "attenuated" (i.e., they do not have all the required characteristics specified above), people do not have strong incentives to see that long-run productivity is maintained.

Transactions Costs

We saw previously that the efficient use of the lake depended on negotiations and agreement between the two interested firms. Negotiating costs, together with the costs of policing the agreement, could be expected to be fairly modest. What we are referring to here is **transactions costs,** the idea that we introduced in the preceding section. In the simple lake case, transactions costs would probably be low enough that the firms would be able to negotiate on the efficient level of emissions. But suppose Firm A, the firm using the lake as a water supply source, is replaced with a community of 50,000 people who use it not only for a water supply, but also for recreational purposes. Now the negotiations must take place between a single polluting firm on one side and 50,000 people, or their representatives, on the other side. For each of these individuals the value of improved water quality is small relative to the value to the firm of polluting the lake. Moreover, the level of water quality in the lake is a public good for these individuals. This seriously increases the transactions costs of negotiating an agreement among different users.

To make matters worse, suppose that instead of one polluting firm there are 1,000 polluting firms, together with a few thousand homeowners who are not yet hooked into the public sewer system and so are using septic tanks on the shores of the lake. Here the possibilities of vesting the ownership of the lake in one person, and expecting negotiations between that person and prospective users to find the efficient levels of use, essentially vanish. This is another way of saying that in large and complex cases of environmental degradation, where free-rider problems abound, very high transactions costs will seriously reduce the potential of the private property approach to identify the efficient level of emissions.

The Absence of Markets

For private property institutions to ensure that an environmental asset is put to its best use, the process also must work in such a way that the owner is able to capture the full social value of the resource in that use. Suppose you own a small island in the Florida Keys. There are two possible uses: Develop a resort hotel or devote it to a wildlife refuge. If you build the hotel, you get a direct flow of monetary wealth because the tourism market is well developed in that part of the world and you can expect customers to find your hotel and pay the going rate for your services. But there is no comparable "market" for wildlife refuge services. The value of the island as refuge may well be much higher than its value as resort, in terms of the actual aggregate willingness to pay of all the people in the country and the world. But there is no good way for them to be able to express that value; there is no ready market such as the one in the tourism market where they in effect can bid against the tourists who would visit the island. You might think that a **nature conservancy** could buy up the island if its value as refuge really is higher than its value as hotel. But nature conservancies run on the basis of voluntary contributions, and islands and other lands are in effect public goods.[6] We saw earlier that when public goods are involved, voluntary contributions to make something available are likely to be a lot less than its true value because of **free-riding behavior.** The upshot is that, while you as an owner could certainly expect to reap the full monetary value of the island as resort, you would not be able to realize its full social value if you held it as a preserve.

Exhibit 10-2 discusses an interesting example of a situation in which a market for previously unvalued environmental assets may be developing. Growing forests produce many services, one of which is the sequestering, or storing up, of CO_2 in the atmosphere. This would work in the direction of alleviating an important causal factor in global warming. Historically, owners of forest land have been unable to realize this particular value of their trees; there has been no market in which they could sell the carbon-sequestering services of their forests, thus making the forest conservation incentive weaker than it otherwise might be. The exhibit discusses the efforts of a Northern California conservation group to work towards making a market in which these services could be priced.

Another example of this is the conservation of biological diversity and the stock of unique genetic material contained in the millions of animal and plant species worldwide. A disproportionately large share of these species are located in developing countries, but these are countries also where development pressures have led to high rates of land clearance and habitat destruction. When landholders in these countries are considering their options, they weigh the value of the land in different uses. Unfortunately, there is no way at present that they can capture the value of the land left as species habitat. No ready economic markets exist where these services can be sold; if they did, landholders could reap private benefits from keeping land undeveloped or using land in ways that are consistent with the preservation of species.

One role for public authorities in this situation might be to create the demand side for such a market. This could be done by offering to pay the landowners an amount equal to the wider ecological value of the land, provided these ecological values were not impaired by the landholders' use of the land. Of course, this would involve enormous difficulties in measuring these ecological values with some degree of accuracy, as well as in finding sources of funds to pay for these services. But without these kinds of market or marketlike

---

[6]The Nature Conservancy is a national group that seeks to protect sensitive resources from damage by buying them outright. Over the last 50 years, they have helped to protect more than 11 million acres of ecologically sensitive land in the United States; some has been transferred to other public and private conservation groups; the rest still belongs to the Nature Conservancy. Many individual states also have conservancy groups.

EXHIBIT 10-2

CALIFORNIA AND THE WEST; HISTORICAL DEAL IS BASED ON TREES' VALUE IN ENVIRONMENT

By Katherine Ellison

In a landmark—though mostly symbolic—deal announced Thursday, a Northern California conservation group has sold the air-cleansing capacity of trees on 5,000 acres to a Texas energy company. The aim of the sale is to help deter global warming and to win some public relations points for clean energy and old-growth forests.

In the deal, Pacific Forest Trust, based in Santa Rosa, sold $6,000 worth of "carbon emissions reduction credits" to Green Mountain Energy Co., a Texas-based energy provider that sells power from environmentally friendly sources.

The credits are based on the work of trees at four sites in California and Oregon, including a 700-acre, partly old-growth redwood forest in San Mateo County. On each of the sites, private forest owners have donated rights to the trees' photosynthetic capacity to the trust, which in turn will sell them to Green Mountain.

When trees perform photosynthesis, they emit oxygen while absorbing carbon dioxide, a heat-trapping "greenhouse gas," to make their bark, roots, branches, and leaves.

Environmentalists increasingly argue forests play a useful role in reducing the risk of climate change, which many scientists believe has been aggravated by emissions of carbon dioxide through the burning of fossil fuels.

The potential sale of photosynthesis may give trees a new lease on life by establishing a value for standing forests independent of their worth as cut timber.

Forest loss is thought to be the second largest source of world carbon-dioxide emissions, next to the burning of fossil fuels. Trees release stored carbon dioxide when they die. The idea of such purchases is to leave the forests standing.

Over the past several years, a few big utility companies from Europe, Japan, and the United States have been buying "carbon rights" from forests, mostly in developing countries, where forest land is relatively cheap. They've done so in the hope that such purchases will count to their credit if laws are passed setting limits on their carbon dioxide emissions.

Similarly, Green Mountain is buying credits in expectation of future regulatory requirements, as well as for the publicity value.

As an energy provider, the company doesn't emit the great quantities of carbon dioxide that energy generators do. But it is trying to offset emissions attributable to its corporate travel, paper use, and employee commuting.

Company spokeswoman Suzie Quinn said those emissions amount to about 5,000 metric tons of carbon dioxide per year. The purchase of carbon rights will offset about half of that for 1999–2000.

To be sure, these numbers are drops in the bucket since humans worldwide pump more than 6 billion tons of carbon dioxide into the atmosphere per year. But Pacific Forest Trust's co-founder, Laurie Wayburn, maintained the deal is a significant step forward. "This is a pilot project," Wayburn said. "It shows it can be done. In the meantime, we've had very significant interest from some of the major power producers in the country."

Source: Los Angeles Times, November 10, 2000. Reprinted by permission.

institutions, private property rights institutions are unable to give society the fully efficient amounts of preservation and environmental quality.[7] The strongest feature of a property rights system is that it gives owners the incentive to protect and manage their assets so as to maximize their market value. For this to result in socially efficient levels of resource use, property rights must be well defined and defensible, transactions costs must be reasonably low, and there must exist markets through which the owners can actually realize the full social values of their decisions.

VOLUNTARY ACTION

By **voluntary action** we mean cases where individuals (including individual firms) engage in pollution-control behavior in the absence of any formal, legal obligation to do so. One might think that in this market-driven, competitive world, voluntary pollution control would be quite scarce, but this may not be true. There are many who feel that programs based on voluntary restraint can be used quite effectively. One of the key issues is establishing the **initial conditions** that will motivate voluntary pollution reductions.

We might distinguish two types of voluntary action. One is **moral suasion,** where behavior is based on a person's sense of moral values and civic duty. The other is action that is motivated by **informal community pressure.**

Moral Suasion

A classic case of moral suasion is the Smokey Bear (and now Woodsy Owl) effort of the National Forest Service, a publicity campaign aimed at getting people to be more sensitive about littering in the woods and about avoiding things that would raise the risk of forest fires. While there are fines and penalties for doing these things, the campaign was not based on threats of penalties as much as it was on appealing to people's sense of civic morality. "Don't Be a Litterbug" campaigns are essentially the same type of approach.

In the early days of recycling, communities often mounted voluntary efforts, where appeals were made on the basis of civic virtue. In some cases these efforts were successful; in others they fell flat. Today we are moving in the direction of more mandatory recycling programs, although it is true that they still must rely heavily on moral suasion to get high rates of compliance. Other situations clearly exist where appeals to civic morality may be effective public policy. This is especially the case with "emissions" such as litter, where violators are normally scattered throughout a population in a way that makes it impractical to monitor them and detect violations as they occur.

---

[7]Recently a private U.S. drug company agreed to pay the government of a Latin American country certain sums of money for plant species useful in drug development. We will discuss this in Chapter 20.

The good thing about moral suasion is that it may have widespread spillover effects. Whereas an effluent tax on a single type of effluent will have no impact on emissions of other types of waste products, appeals to civic virtue for one problem may produce side effects on other situations. People who, through a special publicity campaign, are brought to feel a greater sense of civic virtue when they refrain from littering may find themselves having the same feelings when they, for example, refrain from sneaking dead flashlight batteries into their household waste, or keep the pollution-control systems on their cars in a good state of repair.

Of course not all people are equally responsible from an ethical standpoint. Some people will respond to moral arguments; others will not. The burden of this policy will fall, therefore, on the part of the population that is morally more sensitive; those who respond less to moral arguments will be free riding on the others, enjoying the benefits of others' moral restraint but escaping their rightful share of the burden. What is especially bad about this is the long-run demonstration value. If those who would be responsive to moral arguments are confronted with the sight of widespread moral free riding, this may in the long run tend to erode the general level of civic and moral responsibility. Thus, appeals to the moral responsiveness of people, although perhaps effective in the short run, could actually have the opposite effect in the long run. This is similar to the cynicism that people often feel when new environmental laws are continually put on the books but never enforced.

It is easy to be cynical about moral suasion as a tool for environmental improvement. In this era of increasing mass society and heightened environmental destruction, tough-minded policymakers are naturally drawn toward environmental policies that have more teeth in them. This would probably be a mistake. It perhaps is true that we cannot rely very heavily on moral suasion to produce, for example, a significant reduction in air pollution in the Los Angeles basin or substantial drops in the use of groundwater-contaminating farm chemicals. But in our search for new, effective, public policy devices to address specific pollution problems, we perhaps underestimate the contribution of the overall climate of public morality and civic virtue. A strong climate in this sense makes it possible to institute new policies and makes it easier to administer and enforce them. From which we can also deduce the importance of politicians and policymakers doing things that replenish this moral climate rather than erode it.

Informal Community Pressure

Another sense in which voluntary actions can be important is when communities can put **informal pressure** on polluters to reduce their emissions. It is informal because it is not exercised through statutory or legal means, and it is pressure because it attempts to inflict costs on those who are responsible for excessive pollution. The costs in this case are in terms of such things as loss of reputation, the loss of local markets (perhaps going so far as to involve boycotts), or a loss of public reputation leading to declines in the stock values of firms that are publicly owned. The pressure is exercised through activities of local citizens groups, newspaper stories, demonstrations, discussions with polluters, and so on.

A major factor in voluntary actions of this type is the **information** that is available about polluters' emissions. If good data are lacking on the quantity and quality of emissions from particular sources, it will be difficult to mobilize public concern and focus it on the responsible parties. This is one of the motivations behind the U.S. Toxic Release Inventory, a program established under the **Emergency Planning and Community Right to Know Act** (1986) and the **Pollution Prevention Act** (1990), whereby polluters are required to report their toxic emissions, which are then published in a way that communities can identify emissions that directly affect them. This approach is being pursued also in other countries (see Exhibit 10-3).

SUMMARY

In this chapter we began the exploration of different types of public policies that might be used to combat environmental pollution. The chapter discusses two main decentralized types of approaches to environmental quality improvement. The first was to rely on liability rules, which require polluters to compensate those they have damaged. In theory, the threat of liability can lead potential polluters to internalize what would ordinarily be external costs. By weighing relative compensation and abatement costs, polluters would be brought to efficient emission levels. While liability doctrines may work well in simple cases of pollution where few people are involved and cause-and-effect linkages are clear, they are unlikely to work reliably in the large-scale, technically complicated environmental problems of contemporary societies.

The second major approach we discussed was reliance on the institution of private property rights. Looked at from this perspective, environmental externalities are problems only because ownership of environmental assets is often not clearly defined. By establishing clear property rights, owners and others who would like to use environmental assets for various purposes can negotiate agreements that balance the relative costs of different alternatives. Thus, negotiations among parties theoretically could bring about efficient emission rates. But problems of transactions costs, especially related to the public goods aspects of environmental quality, and lack of markets for environmental services work against relying primarily on traditional property rights institutions in environmental quality issues. We will see in a subsequent chapter, however, that some new types of property rights approaches may hold greater promise.

Finally, we mentioned the idea of moral suasion, which may be useful when it is impossible to measure the emissions stemming from particular sources. The problem of moral free riding was discussed, as was the problem of public disclosure as a means of encouraging ethical behavior in environmental matters.

EXHIBIT 10-3

U.S. TOXICS RELEASE INVENTORY

The U.S. Toxics Release Inventory (TRI) has annually reported polluters' emissions of more than 350 toxic chemicals for a decade. Since Congress established the program in 1986, TRI has published the names, locations, and toxic emissions—by chemical and medium of release—of plants with 10 or more employees that use at least 10,000 pounds of any listed chemical. The media and environmental groups provide extensive coverage of the yearly announcements. As the accompanying table shows, U.S. toxic emissions have declined substantially since TRI's beginning.

Programs like TRI use information differently from programs like PROPER. In the Indonesian case, a poor rating informs the public that a firm is not in compliance with national environmental standards. Disclosure programs such as TRI, by contrast, disseminate "raw" information on toxic emissions with no interpretation or risk assessment.

One problem is that some chemicals covered by TRI are quite dangerous, even in small doses, while others are hazardous only after long exposure at very high levels. By treating all chemicals the same, raw disclosure programs may sometimes alarm the public unnecessarily and pressure industry into adopting high-cost abatement programs that yield few social benefits. Academic researchers and NGOs have used media such as the Internet to inform the public of the relative risks of different chemicals, and to assist communities in identifying large polluters and assessing their overall pollution problems. (The Environmental Defense Fund maintains the most complete such Web site at *http://www.scorecard.org.*)

Community pressure is only one of several channels through which TRI exerts its effects; the financial community has also responded strongly. Research by Hamilton (1995) and Konar and Cohen (1997) has shown significant negative market returns for publicly traded firms when TRI first reports their pollution. Firms' market valuation also responds to information about changes in the volume of toxic pollution relative to toxic emissions from other firms. These results, in turn, create significant incentives to clean up: Firms with the largest stock market declines reduce emissions more than other firms. Numerous case studies have also shown that TRI induces firms to improve their ability to manage materials and waste.

These successes have inspired similar efforts in other countries, including the Chemical Release Inventory in the United Kingdom and OECD sponsorship of pilot Pollutant Release and Transfer Registers (PRTRs) in Egypt, the Czech Republic, and Mexico. The PRTR programs use the same format as TRI but restrict listed chemicals to those with relatively high hazard ratings.

TOTAL RELEASES OF TRI CHEMICALS, 1988–1994 ('000 METRIC TONS)

	1988	1992	1993	1994	% Change 1988–1994
Total air emissions	1,024	709	630	610	−40
Emissions to surface water	80	89	92	21	−73
Underground injection	285	167	134	139	−51
On-site land releases	218	149	125	128	−41
Total releases	1,607	1,113	981	899	−44

Source: David Wheeler, *Greening Industry: New Roles for Communities, Markets and Governments,* published for the World Bank by Oxford University Press, New York, 2000, p. 70. (The text reference is to the PROPER program in Indonesia, in which pollution control authorities rate and announce publicly the environmental performance of industrial polluters.)

QUESTIONS FOR FURTHER DISCUSSION

1 It would seem that neighbors could easily negotiate among themselves to settle problems of local externalities such as noise and unsightly land uses. Yet most communities control these problems with local laws and regulations. Why?

2 Suppose courts changed rules regarding burden of proof, requiring polluters to show that their emissions are harmless, rather than pollutees to show that they have been harmed. What impact might this have?

3 Suppose a community weighed each resident's solid waste disposal when it was picked up and published the individual totals each year in the local newspaper. Do you think this would lead to a reduction in the total quantity of solid waste disposed of in the community?

4 For what types of pollution problems is voluntary action likely to be the most effective policy approach?

5 Accidents with trucks carrying hazardous wastes are fairly common. Suppose regulators enact a rule requiring that the perpetrators of such an accident be liable for a sum equal to the average damages of all such accidents in the industry. Would this lead trucking companies to take the socially efficient amount of precaution against such accidents?

WEBSITES

The Environmental Law Institute, **www.eli.org,** has much information on the legal aspects of pollution control; the Political Economy Research Center, **www. perc.org,** has a strong leaning towards market-based solutions to natural resource and environmental issues. See also the sites listed on the website of this book: **www.mhhe.com/economics/field3.**

SELECTED READINGS

Anderson, Terry L.: "The Market Process and Environmental Amenities," in Walter E. Block (ed.), *Economics and the Environment: A Reconciliation,* The Fraser Institute, 1990, pp. 137–157.

Anderson, Terry L., and Donald R. Leal: *Free Market Environmentalism,* Pacific Research Institute, San Francisco, 1991.

Bartsch, Elga: *Liability for Environmental Damages: Incentives for Precaution and Risk Allocation,* Türbinger, Mohr (Siebeck), 1998.

Coase, Ronald H.: "The Problem of Social Cost," *Journal of Law and Economics,* Vol. 3, October 1960, pp. 1–44.

Dales, J. H.: *Pollution, Property and Prices,* University of Toronto Press, Toronto, 1968.

Kneese, Allen V., and William D. Schulze: "Ethics and Environmental Economics," in Allen V. Kneese and James L. Sweeney (eds.), *Handbook of Natural Resource and Energy Economics,* Vol. 1, North-Holland, Amsterdam, 1985, pp. 191–220.

Rothbard, Murray N.: "Law, Property Rights, and Air Pollution," in Walter E. Block (ed.), *Economics and the Environment: A Reconciliation,* The Fraser Institute, 1990, pp. 233–279.

Zweifel, Peter, and Jean-Robert Tyran: "Environmental Impairment Liability as an Instrument of Environmental Policy," *Ecological Economics,* Vol. 11, 1994, pp. 43–56.

CHAPTER 11

COMMAND-AND-CONTROL STRATEGIES: THE CASE OF STANDARDS

A **command-and-control (CAC)** approach to public policy is one where, in order to bring about behavior thought to be socially desirable, political authorities simply mandate the behavior in law, then use whatever enforcement machinery—courts, police, fines, and so on—are necessary to get people to obey the law. In the case of environmental policy, the command-and-control approach consists of relying on **standards** of various types to bring about improvements in environmental quality. In general, a standard is simply a mandated level of performance that is enforced in law. A speed limit is a classic type of standard; it sets maximum rates that drivers may legally travel. An emission standard is a maximum rate of emissions that is legally allowed. The spirit of a standard is, if you want people not to do something, simply pass a law that makes it illegal, then send out the authorities to enforce the law.

Figure 11-1 is our familiar graph showing marginal abatement costs and marginal damages related to the rate at which some production residual is emitted into the environment. Suppose that initially the actual level of effluent is at e_1, a rate substantially above the efficient rate of e^*. To achieve e^* the authorities set an emission standard at that level; e^* becomes a mandated upper limit for the emissions of this firm. The standard is then enforced by sending out whatever enforcement authorities are necessary to measure and detect any possible violations. If infractions are found, the source is fined or subject to some other penalty. Assuming the firm reduces emissions in accordance with the standard, it would be incurring an amount equivalent to area a per year in total abatement costs. These total abatement costs are the **compliance costs** of meeting the standard.

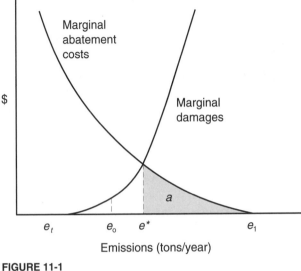

FIGURE 11-1
Emission Standards.

Standards are popular for a number of reasons. They appear to be simple and direct. They apparently set clearly specified targets. They appeal, therefore, to the sense that everybody has of wanting to come directly to grips with environmental pollution and get it reduced. Standards also appear to be congenial to our ethical sense that pollution is bad and ought to be declared illegal. The legal system is geared to operate by defining and stopping illegal behavior, and the standards approach conforms to this mindset.

We will see, however, that the standards approach is a lot more complex than might first appear. Standards appear to offer a method to take away the freedom of sources to pollute, replacing it with mandated changes in behavior. In fact, a very practical reason for the popularity of standards is that they may permit far more flexibility in enforcement than might be apparent. What appears to be the directness and unambiguousness of standards becomes a lot more problematic when we look below the surface.

TYPES OF STANDARDS

There are three main types of environmental standards: **ambient, emission,** and **technology.**

Ambient Standards

Ambient environmental quality refers to the qualitative dimensions of the surrounding environment; it could be the ambient quality of the air over a particular city or the ambient quality of the water in a particular river. So an **ambient**

standard is a never-exceed level for some pollutant in the ambient environ-ment. For example, an ambient standard for dissolved oxygen in a particular river may be set at 3 parts per million (ppm), meaning that this is the lowest level of dissolved oxygen that is to be allowed in the river. Ambient standards cannot be enforced directly, of course. What can be enforced are the various emissions that lead to ambient quality levels. To ensure that dissolved oxygen never falls below 3 ppm in the river, we must know how the emissions of the various sources on the river contribute to changes in this measure, then intro-duce some means of controlling these sources.

Ambient standards are normally expressed in terms of average concentra-tion levels over some period of time. For example, the current national primary ambient air quality standard for sulfur dioxide (SO_2) is 80 $\mu g/m^3$ on the basis of an annual arithmetic mean and 365 $\mu g/m^3$ on a 24-hour average basis.[1] The standard, in other words, has two criteria: a maximum annual average of 80 $\mu g/m^3$ and a maximum 24-hour average of 365 $\mu g/m^3$. The reason for taking averages is to recognize that there are seasonal and daily variations in meteoro-logical conditions, as well as in the emissions that produce variations in ambi-ent quality. Averaging means that short-term ambient quality levels may be worse than the standard, so long as this does not persist for too long and it is balanced by periods when the air quality is better than the standard.

Emission Standards

Emission standards are never-exceed levels applied directly to the quantities of emissions coming from pollution sources. Emission (or effluent) standards are normally expressed in terms of quantity of material per some unit of time; for example, grams per minute or tons per week. Continuous emissions streams may be subject to standards on "instantaneous" rates of flow; for example, upper limits on the quantity of residuals flow per minute or on the average residuals flow over some time period.

It is important to keep in mind the distinction between ambient standards and emission standards. Setting emission standards at a certain level does not necessarily entail meeting a set of ambient standards. Between emissions and ambient quality stands nature, in particular the meteorological and hydrologi-cal phenomena that link the two.

Research to study the linkage between emission levels and ambient quality levels is an important part of environmental science. The environment usually transports the emissions from point of discharge to other locations, often dilut-ing and dispersing them along the way. Chemical processes occur in all envi-ronmental media that often change the physical character of the pollutant. In some cases this may render the emitted substance more benign. Organic wastes put in rivers and streams will normally be subject to natural degradation processes, which will break them down into constituent elements. Thus, the ambient quality of the water at various points downstream depends on the

---

[1] $\mu g/m^3$ stands for micrograms per cubic meter.

quantity of emissions as well as the hydrology of the river: its rate of flow, temperature, natural reaeration conditions, and so on.

The link between emissions and ambient quality also can be vitally affected by human decisions. A classic case is automobiles. As part of the mobile-source air-pollution program, emission standards have been set for new cars in terms of emissions per mile of operation. But because there is no effective way of controlling either the number of cars on the roads or the total number of miles each is driven, the aggregate quantity of pollutants in the air and, thus, ambient air quality, is not directly controlled.

Emission standards can be set on a wide variety of different bases. For example:

1 Emission rate (e.g., pounds per hour).
2 Emission concentration (e.g., parts per million of biochemical oxygen demand, or BOD, in wastewater).
3 Total quantity of residuals (rate of discharge times concentration times duration).
4 Residuals produced per unit of output (e.g., SO_2 emissions per kilowatt-hour of electricity produced).
5 Residuals content per unit of input (e.g., SO_2 emissions per ton of coal burned in power generation).
6 Percentage removal of pollutant (e.g., 60 percent removal of waste material before discharge).

In the language of regulation, emission standards are a type of **performance standard** because they refer to end results that are meant to be achieved by the polluters who are regulated. There are many other types of performance standards; for example, workplace standards set in terms of maximum numbers of accidents or levels of risk to which workers are exposed. A requirement that farmers reduce their use of a particular pesticide below some level is also a performance standard, as is a highway speed limit.

Technology Standards

There are numerous standards that don't actually specify some end result, but rather the technologies, techniques, or practices that potential polluters must adopt. We lump these together under the heading of "technology standards." The requirement that cars be equipped with catalytic converters, or seat belts, is a technology standard. If all electric utilities were required to install stack-gas scrubbers to reduce SO_2 emissions,[2] these would be in effect technology standards because a particular type of technology is being specified by central authorities. This type of standard also includes what are often called "design standards" or "engineering standards." There are also a variety of product standards specifying characteristics that goods must have and input standards that require potential polluters to use inputs meeting specific conditions.

[2]A "scrubber" is a device that treats the exhaust gas stream so as to remove a substantial proportion of the target substance from that stream. The recovered material then must be disposed of elsewhere.

At the edges the difference between a performance standard and a technology standard may become blurred. The basic point of differentiation is that a performance standard, such as an emission standard, sets a constraint on some performance criterion and then allows people to choose the best means of achieving it. A technology standard actually dictates certain decisions and techniques to be used, such as particular equipment or operating practices to be used by polluters. For illustrative purposes, Exhibit 11-1 shows a list of federal standards applicable to retail dealers of agricultural chemicals. Some are emission standards (reducing pesticide and fertilizer application), but most are technology standards of various types.

THE ECONOMICS OF STANDARDS

It would seem to be a simple and straightforward thing to achieve better environmental quality by applying standards of various types. Standards appear to give regulators a degree of positive control to get pollution reduced, but standards turn out to be more complicated than they first appear. The discussion in the rest of this chapter will focus on the efficiency and cost-effectiveness of standards, as well as the problem of enforcement.

Setting the Level of the Standard

Perhaps the first perplexing problem is where to set the standard. We saw in the case of the decentralized approaches to pollution control—liability laws and property rights regimes—that there was, at least, the theoretical possibility that the interactions of people involved would lead to efficient outcomes. But with standards we obviously can't presume this; standards are established through some sort of authoritative political/administrative process that may be affected by all kinds of considerations.

The most fundamental question is whether, in setting standards, authorities should take into account only damages or both damages and abatement costs. Look again at Figure 11-1, particularly at the marginal damage function. One approach in standard setting has been to try and set ambient or emission standards by reference only to the damage function. Thus, one looks at the damage function to find significant points that might suggest themselves.

A principle used in some environmental laws has been to set the standard at a "zero-risk" level; that is, at the level that would protect everyone, no matter how sensitive, from damage. This would imply setting emission standards at the **threshold** level, labeled e_t in Figure 11-1. This concept is fine as long as there is a threshold. Recent work by toxicologists and other scientists, however, seems to indicate that there may be no threshold for many environmental pollutants; that in fact marginal damage functions are positive right from the origin. In fact, if we followed a "zero-risk" approach, we would have to set all standards at zero. This may be appropriate for some substances, certain highly toxic chemicals, for example, but it would be essentially impossible to achieve for all pollutants.

EXHIBIT 11-1

STANDARDS APPLICABLE TO RETAIL CHEMICAL HANDLERS, 1992

FIFRA '88 STORAGE DISPOSAL[a]
(Requires dealer to build dikes, rinse pads, fireproof warehouses, etc.)

PESTICIDE RECORD KEEPING
(Requires dealer to keep detailed records of pesticides sold and applied. The 1990 Farm Bill increases this requirement.)

CERTIFICATION AND TRAINING REQUIREMENTS
(Requires dealer and employees to obtain training in various areas of pesticide application.)

OTHER FIFRA REGULATIONS
(Special state laws and EPA policy requirements.)

FARM WORKER PROTECTION
(Requires dealer to train applicators.)

SARA TITLE III COMMUNITY RIGHT-TO-KNOW[b]
(Requires dealers of chemicals to report quantities of all chemicals held on site.)

OSHA REGULATIONS[c]
(Requires training of employees and safety equipment.)

DOT HAZARDOUS MATERIALS REGULATIONS[d]
(Requires 24-hour hotline, manifest placarding of hazardous material being shipped.)

COMMERCIAL DRIVERS' LICENSES
(Requires drivers to obtain CDL and drug testing.)

STORM WATER PERMITTING
(Requires dealers to hire consultants to perform engineering and testing of storm water runoff at individual facilities.)

EFFLUENT GUIDELINES
(Requires dealers to build pesticide wastewater treatment systems.)

PESTICIDE WASTE REMOVAL
(Required under CWA, CERCLA, and RCRA.[e])

PESTICIDE FEES (PER YEAR)
(State fee for licensing and environmental programs.)

ENDANGERED SPECIES ACT
(Requires reduction or elimination of pesticide application in some areas.)

PESTICIDE ILLNESS REPORTING
(Requires dealers to report illness related to pesticide exposure in some states.)

GROUNDWATER
(Requires dealers to reduce or eliminate pesticide and fertilizer application in some areas under the Clean Water Act, special USDA programs, and the 1990 Farm Bill.)

[a]FIFRA: Federal Insecticide, Fungicide and Rodenticide Act.
[b]SARA: Superfund Amendments and Reauthorization Act of 1986.
[c]OSHA: Occupational Safety and Health Administration.
[d]DOT: Department of Transportation.
[e]CWA: Clean Water Act; CERCLA: Comprehensive Environmental Response, Compensation and Liability Act; RCRA: Resource Conservation and Recovery Act.
Source: Statement of Chris Myrick, National AgriChemicals Retailers Association, in *Water Pollution Prevention and Control Act of 1991,* Hearings before the Subcommittee on Environmental Protection of the Committee on Environment and Public Works, U.S. Senate, 102nd Congress, 1st Session, Washington, DC, 1991, p. 623. Reprinted by permission.

The standard might instead be set at a level that accepts a "reasonably small" amount of damages, for example, e_0, the point where the marginal damage function begins to increase very rapidly. Here again, however, we would be setting the standard without regard to abatement costs. A different logic might suggest that in setting the standard, damages ought to be balanced with abatement costs. This would put us squarely within the logic used in discussing the notion of economic efficiency and, in this way, lead us to set the standard at e^*, the efficient emission level. Exhibit 11-2 discusses some of these issues in the context of the recent controversy about how the EPA sets ambient air quality standards.

EXHIBIT 11-2

THE SEARCH FOR AN INTELLIGIBLE PRINCIPLE:
SETTING AIR QUALITY STANDARDS UNDER THE CLEAN AIR ACT

By Heather L. Ross

When the core environmental statutes we rely on today were crafted in the 1970s, the fundamental answer to the question "What should we do to protect human health and the environment" was clear. It was "more." Now, after decades of effort, expenditure, and success in improving environmental quality, a new question has reached the forefront—"How do we know when we've done enough?" And to this we have no fundamental answer.

Most people agree that zero is too small a number to set as a target for pollution reduction. It is often physically unattainable given existing background levels, seldom medically necessary for good health, and potentially economically ruinous in terms of the clean-up costs required and productive activities forgone. But we have no generally agreed-upon basis for setting any other number.

Into this gap, in May 1999, stepped the U.S. Court of Appeals for the District of Columbia (the Appeals Court). In a novel ruling, it found that the U.S. Environmental Protection Agency's (EPA) setting of National Ambient Air Quality Standards for ozone and particulate matter under the Clean Air Act relied on a construction of that act "that effects an unconstitutional delegation of legislative power." . . . EPA appealed to the Supreme Court, which agreed in May of this year to accept the case for review.

Declaring unconstitutional EPA's approach to setting air quality standards could be compared to a lightning strike from a clear sky—very forceful and entirely unexpected. And lightning was about to strike twice. The Supreme Court, shortly after accepting EPA's appeal, also agreed to review the Appeals Court's longstanding opinion, first issued in

1980 and reiterated in this case, that costs cannot be considered in setting air quality standards. When it comes to the Clean Air Act, cost–benefit analysis ranks right up there with unconstitutionality for shock value.

The Clean Air Act requires that EPA set air quality standards "requisite to protect the public health" with "an adequate margin of safety," which are based on criteria that "accurately reflect the latest scientific knowledge." Students of the statutes say that when this language was originally written in 1970, the prevailing view of the relevant science was that thresholds existed below which concentrations of pollutants had no adverse effect on human populations. Scientists now say, and EPA concurs, that for many pollutants, including ozone and particulate matter, there is no identifiable non-zero threshold below which human health is unaffected.

EPA also says, and the Appeals Court concurs, that factors other than health may not be considered in setting air quality standards. But if health is improving all the way to zero concentration, it is hard to come up with an "intelligible principle" for setting an above-zero standard based on health factors alone. Were EPA to declare zero the only acceptable level "requisite to protect . . . with an adequate margin," it would be hard to say that it was acting outside its statutory authority.

Talk about a delegation of power! Operating within the prevailing interpretation of its delegated authority under the Clean Air Act, EPA has the discretion to virtually shut down the U.S. economy! While it has never come remotely close to doing so, EPA has long faced charges that it was going too far, or not far enough, down the lengthy road between unfet-

Note that there is, in effect, a certain amount of "balancing" going on when standards are set on the basis of an average over some time period. In this case short-run periods, when ambient quality is relatively low, are considered acceptable as long as they do not last "too" long. A judgment is being made, in effect, that it is not necessary to install enough abatement technology to hold

tered economic activity on the one hand and pristine environmental quality on the other. As EPA has moved down that road, the question of how much is enough has become more important, but the social consensus, political convergence, and legal underpinning for a suitable stopping point—neither too much nor too little—has made little headway.

Current case law, established in 1980 by this Appeals Court, rules out cost as a factor in setting air quality standards . . . a number of commenters have suggested alternative approaches, including:

1 Significant improvement. Does the new standard appreciably benefit public health, as opposed to making only a marginal improvement because health harms have already been reduced close to a minimum?

2 Knee-of-the-curve. As emissions standards are tightened, is there a point where the health gains from going further, what economists call marginal benefits, crop markedly?

3 De minimis rules. Are there terms in the statute—for example, "requisite," "protect," "health," "adequate," and "safety"—which can be defined through regulation to convey society's judgment that some risks are too small to worry about?

4 Health–health trade-offs. Are there harms from reducing emissions as well as gains—for example, increased risk of cancer from ozone reduction as well as better respiratory health—such that too much reduction results in poorer health overall rather than better health?

As they do not explicitly involve costs, all of these approaches are possible candidates for the intelligible principle that Judge Williams asked EPA to enunciate. But all of them rely implicitly on the concept of costs. If costs were zero, or were irrelevant, there

would be no reason to stop at the stopping points suggested by these rules. No benefit would be too small to go after. These rules reflect the world we actually live in, where costs are not zero, and are not irrelevant. In whatever units we express those costs, in dollars or health units or something else, this is a world where we decide what to do by weighing costs and benefits.

Here we come to the great irony of environmental regulation. While people can, and do, make up complicated decision rationales all the time, there is actually only one intelligible principle for determining how much is enough, and everybody knows it. What's more, they can state it quite simply: "Is it worth it?"

To answer that question, people weigh the factors, both positive and negative, that they think bear on it. In 1970, Congress was thinking about the positive health-related benefits of establishing air quality standards, and it wrote those into law. In its estimation, the value of those benefits made it worthwhile to take steps to improve air quality from its then-prevailing level. However, as Judge Williams has said, how far Congress thought such clean up could go and still be beneficial is not "apparent from the statute." Answering the "how far" question is thus a matter of interpretation, but two things are clear. The first is that Congress did not intend to harm society by passing the Clean Air Act. The second is that, in the real world, all benefits are net benefits, that is, benefits minus costs. The only way to uphold the first truth is to recognize the second. Neither judicial deference to EPA's interpretation, nor satisfaction with EPA's implementation thus far, nor concern about overturning established law and policy can undermine the basic soundness of that logic.

Source: Resources for the Future Issues Brief, RRF, Washington, October 2000.

ambient quality within the standard under all conceivable natural conditions. In other words, an implicit trade-off is being made between the damages that will result from the temporary deterioration of ambient quality below the standard and the high costs that would be necessary to keep ambient quality within the standard under all conditions.

Uniformity of Standards

A very practical problem in standard setting is whether it should be applied uniformly to all situations or varied according to circumstances. This can be illustrated by using the problem of the spatial uniformity of standards. The ambient air-quality standards in the United States, for example, are essentially national. The problem with this is that regions may differ greatly in terms of the factors affecting damage and abatement cost relationships, so that one set of standards, uniformly applied across these local variations, may have serious efficiency implications.

Consider Figure 11-2. It shows two marginal damage functions, one of which (labeled MD_u) is assumed to characterize an urban area, whereas the other (labeled MD_r) applies to a rural area. MD_u lies above MD_r because there are many more people living in the urban area, so the same quantity of emissions will affect the health of more people there than in the rural region. Assume that marginal abatement costs (labeled MAC) are the same in the two regions. Since the marginal damages are much higher in the urban than in the rural area, the efficient ambient level of benzene is much lower in the former than in the latter region; the efficient level is e_r in the rural region and e_u in the

FIGURE 11-2
Regional Variation in Efficiency Levels.

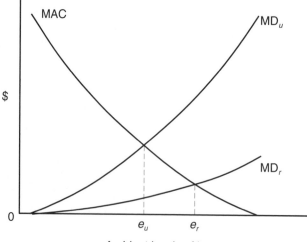

urban area. Thus, a single, uniform standard cannot be efficient simultaneously in the two regions. If it is set at e_u, it will be overly stringent for the rural area, and if it is set at e_r, it will not be tight enough for the urban region. The only way to avoid this would be to set different standards in the two areas. Of course, this confronts us with one of the great policy trade-offs: The more a policy is tailored so that it applies to different and heterogeneous situations, the more efficient it will be in terms of its impacts, but also the more costly it will be in terms of getting the information needed to set the diverse standards and enforcing them once they have been established.

The curves in Figure 11-2 could be used to represent other heterogeneous situations as well as differences in geographical regions. For example, MD_u might represent marginal damages in a particular region under some meteorological conditions, or in one season of the year, whereas MD_r could represent the marginal damage function for the same area but under different meteorological conditions or at a different time of year. Now a single standard, enforced throughout the year, cannot be efficient at all points in time; if it is efficient at one time, it will not be at the other.

Standards and the Equimarginal Principle

Having discussed the issue of setting the standard at the efficient level of emissions, it needs to be remembered that the efficient level itself is defined by the minimum marginal abatement cost function. This means that, where there are multiple emissions sources producing the same effluent,[3] the **equimarginal principle** must hold. The principle states that in order to get the greatest reductions in total emissions for a given total abatement cost, the different sources of emissions must be controlled in such a way that they have the same marginal abatement costs. This means that different sources of a pollutant would normally be controlled to different degrees, depending on the shape of the marginal abatement cost curve at each source. A major problem with standards is that there is almost always an overwhelming tendency for authorities to apply the same standards to all sources. It makes their regulatory lives much simpler, and it gives the impression of being fair to everyone because all are apparently being treated alike. But identical standards will be cost-effective only in the unlikely event that all polluters have the same marginal abatement costs.

Consider Figure 11-3, showing the marginal abatement cost relationships for two different sources, each emitting the same waste material. Note that the marginal abatement cost functions differ; for Firm A they increase much less rapidly as emissions are reduced than they do for Firm B. Why the difference? They may be producing different outputs with different technologies. One firm might be older than the other, and older technology may be less flexible, making it more costly to reduce emissions than at the plant with the newer equipment. One plant may be designed to use a different type of raw material input

---

[3]That is, in cases of "uniformly mixed" emissions.

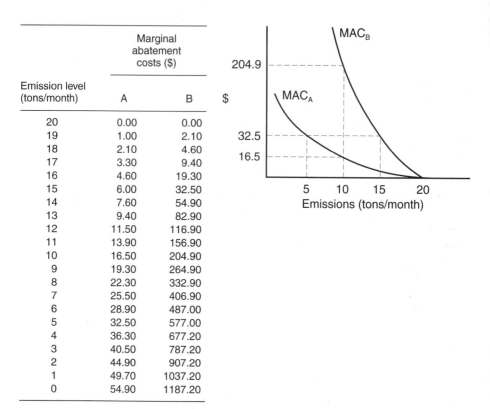

Emission level (tons/month)	Marginal abatement costs ($)		
	A	B	$
20	0.00	0.00	
19	1.00	2.10	
18	2.10	4.60	
17	3.30	9.40	
16	4.60	19.30	
15	6.00	32.50	
14	7.60	54.90	
13	9.40	82.90	
12	11.50	116.90	
11	13.90	156.90	
10	16.50	204.90	
9	19.30	264.90	
8	22.30	332.90	
7	25.50	406.90	
6	28.90	487.00	
5	32.50	577.00	
4	36.30	677.20	
3	40.50	787.20	
2	44.90	907.20	
1	49.70	1037.20	
0	54.90	1187.20	

FIGURE 11-3
Marginal Abatement Costs for Two Sources.

than the other. This, in fact, mirrors the situation in the real world. Normally one can expect considerable heterogeneity in abatement costs among groups of firms even though they are emitting the same type of residual.

Assume that emissions are currently uncontrolled. Thus, they are at 20 tons/month at each firm, or a total of 40 tons/month. Assume now that authorities wish to reduce total emissions to 20 tons/month by setting emission standards. How should the standards be set? The procedure that may seem most obvious—it certainly has to most environmental regulators—is to apply the same standard to each source; in this case, 10 tons/month. This has the superficial appearance of being fair, of treating these sources alike, because each would be reduced in the same proportion from their current levels. Of course, the problem is that the sources are economically *unlike* in that they have significantly different marginal abatement costs. By applying uniform standards to dissimilar sources we violate the equimarginal principle and end up getting far less total emission reduction than we might for the costs involved. At emission levels of 10 tons/month Source A has marginal abatement costs of $16.50/ton, whereas Source B has marginal abatement costs of $204.90/ton. Remembering that total costs are the sums of the marginal costs, we calculate total compliance costs as $75.90 for A and $684.40 for B, or a grand total of $760.30.

How much higher is this than the costs that would result from a program satisfying the equimarginal principle? A look at Figure 11-3 shows that we could achieve the total reduction we want and satisfy that principle by having Firm A cut its emissions to 5 tons/month and Firm B to 15 tons/month. At these levels their marginal abatement costs would be the same ($32.50/ton) and the total cost of the cutback would be $272.30 ($204.40 for A and $67.90 for B), a 64 percent reduction in total costs from the equal-standards case. To put it perhaps more dramatically, for the $760.30 cost of the equal-standards case, we could achieve a much larger reduction in total emissions by cutting back sources in accordance with the equimarginal principle. In fact, cutting Firm A back to zero emissions (total cost: $430.70) and Firm B back to emissions of 12 tons/month (total cost: $322.60) would give total compliance costs about the same as the equal-standards case but with substantially lower total emissions (12 tons/month rather than 20 tons/month).

To summarize: Standards are usually designed to be applied uniformly across emission sources. This practice is almost inherent in the basic philosophy of the standards approach, and to many people this strikes them as an equitable way to proceed. But if marginal abatement costs in the real world vary across sources, as they usually do, the equal-standards approach will produce less reduction in total emissions for the total compliance costs of the program than would be achieved with an approach that satisfied the equimarginal principle. The greater the differences in marginal abatement costs among sources, the worse will be the performance of the equal-standards approach. We will see in the chapters ahead that this difference can be very large indeed.

Could standards be set in accordance with the equimarginal principle? Unless the applicable law required some sort of **equiproportional cutback** there may be nothing to stop the authorities from setting different standards for the individual sources.[4] To get an overall reduction to 20 tons/month in the previous example, they could require Source A to reduce to 5 tons/month and Source B to cut back to 15 tons/month. The difficult part of this, however, is that to accomplish this the authorities must know what the marginal abatement costs are for the different sources. This point needs to be stressed. For almost any real-world pollution problem, there will normally be multiple sources. For a public agency to set individual standards in accordance with the equimarginal principle *it would have to know the marginal abatement cost relationship for each of these sources*. It would take a prodigious effort for any agency to get high-quality information on marginal abatement costs for many different sources, each perhaps producing different outputs using different production technology and methods. The primary source of data would have to be the polluters themselves, and there is no reason to believe they would willingly share this information. In fact, if they realize, as they certainly would, that the information would be used to establish individual source standards, they would have every incentive to provide the administering agency with data showing that

---

[4]An equiproportionate cutback is one that reduces each source by the same percentage of its original emissions. In the example in the text, the 10-ton cutback for each source was equal in absolute terms and also equiproportionate, as each source was assumed to be initially at an emission level of 20 tons per month.

their marginal abatement costs rise very steeply with emission reductions. Thus, there are real problems with authorities attempting to establish source-specific emission standards. *Nevertheless,* a considerable amount of this is done informally, through the interactions of local pollution-control authorities, charged with enforcing common standards, and local sources, each of whom is in somewhat different circumstances. We will come back to this later when we discuss issues of enforcement.

STANDARDS AND INCENTIVES

As discussed in Chapter 9, in evaluating any policy approach it is critical to look at how it affects the **incentives** of the firms subject to regulation. In the case of standards we can usefully divide the discussion into **short-run** and **long-run** incentive effects.

Short Run

In the short run, the question is whether the policy creates incentives for sources to reduce emissions to efficient levels and in cost-effective ways. The command-and-control approach based on standards is seriously deficient in this regard. A basic problem is that standards are all or nothing, either they are being met or they are not. If they are being met, there is no incentive to do better than the standard, even though the costs of further emission reductions may be quite modest. By the same token, the incentives are to meet the standards, even though the last few units of emission reduction may be much more costly than the damages reduced.

In addition, standards in practice tend to take decision flexibility away from polluters. This is certainly the case with technology standards, which dictate the procedures that polluters must follow, even though other procedures may be available to achieve the goal at lower cost. In fact, they may be motivated to avoid other techniques in order to protect themselves against charges of non-compliance, even if these other approaches show considerable promise. Better to play it safe, adopt the technology specified by the standard, and let the public control authorities themselves be saddled with the job of defending the correctness of the choice. Rather than leave firms free to use their own creativity in devising the technological means to achieve a goal, a technology standard instead places the burden on the public authority to make the correct technology decisions. Perverse effects of this type are a major reason why, in recent years, environmental policy has moved strongly toward incentive-based systems, as we shall discuss in the next chapter.

Long Run

In the long run, a desirable quality for pollution-control policies is that they produce strong incentives to search for the kinds of technical and managerial changes that will make it less costly to achieve reductions in emissions. How well do standards perform according to this criterion?

It is easy to deal with the case of technology standards. Here the incentives to find cheaper ways (considering all costs) of reducing emissions are effectively zero. If control authorities dictate in detail the specific technology and practices that polluters may legally use to reduce emissions, there are no rewards to finding better approaches.

Now consider emission standards. Figure 11-4 shows marginal abatement costs of a firm in two situations: MAC_1 refers to such costs before a given technological improvement; MAC_2 is the marginal abatement cost curve the firm could expect to have after investing some large amount of resources in an R&D effort to develop better treatment or recycling technology. Without any pollution-control program at all there is absolutely no incentive to spend the money on the R&D. But suppose the firm is now faced with having to meet emission standards of e_2 tons/year. With the original marginal abatement costs the total annual cost of compliance for this firm is $(a + b)$ per year. If the R&D program is successful, compliance costs would be only b/year. The difference, a/year, is the amount by which compliance costs would be reduced and represents, in fact, the incentive for engaging in the R&D effort. We will see in the next chapter that this is a weaker effect than is provided by economic-incentive types of programs. Nevertheless, it is an incentive, which is more than we could say for technology standards.

To understand fully the incentive effects of standards, one has to look closely at the details. Figure 11-4 depicts a standard applied to total emissions. Historically, most standards have been applied to emissions **per unit of input or output** of industrial firms. For electric utilities, an emission standard per unit of fuel burned is a standard per unit of input. There are important incentive implications of setting standards this way. Consider the following expression,

FIGURE 11-4
Cost Savings from Technological Change: The Case of Standards.

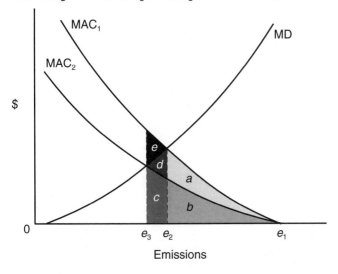

Emissions

showing how total emissions from an industrial operation are related to underlying performance factors:

$$
\frac{\text{Total}}{\text{emissions}} = \frac{\text{Total}}{\text{output}} \times \frac{\text{Inputs used per}}{\text{unit of output}} \times \frac{\text{Emissions per}}{\text{unit of input}}
$$

Suppose authorities apply an input standard to, for example, coal-burning power plants. The standard could be expressed in terms of maximum amounts of SO_2 emissions allowed per ton of coal burned. This is a standard applied to the last term of the equation, and so the power plant will presumably reduce its emissions per unit of input to the level of the standard. But there are two other ways of reducing total emissions, as depicted in the first two terms to the right of the equals sign. One is to reduce total output through, for example, encouraging consumers to conserve electricity. The other is to reduce the amount of coal needed per unit of electricity generated, in other words for the plant(s) to increase **fuel efficiency.** But the plants will have no incentive to reduce emissions in these last two ways because the standard has been written in terms only of the last factor in the expression.

In recent years regulators have been moving more toward **output-based standards,** that is, standards expressed in terms of allowable emissions per unit of output.[5] If you multiply together the last two terms of the expression, you get **emissions per unit of output.** If you now place a standard on this factor, note that polluters can reduce it in two ways: by reducing inputs per unit of output and by reducing emissions per unit of input. The incentives of the polluters have been broadened. So in the case of a power plant, an output-based standard would involve both incentives: to reduce emissions per unit of coal burned (perhaps by switching to low-sulfur coal) and to become more fuel efficient (perhaps by upgrading the boilers of the plant).

Political-Economic Aspects of Standards

The theory of standards is that they are established by regulatory authorities, then responded to by polluters. In fact, this process can lead to patterns of political give and take between the parties that substantially affects the outcome. Suppose that the authorities are making every effort to set the standard at something approaching the efficient level of emissions. In Figure 11-4, e_2 is their view of the efficient level before the technical change. But the new technology lowers the marginal abatement cost curve, and we know from Chapter 5 that this will reduce the efficient level of emissions. Suppose the authorities estimate that, given their view of marginal damages, the new technology shifts the efficient emission level to e_3 in Figure 11-4, and that they now change the standard to reflect this. Now the firm's compliance cost will be $(b + c)$ per year. The difference is now $(a - c)$. So the firm's cost savings will be substantially less than

---

[5]Automobile emission standards have always been in terms of output, for example, grams of pollutant per mile driven. We will talk about this in Chapter 15.

when the standard was unchanged; in fact, compliance costs may actually be higher than before the R&D program. In other words, the firm could suppose that because of the way regulators may tighten the standards, they would be worse off with the new technology than with the old methods. The standard-setting procedure in this case has completely undermined the incentive to produce new pollution-control technology. This is a case of what might be called **perverse incentives.** A perverse incentive is one that actually works against the objectives of the regulation. In this case, standard setting can work against long-run improvements in pollution-control technology.[6]

If emission standards create incentives for technological change, is it not desirable to establish very stringent standards so as to increase that incentive? This is another place where political considerations come into play. If, in Figure 11-4, the standard is set at e_3 right at the beginning, this would mean cost savings of $(a + d + e)$ with the new technology rather than just a as it would be with the standard set at e_2. This type of approach goes under the heading of **"technology forcing."** The principle of technology forcing is to set standards that are unrealistic with today's technology in the hope that it will motivate the pollution-control industry to invent ways of meeting the standard at reasonable cost. By "unrealistic with today's technology," we mean simply so costly that it would lead to widespread economic hardship.

But stricter standards also create another incentive: the incentive for polluters to seek relief from public authorities by delaying the date when they become applicable. In an open political system, firms may take some of the resources that might have gone for pollution-control R&D and devote them instead to influencing political authorities to delay the onset of strict standards. The stricter and more near-term the standards, the more of this activity there is likely to be. Thus, technology forcing is another one of those strategies where the effectiveness of moderate amounts does not imply that more will be even more effective.

It needs to be remembered also that to a significant extent new R&D for pollution control is carried out by a pollution-control industry rather than the polluting industries themselves. Thus, to draw conclusions about the incentives of pollution-control policy for technological change means to predict how these policies will contribute to the growth and productivity of the pollution-control industry. Technology standards are stultifying on these grounds because they substantially drain off the incentives for entrepreneurs in the pollution-control industry to develop new ideas. Emission standards are better in this respect, as we have seen. The evidence for this is the fact that representatives of the pollution-control industry usually take the side politically of stricter environmental standards; in fact, they see the fortunes of their industry tied almost directly to the degree of stringency in the emissions standards set by public authorities.

---

[6]There is another perverse incentive lurking in equiproportionate reductions. If polluters realize that they will be subject to an equiproportionate cutback in the future, it is better for them to increase their base now by increasing their emissions. When the cutback is imposed, they will be able to emit higher amounts than they would have had they not inflated their base.

THE ECONOMICS OF ENFORCEMENT

The typical pollution-control law incorporates standards calling for some degree of emissions reduction from current levels or the adoption of specified pollution-control technologies. In evaluating these policies ex ante, it is often assumed implicitly that the penalties written into the law will be sufficient to produce complete compliance, but this is in fact never the case. Pollution-control laws, like any others, require enforcement, and this takes resources. Because public enforcement agencies always work under limited budgets, it is not a forgone conclusion that enough resources will ever be devoted to enforcement to achieve acceptable levels of compliance. In fact, the notion of "acceptable" is itself subject to debate.

Similar to lots of other problems in economics and the allocation of resources, enforcement involves a trade-off, in this case between the resources used for this activity, which have opportunity costs, and benefits in the form of greater degrees of compliance. This trade-off is depicted conceptually in Figure 11-5. MD is the relevant marginal damage curve for this case, whereas MAC is the conventional marginal abatement cost function, showing the marginal costs required by sources to reduce emissions. The curves labeled C_1 and C_2 are curves that combine marginal abatement costs and **marginal enforcement costs.** Note that these begin at e_0, which is somewhat to the left of the uncontrolled emission rate e. When an emission standard is set at e^*, some degree of voluntary compliance may be expected to occur—in this case from e to e_0. But to get emission reductions beyond e_0 requires explicit enforcement resources. Curves C_1 and C_2 correspond to different technologies of enforcement. We have normally thought of e^* as the efficient level of emissions, but when enforcement costs are present this is no longer the case. With relatively high enforcement

FIGURE 11-5
The Economics of Enforcement.

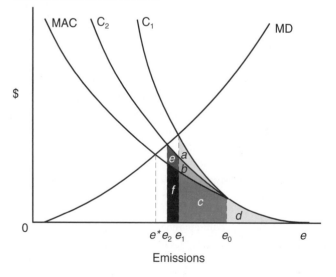

costs (curve C_1), the socially efficient rate of emissions is e_1. At this point total emission reduction costs are equal to $(a + b)$ of enforcement costs and $(c + d)$ of abatement costs. The technology of enforcement includes many things: the monitoring of equipment, the expertise of personnel, the operation of the court system, and so on. When changes occur in any of these factors, the effect is to shift the combined cost curve; in Figure 11-5 it shifts to C_2. This leads to a change in the efficient level of emissions to e_2; at this point, total emission reduction costs would be made up of $(e + b)$ of enforcement costs plus $(f + c + d)$ of abatement costs.

When enforcement costs are included in the analysis, it brings up the question of whether standards should be set, at least in part, with enforcement costs in mind. Stricter standards may involve larger enforcement costs because they require larger operating changes on the part of sources. Less strict standards may be achievable with fewer enforcement resources for the opposite reason. Public environmental agencies are usually faced with budget stringencies. In some cases, greater overall reductions in emissions may be obtained by using less strict standards that can be easily enforced than by stricter standards involving higher enforcement costs.

However, it needs to be stressed that the "strictness" of the standard is not the only factor affecting enforcement costs. A critical element in enforcement is the size of the sanction written into the laws. Most pollution-control statutes contain provisions on the size of the fine (or jail term) that may be levied against violators, if and when they are caught and found guilty. In many cases, fines have been set too low, lower than the abatement costs required to meet the standards.[7] In these situations firms can actually save money by dragging their feet on compliance. With low sanctions such as this, enforcement is therefore likely to be much more difficult and costly than if sanctions are higher. Sources faced with the possibility of having to pay substantially higher fines would presumably have a stronger incentive to come into compliance. We need to keep in mind, however, the paradoxical effect mentioned earlier: If laws attempt to set fines that are extremely high, this could actually dissuade local administrators and courts from pursuing violators vigorously, because of the economic dislocation that would result.

Stringency in enforcement budgets helps explain the attractiveness of public authorities to policies of standards. The essential characteristic of most standards approaches is that they do not require, nor automatically commit, a public agency to a costly enforcement process, especially a costly monitoring program. It is true that the more resources devoted to enforcement the more likely it is that the standards will be met, but standards programs can be put on the books while still leaving open the question of how much money and effort will be put into enforcement. Consider an emission standard that specifies an upper limit on the daily or hourly emission rate. To enforce this perfectly, one

[7]U.S. Environmental Protection Agency, *Consolidated Report on the National Pollution Discharge Elimination System Permit Enforcement Program* (EPA/IG E1H28-01-0200-0100154), Washington, DC, 1990.

would have to monitor the emission rate continuously. For a public agency charged with monitoring thousands of sources, this would be totally impossible. In the United States, this has led to a system of **self-monitoring,** where sources themselves keep the books on emissions flows over time. This permits the agencies to visit periodically to audit the records at each source. Agencies also can make random checks to measure emissions. The rate of auditing and random visits can be varied according to agency budgets. Needless to say, the rate of compliance would worsen as fewer resources are devoted to monitoring, but tolerable levels of compliance may still be attainable with fairly modest efforts at monitoring. A cynic, or a political realist, might conclude that standards approaches are favored because of the very fact that in the real world of tight public agency budgets, they permit partial or incomplete compliance.

One very common feature of environmental standards is that they are usually set and enforced by different groups of people. Standards often are set by national authorities; enforcement usually is done by local authorities. For example, the air quality standards established under the Clean Air Act are set at the federal level, but enforcement is mostly carried out by state-level agencies. This has a number of important implications. One is that standards often are set without much thought to costs of enforcement; it is more or less assumed that local authorities will find the necessary enforcement resources. Of course, this is not the case in practice. With limited enforcement budgets, local authorities may react to new programs by reducing resources devoted to other programs. Another implication is that, in practice, environmental policies incorporating standards end up having a lot more flexibility than might at first appear. Laws written at national levels are specific and apparently applicable everywhere. But at the local level, "where the rubber meets the road," as they say, it's a matter of local pollution-control authorities applying the law to local sources, and in this process there can be a great deal of informal give-and-take between the authorities and local plant managers, with participation by local environmental groups as well.

Technology standards allow the same flexibility in enforcement. Here we have to distinguish between **initial compliance** and **continued compliance.** Initial compliance is where a polluter charged with meeting a particular technology standard installs the appropriate equipment. To monitor initial compliance it is necessary to have inspectors visit the site, check to see that the equipment is installed, and make sure it will operate in accordance with the conditions of the standard. Having ascertained this, the administering agency can then give the firm the necessary operating permit, but this does not ensure that the equipment will continue to be operated in the future in accordance with the terms of the permit. It may deteriorate through normal use, it may not be maintained properly, future operating personnel may not be properly trained, and so on. Without some amount of monitoring, therefore, there is no assurance that the source will continue to be in compliance. But here again the administering agency has great flexibility in setting up a monitoring program. It can vary from very infrequent visits to randomly selected sites all the way up to permanent observers stationed at each source. While more monitoring will undoubtedly lead to higher rates of compliance, the standards approach essentially leaves open the question of the amount of time, effort, and money to be put into enforcement. It is clearly one of the advantages (some might say disadvantages) of the standards approach that it permits this flexibility in monitoring and enforcement.

SUMMARY

The most popular approach to environmental pollution control historically has been the setting of standards. This has been called the "command-and-control" approach because it consists of public authorities announcing certain limits on polluters, then enforcing these limits with appropriate enforcement institutions. We specified three primary types of standards: ambient, emission, and technology. Initial discussion centered on the level at which standards should be set and the regional uniformity of standards.

A leading problem with standard setting is the question of cost-effectiveness and the equimarginal principle. In most standards programs the administrative bias is to apply the same standards to all sources of a particular pollutant. But pollution control can be cost-effective only when marginal abatement costs are equalized across sources. When marginal abatement costs differ among sources, as they almost always do, uniform standards cannot be cost-effective. In practice, differences among sources in their marginal abatement costs often are recognized informally by local administrators in applying a uniform national standard.

We dealt at length also with the question of the long-run impact of standards through their effects on the incentives to look for better ways of reducing emissions. Technology standards completely undermine these incentives. Emission standards do create positive incentives for R&D in pollution control, although we will see that these are weaker than those of economic-incentive types of pollution-control policies, the subject of the next two chapters. Finally, we discussed the all-important question of enforcement.

QUESTIONS FOR FURTHER DISCUSSION

1 Environmental protection programs are frequently designed to require all polluters to cut back emissions by a certain percentage. What are the perverse incentives built into this type of program?

2 If emission standards are ruled out because of, for example, the impossibility of measuring emissions (as in nonpoint-source emissions), what alternative types of standards might be used instead?

3 In Figure 11-2, show the social cost of setting a uniform national standard, applicable to both rural and urban areas (to do this, you can assume that the national standard is set at either e_u or e_r).

4 Consider the example of Figure 11-3. Suppose we define as "fair" a cutback in which the two sources have the same total costs. Would an equiproportionate reduction be fair in this sense? A reduction meeting the equimarginal principle? Is this a reasonable definition of "fair"?

5 It is sometimes suggested that the most equitable way to resolve the trade and environment problem would be for all countries to adopt the same emission standards. What are the pros and cons of this from an economic standpoint?

WEBSITES

For a good summary of all the standards that are included in U.S. environmental laws, see the "Summaries of Environmental Laws Administered by the EPA," put together by the Congressional Research Service, at **www.cnie.org/nle/leg-8/**; a good compendium of material on enforcement of environmental regulations is that of the Environmental Law Net, **www.environmentallawnet.com** (see the section Enforcement & Litigation); see also the links listed on the website of this book, **www.mhhe.com/economics/field3**.

SELECTED READINGS

Crandall, Robert W.: *Controlling Industrial Pollution*, The Brookings Institution, Washington, DC, 1983.

Hahn, Robert W. (ed.): *Risks, Costs and Lives Saved: Getting Better Results from Regulations*, Oxford University Press, NY, 1996.

Hawkins, Keith: *Environment and Enforcement*, Clarendon Press, Oxford, England, 1984.

Luken, Ralph A., and L. Clark: "How Efficient are National Environmental Standards? A Benefit-Cost Analysis of the United States Experience," *Environmental and Resource Economics*, Vol. 1, 1991, pp. 385–414.

McKean, Roland N.: "Enforcement Costs in Environmental and Safety Regulation," *Policy Analysis*, 6(3), Summer 1980, pp. 269–289.

Richardson, Genevra, with Anthony Orgus and Paul Burrows: *Policing Pollution*, Oxford University Press, Oxford, England, 1983.

Russell, Clifford S.: "Monitoring and Enforcement," in Paul Portney (ed.), *Public Policies for Environmental Protection*, Resources for the Future, Washington, DC, 1990, pp. 243–274.

Russell, Clifford S., Winston Harrington, and William J. Vaughan: *Enforcing Pollution Control Laws*, Resources for the Future, Washington, DC, 1986.

Viscusi, W. Kip: *Risks by Choice: Regulating Health and Safety in the Workplace*, Harvard University Press, Cambridge, MA, 1983.

Wallace, David: *Environmental Policy and Industrial Innovation*, Earthscan Publications, London, 1995.

CHAPTER 12

INCENTIVE-BASED STRATEGIES: EMISSION CHARGES AND SUBSIDIES

To build a house it is usually necessary to buy some building materials; nobody is likely to supply them for free. Architects and carpenters will have to be hired; they won't ordinarily work without compensation. In other words, to use the services of these inputs, we have to pay for them. We are used to doing this because they are bought and sold in well-developed markets. The fact that these inputs are costly gives users an incentive to use them as sparingly and efficiently as possible. The economic incentive approach to environmental policy works in much the same way. Until recently people have been able to use the waste-disposal services of the environment virtually without cost, so there has been little incentive for them to think about the environmental consequences of their actions and to economize on the use of these environmental resources. The incentive approach seeks to change this situation.

There are basically two types of incentive policies: (1) **charges and subsidies** and (2) **transferable discharge permits.** Both require centralized policy initiative to get started but rely on flexible firm responses to attain efficient pollution control. In the first, firms are given latitude to respond however they wish to what is essentially a new price for using the services of the environment. The second is designed to work more or less automatically through the interactions among polluters themselves or between polluters and other interested parties. In recent years U.S. environmental laws have begun to incorporate many types of transferable discharge permit systems. In other countries, particularly those of Europe, greater reliance is being put on programs of emission charges. Exhibit 12-1 discusses emission charges for water pollution in the Netherlands. In this chapter we examine the economics of emission charges and subsidies. In the next chapter we will consider the technique of transferable discharge permits.

EXHIBIT 12-1

EMISSION CHARGES IN THE NETHERLANDS

Among the OECD countries, the Netherlands has had the most extensive and successful experience with the charges for water pollution. By 1969, organic water pollution had mounted to the point where many Dutch waterways were biologically dead. Together industry and households were dumping 40 million populations-equivalents, or PE—the average organic pollution caused by one person in a normal household—into Dutch sewers and waterways every year. Heavy-metals emissions from industry had also increased to dangerous levels.

The Dutch responded with the Pollution of Surface Waters Act (PSWA) in 1970, which prohibited unlicensed discharges into surface waters and imposed charges on polluting emissions. Industry had to pay for emissions of heavy metals, and all sectors of society were assessed for estimated organic discharges: urban households, 3 PE; farm households, 6 PE; small enterprises, 3 PE; medium enterprises, PE estimated from engineering models; and large enterprises, directly measured PE. Authorities granted rebates to small and medium enterprises if they could prove that their actual emissions were lower than official estimates.

The Dutch system began as a command-and-control exercise, in which pollution charges were simply intended to finance construction of waste treatment facilities mandated by the PSWA. However, pollution-reduction efforts required construction of high-cost facilities in some areas, and charges escalated as construction costs mounted. At some point, many Dutch factory managers found themselves confronted with charges equal to marginal abatement costs at very high levels of cleanup. A careful statistical analysis by Bressers (1988) has shown that these high charges were much more important than the permitting process in promoting reductions in emissions. By 1990, the system had halved both heavy-metals emissions and total organic discharges into waterways and sewers, and waste treatment facilities had expanded sufficiently to reduce organic pollution of waterways to about 6 million PE. Industry displayed the strongest response to pollution charges from 1969 to 1990, reducing its annual organic emissions from 33.0 to 8.8 million PE (Jansen, 1991).

Source: David Wheeler, *Greening Industry: New Roles for Communities, Markets, and Governments,* Oxford University Press for the World Book, Washington, DC, 2000, p. 38 (cited references are H. Bressers, "The Impact of Effluent Charges: A Dutch Success Story," *Policy Studies Review,* 7(3), 1988, pp. 500–518; and H. Jansen, "West European Experiences with Environmental Funds," Institute for Environmental Studies, The Hague, The Netherlands, January 1991).

Environmental economists have long favored the idea of incorporating incentive-based policies more thoroughly into environmental policies. These can serve to put more teeth into environmental policies in many cases and substantially improve the cost-effectiveness of these policies. But keep in mind something said before: No single type of policy is likely to be the best in all circumstances. Incentive-based policies are no exception. They have strengths and they have weaknesses. The strengths are sufficiently strong to encourage greater reliance on them in many circumstances. But there are many types of environmental problems where they may not be as useful as other approaches.

EMISSION CHARGES

The most straightforward **incentive-based** approach to controlling emissions of a particular residual is to have a public agency offer a financial incentive to change those emissions. This can be done in two ways: by charging for each unit of emissions or by giving a subsidy for each unit of emissions that the source cuts back.

We deal first with **emission charges,** sometimes also called **"emission taxes."** In a charge system polluters are told: "You may discharge any amount of residuals you wish, but your emissions will be measured and you will be required to pay a certain charge for every unit (e.g., ton) of effluent you discharge." For example, one of the first emission charges proposed in the United States was in 1970, when President Nixon recommended a tax of 15 cents per pound on sulfur emissions from large power plants. It was never adopted. When an emission charge is put into effect, firms responsible for emissions must essentially pay for the services of the environment—transportation, dilution, chemical decomposition, and so on—just as they must pay for all other inputs used in their operations. And just as they have always had an incentive to conserve on scarce labor and other conventional production inputs, they will now have an incentive to conserve on their use of environmental services. How do they do this? Any way they wish (within reason). This may sound flippant but in fact it represents the main advantage of this technique. By leaving polluters free to determine how best to reduce emissions, this type of policy attempts to harness their own energy and creativity and their desire to minimize costs, to find the least-cost way of reducing emissions. It could be any combination of treatment, internal process changes, changes in inputs, recycling, shifts to less polluting outputs, and so on. The essence of the charge approach is to provide an incentive for the polluters themselves to find the best way to reduce emissions, rather than having a central authority determine how it should be done.

The Basic Economics

The essential mechanics of an emission charge are depicted in Figure 12-1. The numbers refer to a single source of a particular pollutant. The top panel shows the analysis numerically, while the bottom shows essentially the same information graphically. The tax has been set at $120/ton/month. The second column in the top panel shows the firm's marginal abatement costs and the third column shows total abatement costs. The last two columns show the total monthly tax bill the firm would pay at different emission levels, and the total cost, consisting of the sum of abatement costs and the tax bill. We see that the minimum total cost of $850 occurs at an emission rate of 4 tons/month. Let's pursue the logic of this by considering marginal abatement costs. Suppose the firm is initially emitting 10 tons/month; if it were to cut emissions to 9 tons, it would cost $15 in abatement costs, but it would save $120 in total charges, clearly a good move. Following this logic, it could improve its bottom line by continuing to reduce

Emissions (tons/month)	Marginal abatement cost	Total abatement cost	Total tax bill at $120/ton	Total costs
10	0	0	1,200	1,200
9	15	15	1,080	1,095
8	30	45	960	1,005
7	50	95	840	935
6	70	165	720	885
5	90	255	600	855
4	115	370	480	850
3	135	505	360	865
2	175	680	240	920
1	230	910	120	1,030
0	290	1,200	0	1,200

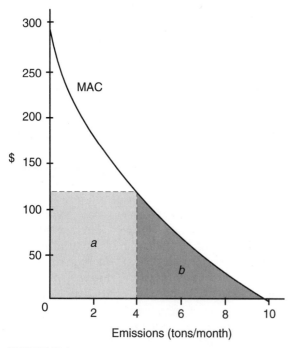

FIGURE 12-1
An Emissions Charge.

emissions as long as the tax rate is above marginal abatement costs. The rule for the firm to follow is, thus: Reduce emissions until marginal abatement costs are equal to the charge on emissions. This is shown diagrammatically in the bottom part of Figure 12-1. With a continuous marginal abatement cost function, it's possible to talk about fractions of tons of emissions, something we could not do in the upper panel. So the graph is drawn to agree with the integer values above; that is, the charge of $120 leads the firm to reduce emissions to exactly 4 tons/month.

After the firm has reduced its emissions to 4 tons/month, its total (monthly) tax bill will be $480. Its monthly abatement costs will be $370. Graphically, total abatement costs correspond to the area under the marginal abatement cost function, labeled *b* in the figure. The total tax bill is equal to emissions times the tax rate, or the rectangle labeled *a*. Under a charge system of this type, a firm's total cost equals its abatement costs plus the tax payments to the taxing authority.

Why wouldn't the firm simply disregard the charge, continue to pollute as it has been doing, and just pass the charge on to consumers in the form of higher prices? If the firm stayed at 10 tons of emissions, its total outlay would be $1,200/month, consisting entirely of tax payment. This is much higher than the $850 it can achieve by cutting back to 4 tons/month. The assumption in an emissions charge program is that **competitive pressures** will lead firms to do whatever they can to minimize their costs. Thus, when there is competition in the industry subject to the emission tax, it will lead firms to reduce emissions in response to the tax. By the same token, however, we must recognize that if competition is weak, firms may not respond in this way. Electric power plants, for example, are usually operated by regulated monopolies subject to oversight by public utility commissions. They may not respond to charges on SO_2 emissions in the same way as firms that operate in more competitive economic climates.

For competitive firms, the amount of the response will depend on several factors. The higher the charge, the greater the reduction, and vice versa. In the example of Figure 12-1, a tax of $50 would have led the source to reduce emissions only to 7 tons/month, whereas one of $180 would have produced a cutback to 2 tons/month, and so on. Also, the steeper the marginal abatement cost function, the less emissions will be reduced in response to a tax. We will come back to this later.

Compare the charge approach with an emission standard. With the tax the firm's total outlay is $850. Suppose that, instead, the authorities had relied on an emission standard to get the firm to reduce emissions to 4 tons/month. In that case the firm's total outlay would be only the $370 of abatement costs. Thus, the charge system ends up costing the firm more than the standards approach. With a standard the firm has the same total abatement costs as in the charge system, but it is still essentially getting the services of the environment free, whereas with a charge system it has to pay for those services. But while polluting firms would thus prefer standards to emission charges, there are good reasons, as we shall see, why society would often prefer charges over standards.

The Level of the Charge

In competitive situations, higher charges will bring about greater reductions in emissions, but just how high should the charge be set? If we know the marginal damage function, the answer presumably would be to set the charge so as to produce the efficient level of emissions, as in Figure 12-2. At a charge rate of t^*, emissions are e^*, and marginal damages equal marginal abatement costs. The firm's total costs of emission control are divided into two types: total abatement

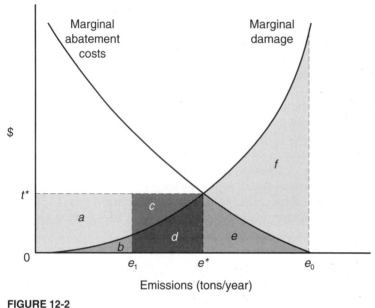

FIGURE 12-2
An Efficient Emission Charge.

costs (compliance costs) of e and total tax payments of $(a + b + c + d)$. The former are the costs of whatever techniques the firm has chosen to reduce emissions from e_0 to e^*, whereas the latter are payments to the control agency covering the charge on the remaining emissions. From the standpoint of the firm, of course, these are both real costs that will have to be covered out of revenues. From the standpoint of *society*, however, the tax payments are different from the abatement costs. Whereas the latter involve real resources and therefore real social costs, the emission charges are actually **transfer payments,** payments made by the firms (ultimately by people who buy the firms' output) to the public sector and eventually to those in society who are benefited by the resulting public expenditures. When a firm considers its costs, it will include both abatement costs and tax payments; when considering the social costs of a tax program, it is appropriate to exclude transfer payments.

The reduction of emissions from e_0 to e^* has eliminated damages of $(e + f)$. Remaining damages are $(b + d)$, an amount less than the firm pays in taxes. This underscores the idea that the emission charge is based on the right to use environmental resources, not on the notion of compensation. But a "flat tax" like this (one tax rate for all emissions) has been criticized because it would often lead to situations where the total tax payments of firms would substantially exceed remaining damages. A way around this is to institute a **two-part emission charge.** We allow some initial quantity of emission to go untaxed, applying the charge only to emissions in excess of this threshold. For example, in Figure 12-2 we might allow the firm e_1 units of emissions free of tax and apply the tax rate of t^* to anything over this. In this way the firm would still have the incentive to reduce emissions to e^*, but its total tax payments would be only $(c + d)$. Total abatement costs, and total damages caused by the e^* units of emissions, would still be the same.

How might the charge be set if regulators did not know the marginal damage function? Emissions are connected to ambient quality; the lower the emissions the lower the ambient concentration of the pollutant, in general. So one strategy might be to set a tax and then watch carefully to see what this did in terms of improving ambient quality levels. We would have to wait long enough to give firms time to respond to the tax. If ambient quality did not improve as much as desired, increase the charge; if ambient quality improved more than was thought appropriate, lower the charge. This is a successive approximation process of finding the correct long-run emissions charge. It is not at all clear whether this approach would be practicable in the real world. In responding to a charge, polluters would invest in a variety of pollution-control devices and practices, many of which would have relatively high up-front costs. This investment process could be substantially upset if, shortly afterward, the authorities shift to a new tax rate. Any agency trying to use this method to find the efficient charge rate would undoubtedly find itself embroiled in a brisk political battle. Rather than planning to make successive adjustments in the tax rate, there would be a strong incentive for policymakers to determine the correct rate at the beginning. This would put a premium on prior study to get some idea of the shapes of the aggregate abatement and damage cost curves.

Emission Charges and Cost-Effectiveness

Perhaps the strongest case for a policy of effluent charges is to be made on grounds of their effects in controlling multiple sources of emissions in a way that satisfies the **equimarginal principle.** If the same tax rate is applied to different sources with different marginal abatement cost functions, and each source reduces its emissions until its marginal abatement costs equal the tax, then marginal abatement costs will automatically be equalized across all the sources.

This is depicted in Figure 12-3.[1] We assume here that there are two sources of a particular type of emission, labeled Source A and Source B. Also assume that these emissions, after they leave the respective sources, are uniformly mixed together, so that the emissions of the two plants are equally damaging in the downstream, or downwind, impact area. The marginal abatement costs for the two sources are the same as those we used in the last chapter. They are shown in graphical form at the bottom of Figure 12-3. The marginal abatement costs of Source A increase much less rapidly with reductions in emissions than do those of Source B. In the real world, differences like this are normally related to the fact that the firms are using different production technologies. They may be producing different outputs (e.g., a pulp mill and a food-canning firm), or they may be plants in the same industry but using different production techniques (e.g., coal-fired and oil-fired electric power plants).

[1]We have seen a graph like this several times before, for example, in Figures 11-3 and 5-5.

Emission level (tons/month)	Marginal abatement costs	
	Source A	Source B
20	0.0	0.0
19	1.0	2.1
18	2.1	4.6
17	3.3	9.4
16	4.6	19.3
15	6.0	32.5
14	7.6	54.9
13	9.4	82.9
12	11.5	116.9
11	13.9	156.9
10	16.5	204.9
9	19.3	264.9
8	22.3	332.9
7	25.5	406.9
6	28.9	487.0
5	32.5	577.0
4	36.3	677.2
3	40.5	787.2
2	44.9	907.2
1	49.7	1,037.2
0	54.9	1,187.2

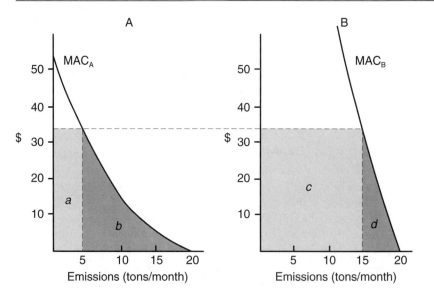

FIGURE 12-3
Emission Charges and the Equimarginal Rule.

According to the graphs, the production technology used by Source B makes emission reduction more costly than it is at Source A. If we impose an effluent charge of $33/ton on each source, the operators of Source A will reduce their emissions to 5 tons/month; those at Source B will cut back to 15 tons/month (dealing only with integer values). After these reductions, the two sources will have the same marginal abatement costs. The total reduction has been 20 tons per month, which the effluent charge has automatically distributed between the two firms in accordance with the equimarginal principle.

Note very carefully that the emission tax has led Source A to reduce its emissions by 75 percent, whereas Source B has reduced its emissions by only 25 percent. The emissions tax leads to larger proportionate emission reductions from firms with lower marginal abatement costs. Conversely, firms having steeper marginal abatement costs will reduce emissions less, in proportionate terms. Suppose that instead of the charge the authorities had instituted a **proportionate** cutback on the grounds that "everybody should be treated alike"; therefore, they require each source to reduce emissions by 50 percent. Our two sources in Figure 12-3 both reduce emissions to 10 tons/month. At this point their marginal abatement costs would be different. Furthermore, we can calculate total abatement costs by remembering that total cost is the sum of marginal costs. Thus, for example, for Source A the total costs of 10 tons of emissions would be $(1.0 + 2.1 + . . . + 16.5 = 75.9)$.

The following tabulation compares the compliance costs of the equiproportionate reduction and the effluent charge.

	Total compliance costs ($/month)	
	Equiproportionate reduction	Effluent charge
Source A	75.9	204.4
Source B	684.4	67.9
Total	760.3	272.3

Note how much the totals differ. The total compliance cost of an equiproportionate cutback is about 2.8 times the total cost of an emission charge. The simple reason is that the equiproportionate cutback violates the equimarginal principle; it requires the same proportionate cutback regardless of the height and shape of a firm's marginal abatement costs. The difference in total costs between these two approaches is quite large with these illustrative numbers. We will see in later chapters that in the real world of pollution control these differences are often much larger.

The higher the tax rate, the more emissions will be reduced. In fact, if the tax rate were increased to something over $55/ton, Firm A would stop emitting this residual entirely. The marginal abatement cost function for Firm B increases so rapidly, however, that an extremely high charge (more than $1,187/ton) would be required to get this source to reduce emissions to zero. A single effluent charge, when applied to several firms, will induce a greater reduction by firms whose marginal abatement costs increase less rapidly with emission reductions than from firms whose marginal abatement costs increase more rapidly. Because the firms are paying the same tax rate, they will have different total abatement costs and different tax bills. In Figure 12-3 the total abatement costs are equal to area *b* for Source A and area *d* for Source B. On the other hand, the monthly tax bill sent to Source A would be only *a*, compared to a bill of *c* sent to Source B. Thus, the less steeply the marginal abatement cost of a firm increases, the larger that firm's emission reduction will be and the smaller its tax bill.

It needs to be emphasized that the efficiency results of the emission charge approach (i.e., that it satisfies the equimarginal principle) are achievable *even though the administering agency knows nothing about the marginal abatement costs of any of the sources.* This is in clear contrast with the standards approach, where the public agency has to know exactly what these marginal abatement costs are for each firm in order to have a fully efficient program. In a charge approach the only requirement is that firms pay the same tax and that they are cost minimizers. After each one has adjusted its emissions in accordance with its marginal abatement costs (which we can expect them to know themselves), they will all be emitting at the appropriate rates to satisfy the equimarginal principle.

Emission Taxes and Nonuniform Emissions

So far the discussion has proceeded under the assumption that the emissions of all sources are uniformly mixed together; that is, the emissions from one source have the same marginal impact on ambient quality levels as those from other sources. In the real world this is not always the case. Very often the situation is something like, although of course more complicated than, that depicted in Figure 12-4. Here there are two sources. Source A, however, is about twice as far away from the center of population as Source B. This means that emissions from Source A do not produce as much damage in the urban area as emissions from Source B. If the two sources are emitting some material into a river that

FIGURE 12-4
Nonuniform Emissions.

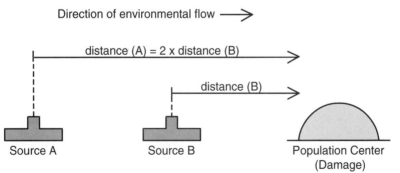

Direction of environmental flow ⟶

distance (A) = 2 x distance (B)

distance (B)

Source A   Source B   Population Center
                                    (Damage)

flows toward the city, the emissions of Source A have a longer time in the water to be broken down and rendered less harmful than do the emissions from Source B. Or if it is an air pollution problem, Source A is much farther upwind than Source B, so there is more time for its emissions to be spread out and diluted than there is for the emissions from Source B. There could be other reasons than location differences for the different impacts; for example, they may emit residuals at different times of the year when wind patterns are different. Studying the location problem will allow us to examine the general problem of nonuniform emissions.

In this case a single emission charge applied to both sources would not be fully efficient. A single charge addresses only the problem of differences in marginal abatement costs, not differences in damages caused by the emissions from different sources. In Figure 12-4, a one-unit reduction in emissions from Plant B would improve environmental quality (reduce damages) in the urban area more than a one-unit reduction in emissions from Plant A, and this fact must be taken into account in setting emission charge rates. Suppose emission reductions at Source B are twice as effective at reducing damages as reductions in emissions at Source A. This means, in effect, that the effluent tax paid by Source B must be twice as high as the effluent charge paid by Source A.[2] Thus, after adjusting to these tax levels the marginal abatement cost of Source B would be twice the marginal abatement cost of Source A. But the damage reduction *per dollar spent in reducing emissions* would be equalized across the two sources.

The logic of the preceding discussion would seem to imply the conclusion that in these cases we would have to charge different emission charges to each source. To do this we would have to know the relative importance of the emissions from each source in affecting ambient quality. But finding out exactly what these relative differences are would be a difficult job, as would the administrative task of charging a different tax rate to each firm. The best response here might be to institute what is called a **zoned emission charge.** Here the administering agency would divide a territory into separate zones; the actual number of zones would depend on the circumstances of the case. Within each zone the agency would charge the same emission charge to all sources, whereas it would charge different charges in different zones.

Naturally the zones would be identified by grouping together sources whose emissions have similar effects on ambient quality levels. Figure 12-5, for example, shows the schematic of a river with a dozen different sources of emissions and one urban area where water quality is measured and water quality targets are established. The 10 upstream sources are strung along the

---

[2]The technical concept here is called a "transfer coefficient." A transfer coefficient is a number that tells how the emissions from any particular source affect ambient quality at some other point. In the example above, suppose 1 ton of SO_2 emitted by B would increase SO_2 concentration over the urban area by 0.1 ppm. Then a ton emitted from Source A would increase the ambient concentration by 0.05 (assuming an effect that is strictly proportional to distance). If the transfer coefficient for Source B is 1, that for Source A is 0.5, so the tax at A has to be half the tax at B.

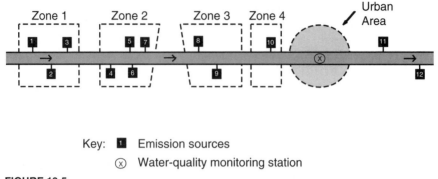

Key: ■ Emission sources
      ⊗ Water-quality monitoring station

FIGURE 12-5
Zoned Emissions Charge.

river at increasing distances from the urban area. Thus, each has a different impact on measured water quality at the monitoring station, and a fully cost-effective program of emissions reductions would have to account for this fact *in addition to* their different marginal abatement costs. But it would be administratively very costly to apply a different emissions charge to each source. We might, in this case, fall back on a zoned emission charge.

We first define different zones along the river, then apply the same tax to all sources within the same zone, but different taxes to sources in different zones. Each zone would contain sources whose emissions have roughly the same impact on measured water quality. In Figure 12-5, for example, four upstream zones along the river are sketched out. The three sources in Zone 1 would pay the same charge, as would the four sources in Zone 2, and so on. Sources 11 and 12 are downstream from the urban area and may not get taxed at all. Of course, this is a simplified diagram to show the basic idea; in the real world, there would also very likely be downstream damages. By using a zone system we can achieve a certain amount of administrative simplification while recognizing differences in the locations of different groups of sources.

Emissions Taxes and Materials Balance

It's important at this point to remind ourselves about the fundamental **materials balance** aspects of residuals. Given a certain quantity of residuals, if the flow going into one environmental medium is reduced, the flow going to others must increase. If we forget this, we might run into situations in which, for example, firms respond to a tax on a certain waterborne residual by adopting a relatively cheap (from their standpoint) method of incineration that substantially increases airborne emissions. This implies that if charges are put on residuals going into one environmental medium, there needs to be some means of coordinating this with discharges of these emissions to other media. This could be done in several ways. One way might be to put the same tax on a residual no matter into which medium it was discharged. But if the marginal damages of the residual were different across media, we would want to charge different taxes for different media if we had enough information to determine what they should be. If the administering agency couldn't do this, it might fall back on simply proscribing certain courses of action; it might, for example, simply rule out any increases in airborne emissions from sources subject to a tax on water-borne emissions of the same residual. This should alert us to the problems of coordination implied by the materials-balance principle.

Emissions Charges and Uncertainty

Pollution-control policies have to be carried out in a world of **uncertainty.** Administrating agencies often do not know exactly what emissions are being produced by each source nor exactly what the human and ecosystem impacts are. Another source of uncertainty is the shape of the marginal abatement cost curve of the sources subject to control; these may be known reasonably well by the polluters themselves, but administrators usually will be very unsure of how high they are, how steep they are, how much they differ from source to source, and so on. It is one of the advantages of emissions charges that they can bring about cost-effective results even within that state of uncertainty.

Nevertheless, when administrators set taxes at certain levels, they normally will be uncertain about how much emission reduction will ensue, for that depends on how sources respond to the tax. This is one of the drawbacks of emission charges. It may be difficult to predict accurately how much total emissions will decrease because exact knowledge of marginal abatement costs is often lacking. Observe Figure 12-6. It shows two different marginal abatement cost functions, a steep one (MAC_1) and one that is much less steep (MAC_2). Consider MAC_1. If the charge were set at the relatively high rate of t_h, this source would reduce emissions to e_1, whereas if it were set at the low rate of t_l, it would adjust emissions to e_2. These two emission rates are relatively close together. In other words, whether the charge is high or low, the emissions rate

FIGURE 12-6
Emission Charges, Uncertainty, and Tax Revenues

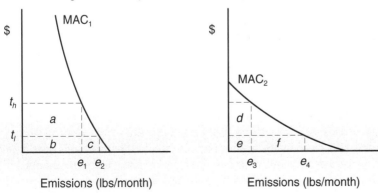

Emissions (lbs/month)

of this source would not vary much; we could count on having an emissions rate of something in the vicinity of e_1 and e_2.

But for the firm with the less steep marginal abatement costs (MAC_2) things are much more unstable. If the charge were set low, it would change emissions to e_4, whereas with a high charge emissions would go all the way down to e_3. In other words, for given changes in the tax rate, this firm would respond with much larger changes in emission rates than would the source with the steeper MAC curve.

The upshot of this discussion is that if most firms in a particular pollution problem have relatively flat MAC functions, regulators may have trouble finding the charge rate that will give us just the amount of reduction in total emissions we want. Since they don't know exactly where the MAC functions really are, they don't know exactly how high to set the tax. If they set it a little high or a little low, these firms will respond with large changes in their emissions. This is one of the main reasons administrators opt for standards: They seem to offer a definite control on quantities of emissions produced. In the next chapter, we will discuss an incentive approach that addresses this problem.

Emission Charges and Tax Revenues

Another important aspect of emission charges is that they lead to **tax revenues** accruing to the government (see Example 12-1). Carrying this line of thought further has suggested to many people that society could benefit by replacing certain existing taxes with emission taxes. Many countries tax employment, for example. When firms hire workers, they must pay employment taxes to cover such things as the public costs of unemployment insurance and social security payments. But employment taxes lead to reduced levels of employment because, in effect, they make hiring workers more expensive. A government, therefore, might reduce its employment taxes and increase emission taxes in such a way as to keep its total tax revenue the same. This action has come to be known as the **double-dividend hypothesis.** This refers to the fact that society would gain both from the emissions taxes (through reduced emission damage) and from reduced employment tax (through increased employment).

But predicting the revenue impacts of emission taxes may be difficult. Suppose, in Figure 12-6, an emission tax was increased from t_l to t_h. If the aggregate marginal abatement costs of the affected firm is MAC_1, total tax revenue will increase from $(b + c)$ to $(a + b)$. But if the marginal abatement cost is actually MAC_2, raising the emission tax will cause tax revenues to decrease from $(e + f)$ to $(d + e)$. This is because in the case of MAC_2 the tax increase leads to a large decrease in emissions, while in the case of MAC_1 it does not. Thus if the tax authorities don't know much about the shape and location of the relevant marginal abatement, they may be in for some major surprises in terms of changes in tax revenues.

EXAMPLE 12-1

CHARGES FOR POLLUTION CONTROL VERSUS CHARGES FOR RAISING REVENUE

Because emission charges generate monetary tax receipts by government, they often have been thought of as a useful way of raising money to cover costs rather than as a way to motivate reductions in emissions. In recent years there has been some small movement toward emission charges in the United States. The Clean Air Act of 1990 requires states to use permit fees (in Chapter 14 we will study this program and the permit system it incorporates) to recover the administrative costs of running the permit program. Permit fees are simply the charges polluters have to pay in order to procure their operating permits from the environmental regulatory authorities. Some states have set permit fees that vary by quantity of emissions; thus the fees effectively become emission charges. Maine, for example, has installed a three-part emission fee for sulfur

oxides, NO_x, volatile organic compounds, and particulate matter. The current values are $5.28 per ton for up to 1,000 tons per year, $10.57 per ton for total annual emissions between 1,000 tons and 4,000 tons, and $15.85 per ton for sources emitting more than 4,000 tons per year. New Mexico charges $10 per ton for these types of pollutants, but $150 per ton for emissions of toxic pollutants.

Emission permit charges like these, and similar ones for waterborne discharges in many states, may sound rather substantial, but probably are much more effective at raising revenues than at producing reductions in emissions. We are probably in a situation as depicted in the accompanying graphic.

The initial emission level is e_1, and the authorities set a maximum target of e^* for the firm. An emission tax rate of t^* would provide the incentive needed to bring about a reduction of emissions to e^*. But this would entail a substantial tax obligation for the firm. Instead, the authorities establish a charge at a rather low level, for example, t_1. This has very modest incentive effects; it leads the firm to reduce emissions from e_1 to e_2. But it provides a tax revenue to the regional agency equal to the cross-hatched area, which is enough to fund the public agencies that are running the program.

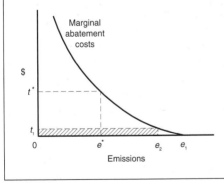

Emission Charges and the Incentives to Innovate

In a dynamic world, it is critical that environmental policies encourage technological change in pollution control. One of the main advantages of emission charges is that they provide strong incentives for this. This is shown in Figure 12-7, which shows two marginal abatement cost curves for a single firm. MAC_1 represents the current condition. It shows the costs the firm

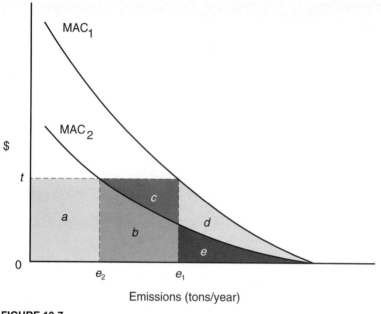

Emissions (tons/year)

FIGURE 12-7
Emission Charges and the Incentive for R&D.

would experience in cutting back its emissions with the particular technology it currently uses. MAC_2, on the other hand, refers to abatement costs that the firm would experience after engaging in a relatively expensive R&D program to develop a new method of reducing emissions. Assume the firm has a reasonably good idea of what the results of the R&D will be, although of course nothing is ever a sure thing. We can use it to measure the strength of the incentives for this firm to put money into the R&D program.

Suppose the firm is subject to an effluent charge of t/ton of emissions. Initially it will reduce emissions to e_1; at this point its total pollution-related costs will consist of $(d + e)$ worth of abatement costs and a tax bill of $(a + b + c)$. If it can lower its marginal abatement cost curve to MAC_2 through the R&D activities, it would then reduce its emissions to e_2. At this point it would pay $(b + e)$ in abatement costs and a in taxes. The reduction in total costs has been $(c + d)$. If the firm had instead been faced with an emissions standard of e_1, its cost savings with the new technology would have been only d, as we saw in the last chapter. Also, as we saw in the last chapter, if public authorities shift the standard to e_2 when the new technology becomes available (giving the same emissions reduction as the tax would have), the firm could actually experience an *increase* in costs because of its R&D efforts.

Thus, the firm's R&D efforts will lead to a bigger reduction in its pollution-control–related costs (abatement costs plus tax payments) under a policy of emission charges than under a standards approach. *Additionally, under the charge system the firm would automatically reduce its emissions as it found ways to shift its marginal abatement cost function downward, whereas under the standard no such automatic process would result.* The difference is that under a charge approach, polluters must pay for emissions as well as for abatement costs, whereas with standards they only need to pay abatement costs. So their potential cost savings from new pollution-control techniques are much larger under the charge program.

Emission Charges and Enforcement Costs

Charges pose a different type of **enforcement** problem than standards. Any charge system requires accurate information on the item to be taxed. If emissions are to be taxed, they must be measurable at reasonable cost. This means that residuals flowing from a source must be concentrated in a small enough number of identifiable streams that monitoring is possible. This rules out most nonpoint-source emissions because they are spread thinly over a wide area in a way that makes them impossible to measure. It would normally be impossible to tax the pollutants in agricultural runoff because the diffuse nature of the "emissions" makes them impossible to measure. This also may rule out certain toxic chemical emissions, which, in addition to being nonpoint source, often involve such small quantities that their flow rates are difficult to measure.

With emission charges the taxing authorities would be sending a tax bill to the polluting firms at the end of each month or year, based on their total quantity of emissions during that period. So the agency would require information on cumulative emissions from each source. This is more involved than just information on rate of discharge because cumulative discharge is rate times duration. There are several ways of getting this information. Perhaps the most ideal would be to have permanent monitoring equipment that measures emissions continuously over the time period in question. Lacking such technology, one could fall back on periodic checking of the rate of emissions, with an estimate of the duration based on normal business considerations or perhaps self-reporting by firms. Alternatively, engineering studies might be carried out to determine prospective emission quantities under specified conditions of operation, inputs used, and so on.

It is probably fair to say that the **monitoring requirements** of an emissions charge policy are more stringent than those for the typical standards program. Polluters, of course, have incentives to find ways, legal and otherwise, to get their tax bills reduced. One way to do this is to influence the monitoring process enough so that reported emissions are smaller. Once they do get their tax bills, recipients will have every incentive to contest them if they appear to be based on uncertain data or have other technical weaknesses. The lack of high-quality monitoring and reporting procedures has undoubtedly contributed to the unpopularity of effluent charge policies for environmental quality control.

Other Types of Charges

So far we have discussed only one type of charge, an effluent or emissions charge. Because it is the emission of residuals that leads directly to environmental pollution, charges on emissions presumably have the greatest leverage in terms of altering the incentives of polluters. But it is often impossible or impractical to levy charges directly on emissions. In cases where we can't measure and monitor emissions at reasonable cost, charges, if they are to be used, would obviously have to be applied to something else. A good case of this is the problem of water pollution from fertilizer runoff in agriculture. It is impossible to tax the pounds of nitrogen in the runoff because it is a nonpoint-source pollutant and thus not directly measurable. The same problem applies to agricultural pesticides. What may be feasible instead is to put charges on these materials as they are bought by farmers; that is, a charge per ton of fertilizer or per 100 pounds of pesticide purchased. The charge is to reflect the fact that a certain proportion of these materials ends up in nearby streams and lakes. Because they are paying higher prices for these items, farmers would have the incentive to use them in smaller quantities. Higher prices also create an incentive to use the fertilizer in ways that involve less wastage; for example, by reducing the amounts that run off.

Placing a charge on something other than emissions is usually a "second-best" course of action made necessary because direct emissions can't be closely monitored. In cases such as this we have to watch out for distortions that can come about as people respond to the charge, distortions that can substantially alleviate the effects of the tax or can sometimes make related problems worse. We mentioned in Chapter 1 the move by many U.S. communities to tax household trash. One technique is to sell stickers to the residents and require that each bag of trash have a sticker on it. The rate of tax is determined by the price of the stickers, and it is relatively easy to monitor and enforce the system through the curbside pickup operations. But the per bag tax will produce an incentive to pack more into each bag, so the reduction in total quantity of trash may be less than the reduction in the number of bags collected.

Distributional Impacts of Emission Charges

There are two primary impacts of effluent charges on the distribution of income and wealth:

1 Impacts on prices and output of goods and services affected by the charges.
2 Effects stemming from the expenditure of tax funds generated by the charges.

Businesses subject to a charge will experience an increase in costs because of both abatement costs and the tax payments. From the firm's standpoint these constitute increases in production cost, which they will presumably pass on to consumers like any cost of production. Whether and how much they can do this depends on competitive conditions and the conditions of demand. If the charge is applied to a single firm or small group of firms within a competitive industry, it will not be able to push its price up above the industry price, and so will have to absorb the cost increase. In this case the impacts will be felt entirely by owners of the firm and the people who work there. Many firms fear, or pretend to fear, being in precisely this situation and base their public objections to taxes on this outcome. If the charge is applied to an entire industry, prices will go up and consumers will bear part of the burden. How much prices go up depends on demand conditions.[3] Price increases often are thought of as regressive because, for any given item, an increase in its price would affect poor people proportionately more than higher-income people. For something that both poor and well-off people consume, such as electricity, this conclusion is straightforward. For price increases in goods consumed disproportionately by more well-to-do people (e.g., airline travel), however, the burden would be mostly on them.

The burden on workers is tied closely to what happens to the rate of output of the affected firms. Here again, the extent of the output effect depends on competitive conditions and the nature of the demand for the good. If the emission tax program is applied to a single firm in a competitive industry or if the demand for the output of an industry is very responsive to price, output adjustments will be relatively large and workers could be displaced. The long-run burden is then a matter of whether good alternative sources of employment are available.

While burdens because of price and output changes may be real, we have to remember that, on the other side, the charge program is creating substantial benefits in the form of reduced environmental damages. To know how a program affects any particular group, we would have to account also for how these benefits are distributed.

Effluent charges also could involve substantial sums going from consumers of the goods produced by the taxed industry to the beneficiaries, whomever they may be, of the funds collected by the taxing authorities. These funds could be used for any number of purposes; how they are used would determine their impacts. They might, for example, be distributed to lower-income people to offset the effects of price increases. They even might be returned in part to the firms paying the effluent taxes. This is done in some European countries to help finance the purchase of pollution-control technology. As long as the return payments do not make the marginal emissions tax rate effectively lower, the incentive effects of the charge are not affected. Alternatively, they might be used to pay for other environmental initiatives in places where direct public action is called for. They even might be used to reduce overall budget deficits, with benefits flowing to general taxpayers.

---

[3]This was discussed in greater detail in Chapter 8.

TABLE 12-1
AN ABATEMENT SUBSIDY

Emissions (tons/month)	Marginal abatement cost	Total abatement cost	Total subsidy at $120/ton	Total subsidy minus total abatement costs
10	0	0	0	0
9	15	15	120	105
8	30	45	240	195
7	50	95	360	265
6	70	165	480	315
5	90	255	600	345
4	115	370	720	350
3	130	500	840	340
2	180	680	960	280
1	230	910	1,080	170
0	290	1,200	1,200	0

ABATEMENT SUBSIDIES

An emission charge works by placing a price on the environmental asset into which emissions are occurring. Essentially the same incentive effects would result if, instead of a charge, we instituted a **subsidy** on emission reductions. Here a public authority would pay a polluter a certain amount per ton of emissions for every ton it reduced, starting from some benchmark level. The subsidy acts as a reward for reducing emissions. More formally, it acts as an **opportunity cost;** when a polluter chooses to emit a unit of effluent, it is in effect forgoing the subsidy payment it could have had if it had chosen to withhold that unit of effluent instead. Table 12-1 shows how this works in principle, using the same numbers as in the preceding discussion on emission charges. The firm's base level is set at its current emissions rate: 10 tons/month. It receives $120 per ton for every ton it cuts back from this base. The third column shows its total subsidy revenues, and the last column shows total subsidies minus total abatement costs. This net revenue peaks at 4 tons/month, the same emissions level the firm would choose with the $120 tax. In other words, the incentive for the firm is the same as for the tax.

Although an abatement subsidy like this would have the same incentive for each individual source, however, total emissions may actually increase. To understand why, note the difference in the financial position of this firm when it emits 4 tons of pollutant under the two programs: With the tax it has total costs of $850 (see Figure 12-1), whereas with the subsidy it has a total *revenue* of $350. Thus, the financial position of the firm is much different. In effect, it will be earning higher profits after the imposition of the subsidy, and this can have the effect of making this industry more attractive for potential new firms. There is the possibility, in other words, of having the emissions per firm go down but the number of firms in the industry increase, and therefore total emissions increase. This feature is a major drawback of simple subsidies like this.

EXHIBIT 12-2

SUBSIDIES FOR SCRAPPING OLD CARS

In 1992 two pilot projects were launched in Chicago and Delaware non-attainment areas, retiring a few hundred old cars. Several other local scrappage programmes were implemented in California from 1993 in the Joaquin Valley, San Diego and Los Angeles areas. Similar schemes currently operate in Phoenix and Chicago. The schemes are usually privately funded but in a few cases (e.g. in the San Joaquin Valley) a local authority pays. In most cases the bonuses given were US $500–600 per eligible car. The minimum age required for a car to be eligible for the scrappage programmes is usually 15 to 20 years (the lowest limit, in the Delaware scheme, was 12 years). The eligible vehicles were selected mostly among those that had recently failed an Inspection and Maintenance (I&M) test. *Not one* of the implemented programmes required the owner of the vehicle for scrapping to buy a *new* car in order to get the bonus.

France implemented its first scrappage scheme (*Prime à la casse*) in February 1994. An incentive of Fr 5,000 (about US $950) was awarded if people scrapped cars that were older than ten years and replaced them with new models. This corresponded roughly to 6% of the average cost of a new car in 1994. Further discounts were offered by car manufacturers and car dealers. The scheme ended in June 1995. A second scheme (*Prime qualité automobile*) worth a bonus of Fr 7,000 ran from October 1995 to the end of September 1996. The minimum age was lowered to eight years. The bonus

was reduced to Fr 5,000 for the replacement of relatively small sized cars. The two schemes retired an overall number of 1,560,000 vehicles. A maximum scrappage rate of 8% was reached in 1996. The number of cars retired *net* of those that would have been retired even without the scheme was estimated at about 700,000.

In **Ireland,** from June 1995 those who scrapped their cars (with a minimum age of ten years) and replaced them with a new-model vehicle could reclaim £ 1,000 (US $1,600) of the registration tax on the new car. The scheme—initially supposed to last until December 1996—was extended to the end of 1997. In 1995, 1996 and 1997, respectively, 5,140, 19,400 and 35,000 vehicles were scrapped—out of a fleet that had roughly 990,000 cars in 1995 and grew to 1,134,000 in 1997. The majority of the vehicles scrapped under the scheme were 10–12 years old.

In **Norway,** a scrappage incentive was introduced in 1996. NKr 5 000 (US $800) was given for scrapping a vehicle older than ten years. There was no compulsory replacement for the scrapped car. A considerable part of the scrapped cars were replaced with second-hand vehicles. The incentive caused an *extra* 150,000 vehicles to be scrapped (7% of the fleet) with respect to the "natural" annual scrapping rate.

Source: Organization for Economic Cooperation and Development, "Cleaner Cars, Fleet Renewal and Scrappage Schemes," OECD, Paris, 1999.

Subsidies to reduce emissions can take numerous forms. One type of subsidy used in several countries is cash payments to automobile owners in return for retiring their old cars. Stricter automobile pollution-control regulations are typically put on new cars, which means that of the entire fleet of cars the older cars account for a disproportionately high amount of overall car emissions. To get these old cars off the roads, many countries have put programs into effect in which owners of older cars earn payments for scrapping them. Exhibit 12-2 discusses some of these programs.

Deposit-Refund Systems

One place where subsidies may be more practical is in deposit-refund systems. A deposit-refund system is essentially the combination of a tax and a subsidy. For example, a subsidy is paid to consumers when they return an item to a designated collection point. The purpose of the subsidy is to provide the incentive for people to refrain from disposing of these items in environmentally damaging ways. The funds for paying the subsidy are raised by levying taxes on these items when they are purchased. In this case, the purpose of the tax is not necessarily so much to get people to reduce the consumption of the item, but to raise money to pay the subsidy. Of course, the tax is called a deposit and the subsidy a refund, but the principle is clear.

Deposit-refund systems are particularly well suited to situations where a product is widely dispersed when purchased and used, and where disposal is difficult or impossible for authorities to monitor. In the United States, a number of individual states[4] have enacted deposit-refund systems for beverage containers, both to reduce litter and to encourage recycling. This approach also has been widely used in Europe. But many other products could be handled effectively with this type of system.

In the late 1960s, Germany instituted a deposit-refund on waste lubricating oil. Each year very large quantities of waste oil are disposed of improperly, putting many air, water, and land resources under threat. In the German system, new lubricating oil is subject to a tax (a deposit), the proceeds of which go into a special fund. This fund is then used to subsidize (the refund side) a waste oil recovery and reprocessing system. The terms of the subsidy are set so as to encourage competition in the recovery/reprocessing system and to provide an incentive for users to reduce the extent to which oil is contaminated during use.[5]

In Sweden and Norway, deposit-refund systems have been instituted for cars. New-car buyers pay a deposit at time of purchase, which will be refunded when and if the car is turned over to an authorized junk dealer. Experience with these systems shows that success depends on more than just the size of the deposit-refund. For example, it is essential that the collection system be designed to be reasonably convenient for consumers.

Other items for which deposit-refund systems might be appropriate are consumer products containing hazardous substances, such as batteries containing cadmium and car batteries. Automobile tires also might be handled this way. The deposit-refund system also might be adaptable to conventional industrial pollutants. For example, users of fossil fuels might pay deposits on the quantities of sulfur contained in the fuels they purchase; they would then get refunds on the sulfur recovered from the exhaust gas. Thus, they would lose their deposit only on the sulfur that went up the stacks.

---

[4]As of 1990 these were Connecticut, Delaware, Iowa, Maine, Massachusetts, Michigan, New York, Oregon, and Vermont.

[5]Peter Bohm, Deposit-Refund Systems, Johns Hopkins Press for Resources for the Future, Baltimore, MD, 1981, pp. 116–120.

SUMMARY

Emission charges attack the pollution problem at its source, by putting a price on something that has been free and, therefore, overused. The main advantage of emission charges is their efficiency aspects: If all sources are subject to the same charge, they will adjust their emission rates so that the equimarginal rule is satisfied. Administrators do not have to know the individual source marginal abatement cost functions for this to happen; it is enough that firms are faced with the charge and then left free to make their own adjustments. A second major advantage of emission charges is that they produce a strong incentive to innovate, to discover cheaper ways of reducing emissions.

The apparent indirect character of emission charges may tend to work against their acceptance by policymakers. Standards have the appearance of placing direct control on the thing that is at issue, namely emissions. Emission charges, on the other hand, place no direct restrictions on emissions but rely on the self-interested behavior of firms to adjust their own emission rates in response to the tax. This may make some policymakers uneasy because firms apparently are still allowed to control their own emission rates. It may seem paradoxical that this "indirect" character of effluent taxes can sometimes provide a stronger inducement to emission reductions than seemingly more direct approaches.

But emission charges require effective monitoring. They cannot be enforced simply by checking to see if sources have installed certain types of pollution-control equipment. If emission charges are to have the appropriate incentive effects, they must be based closely on *cumulative emissions.* Thus, point sources where emissions can be effectively measured are the likely candidates for pollution control via emissions charges.

An advantage of emission charges is that they provide a source of revenue for public authorities. Many have recommended that tax systems be changed, relying less on taxes that have distorting economic effects and more on emissions charges. This requires that authorities be able to predict with accuracy the effects of particular emissions charges on rates of emissions.

Emissions subsidies would have the same incentive effect on individual polluters, but they could lead to increases in total emission levels. One place where subsidies have been used effectively is in deposit-refund systems, which are essentially tax and subsidy systems in combination.

QUESTIONS FOR FURTHER DISCUSSION

1 How might an emission charge program be designed to address the problem of automobile emissions?

2 Explain how emission charges solve the equimarginal problem.

3 Opponents of emission charge policies sometimes assert that they are simply a way of letting firms buy the right to pollute. Is this a reasonable criticism?

4 When emission charges are put into effect, who ultimately ends up paying for them? Is this fair?

5 Emission charges are sometimes seen as creating a "double burden": Firms must pay the costs of reducing emissions and also pay the government for polluting discharges. How might a charge system be designed to reduce this "double burden"?

WEBSITES

The Environmental Tax Program is discussed on a site dealing with environmental taxes, **www.solstice.crest.org/sustainable/etp,** see also Friends of the Earth, **www.foe.org/envirotax/taxbooklet.** Other websites on this topic are listed on the web page of this textbook, **www.mhhe.com/economics/field3.**

SELECTED READINGS

Anderson, Frederick R., Allen V. Kneese, Phillip D. Reed, Serge Taylor, and Russell B. Stevenson: *Environmental Improvements Through Economic Incentives,* Johns Hopkins University Press, Baltimore, MD, 1978.

Anderson, Robert C., Lisa A. Hofmann, and Michael Rusin: *The Use of Economic Incentive Mechanisms in Environmental Management,* American Petroleum Institute, Washington, DC, June 1990.

Bohm, Peter: *Deposit-Refund Systems: Theory and Application to Environmental, Conservation and Consumer Policy,* Johns Hopkins Press for Resources for the Future, Baltimore, MD, 1981.

Brännlund, Runar, and Ing-Marie Gren: *Green Taxes, Economic Theory and Empirical Evidence from Scandinavia,* Edward Algar, Cheltenham, England, 1999.

Brown, Gardner M., Jr., and Ralph Johnson: "Pollution Control by Effluent Charges: It Works in the Federal Republic of Germany, Why Not in the U.S.?," *Natural Resources Journal,* 24(4), October 1984, pp. 929–966.

Hahn, Robert W., and Robert N. Stavins: "Incentive-Based Environmental Regulation: A New Era for an Old Idea?," *Ecology Law Quarterly,* 18(1), 1991, pp. 1–42.

Moore, John L., Larry Parker, John E. Blodgett, James E. McCarthy, and David E. Gushee: *Using Incentives for Environmental Protection: An Overview,* U.S. Congressional Research Service, Washington, DC, June 1989.

Organization for Economic Cooperation and Development: *Environmental Taxes: Recent Developments in China and OECD Countries,* Paris, 1999.

Repetto, Robert, Roger A. Dower, Robin Jenkins, and Jacqueline Geoghegan: *Green Fees, How a Tax Shift Can Work for the Environment and the Economy,* World Resources Institute, Washington, DC, 1992.

Tietenberg, Tom H.: "Economic Instruments for Environmental Regulation," *Oxford Review of Economic Policy,* 6(1), Spring 1990, pp. 17–33.

U.S. Environmental Protection Agency: *Economic Incentives, Options for Environmental Protection,* Washington, DC (21P-2001), March 1991.

Wallart, Nicolas: *The Political Economy of Environmental Taxes,* Elgar, Cheltenham, England, 1999.

CHAPTER 13

INCENTIVE-BASED STRATEGIES: TRANSFERABLE DISCHARGE PERMITS

An effluent charge requires that some central public authority establish a charge rate, monitor the performance of each polluter, and then collect the tax bills. It is essentially an interaction between polluters and public authorities in which we might expect the same type of adversarial relationship we get in any tax system. In this chapter we take a look at a policy approach that, while incorporating economic incentives, is designed to work in a more decentralized fashion. Rather than leaving everything to a centralized public agency, it works through the decentralized market interactions of polluters themselves. It's called the system of **"transferable discharge permits."**

GENERAL PRINCIPLES

In a transferable discharge permit (TDP) system, a new type of **property right** is created. This property right consists of a permit to emit pollutants. Each permit entitles its holder to emit one unit (pound, ton, however the permit is calibrated) of the waste material specified in the right. Rights holders would ordinarily have a number of such permits at any point in time. If a discharger owned 100 permits, for example, it would be entitled to emit, during some specified period of time, a maximum of 100 units of the designated type of effluent. Thus, the total number of permits held by all sources puts an upper limit on the total quantity of emissions. These discharge permits are **transferable;** they can be bought and sold among anybody allowed to participate in the permit market, at whatever price is agreed upon by the participants themselves.

A TDP program begins by a centralized decision on the total number of discharge permits to be put into circulation. These permits are then distributed among the sources responsible for the emissions. Some formula must be used to determine how many permits each source will receive; we will come back to this problem later. Assuming that the total number of permits is less than current total emissions, some or all emitters will receive fewer permits than their current emissions.

Suppose, for example, that a TDP program has been instituted to reduce the amount of sulfur emitted by a group of power plants. Current total emissions are, say, 150,000 tons of sulfur per year, and policymakers have decided that this must be reduced to 100,000 tons per year. Let's focus on the situation of one of the power plants, which we suppose to be emitting 7,000 tons of sulfur currently. This plant is initially given 5,000 discharge permits. The plant manager now has three choices.

1 Reduce the emissions to the level covered by the number of permits the plant was initially awarded.
2 Buy additional permits and emit at levels higher than the original award level (e.g., buy 1,000 permits to add to its 5,000 initial distribution, so its emissions would now be 6,000 tons/year).
3 Reduce emissions below the level of the original award, then sell the permits it doesn't need (e.g., reduce emissions to 4,000 tons/year and sell 1,000 permits).

It may not be obvious that the buying and selling of permits among polluters (and perhaps others) would lead to the distribution of total emissions among polluters in a way that satisfies the **equimarginal principle.** We can examine this with the help of Figure 13-1. Here there are two polluters whose emissions are uniformly mixed together (we will treat the case of nonuniform emissions later). They have different marginal abatement costs; costs go up much more rapidly for B than for A as emissions are reduced. Assume that initially neither firm is controlling any of its emissions; therefore, total emissions are 210 tons per year, 120 tons from A and 90 tons from B. Suppose regulators now wish to reduce total emissions by 50 percent, that is, to 105 tons per year. They create 105 transferable discharge permits, each one of which entitles its possessor to emit 1 ton/year. They then distribute these permits to the two sources, using some agreed-upon allocation rule. Let's assume that each is allocated permits in proportion to its current emission rates. Thus, A gets 60 permits and B gets 45 permits in the original distribution.

Firm A will have to cut back to 60 tons/year and Firm B will have to reduce to 45 tons per year, unless they can agree to redistribute the permits among themselves through buying and selling. Suppose Firm B were to cut back to 45 tons; at this point its marginal abatement costs would be $4,000/ton. If it could buy an extra discharge permit for some price less than $4,000, it would be better off because this would allow it to save the difference in abatement costs. Firm A's marginal abatement cost would be $1,200 per ton if it reduces emissions in accordance with its original holding of 60 permits. If A could sell a permit for

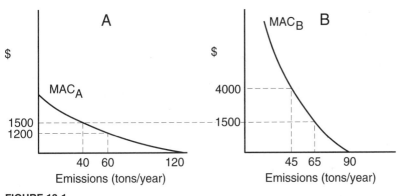

FIGURE 13-1
How Transferable Discharge Permits Work.

some price above $1,200, it would be better off because the revenue from the sale would more than cover the added abatement costs required to reduce its emissions by that unit. Thus, A would be willing to sell a permit for anything above $1,200 and B would be willing to buy a permit for anything below $4,000. Each would obviously be better off by trading the permit, at whatever price they could agree upon between these two extremes. A way of saying this is that there are **"gains from trade"** for these two polluters in trading a permit from A to B.

After this trade, A will be emitting 1 ton less, or 59 tons per year; and B will be emitting 1 ton more, or 46 tons. But in this situation their marginal abatement costs will still be different. As long as this is true, there will continue to be gains from trade for each of them through trading additional permits. Gains from trade would continue to exist and permits would continue to be traded until marginal abatement costs are equalized. This occurs at emission levels of 40 tons for A and 65 tons for B. At this point Source A has reduced its holdings of discharge permits to 40 (the 60 permits it was initially awarded minus the 20 sold to B), whereas B has increased its holdings to 65 permits (45 from the original allocation plus the 20 bought from A). Note, however, that as long as the *total* number of permits in circulation is constant, *total* emissions will be constant.

Of course, in the bargaining process between A and B it is unlikely that they would have proceeded just one permit at a time. More than likely they would have some idea of the prices for which permits could be bought and sold and the level of their marginal abatement costs, so they could trade blocks of permits for agreed-upon prices. But the essential point is that as long as marginal abatement costs are unequal between these sources, they can both become better off by trading permits at some price between these marginal abatement costs. Thus, in the trading of permits and the adjusting of emissions in accordance with their permit holdings, these sources would be led to an outcome that satisfies the equimarginal principle.

In order for the equimarginal principle eventually to be satisfied in this case, it is obviously necessary that all permit buyers and sellers be trading permits at the same price. What this requires is a single overall **market for permits** where

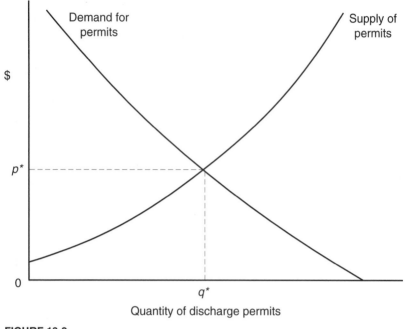

FIGURE 13-2
A Market for Discharge Permits.

suppliers and demanders may interact openly and where knowledge of transactions prices is publicly available to all participants. The normal forces of competition would then bring about a single price for permits. The permits would
in general flow from sources with relatively low to those with high marginal
abatement costs. Although the previous example shows how two sources
would redistribute permits among themselves, we would expect that in markets with many sources participating, trading would be a continuous phenomenon because of the built-in incentive for polluters to look for better ways of
reducing emissions and because of natural changes in a growing economy.

We would also anticipate the development of standard market institutions—
permit brokers and bankers, permit trading on stock exchanges, and so on—
that develop on any market dealing with rights like this, giving us a fully
developed market in traded discharge permits, as pictured in Figure 13-2. The
demanders in this market would be new firms that wish to begin operations in
the trading area or existing sources that wish to expand their operations and
require more permits to cover expected increases in emissions. Suppliers of permits would include firms leaving the area or going out of business, and most
especially firms who have invested in better abatement techniques and now
have excess permits to sell. In any particular year there would be a tendency for
a market price to establish itself, such as p^* in Figure 13-2, and for a certain
number of permits to change hands, such as q^* in the figure.

In recent years the idea of transferable discharge permits has become quite popular among some environmental policy advocates, as well as among policymakers themselves. Unlike effluent charge approaches, which basically make people pay for something they were once getting free, TDP programs begin by creating and distributing a new type of property right. These property rights will have a market value as long as the total number of permits created is limited. From a political standpoint, it is perhaps easier for people to agree on a pollution-control policy that begins by distributing valuable new property rights than by notifying people they will be subject to a new tax. Of course, like any pollution-control policy, TDP programs have their own set of problems that have to be overcome if they are going to work effectively. What looks in theory like a neat way of using market forces to achieve efficient pollution reduction must be adapted to the complexities of the real world.

The Initial Rights Allocation

The success of the TDP approach in controlling pollution depends critically on limiting the number of rights in circulation. Because individual polluters will no doubt want as many as they can get in the first distribution, the very first step of the program is one of potentially great controversy: what formula to use to make the original distribution of emission rights. Almost any rule will appear to have some inequities. For example, they might be distributed equally among all existing sources of a particular effluent. But this would encounter the problem that firms vary a lot in size. Some pulp mills are larger than others, for example, and the average size of pulp mills, in terms of value of output, may be different from the average size of, say, soda bottling plants. So giving each polluter the same number of permits may not be fair.

Permits might be allocated in accordance with the existing emissions of a source. For example, each source might get permits amounting to 50 percent of its current emissions. This may sound equitable, but, in fact, it has built-in incentive difficulties. A rule like this does not recognize the fact that some firms already may have worked hard to reduce their emissions. One easily could argue that those firms who, out of a good conscience or for any reason, have already invested in emission reduction should not now be penalized, in effect, by receiving emission permits in proportion to these lower emission levels.[1] This tends to reward firms who have dragged their feet in the past.[2] It could go even further. If polluters believe that permits will soon be allocated in this way, they may have the incentive to *increase* today's emission rate because this would give them a larger base for the initial allocation of permits.

Each allocation formula has its problems, and policymakers must find some workable compromise if the approach is to be widely accepted. Closely related

---

[1]When we study (in Chapter 15) the Clean Air Act of 1990, we will see that this was the source of great conflict when the details of the SO_2 trading program were being hammered out.
[2]This is just another example of the perverse incentives built into any program that asks everybody to cut their consumption by x percent from their current rate. It favors those who have consumed at high rates in the past and hurts those who have tried hard to live frugally.

to this issue is the question of whether the rights should be given away or perhaps sold or auctioned. In principle it doesn't matter as long as the permits get distributed fairly widely. Subsequent market transactions will redistribute them in accordance with the relative marginal abatement costs of polluters whatever the original distribution may have been. What a sale or auction would do, however, is transfer some of the original value of the rights into the hands of the auctioning agency. This might be a good way for public agencies to raise funds for worthy projects, but it has to be recognized that a plan like this would create political objections. A hybrid system would be to distribute a certain number of permits free and then auction some number of additional permits. Or a small surcharge might be put on permits in the original distribution.

Establishing Trading Rules

For any market to work effectively, clear rules must exist governing who may trade and the trading procedures that must be followed. Furthermore, the rules should not be so burdensome that they make it impossible for market participants to gauge accurately the implications of buying or selling at specific prices. This implies a "hands-off" stance by public agencies after the initial distribution of the rights. Working against this is the normal tendency for environmental agencies to want to monitor the market closely and perhaps try to influence its performance. The supervising agency, for example, may want to have final right of approval over all trades, so as to be able to stop any trades it considers undesirable in some way. The problem with this is that it is likely to increase the uncertainty among potential traders, increase the general level of **transactions costs** in the market, and interfere with the efficient flow of permits. The general rule for the public agency should be to set simple and clear rules and then allow trading to proceed.

One basic rule that would have to be established is who may participate in the market. Is this to be limited to polluters or may anyone trade? For example, may environmental advocacy groups buy permits and retire them as a way of reducing total emissions? One's first reaction is to say that such groups ought to be allowed to buy permits, because that is evidence that society's willingness to pay for lower total emission levels exceeds the price of the permits, which should be the same as marginal abatement costs. This conclusion is probably valid if we are dealing with a local or regional environmental group whose membership is roughly coincidental with the trading area and that has raised money specifically to buy discharge permits in that region. It may not be valid if large, national advocacy groups were to use their resources to buy permits on a regional market, because the amount they were willing to pay for permits might have no close relationship to underlying true social willingness to pay. Of course if the trading areas are essentially national in size, or very large, this will not be a problem.

These and other trading rules will have to be worked out for particular programs in particular circumstances. A body of common law governing discharge permit transactions also will develop over time. The rest of this chapter deals with some of the important economic dimensions of these trading institutions.

Reducing the Number of Permits

In most TDP programs the total number of permits and their initial distribution are established by a public agency like the EPA. Then the sources are allowed to trade with one another, and perhaps with other groups who are not polluters. One question that presents itself is, how does the total number of permits get reduced over time? If the efficient level of emissions is going down because of technological change, how do authorities reduce the overall number of permits in circulation?

There are essentially two ways this can be brought about. One is through the market. Public agencies could buy back permits and essentially retire them, in the sense of making them unavailable for future sale. The same result can be encouraged by allowing other organizations or individuals, particularly those from the environmental community, to purchase permits. Exhibit 13-1 recounts how SO_2 permits have been purchased by certain private groups.

EXHIBIT 13-1

LAW STUDENTS BUY AND HOLD POLLUTION RIGHTS

It was an unlikely scenario: Law school students bidding against corporate giants for pollution rights. But at the Chicago Board of Trade on Monday, students from seven law schools vied with representatives of electric utilities for government-issued allowances to emit sulphur dioxide.

The law students had pooled $3,256 to buy 18 of the auction's 176,400 allowances, each of which permits the emission of one ton of sulphur dioxide. Instead of selling the allowances for a profit at a future auction, the students said they would let them expire unused—yielding a reduction, albeit a small one, in pollution.

"We're also trying to force the price up by taking as many off the market as we can," said Richard Facclolo, president of the Environmental Law Coalition at the University of Maryland, which enlisted six other schools in the bidding effort. "If allowances cost more than pollution control equipment, companies will have a great incentive to invest in that equipment and there will be even less pollution."

The other law schools that bought allowances this year were at the City University of New York, Detroit, Duke, Michigan, Hamline in St. Paul, Minn., and New England in Boston.

The notion of law students joining in the auction originated with Robert Percival, an environmental law professor at the University of Maryland, who has written several textbooks on the subject.

Sulphur dioxide, a chemical component of acid rain, contaminates the environment and can cause respiratory and other health problems. In an effort to halve sulphur dioxide emissions by the year 2000, Congress, in the Clean Air Act of 1990, authorized the Environmental Protection Agency to issue allowances, not to exceed 9 million a year, to electric utilities nationwide.

Utilities that exceed mandated pollution reductions, either through the use of cleaner fuels or the installation of enhanced pollution control equipment, can sell their unused allowances for a profit to other companies.

Source: The New York Times, March 31, 1995. Copyright © 1995 by the New York Times. Reprinted by permission.

Another way of producing a reduction in permits over time is to date the permits, that is, have each permit apply to emissions during a particular time period, say a given year. Then individual sources could be awarded, not a single number of permits applicable to each future year, but a declining sequence of permits, each applicable to a particular future year. In other words, instead of a source holding 100 permits for all future years, they might be given 100 permits for year 1, 95 permits for year 2, 90 for year 3, and so on.

Nonuniform Emissions

Suppose we are trying to design a TDP program to control total airborne SO_2 emissions in a region where there are numerous different sources, power plants, industrial plants, and so on, scattered rather widely around the area. A schematic of this situation is depicted in Figure 13-3. All the emission points are not equally situated relative to the prevailing wind or to the area of highest population density. Some sources are upwind, others are downwind, of the populated area. We assume they are not all equal in terms of marginal abatement costs, but neither are they equal in terms of the impact of their emissions on ambient SO_2 levels over the populated area. In technical terms, they have different **transfer coefficients** linking their own emissions with damages in the urban area.

FIGURE 13-3
Nonuniform Emissions and TDP Programs.

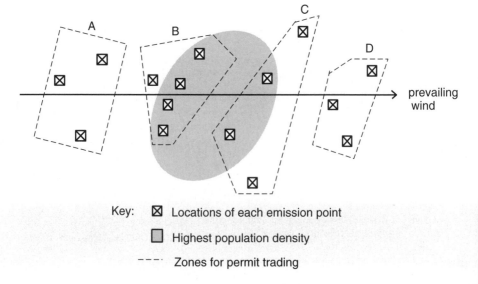

Key: ☒   Locations of each emission point

         ☐   Highest population density

- - - -   Zones for permit trading

Having distributed discharge permits we now allow them to be traded. As long as the number of permits in circulation is held constant, we have effectively controlled total SO_2 emissions. But if we allow straight trading, unit for unit, of permits among all sources, the damage caused by that total could change. For example, if a downwind firm sold permits to an upwind firm, the total number of permits would remain the same but there would now be more emissions upwind of the population and, therefore, more damage.[3]

The problem is similar to the one encountered under the effluent charge policy; in effect each firm is differently situated relative to the damage area, so the emissions of each will have a different impact on ambient quality in that area. If the program were simply to allow trading of permits among all sources on a one-for-one basis, it could easily come to pass that a firm or group of firms with higher transfer coefficients, whose emissions therefore have a greater impact on ambient quality, could accumulate larger numbers of permits. For example, some people feel that the SO_2 trading program established pursuant to the 1990 Clean Air Act has led to a concentration of permits in the hands of midwestern power plants, with negative impacts on cities of the northeast. (See Exhibit 13-2.)

One way to get around this might be to adjust the trading rules to take into account the impacts of individual sources. Suppose the emissions from Source A were twice as damaging as the emissions of Source B simply because of the location of the two sources. Then the administrators of the program might set a rule that if Source A is buying permits from Source B, it must buy two permits to get one. If this principle is extended to a situation with many sources, things can quickly get very complicated. Authorities would have to determine, for each source, how many permits would have to be purchased from each other source in order for the purchasing source to be credited with one new permit. If there were five sources, the agency would have to figure out only 10 such trading ratios, but if there were 20 different sources, it would have to estimate 190 of these ratios.[4] One way around this would be to use a zoned system, analogous to the zoned effluent charge we talked about earlier. Authorities would designate a series of zones, each of which would contain sources that were relatively similar in terms of their location and the impact of their emissions on ambient quality. Four such zones are shown in Figure 13-3. Authorities then could do one of two things: (a) allow trading by firms only with other firms in the same zone or (2) make adjustments for all trades across zone boundaries similar to the technique discussed previously. Thus, for example, if sources in Zone A were judged to have transfer coefficients twice the size, on average, as sources in Zone B, any trade between sources in these two zones would be adjusted by that same factor of two: Any firm in Zone A buying permits from any firm in

---

[3]This is sometimes called the "hot spot" problem.
[4]In general, if there were n sources, there would have to be $[n(n - 1)]/2$ trading ratios established.

EXHIBIT 13-2

ALBANY BATTLES ACID RAIN FED BY OTHER STATES

By Raymond Hernandez

Albany, May 1—The New York State Legislature today completed passage of a bill that seeks to reduce the amount of air pollution that drifts into New York from coal-burning power plants in Midwestern and Southern states.

The measure would stop New York companies from keeping the money they make by selling pollution credits, earned by cleaning their own smokestacks, to major polluters in the Midwest and the South. The credits are now sold on the open market to companies with older power plants that find it cheaper to buy such credits instead of modernizing their plants and cutting their emissions.

The action is the first by a state that directly challenges a major provision in the federal Clean Air Act of 1990: setting up a marketplace in which companies can trade the right to pollute, in the form of credits, a commodity. Some New York utility companies immediately threatened a court challenge to the new legislation, saying the law could violate constitutional protections for interstate commerce.

It is not clear the degree to which the legislation will reduce pollution and acid rain in New York State, in large part because polluters in the South and the Midwest could turn to other companies in other states to buy their pollution credits. But experts say the legislation will ultimately limit the amount of pollution credits available to polluters in the Midwest and the South and thereby force up the price of such credits.

The federal Environmental Protection Agency, which administers the credit program, said it supported New York's attempt to regulate pollution credit trading by companies within its own borders.

Federal regulations permit a company that cuts pollution below federal levels to sell credits it has earned to a company unable or unwilling to meet those federal emission lev-

els. The goal is to reward companies that reduce their toxic emissions below the federal standard, while forcing companies that exceed the standard to buy the right to continue polluting.

Over all, the free-market approach has resulted in cleaner air nationwide. But there has been a glaring glitch, according to environmental experts. Major polluters in the South and the Middle West have found it cheaper to buy pollution credits instead of cutting toxic emissions that have blown downwind into New York and contributed to the state's acid rain problem.

The legislation adopted today is intended to help correct that problem, essentially penalizing power companies in New York when they sell pollution credits to coal-burning power plants in the Midwest and in the South, whose pollution is a major cause of acid rain in the state.

The measure essentially calls for the state to seize all proceeds that a utility would receive from such polluters as part of a transaction for pollution credits. The bill allows state regulators to impose a fine equal to the amount of such a sale; the fine would be used to promote development and use of nonpolluting energy sources like solar power.

The measure drew harsh rebukes from representatives of the state's powerful utility industry, who said it potentially violated the interstate commerce clause of the Constitution prohibiting states from enacting laws that restrict trade outside their borders. Proponents o the measure say companies still have the ability to sell credits to whomever they want but run the risk of incurring penalties when the credits go to out-of-state companies that contribute to New York's acid rain problem.

Source: New York Times, May 2, 2000. Copyright © 2000 by *New York Times.* Reprinted by permission.

Zone B would have to buy two permits in order to get credit for one new one; any source in Zone B would have to buy only half a permit from a firm in Zone A to get credit for one new permit.

TDPs and Problems of Competition

The question of allowing trading across zone boundaries or, on the contrary, restricting it to within zones has a much wider importance than might first appear. TDP programs work through a trading process in which buyers and sellers interact to transfer title to valuable property rights. Markets work best when there is substantial **competition** among buyers and among sellers; they work significantly less well if there are so few buyers or sellers that competitive pressures are weak or absent. In cases where there are few traders, one of them, or perhaps a small group, may be able to exercise control over the market, colluding on prices, perhaps charging different prices to different people, using the control of discharge permits to gain economic control in its industry, and so on. From the standpoint of fostering competition, therefore, we would like to set our trading zones as widely as possible, to include large numbers of potential buyers and sellers.

But this may work against the ecological facts. In many cases there may be meteorological or hydrological reasons for limiting the trading area to a relatively narrow geographical area. If the objective was to control airborne emissions affecting a particular city, for example, we would probably not want to allow firms located there to trade permits with firms in another city. Or if our concern is controlling emissions into a particular lake or river, we could not allow sources located there to trade permits with sources located on some entirely different body of water. Thus, for environmental reasons it may well be desirable to have trading areas restricted,[5] whereas for economic reasons we would want to have trading areas defined broadly. There is no magic rule to tell exactly how these two factors should be balanced in all cases. Authorities can only look at specific cases as they arise and weigh the particularities of the environmental features with the subtleties of the competitive conditions in the industries where trading will occur.

TDP Programs and Enforcement

The directly controlling aspect of a TDP program is that sources are constrained to keep their emissions at a level no greater than the total number of discharge permits in their possession. Thus, an administering agency would essentially have to keep track of two things: (1) the number of permits in the possession of each source and (2) the quantity of emissions from each source. Since the initial permit distribution will be well known, the agency must have some way of

---

[5]Although not always; we will discuss later the national trading market in lead permits used in the introduction of leaded gasoline into the U.S. economy.

keeping track of permit transactions among market participants. Trades, in fact, could become complicated with multiple buyers and sellers and with different types of transactions, such as temporary rentals and long-term leases in addition to permanent transfers. Because permit buyers (or renters) would have a strong incentive to have their purchases revealed to the agency and because all purchases imply sellers, a system of self-reporting, coupled with modern means of information transfer, may be sufficient to provide reliable information on which sources have the permits.

As regards **monitoring,** the administrative agency must be able to monitor polluters to see whether emissions at each source exceed the number of permits it holds. If permits are expressed in terms of total emissions over some period of time, a means has to be available to measure cumulative emissions at each source. This is the same requirement as with an effluent charge. If there were reasonable certainty that emissions were fairly even throughout the year, authorities could get a check on cumulative emissions by making spot checks of instantaneous rates. For most industrial sources of pollution, however, there are considerable daily, weekly, or seasonal variations in emissions; therefore, more sophisticated monitoring would be required.

One desirable feature of TDP programs is that there may be an incentive for sources to monitor each other, at least informally. When, and if, some sources emit more than they have permits for, they are essentially cheating by not buying sufficient permits to cover all of their emissions. In effect this reduces the demand for permits below what it would otherwise be. And this has the effect of lowering the market price of permits. This clearly works against the interest of any firm holding large numbers of permits, which gives it an incentive to see that other firms don't cheat on emissions.

TDPs and the Incentive for R&D

One of our main criteria for judging an environmental policy is whether or not it creates strong incentives for firms to seek better ways of reducing emissions. Emission standards were weak in this regard, whereas emission charges were much stronger. TDP programs in this respect are identical to emissions charges, at least in theory. Consider the firm in Figure 13-4. Suppose that at present the firm's marginal abatement cost function is MAC_1. Emission permits sell for p each, and let us assume that this price is not expected to change. The firm has adjusted its holdings so that it currently owns e_1 permits.[6] Its emissions are therefore e_1 and its total abatement costs are $(a + b)$. The incentive to do R&D is to find a less costly way of con-

---

[6]These marginal abatement cost functions apply to a year; that is, they are the costs per year of changing emissions. The price p is therefore a one-year purchase (or sale) price—what it would cost to buy or sell a permit for just one year. If a firm is buying a permit to hold permanently, the price will be some multiple of the annual value, much as the purchase price of a rental house is some multiple of its annual rental income.

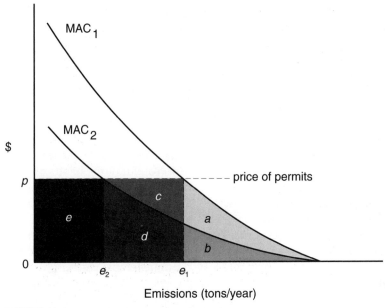

FIGURE 13-4
TDP and Technological Change.

trolling emissions, so the firm can cut emissions and sell the surplus permits. How much would it be worth to get marginal abatement costs shifted to MAC_2? With MAC_2, the firm would shift to an emissions level of e_2. Its total abatement costs here would be $(b + d)$, but it would be able to sell $(e_1 - e_2)$ permits for a revenue of $p(e_1 - e_2) = (c + d)$. The change in its position would thus be:

$$
\begin{array}{ccc}
\text{Total abatement costs} & \text{Total abatement costs} & \text{Receipts from} \\
\text{with } MAC_1 & - \quad \text{with } MAC_2 & + \quad \text{TDP sale}
\end{array}
$$

or $(a + b) - (d + b) + (c + d)$, which equals $(a + c)$. Check this with the savings under an effluent charge (see Chapter 12). It is exactly the same. The market price of the permit has the same incentive as a pollution charge; by not reducing their emissions, firms are forgoing the increased revenues they could have obtained by selling some of their permits.

SUMMARY

Programs of transferable discharge permits have become very popular among U.S. environmental policymakers in recent years. The Clean Air Act Amendments of 1990 contain a TDP program for SO_2 reduction among electric power producers; we will discuss this in Chapter 15. TDP programs have been proposed for control of solid waste and even for global CO_2 reduction. The spirit behind this approach, the transfer of emission rights from sources with low control costs to those with high costs, is also behind some recent developments in the control of nonpoint-source waterborne emissions; we will discuss these later in the chapter on water pollution (see Chapter 14). There is the expectation that this approach could give us pollution control at a substantially lower cost than the current system of technology-based effluent standards, and also a sense that, politically, they would be more acceptable than emission charges.

But TDP programs come with their own set of problems. Most especially, TDP programs take some of the burden of pollution control out of the hands of engineers and place it under the operation of a market. How that market operates is obviously critical to whether this type of policy will work. There are a host of important factors: who gets the permits at the beginning, the strength of their incentives to minimize costs, the degree of competition in the market, the transaction rules set by the administering public agency, the ability to monitor and enforce compliance, and so on. Nevertheless, the transferable discharge permit system seems to be an idea whose time has come, at least in the United States.

Both transferable discharge systems and emission charge systems seek to take the burden and responsibility of making technical pollution-control decisions out of the hands of central administrators and put them into the hands of polluters themselves. They are not, we should stress, aimed at putting pollution-control *objectives* themselves into the hands of the polluters. It is not the market that is going to determine the most efficient level of pollution control for society. Rather, they are means of enlisting the incentives of the polluters themselves in finding more effective ways of meeting the overall objective of reducing emissions.

QUESTIONS FOR FURTHER DISCUSSION

1 How might you design a transferable discharge permit system for solid waste? For phasing out of use a certain type of plastic? For phasing in a program for using recycled newsprint in newspapers?

2 Explain how a program of transferable discharge permits works to satisfy the equimarginal principle.

3 Below are marginal abatement costs of two sources. They currently emit 10 tons each.

(a) What would the total abatement costs be for an equiproportional cutback to a total of 10 tons?

(b) Suppose we print up 10 transferable discharge permits, each of which entitles the holder to 1 ton of emissions. We distribute them equally to the two sources. What will the final emissions be for each of the two sources, and the total abatement costs after all adjustments have been made?

(c) Show that if the permits are originally distributed in a different way (say all to one source and none to the other), the final results will be the same in terms of total and individual emissions, but the distribution of the gains from trade will be different between the two sources.

Emissions (tons)	Marginal abatement costs	
	Source A	Source B
10	0	0
9	2	4
8	4	8
7	6	14
6	8	20
5	10	30
4	12	42
3	14	56
2	18	76
1	28	100
0	48	180

4 What are the pros and cons of letting *anybody* (banks, private citizens, environmental groups, government agencies, etc.) buy and sell transferable discharge permits, in addition to emission sources themselves?

WEBSITES

A very good website for learning about TDP programs is Emissions Trading Education Initiative, **www.etei.org**; there are also many private firms and organizations in this space, for example, Emissions Marketing Association, **www.emissions.org**. For additional sites, see the web page associated with this text, **www.mhhe.com/economics/field3**.

SELECTED READINGS

Chichilnisky, Graciela, and Geoffrey Heal (eds.): *Environmental Markets*, Columbia University Press, New York, c.2000.

Hahn, Robert W.: "Economic Perspectives for Environmental Problems: How the Patient Followed the Doctor's Orders," *Journal of Economic Perspectives*, 3(2), Spring 1989, pp. 95–114.

Hahn, Robert W.: *A Primer on Environmental Policy Design*, Harwood Academic Publishers, Chur, Switzerland, 1989.

Hahn, Robert W., and Gordon L. Hester: "Marketable Permits: Lessons from Theory and Practice," *Ecology Law Quarterly*, 16(1), Winter 1989, pp. 361–406.

Kosobud, Richard F., and Jennifer M. Zimmerman: *Market-Based Approaches to Environmental Policy, Regulatory Innovation to the Fore*, John Wiley, New York, 1987.

Organization for Economic Cooperation and Development: *Implementing Domestic Tradable Permits for Environmental Protection*, OECD, Paris, 1999.

Project 88—Round II Incentives for Action: Designing Market-Based Environmental Strategies: A Public Policy Study sponsored by Senators Timothy E. Wirth and John Heinz, Washington, DC, May 1991.

Roberts, Marc J.: "Some Problems in Implementing Marketable Pollution Rights Schemes: The Case of the Clean Air Act," in Wesley A. Magat (ed.), *Reform of Environmental Regulation,* Ballinger Publishing Company, Cambridge, MA, 1982, pp. 93–118.

Rose-Ackerman, Susan: "Market Models for Water Pollution Control: Their Strengths and Weaknesses," *Public Policy,* 25(3), Summer 1977, pp. 383–406.

Tietenberg, Tom H.: *Emissions Trading: An Exercise in Reforming Pollution Policy,* Resources for the Future, Washington, DC, 1985.

Tripp, James T. B., and Daniel Dudek: "Institutional Guidelines for Designing Successful Transferable Rights Programs," *Yale Journal of Regulation,* 6(2), Summer 1989, pp. 369–392.

U.S. Council of Economic Advisors: "Making Markets Work for the Environment," Chapter 7, *Economic Report of the President,* February 2000, pp. 239–275.

ENVIRONMENTAL POLICY
IN THE UNITED STATES

Having looked at the principles of designing effective environmental policy, we now turn to an examination of actual policies. In fact, most of the remainder of the book consists of chapters about public policies that have been put in place to deal with environmental problems of various types. This section contains four chapters on U.S. environmental policies. There are three chapters on federal policy on problems of water, air, and hazardous materials. Then there is a chapter on environmental policies of the states. Each of these policy areas is extremely complex, with its own history, character, and vocabulary. What the chapters aim for is a summary of the main elements of each policy area, utilizing the ideas discussed in the preceding chapters.

CHAPTER 14

FEDERAL WATER POLLUTION–CONTROL POLICY

Water is biologically necessary for life, but, beyond this, water resources play a vital and pervasive role in the health and welfare of a modern economy. Water for direct human consumption is a small but critical part of the domestic system, which also includes water used in food preparation, cleaning, and sewage disposal. Water is an essential element in many industrial and commercial production processes, again both as an input and as a medium of waste disposal. Large amounts of water are used by farmers for irrigation, especially in the western United States. And in recent decades water-based sports and recreation, both freshwater and saltwater, have become very popular.

The water resource system itself consists of a vast array of interconnected components, from the grandiose to the tiny. The surface-water system includes the huge main-stem rivers and Great Lakes, as well as the thousands of small neighborhood streams and ponds. Add to these the innumerable person-made components, from the mill ponds of the first industrial era to the vast reservoirs and canals of today. Swamps and wetlands abound, ranging from small local bogs to the huge Everglades in southern Florida. And then there is the vast, but unseen, system of groundwater aquifers, exceeding surface waters in terms of sheer quantity of water. Saltwater resources are also of vital importance. Marshes and coastal lowlands are critical for fish and wildlife resources; beaches and scenic coasts are important recreational resources; coastal waters provide transportation and pleasure boating services; and saltwater fisheries are a major source of food.

Efforts to protect these water resources have gone on for a long time but with increasing vigor in the last few decades. In this chapter we look at federal water pollution-control policy. Our objective is to review the main elements of that policy with the economic concepts developed in preceding chapters. We also look at some recent policy innovations that seek to make use of economic incentives to achieve improvements in water quality. Most states and localities also have active water pollution-control efforts, some of which are tied into the federal programs; we will consider some of these in a later chapter.

TYPES OF WATER POLLUTANTS

There are many different types of waterborne pollutants. Within the policy arena it is common to differentiate the following categories:

Conventional pollutants: These represent some of the first water pollutants that were subject to control. They include biochemical oxygen-demanding wastes (BOD), total suspended solids (TSS), bacteria, fecal coliform (FC), oil, grease, and pH.

Nonconventional pollutants: These include chemical oxygen demand (COD), total organic carbon (TOC), nitrogen, and phosphorous. Fertilizers, sewage, manure, and detergents are sources of these substances.

Toxic pollutants: These include 65 named (in the Clean Water Act) chemicals, consisting of natural and synthetic organic chemicals as well as metals discharged from industrial sources.

Waterborne emissions include all the different types of discharges discussed in Chapter 2. **Point sources** include outfalls from industry and domestic wastewater treatment plants. **Nonpoint sources** include agricultural runoff of pesticides and fertilizers and the chemicals and oils that are flushed off urban streets by periodic rains. Many sources, especially point sources, have **continuous** emissions related to the rate of operation of the industrial plant or the domestic sewer system. There are also many **episodic emissions,** such as accidental releases of toxic materials, oil-tanker accidents, or occasional planned releases of industrial pollutants.

In Chapter 2 we also spoke of cumulative and noncumulative pollutants. In water pollution control it is more common to speak of **persistent** and **degradable** pollutants. Degradable waterborne pollutants undergo a variety of biological, chemical, and physical processes that change their characteristics after emission. Especially important are the oxygen-using chemical processes that rely on the oxygen contained in receiving waters to degrade the wastes.[1] The reason for focusing on oxygen requirements is that oxygen plays a critical role in water quality. High levels of dissolved oxygen (DO) are usually associated with high-quality water, water that will support high-quality recreational uses and that can be used in domestic water-supply systems.

Since DO is used up in the degradation process, one way of measuring the quantity of waste emitted is through **"biochemical oxygen demand,"** or BOD,

---

[1]Degradable wastes also include a variety of infectious bacterial agents that can cause such diseases as typhoid, cholera, and dysentery. Waste heat is also a degradable pollutant; it comes mostly from large-scale industrial processes that use water for cooling purposes.

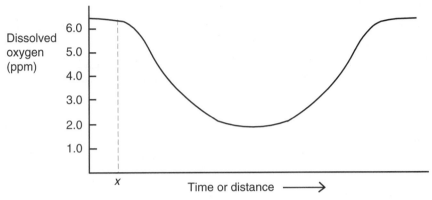

FIGURE 14-1
Dissolved Oxygen Profile in Water after a BOD Load Has Been Introduced.

the amount of oxygen required to decompose the organic material under specified conditions of temperature and time.[2] A substantial proportion of the BOD
load introduced into the water resources of the country comes from municipal
waste-treatment plants. Much of this consists of wastewater from treated
domestic waste, which contains a variety of degradable organic compounds.
Industrial sources also contribute large amounts of BOD, some stemming from
the sanitary facilities within the plants, but more importantly from the great
variety of water-using steps in the production processes, such as cleaning,
product formation, waste removal, and product transport.

When a BOD load is put into a river or body of water, it produces a temporary
reduction in the DO level of that water as the oxygen is used up to degrade the
waste. But over time, through natural aeration processes, the DO content of the
water will normally recover. The **DO "profile"** would thus look like Figure 14-1
(where the discharge point is marked x). This can be thought of as the average
DO level at various distances downstream from the point at which a BOD load
is introduced, or the DO level at various times after a BOD load has been introduced into a lake. This is called a DO "sag," and it illustrates the degradation
process by which the water body is assimilating the BOD load. The important
thing to see is that the DO reduction is reversible. It is also noncumulative—if
the BOD source were stopped, the DO sag would shortly disappear.

Early water pollution-control efforts were centered on conventional pollutants such as BOD, suspended solids, and so on for which there are common
water quality measures such as DO, turbidity, acidity, and coliform count. More
recent programs also focus on **toxic pollutants.** Toxicity is often a matter of concentration; substances that are toxic at high concentrations may not be at low
concentrations. This implies that the diluting ability of water is a valuable quality in addition to its capacity to transform degradable substances.

---

[2]For example, 10 pounds of BOD_{10} is a quantity of material requiring 10 pounds of oxygen in
order to be completely converted to its constituent elements during a period of 10 days and at a
temperature of 20°C.

TABLE 14-1
MAJOR FEDERAL LEGISLATION ON WATER POLLUTION CONTROL

1899 Refuse Act
Required permit from the U.S. Army Corps of Engineers before refuse of any kind could be put into a navigable water. Primary purpose was to ensure navigability, but it had a brief, and not very successful, reincarnation in the 1960s as a water-quality measure.

1948 Water Pollution Control Act (WPCA)
Federal government was authorized to conduct investigations, research, and surveys; however, no federal authority was established to enforce laws, set standards, or limit discharges. Authorized federal government to make loans to municipalities to construct sewage treatment facilities.

1956 WPCA Amendments
Authorized the states to establish criteria for determining desirable levels of water quality; introduced the idea of an "enforcement conference," sponsored by federal agencies to bring together state and local interests to develop enforcement plans. Authorized federal government to make grants for municipal waste treatment facilities, with federal share up to 55 percent of construction costs.

1965 Water Quality Act
Required the states to develop *ambient quality standards* for interstate water bodies and implementation plans calling for effluent reductions from specific sources. State actions required federal approval, with a strengthened "enforcement conference" procedure.

1972 WPCA Amendments
Provided for a federally mandated system of *technology-based effluent standards,* with federal enforcement through the granting of discharge permits. Phase I (starting in 1977) permits were based on "Best Practicable Technology" (BPT); Phase II (starting in 1983) based on "Best Available Technology" (BAT); states could ultimately take over permitting process. Declared a goal of zero discharge to be attained by 1985. Made a large increase in the municipal treatment plant grant program, with federal share increased to 75 percent of construction costs. Mandated secondary treatment in municipal treatment plants.

Persistent water pollutants are those that remain for a long period of time, either because they are nondegradable or because the rate of degradation is very slow. This category includes thousands of inorganic and organic chemicals of various descriptions—the wastes of a modern, chemical-based economy. Industrial wastes contain many such persistent pollutants. Wastes from mining operations can contain various metals as well as acid-mine drainage. Agriculture is the source of a variety of pesticides, fertilizers, and soil runoff. The concept of "persistent" does not mean permanent in a technical sense; many chemicals, oils, solvents, and so on, break down, but over a long period of time. In the process they pose a persistent threat. Radioactive waste is physically degradable over very long periods, but measured in terms of a human scale it is essentially a persistent pollutant. Viruses are apparently also in this category.

TABLE 14-1
MAJOR FEDERAL LEGISLATION ON WATER POLLUTION CONTROL (CONTINUED)

1974 Safe Drinking Water Act
Requires the EPA to set maximum contaminant levels for drinking water; requires public authorities to protect, monitor, and test water supplies. Amended in 1986 and 1996.

1977 Clean Water Act
Established procedures for control of toxic effluent in addition to conventional effluent on which previous acts had focused; sources were required to meet "Best Conventional Technology" (BCT) for conventional pollutants and BAT for toxics, starting in 1984; increased authorization for treatment plant subsidies.

1981 Municipal Wastewater Treatment Construction Grant Amendments
Reduced federal share to 55 percent and substantially decreased the authorized funding level.

1987 Water Quality Act
Postponed some of the deadlines for adopting *technology-based effluent standards;* changed the waste treatment subsidy program from federal grants to federal contributions to state revolving funds.

Sources: Allen V. Kneese and Charles L. Schultz, *Pollution, Prices and Public Policy,* Brookings Institution, Washington, DC, 1973, p. 31; Tom H. Tietenberg, *Environmental and Natural Resource Economics,* 2nd ed., Scott, Foresman, Glenview, IL, 1988, pp. 410–411; A. Myrick Freeman III, "Water Pollution Control," in Paul R. Portney (ed.), *Public Policies for Environmental Protection,* Resources for the Future, Washington, DC, 1990, pp. 100–101.

FEDERAL POLICY: A BRIEF HISTORY

Prior to the 20th century the only public policy initiatives taken toward water pollution control were at the state level. In the "sanitary awakening" of the mid-19th century, the public began to appreciate the importance of water quality for human health. Many states instituted public boards of health in response.[3] The first federal law of any note covering water pollution control was actually enacted at the very end of the 19th century (see Table 14-1). This was the **1899 Refuse Act** empowering the U.S. Army Corps of Engineers to grant permits to anyone desiring to put refuse of any kind into any navigable waterway. The primary objective of this act was to ensure navigation, not to control water pollution per se.

Very little happened, therefore, until after World War II. Then the Water Pollution Control Act of 1948 was enacted, which authorized federal authorities to assist the states in water pollution–control matters. Primary responsibility, however, was to remain at the state level. The 1948 Act also authorized a program that over the years would become a major element of the federal effort: subsidies to municipalities to construct waste treatment facilities. That

[3]The first such agency was in Massachusetts in 1869.

act also sought to develop new enforcement institutions, so-called enforcement conferences, where federal, state, and local administrative authorities would come together and hammer out water pollution–control policies. In 1965 came the Water Quality Act, which, besides extending many provisions of past laws and refunding the municipal waste-treatment subsidy program, sought to encourage the states to develop **ambient standards** for water quality.

The early 1970s saw a rapid growth in the environmental movement and in environmental advocacy in Washington, D.C. There was at the time a feeling among environmental interest groups that past policy had not worked well enough and quickly enough to respond to growing pollution problems. The Environmental Protection Agency (EPA) had recently been formed (1970) and this gave environmental issues more visibility and greater political representation. One result was the 1972 Water Pollution Control Act Amendments. This Act did several things; it set a goal of **zero discharges** to be attained by 1985, and it substantially increased the amount of money for the municipal waste-treatment subsidy program. More importantly, however, it established a powerful, direct federal role in water pollution control.

The primary approach before then was an ambient-based one. States were supposed to establish ambient water quality standards, then translate these into specific emission reductions by the many firms and treatment plants contributing to the problem. The new approach was for federal authorities to set specific effluent standards for individual point sources of water pollutants. To enforce these standards the law reached all the way back to the 1899 Refuse Act, based on federally issued **discharge permits.** Each source of waterborne emissions would require a permit specifying the time, place, and maximum quantity of emissions. To provide the basis for these permits, the EPA would promulgate what are called **technology-based effluent standards** for all sources discharging wastes into the nation's waters. As we discuss in more detail later, these are essentially emission standards that are tied to particular types of pollution-control technology. Thus, the primary approach to water pollution control was changed from an ambient-based to a **technology-based system.**

While the deadlines have been pushed back several times, there is now a substantially completed system in place for establishing and enforcing technology-based effluent standards for point sources. More recently, attention has been directed to **nonpoint sources.** In this case much of the initiative has been left to the states. A substantial focus of the program has been to encourage operators (especially farmers, whose operations account for a large part of nonpoint-source emissions) to adopt **best-management practices** (BMPs). A BMP is a federally approved (and often subsidized) procedure or technique whose adoption will reduce the runoff of nonpoint-source water pollutants. Agricultural BMPs might include, for example, changes in certain cultivation practices, construction of dikes or barriers, or planting of buffer zones around fields. Clearly this is strictly a technology-based approach to pollution control. The other major part of the Clean Water Act has been the program of **federal grants** to municipalities for the construction of **public wastewater treatment plants.** We will discuss this program later in the chapter.

TECHNOLOGY-BASED EFFLUENT STANDARDS

A technology-based effluent standard (TBES)[4] is an effluent standard set at the level of emissions that a source would produce if it were employing a particular type of abatement technology. Firms emitting waste materials or energy usually face a choice among different technologies and methods for reducing emissions. From among these possibilities each source must choose one particular package, which may involve, for example, particular types of equipment, raw materials, internal operating procedures, recycling machinery, treatment processes, or effluent removal techniques. Different packages of technologies and operating procedures lead to different costs as well as a different level of emissions. To establish a TBES, the EPA studies the effluent abatement technologies and procedures available to a particular type of industrial operation; after having selected one technology from among the many available, it sets the emission standard at the level of emissions that are produced when that technology is used by firms in that industry.

It would require enormous effort to establish effluent standards for each and every individual source. Thus, the EPA sets standards for categories of polluting sources. Take, for example, sugar-beet processing plants.[5] This is a process that uses a large amount of water for cleaning purposes; thus, the wastewater may contain large amounts of suspended solids and BOD. Table 14-2 shows the costs and emissions performance of five different technology options for plants in this industry. These are not costs and emissions for any particular plant; they are anticipated costs and emissions for a "representative" plant of each type. Each technological option refers to a particular collection of treatment equipment, operating procedures, fuels, and so on, that the plants might adopt. The EPA, after having developed these estimates,[6] must now choose a particular level of emissions for the standard.

Clearly, lower levels of emissions can be obtained with greater costs; in fact, emissions into water bodies could be reduced to zero at a very high cost. To pick one set of emission levels for the standard requires that the EPA use some sort of criterion. The Water Pollution Control Act of 1972 states that the EPA should initially set emission standards on the basis of the **"best practicable technology"** (BPT) currently available to the firms. This was Phase I, to be achieved by 1977. Then starting in 1983, firms would be subject to Phase II effluent standards, based on **"best available technology"** (BAT).

---

[4]Pollution-control policy is rife with acronyms. The appendix beginning on page 483 contains a list of acronyms used in the book.

[5]Sugar-beet processing uses substantial quantities of water. Some is used simply to move the product around the plant, whereas some is used in actual processing. Hydrated lime is used as a purifying agent, which leaves a large amount of "lime mud" to dispose of. Emission control can be done with a variety of water recycling and recirculation, screening, settling, stabilization ponds, and land disposal.

[6]In fact, these numbers would more than likely have been provided by an engineering consulting firm hired by the EPA. An agency that regulates thousands of plants in dozens of different industries has to look outside for technical help.

TABLE 14-2
ESTIMATED TOTAL COSTS AND EMISSIONS FROM SUGAR-BEET PLANTS
USING ALTERNATIVE EMISSION ABATEMENT TECHNOLOGY

		Technological option				
	No control	A	B	C	D	E
Emissions (kg/kkg of raw product processed)						
BOD*	5.8	3.6	2.2	1.05	.23	0.0
TSS†	10.2	5.7	2.5	1.02	.30	0.0
Total costs ($ mil/year)	0.0	8.0	14.4	23.40	36.50	78.8

*Biochemical oxygen demand.
†Total suspended solids.

Thus, to set the Phase I emission standard for sugar-beet processing plants, EPA would have to determine which of the technologies displayed in the table represented the "best practicable" level of technology. Clearly, this is open to interpretation because the notion of "practicable" is not precise by any means. "Practicable" apparently refers to technology that is reasonably well known and readily available without excessive costs. Suppose EPA decides that technology C, with an estimated cost of $23.4 million per year, represents the best practicable technology for this type of processing industry. Then it would set emission standards at 1.05 kg/kkg for BOD and 1.02 kg/kkg for total suspended solids. All sugar-beet processing plants would then be subject to this emission standard. In Phase II EPA would be called on to select the "best available technology" (BAT) for this type of industry. BAT would appear to be a more stringent standard than BPT because it includes all technologies that are available whether or not they are practicable. But the rules also specify that BAT has to be "economically achievable." On this basis, technology E in Table 14-2 might be regarded as the BAT for sugar-beet processing plants. On the other hand, some (especially those in the industry) might argue that such technology doesn't realistically exist, that it is too costly to be considered "available" in any economic sense, in which case EPA might select D as the BAT.

Setting technology-based effluent standards for an industry is obviously a time-consuming business. It requires large amounts of economic analysis and hinges on an agency judgment about what "available" and "practicable" mean when applied to pollution-control technology. It is also politically controversial, with industries ready to challenge in court when they feel the standards are too constraining. It is no wonder that the EPA made very slow progress in setting TBESs after the 1972 law was enacted.

In the 1977 Clean Water Act the criteria for selecting emission standards were changed. After 1984 sources were to meet standards based on **"best conventional technology"** (BCT). The notion of "conventional" technology is different, and weaker, than the idea of "available" technology; it presumably allows more weight to be put on the costs of installing and operating the technology.[7] In some cases the EPA has set BCT equal to BPT. The EPA also sets TBESs, called "pretreatment standards," for firms discharging wastes into public sewer systems. Their role is to reduce the burden on public wastewater treatment plants.

Technology-based effluent standards to control water pollution stem from the desire to find a technological fix for pollution problems. The original notion behind the 1972 act was that engineering studies by the EPA would identify preferred pollution-control technologies, and because emission standards would be based on these technologies, there would be few practical obstacles in the way of their timely adoption by firms. In fact, the very ambiguity of words like "practicable" and "conventional" means that a great amount of discretion and judgment must be used by people developing the standards. Over the years EPA has struggled valiantly to clarify the role of discretion and judgment in setting the standards. Industrial firms also have had views about what these words mean, which has led through the years to vast amounts of conflict and litigation.

Efficiency and Cost-Effectiveness of TBESs

For a policy to be efficient, it must balance damages and control costs. The technology-based effluent standards are designed, however, to be applied on a national basis. The same standards for, say, leather processing plants will be applied to all leather plants in the country, whether they are located on a river just upstream from a large urban area or on a river in some remote part of the country. This is the result of a totally technology-based approach to pollution control, where questions of economic efficiency have been excluded from consideration.

Cost-effectiveness, as we have discussed many times so far, is a question of whether society is getting the maximum effect, in terms of reduced emissions, for the money spent. The simple key to this question is whether the policy is designed so that when sources are in compliance they will have the same marginal abatement costs. There is nothing in the logic of the TBES process that moves water-pollution sources in the direction of meeting the equimarginal condition. The procedure leads instead to the application of the same standards to all firms within each subcategory. For example, all sugar-beet processing plants in the country are subject to the same effluent standards. These will be cost-effective only if all individual plants in each category have exactly the same marginal abatement costs. This is unlikely to be the case. The EPA has designated around 600 subcategories of water-polluting industries, for each of which TBESs have been promulgated. But there are tens of thousands of individual industrial water-pollution sources, so some of the subcategories must

---

[7]The ambiguities of using these criteria to choose specific technology options led the EPA at one time to establish a benchmark for BCT of $1.15 per pound of pollutant removed. Anything above this was considered too costly to be "conventional."

contain very large numbers of sources. There can be little doubt that the sources in most subcategories are heterogeneous in terms of the production technology they are using, so we would expect them to be heterogeneous in terms of their marginal emission abatement costs. Thus, applying the same emission standards to each firm cannot be cost effective.

Experience with TBESs

In assessing the actual experience with technology-based effluent standards, there are two questions to consider:

1 How much has the nation's water quality been improved as a result of the system?
2 How bad has the cost-effectiveness problem been; in particular, how much greater improvement could have been obtained with a more cost-effective regulatory approach?

Both of these questions are extremely complicated. The country's waters are very diverse, consisting of many different streams, rivers, lakes, estuaries, and aquifers all variously situated with respect to both natural and human factors. It's reasonably easy to draw conclusions of a single, small water body, but very hard to do it for the entire system. Analysts in the EPA have recently undertaken a large-scale study to try and answer the question: What would the water quality of U.S. waters be at the present time if the Clean Water Act and its subsequent regulations had never been adopted?[8] Some of their first results are shown in Table 14-3. This refers to **conventional pollutants** in the nation's **rivers and streams.** The water quality characteristics of these water courses have been aggregated into recreational use categories: swimmable waters are those having high enough water quality to support this type of activity; it also will support the other two activities, fishing and boating. Fishable waters will support this together with boating, while boating waters will support only this activity and not the other two. The nonsupport category represents the lowest quality; waters that are so degraded they will support none of the recreational categories. The last three columns show the increases in mileage of rivers and streams that will support the given activities, first in terms of total mileage, then as a percent of the without–Clean Water Act (CWA) provisions, and then as a percent of what would have occurred if it had been possible to reduce all point-source emissions to zero. Note that the CWA regulations have increased the number of swimmable, fishable, and boatable miles by, respectively, 7.4 percent, 6.2 percent, and 4.8 percent over what they would have been without the CWA. Waters that will support none of these activities have decreased 12.2 percent. While these percentages may seem quite modest, note that the increases are about 50–60 percent of what the increases would have been if all point-source emissions had been reduced to zero. In other words, the Clean Water

[8]Note that this is a with/without question, not a before/after question. See the discussion of this issue in Chapter 8.

TABLE 14-3
RIVERS AND STREAMS (632,552 MILES) SUPPORTING RECREATIONAL USES:
COMPARISON OF WITH–CLEAN WATER ACT (CWA) AND WITHOUT–CLEAN WATER
ACT (CWA) CONDITIONS IN THE MID-1990S

			Increase in use support		
Highest use supported	Without–CWA conditions (miles)	With–CWA conditions (miles)	Miles	Percent increase	Percent of maximum increase[a]
Swimmable	222,120	238,627	16,507	7.4	49.5%
Fishable	399,999	424,712	24,713	6.2	57.8%
Boatable	454,038	475,894	21,856	4.8	59.4%
Nonsupport	178,514	156,658	−21,856	−12.2	59.4%

[a]Analysts estimated the mileage of rivers and streams that would support the various uses if all point-source emissions had been reduced to zero.
Source: Mahesh Podar, *A Benefits Assessment of Water Pollution Control Programs Since 1972: Part 1, The Benefits of Point Source Controls for Conventional Pollutants in Rivers and Streams,* Final Report, U.S. Environmental Protection Agency, Office of Water, Office of Policy, Economics, and Innovation, Washington, DC, January 2000.

Act, which has been primarily aimed at point sources, has moved us 50-60 percent of the way toward zero discharge levels for point sources. This is a significant accomplishment. But it is apparent also that there are limits to the extent to which all watercourses could be restored to swimmable category solely through point-source control. We must also recognize that the results of Table 14-3 cover only part of the overall water quality problem. It does not touch on water pollution in other parts of the water system, namely ponds, lakes, coastal areas, estuaries, and underground aquifers. Further analysis will be needed to cover these resources.

The next important question is the one on cost-effectiveness. Has this amount of improved water quality been achieved at something approaching minimum cost? Or, to say the same thing in a different way, for the amount of money devoted to point-source water-pollution control, have we achieved the maximum possible in terms of improved water quality? It's impossible to examine the entire system to answer this, but studies have been done of particular river basins to compare the costs of the EPA technology-based approach to point source control with the least cost means of attaining the same objectives. These use large-scale models of individual river basins, incorporating the different estimated marginal abatement costs of various sources of pollution, together with the main hydrological features of the basins' water resources. They compare the costs of water pollution-control programs in which all sources were treated alike to those where sources are controlled in accordance with relative marginal abatement costs.

Some results are shown in Table 14-4. The interesting ones are in the last column. This shows, for each study, the ratio of program cost using equiproportionate reduction (which is close to the actual requirements of the Clean Water

TABLE 14-4
COMPARISON OF POINT-SOURCE WATER POLLUTION–CONTROL COSTS, TECHNOLOGY-BASED SYSTEM VERSUS LEAST-COST SYSTEM FOR CONTROLLING WATER POLLUTANTS

Study	Water resource	Water quality target (mg/liter)	Ratio of technology-based system to least-cost control system[a]
Johnson[b]	Delaware Estuary	2.0 mg/liter DO	3.13
		3.0 mg/liter DO	1.62
		4.0 mg/liter DO	1.43
O'Neill[c]	Fox River (Wisconsin)	2.0 mg/liter DO	2.29
		4.0 mg/liter DO	1.71
		6.2 mg/liter DO	1.45
		7.8 mg/liter DO	1.38
Eheart, Beill, and Lyon[d]	Willamette River	4.8 mg/liter DO	1.12
		7.4 mg/liter DO	1.19
	Delaware Estuary	3.0 mg/liter DO	3.00
		3.6 mg/liter DO	2.92
	Hudson River	5.1 mg/liter DO	1.54
		5.9 mg/liter DO	1.62
	Mohawk River	6.8 mg/liter DO	1.22
Kneese and Bower[e]	Delaware Estuary	2 ppm DO	3.1
		3–4 ppm DO	2.9
Kerri[f]	Willamette River	5.0 mg/liter	1.58
Goodman and Dobbins[g]	Merrimack River (MA)	3.0 ppm DO	1.34
Bennett, Thorpe, and Guse[h]	Long Island Sound	Total nitrogen loading (tons)	1.25

[a]The least cost system is the one satisfying the equimarginal role. The technology-based system is one of equiproportionate reduction, which is the one that comes the closest to the system established under the Clean Water Act.
[b]Edwin L. Johnson, "A Study in the Economics of Water Quality Management," *Water Resources Research*, 3(1), 1967, p. 297.
[c]William B. O'Neil, "Pollution Permits and Markets for Water Quality," Ph.D. dissertation, University of Wisconsin–Madison, 1980, p. 65.
[d]J. Wayland Eheart, E. Downey Brill Jr., and Randolph M. Lyon, "Transferable Discharge Permits for BOD Control, An Overview," in Erhard F. Joeres and Martin H. David (eds.), *Buying a Better Environment: Cost Effective Regulation through Permit Trading*, University of Wisconsin Press, Madison, WI, 1983, p. 177.
[e]Allen V. Kneese and Blair T. Bower, *Managing Water Quality: Economics, Technology, Institution*, Johns Hopkins Press for Resources for the Future, Baltimore, MD, 1968, p. 162.
[f]K. D. Kerri, "An Economic Approach to Water Quality Control," *Journal of the Water Pollution Control Federation*, 38(12), December 1966, pp. 1883–1897.
[g]A. S. Goodwin and W. Dobbins, "Mathematical Model for Water Pollution Control Studies," *Journal of the Sanitary Engineering Division, Proceedings*, ASCE, 92(SA6), December 1966, pp. 1–9.
[h]Lynne L. Bennett, Stephen G. Thorpe, and A. Joseph Guse, "Cost-Effective Control of Nitrogen Loadings in Long Island Sound," *Water Resources Research*, 36(12), 2000, p. 3711.

Act) to a least-cost program, that is, one satisfying the equimarginal principle. Thus a ratio of 2.0, for example, indicates that the actual cost is two times higher than the least cost. The costs, and cost ratios, were estimated in most studies for different target levels of dissolved oxygen. Note that most of the ratios lie between about 1.5 and 3.1. From these results we can draw the conclusion that the command-and-control system based on technology-based effluent standards is significantly more costly than is necessary to reach target levels of water quality. Had we installed policies and regulations that met cost-effectiveness criteria, we could have attained substantially greater improvements in water quality than we have over the last three decades or so.

TBESs and Technological Improvements

The discussion in Chapter 12 showed that emission standards lead to weaker incentives to innovate in pollution control than economic incentive–type policies. In the case of TBESs, incentives are made even weaker by linking the emission standards to particular control technologies. When polluters are faced with this type of technology-linked standard, compliance tends to become a matter of adopting the technology the authorities have used to set the standard. Since permanent emissions monitoring is quite costly, administering authorities can check compliance by making periodic inspections to ascertain whether sources are using approved emissions-control technology. To minimize the risk of being penalized for noncompliance, polluters have the incentive to adopt the particular technology that EPA used to establish the standard. The result is that although the TBESs are nominally just emission standards, they end up tending to dictate the particular effluent control technologies chosen by firms. This substantially undermines the incentives to search for other, cheaper ways to meet the standards.

This is another important dimension of these incentive effects. Figure 14-2 shows an abbreviated sketch of a typical residuals and emissions loop. Residuals are generated in the production process, based on inputs used and the production technology in place. These residuals then move to what we can call a residuals treatment phase, where some are perhaps converted into recyclable materials and some are converted in form and quantities, then these enter an emission stream that is introduced into the environment. The primary focus of the program of technology-based effluent standards has been on technology in box (2), that is, on getting point sources to adopt new technological

FIGURE 14-2
End-of-the-Pipe Pollution Control versus Pollution Prevention.

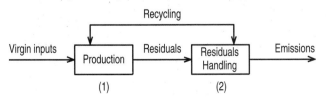

means of handling and testing residuals. This is known as an **end-of-the-pipe** program orientation, because it focuses only on the last step in the residuals/emissions process. It is clear, however, that emissions can be reduced in other ways as well. One is by developing better **recycling technology.** Another is to go back to the production process itself and introduce changes that lower the quantity of residuals that are produced. One way of doing this, for example, is to find ways of using **fewer inputs** in the production process. Another is to reduce the rate of output itself (as in, e.g., efforts to get consumers to conserve energy). As mentioned in Chapter 2, these efforts to reduce the residual stream have come to be called **pollution prevention.** By encouraging firms to concentrate on changing end-of-the-pipe technology, the regulatory program has weakened the incentives to take vigorous steps in the direction of pollution prevention.

TBESs and Enforcement

Effluent standards are enforced through a system of **discharge permits.** To discharge wastes into a river or body of water, a firm must have a permit issued through the relevant EPA-backed state permitting program. The permit specifies the allowable emissions the source may make and is subject to enforcement by state authorities. Given the enormous number of discharge points and the difficulties of monitoring emissions, enforcement becomes a critical program element. One response has been to distinguish between major and minor emitters, using criteria such as quantity, toxicity, conventional pollution load, and impact of emissions. In this way more enforcement resources can be devoted to the major sources, which account for the largest proportion of total emissions.

Lacking high-quality techniques for monitoring emissions, control authorities are forced back on some other means of ensuring compliance. When emission standards are tied to certain technologies, enforcing authorities can try to confirm compliance simply by checking to see if firms have put in place the criterion technology.[9] The problem here is that there is a difference between **initial compliance** and **continued compliance.** The fact that a firm has installed certain pollution-control equipment does not necessarily mean that this equipment will be operated efficiently in the years to come. If operating costs are substantial and if nobody is effectively monitoring emissions, the incentive will be to save on operating costs and let emissions increase.

Technology-based effluent standards have an aura of concreteness and directness. What better way to get pollution reduced than simply to require polluters to adopt certain types of pollution-control technology? But this engineering-based approach is far less effective than it appears. We have seen how, from an economic standpoint, it is likely to be seriously cost-*in*effective; for the money that is being devoted to pollution control under this system, sub-

---

[9]The word "simply" in this sentence may be misleading. Nothing is simple in the world of pollution control. Polluters have challenged virtually every part of the federal pollution-control program, including enforcement procedures. Thus, over the years, legal doctrine has developed regarding such things as the specific procedures for visiting sources to check for compliance.

stantially greater improvements in water quality could be achieved with other policy approaches. The apparent technological definiteness of the approach ("best practicable technology," "best available technology," etc.) is, in fact, far less effective in practice. The EPA is required to make countless engineering decisions in order to develop these standards. Not only is this very difficult for an administrating agency, but each of these decisions is a place where political interests can focus influence. The apparent concreteness of technology-based effluent standards is also substantially undermined by the monitoring and enforcement problem. What looks like a straightforward technological fix becomes, in reality, a policy with a great deal of hidden flexibility.

THE MUNICIPAL WASTEWATER TREATMENT PLANT SUBSIDY PROGRAM

A large proportion of waterborne emissions into the nation's waterways comes not from private industries but from people themselves, especially from the public sewer systems of urbanized areas. Whereas in the case of industrial pollution federal authorities adopted a policy of having polluters themselves pay for reducing emissions, the response toward public-sector pollution has been different. Here the major approach has been **federal subsidies** to construct treatment plants. The inspiration for this type of approach probably comes from two sources: the normal public-works mentality of the Congress and the fact that it is better politics to "get tough" on industrial polluters than on cities, towns, and voters.

Treatment of domestic wastes uses both physical and biological processes and is fairly standardized. The different degrees of treatment are designated *primary, secondary,* and *tertiary,* according to the process used and the extent of treatment given to the wastes. Primary treatment is essentially a set of physical steps built around a basic sedimentation process; it can remove about 35–40 percent of the primary BOD in the original waste stream. Secondary treatment uses biological means (e.g., "activated sludge") to further treat the waste. Primary and secondary processes together can reduce BOD by between 85 and 90 percent. These processes, although quite effective in removing BOD, are less so in handling plant nutrients such as nitrogen and phosphorus. So-called tertiary treatment, making use of a variety of chemical processes, can reduce waste loads even more. The sequence of primary, secondary, and tertiary processes is subject to increasing marginal abatement costs; the greater the reduction one wants in BOD or other pollutants in the waste stream, the higher the marginal cost of getting it.

The 1972 WPCA Amendments mandated that all municipal sewer systems have at least secondary treatment by 1983. To reach this goal Congress authorized a program of federal subsidies to local municipalities to cover the costs of designing and constructing public wastewater treatment plants. These grants had been authorized in the 1956 WPCA Amendments, but they increased markedly in the early 1970s. In the 1972 act, the federal share of construction costs was increased from 55 percent to 75 percent, and in these years large new

TABLE 14-5
PROGRESS IN PUBLIC WASTEWATER TREATMENT FACILITIES

	1960	1970	1980	1988	1996
Total U.S. population (millions)	180	203	224	246	264
Percentage served by waste treatment systems	61	71	71	72	72
Percentage of served population with:					
No treatment	63	41	1	1	<1
Primary treatment only	33	N/A	31	15	9
At least secondary	4	N/A	68	84	91

Source: 1960–1988: Council on Environmental Quality, *Environmental Quality,* 1990, p. 309; and previous issues; 1996: Environmental Protection Agency, *1996 Clean Water Needs Survey, Report to Congress,* U.S. EPA, Office of Water, September 1997, Appendix C. (Figures rounded to the nearest whole number.)

sums were appropriated for the program. From 1960 to 1985, federal grants amounted to about $56 billion in real terms.[10] The figures in Table 14-5 seem to show the impact of the program. From 1960 to 1988 the percentage of public sewer systems discharging untreated waste declined from 63 percent to less than 1 percent, whereas the percentage having at least secondary treatment increased substantially.

It's tempting to attribute this improvement to the federal program, but, as always, we have to look below the surface to find out what really went on. Although the new federal subsidy program added large sums to construct municipal wastewater treatment plants, it was in reality accompanied by substantial reductions of funds for this purpose at the local level. When federal authorities increased funds for the program, local funds were diverted to other things. So although total capital spending for municipal treatment plants did increase during the 1970s, it did not increase by as much as would appear if one looks strictly at the history of the federal program.

There can be little question, however, that the federal grant program for public treatment plant construction has produced results; there can be little doubt also that the program has cost much more than it should have. There are built-in sources of inefficiency that have substantially shaped the program. One is the allocation of the grant funds among municipalities. From an efficiency standpoint, one would want to allocate the funds to municipalities where treatment plant construction would have the maximum impact on water-quality improvement. The EPA has struggled to find a way of doing this in the face of overwhelming political pressures. Its approach has been to allocate grant funds on the basis of a "needs" survey. The needs survey was to take into account existing population, the pollution problem in different bodies of water, and the needs for preserving higher-quality water in these various bodies. The formula was open to interpretation and subject to judgment, especially political judgment. There have been strong pressures to allocate grant funds to states and

---

[10]That is, adjusted for inflation; see the discussion of "real" vs. "nominal" values in Chapter 6.

municipalities more on the basis of their political significance than on water-quality improvement criteria.

Any large subsidy program creates its own set of incentives; some may work toward the objectives of the program, and some probably will not. One problem with the waste treatment plant subsidies is that it created incentives for industrial polluters to solve their emission problems by connecting up to the subsidized public system. Municipalities had the incentive to use these subsidies for economic development purposes, by building really large plants that had excess capacity, then luring companies to locate in their area with the offer of cheap waste disposal. How could the federal government give municipalities a subsidy but keep them from passing it on to business polluters? The answer was to adopt a set of emission standards called **pretreatment standards.** These are standards applied to wastewater streams entering public sewer systems from private business sources. The objective is to get industrial polluters to undertake some treatment themselves before they put their wastes into the public sewer system.

Perhaps the biggest difficulty with the grant program has been the perverse incentives it has tended to create at the local level. When a substantial fraction of design and construction costs is picked up by somebody else, the incentives for grant recipients to seek out the most efficient approach and design for their wastewater treatment problem is substantially weakened. "A community that expects to pay only 5 cents to 25 cents on the dollar will have fewer incentives to control plant costs than if they had to pay the entire investment."[11] In many communities, plants costing tens of millions of dollars have been so heavily subsidized by the federal (and sometimes state) programs that local costs have been only a dollar or two per household. This substantially weakens local incentives to search energetically for the least-cost way of handling their municipal wastewater problem. Cities and towns were motivated instead to line up at the subsidy window and build large plants with "officially approved" treatment technology that qualified for large subsidies. The operating costs of these plants were not subsidized in the federal program; they had to be paid entirely by local groups. This sometimes led to situations where overly large treatment plants were not operated correctly because communities were trying to save costs.

In the 1987 Water Quality Act the treatment plant program was changed. States continue to receive federal grants, but states now must provide matching funds equal to 20 percent of the federal funds. The combined funds are used to establish **state revolving funds** (SRFs), which are used to make loans to communities to build wastewater treatment plants. The loans made from the funds are supposed to be largely paid back (this is why they are called "revolving funds"). This should substantially reshape local incentives because local groups will now be responsible for covering the actual costs of constructing their treatment plants. Although the SRF program was originally designed to

---

[11]U.S. Congressional Budget Office, *Efficient Investments in Wastewater Treatment Plants,* Washington, DC, 1985, p. 12.

expire in 1994, it has proven to be politically popular and has continued to receive federal funding. A similar SRF program has been established to help local communities build drinking water treatment facilities.

RECENT POLICY INNOVATIONS
IN WATER POLLUTION CONTROL

Nonpoint-Source Water Pollution Control

The Environmental Protection Agency estimates that nonpoint-source (NPS) emissions are responsible for more than 50 percent of water quality standards violations at the beginning of the 21st century. Major nonpoint sources are agricultural runoff, urban street runoff, and activities related to land clearance and building construction. The EPA has initiated, in cooperation with the states, a **National Estuaries Program** to develop better pollution-control efforts in the major estuaries and bays of the coastal United States. One result of water-quality studies done under this program is to demonstrate how much of the remaining water-quality problems in these areas is related to nonpoint-source pollutants. The fact that NPS emissions are diffuse and not concentrated into specific outfalls has made them very difficult to control. NPS pollutants are also normally very weather related, which makes the runoff patterns more difficult to monitor. Traditional approaches like emission standards have been problematic because it is difficult to measure emissions accurately. This has pushed back the locus of control directly onto the practices and technologies that typically lead to substantial nonpoint-source runoff.

This is what we earlier called **design standards.** These are standards that require certain techniques or practices to be used by sources whose activities lead to nonpoint-source emissions. Standards that rule out agricultural cultivation on steep, easily eroded land; standards specifying the design of urban storm sewers; and standards requiring home builders to take certain steps to control construction site runoff are types of design standards. The 1987 Water Quality Act, for example, establishes a program of federal subsidies for farmers to adopt **best management practices** (BMPs) to control agricultural pollution. While design standards may be necessary in the case of NPS emissions, we should keep in mind the difficulties inherent in their use. They require administrative determination of what particular technologies and techniques will be allowed in different circumstances. The danger is that they will undermine the incentives among polluters to find new and better ways of reducing NPS emissions.

Another method of controlling NPS emissions is to tax those activities or materials that lead to the emissions, rather than the emissions themselves. Charges might be put on fertilizer used by farmers, for example, or on lawn chemicals used by suburban dwellers. The objective in this case is to induce a reduction in the use of materials that may ultimately end up in rivers, lakes, or groundwater aquifers.

Difficulties of control explain why NPS pollution has not been addressed as vigorously as point-source emissions, despite their importance. Early federal water-quality laws directed state agencies to consider nonpoint-source pollution in their water-quality programs, but did not require that specific steps be taken. The 1987 law gives it somewhat more prominence and authorizes federal money to subsidize local efforts to control NPS pollution. In fact, there is a major contrast between the national, uniform policy that has been followed to control point-source emissions and the policy for nonpoint-source pollution. In the latter case federal authorities have essentially thrown the problem into the hands of the states. Their reasoning is that ". . . the application of uniform technological controls . . . is not appropriate for the management of nonpoint sources. Site specific decisions must consider the nature of the watershed, the nature of the water body, . . . and the range of management practices available to control nonpoint source pollution."[12] So in this case there is a recognition that a uniform national program is not appropriate.

There are many areas of the country where point sources and nonpoint sources exist in close proximity, essentially contributing to the same water-quality problems. The **equimarginal principle** would say in this case that the control of point and nonpoint sources should be balanced so that the marginal emission reduction costs are the same in the two cases. Historically, however, point sources have been controlled much more vigorously than nonpoint sources. What this means is that there may be many regions of the country where shifting more of the burden onto nonpoint sources would be an effective way of lowering the costs of water-quality improvements. One way of doing this is the trading of emission reduction credits between point sources and nonpoint sources, a program that is being tried in several parts of the country. We will discuss these below.

Total Maximum Daily Load (TMDL) Program

The national system of technology-based effluent standards has been criticized from its beginnings, especially by economists, for its relative inflexibility and cost ineffectiveness. A nationally mandated program based on the premise that all sources should be subject to the same standards is bound to make water-quality improvements much more costly than they have to be. Furthermore, there has been a disconnect between the permit program and ambient water-quality improvement goals. It is quite conceivable, for example, that all of the sources on a particular body of water, such as an estuary, could have adopted the legally mandated emission control technologies, but for the water quality in the estuary to be substantially diminished. One way this could happen is through a growth in the number of sources as the economy expands; total emissions would increase even though each individual source had adopted the "best conventional technology." In recent years, therefore, federal water-quality regulators have sought to resuscitate an **ambient-based** orientation into water pollution control.

Although the 1972 Clean Water Act gave federal water pollution control a technology orientation, it also contained a section that in effect also requires an

---

[12]U.S. Environmental Protection Agency, *Nonpoint Source Pollution in the U.S., Report to Congress,* Washington, DC, 1984, pp. xiii–xiv.

ambient approach. In cases where the quality of water bodies is impaired, even after technology-based controls required by the law have been put in place, states are required to develop total maximum daily loads (TMDLs) for these waters; these TMDLs incorporate the following steps:

1 The **total maximum daily load for individual pollutants** that the water body can receive without violating ambient water quality standards set for that water body.
2 The identification of all the sources, both point source and nonpoint source, that contribute to the degraded water quality.
3 An allocation of the total daily load among the relevant sources located on the water body.

According to the law, the states are supposed to take the lead in establishing TMDLs, with backing from the EPA.[13] Because of budget limitations, and attention that was given to technology-based permit programs, little has been done on the TMDL program until the last few years. Regulatory agencies are now beginning to grapple with the considerable problems this approach presents.

TMDLs are, by their nature, applicable to localized bodies of water. Thus, this program will put a tremendous scientific burden on regulatory authorities to obtain accurate information on hydrology, current loadings, the effects of load reductions, and so on, with which to design specific plans. A major reason why this program has not been pursued until quite recently despite being written into the CWA of 1972 is the insufficiency of scientific and planning resources at the state level. Substantial public resources will have to be found if this effort is to be vigorously pursued.

Establishing the **total** maximum daily loading may be the least controversial aspect of the program. To do this requires drawing a connection between total loadings and resulting water quality. In some cases this connection may be reasonably simple, while in others it will be complex. Exhibit 14-1 is an excerpt from the phosphorous TMDL plan for Lake Okeechobee in Florida. The problem here in setting the total loading is that there is expected to be a very long time lag between reducing that loading and reduced phosphorous in the water, due to the accumulated phosphorous in the deposits at the bottom of the lake. Thus authorities must choose a total loading that yields improved water quality in a "reasonable" length of time.

No doubt the much harder job politically will be allocating the total loading among the various pollution sources. There is the standard public goods problem here, since each source will have the incentive to shift as much of the total control cost onto other sources. An added problem is that in many cases nonpoint-source emissions, particularly those from agriculture, are the major contributing factor in water quality degradation. It has been much more difficult to develop effective regulatory programs for nonpoint sources than it has for point sources, a problem that will only intensify with the TMDL program.

---

[13]The EPA maintains a website that has information on all aspects of the TMDL program. See **www.epa.gov/owow/tmdl/index.html.**

EXHIBIT 14-1

ESTABLISHING THE LAKE OKEECHOBEE TMDL

Today, under the Total Maximum Daily Load (TMDL) Program, the Environmental Protection Agency Region 4 (EPA-R4) is proposing a total annual load for total phosphorus for Lake Okeechobee in South Florida. In developing the proposed total annual load, EPA-R4 worked closely with the State of Florida Department of Environmental Protection (FDEP), the South Florida Water Management District (SFWMD), the EPA's Office of Wetlands, Oceans and Watersheds in the Office of Water, EPA Headquarters. A specific allocation of the TMDL to the major pollutant sources in the basin and the implementation plan for the TMDL are to be established in future efforts. EPA is proposing that a collaborative process with the State and local stakeholders be established to accomplish this.

Lake Okeechobee is a large, shallow (average depth 2.7 meters) freshwater lake with a surface area covering 730 square miles. It is the largest freshwater lake in Florida and the second largest freshwater lake in the contiguous United States excluding the Great Lakes.

The Lake has been significantly impacted over the past 60 or more years by hydraulic and land-use modifications to its drainage basin and by the construction of the Hoover Dike and Lake-level manipulation. These watershed land use practices include farming that increased the nutrient and sediment load into the Lake. Historically, the Lake had few natural outlets that drained the Lake. As water levels increased in the Lake, the water would flow over the natural low berm, and move south into the Everglades. This provided natural seasonal flows into the Everglades system and allowed the Lake to be periodically flushed out.

In order to restore the Lake (bring it into compliance with water quality standards), the maximum amount of phosphorus that the Lake can receive and reach this goal must be identified.

A water quality standard establishes the water quality goals of a water body by identi-fying the designated use(s) of the water and setting water quality criterion to protect those uses.

There are various categories of designated uses that determine the level of water quality protection that is necessary for a body of water. In this case, the State has identified the designated use of Lake Okeechobee as a Class I water body, a source of drinking water since it supplies the drinking water for many surrounding communities.

TMDLs are typically developed using a computer-based model. In this case, the TMDL was calculated using the South Florida Water Management District's (SFWMD's) Lake Okeechobee Water Quality Model (LOWQM) which was developed by the SFWMD as part of their ongoing lake restoration program. EPA chose to use this model since it had been peer reviewed and had already been calibrated by the SFWMD for the Lake. The model takes a restoration target goal (or numeric water quality standard if available), and using the data available on the Lake, calculates the amount of phosphorus load the Lake can receive and meet the goal or standard. It can then be used to predict the length of time it will take the Lake to reach this goal.

As discussed above, Lake Okeechobee is a large and complex ecosystem that contains distinct ecological regions. It has been impacted for over 60 years by increased nutrient and sediment loads, and changes in the hydrology of the Lake. There is still a substantial phosphorus load (624 metric tons in 1997) entering the system from the watersheds that needed to be considered. Reducing this external source of phosphorus is critical since studies have shown that this load has a negative impact on water quality in the Lake. Reducing this source will also prevent additional accumulation of phosphorus-laden sediments in the Lake. However, due to the existing internal recycling of phosphorus sequestered in the

(Continued)

EXHIBIT 14-1

ESTABLISHING THE LAKE OKEECHOBEE TMDL (CONTINUED)

sediments, it will take a substantial period of time for the Lake to be restored in response to the reduction of the phosphorus load entering the Lake from watershed alone.

EPA next utilized the computer model to evaluate a range of loading scenarios, and the resulting time period required for Lake restoration at these various loads. EPA chose this approach to allow the public to see the effect different loading scenarios have on the restoration time frame. Using 40 ppb of phosphorus as the in-lake target, the model produced a series of loading scenar- ios from a zero in-flow loading (allowing for atmospheric deposition only) to the maxi- mum assimilative capacity load of 285 metric tons. This resulted in predicted restoration time periods ranging from approximately 20 to 30 years (assuming the only load entering the system is the estimated 71 metric tons per year of atmospheric deposition) to approximately 1000 to 1500 years for the "maximum assimilative capacity" load of 285 metric tons per year (including atmospheric deposition).

EPA assessed the option of establishing the TMDL at zero for the in-flow loading (assuming the estimated atmospheric depo- sition only). This is predicted to allow the Lake to meet the water quality target in approximately 20 to 30 years. While this is the fastest time frame for restoration, EPA realized it is not possible to achieve a zero load from external land-based sources because of the significant amounts of phos- phorus currently sequestered in the water- shed. This option would also require all existing sources to essentially cease dis- charging. EPA concluded a TMDL of zero loading was not realistically achievable and therefore not reasonable. EPA reviewed the modeling results and considering the range of loadings and restoration time periods pro- duced by the model (see Table 4 in the TMDL document), *EPA selected a TMDL of 198 metric tons per year which the model predicts will restore the Lake in approxi-*

mately 200 to 220 years. EPA recognizes this is a long period of time but believes if the external load is reduced to 198 metric tons per year, and this action is combined with other remedial actions (such as sediment removal) that are being investigated, the restoration time period may be reduced. EPA also considered in its decision (using best professional judgment), that the loading of 198 metric tons is likely achievable, consid- ering the current watershed phosphorus loads that are discharged into the Lake.

Since the sources of the impairment that flow directly into the Lake are all non-point sources, EPA has not specifically allocated the TMDL to any one source. Allocation of the TMDL to the watersheds and the devel- opment of the implementation plan designed to achieve the TMDL are the final steps in the TMDL process, and EPA has proposed that these be developed through a collabo- rative process. Allocation and implementa- tion are critical to the ultimate success of the TMDL.

EPA is proposing that a collaborative process be established, starting with an existing broad based group (the Lake Okeechobee Issue Team), which has already brought together representatives of the major stakeholder group. The Lake Okeechobee Issue Team, formed by the South Florida Ecosystem Restoration Working Group, has established a strong consensus on Lake restoration issues. The Issue Team includes state and local repre- sentatives involved in management of the Lake, environmentalists, members of the agricultural community and federal repre- sentatives. EPA is proposing that this group form the core stakeholders for the collaborative-process, with additional parties included as needed so that all the relevant interests are represented.

Source: Overview of Total Phosphorus TMDL Lake Okeechobee, Florida, January 3, 2000, avail- able at www.epa.gov/region04/water/tmdl/florida/ lake_o/index.htm.

As we have discussed numerous times, designing a cost-effective pollution control program requires that the equimarginal principle be satisfied. This principle is certainly applicable to the issue of allocating emission reductions among the various sources so as to achieve the maximum total daily loadings. The 1972 CWA does not specify any new type of implementation strategy for TMDLs, so the expectation presumably was that it would make use of the same types of technology-based regulations that have been used so far under the law. On the other hand, achieving TMDL cost-effectively could create a major opportunity for incentive-based regulations in worker pollution control.

Incentive-Based Approaches to Water Pollution Control

The two main incentive based approaches are **emission charges** and **transferrable discharge permits.** Emission charges have never been particularly popular among U.S. regulators, perhaps because of the social aversion to taxes in general that exists among the population. They do have their strong advocates, however, so they may become more popular in the future. Transferrable discharge permits, on the other hand, have been embraced with some vigor by regulators as well as some environmental interests. This has been especially true in air pollution control, but their use in water pollution control also has been touted.[14] Under the TMDL program, trading might be encouraged if the total load is initially allocated among identified sources in the form of tradable permits, and if emission and emission changes can be monitored closely enough. Under the existing permit program, permitted emissions also could be defined in terms of tradable quantities. This again would require good monitoring capabilities.

Some water-quality tracking programs have already been attempted. One of the best known is that involving Dillon Reservoir in Colorado. The large impoundment is a major water source for Denver. In the early 1980s it was recognized that phosphorous loadings in the reservoir were causing water-quality problems. Although some of the phosphorus was of natural origin, about half was from human activity. Somewhat more than half of this was from nonpoint sources: urban runoff, golf courses, construction sites, septic tanks, and so on. The rest was from four municipal waste treatment facilities. Researchers determined that point-source control by itself would not be sufficient to avoid water-quality problems; even if municipal phosphorous emissions were reduced to zero, there would still be enough phosphorus to cause eutrophication in the reservoir.[15] Besides the very high direct abatement costs it would require, this would severely constrain future population growth in Summit county, which in the 1970s was the fastest growing county in the United States.

---

[14]See, for example: U.S. Environmental Protection Agency, *Draft Framework for Watershed-Based Trading,* April 18, 2000, available at www.epa.gov/owow/watershed/framwork.html.
[15]Lane Wyatt, "A Basinwide Approach to NPS Management," Northwest Colorado Council of Governments, n.d. "Eutrophication" refers to the buildup of plant nutrients, leading to excess growth in underwater plants and algae.

The answer has been to initiate a phosphorus trading program between point and nonpoint sources of phosphorus. The program allocated baseline phosphorous loads to different polluters and then allowed phosphorous emission permits to be traded. The intention is to allow point sources, especially the municipal treatment plants, to buy phosphorous emission permits from nonpoint-source polluters whose marginal phosphorous abatement costs are lower. Those responsible for nonpoint-source emissions have a variety of means available to reduce their phosphorous loadings, such as sewering housing developments that are now using septic tanks, routing underground storm sewers through a series of storage tanks, and detention basins. Of course, the trading program requires that administrative authorities be able to monitor the nonpoint-source emissions at reasonable cost. Several trades have been made, under the management of the Summit Water Quality Committee, composed of representatives from towns in the region as well as other public agencies. If the full trading potential is realized, it has been estimated that the program will allow the participants to solve the phosphorous problem in the reservoir at a cost savings of more than $1 million a year. Similar point/nonpoint-source trading programs have been initiated in the Cherry Creek reservoir of Colorado and the Tar-Pamlico basin of North Carolina (see Exhibit 14-2). The idea is also being explored in other regions.[16]

State environmental regulators also have shown interest in trading to improve the cost effectiveness of water pollution control. In 1981 the state of Wisconsin initiated a limited program of tradable BOD emission permits on the Fox River. This river is used for wastewater disposal by numerous groups, especially pulp mills and municipal treatment plants. Emissions to the river already were subject to control through the regular EPA technology-based effluent standards and emission permits. Allowable discharges vary over the year because variations in temperature and stream flow alter the river's BOD assimilative capacity. The goal of the trading program is to get the same level of water-quality improvement at a substantially reduced cost.

The trading scheme is aimed solely at BOD discharges. Initial distribution of emission rights was based on historic levels of emissions by the major polluters. The rights were distributed free and they are valid only for five years; after that they must be reissued by the administering agency. Traded emission permits also have a maximum life of five years.[17] The designers of the plan hoped that by allowing permits to be traded, firms or municipalities with relatively high marginal BOD abatement costs would buy permits from those with low marginal abatement costs. Some researchers had estimated that this would result in substantial cost savings in cleaning up the river.[18]

[16]David Letson, "Point/Non-Point Source Pollution Reduction Trading: An Interpretive Survey," *Natural Resources Journal*, 32(2), Spring 1992, pp. 219–232.
[17]See Martin H. David and Erhard F. Joeres, "Is a Viable Implementation of TDP's Transferable?" in Erhard F. Joeres and Martin H. David (eds.), *Buying a Better Environment, Cost Effective Regulation through Permit Trading*, University of Wisconsin Press, Madison, WI, 1983, pp. 233–248.
[18]William B. O'Neil, "The Regulation of Water Pollution Permit Trading under Conditions of Varying Stream Flow and Temperature," in Erhard F. Joeres and Martin H. David (eds.), *Buying a Better Environment, Cost Effective Regulation through Permit Trading*, University of Wisconsin Press, Madison, WI, 1983, pp. 219–232.

EXHIBIT 14-2

ALBEMARLE-PAMLICO: CASE STUDY IN POLLUTANT TRADING

By John Hall and Ciannat Howett

The Albemarle-Pamlico estuary of North Carolina is the second largest and one of the most productive estuarine systems in the country. Over the past two decades, excess nutrients entering the estuary from the Tar-Pamlico River have caused algae levels to increase. These increased levels can lead to fish kills, odors, and habitat loss and can generally diminish water quality.

To reverse the degradation of the estuary, in 1989 North Carolina's Department of Environmental Management decided to increase control of municipal and industrial point-source dischargers along the river. Estimated capital cost for the facilities was approximately $50 million.

The problem with the state's strategy was that almost 80 percent of the nutrient pollution entering the Tar-Pamlico River was discharged *not* from point-sources, but from agricultural and urban runoff and other nonpoint-sources of pollution. The state's strategy provided for only minimal increased attention to reducing nonpoint-source and did not earmark additional funding or staffing for such efforts. Technical analyses indicated that little, if any, actual improvement in water quality would occur from the point-source control measures.

In 1989, a group of municipalities and industries located along the Tar and Pamlico Rivers joined together to form the Tar-Pamlico Basin Association, Inc. Their purpose was to develop an alternative strategy that addressed both point and nonpoint sources of pollution in the entire Tar-Pamlico watershed on a cost-effective basis.

Under the Tar-Pamlico agreement, the Association is given group nutrient-reduction goals, rather than individual nutrient limitations being placed in each member's discharge permit. The goals are set at increasingly stringent levels each year for the first five years of the project.

The agreement requires members of the Association to evaluate their facilities to identify operational or minor capital improvements that could reduce nutrient discharge levels. Once they have optimized existing facilities, they are given the choice of achieving the group limitations by making major improvements to their facilities, "trading" discharge levels between themselves, or by funding implementation of nonpoint-source pollution controls.

As a result of the initial evaluation, Association members were able to meet almost 80 percent of their group nutrient-reduction targets through operational changes alone. By working together as a group, they were able to finance a sophisticated engineering evaluation of their plants which as individuals—particularly the small towns that are members of the Association—they never could have afforded.

If the Association members had not been able to reach their group nutrient reduction goals, the Tar-Pamlico strategy would have allowed them to pay into a fund to implement nonpoint-source controls. The arrangement was for them to pay $56 for each kilogram of nutrients they discharged over the target level. A 10-year credit was to be given for each kilogram funded by this approach. The flexibility of this arrangement is important because, once plant performance is optimized, preventing nutrient pollution through nonpoint-source controls, such as agricultural best management practices (BMPs), is far less costly than it is through advanced wastewater treatment. Further, it also promotes habitat restoration, wetlands preservation, soil-quality control, and those other benefits that come with agricultural BMPs.

Source: EPA Journal, Summer 1994, pp. 27–29.

To date there have been relatively few trades of BOD emission permits among dischargers on the Fox River. A major difficulty with the Fox River program has been the relatively small number of potential participants. The pulp mills are few enough in number that they can potentially act as oligopolists instead of competitive bidders.[19] The municipalities are also relatively few in number, coupled with the fact that being publicly controlled wastewater treatment facilities, they don't necessarily have to make decisions on the basis of strict cost-minimization objectives. Municipal dischargers also could qualify for public subsidies, further undermining the incentives to minimize costs.

Another important factor working against trades was that the original permit allocations were too liberal. If polluters are to have incentives to trade, the quantity of permits initially allocated must be substantially less than current, or easily achievable, emission levels. In the Fox River case, the number of permits given out did not imply a significant reduction of BOD emissions beyond what could be obtained by standard and easily available control techniques. In addition, municipal dischargers had historically been able to get waivers of emission limitations if they found them too costly to achieve. Also working against permit trades have been the rules that administrative authorities have established to govern transactions. In principle, trades should be allowed whenever market participants wish to make them; it is their cost calculations and objectives that should be allowed to govern their market participation. In the Fox River case, however, firms are required to justify the need for permits, and trades that "simply" reduce operating costs are not allowed. This substantially limits the number of potential traders. In addition, the fact that the administering agency must reissue permits every five years creates uncertainty over whether purchased permits will be counted in a firm's new base when reauthorization occurs. All these factors have worked to reduce the number of trades that might otherwise have occurred. We perhaps can look at the Fox River case as providing a good laboratory for learning about designing and administering transferable discharge permit programs.

SUMMARY

Current federal water pollution–control policy centers on the promulgation and enforcement of technology-based effluent standards (TBESs). These are emission standards stemming from the EPA's findings as to the "best available technology," or "best practicable technology," for specific industries. These technology-based standards, although appealing as "technological fixes," have a number of drawbacks. They are likely to give far less pollution control for the money spent than alternative approaches because they normally violate the equimarginal principle. They also have negative impacts through reducing the long-run incentives polluters might have to find better ways of controlling waterborne emissions.

---

[19]An "oligopoly" is an industry containing just a few dominant firms. The auto and airline industries are oligopolies. In this example, although there may be many pulp mills nationwide, the Fox River TDP market included a relatively small number of them.

We also discussed in the chapter the federal program of subsidies for municipal waste treatment facilities. Over the last several decades the proportion of the U.S. population being served by advanced (secondary or tertiary) treatment facilities has been substantially increased. Again, however, because of the perverse incentives built into the program, substantially greater progress could have been made with the money spent.

As of this writing, federal authorities are considering a major new revision of federal water pollution–control policy. One objective will be to try and find greater opportunities for using incentive-based strategies to combat water pollution. Most water pollution problems are local, or regional, implying that the permit markets in water pollution control will have to operate with relatively small numbers of traders.

QUESTIONS FOR FURTHER DISCUSSION

1 Distinguish between a "technology-based" water pollution control program and a "media- based" program.

2 In order to meet TMDL limits in a cost-effective manner, what is the appropriate role of the equimarginal principle? What about the economic efficiency principle?

3 Controlling the residuals from the production of bleached tissue paper is about five times costlier than controlling the residuals from unbleached tissue paper. Analyze this difference with our standard pollution-control model. What does it suggest in terms of public policy toward water pollution control?

4 Achieving technological improvements in water pollution control is a very desirable objective. Yet technology-based programs are unlikely to be cost-effective. Are these two ideas inconsistent?

5 Can you think of a way of designing a water pollution–control policy that combines a media-based approach with a technology-based approach?

WEBSITES

The EPA maintains web sites for vast quantities of data on water quality throughout the U.S.; see **www.epa.gov/storet.** Much useful material is contained in the water policy position papers of the Congressional Research Service, **www.cnie.org/nle/crsh2o.html.** See also the sites listed in the web page associated with the text, **www.mhhe.com/economics/field3.**

SELECTED READINGS

Bergstrom, John C., Kevin Boyle, and Greg Poe: *The Economic Valuation of Water Quality,* Edward Elgar, 2001.

Bingham, Tayler H., Timothy R. Bondelid, Brooks M. Depro, Ruth C. Figueroa, A. Brett Hauber, Suzanne J. Unger, and George L. Van Houtven: "A Benefits Assessment of Water Pollution Control Programs Since 1972," Report to the EPA by the Research Triangle Institute, Research Triangle Park, NC, 1998.

Freeman, A. Myrick III: "Water Pollution Policy," in Paul R. Portney and Robert N. Stavins (eds.), *Public Policies for Environmental Protection,* Resources for the Future, Washington, DC, 2000, pp. 169–214.

Harrington, Winston, Alan J. Krupnick, and Henry M. Peskin: "Policies for Nonpoint-Source Water Pollution Control," *Journal of Soil and Water Conservation*, 40(1), January–February 1985, pp. 27–32.

Kneese, Allen V., and Blair T. Bower: *Managing Water Quality: Economics, Technology, and Institutions*, Johns Hopkins Press for Resource for the Future, Baltimore, MD, 1968.

Luken, Ralph A.: *Efficiency in Environmental Legislation: A Benefit–Cost Analysis of Alternative Approaches*, Kluwer Academic Publishers, Boston, 1990.

Schneider, Paul: "Clear Progress: 25 Years of the Clean Water Act," *Audubon*, 99(5), 1997, pp. 36–47, 106–107.

Spulber, Nicolas, and Asghar Sabbaghi: *Economics of Water Resources: From Regulation to Privatization*, Kluwer Academic Publishers, Boston, 1998.

U.S. Environmental Protection Agency: *A Benefits Assessment of Water Pollution Control Programs Since 1972, Part I. The Benefits of Point Source Controls for Conventional Pollutants in Rivers and Streams*, Office of Water, 2000.

U.S. Environmental Protection Agency: *A Retrospective Assessment of the Costs of the Clean Water Act, 1972 to 1997*, Washington, DC, 2000.

CHAPTER 15

FEDERAL AIR
POLLUTION–CONTROL
POLICY

As it travels through space, planet earth takes along with itself an enveloping, but relatively thin, layer of gases, without which it would be a cinder. That layer of atmospheric gases provides two critical services: direct life support for living organisms on the earth's surface and control over the radiation exchange between earth and space. Both of these services can be upset by human activity.

For human beings and other living organisms, the air is what water is for fish. Unless you wear a gas mask, there is no escaping what the air has to offer. The surface air (the troposphere) normally contains about 78 percent nitrogen, 21 percent oxygen, small amounts of other gases, and varying amounts of water vapor. It also may have many, many other things put there through special acts of nature and the activities of human beings. The upper layers of the earth's atmosphere (the stratosphere) contain only about 5 percent of the planet's air, but it has a critical role to play in making it habitable. Trace gases in the stratosphere, particularly ozone, filter out about 99 percent of incoming ultraviolet radiation, acting like a giant sun block, without which we would be exposed to damaging levels of radiation. Other trace gases in the stratosphere provide greenhouse services; they trap some of the infrared radiation that is reflected back from the earth's surface, warming it and making it more hospitable to living organisms. As we have recently found out, both of these vital phenomena can be disrupted by human activity.

Human disruptions of the atmosphere are not new; instances of local smoke pollution have occurred for centuries. But in the last few decades, the potential severity of air pollution problems has grown more acute, owing to the sheer scale of airborne residuals released and the exotic nature of some of the emitted substances. There are thousands of potential air pollutants, for example, oxides of carbon, nitrogen and sulfur, volatile organic compounds, suspended particulate matter, photochemical oxidants, radioactivity, heat, and noise. These pollutants cause a diverse set of damages. Perhaps the most important are human health impacts. Prolonged exposure to airborne substances can lead to lung cancer, bronchitis, emphysema, and asthma; accidental releases can have acute impacts. Air pollution also causes damage to plants, as in, for example, the destruction of forests and reduced crop yields stemming from acid deposition. Air pollution can lead to severe damage of exposed materials, such as the surface erosion and discoloration of stone and concrete work and the corrosion of metals. Stratospheric ozone depletion and enhanced global warming have significant implications for humans and the earth's ecosystem. Not all air pollution is outdoors; in fact, indoor air pollution is a critical problem in many homes, factories, mines, and farms.

Many airborne pollutants are emitted on a continuous basis. The sulfur dioxide (SO_2) emissions from power plants, for example, are continuously produced as long as the plants are in operation. For individual motor vehicles, emissions start and stop with their operation, although for an entire urban area, auto and truck emissions vary continuously throughout the days and seasons according to the rhythms of economic activity. Episodic, especially accidental, emissions have been the cause of severe air pollution incidents; for example, the Bhopal disaster in India and, to a much lesser degree, the numerous transportation accidents that occur in many countries. The links between emissions and ambient air–quality levels can be complicated because of the complexities of meteorological phenomena. The best-known example of this is the creation of local weather conditions that trap air pollutants, sometimes for extended periods of time. The infamous "temperature inversions" over urban areas are well known.

Annual expenditures in the United States for air pollution control have increased substantially since the early 1970s. Has this had an impact? Table 15-1 shows aggregate U.S. emissions for major air pollutants in 1970, 1980, 1990, and 1997. These are divided into emissions from stationary sources and emissions from mobile sources. Most emissions have decreased, or stayed about the same, during this period. The only ones to increase substantially are particulate matter, especially from stationary sources, and carbon monoxide from mobile sources. Sulfur dioxide emissions are largely from stationary sources, and these have decreased substantially over this time period. Nitrogen oxides, on the other hand, are largely from mobile sources, and these have shown a slight increase. The biggest success story has been with lead emissions; these have decreased dramatically from both mobile and stationary sources.

Emission data like this do not tell us directly whether pollution-control policies have been effective. To know this, one needs a with/without analysis: what emissions were compared to what they would have been if the policies had not been pursued. As it happens, the EPA was instructed to do such an analysis to access the impacts of the Clean Air Act Amendments of 1990. Table 15-2 shows a part of their results. For the major air pollutants, it shows actual 1990 emissions and projected 2000 emissions with and without the 1990 law. Note that if there had been no 1990

TABLE 15-1
STATIONARY AND MOBILE SOURCE OF CRITERIA POLLUTANTS IN UNITED STATES, 1970, 1980, 1990, 1997*

	Emission (million short tons)			
	1970	1980	1990	1997
Carbon monoxide				
Stationary	29.5	24.9	22.6	20.4
Mobile	10.7	13.8	15.4	16.8
Nitrogen oxides				
Stationary	11.6	12.3	12.2	12.0
Mobile	9.6	12.6	11.2	11.6
Volatile organic compounds				
Stationary	16.1	15.1	12.1	11.6
Mobile	14.6	11.1	8.8	7.6
Sulfur dioxide				
Stationary	30.7	25.2	22.3	19.0
Mobile	0.5	0.7	1.4	1.4
Particulate matter (PM_{10})				
Stationary	12.4	6.3	29.0	32.8
Mobile	0.7	1.0	0.8	0.8
Lead**				
Stationary	39.2	9.5	3.8	3.4
Mobile	181.7	64.7	1.2	0.5

*"Criteria pollutants" are discussed in the section on the history of federal air pollution control.
**Thousand short tons.
Source: U.S. Environmental Protection Agency, *National Air Pollutant Emissions Trends Update, 1970–1997,* available at www.epa.gov/ttn/chief/trends/trends97/index.html.

law, total emissions of most pollutants would have increased somewhat, while emissions of carbon monoxide actually would have decreased. This is attributable both to the impacts of previous policies, as well as basic changes at work in the economy. Emissions with the 1990 program, however, are substantially lower, with the exception of those of particulate matter. From data like these we can

TABLE 15-2
ESTIMATED IMPACTS OF 1990 CLEAN AIR ACT (CAA)

	Emissions (hundred tons per day)		
	1990 actual	2000 without CAA	2000 with CAA
Volatile organic compounds	62.2	66.0	46.8
Nitrogen oxides	67.3	67.8	49.5
Carbon monoxide	258.6	242.1	201.5
Sulfur dioxide	61.3	64.8	48.5
Particulate matter (PM^{10})	77.5	78.8	76.9

Source: U.S. Environmental Protection Agency, *The Benefits and Costs of the Clean Air Act 1990 to 2010,* Washington, DC, November 1999, pp. C-13, C-46.

conclude that the public policies have led to substantial emission reductions and no doubt to improved ambient air quality. What needs to be asked, however, is whether the sums of money the nation has put into air pollution control have bought as much improvement in air quality as they could have and should have. To answer this we have to look more closely at the policies themselves.

FEDERAL AIR POLLUTION–CONTROL LAWS: A BRIEF SKETCH

There was little federal concern or statutory activity in air pollution matters prior to the late 1960s; in this respect, it was similar to water pollution. Air pollution was regarded as primarily a local concern, to be dealt with under **local nuisance laws.** Federal laws dealt mainly with providing funds for research and for state grants to train personnel and obtain technical assistance. However, in the 1967 Air Quality Act, the Department of Health, Education and Welfare was charged with establishing criteria through which ambient air–quality standards could be set for six common air pollutants: sulfur dioxide (SO_2), nitrogen oxides (NO_x), ozone, particulate matter, carbon monoxide, and lead. These became known as the **"criteria" pollutants,** and ambient standards for these six were to be set by the states. By the end of the 1960s, however, frustration was widespread over the perceived weakness of this federal/state approach. The Clean Air Act Amendments of 1970 represented a much more aggressive assertion of federal power into air pollution matters. It established the basic contours of air pollution policy that persist to the present: uniform national ambient air–quality standards, a variety of technology-based emission standards, and stricter emission standards for automobiles.

In the Clean Air Act Amendments of 1977, federal legislators addressed some of the problems created by the uniform ambient standards of the 1970 Act. Air quality was worse in some cities than others, and better in rural areas. There was widespread concern after the 1970 law that cities in areas with air quality already better than the national ambient standard could compete unfairly for new industrial development. New firms might be attracted to these areas by the promise of less strict emissions controls than firms would face in areas where air quality was already worse than the standards. The 1977 CAA amendments differentiated PSD areas (PSD stands for "prevention of significant deterioration"—for a list of acronyms used in this chapter, see the appendix starting on page 483) and *nonattainment* areas. Different technology-based effluent standards would apply to PSD regions, where air quality was already better than the standard, than to nonattainment regions.[1]

After the 1977 act there were no new federal air pollution statutes until 1990, a reflection of the Reagan administration's desire to reduce the "burden" of regulations on the U.S. economy. There were, however, some significant policy innovations that occurred during this period within the existing laws. These were programs based on the trading of **emission reduction credits,** which we will discuss in more detail later in this chapter.

---

[1]The PSD regions were differentiated into three classes; see the detail in Table 15-3.

TABLE 15-3
MAJOR FEDERAL AIR POLLUTION LAWS

Air Pollution Control Act (APCA) of 1955

Authorized the Secretary of Health, Education and Welfare to spend up to $5 million a year to do research and to help the states in training and technical assistance on matters of air pollution. Extended in 1959 and 1962.

Motor Vehicle Exhaust Study Act of 1960

Directed the Secretary of HEW to do a study on "Motor Vehicles, Air Pollution and Health" within two years.

Clean Air Act (CAA) of 1963

Authorized federal grants to states to develop state and local air pollution–control programs; established a conference system to deal with problems of interstate air pollution; extended authorization for federal research on air pollution.

Motor Vehicle Air Pollution Control Act of 1965

Authorized the Secretary of HEW to set *emission standards* for new cars (but no deadline was established); dealt with international air pollution and called for more research.

CAA Extension of 1966

Extended the CAA of 1963 and added authority to make grants to states to support air pollution–control programs.

Air Quality Act (AQA) of 1967

Provided for additional grants to states to plan air pollution–control programs; provided for interstate air pollution–control agencies, expanded research on fuels and vehicles; required HEW to establish air–quality regions of the country, publish air–quality criteria and control technology reports for the common pollutants; required states to establish ambient air–quality standards for the "criteria" pollutants and develop attainment programs; authorized HEW to give financial assistance to states to establish motor-vehicle inspection programs.

CAA Amendments of 1970

Established *national* ambient air–quality standards (NAAWSs) for criteria pollutants; required the establishment of new-car emission standards along with certification programs; EPA was to establish emission standards for major toxic or hazardous pollutants; EPA to establish technology-based emission standards for all *new sources* (NSPS) of the common air pollutants; required state implementation plans (SIPs) to control existing stationary sources of air pollutants.

CAA Amendments of 1977

Established the goal of "prevention of serious deterioration" (PSD) in areas already cleaner than the national standards; established three classes of already clean areas:

Class I areas: no additional air–quality deterioration permitted (includes national parks, etc.).
Class II areas: some air–quality deterioration to be permitted (includes most PSD regions).
Class III areas: air quality to be allowed to deteriorate to level of NAAQSs.

Established a technology standard "lowest achievable emission rate" (LAER) for new sources in nonattainment areas and "best available control technologies" (BACT) for new sources in PSD regions.

(Continued)

TABLE 15-3
MAJOR FEDERAL AIR POLLUTION LAWS (CONTINUED)

CAA Amendments of 1990
Established tougher tailpipe standards for new cars, with longer warranty period; mandated pilot program of "clean" cars in some cities; reformulated fuels in some cities; Phase II pumps at gas stations; onboard fume canisters on cars; streamlined stationary-source permitting procedures; provided for reduction of 189 toxic airborne emissions through TBES ("maximum achievable control technology," MACT); provided for stricter local plans to reduce ozone, carbon monoxide, and particulates in the worst cities; further rules for phasing out of CFCs; provided for a system of transferable discharge permits among power plants to reduce sulfur dioxide emissions.

Sources: Arthur C. Stern, "History of Air Pollution Legislation in the United States," *Journal of Air Pollution Control Association,* 32(1), January 1982, pp. 44–61; Paul R. Portney, "Air Pollution Policy," in Paul R. Portney (ed.), *Public Policies for Environmental Protection,* Resources for the Future, 1990, Chapter 3; *EPA Journal,* January/February 1991, pp. 8–9.

In 1990, after many years of negotiation and political conflict, Congress passed, and the president signed, the Clean Air Act Amendments of 1990. This statute contains five main sections, dealing with (1) motor vehicles and fuels, (2) acid rain, (3) urban air quality, (4) air toxics, and (5) stratospheric ozone problems. The law is notable for including an innovative transferable discharge permit system for SO_2 emissions; it also continues many of the command-and-control approaches that have characterized federal programs to date.

The continued problem of motor-vehicle pollution was addressed by a further tightening of new car emission standards and expansion of state inspection and maintenance (I&M) programs. In addition, the law mandates many new technologies, such as reformulated fuel, fume-catching nozzles at gas stations, and the development of a generation of clean cars.

The law also attempts to deal more directly with **toxic air pollutants.** In earlier laws, the EPA had been directed to address the problem of airborne toxics, but over the years they had made relatively little progress. The 1990 Act specifically lists 189 toxic materials that are to be controlled and requires that the EPA establish technology-based effluent standards to apply to sources emitting more than 10 tons/year of a single toxic or 25 tons/year of any combination of toxic compounds. The standard is to be the "maximum achievable control technology" (MACT), defined as technology based on the "best control technologies that have already been demonstrated"[2] in the designated industrial categories. The EPA has become aware over the years of some of the negative side effects of specifying too closely the technologies that polluters must use to reduce emissions; it claims that in the case of these MACT standards, it will aim at ". . . setting standards the industry must achieve, rather than dictating equipment that industry must install."[3] Only time will tell if this more flexible regulatory approach will bear fruit.

[2]*EPA Journal,* 17(1), January/February 1991, p. 32.
[3]Ibid.

Regarding criteria pollutants, the 1990 Act seeks to come to grips with the continuing nonattainment problem. In the 1977 law the metropolitan areas of the country had been given until 1987 to come into compliance with ambient standards. Although some progress had been made, many cities still failed to meet the standards at the end of the 1980s. Previous laws treated all these regions alike, but in 1990 an effort was made to recognize degrees of nonattainment. A system was established in the law to classify cities in terms of the severity of their air pollution problems. The law specifies five classifications for ozone, two for carbon monoxide, and two for particulate matter. Control programs of increasing severity are specified for cities in increasingly serious nonattainment categories. For example, emissions of volatile organic compounds and nitrogen oxides produce ground-level ozone, which, in turn, is instrumental in producing urban smog. In 1990, 96 cities failed to meet the national air-quality standard for ozone. The 1990 act places these cities into five categories according to the severity of their ozone levels: "marginal," "moderate," "serious," "severe," and "extreme." Only one city—Los Angeles—is in the extreme category. The law then specifies increasingly stringent control techniques for cities according to which category they are in. These techniques are based primarily on the enforcement of technology-based effluent standards and the outright specification of technologies that must be adopted in the various regions.

Current federal air pollution statutes are long and complex, but they can be boiled down to the following:

- National ambient air–quality standards for criteria pollutants, with pollution–control programs of varying stringency based on the severity of the air pollution in different regions.
- Technology-based effluent standards for stationary sources of airborne emissions on (1) all new sources, (2) existing sources in nonattainment regions, and (3) sources of toxic emissions.
- Emission standards for new cars, with inspection and maintenance programs (I&M) in some states.
- A variety of new technology specifications for automobile pollution ("clean cars," reformulated fuel, on-board vapor-catching devices, etc.).
- A number of transferable discharge programs targeted at specific airborne emissions.
- The phaseout of CFCs.

In the next few sections we look more closely at these major parts of the air pollution–control program (the discussion of the CFC phaseout is postponed until Chapter 20).

NATIONAL AMBIENT AIR–QUALITY STANDARDS

The 1970 Clean Air Act specifies a system of **national ambient air–quality standards** (NAAQS) for criteria pollutants, to be applied uniformly across the country. In Chapter 11 we discussed the question of uniformity in standards. Unless marginal damage and marginal abatement costs happen to be the same in all regions, uniform national standards will not be efficient. They will be overly stringent where marginal damages are relatively low and/or marginal abatement costs relatively high, or not stringent enough where marginal damages are relatively high and/or marginal abatement costs relatively low.

A fundamental issue is how the level of the standard is chosen. The current standards for criteria pollutants are shown in Table 15-4. From an efficiency point of view, standards cannot be socially optimal unless they are established with an eye to both marginal damages and marginal control costs. There are two levels of standards established in the CAA: primary and secondary. The legal criteria to be used by the EPA in establishing these are as follows:

- **Primary standards:** To be set at whatever level is required to protect the **public health,** with an "adequate margin of safety." The latter clause has been interpreted to require that the standards be set to protect the health of the more sensitive members of the population, such as children, asthmatics, and the elderly,

TABLE 15-4
NATIONAL PRIMARY AND SECONDARY AMBIENT AIR–QUALITY STANDARDS AS OF 2000*

Pollutant	Primary standard	Secondary standard
Particulate matter (PM_{10})		
Annual mean	$50\ \mu g/m^3$	Same as primary
Daily mean	$150\ \mu g/m^3$	Same as primary
Particulate matter ($PM_{2.5}$; proposed in 1997)		
Annual mean	$15\ \mu g/m^3$	Same as primary
Daily mean	$65\ \mu g/m^3$	Same as primary
Carbon monoxide		
8-hour mean	9 ppm	None
1-hour mean	35 ppm	None
Nitrogen dioxide		
Annual mean	0.053 ppm	Same as primary
Ozone		
1-hour mean	0.12 ppm	Same as primary
8-hour mean (proposed in 1997)	0.08 ppm	Same as primary
Lead		
Quarterly mean	$1.5\ \mu g/m^3$	Same as primary
Sulfur dioxide		
Annual mean	0.03 ppm	Same as primary
24-hour mean	0.14 ppm	Same as primary
3-hour mean	None	0.50 ppm

*ppm stands for parts per million; $\mu g/m^3$ stands for micrograms per cubic meter. The standards are established over averaging times; that is, they are expressed in terms of maximum average concentrations of the pollutants over some time period. For most of the pollutants, several such maxima, pertaining to different time periods, are stated.

Source: U.S. Environmental Protection Agency, Office of Air Quality Planning and Standards, available at www.epa.gov/airs/criteria.html.

- **Secondary standards:** To be set at the level necessary to protect the **public welfare.** This has been interpreted to include such things as protection from decreased visibility, damage to crops, animals, vegetation, and buildings.

According to a strict reading of the law, therefore, these standards are to be established by reference only to damages; considerations of costs apparently are not permitted. Only one unique secondary standard has been created—that for sulfur dioxide. The standards as set imply that the damage functions associated with these criteria pollutants have **thresholds,** below which damages are minimal or nonexistent. When the standards were set, relatively little was known about the damage functions. Even today we are unsure if these thresholds exist. Recent results suggest that they may not, that in fact damages may occur even at very low levels of these pollutants. But the costs of achieving zero levels of these pollutants would be enormous.

The implication of this is that in setting the national standards some informal recognition undoubtedly has been given to abatement costs. Implicit concern with abatement costs also has occurred in enforcement. Despite the unambiguous nature of the standards, there are many urban areas of the country where ambient air quality is still worse than the standards, two decades after their establishment. Strict enforcement of the standards in a short period of time would simply have cost too much. **Enforcement** has involved an implicit trade-off of marginal damages and marginal abatement costs, according to the particularities of the different urban areas, the appearance of new abatement technology, and the willingness to pay for air pollution control, as manifested primarily in the ongoing political struggle in local areas.

The issue of how the EPA decides on the standards has recently become very controversial. In 1997 the EPA announced tighter standards for ozone and small particulate matter.[4] These were invalidated in the ensuing court case, essentially on the grounds that the CAA law allows too much discretion to the EPA in setting the standards. The continued conflict over this issue may lead the EPA more overtly toward a benefit–cost perspective in justifying future standard changes. This may require that the U.S. Congress revise the statute.

STATIONARY-SOURCE CONTROL

Federal policy toward stationary-source air pollution control is intertwined with policy actions and administration by the states. The 1970 Clean Air Act Amendments require the EPA to establish national ambient standards and states to develop **state implementation plans** (SIPs), which, when enforced by the states, will decrease emissions enough to meet the standards. These SIPs are to be specified for designated geographical areas called **Air Quality Control Regions** (AQCRs). In those states where for one reason or another no SIP is

---

[4]Large particulate matter, designated PM_{10}, consists of particles smaller than 10 micro meters in diameter; small particulate matter, or $PM_{2.5}$, consists of particles less than 2.5 micro meters in diameter.

TABLE 15-5
TECHNOLOGY-BASED EFFLUENT STANDARDS (TBES) FOR CONTROL
OF LARGE STATIONARY SOURCES OF AIR POLLUTANTS

	Nonattainment Regions
Existing sources:	RACT: "Reasonably Available Control Technology"
New sources:	LAER: "Lowest Achievable Emission Rate"
	Prevention of Significant Deterioration (PSD) Regions
Existing sources:	None
New sources:	BACT: "Best Available Control Technology"

developed, the EPA is authorized to administer the air pollution–control program through its regional office. The SIP plans are subject to approval by the EPA. To be approved, the SIPs must include a set of **technology-based effluent standards** (TBESs) to be applied to firms in various industrial categories and subcategories.

Technology-Based Effluent Standards

The stationary-source program contains several different types of TBESs, as shown in Table 15-5. The standards differ between existing and new sources and between nonattainment and PSD regions. Distinctions between existing and new sources are a prominent feature in environmental control programs. New sources, or existing sources that are modified in some major way, are usually held to stricter standards than existing, established sources. In the air-quality program, new sources in nonattainment areas are subject to a LAER (lowest achievable emission rate) standard,[5] which is meant to be more restrictive than the RACT (reasonably available control technology) standard applied to existing sources in those areas. In PSD regions, new sources are held to standards based on BACT (best available control technology), whereas existing sources are in effect not subject to any standard.[6]

The case for holding new sources to stricter standards (a **new-source bias**) than those applied to existing sources is usually made on the basis of cost; it normally costs more to retrofit existing plants with pollution-control equipment than to incorporate the equipment into new plants when they are being built. In effect the argument is that the marginal abatement costs of existing plants are normally higher than those of new plants, so cost-effectiveness justifies more restrictive emis-

---

[5]LAER is defined as the lowest emission rate specified in any state implementation plan, whether or not any source is currently achieving that rate.

[6]In giving the states the primary responsibility to set TBESs, there was some fear among federal policymakers that economic competition among them would motivate some to set less restrictive standards to attract business. Thus, the EPA is empowered to set a floor level for standards applying to new or modified stationary sources. These are called new-source performance standards (NSPS).

sion standards for the former than for the latter. To a large extent, this is probably an economic argument being used to justify a course of action that is politically expedient. It is easier to put stricter limits on new sources than on existing ones because, by definition, the former will have less political clout than the latter. And existing firms may not be so opposed to applying stricter controls that make it relatively costly for new competitors to get into business. From an administrative standpoint a new-source bias is also easy to understand. In any given year there are many times more existing sources than there are new or modified sources, so more administrative resources may be concentrated on the latter. A focus on new sources also implies a gradualist approach because it means that stricter standards will gradually spread through the various industries as old capital is replaced with new.

But the price paid for holding new sources to stricter standards may be high. The problem is that a new-source bias creates incentives to hold on to existing plants because they will be subject to less strict environmental standards than new or modernized plants. So in trying to ease the transition to lower pollution levels through a new-source bias, the regulations may inadvertently slow up the rate of adoption of pollution abatement technology. This is no doubt one of the main reasons so many urban regions of the United States continue to suffer from substantial air pollution problems many years after the beginning of the federal program.

Virtually all of the observations we made about technology-based effluent standards in water pollution control are also applicable to air pollution–control policy. It is an approach that tends to put the initiative and responsibility for pollution control in the hands of administrative agencies rather than the polluters themselves. Too much of the energy and creativity of polluting firms is devoted to finding ways of avoiding compliance rather than devising better means of controlling emissions. The incentives for R&D to develop new techniques of pollution control or to reach back into the production process to reduce residuals in the first place are weakened. But most importantly, TBESs have the effect of encouraging uniform compliance measures among sources. In a world where marginal abatement costs differ substantially across sources, this cannot be a cost-effective policy.

Cost-Effectiveness of the TBES Approach

Numerous studies have been done by environmental economists to estimate excess costs of the command-and-control approach to air pollution control inherent in technology-based effluent standards. These studies involve complex models that incorporate economic factors, such as control costs at each source, with emission and meteorological factors that show how ambient air quality is affected by various patterns of emissions. The models can be run to determine the costs and ambient quality levels achieved with the CAC approach, then run again without the TBESs to see what the total control cost would be of a program that achieved the same ambient air quality but with a cost-effective distribution of emission reductions among firms. Table 15-6 summarizes the main results of some of the studies. The last column shows the ratio of the CAC program costs, incorporating various technology-based effluent

TABLE 15-6
COMPARISON OF CAC CONTROL COST WITH LEAST-COST PROGRAMS
IN AIR POLLUTION CONTROL

Study	CAC benchmark	Ratio of CAC costs to least cost
1 Particulates, St. Louis (1974)	SIP regulations	6.00
2 Sulfur dioxide, four corners region (Utah, Colorado, Arizona, and New Mexico) (1981)	SIP regulations	4.25
3 Sulfates, Los Angeles (1982)	Applicable Clean Air Act emission standards	1.07
4 Nitrogen dioxide, Baltimore (1983)	RACT regulations	5.96
5 Nitrogen dioxide, Chicago (1983)	RACT regulations	14.40
6 Particulates, Baltimore (1984)	SIP regulations	4.18
7 Sulfur dioxide, Delaware Valley (1984)	Uniform percentage reduction	1.78
8 Particulates, Delaware Valley (1984)	Uniform percentage reduction	22.00
9 Airport noise, U.S. (1983)	Mandatory retrofit	1.72
10 Hydrocarbons, all domestic Du Pont plants (1984)	Uniform percentage reduction	4.15
11 CFC emissions, U.S. (nonaerosol) (1980)	Proposed emission standards	1.96

Sources: Adapted from T. H. Tietenberg, *Emissions Trading: An Exercise in Reforming Pollution Control,* Resources for the Future, Washington, DC, 1985, pp. 42–43. Individual studies are as follows: **1** Scott E. Atkinson and Donald H. Lewis, "A Cost-Effective Analysis of Alternative Air Quality Control Strategies," *Journal of Environmental Economics and Management,* 1(3), November 1974, pp. 237–250; **2** Fred Roach et al., "Alternative Air Quality Policy Options in the Four Corners Region," *Southwestern Review,* 1(2), Summer 1981, pp. 44–45; **3** Robert W. Hahn and Roger G. Noll, "Designing a Market for Tradeable Emission Permits," in Wesley A. Magat (ed.), *Reform of Environmental Regulation,* Ballinger, Cambridge, MA, 1982, pp. 132–133; **4** Alan J. Krupnick, "Costs of Alternative Policies for the Control of NO₂ in the Baltimore Region," Resources for the Future, Washington, DC, 1983, p. 22; **5** Eugene P. Seskin, Robert J. Anderson Jr., and Robert O. Reid, "An Empirical Analysis of Economic Strategies for Controlling Air Pollution," *Journal of Environmental Economics and Management,* 10(2), June 1983, pp. 117–120; **6** Albert M. McGartland, "Marketable Permit Systems for Air Pollution Control: An Empirical Study," Ph.D. dissertation, University of Maryland, 1984, p. 67a; **7** Walter O. Spofford Jr., "Efficiency Properties of Alternative Source Control Policies for Meeting Ambient Air Quality Standards: An Empirical Application to the Lower Delaware Valley," Resources for the Future, Washington, DC, 1984, p. 77; **8** Ibid.; **9** David Harrison Jr., "Case Study 1: The Regulation of Aircraft Noise," in Thomas C. Schelling (ed.), *Incentives for Environmental Protection,* MIT Press, Cambridge, MA, pp. 81–96; **10** Michael T. Maloney and Bruce Yandle, "Estimation of the Cost of Air Pollution Control Regulation," *Journal of Environmental Economics and Management,* 11(3), September 1984, pp. 244–264; **11** Adele R. Palmer, W. E. Mooz, T. H. Quinn, and Kathleen A. Wolf, *Economic Implications of Regulating Chlorofluorocarbon Emissions from Nonaerosol Applications,* Rand Corporation, Report No. R-2524-EPA, June 1980, p. 225.

standards, as indicated, to least-cost programs that would provide the same improvement in air quality. If the actual programs were also cost-effective, these ratios would be at or near 1.0. In fact, they vary from 1.07 to 22.0.

Four of the studies show CAC/least-cost ratios between 1.0 and 2.0. These are CAC programs that also come close to achieving minimum costs. The most likely explanation for this is that these cases involve multiple sources that have relatively small differences in marginal abatement costs. Most of the other ratios, however, are around 4.0 to 6.0, meaning that the actual programs involving TBESs were four to six times more costly than they would have been had they been designed to be cost-effective. The problem with this is not just that society is paying much more than is necessary to get the improvements in air quality, although this is certainly a serious shortcoming. The real problem is that because the actual control programs are so much more costly than they need be, the apparent aggregate marginal abatement cost function is much higher than it need be, and therefore we are probably settling for smaller improvements in ambient quality than might be achieved if control programs were fully cost-effective.

New Directions in Stationary-Source Control

Of course it was recognized very early that the CAC types of policies favored by current laws would produce far less improvement in ambient quality for the money spent than we would get with more efficient policies. In the mid-1970s the EPA began to experiment with alternatives that might be more flexible and cost-effective in meeting air-quality goals. The 1977 Clean Air Act authorized a limited type of emission permit trading, based on the idea of **emission reduction credits** (ERCs). Sources obtain ERCs by reducing their emissions below a baseline level set by authorities. These ERCs may then be traded to other firms, or used by other units of the same firm.

More recently a number of complete **transferrable discharge programs** have been developed and put into place to address some of the nation's most significant air pollution problems:

- Pollution control authorities in Southern California began the Regional Clean Air Incentive Market (RECLAIM) in 1993. It applies to emissions of nitrogen oxide (NO_x) and sulfur dioxide (SO_2). Transferrable discharge permits (called RECLAIM trading credits in the program) were initially distributed to over 300 sources. Each permit has a denomination of one pound of RECLAIM pollutant and applies to a specified year. In the original distribution, sources received a time profile of permits, with the number applicable to each year declining to a minimum in year 2003. The final permit holdings imply reductions in total NO_x and SO_2 emissions by, respectively, 71 percent and 60 percent from their 1994 levels. Sources may buy and sell permits for the current year or future permits applicable to a later year.
- In the 1990 Clean Air Act Amendments, a very substantial TDP program was put into effect to control SO_2 emissions in the United States. This is a national market involving large electricity-generating plants, and we will examine it in some depth in the next section.
- Beginning in 1999, 13 northeastern U.S. states/regions began a transferable discharge program to control emissions of NO_x.[7] By interstate agreement

---

[7]These are the states of the Ozone Transport Committee, a group set up to determine how best to reduce ozone pollution in the northeast. The group includes the states Connecticut, Delaware, Maine, Maryland, Massachusetts, New Hampshire, New Jersey, New York, Pennsylvania, Rhode Island, and Vermont; the northern counties of Virginia; and the District of Columbia.

the total NO_x emissions for the group are allocated among the states, then each state allocates its total emissions as tradeable permits among sources in the state. Trading among sources, which are mostly electric utilities and large industrial boilers, may be both intra- and interstate. The EPA is developing a similar NO_x TDP program that would cover these 13 states/regions plus 10 others. It's expected that eventually the plans will be melded into a single program.

- Many individual states are establishing TDP programs to deal with air pollution problems within their borders. One of these, for example, is the market for volatile organic material (VOM) emissions in northeastern Illinois. The purpose of this market is to allow Chicago to achieve attainment of the NAAQS ozone standard in a cost-effective way. Major sources of VOM omissions are assigned baseline emission levels on the basis of their historical VOM emissions during recent years. They are then allocated TDPs (called allotment trading units, ATUs, in this program) equal to 88 percent of their baseline levels. Each ATU corresponds to 200 pounds of VOM per ozone season (May 1 to September 30) and is tradable in keeping with the fundamental principles of TDP programs.[8]

Space precludes a detailed review of all these plans. So we will look more closely at one of them, the SO_2 program under the 1990 Clean Air Act Amendments. This is the largest program, in terms of geographical spread, and probably the one that has received the greatest public scrutiny.

THE TDP PROGRAM OF THE 1990 CAA

Emissions of sulfur dioxide from power plants are a major source of acid precipitation, especially in the northeastern United States and eastern Canada. The purpose of the program is to achieve a reduction in total SO_2 emissions at much lower cost than if all plants were required to meet the same proportionate reductions or if all firms were held to the same TBESs. The law calls initially for a reduction of approximately 20 percent from estimated total sulfur emissions of 1980, and a further 20 percent reduction in later years. The program represents a very substantial departure from the "command-and-control" approaches of the past. If it works according to expectations, at least the expectations of many environmental economists, it should save considerable amounts of money and give a big boost to the application of incentive-type measures to other environmental problems.

How It Works

The program has two phases. Phase I ran from 1995 to 2000 and involved 110 electric power plants located in 21 eastern and midwestern states. Phase II starts in 2000 and includes about 1,000 power plants throughout the country.

[8]Additional information on this market is available at www.epa.state.il.us/air/erms/index.html.

The program began by EPA allocating to each Phase I plant a **time profile of discharge permits.**[9] Each permit is for a particular year and can be used either in that year or in any subsequent year (in other words, a permit dated for one year can be banked and used in a later program year). The permits are tradable and may be bought and sold by SO_2 sources, as well as anybody else who might wish to participate in the permit market. The EPA collects detailed data on the SO_2 emissions of each source and the number of permits held by each source. At the end of each year the EPA deducts from the permit holdings of each source an amount equal to the total tons by SO_2 the source has emitted in that year. If a source does not hold enough permits to cover their emissions, they are subject to a fine of $2,000 per ton of excess emissions.[10]

Initial Permit Distribution

Each of the participating power plants was given an initial allocation of permits (or "allowances," as they are called in the program) based on the following formula:

$$\text{Number of permits} = \text{Average Btus of fuel used 1985–1987 (in millions)} \times \text{2.5 pounds of } SO_2 \text{ per million Btus}$$

The formula gave more permits to larger plants, as measured by the average quantity of fuel used during the base period 1985–1987. It is not exactly an equiproportionate system, but it moves in that direction by using a common sulfur conversion factor—2.5 pounds of SO_2 per million Btus of fuel—to calculate initial allowances. Two plants burning the same amount of fuel end up with the same permit allocation, even though one of them may have put more effort than the other into reducing SO_2 emissions. But because the plants are all large coal-burning plants, the formula in effect treats them roughly the same.

This initial allocation totalled 5,489,335 permits. About 57 percent of these went to power plants in five states: Ohio, Indiana, Georgia, Pennsylvania, and West Virginia. An additional special Phase I allocation of permits was given to power plants in Illinois, Ohio, and Indiana.[11] The EPA also held back large quantities of permits. It has a "bonus reserve" of up to 3.5 million permits, which can be used to allow certain states to accommodate growth in their electricity-producing sectors or to provide temporary delays to power plants that wish to install scrubbers[12] to reduce SO_2 emissions. It also may auction off

---

[9]In other words, a source might be given a profile such as 5,000 permits applying to emissions in 1996; 4,900 permits for 1997; 4,800 permits for 1998; 4,700 permits for 1999; 4,600 permits for 1999; and 4,500 permits for 2000 and every subsequent year. This allows for a gradual reduction in the overall level of SO_2 emissions.

[10]The fine is indexed to inflation; in 1998 it was $2,581 per ton, for example.

[11]The initial allocation of permits was probably the most controversial issue when the law was being hammered out because it determines how the overall cost burden of SO_2reduction will be distributed among plants, states, and regions. The extra allocation to the three midwestern states was simply a way to help get their political support for the program.

[12]A "scrubber" is a device for treating stack gases; it can remove up to 95 percent of the sulfur in the gas.

a number of permits, as well as sell a certain number at a fixed (real) price of $1,500/permit. The EPA has an additional reserve of permits that it may allocate to utility firms that undertake approved programs in energy conservation or renewable energy development.

In Phase II, starting in 2000, the program was expanded to cover power plants throughout the country. At this point it covers about 1,000 power plants burning coal, oil, or natural gas. The formula for allocating permits was much the same as in Phase I except that the SO_2 index was lowered to 1.2 pounds of SO_2 per million Btus of fuel used. Furthermore, in Phase II there is an overall cap of 8.95 million permits given out by the EPA.

Trading Rules

Emission permits are **tradable.** Managers of an individual plant may do one of three things. They may simply hold on to the permits they were originally allocated and reduce their sulfur emissions to or below that level.[13] They could reduce their emissions below their permit holdings and sell the surplus permits. Or they could reduce their emissions to something more than their initial permit holdings and buy extra permits to cover the overage. Thus, market participants—buyers and sellers—will consist of these utility plants adjusting their permit holdings to match their emission rates, as well as other participants who may buy and sell permits. Other utilities that might wish to expand their electricity output, but are held in check by SO_2 emission limitations, may buy additional permits, as may new plants starting operations after the program is put into effect. The law also allows permits to be traded and held by private citizens, brokers, speculators, environmental groups, other types of business enterprises, and so on. As an environmental group, you might wish to buy permits simply to get total SO_2 emissions reduced.[14] As a manufacturer of pollution-control equipment, you might wish to buy a stock of permits that you could lend to your customers while they were installing your equipment. As a speculator, you might want to buy and hold permits because you think their price is going to rise.

The Role of the EPA

The role of the EPA is quite different from typical command-and-control type pollution–control programs. It is to keep track of permit trades so that it knows at all times how many emission permits are held by each plant. It also must monitor emissions to ensure that no plant emits more than it is entitled to by the number of permits it holds. The law specifies that each source is to install and maintain continuous monitoring devices. Emissions and permit data are collected via the Internet. In theory the EPA will be concerned only with

---

[13]They might reduce emissions below their permit holdings in order to have a reserve of surplus permits on hand for future contingencies.

[14]One group that facilitates this type of transaction is the Clean Air Conservancy (**www. cleanairconservancy.org**).

TABLE 15-7
EMISSIONS AND PERMIT HOLDINGS, SO_2 TDP PROGRAM
(millions of tons of SO_2)

Year	Permit allocations	Emissions	Permits banked	Total permits held
1990	—	9.96		
1994	—	8.50		
1995	8.74	5.30	3.44	8.74
1996	8.30	5.44	6.30	11.74
1997	7.15	5.47	7.98	13.45
1998	6.97	5.29	9.66	14.95

Source: U.S. Environmental Protection Agency, Acid Rain Program Annual Reports; available at: www.epa.gov/airmarkets/cmprpt/index.html.

whether emissions exceed allowances; its only direct control over technology choices is to approve for each plant " . . . a compliance plan that specifies the company's choice of one or more of the compliance methods authorized under the act."[15]

Will It Work?

Will the program run smoothly and produce reductions in SO_2 emissions at a substantial cost savings over a CAC-type program? After a few years of experience, the national SO_2 TDP program appears to have been quite effective. In fact judging by emission reduction that has taken place, one would have to judge it to have been super effective. Table 15-7 shows some interesting data on the program. The first column shows the total number of TDPs allocated to the power plants in the program, from 1995, the first year of the program, to 1998. The second column shows total SO_2 emissions for these plants, for two years prior to the program (1990 and 1994), and then for the years 1995 to 1998. There are two interesting things: first, there has been a substantial reduction in emissions from these power plants since before the program became operational and, second, during the program years emissions have actually been lower than the permit allocation for those years. What this means is that banked permits, the difference between permits held and emissions, have increased markedly over the first few years of the plan. We now have a situation in which the number of permits available to be used by source is substantially higher than their current emissions. A major part of the explanation for this is probably that sources invested fairly heavily in the beginning in new SO_2 control technology, shifting their marginal abatement costs downward in the expectation that this would allow them to sell excess permits. These cost savings were realized even before there was much activity in permit trading, as Example 15-1 discusses.

[15]*EPA Journal,* 17(1), January/February 1991, p. 23.

EXAMPLE 15-1

COST SAVINGS WITHOUT PERMIT TRADING

When the 1990 CAA program of TDPs was enacted, most people thought that an active trading market would develop and permits would trade at relatively high prices, perhaps $1,000 per ton. An active market in permits, according to theory, would allow electric utilities as a group to achieve significant cost savings through the gains from trade inherent in permit trading. This has not happened; relatively few trades have taken place, and prices of permits have been much lower than predicted (around $150 per ton). Yet significant emission abatement cost savings have occurred anyway. How has this happened?

In addition to the permit trading system, the CAA of 1990 broke with past laws by allowing utilities much more flexibility in their choice of ways to reduce emissions. The original air pollution control laws had effectively required utilities to install stack-gas scrubbers in order to reduce emissions. But the 1990 law allows them to seek cheaper ways of controlling emissions. One effective way of doing this is to switch to low-sulfur coal. For many utilities, it has been more profitable to switch to low-sulfur coal, thereby bringing abatement costs down, than to buy permits with the older, higher abatement cost technologies.

Suppose a utility has the marginal abatement cost labeled MAC_1 in the following model.

Initially, the firm is given e_1 permits. If it could purchase permits at a price of

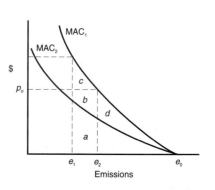

p_0, it could buy $e_2 - e_1$ permits, at a total cost of $(a + b)$. With abatement cost savings of $(a + b + c)$, their gains from the permit purchase would be c. But suppose, because of newly available and relatively inexpensive technologies for reducing emissions, they could shift their abatement costs down to MAC_1 at a relatively low cost. At an emissions level of e_1, this would entail total savings in abatement costs of $(b + c + d)$, which, depending on the cost of making the shift from MAC_1 to MAC_2, could yield them substantially higher profits than they could have obtained by buying permits and emitting at a higher level. This is apparently what has happened in the early stages of the CAA of 1990: relatively few permit trades but substantial reductions in emission abatement costs.

Source: See Dallas Burtraw, "Cost Savings Sans Allowance Trading? Evaluating the SO_2 Emission Trading Program to Date," Resources for the Future Discussion Paper 95-30, Washington, DC, September 1995.

It seems very likely that too many permits were allocated to sources at the beginning of the program. Observers to date have been surprised at the relatively low market prices for permits that have pertained in the early years of the market and the relatively small number of trades. In Chapter 13 we discussed the important problem of setting limits on the initial distribution of permits. If the total number of permits put into circulation is too large, their price will obviously be relatively low. The initial supplies of permits is likely to be based in large part on assertions by polluters themselves about their abatement costs and the difficulties of reducing emissions. In the 1990 program, authorities may have been misled into issuing too many TDPs at the beginning of the program. Another problem that bears watching stems from the fact that the main participants in the program are large electric-generating plants. TDP programs depend for their success on firms being cost minimizers, which, if they are in a competitive industry, can be reasonably expected to be true. But the electric-generating business has historically been a **regulated monopoly** rather than a competitive industry. So **public utility commissions,** which perform oversight in these industries, may have a role in TDP sales and/or purchases of firms they oversee. The effects of this are difficult to predict.

A major controversy also has developed in the program over the **hotspot** issue, as mentioned briefly in Chapter 13. The power plants in Phase I of the program were spread throughout the eastern part of the country, while in Phase II these are power plants throughout the United States. Thus, unrestricted trading could conceivably concentrate permits in a single region, for example, the Midwest. States of the northeast are convinced that this is in fact happening, and that it is leading to diminished air quality in the northeastern part of the country. The issue is quite contentious and has not yet been resolved on either the political or scientific level.

Despite these possible problems, the program represents a considerable innovation in U.S. pollution-control policies. It is the first large-scale example of a system of transferable discharge permits tried in the country and, in that sense, represents a kind of laboratory for environmental economists, who have been talking for many years about the advantages of moving to economic incentive programs to combat pollution.

MOBILE-SOURCE AIR POLLUTION CONTROL

The other major part of the federal air-quality program is control of mobile-source emissions. Although there are thousands of stationary sources of air pollution, there are many millions of mobile sources. Furthermore, the political fundamentals of mobile-source control are totally different from stationary-source emissions. It is often good politics to be seen chastising the polluting behavior of the businesses, especially corporations, responsible for stationary sources. It is quite different to take an aggressive stance against the millions of people whose cars cause the pollution but who also vote. So the spirit of the mobile-source program has been to reduce emissions, but in a way that avoids placing an obvious burden on individual drivers. The EPA counts it as a benefit of the mobile-source provisions of the 1990 Act that "Most car owners probably will not be aware of the many vehicle and fuel changes that auto and oil companies make in response to the Clean Air Act."[16]

---

[16]Ibid., p. 17.

To examine the mobile-source program, it will help to set the stage. The total quantity of mobile-source emissions in a given period can be expressed in the following way:

$$\text{Total quantity of emissions} = \text{Number of vehicles} \times \text{Average miles traveled} \times \text{Emissions per mile}$$

If we were devising a cost-effective way of reducing the total quantity of emissions, we would want to balance the three factors on the right side of this equation according to the **equimarginal principle.** In fact, the federal mobile-source pollution–control program has focused almost completely on the last of these factors. And a major reason air pollution is still a serious problem in many regions is that although car makers have been quite successful in producing cars with ever-smaller emissions per mile, the first two factors in the equation have continued to grow relentlessly and virtually without control.

The federal mobile-source pollution–control program consists of the following major elements:

- At the manufacturing level, a "new-car certification" program that essentially sets emission standards on new cars, together with a warranty program that is meant to ensure the continued emissions performance of automobiles after they have left the plant.
- At the state level, inspection and maintenance (I&M) programs aimed at ensuring that the emissions performance of automobiles does not deteriorate as they are used.
- In nonattainment areas, a variety of technological specifications dealing with vehicles, fuels, and other components of the transportation system.

New-Car Emission Standards

The main emissions from mobile sources are hydrocarbons (sometimes called "volatile organic compounds" or VOCs), nitrogen oxides (NO_x), carbon monoxide (CO), and particulate matter. Lead used to be a major mobile-source pollutant but, since the advent of lead-free gas, this is no longer the case.[17] The first two of these (VOCs and NO_x) are smog precursors; that is, after they are emitted, they react with sunlight and among themselves to form the smog and elevated ozone levels that characterize so many urban areas.

The primary federal approach to controlling mobile-source emissions was set in the 1970 Clean Air Act. It consists of a **new-car certification program**— essentially a program of mandated emission standards on new cars. Manufacturers are required to certify that the emissions of new cars do not violate the legally mandated standards. Violations may lead to a variety of penalties, up to and including shutting down the assembly lines that produce the offending vehicles. Table 15-8 shows the emission standards established in fed-

---

[17]We will discuss the lead-reduction program later.

TABLE 15-8
AUTOMOBILE EMISSION STANDARDS ESTABLISHED IN FEDERAL LAW 1974–2004*

	VOC	CO	NO$_x$	PM	HCHO
	Grams per mile				
Uncontrolled emissions (c. 1970)	8.7	87.0	3.5		
Federal standards:					
1974	3.0	28.0	3.1	n/a	n/a
1978	1.5	15.0	2.0	n/a	n/a
1980	0.41	7.0	2.0	n/a	n/a
1990	0.41	3.4	1.0	n/a	n/a
1994**					
Cars (<3,751 lbs.)	0.25	3.4	0.4	0.08	n/a
Trucks (3,751–5,750 lbs.)	0.32	4.4	0.7	0.08	n/a
Trucks (>5,750 lbs.)	0.39	5.0	1.1	n/a	n/a
2004†					
All vehicles‡	0.09	4.2	0.07	0.01	0.18

*VOC: volatile organic compounds, now called "non-methane organic gas"; CO: carbon monoxide; NO$_x$: nitrogen oxides; PM: particulate matter; HCHO: formaldehyde.

**To be met by 40 percent of all light vehicles manufactured in 1994, 80 percent in 1995, and 100 percent in 1996 and beyond.

†This is the year in which the new standards will begin to be phased in; the final standards will not be reached until 2009. These standards have been announced by the current administration and are currently (summer 2000) under discussion and debate.

‡These are the "full useful life standards," that is, the standards that cars are expected to meet after 120,000 miles. The standards for new cars are slightly more restrictive. The standards for VOC, CO, PM, and HCHO may vary slightly from the numbers shown because manufacturers are allowed some flexibility to certify cars with varying profiles of emission standards, as long as the fleet average for NO$_x$ is less than 0.07 grams per mile.

eral laws over the last several decades. The first row shows emissions for a typical car of around 1970, based on average performance and gas mileage data. As of 1990 the mandated emission standards were quite small relative to these early performance data. The 1990 standard for VOCs, for example, was only about 5 percent of the actual emissions of two decades earlier. The CO and NO$_x$ percentages are, respectively, 4 percent and 29 percent. What these numbers show are the very substantial reductions in new-car emissions (with the exception perhaps of NO$_x$) that have been achieved during the last 20 years. The Clean Air Act Amendments of 1990 mandated further drops in emission standards. A first round began in 1994, and a second round of tightening is now (2000) under public discussion.

These reductions in standards have been controversial. Critics, especially automobile companies, maintained that they were unrealistic when they were enacted. But advocates held that unrealistic standards were useful because they provided the incentive for car companies to search for new control technologies. This approach goes under the name of **"technology forcing."** Technology forcing is one of those things, of which there are many others, that are good in moderation but perhaps counterproductive if used in excess. The very stringent emission standards written into the 1970 clean-air legislation were in fact not met; rather, they were postponed and not finally achieved until the early 1980s.

We do not know whether more realistically timed emission standards might have led the automobile companies to spend more money on research and less on political efforts to get the standards postponed.

Although the emission standards have been progressively lowered through time, this trend actually overstates the reduction in emissions performance by cars in actual operation. The problem is that emissions performance of cars progressively deteriorates as the cars age and accumulate mileage. The federal program attempts to attack this problem in two ways. First it requires pollution-control equipment on automobiles to be long-lived enough to ensure that emissions standards will continue to be met for a given number of miles (the "warranty" program). In addition, it mandates that states with severe air-pollution problems initiate **inspection and maintenance** (I&M) programs, whereby individual cars can be checked for emissions. Owners whose cars exceed emission standards can then be held liable for repairs to bring them into compliance.

Lead Trading and the Switch to Lead-Free Gas

In the 1950s the practice of adding lead to fuel to augment its performance became common among gasoline refiners. As leaded gas became popular, the lead content of urban air began to show an alarming increase and concern mounted over the resulting health effects. In addition, lead in gasoline interfered with catalytic converters, the technology of choice for reducing other emissions. The federal response was to establish a timetable for the elimination of lead in gasoline. The program included a **trading system** to help reduce the overall cost of a transition to lead-free gasoline. To decrease the lead content of gas but maintain normal octane ratings, refineries had to install new equipment and operating procedures. But conversion costs differed among refineries, especially between large and small operations. Some could switch to lead-free gas quickly and at reasonably low cost, whereas for others conversion would take longer and be more costly. A **proportional cutback** program would have required each refinery to reduce the lead content of its gas according to a common timetable. Instead, a lead trading program was introduced to allow more flexibility and lower costs in the conversion process. **Lead credits** were earned by refineries reducing the lead content of their output in advance of the EPA timetable.[18] In 1982, for example, the EPA standard was 1.1 grams of lead per gallon of gasoline produced. Suppose a refinery instead produced 10,000,000 gallons of gas in that year containing an average of 0.9 gram of lead per gallon.[19] It would then have $10,000,000 \times (1.1 - 0.9) = 2,000,000$ grams of lead credits that it could sell to somebody else. Who would buy the credits? Other refineries who, because of their higher conversion costs, were moving more slowly in changing over their operations to low-lead gas.

---

[18]For a good discussion of this program, see Robert W. Hahn and Gordon L. Hester, "Marketable Permits: Lessons for Theory and Practice," *Ecology Law Quarterly*, 16(1), Winter 1989, pp. 361–406.

[19]This discussion draws on Robert W. Hahn, *A Primer on Environmental Policy Design*, Harwood Academic Publishers, Chur, Switzerland, 1989, pp. 41–44.

This might sound as if some refineries were given a chance to drag their feet in converting to low-lead gas, but the times involved were small. In fact, the lead trading had to be balanced out each quarter. That is, at the end of each quarter every refinery had to have a nonnegative balance of lead permits. So if a refinery did buy lead permits at some point in time, it still had to convert enough of its capacity to low-lead gas to account for those purchased lead rights. Thus, a refinery could gain only a few weeks, at most several months, of flexibility by purchasing lead rights. In 1985 banking was allowed. Firms after that could bank credits produced in a certain quarter, then use or sell them in a later quarter.

Despite what might look like limited trading possibilities, the lead market, which was national in scope, was widely used in the transition to low-lead gas. The national transition was essentially completed in 1988, and EPA estimates that it probably saved several hundreds of millions of dollars in total transition costs. Its success has been chalked up to two main points: initial widespread agreement on the overall goal of phasing out leaded gas and the ease of monitoring the amount of lead in gas.

Although the lead trading program was a success in easing the lead "phase-down," getting lead out of gas was not achieved without compensating environmental costs. People wanted less lead, but they also still wanted high engine performance. Thus, the octane rating of gasolines was to some extent maintained by substituting other compounds for lead. Some of these, like benzene, toluene, and the xylenes, are known carcinogens in their own right, and also have increased the aromatic qualities of gasoline, which increases VOC emissions.

The 1990 Clean Air Act

Despite the apparent progress in lowering new-car emissions over the years, many urban areas of the country continue to exceed ambient standards, particularly for NO_x and VOCs. The reason is that the number of cars and the total mileage driven in these areas continue to increase unrelentingly. In the 1970s there had been for a short time an effort to introduce direct transportation controls in some urban areas. At that time, states were supposed to develop state implementation plans (SIPs) incorporating such things as parking restrictions, exclusive bus and car pool lanes, road user charges, and so on that would control car use. But, with few exceptions, states were never able to develop these transportation plans. Owing to very strong political forces behind the idea of free car use, mileage has continued to increase unabated throughout the last few decades.

The 1990 Clean Air Act, besides tightening emission standards, also incorporates a large number of federally mandated technology standards that are supposed to allow nonattainment areas to move toward attainment even without any direct controls on the overall number of cars. These standards include

- "Reformulated" fuels: less volatile gas, oxygenated fuels, and so on.
- Alternative fuels: requiring vehicles that run on methanol, natural gas, and so on.

- Clean cars: low, ultra-low, and zero-emission (electric) vehicles.
- VOC capturing equipment: installed on cars, with analogous equipment at filling stations.

Elaborate rules have been specified for the conditions and means by which these technologies are supposed to be phased into use in nonattainment areas. In addition, I&M programs are to be put into place in areas where they do not exist and "enhanced" in areas that do have them. In some of the worst areas attention is also to be given to increased transportation planning to combat the VMT (vehicle miles traveled) problem.

The mobile-source parts of the 1990 law are a veritable jungle of technological specifications and requirements. In this it carries on the historic command-and-control tradition of pollution-control policy. It is an ongoing arena of great conflicts over detailed technical specifications and regulations in which economic and political incentives are thoroughly intertwined and opaque to the outsider. An instance of this is discussed in Example 15-2. The program is, however, starting to be sprinkled with certain modest incentive-based mechanisms. For example, the 1990 act requires that oxygenated fuels be used in certain nonattainment areas. Oxygenated fuels are fuels containing more than 2.7 percent oxygen by weight. The act provides that credits may be earned for gasolines that exceed the minimum oxygen threshold. These credits may then be traded to other fuel suppliers within the same nonattainment area for the purpose of complying with the reformulated gasoline requirement. The act also permits fleet owners, who are subject to minimum numbers of clean-fuel vehicles, to obtain tradable credits by purchasing more than the minimum number of these vehicles. These credits may then be sold to other sources, where they may be used to demonstrate compliance under the program in the same nonattainment area.

Clean Cars

As discussed above, mobile-source pollution control has focused almost completely on developing **clean cars.** If emissions per mile can be lowered enough, according to this line of thought, then total emissions will be reduced even if the total number of cars and total miles driven keep on increasing. Gradually lowering the mandated new-car emission standards represents an evolution in the direction of cleaner cars. Efforts also have been directed at getting automobile companies to develop new technologies that would represent a greater leap in automobile emission performance. The ultimate expression of this is the **zero-emission** vehicle (ZEV). At present the only practical ZEV would appear to be the electric vehicle (EV). As part of the Clean Air Act of 1990, California[20] sought to employ a **technology-forcing** approach, by mandating that auto makers make EVs available in that state starting in 1998. This date has now been pushed

[20]Since California began controlling auto emissions prior to the original Clean Air Act (1970), it is grandfathered in, in the sense that it is allowed to have stricter emission-control provisions than other states. The California regulation required that at least 2 percent of auto sales in the state be ZEVs between 1998 and 2000, 5 percent in 2001 and 2002, and 10 percent in 2003 and thereafter.

EXAMPLE 15-2

THE POLITICAL ASPECTS OF TECHNOLOGY STANDARDS

One of the benefits of incentive-based policies is that they leave to the people who should best know the decisions on how to reduce emissions cost-effectively. Thus the political opportunities for purveyors of particular technologies to entrench themselves in the regulatory process is minimized. On the contrary, when laws are written that contain specific technology choices embedded within them, two things happen: (1) the ability to meet cost-effective goals is compromised and (2) future policy decisions can get warped by the combat that takes place between the economic interests representing different technologies.

One of the major objectives of the 1990 Clean Air Act was to reduce automobile emissions, especially in those areas of the country that are in nonattainment with respect to ambient air–quality standards. This is a very straightforward goal, and might have been promulgated as such. But the EPA, and Congress, became convinced that one of the ways this could best be done was to require refiners to produce and make available in these regions gasoline that produces fewer emissions. Even more specifically, a requirement was added that gas sold in these areas contain at least 2 percent oxygen. To meet this very detailed technology specifica-

tion, refiners began to add the oxygenating material called MTBE (methal tertiary-butyl ethyl) to gasoline. Subsequently, it has been found that this substance may have caused significant environmental damage itself, and now efforts are underway at state and federal levels to require that MTBE specifically not be added to gasoline. From a cost-effective standpoint, the best thing would be to drop entirely the emphasis on reformulated gasoline. Establish emission requirements and then let consumers and industry figure out the most cost-effective ways of reaching them (for example, maybe one of the best ways of reaching them is to get people to drive less). But the 2 percent oxygen requirement now has become politically sensitive. Makers of ethanol, especially corn farmers, see a potentially lucrative market (ethanol is also a gasoline oxygenate) if MTBE is disallowed but the 2 percent oxygen requirement is maintained, because refiners would then likely turn to their product. Pollution control should be a contest where the race goes to those with the most cost-effective means of controlling emissions. By writing such specific technology requirements into the laws, however, it becomes instead a political contest where the race goes to the people who have the most political clout.

---

back to 2003 because of difficulties in developing EVs that have power and endurance performance that customers will find attractive. It may be pushed back again if technological development of EVs continues at the same pace.

Meanwhile, attention has shifted to low-, but not zero-, emission vehicles. Carmakers have been given a variety of incentives to develop cars that produce emissions that are substantially lower than current standards, and perhaps even the stricter standards that will come into effect in 2003. Attention centers both on changes in existing internal combustion technologies and on developing new technologies such as the combined gas and electric power system.

Incentive Issues in Mobile-Source Programs

The mobile-source air pollution–control program is substantially a technology-based program, in which improvements are sought through a series of techno-logical fixes. Little attention has been directed at behavioral factors associated with the fully mobile lifestyle, such as multiple-car families, dispersed living patterns, and long-distance voyaging. The basic fact is that mobile-source emissions are linked not only to the technical characteristics of cars and fuel systems, but also to the millions of decisions that individuals make about where, when, and how to travel. So far the technology approach has been reasonably effective; the massive increase in total **vehicle miles traveled** (VMT) in the last five decades has not been accompanied by a large increase in total emissions because individual cars are much cleaner now than they were in the 1970s. Theoretically, it would be possible to reduce mobile-source emissions to zero if all cars were ZEVs. But achieving this in practice is not possible in the near or intermediate future.

This implies that there is a need for incentive-based policies that impact peoples' decisions about automobile use. One approach that has been suggested is to levy a significantly higher tax on gasoline. With gasoline more expensive, motorists would have the incentive to think more about their driving habits, organize their driving more coherently, reduce total miles traveled, shift to more fuel-efficient vehicles, use mass transit to a greater extent, and so on. The effects of the higher fuel price would filter throughout the transportation system and lead people to shift their behavior in places where the marginal costs of doing so are lowest, much as they did in the energy "crisis" of the 1970s. Gasoline taxes also might help reduce traffic congestion in some cases. Taxes on gas have historically been levied at the state level. This might make it possible to adapt the tax to the level of air pollution in the region, but it also complicates the policy from a political point of view.

Another suggestion is to place a charge directly on vehicle emissions. As part of the state I&M programs, inspectors could record each year the total mileage that a vehicle had been driven. This total mileage could be multiplied by the emissions per mile, also measured at the time of inspection, to yield an estimate of total emissions in the preceding year. A charge could then be levied on these emissions. Unlike a fuel tax, which would have no direct incentive for drivers to worry about emissions, a charge on emissions would create an incentive to look at all the ways of lowering them, including reducing total miles driven, driving low-polluting vehicles, and so on. One attractive aspect of this approach is that the charge could be varied among regions to match the severity of regional air-quality problems.

Another place where incentives need to be more closely examined is in the **inspection and maintenance** (I&M) programs. This is the other major part of the mobile-source emission control program. The new-car certification program applies to cars as they roll off the assembly line, while the I&M programs put in place by the states are meant to identify cars that fall below the standards during their useful lives. It is then the responsibility of the owners to get them repaired. The 1990 Clean Air Act requires **enhanced I&M** programs in which more sophisticated, and costly, testing technology is used.

I&M, as currently pursued, is a case where the apparent ethical attractiveness of a program—making owners responsible for keeping their vehicles in repair—may be in conflict with its cost-effectiveness. The failure rate for tested cars appears to be quite low; in a major study of the Arizona enhanced I&M program, the failure rate was about 12 percent.[21] This means that, on average, 8.3 cars have to be inspected in order to find each of the nonconforming vehicles. And this means that the majority of the total cost of the I&M program goes to simply trying to find the problem vehicles. This substantially lowers the cost-effectiveness of the program, that is, the amount of emission reduction we get per, say, million dollars of program cost.

The incentive issue here is that owners of cars needing repair have no particular desire to be identified. In fact their incentive is to avoid the repairs if the cost of doing so is less than the expected repair costs. The question is whether an I&M program can be designed that would substantially reduce this perverse incentive or, if this is not possible, might it be better to approach the problem in an entirely different way? One possibility, for example, would be for the public to subsidize repair costs. This would make the individuals with nonconforming cars much less reluctant to have them tested, though it would still be necessary to test all cars in order to find the few that don't meet emission standards. A more cost-effective approach might be to shift responsibility more completely to automakers, by requiring that new cars be made so as to be able to meet more stringent emission standards over the life of the vehicles. The invention of better technology for identifying nonconforming cars, such as **remote sensing** or **on-board diagnostics,** may help alleviate the task of identifying, from among the millions of cars in use, the relatively small number that do not meet emission standards.[22]

SUMMARY

The federal effort to control airborne emissions has had several main elements. National ambient air–quality standards have been established, not on the basis of efficiency considerations as we have discussed them, but "to protect the public health," with an "adequate margin of safety," irrespective of the costs. In fact, the essential trade-offs between costs and benefits were left for administrators to work out behind the scenes. A distinction is made between nonattainment areas, where ambient standards are not met, and PSD regions, where they are. To meet the ambient standards, primary reliance is placed on technology-based emission standards. These TBESs are based on a number of different concepts, such as lowest achievable emission rate (LAER) for new sources in nonattainment areas and maximum achievable control technology (MACT) for hazardous emissions. Most economic studies of these TBESs in air pollution control show that for the total amount of money spent on pollution control,

---

[21]See the EPA report, *Analysis of the Arizona IM240 Test Program and Comparison with the TECH5 Model*, at www.epa.gov/otaq/regs/im/az-rpt/az-rpt.htm.
[22]For greater discussion of this issue see Winston Harrington and Virginia D. McConnell, *Coase and Car Repair: Who Should Be Responsible for Emissions of Vehicles in Use?*, Resources for the Future, Washington, DC, Discussion Paper 99-22, February 1999.

they achieve only a fraction of the emission reduction that a fully cost-effective program would attain.

The 1990 CAA contains an innovative national program of transferable emission permits, in this case applied to SO_2 emissions from large power plants. Emission permits were allocated to existing power plants; these permits may then be traded. The objective is to achieve a roughly 50 percent reduction in total SO_2 emissions in a cost-effective way. Substantial uncertainties surround this new market for discharge permits, and additional regulatory oversight and legal evolution will determine how well the system succeeds.

Mobile-source emission reductions have been sought almost entirely through establishing emission standards for new cars, and then trying to ensure that emissions do not increase as the cars are being used. The 1990 Clean Air Act attempts to mandate a number of technological changes, such as reformulated fuel and low-polluting vehicles. Less attention has been given to the important problem of reducing total vehicle miles in urban areas with seriously degraded air quality.

QUESTIONS FOR FURTHER DISCUSSION

1 The actual market price of permits in the SO_2 transferable permit program have been much lower than was predicted before the plan went into effect. What are the possible reasons for this?

2 Suppose that engineers invented an accurate and reliable means of monitoring and measuring the emissions from individual automobiles throughout the year. What possibilities would this open up for new types of mobile-source emission control programs?

3 The federal mobile-source air pollution program means that new cars sold in rural regions meet the same emissions standards as cars sold in urban areas. Because there are a lot fewer cars in rural areas, this means that air quality will be a lot better there than in the cities. Is this efficient? Is it equitable?

4 What are the advantages and disadvantages of a "new-source" bias in stationary-source air pollution control? Consider especially its impacts on the incentives of the operators of existing sources.

WEBSITES

Details about the SO_2 TDP program are available at **www.epa.gov/airmarkets/**. Technical issues related to the control of mobile-source emissions are covered well by the National Center for Vehicle Emissions Control and Safety, **www. colostate.edu/depts/ncvecs/ncvecs1.html**. For additional sites see the web page connected to this book, **www.mhhe.com/economics/field3**.

SELECTED READINGS

Crandall, Robert W., Howard K. Gruenspecht, Theodore E. Keeler, and Lester B. Lave: *Regulating the Automobile,* Brookings Institution, Washington, DC, 1986.

Ellerman, A. Denny: *Markets for Clean Air, the U.S. Acid Rain Program,* Cambridge University Press, Cambridge, England, 2000.

Hahn, Robert W., and Gordon L. Hester: "Where Did All the Markets Go? An Analysis of EPA's Emission Trading Program," *Yale Journal of Regulation*, 6(1), Winter 1989, pp. 109–153.

Krupnick, Alan J., and Paul R. Portney: "Controlling Urban Air Pollution: A Benefit–Cost Assessment," Science, Vol. 252, April 26, 1991, pp. 522–528.

National Research Council: *Rethinking the Ozone Problem in Urban and Regional Air Pollution*, National Academy Press, Washington, DC, 1991.

Nivola, Pietro S., and Robert W. Crandall: "The Extra Mile: Rethinking Energy Policy for Automotive Transportation," *Brookings Review*, Vol. 13, Winter 1995, pp. 30–33.

Portney, Paul R.: "Air Pollution Policy," in Paul R. Portney and Robert N. Stavins (eds.), *Public Policies for Environmental Protection*, Resources for the Future, Washington, DC, 2000, pp. 77–124.

Tietenberg, Tom H.: *Emissions Trading, An Exercise in Reforming Pollution Policy*, Resources for the Future, Washington, DC, 1985.

U.S. Environmental Protection Agency: *The Benefits and Costs of the Clean Air Act Amendments of 1990*, EPA 410-R-99-001, Washington, DC, 1999.

16

FEDERAL POLICY ON TOXIC AND HAZARDOUS SUBSTANCES

Within the general domain of environmental analysis and policy there is a class of pollutants that have come to be called "toxic" substances and "hazardous" materials. Although all pollutants are damaging to some extent, these have been singled out for their special short- or long-run potency. Most are chemicals, the person-made organic and inorganic compounds that are now ubiquitous throughout all industrialized economies, and even widespread in developing countries. Figure 16-1 shows the rise of that industry in the United States. From virtually nothing 70 years ago, it has grown in exponential fashion, and today chemicals and chemical products have permeated into every corner of the economy. In product improvements, new materials, food safety, health innovations, and many other dimensions, chemicals have enriched the lives of almost everyone. There is, however, a downside. A large number of these substances may cause human and ecosystem damages, certainly from exposure to concentrated doses, but also from long-run exposure to the trace amounts that show up virtually everywhere in workplaces, consumer products, and the environment.

The call to arms on chemicals in the environment was made by Rachel Carson in her book *Silent Spring*. She documented the ecosystem damage caused by the popular pesticide DDT and was largely responsible for getting it banned in the United States. Other events have multiplied concern. Health damages to workers exposed to chemicals in the workplace, such as vinyl chloride and certain potent agricultural chemicals, have occurred with disconcerting frequency. In 1978, in the celebrated case of Love Canal, people found chemicals oozing into their houses built on top of an abandoned hazardous

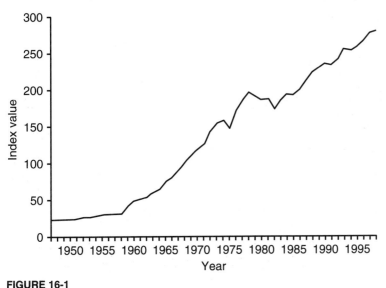

FIGURE 16-1
Chemical Production Index, United States, 1947–1998. (*Source:* U.S. Federal Reserve Bulletin, *Washington, DC, annual issues.*)

waste disposal site. Accidental releases of chemicals have become a growing problem, from the large-scale episodes like those in Milan, Italy, in 1976, and Bhopal, India, in 1984, to innumerable smaller airborne and waterborne accidents.[1] There is rising concern about the damages from long-term exposure to chemical residues in food, clothing, and other consumer products.

The primary concern is the impact of chemicals on human health. Health damages from accidental releases and workplace exposure are relatively easy to identify. Those from long-run exposure to trace amounts of chemicals in water, air, and soil are much harder to measure. Ecosystem damages are also important. Accidental waterborne chemical releases have wreaked havoc among fish and other organisms in enclosed bodies of water. Agricultural and industrial runoff has substantially damaged many rivers and estuaries around the world.

Hazardous and toxic materials have characteristics that present unique problems for monitoring and control.

1 They are **ubiquitous** in the modern economy; each year sees the development of new chemicals. This makes it difficult even knowing what substances are being used and in what quantities. It accounts for the fact that much public policy has been directed at simply getting better information about quantities of hazardous and toxic materials at various places in the system.

---

[1]An appreciation for the ongoing seriousness of this problem can be gained by looking at the website of the National Response Center,**www.nrc.uscg.mil.**

2 With the thousands of substances in use, each with different chemical and physical properties, it is virtually impossible to be fully informed about the **levels of danger** that each one poses to humans and other parts of the ecosystem.

3 In many cases the quantities used are **relatively small,** as are the quantities that end up as effluent. This substantially increases monitoring problems. It also makes it easier for users to carry out surreptitious disposal. It is easy to see the plume of smoke coming out of the stack of an industrial plant; it is harder to track the much smaller quantities of chemicals used in production.

4 The damages caused by exposure to hazardous materials often can take many years, even decades, to show up. And whenever there is a **long time gap** between cause and effect, there is a tendency to downgrade the overall seriousness of the problem.

In the next few sections we consider federal policy on hazardous and toxic substances and some of the major economic issues in the management of these materials. The policy world governing these materials is a jungle. There are numerous major and minor laws at the federal level, each applying to a piece of the total picture. Many federal agencies are involved, with territories staked out and objectives pursued in ways that are often inconsistent. Then there are public agencies at state and local levels that are actively pursuing efforts to come to grips with these types of pollutants. And all of this is within a setting where thousands of different substances are in use, hundreds more introduced each year, massive uncertainties about the human and nonhuman effects of most of them, and public concerns that flare up and die down in unpredictable ways.

To help sort out these complexities the following discussion is organized into three sections: (1) laws governing the use of chemicals in industrial and agricultural production processes and in consumer goods, (2) laws governing airborne and waterborne emissions of toxic materials, and (3) laws governing the handling, treatment, and disposal of hazardous wastes. Table 16-1 lists the major federal laws in each category. There is not enough space or time here to deal with each law in detail, so the following sections first give short sketches of the most important of the laws in each category, then discuss some of the major economic issues they present.[2]

FEDERAL LAWS GOVERNING CHEMICALS IN PRODUCTION AND CONSUMER PRODUCTS

At issue here is the management of chemicals in consumer products and in the workplace, with the objective of ensuring that these products and workplaces are "reasonably" safe. What "reasonably" means is a matter of public debate.

---

[2] For good discussions of toxic and hazardous substance laws, see Mary Devine Worobec and Girard Ordway, *Toxic Substances Control Guide,* Bureau of National Affairs, Washington, DC, 1989; Hilary Sigman, "Hazardous Waste and Toxic Substance Policies," in Paul R. Portney and Robert N. Stavins (eds.), *Public Policies for Environmental Protection,* 2nd ed., Resources for the Future, Washington, DC, 2000, pp. 215–260.

TABLE 16-1
FEDERAL LAWS DEALING WITH TOXIC AND HAZARDOUS SUBSTANCES

Policy and statute	Responsible agency	Coverage
A. Policies on Chemicals Used in Production and Consumer Products		
Federal Insecticide, Fungicide, and Rodenticide Act (1972)	EPA	Pesticides
Food, Drug, and Cosmetic Act (1938)	FDA	Basic coverage of food, drugs, cosmetics
Food additives amendment	FDA	Food additives
Color additives amendments	FDA	Color additives
New drug amendments	FDA	Drugs
New animal drug amendments	FDA	Animal drugs and feed additives
Medical device amendments	FDA	Medical devices
Section 346(a) of the Food, Drug, and Cosmetic Act	EPA	Tolerances for pesticide residues in human food and animal feeds
Federal Hazardous Substances Act (1960)	CPSC	"Toxic" household products (equivalent to consumer products)
Consumer Product Safety Act (1972)	CPSC	Dangerous consumer products
Poison Prevention Packaging Act (1970)	CPSC	Packaging of dangerous children's products
Lead-Based Paint Poison Prevention Act (1991)	CPSC	Use of lead paint in federally assisted housing
Federal Meat Inspection Act (1907)	USDA	Food, feed, and color additives and pesticide residues in meat and poultry products
Poultry Products Inspection Act (1957)	USDA	Poultry products
Egg Products Inspection Act (1970)	USDA	Egg products
Federal Mine Safety and Health Act (1977)	MSHA	Coal mines or other mines
Toxic Substances Control Act (1976)	EPA	Requires premanufacture evaluation of all new chemicals (other than food, food additives, drugs, pesticides, alcohol, tobacco); allows EPA to regulate existing chemical hazards
Occupational Safety and Health Act (1970)	OSHA	Workplace toxic chemicals
Food Quality Protection Act of 1996	EPA	Pesticides in food

(continued on next page)

TABLE 16-1
FEDERAL LAWS DEALING WITH TOXIC AND HAZARDOUS SUBSTANCES (CONTINUED)

Policy and statute	Responsible agency	Coverage
B. Policies on Chemical Emissions		
Clean Air Act (amended 1970)	EPA	Hazardous air pollutants
Clean Water Act (amended 1972)	EPA	Toxic water pollutants
Safe Drinking Water Act (1974)	EPA	Drinking water contaminants
C. Policies on Handling, Storage, Transportation, Treatment, and Disposal of Hazardous Wastes		
Resource Conservation and Recovery Act (1976)	EPA	Hazardous wastes
Maritime Protection, Research, and Sanctuaries Act (1972)	EPA	Ocean dumping
Comprehensive Environmental Response, Compensation, and Liability Act (1980)	EPA	Hazardous waste sites
Hazardous Materials Transportation Act (1975)	DOT	Transportation of toxic substances generally
Federal Railroad Safety Act (1970)	DOT	Railroad safety
Ports and Waterways Safety Act (1972)	DOT	Shipment of toxic materials by water
Dangerous Cargo Act (1871)	DOT	Shipment of toxic materials by water

EPA = Environmental Protection Agency; FDA = Food and Drug Administration; OSHA = Occupational Safety and Health Administration; CPSC = Consumer Product Safety Commission; DOT = Department of Transportation; USDA = Department of Agriculture; MSHA = Mine Safety and Health Administration.

Sources: Michael Shapiro, "Toxic Substances Policy," in Paul R. Portney (ed.), *Public Policies for Environmental Protection*, Resources for the Future, Washington, DC, 1990, pp. 198–199; original sources are Toxic Substances Strategy Committee, *Toxic Chemicals and Public Protection*, Washington, DC, 1980, and Council of Environmental Quality, *Environmental Quality—1982*, Washington, DC, 1982.

Some might argue that these matters are not properly part of environmental economics. **Household and work environments** are not, properly speaking, parts of the *natural* environment and, in these cases, the relations of consumers to producers, and of workers to firm owners, are played out directly through markets. Nevertheless, environmental concerns have to some extent reached out to subsume certain elements of the private environment as well as the world of nature properly speaking, so we follow that lead here. Homeowners exposed to formaldehyde leaking from insulation or a worker exposed to asbestos fibers in the workplace is subject to the same kind of actual and potential damages as are individuals exposed to toxic emissions coming from a neighborhood factory.

Consumer product safety is an issue that has been around for a long time. In the time of rapid industrial growth of the 19th and early 20th centuries, the free-for-all business atmosphere led to many cases of intentional or inadvertent product adulteration, often with dire results. Then in the latter 20th century, the rise of the chemical economy produced markets so scientifically complex that they are beyond the powers of the average consumer. These developments have led to a number of federal laws, the most important of which are sketched out in the following sections.

Federal Insecticide, Fungicide, and Rodenticide Act (FIFRA)

There are about 48,000 different pesticide products available for use in the United States, although these products contain only about 600 active chemical ingredients. A pesticide is a general term used to designate any substance meant to kill, repel, or control any nonhuman organism, from bacteria to bugs to oak trees. In fact, the law also covers certain noninsecticide products such as growth hormones and new organisms developed through recombinant DNA research. The present act was first passed in 1947, but it has predecessors that go back to the early decades of this century.

FIFRA works through a straightforward **command-and-control** approach. In order for a pesticide to be used, it must be registered with the EPA. Thus, in setting registration requirements the agency can control where and how a pesticide is used. The EPA has established a complex registration procedure, with standards applying to evidence that must be presented by manufacturers seeking approvals. FIFRA is a **balancing** law: It directs the EPA to make registration decisions so as to prevent **unreasonable adverse effects** on people or the environment, taking into account the economic, social, and environmental impacts of the pesticide. FIFRA also has provisions for establishing acceptable pesticide residue levels in raw foods. Normally these levels are nil, unless a **tolerance** level has been established or special exemption issued. To enforce the provisions of FIFRA, EPA may issue fines or criminal penalties, inspect facilities, seize products, or require product recalls. Enforcement of residue levels also is carried out by the Food and Drug Administration and the U.S. Department of Agriculture.

Food, Drug, and Cosmetic Act (FDCA)

Whereas the previous law worked through a chemical registration technique, the FDCA works through **legal prohibition** of foods, drugs, or cosmetics that do not meet certain criteria. In effect, the law prohibits the sale of any food, drug, or cosmetic that is "adulterated" or "mislabeled." Foods or drugs are regarded as adulterated if they contain additives that are considered to be harmful. A drug is mislabeled if it is not considered to be safe and effective. A food additive may be several things. It may be a specific chemical, like a preservative or a coloring agent, added to food to give it some quality. It may be the residue from a pesticide used when the crop was in the field. It may be a chemical that migrated into the food from the packaging material in which it is enclosed. Naturally occurring substances are not included; thus, for example, peanuts are not banned although they naturally contain powerful carcinogenic chemicals called aflatoxins. The FDCA also covers the regulation of food treated with irradiation.

Until 1996 processed foods were governed by the "Delaney Clause" of the FDCA. This prohibited in processed food any additive, including a pesticide, shown to cause cancer in animals. In the **Food Quality Protection Act of 1996** the criterion for allowing presticide residues in processed foods was made consistent with that for pesticides on raw foods. The 1996 law requires most pesticide levels in raw and processed foods to be set at a "safe" level, which is defined as a level at which there is "a reasonable certainty of no harm" from the exposure allowed by the tolerance.

A closely related issue in food safety is the question of **genetically modified food plants and animals.** This is not a conventional pollution-related problem, but it is one that has been subsumed to some extent within the orbit of environmental interest groups and environmental politics. With advances in **biotechnology,** the genetic structures of organisms can, to some extent, be manipulated through gene-splicing techniques. Through this means plant and animal species may be given characteristics and qualities that they would not be expected to have under normal circumstances. A certain plant might be given a gene that renders it impervious to a certain pesticide, for example. Or a food animal might be given a gene from another organism that increases its rate of growth.

The fear is that genetically modified organisms may represent threats to human health and/or the normal functioning of the ecosystem. Suppose a food plant is made resistant to a certain pesticide through genetic manipulation. Might not this resistance be picked up by a weed plant that is closely related to the food plant? Or suppose a food animal is altered to make it less susceptible to certain diseases that afflict livestock raised in modern conditions. Might this pose a health threat to humans who consume the products of this animal over an extended period?

To date there are many unanswered questions about the environmental impacts of biotechnology products. Advocates are enthusiastically asserting their benefits; skeptics are just as vigorously warning about potential negative impacts. A great deal of research is underway to clarify the situation. Regulatory action is being pursued by the Environmental Protection Agency, the Food and Drug Administration, and the U.S. Department of Agriculture. It promises to be a major issue well into the future.

Toxic Substance Control Act (TSCA)

TSCA was intended to give federal authorities a comprehensive legal tool with which to control the manufacture and use of chemicals in the United States, especially many industrial chemicals that could not be regulated effectively under other statutes. TSCA directs the EPA to carry out several functions:

- Complete an inventory of all chemicals produced or imported during the period 1975–1977, using information supplied by manufacturers and processors.
- Test existing chemicals for safety.
- Screen new chemicals.
- Regulate chemical use, for example, specifying conditions under which they may be used, setting labeling requirements, requiring additional testing, and so on.

Like FIFRA, TSCA is a "balancing" law; that is, it says that EPA is to make decisions on any chemical by comparing the risks it may pose with the benefits it produces for firms and consumers.

Consumer Products Safety Act (CPSA)

The CPSA of 1972 established the Consumer Products Safety Commission, which is authorized to conduct safety studies of consumer products, promulgate mandatory safety standards for products, and ban products determined to be hazardous. These regulations apply to all characteristics of particular products, including any chemicals they may contain.

Occupational Safety and Health Act (OSHA)

The goal of this law is to ensure safe working conditions, and the technique used is setting **workplace standards.** These are of two types: **health standards,** which are supposed to protect workers against exposure to harmful agents in the workplace, and **safety standards,** which are supposed to protect workers from imminent physical harms, such as falls, fires, or electrocution. Chemical exposure comes under the safety-standard rubric. Thus, under OSHA, the Occupational Health and Safety Administration sets workplace exposure standards (called "permissible exposure levels," or PELs; see the Appendix starting on page 483 for a list of acronyms used in this chapter) for specific chemicals that have been deemed dangerous. Since its enactment, for example, standards have been set for such chemicals as vinyl chloride, lead, benzene, cotton dust, and coke oven emissions. The standards are in the form of maximum ambient workplace concentrations of the chemical, and many of the standards also include "action levels" that trigger medical monitoring and surveillance of workers under certain conditions.

Another major part of OSHA is the system for informing workers of the hazards posed by chemicals in the workplace. As we will discuss later, the way labor markets adapt to the presence of chemicals in the workplace and, thus, the need for various types of public policy depend critically on how much information is available to workers on the health risks associated with exposure to various chemicals. With this in mind, EPA promulgated under OSHA a **"hazard communication standard"** that requires chemical manufacturers and users to assess the hazards of chemicals they use and notify workers of these hazards in their work area. This is aimed at getting firms to develop chemical hazard assessment data and then make them available to workers.

ECONOMIC ISSUES IN CHEMICAL PRODUCTION AND EXPOSURE

The "Balancing" Issue

Perhaps the most important question in the use of chemicals is the criterion for determining acceptable levels of exposure or protection. In setting the benzene or cotton dust standards in workplaces or the formaldehyde regulations for building materials, what principle should regulating agencies follow in setting

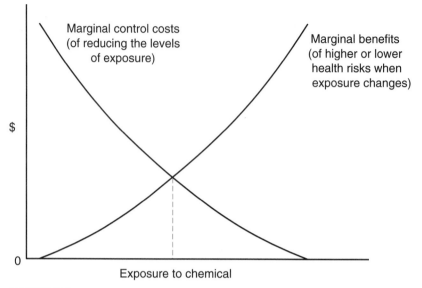

FIGURE 16-2
Cost–Benefit Balancing in Regulating Exposure to a Chemical.

exposure standards? In discussing our general model of environmental pollution control in Chapter 5, we developed the idea of the efficient level of environmental pollution as being a trade-off between control costs and damages. Applying the same logic to the case of chemicals means that in setting chemical exposure levels society should try to determine the point where the benefits of reducing health or other risks are just balanced by the costs of decreasing the production and use of the chemical. This trade-off is pictured in Figure 16-2.

A balancing approach is allowed under TSCA. In setting regulations for use of a chemical, the EPA may take into account both the health risks of using the chemical and the costs to the economy if the chemicals are banned or regulated. Until recently, FIFRA also permitted balancing, while the FDCA for the most part did not. These two laws were changed in 1996, however.[3] They now use a consistent health-based criterion for setting pesticide tolerances in all food. The criterion is phrased as "a reasonable certainty that no harm will result." Exhibit 16-1 describes a recent EPA decision under this standard. OSHA does not permit a balancing approach.

Many objections have been made against a balancing approach in managing chemicals: that scientific results are often too weak to show benefits and costs (especially costs) clearly; that matters of life and death are moral issues and ought to be treated as such; that it's the job of politicians, not economists, to determine the values that society ought to put on different outcomes; and so on. There is not the space to deal with all the issues here. They are basically the same questions that arose in our previous discussions of the concept of the efficient level of emissions, or ambient quality.

[3]In the Food Quality Protection Act of 1996.

EXHIBIT 16-1

COMMON PESTICIDE TO BE PULLED FROM MARKET

The U.S. Environmental Protection Agency announced on June 8, 2000, that it entered into an agreement with Indianapolis-based Dow AgroSciences to effectively eliminate the **pesticide** chlorpyrifos for nearly all household purposes.

Chlorpyrifos, which is sold under the trade names Dursban, Equity, Lorsban, and others, is one of the most widely used organophosphate insecticides in the United States with more than 20 million pounds applied annually. Approximately 50 percent is used around homes, gardens, and lawns to control a variety of insects, including termites. The remaining 50 percent is used on 40 different agricultural crops. Dow Agro-Sciences is the primary registrant and the only U.S. manufacturer.

There are approximately 825 registered products containing chlorpyrifos. Approximately 11 million pounds of the **pesticides** are used each year by farmers and fruit growers; about five million pounds by industrial, commercial, and government buyers; and about three million pounds by the home-and-garden market. Sales in the mid 1990s were about $500 million per year, according to the National Center for Food and Agricultural Policy, a research firm in Washington.

Food Quality Protection Act

EPA is taking this action under the Food Quality Protection Act, which was passed unanimously by Congress and signed by the president in 1996. The Act requires a systematic review of all pesticides to ensure they meet the tough new safety standards that—for the first time—must be protective of children, who are among the most vulnerable to adverse health effects from pesticide residues.

Congress passed the FQPA four years ago, requiring the review to be completed by October 1999; but so far, only a handful of chemicals have been examined. Under the Act, EPA is required to restrict or ban a pesticide's use if it poses a specific threat to children. The FQPA substitutes the risk/benefit methodology formerly used to regulate the pesticides for the Food and Drug Administration standard of "reasonable certainty of no harm."

The agreement between EPA and Dow AgroSciences will: stop production of and phase out all home, lawn, and garden uses; stop production of and phase out the vast majority of termite-control uses; and significantly lower allowable pesticide residues on several foods regularly eaten by children. Specifically, the agreement will halt the manufacture of chlorpyrifos by December 2000 for nearly all residential uses. It will require that virtually all residential uses be deleted from existing product labels prior to that time, including use for home and garden sprays, termite control use in completed houses, and use on lawns.

In addition, by the beginning of the next growing season, allowable residues will be canceled or significantly lowered for several foods regularly eaten by children, such as tomatoes, apples, and grapes.

Normally, EPA sets a safe-exposure level for a pesticide such as chlorphyrifos at 1/100 of the maximum concentration at which there are no detectable effects on an adult animal. Under the 1996 law, that 1/100-fold safety margin is increased tenfold if there is evidence that infants or children are especially vulnerable to a pesticide. The level of chlorpyrifos that will now be deemed safe for children will be 1/1000 of the no-effect level.

Source: Indiana Environmental Compliance Update, M. Lee Smith Publishers, July 2000. Reprinted by permission.

There is no question that the data and analytical requirements of a balancing approach are high. This approach requires good dose—response information, exposure data, and estimates of the benefits of reducing risks to workers and consumers. Some would argue that sheer numbers make the balancing approach impossible. Can we ever expect to have enough information to permit an effective balancing approach for all the chemicals to which workers and consumers may be exposed? The problem is compounded by the fact that to regulate one substance, we need more than just information on the risks and benefits of that one material. If a chemical is banned, either altogether or in particular uses, the full impact depends on what other substance might be used as a **replacement**. Thus, to assess a particular substance we have to know not only its own characteristics, but also what products would replace it if it were controlled, and what the full characteristics of these substitutes are.

One answer to this is that not all chemicals are of equal importance. It is possible to focus attention on substances that are in wide use or are used in relatively large quantities. Between 1975 and 1989, for example, the EPA reviewed 19 cancer-causing pesticides widely used in raising agricultural crops. Of the 245 registered food uses permitted with this group of pesticides, 96 were canceled as a result of the EPA review. According to the researchers who studied this EPA experience, "balancing" considerations played an important role in these decisions.[4] Not exclusively, however. The decisions were made partly in response to political activity ("lobbying") by environmental groups on one side and industry groups on the other.

The problem of **testing** a very large number of chemicals has focused attention on the deficiencies of current testing procedures and the risk estimates that arise from them. Results are hard to get from studies of humans, mainly because it is virtually impossible to get accurate exposure data. That means most risk information must come from laboratory experiments with animals, particularly mice and rats. The biggest problem here is one of extrapolating test results, from one organism to another with an entirely different metabolism, and from one dosage rate to another. A typical chemical in the human environment—for example, a pesticide residue in a certain type of food—might expose the average person to 1 or 2 µg of the substance each day. If mice were tested at this exposure level, an experimenter might need to test half a million mice to detect the one or two in a million probability of, say, getting cancer from the chemical. This is simply not practical, and to get around it researchers typically expose animals to much larger doses of the chemical under test. Although these exposure rates may be several thousand times higher than humans are typically subjected to, the results of the studies are nevertheless extrapolated to humans. In other words, animal experiments using massive doses are used to predict the effects on humans of exposure to tiny doses. There has been much controversy over whether this procedure gives accurate results.

Chemical testing procedures have improved over the last several decades. The future no doubt will see further changes, and we may hope that at some point we

[4]Maureen L. Cropper, William N. Evans, and Paul R. Portney, "An Analysis of EPA Pesticide Regulation," *Resources*, 102, Winter 1991, pp. 7–10.

will develop cheap, effective ways of testing a chemical for toxicity to humans. In the meantime, it has to be recognized that there is still a lot of uncertainty surrounding the average estimate of risk arising from using a particular chemical, and this has to be taken into account in making balancing decisions about its use.

As for letting the **political process** determine the trade-offs implicit in managing chemicals in the workplace and in consumer goods, this is clearly the way it should be. But not in the absence of the **best available data** from science, including economics. The political process responds to all kinds of real or imaginary influences, usually in the short run. Laws often get written in terms of absolutes; political representatives normally strive to avoid giving the impression that they are trading off human lives for anything else, especially economic values. Statutes written in absolute terms, or even in general qualitative terms,[5] essentially drive the balancing process underground, or into the administrative agencies, where trade-offs get made through implicit comparisons and unseen variations in enforcement. For example, whereas the OSHA statute requires workplace standards to protect workers' health without regard to cost, it is in fact impossible to do this in practice. Rather, balancing takes place, without describing it as such, in the setting of the standards. Even more importantly, balancing occurs through enforcement; seemingly tough standards are promulgated but with weak enough enforcement that balancing is pursued in effect. Under these circumstances it may be better to follow an explicit balancing standard.

Uniform Standards

The problem of toxic materials in the workplace and in consumer products has been addressed largely by establishing standards of various types. This brings up several important issues. One is the issue of whether the standards should be **uniform.** Another is the issue of how **markets** ordinarily function to take account of risks present in workplaces and consumer products. We can illustrate these with a discussion of workplace standards, of the type that would be established by OSHA.

Consider Figure 16-3. It applies to a case of workplace exposure where workers are faced with the risk of accidental exposure to a chemical used in production. The horizontal axis shows the level of risk, starting at zero and increasing to the right. Higher risks are associated with increasing marginal damages, through the health effects of exposure to the chemical. There are two MC curves, each showing the marginal control costs of reducing workplace risk. Risk can be reduced through a variety of means: introducing safety equipment, rearranging the workplace, policing safe procedures, and so on. But the costs of

---

[5]OSHA states that toxic materials in the workplace are to be controlled if they lead to " . . . material impairment of health or functional capacity. . . ." The Consumer Products Safety Act is aimed at products that constitute an "unreasonable risk of injury. . . ." The Comprehensive Environmental Response, Compensation and Liability Act (see later in this chapter) applies to hazardous substances in which there is "substantial danger to the public health . . . ," and so on. See John J. Cohrssen and Vincent T. Covello, *Risk Analysis: A Guide to Principles and Methods for Analyzing Health and Environmental Risks,* U.S. Council on Environmental Quality, Washington, DC, 1989, pp. 13–15.

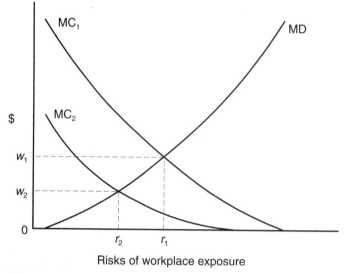

FIGURE 16-3
Management of Workplace Exposure.

achieving reductions in risk vary from one situation to another. Because of different production technologies, workplaces differ, and the marginal costs of decreasing exposure risk also differ. Figure 16-3 shows two such marginal cost curves: MC_1 and MC_2. The former lies well above the latter because we assume it represents a technology that is inherently riskier than the other; that is, it is one where the marginal costs of reducing risk are relatively high.

Suppose a common standard for workplace exposure were set at r_1. In other words, a standard was established saying that all workplaces had to be arranged so that exposure risks were no higher than r_1. This standard is efficient for the workplace whose marginal control costs are MC_1. But it is not restrictive enough for the other one. Because of lower marginal control costs, the efficient level of risk for the latter is r_2. Enforcing a weaker standard in that workplace implies substantial efficiency loss.

There is a wider issue here. Note that if workplace exposure were managed efficiently in the two workplaces, marginal damages would be higher in one than in the other. For the riskier workplace, marginal damages would be w_1, whereas for the less risky workplace they would be w_2. We might expect, if the labor market works smoothly, that wages in Firm 1 would be higher than those in Firm 2; the higher wages would be necessary to attract workers into the riskier work situation of Firm 1. In other words, the normal working of the labor market may function in such a way as to produce higher wages in riskier situations. Then workers contemplating employment would face an array of wages and risks, and each could choose the combination that most closely matched her own preferences. Moreover, this also would produce an incentive for firms to find ways of reducing risks in the workplace because they would gain through the savings in wages this would produce.

If the labor market worked smoothly like this, there would perhaps be no need for public efforts to set standards. To some extent it does, but there are always ways of making it work better. For the labor market to work smoothly, it must be reasonably **competitive** and, to be competitive, people on both sides of the market must have reasonably good alternatives. Often they do not. More importantly, competitive labor markets require that all participants know the risks involved in different job situations. This **knowledge** is often lacking. Very often workers are not fully aware of the chemical risks to which they are exposed, either because they do not know what chemicals are in the workplace, or more likely because they lack knowledge of the effects, especially long-run effects, of these substances. This suggests a strong role for public action, to see to it that workers are more fully informed about workplace risks.

Differentiated Control

The discussions of water and air pollution policy—especially the latter—showed that the major laws have differentiated between "old" sources and "new" sources, regulating the latter more stringently than the former. We also discussed some of the problems this leads to. In toxics control the same thing exists, especially under TSCA. This act differentiates between existing chemicals and new chemicals and, in effect, sets more stringent testing requirements for the latter. This is likely to have the predicted effect: providing an incentive for chemical producers and users to hold on to older, more toxic chemicals, rather than develop replacements that are less toxic but that would have to go through more rigorous testing.

FEDERAL POLICY ON TOXIC EMISSIONS

Toxic emissions come in a great variety of forms, from small airborne releases of cleaning fluid from dry cleaning establishments to large-scale releases of toxics from substantial industrial plants. Also included are the concentrated accidental releases that have helped in the past to spur public concern about toxics in the environment. Not all toxics are chemicals; some, like heavy metals (mercury, cadmium, etc.) are by-products of various industrial and mining operations.

When emissions-control policies at the national level were first being hammered out, the main focus was on the management of conventional airborne and waterborne pollutants. For air this meant the criteria pollutants—SO_2, CO, O_3, NO_x, total suspended particulates, and lead—and for water it meant BOD, suspended solids, coliform count, and so on. Even in these early days, however, it was known that there was a potentially serious class of toxic emissions stemming from industrial production operations, as well as from household sources. But the difficulties with even enumerating all of the possible substances involved, and of knowing what impacts each might have, essentially led to putting off coming to grips with the problem. In addition, the control of conventional pollutants has been effective to some extent in controlling toxics, since they are often closely associated. Indeed, the EPA estimated that, as of the mid-1980s, the criteria pollutant–control programs were responsible for a larger reduction in airborne toxics than were specific toxic reduction programs.[6] In recent years, however, more effort has gone into specific toxic emissions reduction programs.

Water Pollution–Control Laws

The 1972 Water Pollution Control Act Amendments, which established the major thrust of federal water pollution control, contained a section on toxic effluents. In keeping with the time, however, it was so utopian that it led to relatively little in the way of clear accomplishments. The law stated that, similar to conventional pollutants, toxic discharges were to be prohibited, and it gave the EPA just 15 months to come up with a list of toxic pollutants and the regulations that would govern their emissions. After that, polluters would have one year to come into compliance. In a situation so full of uncertainties, these deadlines were completely unrealistic. It was another case where public posturing and looking tough on polluters was more important than the reality of achieving reductions in damaging emissions. In fact, relatively little progress was made in these early years. But another major toxic spill kept the issue in the public eye. A relatively small chemical plant in Virginia discharged quantities of the insecticide Kepone into the James River as well as into a nearby public wastewater treatment plant. It caused serious damage downstream and severely damaged the bacterial process in the municipal treatment plant. This helped to spur Congress to address toxic emissions more vigorously, which it sought to do in the 1977 Clean Water Act. This law identified 65 specific compounds and classes of compounds containing about 125 chemicals. The EPA was directed to determine and promulgate technology-based effluent standards using the criterion of "best available technology" (BAT) for these toxic pollutants.

There are provisions in the 1987 Water Quality Act covering the identification of toxic "hot spots" in navigable waters[7] and the development of state plans to bring these waters up to applicable standards. The law also requires states, when developing their ambient water–quality standards, to set numerical criteria for certain priority toxic pollutants identified by the EPA.

Air Pollution-Control Laws

Airborne emissions of toxic compounds also were addressed in early environmental laws, but, like the waterborne emissions, the pace of progress in actual control has been very slow. Section 112 of the 1970 Clean Air Act Amendments authorized the EPA to establish controls for any airborne emissions it felt were particularly dangerous. On the basis of EPA studies, that agency was first supposed to "list" a substance as hazardous, then develop **technology-based emis-**

---

[6]U.S. Council on Environmental Quality, *Environmental Quality 1984*, Washington, DC, 1985, p. 58.

[7]A "hot spot" in this case is a section of water that does not meet specified ambient standards even when dischargers are brought under control.

sion standards, using BAT, for its control. Progress in listing hazardous pollutants was very slow; over the next two decades, the EPA was able to list and establish emission standards for only seven materials (arsenic, asbestos, benzene, beryllium, mercury, radionuclides, and vinyl chloride). The basic problem has been in getting unambiguous scientific results about the extent to which particular hazardous materials actually cause human health damages. In fact, in 1979 the EPA attempted to change the criterion so that it could use the results of animal (i.e., nonhuman animal) studies to list hazardous materials. In 1985 the EPA announced its intention to list six more substances (1,3-butadiene, cadmium, ethylene dichloride, chloroform, ethylene oxide, and methylene chloride). But the 1990 Clean Air Act Amendments took the matter out of its hands. The law specifically mentions 189 toxic substances that are to be controlled, and the EPA is charged with determining technology-based emission standards, using a concept of **"maximum achievable control technology"** (MACT). The law establishes a timetable that EPA is supposed to meet in developing these standards. The act also contains plans for a program to prevent accidental releases of airborne toxics, the establishment of a National Urban Air Toxics Research Center, and numerous other sections.

Safe Drinking Water Act (SDWA)

This federal law was enacted in 1974 along strictly CAC lines. It directs the EPA to establish standards, in terms of **"maximum contaminant levels"** (MCLs) for any drinking water contaminant that is thought to pose a threat to human health. The EPA also was given some powers in conjunction with the states to enforce the standards in public water supply systems, the primary targets of the law. By 1984, however, the EPA had promulgated only one MCL. Thus, in the SDWA Amendments of 1986, the EPA was specifically given three years to set MCLs for 83 drinking water contaminants. This law also included provisions for developing a drinking water monitoring program, more effective state/federal enforcement actions, and a public notice system whereby community residents can be notified if contaminant levels exceed MCLs. The act specifies a technology standard in terms of BAT, especially for water treatment works, and has other provisions for programs to protect the quality of groundwater resources from which many communities take their drinking water.

ECONOMIC ISSUES IN TOXIC EMISSIONS

The early laws on hazardous waste were aimed at managing the flow of hazardous emissions coming from firms, in order to reduce potential impacts, especially on human health. In this respect it mirrored the approach taken in conventional pollutants. But toxic emissions are more difficult to manage. Smaller quantities make them much more difficult to monitor, even though in many cases small quantities can be quite damaging. This has led policymakers to attack the toxics problems by "moving back up the line"; that is, by trying to reduce the amounts of material that are in need of disposal. This can be done in two ways: (1) by recycling residuals back into the production process and (2) by shifting technologies and operations so that the amount of residuals actually generated by firms is reduced. We call these methods **"waste reduction."**[8]

Waste Reduction

The thought behind waste reduction is that by changing production processes and adopting new technologies and operating procedures, firms can substantially reduce the quantities of hazardous waste they produce per unit of final product. For example, a firm might find a new way to operate a materials cleaning process to get the same effect but with less cleaning solvent. Or a firm might shift from using a process requiring a toxic material to one involving a nontoxic substance. Or an end product might be redesigned in a way that permits its fabrication using smaller quantities of hazardous materials. Waste reduction is obviously very complicated and firm-specific. Different processes lend themselves to different waste reduction procedures, and the costs of achieving significant waste reduction in one situation will be very different from the costs of other cases. This is a setting where it is essentially impossible to achieve efficient controls by having a regulatory agency dictate particular technology choices for firms using toxic substances. The technical aspects of production processes and the situation of each firm are too heterogeneous for this approach. Instead, more effective means need to be found that will give firms themselves strong incentives to reduce toxic emissions in cost-effective ways.

How to give firms the appropriate incentives for waste reduction? Certain recent changes in hazardous-waste disposal laws have moved in this direction. With waste disposal more costly, firms will be motivated to search for better ways of reducing the quantities of waste requiring disposal. A major flaw in this approach, however, is that the vast majority of hazardous waste is not subject to disposal regulations because it never leaves the premises of the firms where it is used. We will come back to this later.

To what extent might we rely on **liability and compensation laws** to provide the necessary incentives? We discussed the issue of liability conceptually in Chapter 10. By requiring polluters to compensate those whom they have damaged, these costs can become internalized, which would lead firms to take them into account in making their decisions. This could also operate through an insurance market, if premiums for hazardous waste damage policies could be set so as to reflect accurately the risks of damage associated with a firm's hazardous waste actions. The real problem is whether enough is known about risks to be able to rely on an efficient insurance market and compensation system. Although there are thousands of chemicals in use, we have very little hard information on exactly how much damage they may cause to humans; most of the dose–response information we have comes from studies on animals, especially mice. Under the circumstances, there is not enough information about risks and the damages to be able to establish consistent compensation awards or insurance premium rates that reflect true risks.

---

[8]Some people prefer to distinguish between "waste reduction" and "recycling" as separate processes, but these are lumped together here.

In the case of conventional pollutants, we have discussed using incentive mechanisms such as emission charges. In applying this to toxics, the biggest problem is accurate emissions monitoring. The widespread **dispersion** of these materials throughout the economic sector, together with the fact that many are emitted in nonpoint modes, makes widespread monitoring by third parties essentially impossible. Also, taxing emissions would provide a strong incentive for firms to dispose of toxics illegally, which would usually be difficult to detect because of the relatively small volumes involved. Taxes on waste disposal, however, may be somewhat more feasible, as will be discussed later. Another possibility is to levy a **tax on the feedstocks** used to manufacture chemicals, as these would be fewer in number and easier to measure than the chemicals themselves once they have moved into production channels. Still another possibility might be to institute **deposit–refund systems** for chemicals. Firms would pay a deposit along with the purchase price when the chemicals were bought. They could recover that deposit, or a portion of it, by documenting a reduction of emissions, that is, of the recovery of the chemical from the normal waste stream.

One way that incentives for waste reduction have been created in recent years is through making **information** more widely available about the presence and release of toxic materials. One reason hazardous wastes have been hard to manage is that with the relatively small quantities often involved, and with most disposal taking place in the same location where the materials were used, it has been difficult for the public to get accurate information on the quantities and qualities of hazardous materials present in the immediate area. This has been addressed in the Emergency Planning and Community Right-to-Know Act of 1986, which requires facilities with 10 or more employees that manufacture, process, or use chemicals in quantities above some threshold level to report their chemical emissions to EPA and state authorities. These are compiled and published periodically in the EPA's Toxic Release Inventory (TRI).[9] Communities can then find out what hazardous materials are being used and discharged in their areas. The negative publicity of this revelation has motivated many firms to seek ways of reducing their use of hazardous materials. The law is a fairly blunt tool, however; it provides no guidance on what actual damages may be coming from the hazardous materials releases and, in some cases, real damages and public concern may not be closely connected.

FEDERAL POLICIES ON THE MANAGEMENT OF HAZARDOUS WASTES

The control of airborne and waterborne toxic residuals does not address the major issue of the large quantities of hazardous materials that are left over after production (and recycling) is completed, and which must then be disposed of.

---

[9]**Environmental Defense,** an environmental advocacy group, has put together a unique website, Scorecard, available at **www.scorecard.org,** where visitors can easily access TRI data for their local areas. The site has data on criteria air pollutants, ambient concentrations of some hazardous chemicals, and hazardous waste sites, organized so that users can see the data for their local regions.

This is the problem of **hazardous wastes.** Hazardous waste consists of a diverse set of materials. In liquid form there are waste oils, solvents, and liquids containing metals, acids, PCBs, and so on. There are hazardous wastes in solid form, such as metals dust, polyvinyls, and polyethylene materials. There are many materials between liquid and solid, called sludges, such as sulfur sludge, heavy metal, solvent and cyanide sludges, and dye and paint sludges. Then there are a variety of mixed substances such as pesiticides, explosives, lab wastes, and the like. In legal terms, the EPA and various state environmental agencies have power to define what is considered a hazardous waste; in past years, the definitional net they have thrown over the full physical list of substances has left out some significant materials (e.g., waste oil).

Hazardous waste generation is not spread evenly over the United States. The largest quantities of hazardous waste are produced in Texas, Ohio, California, Illinois, Louisiana, New Jersey, Michigan, and Tennessee. At the other end of the scale, Vermont, the Dakotas, Hawaii, Alaska, Maine, and Nevada produce relatively small amounts of hazardous waste.

Table 16-2 shows the results of an EPA survey to find out how hazardous wastes were being disposed of in 1997. The greatest proportion was disposed of in injection wells, that is, deep wells driven into underground geologic formations (salt caverns and aquifers). From an industry standpoint this method is relatively cheap and flexible. About 10 percent of hazardous waste generated is subject to some type of recovery (recycling) operation, and about 9 percent is burned, roughly half of which is done to produce useful heat. Although these

TABLE 16-2

HAZARDOUS WASTE QUANTITIES MANAGED IN 1997, BY MAJOR TECHNOLOGY USED

Technology	Tons managed	Percent of total
Recovery operations:		
Fuel blending	1,463,734	3.9
Metals recovery	1,077,691	2.9
Solvents recovery	617,.273	1.6
Other recovery	443,095	1.2
Land disposal:		
Deep well/underground injection	26,182,310	69.4
Landfill	1,526,829	4.0
Surface impoundment	1,011,613	2.7
Thermal treatment:		
Energy recovery	1,697,568	4.5
Incineration	1,656,331	4.4
Other:		
Sludge treatment	411,228	1.1
Land stabilization	1,364,716	3.6
Land treatment/application/farming	19,434	0.1
Other	251,307	0.7

Source: U.S. Environmental Protection Agency, *The National Biennial RCRA Hazardous Waste Report,* Washington, DC, 1999, pp. 2–10.

numbers do not show it directly, about 80 percent of all hazardous waste generated in the United States is disposed of on-site, that is, at the site of the industrial plant where it was manufactured and/or used. Only 20 percent was transported to off-site disposal facilities.

The two major pathways leading to damage are through accidental releases and releases stemming from improper handling, either at the site of use or at waste disposal facilities. Accidents have led to severe and obvious damages, to humans and to other parts of the ecosystem.[10] It has been less easy to document the damages coming from long-run exposure to small amounts of hazardous wastes. Ecosystems in the vicinity of industrial waste dumps are sometimes visibly affected. Human health effects have been harder to show, particularly when what is at issue is long-run exposure to small quantities of hazardous materials. Much more epidemiological and laboratory work remains to be done.

Federal policy has been directed at two types of problems: (1) developing a system to manage the storage, transportation, and disposal of current hazardous wastes, and (2) cleaning up land disposal sites where large quantities of hazardous wastes were dumped in years past. The two major federal hazardous waste laws address these issues.

The Resource Conservation and Recovery Act of 1976 (RCRA)

There are four major parts to RCRA:

1 **Definition of "hazardous wastes."** In an ideal world, with free research resources, we would probably want to define "hazardous" in terms of the potential damages a substance might cause. But we don't live in this kind of world, so EPA has adopted a definition based on physical properties that apparently are capable of causing damage, in particular corrosivity, toxicity, reactivity, and explosivity. If a substance meets the criteria under any of these headings, it is deemed to be hazardous. Politics being what it is, however, certain well-known substances were expressly excluded in the act; in particular, waste lubricating oil, wastes from oil and natural gas exploration, and radioactive wastes.

2 **"Manifest" system.** One of the fundamental problems of controlling hazardous waste emissions is simply knowing how much of the material has been produced and how and where it moves through the system to final disposal. The 1976 act directed EPA to create a paper-trail system to track hazardous waste through the system. When material is generated, transported, stored, treated, or disposed of, it is supposed to be accompanied by a manifest stating the origin, quantities, and destination of the material. As it moves through the economic system, all waste is to be accompanied by its manifest. This would allow regulatory authorities to know the location of the waste at any point in time, which is fundamental to establishing any kind of control program.

---

[10]In Chapter 7 we discussed efforts to develop techniques to estimate ecosystem damages arising from hazardous waste releases.

3   **Standards for treatment, storage, and disposal facilities.** Performance and design standards are to be enforced on operators engaged in handling and disposing of hazardous materials. For example, a performance standard on hazardous waste incinerators is that they destroy 99.99 percent of the organic wastes in the incinerator feedstock. A design standard applied to hazardous waste landfill operators is that the landfills be constructed with approved liners to reduce the risk of contaminating nearby groundwater.

4   A **permit system** to enforce the standards. In order to stay in operation, hazardous waste transporters and disposers must obtain a permit from public authorities. The permit is supposed to be obtained only after all design and operating standards have been met.

Currently there are about 500 licensed commercial treatment, storage, and disposal facilities in the United States. We saw earlier that the vast majority of hazardous waste is actually used and disposed of at the site where it is generated; for this material the manifest system is obviously less useful, although the permit system still applies. There are currently about 2,500 generator-owned treatment, storage, and disposal facilities and 75,000 industrial landfills in the United States.

In 1984 Congress enacted a significant set of amendments to RCRA. The growing efforts to control hazardous emissions under air and water pollution laws were pushing more of these materials toward land disposal. Simultaneously there was increasing concern about the safety of groundwater resources and possible contamination from hazardous waste disposal sites, even at sites that had supposedly been designed expressly to handle hazardous materials. The result was a law that severely restricts land disposal of hazardous wastes and directs the EPA to identify acceptable disposal means for various types of hazardous materials. It also extended control to hazardous waste sources not previously covered, such as underground storage tanks and small sources of hazardous waste (those producing between 100 and 1,000 kg of hazardous waste per month). The 1984 law continued and accelerated the trend in federal law in the direction of direct CAC-type controls: uniform technology and performance standards applied throughout the industry without regard to questions of cost-effectiveness or efficient risk reduction.

The Comprehensive Environmental Response, Compensation and Liability Act of 1980 (CERCLA)

This law is directed at cleaning up past hazardous waste disposal sites and has come to be called **"Superfund,"** perhaps in reference to the massive sums of money involved. CERCLA was enacted in response to heightened public fears about the health impacts of past, and often forgotten, hazardous waste disposal sites. In some cases, as in the notorious Love Canal incident, people were exposed directly to hazardous materials that migrated through the soil; in other cases, the fear was, and is, of groundwater contamination from these old dump sites. CERCLA has several main features:

1 A **financial fund** derived from taxes on petroleum and chemical feed-stocks, a corporate environmental tax, and payments made by partners responsible for past dumping. The fund is used to carry out site investigations and cleanup actions. The legal authority for the taxes expired in 1995, so now the fund is supported entirely by payments from responsible parties.

2 A method for selecting sites for cleanup actions. This is called the **National Contingency Plan** (NCP) and specifies procedures for identifying and investigating sites, determining cleanup plans, and deciding on who will pay for it. Part of the procedure involves a state–federal effort to create the list of sites that are in greatest need of action; this is called the **National Priorities List** (NPL), and it involves a hazard-ranking system taking into account the types and quantities of hazardous materials at the site and the possibility of human exposure.

3 Authority for the EPA to clean up sites itself or to identify responsible private parties to clean up the sites.

4 A **liability provision** for natural resources damage. Besides cleanup liability, CERCLA has a provision for holding responsible parties liable for damages to natural resources stemming from spilled or released toxic materials. Thus, if a chemical is accidentally released into a river, the people causing the spill can be held liable for the damages this causes. Or, if an old landfill leaks toxic compounds, responsible parties may be held liable not only for cleaning up the site but also for damages to surrounding groundwater resources.

In 1986 Congress passed the Superfund Amendments and Reauthorization Act, or SARA. This act extended the fund and broadened the tax to include, along with the feedstock tax, an "environmental tax" on all corporations equal to 0.12 percent of their taxable income over $2 million.

The Superfund cleanup process is very long and complicated, starting with identifying the site and the "potentially responsible parties" (PRPs) who have used the site at some time in the past, then proceeding with cleaning up the site and delisting it from the NPL. Each step involves public authorities at all levels as well as numerous private parties. It is a process full of conflict, and the costs of the legal actions on a site can sometimes rival or even exceed the actual costs of cleaning up the hazardous material. Exhibit 16-2 discusses some of this conflict about who will ultimately bear those costs.

Radioactive Wastes

Radioactive wastes are governed by a separate set of statutes. There are two types of radioactive wastes: **high-level wastes** (HLW) and **low-level wastes** (LLW). HLW is made up primarily of spent fuel from nuclear power plants and wastes from government nuclear processing facilities. LLW comes from a variety of industrial and medical processes that utilize small amounts of radioactive material, and includes the material itself together with all manner of items that have become contaminated in normal production operations.

EXHIBIT 16-2

WHO'LL FOOT THE SUPERFUND BILL?

The debate over the 1980 superfund law is really a fight over money. No one wants to foot the bill for cleaning up the 1,200 hazardous-waste sites that have been ranked as top priorities by the Environmental Protection Agency (EPA). Little wonder, considering that the cost of cleaning up each location is estimated to be about $25 million.

As originally written, superfund asserted a "polluter pays" philosophy, under which every company or individual that handled a site's hazardous waste could be asked to help clean up the toxic aftermath.

Over the years, however, the polluter-pays concept has become blurred as major polluters tried to avoid being stuck with enormous cleanup bills by suing other suspected polluters. By 1993, as much as a third of the money spent on superfund went to litigation and negotiations rather than cleanup. In the worst cases, the superfund liability net extended to those least able to afford it: churches, schools and small businesses.

To eliminate that legal spider web, many business leaders, local government officials and lawmakers want to drop the polluter-pays doctrine for hazardous waste disposed of before 1987.

But if the polluters don't pay to clean up the sites, who will?

That question is the crux of the current controversy in Congress over rewriting the superfund law. Currently, the superfund program costs $2 billion–$2.3 billion each year, about $1.5 billion of which is underwritten by superfund taxes imposed on the chemical and oil industries.

Superfund Reform '95, a coalition organized and led by the insurance industry, has proposed a list of changes to the program, including cutting EPA and Justice Department overhead and enforcement costs, requiring states to pay a greater share of the cleanup costs and calling on the federal departments and agencies that are among the suspected polluters at some superfund sites to directly contribute $150 million a year. Its plan assumes that Congress will continue to appropriate at least $250 million a year in general revenues to the superfund program, and that lawmakers will begin funneling $175 million in interest on past unspent superfund taxes, according to National Strategies Inc., a Washington consulting firm.

But other lawmakers and analysts question whether Capitol Hill will appropriate upwards of $425 million a year at a time when they're scrambling to cut the budget deficit. They also argue that cost savings are based on incomplete information about how much the private sector spends on superfund and about how quickly any savings can be achieved.

"We are all making a lot of assumptions because of an incredible dearth of data," Katherine N. Probst, a senior fellow at Resources for the Future Inc., said. "I think there is a question of reasonable assumptions that you can back up and zany ones."

The primary problem in HLW is to find a secure, *permanent* storage site, because the rate of radioactive decay is so slow that these wastes will be lethal essentially forever by human standards. The Nuclear Waste Policy Act of 1982 requires the Department of Energy (DOE) to find and develop a permanent underground depository for nuclear HLW. This has proved to be an immensely complicated task and one full of political conflict. The effort is funded by a tax of one-tenth of a cent per kilowatt-hour of electricity generated at all nuclear power plants. The standards for storage have been set by the EPA, in terms of the maximum allowable rate of release of radionuclides from the repository for the next 10,000 years! It is difficult, if not essentially impossible, to identify underground geological formations that are sure to be secure for the next 10,000 years. It is even more difficult to convince people living near candidate sites that no damage will come their way and that this is the best use of a portion of their landscape. Thus, the projected year of opening for the depository has been continuously set back, from 1998 at first to 2010 now, and this date will no doubt continue to slip.

Low-level radioactive wastes are disposed of for the most part in approved landfills. Prior to 1980, there were three landfill sites in the United States accepting low-level radioactive waste. These were in South Carolina, Washington, and Nevada. With the volume of these wastes climbing rapidly, these states began to raise objections to being the only recipients. But there were negative incentives for other states to open their own sites, because of their fear that they would be forced to accept LLW from other states. The first result was a 1980 federal law, the Low Level Radioactive Waste Policy Act of 1980, which encouraged states to enter into interstate compacts to open sites that would accept all the waste from states in each compact. Very little happened over the next few years, however, because groups of states could not come to an agreement on these compacts. The law was therefore amended in 1985 to provide greater incentives for groups of states to enter into compacts to develop and operate LLW landfills. The primary incentive was a rapidly increasing surcharge per cubic foot of LLW that the sites in South Carolina, Washington, and Nevada would be authorized to charge, culminating in a complete cutoff of outside LLW after 1990.[11]

A third major nuclear issue is cleaning up Department of Defense nuclear weapons manufacturing sites. Weapons production stopped about a decade ago, after about 50 years of activity. There are more than 100 sites across the country where massively contaminated soil, water, structures and equipment pose serious health threats to nearby people and ecosystems. The Office of Environmental Management (OEM) within the U.S. Department of Energy (DOE) has estimated that cleaning up these sites could cost as much as $200 billion. This is probably a substantial underestimate.[12] There are many serious questions that need to be addressed, having to do with which sites to clean up, how the cleanups should proceed, who should carry them out, and so forth.

---

[11]The incentive for entering into interstate compacts was that by law they could then exclude waste from noncompact states. The compact system has not developed as Congress envisioned, and the full legal ramifications of the approach are still not settled. See L. David Condon, "The Never Ending Story: Low-Level Waste and the Exclusionary Authority of Noncompacting States," *Natural Resources Journal*, 30(1), Winter 1990, pp. 65–86.

[12]For a good discussion of this problem, see Katherine N. Probst and Adam I. Lowe, *Cleaning Up the Nuclear Weapons Complex: Does Anybody Care?*, Resources for the Future, Center for Risk Management, Washington, DC, January 2000.

Transport Laws

Although RCRA and CERCLA are the two main federal laws focused on handling hazardous wastes, we should also mention the Hazardous Materials Transportation Act (HMTA) of 1975, which gave the Department of Transportation authority to regulate the movement of hazardous materials when transported by air, water, highway, or rail. This is done by enforcing a set of packaging, labeling, and handling standards. Hazardous wastes shipped in bulk by sea are regulated by the Coast Guard under the Ports and Waterways Safety Act of 1972.

ECONOMIC ISSUES IN MANAGING HAZARDOUS WASTE

The policy debate on hazardous waste management is fueled by the public fears and alarms that follow the highly publicized exposure incidents, such as Love Canal, Times Beach, and similar events.[13] It is not hard to understand why public authorities have relied on conventional CAC-type operating standards to address these issues. It creates the impression that policymakers have established a system of positive control based on rational technical decisions. There are many elements of the program where an economic perspective can be very useful.

How Clean Is Clean?

Approaching site cleanup as strictly technical is likely to mean that essential trade-offs are ignored and that aggregate remaining risks are higher than they otherwise could be. Criteria as to how to clean up sites have largely been established with the objective of making each site totally risk free under the worst possible future development scenario. Thus, at many sites very costly cleanup techniques have been used in cases where the risk of damage to humans is relatively low. A recent economic analysis of 150 randomly selected superfund sites concludes that the expected number of cancer cases averted at each cleanup site is less than 0.1 and that the cost per cancer case averted was on average greater than $100 million.[14] What this indicates is that perhaps a more explicit benefit–cost approach might be able to adopt cleanup techniques at each site more closely to the benefits to be expected in terms of human exposures. This would allow more sites to be cleaned up with a consequent increase in overall human protection, given the total amount of money that is spent on the program.

---

[13]Times Beach is a community in Missouri in which dioxin-contaminated oil was spread on its roads. The federal government ended up buying all the houses in the community.
[14]James T. Hamilton and W. Kip Viscusi, "How Costly Is 'Clean'? An Analysis of the Benefits and Costs of Superfund Site Remediations," *Journal of Policy Analysis and Management*, 18(1), Winter 1999, pp. 2–27.

Financing Hazardous Waste Site Cleanups

Cleaning up past hazardous waste sites is a lengthy and expensive process that involves complicated issues of liability, technical alternatives, and public risks. The EPA estimates that cleaning up the sites currently listed on the NPL will take more than $30 billion. This substantially exceeds the sums that will be raised under CERCLA through taxes on chemical feedstocks and the general corporate tax. A big question, therefore, is how to get greater resources from past or present dumpers, or their insurers, to help clean up the long list of sites currently on the NPL and new ones that may be listed. Several private insurers have suggested establishing large **environmental trust funds,** from mandatory or voluntary contributions, to be devoted to cleaning up hazardous waste sites. Others have suggested changing the current systems of financing and liability.

Ultimately the success in this effort may depend most critically on introducing changes that increase incentives for private firms to enter into cleanup agreements, among themselves and between themselves and the EPA. The courts have ruled that in pursuing PRPs to obtain cleanup funds, the EPA may use the doctrine of **strict, joint, and several liability** by responsible parties. What this means is that when more than one firm has dumped hazardous wastes into the site, the EPA may nevertheless sue and recover total cleanup costs from just one of the responsible parties. So, for example, a company that has dumped only a small portion of the wastes into a site can nevertheless be held responsible for the total cleanup costs at the site. The effect of this is to provide an incentive for this one firm to identify and recover costs from other parties that were responsible for dumping at the site. But there are also strong negative aspects to this approach. The doctrine can hold individual firms responsible for total cleanup costs of a site even though they may have dumped only a small proportion of total wastes at the site. This no doubt leads firms to hold back because the admission of even partial responsibility opens them up to the risk of having to pay total cleanup costs. This and other features make the process highly litigious, with firms spending enormous amounts of money suing one another, the EPA, municipalities, states, insurance companies, and so on. Exhibit 16-3 is a news clip on this topic.

Environmental Justice

All environmental issues involve **distributional** questions, having to do with which particular individuals or groups from among the whole population bear the costs and experience the benefits of environmental programs. **Environmental justice** is the term used to describe the search for programs that are equitable to the less advantaged members of society. Much of the environmental justice focus has been on the location of hazardous waste sites in relation to communities in which there are relatively large numbers of low-income residents and people of color. This issue gained prominence in the early 1980s, largely as the result of efforts to site a large hazardous waste dump in Warren

EXHIBIT 16-3

THE REAL CLEANUP

Insurers' Superfund Focus: Hiring Lawyers

By Michael Parrish, Times Staff Writer

Nearly 90% of the billions of dollars insurance companies have spent on Superfund toxic waste sites has been sunk into legal battles—mostly with their own policymakers, according to a RAND Corp. study released Thursday.

The money spent in court is enough, according to the study, to clean up 15 Superfund sites a year.

In contrast, the big industrial firms in the study have mostly gone ahead and paid for cleanups without fighting them in court, spending an average of just 21% of their Superfund money on legal costs.

Critics of the Superfund law, which is up for reauthorization by 1994, say the study supports their call for drastic reform.

"The only people cleaning up in Superfund are the lawyers," said Anne Ligon, assistant general counsel of the Superfund Action Coalition, a Washington lobbying group formed in January to represent companies faced with Superfund liabilities.

Insurers generally agreed.

But environmentalists, regulators and the RAND authors themselves found support for the current process in the study.

"It shows you the legal costs are not a big issue—except for the insurance companies," said Doug Wolf, an attorney with the Natural Resources Defense Council. "And I don't think we should let them dictate our policy for cleaning up abandoned waste sites."

The EPA spends about $1.5 billion a year in taxpayer dollars on Superfund cleanups. It has recovered $295 million from responsible parties since 1987 and is seeking $1 billion more.

While no one knows how much these parties have paid out for cleanups, their insurers are spending about $500 million annually in costs associated with the Superfund law.

The RAND researchers found that fully 88% of that $500 million is spent on lawsuits, with 47% of that sum being used to contest the claims of the insurance companies' own customers. Another 42% goes to defending policyholders against the EPA or other parties.

The RAND authors and others predict that some legal expenditures are bound to occur as state case law, which controls many of the legal battles, is sorted out.

And they see some evidence that the system is creating incentives for private companies to undertake cleanups before being forced to by the EPA: The study estimates that fully 10% of all cleanups costing a company more than $100,000 are being done without government involvement.

The large companies "have been willing to step forward and pay remedial costs, which many had doubted at the beginning of the program," noted Lloyd S. Dixon of RAND's Institute for Civil Justice, one of the study's authors.

The insurance companies and such groups as the Superfund Action Coalition want to replace the existing system with one using taxpayer funds to finance a public-works cleanup, much as billions of federal dollars have been spent in recent years to build new sewage treatment plants around the country.

"It's clear as a bell that Superfund's incredibly harsh and inequitable liability scheme has created and is going to continue to create considerable controversies," said Karl S. Lytz, an attorney at Latham & Watkins. He represents Montrose Chemical Corp. of California at one of the first Superfund sites listed in the nation—the Stringfellow acid pits in Riverside County.

Relations between companies such as Montrose and their insurers have grown "only more litigious over recent years," Lytz said. "And that level of fighting will continue."

But environmentalists, particularly, remain opposed to shifting to a public-works scheme.

"This report highlights [the insurance companies'] self-interest in that proposal," said Wolf of the NRDC. "They would benefit more than anyone else."

County, South Carolina, a county with a predominantly African-American population. A 1987 study sponsored by the United Church of Christ came to the conclusion that ". . . in communities where two or more hazardous waste sites were located, or where one of the nation's largest landfills was located, the percentage of the population composed of minorities was, on average, more than three times that of communities without such facilities."

Since this first study many others have been carried out to assess the relationship between the locations of hazardous waste sites and the demographic characteristics of the surrounding population. Results have not always been consistent because of different data sets used (e.g., whether data from countries, census tracks, or zip code area are used) and the time periods covered. But the preponderance of evidence to date does indicate that RCRA sites tend to be located in areas where there are relatively large numbers of low-income and minority populations. Having established this pattern, the next question is, why has it occurred? There are essentially two ways this could have occurred.

1 The siting process itself has worked against people of color and poor people. This could be either because of rank discrimination, in which undesirable activities are foisted onto certain people, or because in the political process surrounding these siting decisions, certain people lack the political influence necessary to ward off these facilities.

2 The dynamics of the land and housing market may lead to this type of pattern, even though the original siting decisions were not discriminatory. If these facilities make local neighborhoods less desirable, the better-off people may be motivated to move out. Furthermore, if the facility works so as to depress land prices, it could make housing there more attractive to low-income families. This could also happen if racial or income discrimination in general relegates certain people to less desirable neighborhoods.

Recent research suggests that both of these factors are at work, though at specific sites one factor may be substantially more important than the other.[15] It is clear that policymakers need to look carefully at the siting decision process to make it more democratic and remove its discriminatory features. It's also clear that economists need to learn much more about how the land and property markets function so that we can identify situations where certain people will end up being unfairly exposed to environmental risks.

Brown Fields

As of the beginning of 2000, there have been 1,432 superfund sites listed on the National Priorities List. Of these, 882 sites have been removed, 676 because cleanup has been completed and 206 for other reasons. One can argue, therefore, that despite its inefficiencies, the superfund program has made a real dent

---

[15]See, for example, Vicki Been, "Unpopular Neighbors Are Dumps and Landfills Sited Equitably?" in Wallace E. Oates (ed.), *The RFF Reader in Environmental and Resource Management,* Resources for the Future, Washington, DC, 1999, pp. 191–196.

in the number of sites needing attention. The EPA also has identified over 10,000 other sites where light to moderate contamination is suspected or has been confirmed. Superfund, as it was originally developed, does not address these many sites that are contaminated to a lesser degree. A substantial portion of these additional sites are within urban and suburban areas and have potential for industrial or commercial redevelopment.

There may be important incentive problems associated with these sites. Developers may avoid them in favor of sites in pristine environments in order to avoid the possibility of being made legally responsible for cleaning them up. This possibility has led the U.S. EPA, and many of the states, to develop special programs dealing with these types of sites, which are called **brown fields.** The programs consist of efforts to relax potential liability problems at the sites, and funding assistance to assess and ameliorate contamination problems at the sites.

Initiatives for Changing Incentives

There may be useful programs that could be installed to reshape the incentives relating to using and disposing of hazardous materials. Taxes on hazardous wastes, levied at the place where they are generated or where they are disposed of, are a feasible way of providing the incentive for reducing the quantities produced, as well as directing the flow of wastes toward various channels. These have come to be called **"waste-end taxes."** The monitoring problem is much less a factor than with toxic emissions because wastes are often in bulk form that lends itself to quantitative measurement. In fact, a tax of $2.13/ton of hazardous waste was at one time charged at approved disposal sites as part of the RCRA program, but this has been abandoned. Many states have established waste-end charges for sites within their jurisdictions. Charges of this type would stimulate industry efforts at waste reduction. They also would lead to increases in the prices of products that produce substantial quantities of waste in their manufacture. They have one unfortunate effect, however, in that they also will create an incentive to dispose of hazardous materials surreptitiously.

A major problem with many hazardous wastes is that they are in quantities that are difficult to monitor. This will continue to be the case even with the manifest system. Any kind of tax placed on hazardous material creates an incentive for disposers to conceal material discharged, perhaps by disposing of it on-site, into a public sewer system, or in some unapproved landfill. One way of turning these incentives around is to offer a subsidy for hazardous materials disposed of in approved ways. This, of course, would require a source of funds. A possibility would be to institute **deposit–refund** systems for hazardous materials. Firms would pay a deposit per unit of hazardous chemical at the time of purchase from a chemical supplier. They would then be paid a refund on materials when they were properly disposed of.[16]

---

[16]For more on this idea, see Clifford S. Russell, "Economic Incentives in the Management of Hazardous Wastes," *Columbia Journal of Environmental Law,* Vol. 13, Spring 1988, pp. 257–274.

SUMMARY

The coming of the chemical society has led to new sources of environmental damage and opened up new requirements for managing toxic and hazardous materials. At the federal level a number of major laws deal with toxic and hazardous substances, and numerous federal agencies are responsible for their administration. For the most part the laws incorporate a variety of command-and-control measures to identify and monitor the use of toxic materials in workplaces and consumer products, to control toxic emissions from production, and to manage the complex process of disposing of hazardous materials.

Important points exist where the management of toxics could be substantially improved. One of these is to improve the procedures for "balancing" the costs and benefits of using chemicals in particular products and processes. We also discussed the new emphasis on waste reduction; that is, changes in production systems that lead to lower quantities of hazardous waste requiring disposal. Finally, we discussed the federal laws governing the handling and disposal of hazardous waste and the cleaning up of past dump sites.

QUESTIONS FOR FURTHER DISCUSSION

1 Handlers of hazardous wastes, that is, firms that accept hazardous materials and transport them for disposal, sometimes dispose of the materials illegally or in unapproved landfills. How might a deposit–refund system be designed to provide incentives to dispose of hazardous materials in approved ways?

2 "The EPA has estimated that the chemical residues on a certain food most likely contribute to 14 excess deaths in the U.S. population each year. Thus, if use of the chemical is banned we can expect the number of excess deaths to decrease by this number." Comment.

3 What are the advantages and disadvantages of using the doctrine of strict, joint, and several liability for superfund sites?

4 What are the two primary alternative explanations for the demographic patterns found in the vicinity of many hazardous waste dump sites?

5 In conducting a "balancing" analysis for a particular chemical or pesticide, what role is played by peoples' attitudes toward risk?

WEBSITES

For recent policy issues on toxic and hazardous substances, the Congressional Research Service, **www.cnie.org/nle/crswaste.html,** has many useful reports; Resources for the Future, **www.rffr.org,** also has many reports and other writings on the economic issues associated with toxic and hazardous materials. See also the sites listed in the website associated with this book, **www.mhhe.com/ economics/field3.**

SELECTED READINGS

Been, Vicki, with Francis Gupta: "Coming to the Nuisance or Going to the Barrios? A Longitudinal Analysis of Environmental Justice Claims," *Environmental Law Quarterly,* 24(1), 1997, pp. 1–56.

Environmental Law Institute: *An Analysis of State Superfund Programs: 50 State Study, 1995 Update,* Environmental Law Institute, Washington, DC, 1996.

Fullerton, Don, and Seng-Su Tsang: "Should Environmental Costs Be Paid by the Polluter or the Beneficiary? The Case of CERCLA and Superfund," *Public Economics Review,* Vol. 1, 1996, pp. 85–127.

Hamilton, James T., and W. Kip Viscusi: "The Benefits and Costs of Regulatory Reforms for Superfund," *Stanford Environmental Law Journal,* 16(2), 1997, pp. 159–198.

Hamilton, James T., and W. Kip Viscusi: "Environmental Equity at Superfund Sites," in *Calculating Risks: The Spatial and Political Dimensions of Hazardous Waste Policy,* MIT Press, Cambridge, MA, 1999, pp. 157–188.

Hamilton, James T., and W. Kip Viscusi: "How Costly Is Clean? An Analysis of the Benefits and Costs of Superfund Site Remediations," *Journal of Policy Analysis and Management,* 18(1), 1999, pp. 2–27.

Harris, Christopher, William L. Want, and Morris A. Ward: *Hazardous Waste, Confronting the Challenge,* Quorum Books, New York, 1987.

Hird, John A.: *Superfund: The Political Economy of Environmental Risk,* The Johns Hopkins University Press, Baltimore, MD, 1994.

Macauley, Molly K., Michael D. Bowes, and Karen L. Palmer: *Using Economic Incentives to Regulate Toxic Substances,* Resources for the Future, Washington, DC, 1993.

Probst, Katherine N., Don Fullerton, Robert E. Litan, and Paul R. Portney: *Footing the Bill for Superfund Cleanups: Who Pays and How?,* Resources for the Future, Washington, DC, 1995.

Sigman, Hilary: "Hazardous Waste and Toxic Substance Policies," in Paul R. Portney and Robert N. Stavins (eds.), *Public Policies for Environmental Protection,* 2nd ed., Resources for the Future, 2000, pp. 215–259.

U.S. General Accounting Office: *Superfund: State Voluntary Programs Provide Incentives to Encourage Cleanups,* Washington, DC, 1997.

CHAPTER 17

STATE AND LOCAL ENVIRONMENTAL ISSUES

In the 1950s and 1960s there was no strong federal presence in U.S. environmental policy; what initiative there was lay mostly at the state level. In the 1970s this changed dramatically, as strong federal laws were written that essentially shifted the policy center of gravity toward Washington. But in more recent years nonfederal involvement in environmental policy issues has grown rapidly. The current trend in Washington is to push many policy problems back to the states for action.

States and communities are playing three primary roles:

- Contributing to federal laws; most federal policies permit, require, or encourage some type of contributing state action, especially in enforcement. About three-quarters of the environmental enforcement actions undertaken in the United States are carried out by the states.
- Adopting companion policies that express the particular environmental values, goals, or circumstances of individual states; these have often been a source of innovative policy ideas.
- Dealing with certain major issues that have been left for the most part to the states.

In this chapter we take a look at some of these state and local issues. Given the diversity among the states, we cannot do a survey of the environmental policies being pursued in each one. After an introductory section dealing with general issues, we take up three problems that have historically been left to the states: solid waste, land-use controls, and groundwater protection.

GENERAL ISSUES

The states vary widely in terms of their commitments to environmental quality, the severity of their environmental problems, and the progress they have made in environmental policy matters. Table 17-1 shows state rankings by total

TABLE 17-1
STATE ENVIRONMENTAL EXPENDITURES, 1994

Ranked by total environmental expenditures ($ millions)		Ranked by per capita expenditures		Ranked by state environmental expenditures as percent of total state expenditures	
1. California	2,103.7	Alaska	338.8	Wyoming	5.15
2. Texas	700.4	Wyoming	189.7	Alaska	3.91
3. Pennsylvania	539.3	Vermont	91.6	Colorado	3.54
4. New York	516.8	Montana	82.6	Idaho	3.45
5. Florida	468.7	Idaho	80.6	Nevada	3.15
6. Illinois	402.7	Delaware	77.4	Vermont	3.00
7. New Jersey	346.4	Colorado	74.2	Montana	2.95
8. Washington	300.3	Nevada	73.6	South Dakota	2.58
9 Colorado	271.1	California	66.9	Oregon	2.46
10. Louisiana	262.2	Oregon	62.3	California	2.29
11. Wisconsin	245.1	South Dakota	62.2	Delaware	2.29
12. Minnesota	234.9	Maine	61.5	Louisiana	2.22
13. Tennessee	211.8	Louisiana	60.8	Maine	2.21
14. Ohio	206.2	North Dakota	57.6	Utah	2.13
15. Alaska	205.4	Washington	56.2	North Dakota	1.95
16. Maryland	197.8	West Virginia	53.8	Tennessee	1.89
17. Michigan	197.7	Rhode Island	53.6	Texas	1.88
18. Massachusetts	194.7	Utah	52.3	West Virginia	1.87
19. Missouri	194.1	Minnesota	51.4	Washington	1.84
20. Oregon	192.2	Wisconsin	48.2	Arkansas	1.84
21. North Carolina	168.9	Pennsylvania	44.7	Missouri	1.83
22. Virginia	164.1	New Jersey	43.8	Mississippi	1.82
23. Kentucky	158.1	Connecticut	42.7	Wisconsin	1.77
24. Georgia	157.8	Arkansas	42.2	Rhode Island	1.74
25. Connecticut	139.9	Mississippi	42.1	Minnesota	1.68

(continued on next page)

environmental expenditures, expenditures per capita, and environmental expenditures as a percentage of total expenditures for 1994. These numbers should be treated with caution, however. The nature and severity of environmental problems vary substantially among states. Air pollution is much more severe in some states than others. Hazardous-waste releases, although occurring in every state, are nevertheless concentrated in certain ones, particularly Texas and Louisiana. Florida has special water-quality problems because of the Everglades and because of its reliance on groundwater. Coastal states have special problems in managing their coastal resources. Mining regulation is a particular problem for some states, as is agricultural runoff in others. Given these great variations, equal expenditures in several states can mean quite different things in terms of achieved results in environmental quality.

TABLE 17-1
STATE ENVIRONMENTAL EXPENDITURES, 1994 (CONTINUED)

Ranked by total environmental expenditures ($ millions)		Ranked by per capita expenditures		Ranked by state environmental expenditures as percent of total state expenditures	
26. South Carolina	139.6	Kentucky	41.3	Maryland	1.68
27. Alabama	126.9	Tennessee	40.9	Pennsylvania	1.66
28. Indiana	114.0	Maryland	39.5	Kentucky	1.65
29. Mississippi	112.3	South Carolina	38.1	Florida	1.56
30. Nevada	107.2	Texas	38.1	Illinois	1.55
31. Arkansas	103.6	Missouri	36.8	South Carolina	1.46
32. Utah	99.8	New Hampshire	35.1	New Hampshire	1.43
33. West Virginia	98.0	Illinois	34.3	New Jersey	1.42
34. Arizona	93.5	New Mexico	33.7	Nebraska	1.37
35. Idaho	91.3	Florida	33.6	Alabama	1.28
36. Wyoming	90.3	Nebraska	32.8	Connecticut	1.25
37. Iowa	90.0	Massachusetts	32.2	Iowa	1.19
38. Oklahoma	81.5	Iowa	31.8	Virginia	1.15
39. Maine	76.3	Alabama	30.1	Oklahoma	1.13
40. Montana	70.7	New York	28.5	Georgia	1.01
41. New Mexico	55.7	Virginia	25.1	New Mexico	1.00
42. Delaware	54.6	Oklahoma	25.0	Arizona	0.98
43. Rhode Island	53.4	Hawaii	24.5	North Carolina	0.96
44. Nebraska	53.2	North Carolina	23.9	Massachusetts	0.95
45. Vermont	53.1	Arizona	22.9	Kansas	0.81
46. Kansas	49.6	Georgia	22.4	New York	0.80
47. South Dakota	44.9	Michigan	20.8	Indiana	0.79
48. New Hampshire	39.9	Indiana	19.8	Ohio	0.77
49. North Dakota	36.7	Kansas	19.4	Michigan	0.76
50. Hawaii	28.9	Ohio	18.6	Hawaii	0.55

Source: The Council of State Governments, Resource Guide to State Environmental Management, 4th ed., Lexington, KY, 1996.

Constitutional and Policy Issues

The U.S. Constitution governs the division of powers between the federal government and the states. In cases where valid (i.e., constitutional) environmental laws have been enacted at the federal level, these normally **preempt** state action. Thus, for example, federal laws to control coastal tanker traffic so as to reduce the threat of oil spills will usually preempt any state actions aimed at the same result. In cases where the federal government has not acted, states may do so provided they do not exceed constitutional limits. The most important of these is that states may not pass laws that discriminate against interstate commerce. In environmental matters, this has been held to bar states from passing laws restricting the importation of solid waste from other states. But virtually all state environmental actions will have some impact on interstate commerce, so the federal courts have become the arena for ongoing controversy about the legitimacy of state environmental actions.

In addition to constitutional issues, there are important policy dimensions to the federal–state balance in environmental law. When environmental issues are truly local—contamination of a groundwater aquifer, for example—state action may be more appropriate because the balancing that is required involves strictly **local** interests; presumably the unique characteristics of the situation are best served by local political bodies. But when **interstate** environmental externalities are involved, federal action is called for to manage the conflicting claims of the different states.

Another situation making state-level environmental actions problematic is that states usually feel that they are in competition among themselves for business growth, which may make them reluctant to pursue vigorous environmental programs. In recent years many states have moved to pull together the disparate environmental programs under their jurisdictions into single, EPA-like environmental agencies. These organizations should be able, at least theoretically, to develop greater expertise and make more coordinated and effective environmental decisions than was possible in the past.

Virtually all federal programs have provisions for substantial state and local participation. Federal water pollution law (incorporating technology-based effluent standards) works through a **permitting system;** sources must obtain permits for waterborne emissions and are supposed to operate in accordance with the terms specified in the permits. For the most part, it is the states that actually operate the permit system, though there are a few (e.g., New Hampshire and Oklahoma) where federal authorities are still responsible. Federal water law also requires the states to establish ambient water–quality standards in the various bodies of water within their boundaries. Traditionally these standards have been expressed in terms of the functions that particular water-quality levels would allow; for example, standards for fishable-swimmable water and standards for drinkable water. In recent laws states also have been given the responsibility of setting ambient standards for waterborne toxics.

States have many responsibilities in controlling air pollution. A major activity is the design and operation of State Implementation Plans (SIPs). These are plans of action through which national ambient air–quality standards are to be reached in current nonattainment regions. The states have permitting authority to achieve these SIPs. The 1990 act allows them to operate **fee systems** for these permits, similar to the water program. Permit fees may be charged, *and these may be based on emission levels;* but fees are only supposed to be high enough to cover the costs of running the permit program. They may not be used, in other words, as full incentive-changing emission charges such as those we discussed in previous chapters. In recent years, this type of "dedicated funding" system is being increasingly relied upon by states to fund their environmental programs. Rather than fund these efforts from general state revenues, they are turning to using sources in particular programs—permit fees, fines, trust funds, and so on—to get the money to run these programs. "Car owners pay for air-pollution control programs with a portion of their license-tag fees, factories pay for water quality efforts with fees for permits to discharge wastewater, recycling programs are funded by special levies on items such as motor oil and batteries, and the fines forked over by violators of environmental rules pay for enforcement efforts."[1]

States also may regulate hazardous wastes, but, according to RCRA, the state regulations must be at least as strict as applicable federal regulations. Many states have done this in various areas: definition of hazardous wastes, standards for incinerators, requirements for the manifest system, location requirements for hazardous waste disposal sites, insurance requirements for hazardous waste facility operators, and so on. State hazardous waste regulations are almost exclusively performance and technology standards. New Jersey's laws on incinerating hazardous wastes, for example, specify such details as minimum operating temperatures allowed and staffing requirements. Arkansas mandates the disposal method for different types of hazardous wastes. California statutes specify detailed design standards for hazardous waste landfills that are more stringent than federal standards. Many states have enacted their own "superfund" laws to supplement the federal law. Many of these are designed in the image of CERCLA, with a response fund, a site priority list, and various action criteria.[2] States also have taken varying degrees of responsibility for actions at some of the NPL sites.

Policy Innovations at the State Level

During the last few decades, the states have been the source of some innovative environmental policy initiatives. This is especially true of California, which has been the source of several policy initiatives that have later spread to other states and the federal level. Chief among these has been mobile-source pollution control. The Los Angeles area was the first in the nation to experience smog, and the California response in the early 1960s was to require technological improvements in cars to reduce emissions. Since that time, vehicles sold in California have had to meet more stringent emission standards. The standards have not been legally preempted by federal emission limits, and in recent years a number of other states have considered adopting the California standards as a way of dealing with increasingly severe urban air pollution.

California also is helping to pioneer the use of tradable emission permits to control airborne emissions. The South Coast Air Quality Management District, a regional organization whose objective is to manage air pollution reductions in the Los Angeles basin, has recently designed a tradable permit program to apply to an estimated 2,000 large sources of reactive organic gases and nitrogen oxides. These sources would be assigned an initial holding of permits equal to their baseline emissions and would be allowed to trade the permits. The total

[1]*Environment Reporter,* Bureau of National Affairs, Washington, DC, March 30, 1992, p. 2580.
[2]See U.S. Environmental Protection Agency, *An Analysis of State Superfund Programs: 50-State Study, 1990 Update,* EPA/540/8-89/011, Washington, DC, 1990.

emission cap for each source would be decreased by 5.8 percent per year for reactive organic gases and 8 percent a year for nitrogen oxides. The District estimates that cost savings of using the tradable permit approach, rather than a conventional command-and-control policy, will be nearly a billion dollars over the next decade.[3]

Many other environmental programs that have become law at the federal level were initially developed by one or more of the states. DDT was first banned by Wisconsin; this later became a national effort. The Federal Strip Mining Control and Reclamation Act of 1977 was substantially modeled after the Pennsylvania strip mining reclamation law. The federal toxics release inventory program is an idea that originated with programs in New Jersey and Maryland.

MUNICIPAL SOLID WASTE

In the rest of this chapter we deal in some detail with several important environmental problems that traditionally have been left to states and localities. The first of these is **solid waste,** the disposal of which has emerged as a leading problem in many cities and towns across the country, especially in the East and along the West Coast. Landfilling, for a long time the preferred disposal method for urban solid waste, has come up hard against rising land shortages in many places, leading some localities to ship their solid wastes long distances for disposal, whereas others are moving into incineration. In addition, rising fears of groundwater contamination from landfills and of air pollutants from incineration have turned what once was a disposal activity to which nobody gave a second thought into a prime environmental concern.

The Nature of the Problem

The **municipal solid waste** (MSW) stream is actually a trickle at the end of a long and very large flow of materials used in the U.S. economy. The EPA estimates that the total quantity of materials generated per person per day is about 300 pounds. Most of this is industrial waste. Municipal solid waste consists of trash or garbage from homes, businesses, and institutions. In 1995 there were an estimated 4.4 pounds per person per day of MSW generated in the country. This was up from 2.7 pounds in 1960 (see Table 17-2). Slightly over half of this MSW was disposed of in landfills in 1995, down from about two-thirds in 1960. Over the last few decades, the amount of MSW that is recycled has increased, from 6.3 percent in 1960 to 27.0 percent in 1995. These are aggregate numbers, which hide substantial variation among states and communities in the country. The MSW problem is not equally acute everywhere. In localities with large populations and/or constrained landfill space, the problem is one of immediate concern; in areas with the opposite characteristics, it is much less so.

---

[3]Laura Mahoney, "Emission Trading Program for Southern California Promises Air Quality Improvements, Big Savings for Industry," *Environment Reporter,* Bureau of National Affairs, Washington, DC, February 21, 1992, pp. 2423–2424.

TABLE 17-2
MUNICIPAL SOLID WASTE, SELECTED DATA

	Year					
	1960	1970	1980	1990	1995	2000*
Total quantity generated (mil. tons)	88.1	121.0	151.6	196.9	208.0	221.7
Quantity generated per capita (lbs./person/day)	2.7	3.3	3.7	4.3	4.4	4.4
Disposal, percent of total:						
Landfill	63.0	72.6	81.4	66.7	56.9	53.7
Combustion	30.6	20.7	9.0	16.2	16.1	16.2
Recycled	6.3	6.6	9.6	17.2	27.0	30.0

*Estimates.
Source: U.S. Environmental Protection Agency, *Municipal Solid Waste Factbook,* Version 4.0, Washington, DC, August 1, 1997, available at www.epa.gov/garbage/facts.htm.

Technical Options for Reducing MSW

We define the following terms: TM is total materials used, by a firm or industry or economy, in a period of time; VM is virgin materials used; and RM is recycled materials used. Then it must be true that for any time period:

$$TM = VM + RM.$$

Materials-balance considerations[4] tell us that all materials inputs taken into an economic system must eventually end up back in the environment in some fashion. The form may change, as when solid materials are burned to yield energy and waste products. The time span can differ; some materials do not lend themselves to reuse and so are discarded almost immediately, whereas others can be recycled, perhaps many times. But recycling can never be perfect because of conversion losses, waste in consumption, and so on. This means we should focus on the quantity of virgin materials used. Rearranging the above expression gives:

$$VM = TM - RM, \quad \text{or} \quad = TM(1 - r),$$

where r is the **rate of reuse,** or RM/TM. There are essentially two ways to reduce the use of virgin materials: (1) reduce the overall quantity of materials (TM) and/or (2) increase the reuse rate r; in other words, waste reduction and recycling.

Total materials use can be reduced in two ways: by reducing the rate of economic activity or by reducing the **materials intensity** of that activity. By "materials intensity" we mean the quantity of materials used per unit of production or consumption. And this in turn can be done in two ways: (1) by rearranging the composition of output and consumption away from products that use rela-

[4]See Chapter 2.

tively large amounts of materials and toward those that use less (e.g., a shift away from tangible goods toward services) and (2) by decreasing the materials intensity of particular products (e.g., reducing the amount of packaging material in consumer electronics or food products).

The other alternative is **recycling.** This means reaching into the waste stream to extract materials that may be reused. Some may be reused directly, as when consumers reuse old boxes. But most require some reprocessing. Of course, the separation, transportation, and reprocessing technologies that are available critically affect the costs of recycled materials, and thus their ability to displace virgin materials.

Current Policy

The present policy picture is very complicated, as you would expect from the nature of the physical problem, the large number of materials involved, and the thousands of municipalities, small and large, searching for solutions. Table 17-3 lists some of the various measures that are, or have been, pursued in various states. For the most part these focus on some facet of recycling. When MSW first became an issue, it was regarded primarily as a disposal issue—people were tak-

TABLE 17-3
MSW REDUCTION AND RECYCLING ACTIONS UNDERTAKEN
IN STATES AND COMMUNITIES

Product bans: plastic nondegradable plastic bags, plastic-coated paper, polystyrene containers, disposable diapers, plastic six-pack rings, cans containing both plastic and metal, plastic bag purchases by state or local agencies, and so on.

Returnable disposal fees: fee on newsprint that is returned for recycling, returnable deposits on tires and car batteries.

Taxes on virgin materials content.

Consumer fees on MSW: fees per bag or can of unsorted MSW.

Prohibitions on landfilling certain products, such as yard clippings, metal, and tires.

Bottle deposits.

Mandatory recycled content of purchased material by public agencies.*

Voluntary or mandatory material separation and curbside recycling.

Recycled or recyclable labels on products.

Technical assistance for recycling programs.

Grants and loans to municipalities for recycling programs.

Public construction of waste separation and reprocessing plants.

Public construction of waste-to-energy plants.

Tax credits and exemptions for recycling equipment and other investments by private businesses.

---

*At the federal level, President Clinton signed Executive Order 13101 in 1998 requiring all federal agencies to purchase only paper that had at least 30 percent recycled content.

TABLE 17-4
MUNICIPAL SOLID WASTE GENERATED AND RECOVERED IN THE UNITED STATES, 1995

	Waste generated (million tons)	Materials recovered (percent of total)
Paper	81.5	40
Yard waste	29.8	31
Plastics	19.0	5
Metals	15.8	39
Wood	14.9	10
Food waste	14.0	4
Glass	12.8	24
Other	20.2	11
Total	208.0	27

Source: U.S. Environmental Protection Agency, *Municipal Solid Waste Factbook,* Version 4.0, Washington, DC, August 1, 1997, available at www.epa.gov/garbage/facts.htm.

ing to the landfill materials and products that could be recycled. Thus, the initial response of most communities was to think about materials recovery and recycling. **Voluntary recycling programs** began in the 1970s (the first was in Oregon). In some communities recycling has become mandatory for items that are recyclable. Recent figures show that about 22 percent of MSW is currently recycled. As Table 17-4 shows, the recycling rate for different materials varies from a high of 40 percent for paper to a low of 4 percent for food wastes. Of the material discarded, about 84 percent is landfilled and most of the remainder is incinerated.

THE ECONOMICS OF RECYCLING

The complete materials recycling loop is actually a complex process involving a number of stages and interconnections. A schematic outline of this loop is depicted in Figure 17-1. It shows the primary actors at each stage and how the flow of materials goes from one stage to the next. At each stage there is also some material disposal, depicted by the dashed arrows. The connections among actors at each stage are worked out through markets; these markets are depicted by small supply/demand figures between each stage of the recycling loop.

The size and composition of the material flows are determined by the many decisions made by the demanders and suppliers in these markets. Producers and packagers design products and the materials used for them; they make decisions on the total quantities of materials used and the amounts of virgin and recycled feedstocks they will use. Consumers choose products that contain different types and amounts of material; they also decide how to dispose of the various materials after the products have been "consumed." There is a stage consisting of collectors: firms who collect, transport, and sort material and make it available to materials reprocessors. The latter, in turn, convert the various

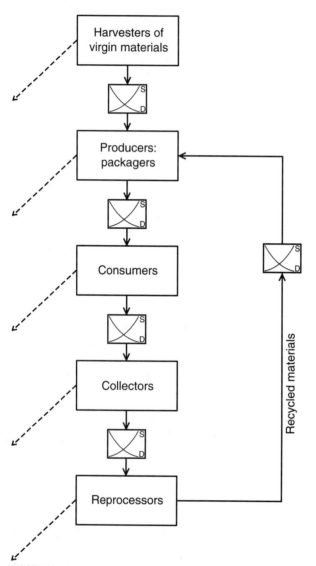

FIGURE 17-1
Recycling Consists of a Number of Markets Linking Generators
and Users.

materials of the solid waste stream into materials that may be reused by pro-
ducers/packagers, thus closing the loop.

Solid waste is a problem because of pricing difficulties in the various markets around the loop. For example,

- The harvesting of virgin materials leads to a variety of economic
  costs. In most cases these costs are external to the harvesting firms,

making the prices of virgin materials too low from the standpoint of social efficiency.[5]

- Because of low prices for virgin materials, it is difficult for would-be entrepreneurs to be competitive in supplying closely competitive products; that is, materials pulled from the waste stream and reprocessed into reusable forms.
- Discarded solid waste involves environmental costs that ought to be reflected in prices paid by consumers facing different disposal options. Solid waste disposal services are paid for in most communities through flat fees levied to cover the cost of collection and disposal. These fees can go up or down to reflect overall disposal costs (fees are going up in many cases because of increased scarcities of landfill space), but the per-family fees do not vary according to the quantities of material discarded per family. Thus, there is no incentive for consumers to be concerned about the amounts of solid waste they discard, nor any incentive to reduce the amounts of "excess" packaging materials that accompany their purchases.[6]

Producer Use of Recycled Material

Let us take a closer look at the top-most market in Figure 17-1, the market in which producers of goods and services use various amounts and types of material. This market is modeled in Figure 17-2. The demand curve applies to a firm or industry; it shows the quantity demanded of a particular type of material in a given period, such as a year. There are two sources of this material: virgin and recycled. We assume that this firm or industry is small relative to the total use of this material; thus, it can obtain virgin material feedstocks in whatever quantity it wishes at a constant price. This price is marked p_v and is shown as a horizontal line intersecting the demand curve at a quantity level q_0. But this material also may be obtained from recycled sources. Here, however, the procurement cost picture is more complicated. Reaching into the waste stream for recycled materials involves a number of special costs—of collection, separation, transportation, reprocessing, and so on. We assume that these costs increase with the amount of recycled material used. The supply curve of recycled material to this firm or industry is therefore an increasing function such as S_1 or S_2. These two supply curves refer to situations with different recycling technology.[7] For S_1, costs go up relatively rapidly; S_2 increases much less rapidly. Consider for the moment the recycled material supply curve labeled S_1. If this is the one faced by this firm or industry, it will end up using q_1 of recycled materials. In other words, the producer will use recycled materials up to the point where its cost is equal to the price of virgin materials. Since the total materials use is q_0, the difference $(q_0 - q_1)$ consists of virgin materials.

---

[5] A variety of public programs also have the effect of lowering the costs of virgin materials.

[6] But remember the very first example discussed in Chapter 1, the "pay per throw" system being instituted by many communities in the last few years.

[7] In recent decades there have been rapid changes in the technologies of collecting, sorting, sifting, and reprocessing of various types of solid waste.

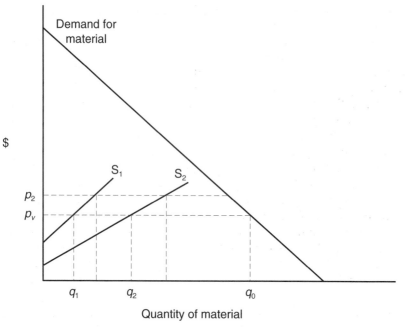

FIGURE 17-2
Use of Recycled Materials in Production.

The reuse ratio, the proportion of total materials coming from recycled feed-stock, is q_1/q_0. This ratio can be increased in three ways: increase q_1 while holding q_0 constant, decrease q_0 while holding q_1 constant, or both. Most community efforts at recycling are aimed at the first of these. For example, public curbside sorting and collection programs are ultimately aimed at making the supply of recycled material more abundant and, hence, less costly to producers. In terms of the model of Figure 17-2, these programs have aimed at shifting the recycled supply curve downward, say, from S_1 to S_2. If this is done, recycled materials use increases to q2 and the recycling rate increases to q_2/q_0.

Another way of increasing the recycling ratio is to reduce the demand for materials in general while holding constant the use of recycled materials. Diagrammatically this means shifting the whole materials demand curve back. This might be done, for example, by finding ways of producing output using fewer materials. It also might simply happen as consumers shift away from materials-intensive products. Finally, there is one way of simultaneously reducing total materials used and increasing recycled materials: Increase the price of virgin materials. If, on Figure 17-2, we lift the virgin materials price to, say, p_2 through a tax, this will lead to a move both up the recycling supply curve and up the materials demand curve. This means an increase in the quantity of recycled materials and a decrease in the quantity demanded of materials in total. Raising the price on virgin materials with a tax thus has a double effect on the reuse ratio, because it works at both ends of the problem.

We can use this simple model to examine recent proposals for **recycled-content standards** in materials-using industries. Early enthusiasm for community recycling efforts led to situations in which the amounts of collected material outstripped technical ability to turn it into useful raw material, and in the absence of demand large quantities of sorted and collected material actually end up in landfills. Thus, recent policy efforts have turned toward trying to increase the strength of demand for the recycled material. A number of states have thought to try this by introducing minimum-content standards for materials-using production processes. Minimum-content standards require that all materials-using products manufactured or sold within a given state contain some specified percentage of recycled material.

We have talked many times of the cost-ineffectiveness of uniform standards in the face of heterogeneous emissions withholding costs. In the case of uniform content standards for materials, the same principle applies, but here the important factor is heterogeneity across materials-using firms in terms of the costs of obtaining and using recycled materials. For a truly cost-effective approach to the problem, we would want to achieve equality across industries and materials in terms of **marginal recycling costs.** What this implies is having higher rates of recycled materials use by industries whose recycling costs are relatively low and lower rates for industries with relatively high recycling costs. One way to achieve this is to apply a tax on virgin materials. As mentioned previously, a tax of, say, $p_2 - p_v$ per unit of virgin materials, charged to all firms, would lead each to increase its recycling ratio in a way that satisfied the equimarginal principle. Another way would be to initiate a tradable permit system in the recycling market. A regulatory agency or statute would set an overall recycling objective for an industry, expressed in terms of the desired recycling rate. Each individual firm would then have three choices: (1) Increase its own recycling rate to the industry standard, (2) increase to a rate higher than the standard and sell "excess" recycling permits, or (3) increase to less than the industry standard, buying however many permits are necessary to make up the difference.

In the real world, of course, things are a lot more complicated than they appear in this simple model. For example, one underlying assumption built into Figure 17-2 is that recycled material and virgin material are physically interchangeable. This is hardly ever true in practice. Although newspaper can be produced largely from recycled newspaper, some virgin newsprint is usually necessary to achieve minimum quality levels. The same is true of many recycled metals. It is also true that the recycling market, like any economic market, is very dynamic, whereas the model displayed in Figure 17-2 is essentially static; that is, it is limited to events happening in a single time period. But producers normally look well into the future when making decisions. For example, even though current virgin materials prices are low, producers may nevertheless invest today in recycling and reprocessing works, if they *anticipate* that prices will increase in the future. But the simple model offers insight into basic recycling economics. In the future, we can expect the markets for recyclables to become better organized and more stable, which will be a growing impetus for the growth of recycling. See, for example, Exhibit 17-1, about the growth of electronic information in the market for reusable materials.

EXHIBIT 17-1

RECYCLABLES MARKET OPENS AT CHICAGO BOARD OF TRADE

The Electronic Market Should Help Small Towns Find Big Buyers for Reusable Materials Like Bottles and Newspapers

By David Dishneau

CHICAGO—Forget junk bonds. Now they're trading junk.

A national marketplace for buying and selling recyclable trash opened yesterday at the Chicago Board of Trade. The first transaction: Weyerhaeuser Co. bought 100 tons of old newspapers from Oswego County, N.Y.

The venture promises to boost recycling by setting quality standards and publicizing prices for used paper, glass and plastics. It can help small towns with curbside collection programs find big buyers of reusable materials.

"This is the biggest shot in the arm for recycling in this country since municipal recycling efforts began in the 1970s," said Mark Lichtenstein, Oswego County's trash manager and president of the National Recycling Coalition, which includes both buyers and sellers of recyclables.

The computerized system already has 60 subscribers who paid $1,000 each for access to its electronic bulletin board. Users can offer or bid for materials or just check the prices at which recyclables are trading.

"With these transactions, America will take its recycling efforts from the current state, which are really not unlike having a national yard sale, to an electronic marketplace for recycled goods," said David

Gardiner, an assistant administrator at the Environmental Protection Agency.

Currently, big companies buy most of their recyclable materials from brokers and commercial trash collectors with whom they have contracts. But small local governments are often at the mercy of local dealers because they lack knowledge of the value of their materials elsewhere.

In Washington state recently, corrugated cardboard was selling for $200 a ton in Seattle but just $35 in Spokane, according to David Dougherty, director of the Clean Washington Center, a state environmental agency.

Weyerhaeuser, a wood-products manufacturer based in Tacoma, Wash., and Oswego County agreed to make the first transaction because their state environmental offices helped create the exchange.

Weyerhaeuser paid $90 a ton for Oswego County newsprint, which it will ship to a paper mill in Italy.

"Recycling is an investment, and whenever you can hook the supplier up to the end user, you minimize the risk involved," said Jason Plut, a spokesman for Weyerhaeuser, which recycled 2 million tons of paper last year.

Source: Springfield Union News, October 18, 1995. Copyright 1995 by the Associated Press. Reprinted by permission.

Consumer Recycling Decisions

Let us now take a look at the second and third markets depicted in Figure 17-1, where consumers purchase goods and services and make solid waste disposal decisions. For environmental activists it is sometimes easy to believe that all we need is sufficiently severe laws to force producers and consumers to behave in certain ways, but laws of that type will be useless if they do not take into account the choices people actually face.

To examine this choice on the part of a consumer, consider some illustrative numbers pertaining to two goods, and the private and social benefits and costs

TABLE 17-5
INDIVIDUAL AND COMMUNITY BENEFITS AND COSTS IN PRODUCT CHOICE
AND RECYCLING (NUMBERS ARE ASSUMED TO BE IN CENTS)

	Product A	Product B
Purchase price	100	100
Value to consumer	140	160
Net value	40	60
Conventional (landfill) disposal alternative		
Disposal costs		
Private	10	10
Social	10	40
Net benefits		
Private	30	50
Social	20	10
Recycling alternative		
Disposal costs		
Private	10	40
Community transport	(cannot be recycled)	10
Environmental damage	10	0
Value of recovered material	0	20
Net benefits		
Private	30	20
Social	20	30

of recycling or discarding the associated packaging material. Assume they are two similar products, but perhaps with different packaging, such as bulk cereal and cereal in boxes, or drinks in plastic and drinks in glass containers. The data are in Table 17-5, and they apply to the situation of a single consumer. Each of Products A and B sells for the same price, but one, because of handling convenience, has a higher value to this consumer. Of course for other consumers the numbers pertaining to "value to consumer" could be different. For this consumer the net value before disposal of these two goods is in favor of Product B.

Disposal Costs   Now introduce the **disposal costs** of materials coming with the product. Consider first the costs of disposal in the conventional way—in the community landfill. Disposal costs are in two parts: private and social. The private costs refer to the consumer's costs of handling and discarding the materials, whereas the social costs refer to the environmental damages caused by the material when disposed of in the community's landfill. The private disposal costs of the two containers are the same—the time it takes to bag up the trash and set it on the curb is the same no matter with which product the consumer is dealing. But the environmental costs for Product B are substantially higher than those of Product A, for example, because there is much more material involved or because it uses a different type of material.

We now can calculate the **net benefits** of the two goods for the consumer and for the community. Remember that the full social costs contain the costs borne by the individual consumer plus the other damage costs. Here we arrive at the nub of the problem, because from the individual's standpoint Product B is the preferred choice, whereas for the community Product A is the preferred choice. The environmental costs stemming from conventional disposal are essentially **external costs;** if consumers do not take them into account when making purchasing decisions, they will make choices that are best from their standpoint but not best from the perspective of the community.

Recycling Now introduce recycling. The products are different in this respect. Product A cannot be recycled for technical reasons; thus, it will continue to be disposed of in the landfill. But Product B may be recycled, and the costs of doing so rest partly on consumers and partly on the community. There are private costs coming from the need to separate trash and handle the recycled goods in the home. The community also faces a transport cost, but offsetting this is the fact that the recycled material has a market value. These costs are shown in Table 17-5. With the items as indicated, we can calculate the benefits of the two goods in the presence of the recycling program. The net benefit of Product A stays the same, since it cannot be recycled. The net benefit of Product B is now substantially higher than it was before the recycling program, primarily because of the avoided environmental damage and the market value of the recycled material.

The Consumer's Choice The consumer now has three alternatives: (a) buy Product A, disposing of it in the community landfill; (b) buy Product B, recycling the associated material; and (c) buy Product B, but dispose of it in the landfill. We can tabulate the net benefits to individual and community as follows:

Option	Net benefits	
	Individual	Community
(a) Buy A	30	20
(b) Buy B, recycle	20	30
(c) Buy B, landfill	50	10

The individual's preferred choice is Product B without recycling; the community's preferred choice is B *with* recycling. The fundamental question is, What can be done to provide the incentive for the individual consumer to adopt the recycling alternative?

Consider one alternative that has been tried by many communities: mandatory recycling. The community enacts a local regulation making it illegal not to recycle the material from B if that product has in fact been purchased. That is, the ordinance requires that all purchased recyclable products in fact must be recycled. What this does, if it is enforced, is to take away option (c) from the consumer. So the consumer falls back on the next best alternative: buying the nonrecyclable Product A. This simple problem illustrates an important point: The recycling process starts back at the choice of purchase made by the consumer, and we have to look at the impacts of recycling ordinances on this purchase decision as well as on recycling decisions themselves. In the present case the mandatory recycling law has the effect of causing the consumer to shift purchasing away from recyclable products to nonrecyclable ones, thus substantially undermining the intent of the law.

Disposal Charges   A basic principle in environmental economics is that emission charges can provide the incentive for polluters to adopt socially efficient rates of emissions. In the present situation the counterpart of emission charges is consumer disposal charges. A completely efficient set of disposal charges would involve a charge on each item at a level equal to the social costs of disposal. A unit of Product A produces damages of 10¢, so its tax would be that much. The tax on a nonrecycled unit of Product B would be 40¢. For a recycled unit of B the tax is a little more complicated. If B is recycled, there is no environmental cost, but there is a community transportation cost of 10¢. But this is more than offset by the fact that the item has a 20¢ market value. Thus, the net tax is actually 10 − 20¢, or −10¢. The tax is actually a 10¢ payment to the consumer. If we levy these taxes on these products at the point of disposal, the net benefits of the various options to the individual consumer would now become (a) 20¢, (b) 30¢, and (c) 10¢, which are the same as the social net benefits of the previous tabulation. Now the consumer will choose (b), the recycling option. In effect, *these taxes have changed the pattern of private net benefits so that they are the same as community net benefits.* When this is done, a consumer will have the incentive to (1) choose the product and (2) make the recycling decision in ways that are efficient from the standpoint of the community.

In fact, a charge based on the social costs of disposal for each item is not going to be feasible in the real world; it would require authorities to evaluate the waste stream of each individual and charge according to the different items identified. What many communities are doing, rather, is establishing a single charge, per bag or can, of undifferentiated waste, and collecting separated and recyclable materials free. In this case the charge on nonseparated trash ought to be some average of the disposal costs of the various items in the waste stream. In our example, the social costs (in terms of environmental damages) of a unit of A are 10¢, and of a unit of B if not recycled, 40¢. If the authorities took an intermediate value, setting a charge of 25¢ per container thrown away, the private net benefits of the different alternatives would be (a) 5¢, (b) 30¢, and (c) 25¢. So in this case the tax would be sufficient to lead the consumer to buy B and recycle.[8] A tax much lower than this, however, would lead the consumer to

---

[8]This is the essence of the "pay per throw" system that we discussed at the beginning of the book.

buy B and dispose of it in the landfill, owing to the relatively high private costs of recycling.

A Deposit Program   We can look also at the effect of a **deposit program** on recyclable items. If a 40¢ deposit were put on item B, reflecting the damages done if it were thrown away rather than recycled, the array of net benefits for the individual would now be (a) 30¢, (b) 20¢, and (c) 10¢. The consumer refrains from throwing out the recyclable item, but also shifts back to (a), the nonrecyclable good. This is the same effect as with mandatory recycling; the bottle bill leads this particular consumer to choose nonrecyclable items when shopping. One way around this is to have a deposit on *all* materials, equal to their disposal costs. For Product A, the nonrecyclable item, this essentially acts as a tax, and gives a result similar to the "perfect" tax discussed previously.

We need to stress that these results depend on the particular numbers shown in Table 17-5. Some of these, such as environmental damage costs and purchase price, would be the same for all consumers, but others, such as private disposal costs, depend on the individual's own subjective valuation of the burdens of handling different types of products. These could differ among consumers and this obviously could lead to differences in response to various solid-waste policies. It is also quite true that many people obtain a certain amount of civic satisfaction from engaging in behavior that is efficient from the community's standpoint. But to get as much benefit as we can from recycling decisions made by consumers, we have to consider the benefits and costs of these decisions through their eyes.

LAND-USE CONTROL POLICIES

Land-use issues, and the public control over **land-use decisions,** are also matters that historically have been left to the individual states and communities of the United States. Although in recent years we have seen certain federal initiatives, especially on the matter of wetlands preservation, the dominant perspective is still that land-use issues are primarily local issues and therefore require **local policy responses.** The environmental issues we have talked about heretofore have been about the management of flows of production and consumption residuals, with the discussion focusing on the various policy tools, standards, emission fees, TDPs, and so on to affect these residual flows. When it comes to land, the problem is somewhat different. The land surface of the earth is fixed in quantity, and human beings spread themselves around on it in accordance with varying incentive patterns and with varying impacts. The key problem, then, is how decisions are arrived at to devote particular pieces of land to particular human and nonhuman uses.

Because almost all environmental externalities have a spatial dimension, it might be tempting to think of all pollution as essentially a land-use issue. But while many of the large cases of air and water pollution are indeed spatial, they do not lend themselves to solutions through altered land-use patterns. The acid rain problem is not a land-use problem, for example. Certain local cases of environmental externalities, however, may be more closely related to decisions on land use. Local air pollution problems may be the result of transportation patterns produced by sprawling housing development. A community faced with noise pollution from a local airport may be able to manage it through land-use controls in the vicinity of the airport.

But many contemporary land-use issues are not pollution related; rather, they are about the human use of land that substantially reduces or destroys its environmental value. Within any localized region there are usually lands that have **special environmental value,** because of strategic ecological linkages or aesthetic values, or both. Some cases of this are

- Wetlands, which provide important environments for plants and animals and are linked into other components of the ground and surface water system.
- Coastal lands, where scenic and recreational qualities are important.
- Critical habitats, where land-use patterns affect the health or survival of plant and animal species.
- Scenic and open land, where people may find vistas and experiences that have spiritual significance and recreational value.

To examine the economic logic of public and private land-use decisions, let us focus on an example involving one particular piece of land. All land parcels are essentially unique and will have varying values in different uses, but illustrative numbers can be used to demonstrate the essence of the problem.

The parcel is currently in open space, with all environmental values intact, and it is owned by a single individual. Suppose there are three mutually exclusive options for the parcel: (a) It may be developed without public restraints, (b) it may be preserved in its current state, or (c) it may be developed but with certain restrictions set by the local environmental agency. The illustrative numbers in Table 17-6 show the **returns and costs** of these different courses of action. Naturally, when land-use decisions of this type are made, there is actually a stream of returns and costs off into the future, so the numbers in Table 17-6 in effect represent the *present values* of these streams of returns and costs.[9]

First consider options (a) and (b). If the owner were to develop the land, he or she would realize a gross return of 100 and have construction costs of 80. But developing the land would have serious environmental costs; namely, the destruction of its **ecological value,** which is set at 50. We assume, and this is critical, that this lost ecological value is a loss to society but not a loss to the individual. There is no way for the landowner to package and sell this value, as it were. Thus, because there is no way for the owner to realize the ecological value of the land, the individual's decisions about using the land will be predicated on its private development value. The private net return is 20, whereas the full social return of developing the land is –30. In the absence of any public

---

[9]For a discussion of the present-value concept, see Chapter 6.

TABLE 17-6
RETURNS AND COSTS OF VARIOUS LAND-USE OPTIONS

	Land use		
	Develop (a)	Preserve (b)	Develop with restrictions (c)
Returns:			
Private	100	—	90
Public	—	50	—
Total	100	50	90
Costs:			
Private	80	20	80
Public	50	—	10
Total	130	20	90
Net return:			
Private	20	−20	10
Public	−30	30	0

land-use policy, the land would presumably be developed even though it represents a net loss to society.

It is instructive to look at it from the reverse perspective, the returns and costs of option (b): preservation. In this case private returns are nil, but public returns from the preserved ecological values of the land are 50. The cost in this case is the forgone net return from developing the land, or 20. Thus, the net social returns from preservation are $50 - 20 = 30$.

Let us now consider certain policy options. The most common local land-use tool is outright prohibition of certain land uses that are thought to have low or negative social returns, even though they may have positive private returns. This is done through the exercise of the **police power,** which is a power that communities have of prohibiting private activities that are detrimental to the wider public. The most common technique is **zoning,** in which communities rule out certain types of land uses where they would be destructive to the surrounding land values; for example, factories in residential areas. Environmental restrictions on development also come under this heading because they contribute to the health and welfare of the community. Thus, a police power approach to our problem would be simply to develop a zoning law or environmental preservation law that rules out option (a).

A major problem with a police power approach like this is that, although it may legally prohibit certain land uses such as option (a), it does not change any of the numbers in the table, so it does not change any of the underlying incentives of the situation. An owner whose land has been subject to a development restriction by public authorities has much to gain by getting the authorities to relax the restraint. In fact it would make sense for the landowner in Table 17-6 to spend some portion of the expected net returns to try and get the authorities to reverse themselves.

Instead of outright prohibition, the police power may be used to place conditions on development. For example, a developer might be required to leave a certain amount of open space, to avoid certain ecologically sensitive areas, or to install a public sewer system. This approach is sometimes called **incentive zoning.** Table 17-6 depicts a third alternative, called "develop with restrictions," to capture this type of option. The owner is allowed to develop, but certain constraints are placed on this process, which have the effect of avoiding some of the ecological costs. Since the restrictions lower the developed value, the private net return is now only 90 – 80 = 10. The social net return is now 90 – 90 = 0, because all but 10 of the ecological costs have been avoided by the development restrictions.

The Takings Issue

One of the most contested issues in using local land-use controls for environmental protection purposes is the **takings** problem. The Fourteenth Amendment to the U.S. Constitution asserts that persons may not be deprived of their property without "due process of law." This requirement serves to restrict the exercise of the police power by local governments. A community may not simply invoke the police power to do anything it wishes. The police power may in general be exercised only when it is reasonable, clearly enhances public welfare, and is not arbitrary or discriminatory. The problem is in knowing when these conditions are met. In the example of Table 17-6, a local restriction that ruled out option (a) but permitted option (c) would lower the net private return from 20 to 10, thus lowering the private value of the land by that amount. Is this a valid exercise of the police power?

A well-known recent case that went all the way up to the U.S. Supreme Court involved a coastal community. The community had put restrictions on the development of certain shoreline property on the grounds that it was subject to flooding by the high water from ocean storms. The landowner sued, saying that the flood danger was exaggerated and that the regulations deprived him of the value obtainable by developing the property. The Supreme Court upheld the landowner.

A major difficulty with cases like this is that although private revenues and costs of land-use restrictions are usually known with accuracy, the same cannot be said about environmental values. In the example of Table 17-6, we assumed we knew exactly how much the environmental attributes were worth, but usually this is not true. So the courts have to try to balance known private values with unknown public environmental values. From the standpoint of public health, there may be little difficulty barring development in sensitive wetlands, on the grounds that these are linked into the hydrological systems on which many people depend for water supply.

But when public health is not so directly involved, things can be much less clear. Suppose that I own a particular farm in a community and that over time the people of the community have come to value the scenic qualities of my land. Clearly the land has environmental (scenic) value, but may the town pass a regulation saying that I can't develop it for that reason? In doing this, the town is essentially putting on me the entire burden of providing these scenic values. Outcomes in takings conflicts depend on the details of the individual cases in the context of legal doctrines regarding the appropriate ways of evaluating and weighing the different values involved. Exhibit 17-2 discusses a recent case.

One way around the takings issue is compensation to the landowner. A straightforward way of doing this is for a public agency or a private environmental group to purchase "in fee simple" the land in question. In the case of Table 17-6 a purchase price of 20 would just compensate the landowner for the lost development opportunities. The land is then taken out of the private market and its environmental values are preserved. This requires that the community or some private group have substantial financial resources. The **Nature Conservancy,** for example, is a private group, funded largely through contributions, that preserves sensitive land by outright purchase. But this option may be too expensive for many local communities faced with development pressures in their region. A less costly approach is to purchase just certain partial rights in the land, not the land in its entirety. In the case of Table 17-6, for example, the community might buy from the landowner just the right to undertake option (a), but not the right to pursue option (c). The value of this one right would be 10, the difference in net returns between the two options. This purchase of just the development right would preserve some, although not all, of the land's environmental values, but it may be a desirable course of action for a community faced with a shortage of resources.

GROUNDWATER PROTECTION

Groundwater supplies about a quarter of all water used in the United States. Most of it is used in agriculture, but it is also a significant source of drinking water for many communities, especially those in rural areas. In recent years the quality of **groundwater resources** has been increasingly threatened from a variety of sources: agricultural runoff, industrial waste disposal, landfill leakage, underground storage tanks, and so on. Groundwater resources are substantially different from surface water in terms of their regenerative capacity; once contaminated, groundwater aquifers are likely to be lost to use for a long time because of the very slow rate at which they are replenished.

Most groundwater pollutants stem from **nonpoint-source** emissions. As we have discussed many times, this essentially rules out any type of emission control policy that requires direct monitoring of emissions. Thus, groundwater pollution-control programs must focus on controlling the various practices and behaviors of sources that normally could be expected to threaten groundwater resources. To do this there is the full array of emission control policies, both CAC types and **economic incentive strategies.** Among

EXHIBIT 17-2

REGULATORY TAKINGS: BATTLE RAGES ON DESPITE TWO DECADES
OF COURT RULINGS

By John M. Armentano

The case began when — purchased a 40-acre tract of undeveloped land on Lower Sugarloaf Key, Fla., in 1973, as part of a much larger real estate purchase. The tract consisted of 32 acres of salt marsh and freshwater wetland and eight acres of uplands.

— began attempting to develop the property in 1980—more than seven years after he had purchased it—and submitted a permit application to the U.S. Army Corps of Engineers in March 1981, as was required for dredging and filling navigable waters of the United States. The Corps granted the requested permit in May 1983 and a modified permit in January 1984. Under both permits, the authorized work had to be completed within five years.

—'s efforts to get state and county approval for his project used up most of the five-year time limit on the two federal permits. — therefore requested that the Corps extend the time limits of the permits. The Corps denied —'s request to reissue the permits without changes, but granted a new permit allowing substantially the same development on October 17, 1988.

Apparently despairing of ever obtaining state approval for his 54-lot plan, — submitted a new, scaled-down plan to the Corps in July 1990. However, between the time the Corps had issued —'s 1988 permit and the time he applied for the 1990 permit, the Lower Keys marsh rabbit was listed as an endangered species under the Endangered Species Act; thereafter, the silver rice rat also was listed as an endangered species. Based on the presence of these two animals on —'s land, the Corps denied —'s 1990 permit application on March 17, 1994. At the same time, the Corps notified — that his 1988 permit had expired.

In July 1994, — filed suit, alleging that the Corps' denial of his permit worked an uncompensated taking in violation of the Fifth Amendment.

In its decision, the Federal Circuit said that it was "common sense" that one who buys with knowledge of a restraint assumes the risk of economic loss. In such a case, the court continued, the owner presumably paid a discounted price for the property. Compensating the owner for a "taking" would confer a windfall, it stated. In this case, the court emphasized, — had known of the necessity and the difficulty of obtaining regulatory approval when he had purchased the land. The court noted that the sales contract specifically stated that — "recognize[s] that . . . as of today there are certain problems in connection with the obtaining of State and Federal permission for dredging and filling operations." In the court's view, — thus had both constructive and actual knowledge that either state or federal regulations ultimately could prevent him from building on the property.

— pointed out, however, that he was only denied a permit based on the provisions of the Endangered Species Act, when two endangered species were found on his property. He argued that because the Endangered Species Act had not existed when he had purchased the land, he could not have expected that he would have been denied a permit based on its provisions.

The Federal Circuit found that —'s position was "not entirely unreasonable," but concluded that it had to be rejected. It stated that in view of the "regulatory climate" that existed when — had acquired his property, — could not have had a reasonable expectation that he would obtain approval to fill ten acres of wetlands in order to develop the land."

Source: New York Law Journal, September 22, 1999.

the latter, for example, would be taxes on nitrogen fertilizers used by farmers, leading to lower rates of fertilizer use and therefore less nitrate runoff. Among the former are various types of **technology specifications** for underground waste disposal to reduce the probabilities of groundwater contamination. Among the states a wide array of protection programs have been undertaken, including performance standards for handling wastes in sensitive aquifer recharge areas; permit programs to govern large-scale wastewater absorption systems, spray irrigation systems, or land spreading of sewage sludge; regulations on bulk storage and waste transport facilities; and regulations on agricultural activities, particularly the use of fertilizers and chemicals.

Many states are moving in the direction of greater reliance on **land-use zoning** as a way of protecting groundwater aquifers. By ruling out, or regulating, various uses in the recharge areas, risks of contamination can be lowered. Florida has pioneered this effort, which is not surprising given the heavy reliance on groundwater of the large population in the southeastern part of that state. Nassau and Suffolk counties in New York also have adopted hydrologic zoning to protect critical groundwater resources.[10]

SUMMARY

In recent years state and local efforts have become more important in environmental policy matters. As greater attention shifts to problems of enforcing environmental policies and regulations, state-level efforts in this respect have become more critical. States also have served as the source of innovation in many areas of environmental policies, spurring federal efforts and trying out new ideas in the control of emissions. The leading role of California in fostering more aggressive air pollution control is especially notable.

States and localities have had the primary responsibility for solid-waste management, land-use controls, and the protection of groundwater resources. Community efforts at recycling are a major part of the effort to address solid waste issues. We saw how recycling decisions depend on complex incentive situations facing consumers in their buying and disposal decisions and producers whose demands for recycled materials may lead them to reach into the solid-waste stream for sources of raw materials. Strong incentive situations also face local authorities when making land-use control decisions. Here the major issue is the change in land values produced by land-use regulations and the fine line between what may be considered a legitimate exercise of the police power and what is an unconstitutional "taking" of private property. These matters continue to evolve in the courts.

---

[10]Peter S. Tell, "Groundwater Protection Zones: United States and European Experiences," *International Environment Reporter,* March 1990, pp. 123–132.

QUESTIONS FOR FURTHER DISCUSSION

1 What are the implications for cost-effective recycling programs of regulations that establish the same recycling ratios for all sectors of the economy?
2 How might a system of transferable permits be designed to achieve an aggregate recycling target cost effectively?
3 Another way of increasing the use of recycled material by industry is to subsidize its purchase of materials taken from the waste stream. How would you analyze this in terms of Figure 17-2?
4 What are the factors, both economic and environmental, that make a problem more properly a local issue rather than a state issue?
5 Many communities are starting "pay-as-you-throw" programs to manage their solid waste. For any particular community, what are the economic factors that will determine how effective a pay-as-you-throw system will be?

WEBSITES

Resources for the Future, **www.rff.org,** has a number of papers available on economic issues of land use; select "Land Use" under "Natural Resources". The U.S. EPA has a good website on various aspects of municipal solid waste: **www.epa.gov/epaoswer/osw/index.htm.** See also the links listed in the website of this book, **www.mhhe.com/economics/field3.**

SELECTED READINGS

Black, Edward G.: "California's Community Right-to-Know," *Ecology Law Quarterly,* 16(4), 1989, pp. 1021–1064.
Boyd, James, Kathryn Caballero, and R. David Simpson: "Carving Out Some Space, A Guide to Land Preservation Strategies," *Resources,* No. 136, Resources for the Future, Washington, DC, Summer 1999, pp. 10–13.
Conservation Foundation: *Groundwater Protection,* Washington, DC, 1987.
Fischel, William: *The Economics of Zoning Laws,* Johns Hopkins Press, Baltimore, MD, 1985.
Fraser, Iain, and Chongwoo Choe: "The Economics of Household Waste Management: A Review," *The Australian Journal of Agricultural and Resource Economics,* 42(3), 1998, pp. 269–302.
Jenkins, Robin R., Salvador A. Martinez, Karen Palmer, and Michael J. Podolsky.: "The Determinants of Household Recycling: A Material Specific Analysis of Unit Pricing and Recycling Program Attributes," Discussion Paper 99-41, Resources for the Future, Washington, DC, May 1999.
Jessup, Deborah Hitchcock: *Guide to State Environmental Programs,* 3rd ed., Bureau of National Affairs, Inc., Washington, DC, 1994.
Lester, James P., and Emmett N. Lombard: "The Comparative Analysis of State Environmental Policy," *Natural Resources Journal,* 30(2), Spring 1990, pp. 301–319.
Malone, Linda A.: *Environmental Regulation of Land Use,* Clark Boardman, New York, 1990.
Menell, Peter S.: "Beyond the Throwaway Society: An Incentive Approach to Regulating Municipal Solid Waste," *Ecology Law Quarterly,* 17(4), 1990, pp. 655–740.

Nestor, Deborah Vaughn, and Michael J. Podolsky: "Assessing Incentive-Based Environmental Policies for Reducing Household Waste Disposal," *Contemporary Economic Policy*, 16(4), 1998, pp. 401–411.

Regens, James L., and Margaret A. Reams: "State Strategies for Regulating Groundwater Quality," *Social Science Quarterly*, 69(1), March 1988, pp. 53–69.

Ringquist, Evan J.: *Environmental Protection at the State Level*, Island Press, Washington, DC, 1993.

U.S. Environmental Protection Agency: *Characterization of Municipal Solid Waste in the United States: 1997 Update*, EPA 530-R-98-007, Washington, DC, 1998.

U.S. Office of Technology Assessment: *Facing America's Trash: What Next for Municipal Solid Waste?*, Washington, DC, 1989.

INTERNATIONAL
ENVIRONMENTAL ISSUES

The prospects for the 21st century are for the world to continue to shrink and nations to become increasingly interconnected. These interactions will grow in environmental matters. Regional and global problems will demand greater levels of cooperation and more effective international institutions. As demonstrated by the 2000 Seattle meetings of the World Trade Organization (WTO), problems of environmental degradation in developing countries and the relationships of growth and environmental values will become more important. As all countries struggle, to a greater or lesser extent, to manage their own environmental problems, greater value will attach to the exchange of information, technology, and policy experience. A look at this international experience can substantially deepen our perspectives on the nature of environmental issues and the way people have thought to address them.

We first review some of the environmental policy efforts being made in other industrialized countries and in developing countries. The discussion then turns to several global environmental problems: stratospheric ozone depletion and the greenhouse effect. Finally, we offer some perspective on the economics of international environmental agreements.

CHAPTER 18

ENVIRONMENTAL ISSUES IN OTHER INDUSTRIALIZED COUNTRIES

We begin by looking at experience in other industrialized countries of the East and the West. In the United States we have seen that there was a great burst of political energy in the early 1970s that launched many of the environmental initiatives at the federal level. Much the same took place in other countries; their primary environmental policies date from around the same time.

INTERNATIONAL COMPARISONS OF ENVIRONMENTAL QUALITY

Perhaps the best place to start is to look at several comparisons among countries in terms of environmental achievements. Good comparative data are not easy to obtain because the monitoring efforts of the countries have not been established with the primary goal of facilitating international comparisons. Each country collects and publishes its own data, using whatever bases, indices, and systems it finds most useful for its purposes. Thus, comparability is a problem. Efforts are slowly under way, especially among the European countries, to achieve some degree of uniformity in monitoring and data reporting.

Another thing making comparisons difficult is that within any country environmental quality can vary substantially among regions. In the United States, southern California and other urban areas have severe air problems. In Germany there is the heavily industrial Ruhr Valley. Japan has the Tokyo–Osaka corridor. This means that international comparisons have to be made with care and confined to situations that are reasonably similar.

The most cogent comparisons are in terms of achieved levels of ambient quality. Table 18-1 shows comparative ambient SO_2 levels for six large cities

TABLE 18-1
AMBIENT LEVELS OF SO_2 FOR SIX MAJOR WORLD CITIES
(annual average concentration, in $\mu g/m^3$)

	New York	Paris	Berlin	London	Tokyo	Montreal
1975	44	115	n/a	119	60	41
1980	38	89	90	69	48	41
1981	40	71	77	72	n/a	n/a
1982	39	68	82	57	42	n/a
1983	36	61	67	49	29	n/a
1984	38	57	n/a	46	27	n/a
1985	n/a	54	n/a	41	n/a	n/a
1995	26	14	18	25	18	10

Sources: U.S. Environmental Protection Agency, *International Comparison of Air Pollution Control,* Washington, DC, 1988, pp. 11–12, as presented in Raymond J. Kopp, Paul R. Portney, and Diane E. DeWitt, *International Comparisons of Environmental Regulation,* Resources for the Future, Washington, DC, 1990, p. 11; World Bank, www.worldbank.org/data/ databytopic/databytopic.html, at air pollution.

around the world over the decade 1975–1985. At the beginning of this period Montreal had the lowest concentration, followed closely by New York. In all cities SO_2 levels have dropped markedly in the two decades 1975 to 1995. Percentage wise the biggest drop was in Paris, and the smallest in New York.

Table 18-2 shows some comparative data on various environmental measures for selected OECD (Organization for Economic Cooperation and Development) countries. The first three rows show per capita emission data for some common pollutants. SO_2 emissions vary from about 100 kg per capita in Australia to 7.3 kg per capita in Japan. Nitrogen oxide emissions are also quite variable, while CO_2 emissions are less so. The fourth row shows the percentage of the total population served by wastewater treatment facilities, and this varies from 22 percent in both Mexico and Hungary to 93 percent in Sweden. Municipal solid waste per capita varies from a low of about 300 kg per capita in Mexico to 720 kg per capita in the United States. The next row partially explains the variations in airborne emissions noted above. Some countries have adopted nuclear power much more widely than others; Canada, France, and Sweden, for example, produce relatively large amounts of high-level nuclear waste from electric power plants.

Interpreting Differences in Environmental Performance

One has to be careful in interpreting these comparative environmental data.[1] The first reaction might be to interpret different environmental indices as indicating the effort each country has put into pollution control, but a moment's reflection shows that this is not necessarily the case. Differences in ambient environmental quality between different countries can be explained in essentially two ways: (1) as differences in the efficient, or desired, levels of ambient quality and/or (2) as differences in the extent to which each country, through policy and its enforcement, have achieved these efficient levels.

[1]The same might be said about comparisons among different regions of the same country.

TABLE 18-2
ENVIRONMENTAL INDICATORS FOR SELECTED COUNTRIES IN RECENT YEARS

	Australia	Canada	France	Hungary	Italy	Japan
Emissions:						
SO_2 (kg/capita)	100.7	88.9	16.2	64.5	23.1	7.3
NO (kg/capita)	118.5	67.1	29.1	19.4	30.9	11.3
CO_2 (tons/capita)	16.6	15.8	6.2	5.7	7.4	9.3
Wastewater treatment (percent of population served)	n/a	78	77	22	61	55
Municipal solid waste generated (kg/capita)	690	490	590	500	460	400
Nuclear waste*	—	5.6	4.6	2.2	—	1.9
Noise**	n/a	n/a	9.4	n/a	n/a	38.0

	Korea	Mexico	Sweden	United Kingdom	United States
Emissions:					
SO_2 (kg/capita)	32.9	23.2	10.3	34.5	69.0
NO (kg/capita)	27.6	16.4	38.1	35.0	79.9
CO_2 (tons/capita)	9.2	3.5	6.0	9.4	20.4
Wastewater treatment (percent of population served)	53	22	93	88	71
Municipal solid waste generated (kg/capita)	400	300	360	480	720
Nuclear waste*	2.1	0.3	4.6	3.6	1.0
Noise**	n/a	n/a	0.3	5.7	17.2

*Waste from spent fuel arising in nuclear power plants, in tons of heavy metal per million tons of oil equivalent of total primary energy supply.
**Million inhabitants exposed to leq>65dB.
n/a: not available.
—: negligible.
Source: Organization for Economic Cooperation and Development, Environmental Data, Compendium, 1999.

These are depicted in Figure 18-1, which shows three familiar marginal damage/marginal abatement cost diagrams, with ambient quality indexed on the horizontal axes. Suppose that e_1 and e_2, indicated on each figure, refer to ambient levels in two countries. Panel (a) shows that this policy could be the result of differences between the two countries in terms of their marginal abatement costs, given the same preferences for environmental quality in the two countries. In the short run this could be the result of different **technological means for pollution control** available in the two countries. But in the long run this factor would be less important because pollution-control technology is mobile; whatever is available in one country can be made available in the other.

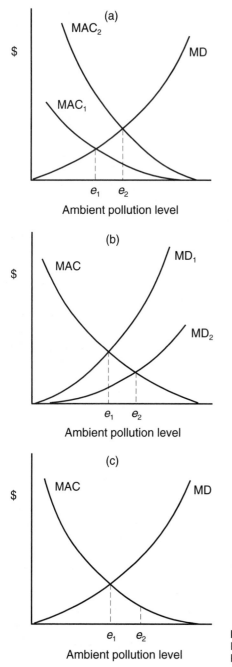

FIGURE 18-1
Interpreting International Differences in Ambient
Pollution Levels.

Of course, the difference in marginal abatement cost functions could arise also because one country has adopted more **cost-effective environmental control policies** than the other.

Other factors also may be at work. As we have stated many times, ambient conditions are the result of **emissions** *and* the **assimilative capacity** of the environment. So a country that has achieved low emissions still may suffer relatively high ambient concentrations because of the way its environment works: Similar emissions in Mexico City and New York will produce much dirtier air in the former because of its prevailing meteorological patterns. By the same token, similar ambient levels do not imply that countries have made similar efforts to control emissions, because in one the assimilative capacity of the environment may be greater.[2] Another real possibility is that there are differences in economic circumstances of the two countries—one relatively rich and the other relatively poor—so that the **opportunity cost** of pollution control in terms of forgone conventional income is higher in one than in the other. Note that the country with the highest ambient concentration actually may have spent more in total on abatement costs than the country with the lower concentration. We will have more to say on this point in Chapter 19, which discusses the relationship of environmental quality to economic development.

Panel (b) depicts the case where the difference between e_1 and e_2 is explained by differences in the damages flowing from ambient pollution loads in the two countries. This could stem, for example, from real differences in willingness to pay for pollution control by people in similar economic and social circumstances, that is, environmental quality as a matter of tastes and preferences, or from the fact that the two countries give a different priority to environmental quality. As an example of the former, consider the following case, which actually applies to the siting of an industrial plant that has some small but nonzero probability of catastrophic accident:

> Recently California and the United Kingdom have approved sites for Liquefied Energy Gas (LEG) terminals. In this, and perhaps this alone, they are the same. After a long drawn-out process in which it proved impossible to approve any of the proposed sites, California finally, with the help of a new statute passed expressly for the purpose, was able to give approval for an LEG facility at the remotest of all the sites on the list of possibles: Point Conception. Scotland has a longer coastline than California and most of the country is very sparsely populated (less than 25 persons to the square mile) and yet the approved site, at Mossmorran and Braefoot Bay on the Firth of Forth, lies within the most densely populated part of the entire country (with a population density of between 250 and 500 persons per square mile). Moreover, laden tankers will pass within a mile or so of Burntisland (an industrial town) and sometimes within four miles of Edinburgh—the capital city of Scotland! If the California siting criteria (explicit in Statute 1081) were to be applied to the Scottish

---

[2]For example, there has been a running dispute between Great Britain and the other members of the European Community (EC) over the basis of water pollution control. It stems from the fact that rivers in Great Britain tend to be short and have very substantial assimilative capacity, whereas those on the continent are longer, with less capacity. Thus, Great Britain has been in favor of an ambient standard approach to water-quality improvement within the EC, whereas other member states have leaned toward emission standards.

case it would be quite impossible to approve the Mossmorran/Braefoot Bay site, and if the United Kingdom criteria (implicit in the Mossmorran/Braefoot Bay approval) were to be applied to the California case, any of the suggested sites could be approved, which means that the terminal would go to the first site to be suggested— Los Angeles harbor.[3]

Finally, panel (c) depicts the situation of different enforcement efforts. Although both have the same desired level of ambient quality, one country has devoted more resources to enforcement, and thus its actual level is lower. Throughout this book we have talked about the importance of enforcement. Most developed countries have significant antipollution laws on the books; most also have significant enforcement problems, as is illustrated in the following comments:

> Some people here say the problem is that there is not an adequate body of environmental law in Ireland. But that is not true. There are 55 or so laws that affect what private industry can do to the environment. They are just not enforced. You can take it for granted that every single law is not being adequately enforced. Local authorities and corporations, too, actually have a pretty good record for responding to citizen complaints about pollution, since by then it is a political matter. But what you very rarely find is a local authority playing watchdog, checking up to see if regulations are being followed.[4]

> In Spain, we have beautiful laws to protect the environment, but nobody is really complying with them. Industry knows that the chances are not very great that the government is going to suddenly crack down and begin enforcing the laws. They say they will gradually get tougher, but in my opinion it would be better to have fewer and simpler regulations and get a better record of compliance from the very beginning.[5]

Of course, when making comparisons among countries all three factors will normally come into play: abatement costs, damages, and enforcement efforts.

ENVIRONMENTAL POLICY IN OTHER COUNTRIES

Regardless of where one lives, there is much to learn through comparing one's own experience with that of others. The rest of this chapter examines some of the distinguishing environmental policy efforts of developed countries other than the United States. It is not intended to offer a catalogue of events in each country; this would be impossible in the space we have, and also because environmental issues and responses are changing so rapidly that a catalogue of this type would quickly be out of date. Instead, we will try to single out particularly noteworthy policies or trends that characterize environmental policy in particular countries or groups of countries.

---

[3]Michael Thompson, "A Cultural Basis for Comparison," in Howard Kunreuthen and Joanne Linnerooth (eds.), *Risk Analysis and Decision Process, The Siting of Liquefied Energy Facilities in Four Countries,* Springer, Berlin, 1983, p. 233.

[4]Interview with Irish water-quality official, quoted in H. Jeffrey Leonard, *Pollution and the Struggle for World Product,* Cambridge University Press, Cambridge, England, 1988, p. 211.

[5]Interview with a private company manager for energy conservation and environmental affairs, quoted in ibid.

National Styles in Environmental Policy

From our discussion of the different policy options available in environmental policy, one might get the impression that policy matters are primarily technical exercises in picking the right approach to match the environmental problem being addressed. But a number of studies have shown that environmental policies in different countries are also a reflection of their unique political cultures and institutions. In one study of air pollution policy in Sweden and the United States, the author characterized the differences between the two countries as the difference between the hare and the tortoise.[6] The United States was the hare, with bursts of speed followed by pauses and rests, while Sweden was the tortoise, with slower but steadier progress. His side-by-side comparison of U.S. and Swedish policy approaches is the following:

United States	Sweden
1. Statutory ambient standards	1. Nonstatutory emission guidelines
2. Strict timetables for compliance	2. Compliance timetables set on basis of economic feasibility
3. Technology-forcing emission standards	3. Adjustments of standards to technological developments

In general, the U.S. style, at least during the 1970s covered in this study, emphasized formal and sharply defined objectives written into public laws, after much political wrangling, with later administrative compromises and delays to accommodate reality. The Swedish approach was to set policy with far less public fanfare, negotiating voluntary agreements that were based on technical and economic feasibility. Despite these differences, the changes through time in ambient air quality were quite similar between the two countries. He concludes: "At this point, the overall result seems very much to be a dead heat. Neither of the two countries seems to have been remarkably more successful than the other in relieving its citizens from the blight of air pollution."[7]

Another interesting study has been done on the introduction of vinyl-chloride (VC) standards into industrial workplaces. VC is used to make polyvinyl chloride (PVC), which in turn is shaped into thousands of products: piping, flooring, food wrapping, credit cards, baby pacifiers, shoes, medical devices, and so on. High levels of VC exposure in the workplace were identified in the early 1970s as a cause of serious health conditions among workers, particularly cancer. So around this time many countries addressed the task of reducing VC exposure in plants producing PVC. The study was a comparison

[6]Lennart J. Lundquist, *The Hare and the Tortoise: Clean Air Policies in the United States and Sweden*, University of Michigan Press, Ann Arbor, 1980.
[7]Ibid., p. 194.
[8]Joseph L. Badaracco Jr., *Loading the Dice, A Five-Country Study of Vinyl Chloride Regulation*, Harvard Business School Press, Boston, 1985.

of the way the policy process worked in five countries: France, Great Britain, Japan, the United States, and West Germany.[8] The basic contrast is between the adversarial style of the United States and the cooperative negotiating style of the other countries. The author characterizes the U.S. effort in the following way:

> . . . the key decisions in the adversarial case were made by agency officials and judges on the basis of virtually secret deliberations. Industry and labor did not cooperate but instead took steps to impede and discredit each other. Industry and government behaved similarly. Lawyers were active from start to finish, and no intermediaries acted as buffers among the parties. The various parties had only an indirect influence on the major decisions, and this was largely confined to public, highly publicized, courtlike hearings. Basic information was communicated through documents, and cost/benefit considerations were not an explicit part of the agency's decision process. In the end, OSHA issued its final regulations and required that industry achieve— under penalty of law—a very strict standard, one which exceeded the industry's technical capability at the time it was promulgated.[9]

By contrast, the cooperative styles of standard setting are characterized in the following way:

> . . . the parties involved directly influenced the critical decisions and actually made many of them. They achieved consensus through negotiations and discussions among middle-level officials over a period of several years. There were important intermediaries, and very few lawyers, involved in the process. Representatives of the major parties developed personal relationships in small working groups. Meetings were held in private—informally, and without rigid timetables. The working parties explicitly discussed cost and benefit. In the end, the decisions that emerged from these multipartite discussions were less formal, they followed technology, and they included flexible open-ended recommendations that companies should seek to achieve the lowest feasible levels of VC exposure.[10]

Having established these two styles, however, the results show that the ambient workplace exposure standards arrived at in the adversarial process (the United States) were stricter than those established through the cooperative process.

A more recent comparative work looked at the environmental policy process in the United States and Great Britain. The author concludes that U.S. policy is based on formal rules and strict enforcement, whereas in Great Britain there is more emphasis on voluntary compliance. But, he concludes, these two approaches led to "roughly" similar environmental outcomes.[11] The British approach, along with similar styles in other European countries, is likely to shift over time more toward formal pollution-control directives and enforcement as a part of the European Community's efforts to harmonize the pollution-control laws in the various member countries.

---

[9]Ibid., pp. 124–125.
[10]Ibid., p. 124.
[11]David Vogel, *National Styles of Regulation, Environmental Policy in Great Britain and the United States,* Cornell University Press, Ithaca, NY, 1986.

The U.S. approach also contrasts with that of Japan. Japanese environmental policy is based on a series of ambient standards that represent objectives, together with specific emission standards to move toward those objectives. National, generic emission standards are set, but at the local, or prefecture, level, particular emission standards are worked out on a source-by-source basis. This approach involves two characteristics that are specific to the Japanese experience. One is a high degree of negotiation between local pollution-control authorities and polluting sources, the results of which are to produce emission standards that are to some extent specific to each source. The other feature is the large amount of "administrative guidance." According to the basic national water pollution–control law, any operating unit that is the source of water-based emissions must submit a detailed plan showing the location, timing, type, and so on of emissions, as well as the methods and technologies to be used to control these emissions. Local pollution-control authorities then become heavily involved in the administrative guidance of these plans, along with the regular plant operators. The Japanese experience includes much more discretion at the local level. Pollution–control agreements may be struck between local authorities and firms. At first,

. . . many contracts were simply "gentlemen's agreements" (shinshi kyotei). For example, many early agreements declared that a company had an abstract duty to prevent pollution, to supply information, or to cooperate with local officials in a factory inspection. The company simply promised to take feasible and "appropriate" measures to prevent pollution. Such contracts in most cases did not contain provisions to handle violations.[12]

But more recently, local agreements have started to be

. . . drafted more precisely, and are richer in content. For example, many agreements require companies to meet emission or effluent standards stricter than national standards; others stipulate that a factory use special low sulfur fuel; some require the use of the most advanced pollution prevention technology, contain stipulations on factory operations, or provide for inspection of the factory. In some cases these contracts also authorize drastic enforcement measures like stop-work orders, emergency enforcement by proxy, strict liability for damages, fines, cancellation of a contract (where a sale of land between local government and a factory is involved), and as previously mentioned, interruption of the municipal water supply upon notice of violation.[13]

It needs to be stressed that these differences in style and institutions, although they may sound significant, may not have significant impacts on the levels of ambient quality actually achieved. They should not be interpreted as better or worse styles from among which a country may choose. Each national style is unique, stemming from a country's own political culture, and the effectiveness of policy has to be considered within the context of these particular styles.

[12]Julian Gresser, Koichiro Fujikura, and Aiko Morishima, *Environmental Law in Japan*, MIT Press, Cambridge, MA, 1981, p. 248.
[13]Ibid.

Guiding Principles of Pollution Control

In some countries, political authorities have attempted to develop **guiding principles** to identify appropriate pollution control policies. A guiding principle is simply an overarching policy criterion that supposedly sets guidelines for determining acceptable policies. In Japan, for example, pollution-control efforts were initially developed under the principle of "harmonization," which was essentially a requirement that pollution-control laws be "harmonized" with the requirements of economic growth. In China, new industrial construction is supposed to be pursued within the principle of "three at the same time." Each new construction plan is supposed to contain a special section on environmental protection showing how pollution-control methods will be designed, installed, and operated.[14]

Countries of the Organization for Economic Cooperation and Development (OECD) have sought to pledge their allegiance to what is called the **polluter pays principle** (PPP). This principle states that it is the polluters themselves who should bear the cost of measures to reduce pollution to levels specified by public authorities. Although this may sound like a rule based on ethical considerations, it is really grounded in political economics. It is meant to rule out situations where governments subsidize pollution-control expenditures of firms or industries in order to give them an economic advantage over competitors who must pay their own compliance costs. This is regarded as especially important among the closely competing firms and industries of the countries of Europe. There are exceptions allowed to the PPP in certain cases of undue economic hardship, short-term transition periods, and cases that have no significant impacts on international trade and investment. Because most countries, in OECD as elsewhere, subsidize pollution reduction to a greater or lesser degree, it has been necessary for political diplomats to find ways of reconciling principle and reality. In general, this has been done by defining the PPP abstractly enough that it can be held compatible with a wide number of arrangements.

Command-and-Control Approaches

It is safe to say that policy authorities in other industrialized countries have most often opted for **command and control** as a primary approach to pollution control. This means, as we have seen in earlier chapters, such things as political and administrative determination of, for example, the pollution-control technologies that are going to be acceptable, what emissions levels will be, where firms may locate, how buildings and equipment should be designed, what fuels and inputs may be used, how certain substances are to be handled, and so on.

---

[14]Rui Lin Jin and Wen Liu, "Environmental Policy and Legislation in China," in *Proceedings of the Sino-American Conference on Environmental Law,* Natural Resource Law Center, University of Colorado School of Law, Boulder, CO, 1989, p. 173.

In most countries, some concept has been adopted to establish the technological level(s) on which to base command-and-control decisions. In Great Britain it is "best practicable means," which refers to "reasonably practicable and technically possible to prevent the emission of gases and render these discharges harmless."[15] Germany relies on the basic idea that pollution-control programs must involve "state-of-the-art" technology. In Sweden the underlying decision criterion is to choose "what is technically feasible using the most effective technical devices and methods that are available in the area in question."[16] Italy has a standard calling for emissions reductions to "the lowest level possible through available technologies."[17] As we have mentioned several times in previous chapters, this approach actually allows regulators to make implicit trade-offs between damage reduction and technical and economic feasibility.

Incentive-Based Policies

Although basic policies continue to be based on command-and-control procedures, there are movements in many other countries in the direction of incentive-based policies, just as in the United States.[18] For the most part, however, other countries are relying on charges, on either emissions or on polluting products, rather than tradable emission permits. This is especially the case in Europe. In recent years many governments in Europe have been moving toward a greater use of charges. Our discussion of emission charges in Chapter 12 focused on charges as a means of bringing about cost-effective emission reductions. These might be called "incentive" charges or, as they are sometimes called in Europe, "balancing" charges. The emission charges employed in Europe are not incentive charges of this type. Rather, they are employed primarily to raise money that then can be used to subsidize pollution-control activities of public and private organizations. Exhibit 18-1 discusses some recent initiatives in incentive-based policies among countries that are members of the OECD.

Environmental Analysis

By **environmental analysis** we refer to the attempts to measure such things as the cost-effectiveness of particular policy actions, the **benefits** of environmental improvements, and the **benefits and costs** of alternative environmental policies and regulations. Significant progress is being made in other countries to develop techniques for measuring the social benefits of environmental improvements. Environmental economists are very active, for example, in Europe. The control

---

[15]Roy Gregory, *The Price of Amenity: Five Studies in Conservation and Government*, Macmillan, London, 1971, p. 12.

[16]Göran A. Persson, "Sweden," in Edward J. Kormondy (ed.), *International Handbook of Pollution Control*, Greenwood Press, Westport, CT, 1989, pp. 219–232.

[17]Giancarlo Pinchera, Silvia Brini, and Mario Cirillo, "Italy," in *European Environmental Yearbook*, 4th ed., Doc Ter, Institute for Environmental Studies, Milan, 1990, p. 415.

[18]For a good summary, see Organization for Economic Cooperation and Development, "Environmental Taxes in OECD Countries," OECD, Paris, 1995.

EXHIBIT 18-1

POLICY DEVELOPMENTS IN OTHER DEVELOPED COUNTRIES

In the early 1970s, when environmental policies were still in their infancy, economic instruments were used in only a few instances and were subject to much controversy. Since then, a slow, but continuous evolution has taken place. The role of economic instruments has increased on several grounds. First, the number of applications has increased as economic instruments are increasingly used in more (in fact, all) OECD countries. Second, the variety of instruments has also grown: while user charges and subsidies were typically already in use in the 1970s, different types of charges (emission charges) have also become common. Other types of economic instruments (e.g., deposit–refund systems, performance bonds, liability payments) have also appeared. Another typical feature of this evolution is the growing role of environmental taxes and an increasing number of applications of tradable permit schemes.

A significant evolution has been the increasing role of environmental taxes in the context of an integration between tax and environmental policies. In more and more countries, "green tax forms" are implemented or contemplated. Environmental charges are increasingly brought under the fiscal framework. This is specifically true for incentive (i.e., not explicitly revenue raising) charges. For instance, the Netherlands have canceled most charges with financing purposes and/or replaced them by taxes paid into the general government budget. In 1998, France started a progressive transfor-

mation of earmarked charges into fiscal taxes aid to the central government budget.

Whilst market creations (tradable permits, transferable quotas) remain relatively scarce, there are more and more applications. This is a clear trend: on the one hand, long standing tradable permit schemes are reaching a level of maturity (smoother implementation, proven environmental effectiveness and economic efficiency); on the other hand, new experiments are being made in various areas. For instance, the U.S. Emissions Trading Schemes that could be considered as forerunners in this field are being succeeded by new and substantial systems, and more are in preparation. A number of initiatives are also being taken for tradable permit schemes in water quality management, but results are modest so far. Other countries, notably Australia, Canada, and Mexico, continue to operate tradable permit systems. Countries that are considering their introduction for the first time include Denmark, Poland, the Netherlands, Norway and the U.K. Furthermore, the potential use of tradable permits for reducing greenhouse gas emissions is high on the international political agenda.

A clear growth in the field of enforcement incentives can be noted. In the 1994 survey, four countries mentioned non-compliance fees and/or performance bonds. The current survey shows that eight countries mention non-compliance fees, five countries operate performance bonds, and eight liability payments. Such enforcement incentives are

---

of air and water pollution there is complicated by the presence of many international boundaries in a relatively small geographical area. Efforts at harmonizing environmental laws, spearheaded by the European Community, can be helped along by the accumulation of results of benefit-measurement studies. Table 18-3 (page 404) shows just a few of the many studies done in other countries to estimate the benefits of environmental policies.[19]

---

[19]For Ståle Navrud (ed.), *Pricing the European Environment*, Oslo Scandinavian University Press, 1992.

EXHIBIT 18-1

POLICY DEVELOPMENTS IN OTHER DEVELOPED COUNTRIES (CONTINUED)

also explicitly mentioned by the new Member countries of the Czech Republic and Poland.

The application of deposit–refund systems has not shown much development in recent years, but still plays a significant role. Many of the systems mentioned were already in place in 1994. Few new products have been brought under deposit systems. Car batteries are one exception. These systems are still quite successful, but the issue of the cost of operating these systems should be addressed.

Many countries report the existence of subsidy schemes of various types: grants, soft loans, accelerated depreciation. A comparison with the 1994 survey is not possible, but it is clear that subsidies still play an important role among economic measures.

The new OECD Member Countries are applying economic instruments to a significant level. The Czech Republic and Poland appear to have full-grown charges-cum-subsidy schemes which play a structural part in bringing environment investments to substantially higher levels (in particular in the context of environmental funds). The number of pollutants addressed in the charge schemes is also larger than found on average in the OECD. Hungary is operating many environmentally-related taxes. Korea and Mexico also apply a range of economic instruments.

It is clear that extensive use is made of economic instruments in natural resources management. Almost all of the countries that

replied to the questionnaire reported the use of one or more economic instruments for natural resource management. Many countries levy water abstraction charges or taxes. A distinctive feature is the use of transferable fishing quotas in five countries. For the management of forestry, two types of economic instruments are generally used: charges and taxes (e.g., stumpage fees) and subsidies (for protection and reforestation). Relatively few economic instruments are used for wetlands protection, while a variety of subsidies are designed for the protection of soil, landscape, etc., sometimes in the context of agri-environmental measures. Wildlife protection is primarily achieved through hunting and fishing fees, subsidies for the protection of biodiversity, and entrance fees for natural parks. The removal of adverse subsidies has also been used for natural resource management.

There is still a lack of evaluation on the environmental effectiveness of economic instruments, as well as their static and dynamic efficiency. However, more information is now available than in the 1994 survey. Effectiveness is rated positively in general, although the substance of this information is meager. Many statements apply to—sometimes remote—proxies for environmental effectiveness, rather than effectiveness itself.

Source: "OECD Economic Instruments for Pollution Control and Natural Resource Management in OECD Countries: A Survey," OECD, Paris, October 1999, pp. 97–99.

ENVIRONMENTAL POLICY IN EX-SOCIALIST COUNTRIES

It may be tempting to think that socialist economic systems would have been better than market economies in managing environmental quality issues because they involved pervasive central direction over all economic decisions. Administrative agencies, apparently with control over all the important variables, could make sure that all "externalities" were properly accounted for in production planning, and plant managers would be directed to pursue courses of action that ensured efficient levels of emissions and ambient environmental quality.

TABLE 18-3

EXAMPLES OF BENEFIT ESTIMATION STUDIES CARRIED OUT BY ENVIRONMENTAL
ECONOMISTS IN OTHER COUNTRIES

Country and study	Results
Australia[a] Contingent valuation (CV) study to measure willingness of people to pay (WTP) to develop biological means of fly control	$13.40/person/yr
Finland[b] WTP for grouse hunting, as a function of the grouse population (CV method)	
Grouse population at current level	604 FIM/person/yr
Grouse population half of current level	462 FIM/person/yr
Grouse population two times current level	786 FIM/person/yr
France[c] WTP to maintain more nearly constant water level in a flood control reservoir to benefit recreationists (CV method)	47 FF/person/yr
Germany[d] WTP to have an improvement in air quality (CV method)	75–190 DM/person/month
Israel[e] WTP for a 50 percent reduction in air pollution in Haifa	
Indirect means (hedonic)	$66.2/household/yr
Direct means (CV)	$25.1/household/yr
Netherlands[f] WTP to prevent further deterioration of the Dutch forests and heath (CV method)	22.83 DFL/person/month
Norway[g] WTP for improved water quality in the inner Oslo fjord (CV method)	
Users	942 NOK/household/yr
Nonusers	522 NOK/household/yr
Sweden[h] WTP for a reduction in the risk of getting lung cancer from radon exposure (CV method)	4300 SEK/household
United Kingdom[i] WTP for an improvement in river water quality (CV method)	£12.08/person/year

[a]B. Johnston, "External Benefits in Rural Research and the Question of Who Should Pay," Presented to 26th Annual Conference of the Australian Agricultural Economic Society, February 9–11, 1982, University of Melbourne.

[b]V. Owaskainen, H. Savolainen, and T. Sievanen, "The Benefits of Managing Forests for Grouse Habitat: A Contingent Valuation Experiment," Paper presented at Biennien Meeting of the Scandinavian Society of Forest Economics, April 10–13, 1991, Gausdal, Norway.

[c]B. Desaigues, and V. Lesgards, *La Valorisation des Actifs Naturels un Example d'Application de la Method d'Evaluation Contingente*, Université de Bordeaux, working paper, 1991.

[d]K. Holm-Müller, H. Hansen, M. Klockman, and P. Luther, "Die Nachfrage nach Umweltqualität in der Bundesrepublik Deutschland" (The Demand for Environmental Quality in the Federal Republic of Germany), *Berichte des Umweltbundesamtes* 4/91, Erich Schmidt Verlag, Berlin, 1991, p. 346.

[e]M. Shechter, and M. Kim, "Valuation of Pollution Abatement Benefits: Direct and Indirect Measurement," *Journal of Urban Economics*, Vol. 30, 1991, pp. 133–151.

[f]J. W. van der Linden, and F. H. Oosterhuis, *De maatschappelijke waardering voor de vitaliteit van bos en heide* (The Social Valuation of the Vitality of Forests and Heath), in Dutch, English summary, Publication by the Ministry of Public Housing, Physical Planning and Environmental Management, VROM 80115/3, Leidschendam, 1987, p. 46.

[g]A. Heiberg, and K.-G. Him, "Use of Formal Methods in Evaluating Countermeasures of Coastal Water Pollution," In H. M. Seip and A Heiberg (eds.), *Risk Management of Chemicals in the Environment*, Plenum Press, London, 1989.

[h]J. Aakerman, *Economic Valuation of Risk Reduction: The Case of In-door Radiation*, Stockholm School of Economics, Stockholm, Sweden, 1988, p. 65.

[i]C. H. Green, and S. Tunstall, "The Evaluation of River Water Quality Improvements by the Contingent Valuation Method," *Applied Economics*, 1991, p. 23.

It did not work out this way, however. Not only did centrally planned economies fail miserably in environmental matters, but their failures even in basic economic planning and administration have led their citizens to move toward market systems. With the opening up of the former Soviet Union and the countries of Central and Eastern Europe, it has become apparent that the state systems have produced extreme environmental damages in many regions. Large environmental assets have been seriously degraded, and in many places ambient air and water quality have deteriorated sufficiently to have severe repercussions on human health.

There are several reasons for this. With the merging of political and economic power and the **priorities** by political leaders on rapid economic growth, the effects of the growth on the environment were frequently simply overlooked.[20] In addition, the systems of economic administration established by a large state-run bureaucracy offered **perverse incentives** to local plant managers, not only on environmental matters but also with regard to basic economic decisions.[21] A third factor is that, because of the closed nature of the political systems of these countries, **public information** on environmental matters was severely lacking. Communist regimes were reluctant to collect, tabulate, and publish data on the state of environmental problems in their countries. Thus, it was impossible for groups to monitor environmental damages and "lobby" for change.[22] Instead, environmental issues were "buried under mountains of paper and streams of declarations and statements."[23]

Another tendency in socialist regimes was what might be called the **grandiose project syndrome.** Authorities, in an effort to "jump start" economic growth, often undertook huge development projects, while overlooking potentially serious environmental side effects. Exhibit 18-2 recounts a particularly egregious case, the destruction of the Aral Sea in the former Soviet Union by a scheme to produce irrigated cotton.

This discussion should not be taken to imply that nothing was ever done in socialist countries to protect the environment. It would be just as false to give the impression that market economies always automatically adjust to give the efficient levels of ambient environmental quality. Any economic system, if it is intent on putting its entire emphasis on material development, will downplay the impacts of this on the natural environment.

The ex-socialist countries of Central and Southern Europe and the former Soviet Union are trying to pull themselves out of a vast economic hole dug for them by many decades of socialism. They must try to achieve improvements in environmental quality even as they try fundamentally to reshape their economic systems and establish more progressive economic institutions. To achieve more

[20]Ann-Marie Satre Ahlander, *Environmental Problems in the Shortage Economy, The Legacy of Soviet Economic Policy*, Edward Elgar, London, 1994.

[21]Barbara Jancar, *Environmental Management in the Soviet Union and Yugoslavia*, Duke University Press, Durham, NC, 1987.

[22]Cynthia B. Schultz, and Tamara Raye Crockett, "Economic Development, Democratization, and Environmental Protection in Eastern Europe," *Environmental Affairs*, 18(1), Fall 1990, pp. 53–84.

[23]Ibid., p. 63.

EXHIBIT 18-2

THE ARAL SEA: LESSONS FROM AN ECOLOGICAL DISASTER

The Aral Sea is dying. Because of the huge diversions of water that have taken place during the past thirty years, particularly for irrigation, the volume of the sea has been reduced by two-thirds. The sea's surface has been sharply diminished, the water in the sea and in surrounding aquifers has become increasingly saline, and the water supplies and health of almost 50 million people in the Aral Sea basin are threatened. Vast areas of salty flatlands have been exposed as the sea has receded, and salt from these areas is being blown across the plains onto neighboring cropland and pastures, causing ecological damage. The frost-free period in the delta of the Amu Darya River, which feeds the Aral Sea, has fallen to less than 180 days—below the minimum required for growing cotton, the region's main cash crop. The changes in the sea have effectively killed a substantial fishing industry, and the variety of fauna in the region has declined drastically. If current trends continued unchecked, the sea would eventually shrink to a saline lake one-sixth of its 1960 size.

This ecological disaster is the consequence of excessive abstraction of water for irrigation purposes from the Amu Darya and Syr Darya rivers, which feed the Aral Sea. Total river runoff into the sea fell from an average 55 cubic kilometers a year in the 1950s to zero in the early 1980s. The irrigation schemes have been a mixed blessing for the populations of the Central Asian republics—Kazakhstan, Kyrghyzstan, Tajikistan, Turkmenistan, and Uzbekistan—which they serve. The diversion of water has provided livelihoods for the region's farmers, but at considerable environmental cost. Soils have been poisoned with salt, overwatering has turned pastureland into bogs, water supplies have become polluted by

pesticide and fertilizer residues, and the deteriorating quality of drinking water and sanitation is taking a heavy toll on human health. While it is easy to see how the problem of the Aral Sea might have been avoided, solutions are difficult. A combination of better technical management and appropriate incentives is clearly essential: charging for water or allocating it to the most valuable uses could prompt shifts in cropping patterns and make more water available to industry and households.

But the changes needed are vast, and there is little room for maneuver. The Central Asian republics (excluding Kazakhstan) are poor: their incomes are 65 percent of the average in the former U.S.S.R. In the past, transfers from the central government exceeded 20 percent of national income in Kyrghyzstan and Tajikistan and 12 percent in Uzbekistan. These transfers are no longer available. The regional population of 35 million is growing rapidly, at 2.7 percent a year, and infant mortality is high. The states have become dependent on a specialized but unsustainable pattern of agriculture. Irrigated production of cotton, grapes, fruit, and vegetables accounts for the bulk of export earnings. Any rapid reduction in the use of irrigation water will reduce living standards still further unless these economies receive assistance to help them diversify away from irrigated agriculture. Meanwhile, salinization and dust storms erode the existing land under irrigation. This is one of the starkest examples of the need to combine development with sound environmental policy.

Source: World Bank, *World Development Report 1992, Development and the Environment,* Washington, DC, 1992, p. 38. Reprinted by permission.

---

effective environmental protection while reviving their stagnated economies will be a difficult balancing act.

The most effective strategies for these countries appear to be

1 To attack cases of large-scale pollution and damage in the short run through straightforward command-and-control (C&C) type intervention and controls.

2 To clarify, in the slightly longer run, the current and likely future situation with respect to where major sources of emissions and damages will likely occur as economic redevelopment plans are put into effect.
3 To begin to establish regulating institutions and environmental policies, which, in the long run, are capable of giving them cost-effective and efficient pollution-control measures.

DEVELOPMENTS IN ENVIRONMENTAL ACCOUNTING

A number of countries have begun to take steps to augment their national income accounts to take into account the effects of economic growth on natural resource and environmental assets. **National income accounting** was developed by governments who felt the need for a way of knowing how the overall economy was doing from year to year. Familiar measures such as gross domestic product, net domestic product, and the rate of unemployment are meant to give us a summary of the total amount of economic activity in a year's time and of the status of certain aggregate variables that affect overall economic welfare. Conventional national income accounting has been criticized because it does not adequately deal with the resource and environmental implications of economic growth. Consider the standard production possibilities curve in Figure 18-2, showing marketed economic output on the vertical axis and environmental quality on the horizontal axis. Aggregate economic activity as reported in the conventional accounts consists only of measured marketed output. Thus, for example, a move from m_1 to m_2 would be regarded as an improvement in

FIGURE 18-2
National Income Accounting and the Neglect of Environmental Quality.

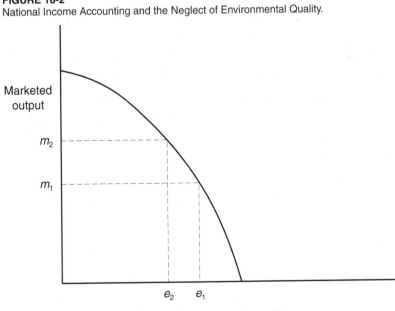

economic welfare. But this improvement has been accompanied by a reduction in environmental quality from e_1 to e_2. To get a complete picture of changes in social welfare we need to take into account both the increase in marketed output and the reduction in environmental quality.

Researchers and public authorities in different countries are approaching this problem in several ways. The basic question is how to measure and treat the "quantity" $e_1 - e_2$ in Figure 18-2. A number of countries, the United States included, have sought simply to measure annual total costs of pollution-control expenditures. The next logical step is perhaps to deduct these costs from measured output, on the grounds that they do not represent a true increase in economic welfare but expenditures necessary to protect ourselves from pollution. This procedure has been undertaken in France and Japan.

But the method of deducting pollution-control expenditures does not get directly at measuring the values of environmental quality change as represented by the distance $e_1 - e_2$ in the figure. The first step in doing this is to measure the *physical* quantities of environmental resources and changes in these quantities over time. Attempts to measure physical changes in the total resource endowments of a nation are being undertaken in several countries, notably France and Norway. The French are trying to develop a complete environmental accounting system: Les Comptes du Patrimoine Natural (natural endowment accounts), which can be used to measure physical changes in natural and environmental resources resulting from economic production and consumption. Exhibit 18-3 shows some results of a study of this type by economists at the World Bank.

To put the quantity $e_1 - e_2$ in value terms, however, requires taking the next step: to place values on the physical changes in environmental resources. Major work on this is being done in the Netherlands. The objective is to put monetary values on the various dimensions of environmental degradation, including the reduced value of resources and the damages from pollution. A valuation approach like this also is being undertaken by the United Nations.

We are just at the beginning of efforts to incorporate environmental values into national income accounts. The conceptual and measurement problems are very difficult, and it will be some time before acceptable procedures can be developed and believable numbers estimated. But if it is successful, this work could have a profound impact on public policy decisions.

SUMMARY

In many other industrialized countries, major pollution-control efforts started in the decade of the 1970s, as they did in the United States. Policy in different countries is pursued through means that are congenial to the political culture and institutional history of each one. For the most part, pollution-control efforts have relied on various command-and-control approaches involving standards of various types. In many European countries, emission charges have been widely used, but historically these have been primarily to raise revenues, which then can be used to subsidize pollution-control efforts. In the future,

EXHIBIT 18-3

GREEN ACCOUNTING

If a country, in the course of producing its conventional goods and services, despoils or depletes its natural resource endowment, the normal GDP accounts will give a distorted view of its economic welfare. To account for changes in **natural capital,** it's necessary to put a value on such things as agricultural and ecologically valuable land, forests, and mineral deposits. Then if these natural assets get degraded or used up, their reduced value can be deducted from normal income measures to find true, or sustainable, measures of income and wealth.

Economists at the World Bank are pursuing a major effort to measure the values of natural capital in countries of the world, and especially to compare natural capital and its changes with other forms of capital, including **human capital** and **produced capital.** Some recent results for selected countries are shown in the accompanying tabulation. Note that the major form of wealth in almost all countries is in human capital (the exception is Saudi Arabia). Natural capital, on the other hand, varies from a low of 3 percent of total capital in France to a high of 42 percent in Saudi Arabia.

ESTIMATES OF NATIONAL WEALTH FOR SELECTED COUNTRIES

Country	Total wealth per capita ($1,000)	Percentage distribution of total wealth		
		Human resources	Natural resources	Produced assets
Australia	147	84	7	9
Bangladesh	22	76	14	10
Chile	148	79	10	12
China	37	77	7	6
Egypt	52	64	5	31
France	297	74	3	24
India	20	58	20	22
Mexico	113	77	6	17
Saudi Arabia	171	40	42	18
United States	401	77	4	19

Source: Arundhati Kunte, Kirk Hamilton, John Dixon, and Michael Clemens, "Estimating National Wealth: Methodology and Results," World Bank, Washington, DC, January 1998.

these could perhaps easily be transformed into incentive taxes with a primary pollution-control objective.

Environmental standards may be set at the national level (as in, e.g., Germany, Italy, and the United States) or at the local level (as in France and England). But their *enforcement* tends to be very local, involving "bargaining" between emitters and local officials—not bargaining in the formal sense, but give-and-take between these parties as to what courses of action are to be undertaken by different sources to control emissions.

The large-scale environmental degradation of the ex-socialist countries bears an instructive lesson for pollution control in all countries. The initial reaction to environmental pollution is to think that it comes about because authorities lack the necessary means of control to bring about emission reductions. But in the ex-socialist countries, authorities presumably had total control and environmental damages have still been massive. This points up the importance of having open political systems, readily available information on what the state of the environment really is, and incentive systems that lead polluters to internalize the damages their emissions produce.

QUESTIONS FOR FURTHER DISCUSSION

1   If two (or more) countries are shown to have the same (total) quantity of emissions, does this mean that they are equally close to the efficient level of emissions for each one?

2   Explain the polluter pays principle. How would this apply to the control of non-point-source emissions?

3   Consider the "European" approach to emission charges. For a single source, is it possible that a low emissions charge could produce enough revenues to pay for all of the abatement costs required to reduce this source's emissions to an efficient level? What factors affect this? (Hint: You will want to explore this with the help of our standard emission-control model.)

4   What factors determine whether it would be more effective to proceed against polluters by hammering them in court or by sitting down with them to try to work things out on a "reasonable" basis?

5   Explain what is meant by "greening the national income accounts."

WEBSITES

For a review of the state of the environment in many countries around the world, see the web page of the National Council for Science and the Environment, **www.cnie.org/stateof.htm.** Pace University **www.law.pace.edu/env/fullcomp.html,** has a virtual environmental law library that contains a comparative summary of environmental laws around the world.

SELECTED READINGS

Barde, Jean-Philippe, and David W. Pearce (eds.): *Valuing the Environment, Six Case Studies*, Earthscan Publications, London, 1991.

Bower, Blair T., Rémi Barré, Jochen Kühner, and Clifford S. Russell: *Incentives in Water Quality Management, France and the Ruhr Area*, Resources for the Future, Washington, DC, 1981.

Brown, Gardner M., Jr., and Ralph W. Johnson: "Pollution Control by Effluent Charges: It Works in the Federal Republic of Germany: Why Not in the U.S.?" *Natural Resources Journal*, 24(4), October 1984, pp. 929–966.

Folmer, Henk, and Charles Howe: "Environmental Problems and Policy in the Single European Market," *Environmental and Resource Economics*, 1(1), 1991, pp. 22–45.

Gresser, Julian, Koichiro Fujikura, and Akio Morishima: *Environmental Law in Japan*, MIT Press, Cambridge, MA, 1981.

Hamilton, Kirk, and Ernst Lutz: "Green National Accounts: Policy Uses and Empirical Experience," World Bank, Paper No. 39, Environmental Economics Series, Washington, DC, July 1996.

Huppes, Gjalt, and Robert A. Kagan: "Market-Oriented Regulation of Environmental Problems in the Netherlands," *Law and Policy*, 11(2), April 1989, pp. 215–239.

Johnson, Stanley P., and Guy Corcelle: *The Environmental Policy of the European Community*, Graham and Trotman, London, 1989.

Kormondy, Edward J.: *International Handbook of Pollution Control*, Greenwood Press, Westport, CT, 1989.

Lutz, Ernst (ed.): *Toward Improved Accounting for the Environment*, The World Bank, Washington, DC, 1993.

Milon, J. Walter, and Jason F. Shogren (eds.): *Integrating Economic and Ecological Indicators*, Praeger, Westport, CT, 1995.

Nordhaus, William D., and Edward C. Kokkelenberg (eds.): *Nature's Numbers, Expanding the National Economic Accounts to Include the Environment*, National Academy of Science, National Research Council, National Academy Press, Washington, DC, 1999.

Peskin, Henry M., and Ernst Lutz: "A Survey of Resource and Environmental Accounting in Industrialized Countries," World Bank, Environment Department Working Paper No. 37, Washington, DC, August 1990.

Probst, Katherine N., and Thomas C. Beierle: "The Evolution of Hazardous Waste Programs: Lessons from Eight Countries," Resources for the Future, Washington, DC, 1999.

Russell, Clifford S.: "Monitoring and Enforcement of Pollution Control Laws in Europe and the United States," in Rüdiger Pethig (ed.), *Conflicts and Cooperation in Managing Environmental Resources*, Springer-Verlag, Berlin, 1992, pp. 195–213.

Wilczynski, Piotr: *Environmental Management in Centrally-Planned Non-Market Economies of Eastern Europe*, Environment Working Paper No. 35, World Bank, Washington, DC, July 1990.

Willis, K. G. (ed.): *Environmental Valuation: New Perspectives*, University of Arizona Press, Tucson, AZ, 1995.

CHAPTER 19

ECONOMIC DEVELOPMENT AND THE ENVIRONMENT

There was a time, several decades ago, when problems of environmental qual-ity were widely regarded as being unique to developed, industrial economies. Industrial development was associated with air and water pollution, overre-liance on chemicals, visual blight, and so on. Developing countries, however, were thought to have fewer environmental problems because their preindus-trial technology was more environmentally benign, and because they had not yet committed themselves to a materialistic style of life, with the negative trade-offs many believe that this implies.

Ideas have changed, however. For one thing, it has become clear that mas-sive environmental degradation in fact has occurred in the developing world. Rural areas have seen large-scale soil erosion and water-quality deterioration, deforestation, and declining soil productivity. Urban areas have experienced seriously diminished air and water quality. Furthermore, this environmental deterioration in developing countries is not just a matter of aesthetics or quality of life, but rather a more serious issue involving the diminishment of economic productivity and the acceleration of social dislocation. Environmental prob-lems in developing countries are much more likely to be matters of life and death than they are in the developed world.

In this chapter we explore the interrelationship of economic development and the environment among the nonindustrialized countries of the world. In keeping with the distinction made in Chapter 2, we approach it on two levels: the positive and the normative. From the positive standpoint, the problem is to understand how development and environmental degradation are reciprocally related and what factors account for this interrelationship. From a normative standpoint, the problem is to deal with questions about the types of public poli-cies that are best under these circumstances.

GENERAL CONSIDERATIONS

It is common to distinguish between **economic growth** and **economic develop-ment**. There is a simple, as well as a more complicated, way of distinguishing between these concepts. In simple terms, growth refers to increases in the **aggre-gate level of output,** whereas development means increases in **per-capita out-put.** Thus, a country could grow, but not develop, if its population growth exceeded its rate of economic growth. The more complicated way is to say that economic growth refers to increases in economic activity without any underlying change in the fundamental economic structure and institutions of a country, while development also includes a wider set of technological, institutional, and social transformations. Changes in such things as education, health, population, transportation infrastructure, and legal institutions are all part of the develop-ment process. This should alert us to the fact that when talking about environ-mental issues in developing countries, we will usually be talking about situations where the social and technological milieu can be very different from that in industrialized countries. At the same time it implies that in environmental policy matters, a wider set of choices may be available because of the more thoroughgo-ing institutional transformations taking place in many developing countries.

In speaking of these issues, there is the tendency to divide the world into just two parts: developed and developing, or **"first" world** and **"third" world.**[1] Of course, any brief classification such as this is an enormous oversimplification of the real world. At the very least we should think not of a simple categorization such as this but of a continuum, running from the poorest to the richest, or along any other dimension of interest. The countries of the world are spread along that continuum, although not necessarily evenly. It's also true that **national aggregates** can tend to obscure some important development prob-lems *within* particular countries. Many countries that look reasonably good on the basis of national macrodata have pockets of poverty and underdevelop-ment that would be sufficient to put these regions in the less developed ranks if national political boundaries were drawn differently.

ENVIRONMENTAL DEGRADATION
IN DEVELOPING ECONOMIES

Many people in the developed world have been brought to a realization of the existence of environmental problems in the developing world through recent global concerns, such as global warming and the rapid pace of species extinc-tion. A disproportionately high number of the world's endangered species are residents of developing countries, so efforts to preserve the habitats of these species have brought people to focus on the development–environment link-ages in nonindustrialized countries. Similarly, the developed world's concern about global warming has heightened concern about deforestation because

---

[1]In the argot of international political economics, the "first" world is used to refer to the devel-oped industrial market economies, whereas the "third" world refers to the group of developing economies. The "second" world referred at one time to the socialist economies.

forests act to absorb atmospheric CO_2. In many developing countries the harvesting of fuel wood and timber and the conversion of forested lands to agricultural uses have led to high rates of deforestation. Thus, large-scale deforestation has the potential to worsen the global greenhouse effect.

But from the standpoint of the developing countries themselves, their worst environmental problems are probably the water and air pollution they suffer, especially in their expanding urban areas. In the developed world, the chemical treatment of water supplies, together with the treatment of wastewater, has largely neutralized the water system as a source of widespread human disease; continued water pollution control is justified on recreational and aesthetic grounds. This is not the case in many developing countries where water pollution is still responsible for vast amounts of disease and death. Lack of treatment facilities leads to widespread exposure to disease-bearing human wastes. In places where there has been an expansion of industry, mining, and the use of agricultural chemicals, rivers have become contaminated with toxic chemicals and with heavy metals. Seepage of hazardous materials from industrial sites and waste dumps is increasingly threatening the groundwater resources toward which many countries are turning as surface waters become more heavily contaminated.

In a review of studies by the U.S. Agency for International Development (USAID) and the World Health Organization (WHO), the World Bank concluded that providing access to safer water and adequate sanitation to those who currently lack it would have the following effects:

- 2 million fewer deaths from diarrhea each year among children under five years of age.
- 200 million fewer episodes of diarrheal illness annually.
- 300 million fewer people with roundworm infection.
- 150 million fewer people with schistosomiasis.
- 2 million fewer people infected with guinea worm.[2]

Air pollution is also a significant problem in developing countries. Data from the United Nations Global Environment Monitoring System (GEMS) indicate that in the mid-1980s about 1.3 billion people around the world were exposed to levels of particulate matter that exceeded WHO standards; most of these were in developing countries. In many countries gasoline is still virtually all leaded, leading to serious damages from airborne lead pollution. Indoor air pollution is also a more serious problem than in developed countries, owing to the continued heavy reliance on biomass fuels for cooking and heating.

ECONOMY AND ENVIRONMENT

Whereas the concern about environmental problems has been of more recent origin, issues related to economic growth in the less-developed world have been uppermost for many years; indeed, historically they have been a defining

---

[2]World Bank, *World Development Report 1992, Development and the Environment*, Oxford University Press for the World Bank, New York, 1992, p. 49.

focus of this group of countries. This emphasis on economic development will continue as they strive to close the economic gap with the developed economies. What needs to be examined, therefore, is the relationship between economic development and environmental quality.

A Static View

Probably the most frequently mentioned viewpoint on these matters is that developing countries simply cannot afford high levels of environmental quality. According to this view, the situation of these countries, in comparison to developed economies, can be pictured by the production possibilities curves (PPCs) of Figure 19-1. **Marketed output** refers to the conventional types of goods and services produced and distributed through economic markets. The PPC labeled A is for a typical developed country, while B refers to a developing nation. Because of past resource exploitation, or population pressures, or less sophisticated technology, B lies entirely within A. Thus, to achieve higher levels of marketed income, which it must if it is to develop, it must be willing to put up with lower levels of environmental quality. For example, for the developing country to reach a level of marketed output of c_1, it must **trade off** environmental quality back to the level e_2. The developed country, because of the factors mentioned previously, can have c_1 of marketed output with a much higher level of environmental quality—e_1 instead of only e_2. As one economist put it:

> . . . the poorer countries of the world confront tragic choices. They cannot afford drinking water standards as high as those the industrial countries are accustomed to. They cannot afford to close their pristine areas to polluting industries that would

FIGURE 19-1
Production Possibilities Curves of Developed and Developing Countries.

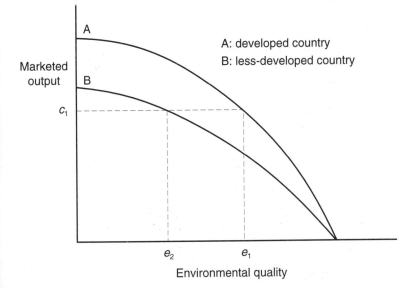

A: developed country
B: less-developed country

Marketed output

Environmental quality

introduce technical know how and productive capital and that would earn urgently needed foreign exchange. They cannot afford to bar mining companies from their unexploited regions. Nor can they afford to impose antipollution requirements on these companies that are as strict and expensive as those in richer industrial countries. They should always realize that environmental protection measures are financed out of the stomachs of their own people; the multinationals cannot be made to pay for them.[3]

Developing countries, according to this view, cannot afford the high levels of environmental quality sought in the developed world because this would mean lower monetary incomes and a lessened capacity to support their populations.

There is another side to this argument, however. The production possibilities curve approach sees marketed output and environmental quality as **substitutes;** more effort devoted to reducing environmental impacts leading to lower monetary incomes. But in the developing world there are clear cases where environmental quality and measured GDP are **complementary.** Most developing countries depend proportionately more on primary industries than do developed ones. For example, they usually have a greater proportion of their population involved in agriculture. Thus, degradation of environmental resources has the potential for being more highly destructive of productive assets in developing countries. In industrial countries, environmental quality issues hinge primarily on matters of human health and the aesthetic quality of the environment. Furthermore, technological developments have **decoupled,** to a considerable extent, the resource-using sector from the rest of the economy. In developing countries, however, environmental issues are related to human health and productivity and also to the degradation of the future productivity of the natural resource base on which many people are and will be directly dependent. According to this argument, the environment and the economy are not so much substitutes as they are complements.

Sustainability

But these are essentially static arguments, and the essence of economic development is long-run change. So the relevant question is: How is long-run economic development likely to affect environmental quality? The normal expectation is that development would shift the production possibility curve of Figure 19-1 outward. As economies change, becoming less tied to natural resources, and as less polluting technologies are adopted, this outward shift would improve the potential trade-offs between marketed output and environmental quality. Developing countries could then devote more resources to improving environmental quality.

Sometimes the opposite has happened, however; the short-run effort to increase or maintain marketed incomes, in effect, tended to shift the PPC curve to the left and worsen the available choices. This has occurred when the search

---

[3]Robert Dorfman, "An Economist's View of Natural Resources and Environmental Problems," in Robert Repetto (ed.), *The Global Possible,* Yale University Press, New Haven, CT, 1985, pp. 67–76.

for short-run economic growth has led to **irreversible** reductions in the productivity of some part of a country's environmental assets. Here we are defining "environmental assets" very broadly, to include such things as soil fertility and forestry resources along with urban air and water pollution. The concept that has become widely used to talk of this phenomenon is **sustainability.** A practice is sustainable if it does not reduce the long-run productivity of the natural resource assets on which a country's income and development depend.[4]

Sustainability is fundamentally a matter of **renewable** resources. When **non-renewable** resources are used, they automatically become unavailable to future generations. The rule to follow here is to use them at the correct rate—neither too fast nor too slow—and to see to it that the natural wealth that they represent is converted into long-lived human-made wealth as they are used. Thus, for example, the petroleum resources of many developing countries must be converted to long-term productive capital, both private and public, if they are to contribute to the long-run economic development of the extracting country. By productive capital we mean not only physical capital (roads, factories, etc.), but also human capital (education, skills) and what we might call "institutional capital" (an efficient legal system, effective public agencies, etc.).

Long-Run Relationships

In the latter part of the 1990s, many developing countries experienced substantial growth slowdowns. As of the beginning of the next decade, however, most countries have recovered and the prospects are good for future growth rates of 4–6 percent a year. With long-run growth rates of this type, what impacts can be expected on environmental quality in these countries? If all technological factors were to stay the same over this period, environmental impacts and damages would increase along with this economic growth. But these factors are unlikely to remain constant. Economic development brings with it many changes. The most obvious is an increase in per-capita incomes, and, as people's income goes up, so does their willingness to sacrifice for improved environmental quality. Developing economies usually also experience a variety of structural changes, often in the direction of replacing relatively high-polluting industries with those that pollute less.

Studies have been done to investigate the relationship between various environmental quality indices and the income levels attained in different countries. The objective is to see if, as income levels change, there are systematic changes also in environmental quality variables. Several of the leading results are shown in Figure 19-2. These are based on "cross-section" analyses of income levels and environmental quality. This involves looking at the environmental characteristics of a large number of countries, with widely varying income

---

[4]The concept of "sustainability" received its major impetus in the influential report put out by the World Commission on Environment and Development: *Our Common Future*, Oxford University Press, Oxford, England, 1987. This report is popularly called "The Brundtland Report" because the Commission, created by the United Nations in 1983, was headed by Mrs. Gro Harlem Brundtland, prime minister of Norway.

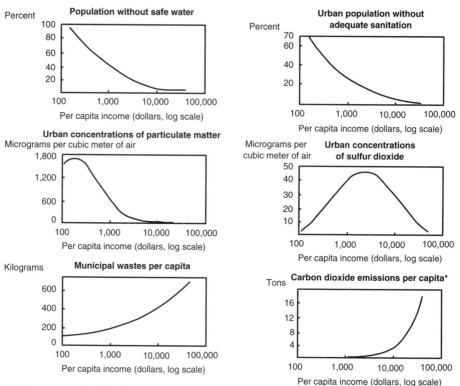

*Emissions are from fossil fuels.

Note: Estimates are based on cross-country analysis of data from the 1980s.

FIGURE 19-2
Environmental Indicators in Relation to Country Income Levels. (*Sources: World Bank,* World Development Report 1992, Development and the Environment, *Oxford University Press for the World Bank, New York, 1992, p. 11, based on a paper by Nemat Shafik and Sushenjit Bandyopadhyay, "Economic Growth and Environmental Quality: Time Series and Cross-Section Evidence"; Gene Grossman and Alan B. Kreuger, "Environmental Impacts of a North American Free Trade Agreement," Discussion Paper No. 158, Woodrow Wilson School, Princeton University, 1991.)*

levels, and then using statistical methods to discover the underlying relationships, if indeed there are any. In fact, studies show clear relationships between income levels and a variety of environmental quality indices. In Figure 19-2, note that there are essentially three types of relationships:

1 Those showing steady declines as incomes increase: This applies to access to safe water and sanitation facilities, which countries can presumably more easily afford as incomes rise, but which also are normal goods in the sense that as incomes increase people are willing to pay larger amounts for them.

2 Those that first increase but then decrease with income: This applies to ambient amounts of particulates and SO_2. This pattern is probably due to the fact that in its early stages industrial development leads to greater air pollution, whereas with continued development there is a shift in indus-

try type toward cleaner industries, as well as a rising public demand in more well-to-do countries for pollution control.

3 Those showing a steady increase with income gains: This applies to municipal solid wastes and CO_2 emissions per capita. The first is a reflection of the growth in material standards of living as incomes increase, whereas the second results from the increasing demand for fossil-based energy that normally accompanies development.

These relationships as pictured are not inevitable. They can be taken as general tendencies, which may be different in particular countries, depending on **technology choices** adopted as well as the **preferences of their citizens.** It points out that for many environmental problems the situation is likely to get better as development occurs; indeed, economic development may be seen as a way of combating these problems, which is why continued efforts need to be directed at encouraging equitable growth and open political processes in the developing world.

THE POLLUTION-HAVEN HYPOTHESIS

In recent years much has been made of the idea that developing countries may be acting as "pollution havens," places where firms can move and operate without the strict environmental controls of the developed countries. The idea essentially has two parts:

- That stringent environmental standards in industrialized countries are causing some firms, especially "pollution-intensive" ones, to flee to countries with less stringent standards.
- That some developing countries have tried, with some success, to attract pollution-intensive firms with the promise of lower pollution-control standards, in the hopes of bolstering their rates of economic growth.

Sometimes these ideas are wrapped into the issue of the **"multinationals";** that is, firms owned in one country but operating establishments in others.

It is surprisingly difficult to get conclusive data on this matter. Most opinions are formed on the basis of anecdotal, or episodic, events like the Bhopal disaster in India. But these are not good sources from which to draw conclusions about general trends. Nor is it possible to approach this question by looking at different environmental regulations in the various countries. Almost all countries, developing and developed, have regulations on the books that appear to place emissions under reasonably strict controls, but that are not usually followed in practice because of weak enforcement. Thus, to prove the pollution-haven hypothesis, it apparently would be necessary to look at data on the emissions performance of firms, or groups of firms, before and after they have moved from developed to developing countries. But data of this kind do not exist.

In a wider context, however, we should look at the rise and decline of **polluting sectors** in countries of the developing world. Some companies in fact do relocate, but much the more relevant economic phenomenon is the expansion and contraction of economic sectors as economies develop and change. Certain

---

EXHIBIT 19-1

EVIDENCE ON THE "POLLUTION HAVEN" HYPOTHESIS

Concern about pollution havens began in the early 1970s, when developed countries rapidly tightened pollution controls and most developing countries had not yet begun formal regulation. Business investment in pollution controls skyrocketed in Japan during that time, and companies in North America and Western Europe made similar investments. If such costs gave an edge to polluting industries in developing countries, the effect should have appeared in international trade patterns: Developing countries' exports of the products of dirty industries should have risen faster than their imports, lowering their import/export ratios for these products. The converse should have been true for developed countries.

[Data show] that the shadow of pollution havens did emerge in five particularly polluting sectors: iron and steel, nonferrous metals, industrial chemicals, pulp and paper, and nonmetallic mineral products. After the early 1970s, Japan's import/export ratio in these industries rose rapidly, while the ratio declined steeply in the newly industrialized economies (NIEs) of the Republic of Korea, Taiwan (China), Singapore, and Hong Kong (China). And the same pattern occurred in mainland China and the other developing countries of East Asia a decade later. However, in each region the pollution haven story was markedly short. Both sets of Asian economies have stabilized their import/export ratios at levels greater than one, and remain net importers of pollution-intensive products from industrial countries.

The story in the Western Hemisphere is similar. In North America, the United States and Canada witnessed a steady climb in import/export ratios for polluting industries from the beginning of the environmental era to the late 1980s, while Latin America experienced the opposite after 1973. However, as in developing Asia, the Latin American ratio leveled off near one by the 1990s.

Why didn't polluting industries continue to shift to developing countries? Economic growth—accompanied by more regulation—provides the best answer. Along with greater prosperity in the newly industrialized countries came increased demands for environmental quality and better institutional capacity to regulate. The same process occurred in the Asian developing countries after a decade's delay. Faced with rising costs from environmental damage, they stabilized the terms of trade through measures to control their own pollution.

Source: David Wheeler, *Greening Industry: New Roles for Communities, Markets, and Governments,* Oxford University Press for the World Bank, New York, 2000, pp. 18–21.

---

basic manufacturing industries (e.g., steel, industrial chemicals) that are "dirty," in the sense that they tend to have relatively high emissions per unit of output, often will expand early in a country's development and decline later as incomes increase. Furthermore, one of the strongest relationships that researchers have found is that as incomes in a country increase, the strictness of environmental regulations increases.[5] Thus, the emissions performance of developing countries is affected much more by their own economic development and public policy factors than by the fact that dirty firms in developed countries are trying to take advantage of weak environmental regulations. See Exhibit 19-1.

---

[5]See Sumitsu Dasgupta, Ashoka Mody, Subhenda Roy, and David Wheeler, "Environmental Regulation and Development: A Cross-Country Empirical Analysis," World Bank, Policy Research Department, Working Paper No. 1448, Washington, DC, April 1995.

ENVIRONMENTAL POLICY CHOICES
IN DEVELOPING COUNTRIES

Although it may be true that development can help to alleviate some environmental problems, there is nothing automatic about this; appropriate public policies are still called for. This is especially true for those factors, like CO_2 emissions and solid waste, that get worse with development. Most discussions of the strengths and weaknesses of alternative policies have been directed toward developed countries. There is an important question about how much the lessons learned in this context apply also to developing countries. Although the environmental problems are in principle the same, involving externalities, common-property resources, public goods, and so on, the sociopolitical situations are markedly different from those in most developed countries.

Benefit–Cost Analysis

The basis of effective policy is in the analysis of the benefits and costs of different courses of action. Much more than in developed countries, damages in developing countries affect economic productivity through impacts on human health, soil fertility, resource depletion, and the like. Thus, there is a critical need for estimates of environmental damages in developing countries. A number of international agencies have sponsored a series of **"country environmental studies"** (CESs) in various developing countries. These have been aimed primarily at taking inventories of the physical dimensions of environmental problems. They have not dealt with policy issues to any great extent, nor have they gotten to the point of trying to value the damages caused by environmental deterioration.[6] Studies of this type would be especially important to pursue in those countries because they would show more clearly the extent of pollution-related damages and provide support for more active public policies.

There are several important issues regarding the use of standard techniques of **benefit–cost** analysis in developing countries. One is the emphasis on willingness to pay as a measure of the benefits of pollution reduction. Willingness to pay reflects not only tastes and preferences, but also ability to pay. In many developing economies, poverty is widespread, so a standard **willingness-to-pay** approach to valuing environmental damages may yield only modest estimates of these damages. In the face of enormous poverty, willingness-to-pay estimates may be quite small despite what look to be high rates of environmental degradation. Thus, if willingness-to-pay approaches are used, they must be used with frank recognition that the **distribution of income** is heavily skewed, and value judgments are called for in making decisions on environmental quality programs. This argues also for putting more emphasis on **lost productivity,** particularly in the **long run,** in assessing the damages of environmental degradation.

---

[6]Walter Arensberg, "Country Environmental Studies, A Framework for Action," in Denizhan Eröcal (ed.), *Environmental Management in Developing Countries,* Organization for Economic Cooperation and Development, Paris, 1991, pp. 279–295.

Another special difficulty in applying benefit–cost analysis of environmental programs to developing countries is **discounting**. In developed economies, discounting is a relatively benign procedure that helps make choices among programs with different time profiles of benefits and costs. But in developing countries the focus is more on long-run development, and here the role of discounting is less clear. It's often asserted that people in developing countries, especially those with lower incomes, discount the future very highly, preferring to emphasize actions that will pay off in the short run because of their immediate need for income. Thus, environmental improvement programs, if they deliver the bulk of their benefits only in the long run, may take lower priority than economic development projects that pay off more quickly. High rates of discount also can lead people to overlook negative environmental impacts that occur far off into the future. The present value of even severe long-run environmental damage can be quite low when it is evaluated with a positive discount rate.[7] For some people these arguments imply using a very low, perhaps even zero, discount rate in evaluating environmental and developmental projects in developing countries. But this would make it impossible to coordinate public policies and development projects with decisions being made in the private sector and would treat a dollar of net benefits 10 years from now as equivalent to a dollar of net benefits today. It is perhaps better to utilize a normal discount rate in evaluating programs, but to augment the typical benefit–cost study in developing countries with an analysis of the impacts of the program on long-run **sustainability**.[8]

Reducing Environmental Disincentives of Current Policies

Environmental policy is usually regarded as requiring activist intervention to remedy the problems of uncontrolled externalities, the undersupply of public environmental goods, and so on. But many times environmental improvements can be had by **altering current policies** that have negative environmental impacts. In many cases these policies have been put in place in the belief that they will spur economic growth. But their impact is to create **distortions** in local economies that lead both to lower growth rates and to environmental degradation.

A good example of this is the practice many governments have of subsidizing pesticide use by farmers. In many cases these subsidies were undertaken in the belief that they would spur farmers to adopt new crop varieties and intensive methods of cultivation. But the subsidies often continue well after their usefulness in this regard has ceased. Table 19-1 shows the estimated annual rate

---

[7]We are not talking here about unpredictable consequences; rather, those that are predictable but far into the future. When CFCs were introduced as refrigerants in the early 20th century, nobody predicted the impacts they would have on the global atmosphere. Likewise, nobody foresaw the negative effects of DDT. At the time these substances were introduced, science was not well enough advanced to have predicted these outcomes. There is a difference, however, between consequences that are not predictable and those that are predictable but far enough in the future to be neglected in today's decision making.

[8]David Pearce, Edward Barbier, and Anil Markandya, *Sustainable Development, Economics and Environment in the Third World,* Edward Elgar Publishing, Aldershot, England, 1990.

TABLE 19-1
ESTIMATED AVERAGE RATE AND VALUE OF PESTICIDE SUBSIDIES
IN EIGHT DEVELOPING COUNTRIES

Country	Percentage of full retail costs	Total value ($ million)
China	19	285
Colombia	44	69
Ecuador	41	14
Egypt	83	207
Ghana	67	20
Honduras	29	12
Indonesia	82	128
Senegal	89	4

Source: Robert Repetto, "Economic Incentives for Sustainable Production," in Gunter Schramm and Jeremy J. Warford (eds.), *Environmental Management and Economic Development*, Johns Hopkins Press for the World Bank, Baltimore, MD, 1989, p. 72.

of pesticide subsidies offered to farmers in eight developing countries. The range is from 19 percent to 89 percent of the retail cost of the pesticide. The result of these subsidies is predictable: the overuse of agricultural chemicals and the damages that result. These include heavy pesticide exposure of farm workers, contamination of nearby surface and groundwater resources, and the rapid development of immunity by target pests. Throughout the developing world, the subsidies involve hundreds of millions of dollars that could be spent better in other ways, or simply left in the private sector.

Other agricultural subsidies, for example, on irrigation water and fertilizer, have similar effects. Much attention also has focused on overly rapid rates of deforestation in developing countries. In many cases this happens because of government policies. Policies that underprice the value of timber concessions offered to logging companies increase the incentive to harvest timber at a high rate. Uncontrolled private access to communal forest resources reduces the incentive to conserve timber stocks. Misguided public road building can open up large areas to timber harvesting. In some cases land grants to individuals cannot become permanent unless and until the land is cleared and put into agricultural production, which obviously creates the incentive to get rid of the trees as soon as possible. The result of these policies is timber harvest that is higher than it should be, pursued in places it should not be, with the resulting impacts in soil loss, polluted water, reduction in the global CO_2 sink, and so on.

We should not think, however, that distorting public policies with negative environmental impacts are features solely of the developing world. In fact, the developed world also has many such policies. In the United States, agricultural price supports coupled with land-use restrictions have led to excessive rates of pesticide use in certain crops. Publicly subsidized flood insurance has led people to develop shoreline property that might best be left undisturbed.

Institutional Policy: Property Rights

Economic development usually implies wide-ranging economic and political transformations. An important part of this is developing modern economic institutions that can provide the appropriate incentive structures to shape the decisions that will lead toward development. Inappropriate property rights institutions often have been singled out for having environmentally destructive consequences. Thus, one major avenue for policy to protect environmental resources is to alter property rights institutions.

In a study of resource depletion in Ethiopia, the author lists a series of stages through which a portion of the rural economy had evolved.[9]

Stage 1: Because of population pressure, the average harvest of fuel wood begins to exceed the average rate of wood production.
Stage 2: Farmers begin to use straw and dung for fuel; thus, less of these are available for maintaining soil fertility.
Stage 3: Almost all tree cover is removed, all dung is sold for cash, and wheat yields begin a serious decline.
Stage 4: Soil erosion becomes dramatic because of reduced tree cover and declining fertility.
Stage 5: There is a total collapse of fertility; farmers abandon their land, swelling urban populations.

The basic question is: Why did this sequence of stages take place? It might be more instructive to ask this the opposite way: Why didn't something like the following scenario happen? Fuel wood harvest increases because of increasing demand, this increases the price of fuel wood because of increased scarcity. Farmers see the increasing incomes to be made by growing and selling fuel wood, so they devote portions of their land to growing fuel wood and act to conserve the remaining supplies in the face of its increasing value. Finally, a substantial fuel wood harvest and market appear, with a considerable proportion of the land devoted to fuel wood production. Why, in other words, did the rising market price of fuel wood lead to wiping out the forest? Why did the farmers not act to make themselves better off by conserving and even increasing the production of an increasingly valuable resource?

One part of the answer is property rights. Most of the forested land was not owned by individuals or small groups, but was essentially an open-access resource. Anyone who wanted to harvest wood from these lands had the right to do so. In Chapter 4 we examined a simple model of an open-access resource showing that individuals making decisions on the basis of benefits and costs to themselves will overlook **common-property externalities** they inflict on others. A resource of this type often will be overexploited. Viewed from another angle, when there is open access to a resource, the incentive that any individual might have to reduce the rate of use and conserve the resource is totally undermined.

[9]Kenneth J. Newcombe, "An Economic Justification for Rural Afforestation: The Case of Ethiopia," in Gunter Schramm and Jeremy J. Warford (eds.), *Environmental Management and Economic Development*, Johns Hopkins Press for the World Bank, Baltimore, MD, 1989, pp. 117–138.

If someone reduces his or her harvest, others will simply take what has been left. Open-access resources promote a "use it or lose it" situation.

Thus, one of the root causes of the deforestation, which began the whole unraveling process in the example, was an institutional one, a property rights system that created incentives for wiping out the resource even though rising scarcity was making it socially desirable to conserve it. This problem has occurred with great regularity in developing countries, especially with land and forest resources. The most straightforward response would seem to be to change the property rights system so that the normal incentives for conservation can operate. This means instituting a system of individual or small-group property rights.

We have to keep in mind that like any single policy recommendation, this one is no panacea for all of the environmental problems of developing countries. It will work in some situations and not in others. Overuse of resources, such as the deforestation mentioned previously, can occur on "private" lands if the owners cannot effectively defend their boundaries and keep out would-be encroachers. This means, among other things, that there have to be effective and equitable **legal institutions** to settle land-use conflicts. Establishing private property rights in developing countries also means facing the **demographic realities.** In places with great population pressure, private property rights would hardly be feasible if that cut off a substantial proportion of the population from resources they need in order to subsist. Even in places without noticeable population pressure, essentially the same problem could occur if the property rights are distributed inequitably in the first place.

There are many other dimensions to the property rights issue. It is a topic of great controversy, and the debate is often carried out in overly simplistic terms. It is clear, however, that a wide range of resource and environmental problems in developing countries have been made much worse by ill-defined property rights and the open-access externalities to which these give rise. In those situations, innovations in property rights institutions can be extremely effective.

Population Policy as Environmental Policy

Many people feel that the only effective way to control environmental destruction in developing countries is to control the **number of people** in those countries. In the simplest possible terms, the total impact of a group of people on their environmental resources can be expressed in the following way:

$$\text{Total environmental impact} = \text{Environmental impact per person} \times \text{Number of people}.$$

It is clear that total environmental impact can increase as a result of increases in either or both of these factors. The contrary is also true: Decreases in total impact can result from decreases in either or both of the factors. More complicated scenarios are possible: Changes in technology, economic structure, and so on that lower the per-capita environmental impacts in a country can be more than offset by population increases. But both factors are involved. Population declines, or declines in the rate of population increase, may be very helpful, but they are not sufficient in themselves to ensure a reduction in aggregate environmental degradation.

The world population is generally expected to increase from the current 6 billion to 7 to 10 billion over the next half century. It's expected that about two-thirds of this increase will occur in countries of the developing world. Whether the increase is at the high end of this range or substantially lower depends in large part on the long-run behavior of **fertility rates** in these developing countries.[10] Although fertility rates in developing countries are sometimes very high, many have started to decline in recent years. To some extent this is a reflection of rising incomes, because increasing incomes are almost always associated with lowered fertility rates. Other important causal factors are a reduction in infant mortality, increased availability of family planning services, and (especially) increases in educational opportunities for women. Continued emphasis on these factors is in the best interest of people in the developing world, not solely for environmental reasons, but also to reduce poverty directly and to make it easier to institute developmental changes.

However, although reductions in population growth rates can certainly help to reduce the overall impacts any group of people has on its environmental resources, it is no substitute for undertaking environmental policies in their own right. For one thing, diminished population growth rates do not necessarily automatically imply diminished environmental damages. Even with comparatively lower populations, for example, it is anticipated that developing countries will experience marked increases in **urbanization** in the next half century and probably beyond. Unless confronted directly, this will lead to more severe air and water pollution in these burgeoning urban areas. As another example, decreases in agricultural populations may not be accompanied by reduced resource damages if, simultaneously, a shift to chemical agriculture occurs without proper safeguards against water pollution and increased pest resistance. In other words, although population policies may facilitate reduced environmental damages, they are no substitute for direct environmental policy itself.

What Types of Environmental Policies?

We come, therefore, to the important question of the types of environmental policies that are most appropriate for developing economies. We have stated several times, in the context of developed economies, that no single policy approach will be the best for all environmental problems: certain problems call for one approach; others call for something else. The same is true of developing

---

[10]The fertility rate is the average number of children born per woman over her lifetime; a rate of 2.0 implies zero population growth. Some developed countries have fertility rates of less than 2.0. In the developing world, fertility rates currently average about 3.8.

countries. But beyond this, it needs to be asked if anything characterizing the developing world might cause policymakers to rely more heavily on one type of policy than another. The main argument in developed economies is the choice between **command-and-control** and **incentive-based** policies. Is this also relevant to the setting of developing countries?

One especially relevant factor is that developing countries can ill afford, given the resource requirements of economic development, to devote more resources to environmental quality improvement than is necessary. This is an argument for making sure that the pollution-control policies adopted are **cost-effective,** and this in turn is an argument in favor of incentive policies. We have seen repeatedly throughout this book that incentive-type policies, in situations where monitoring emissions is possible and where materials-balance problems are addressed, can be expected to be substantially more cost-effective than command-and-control strategies. They make it possible to take advantage of different abatement costs across sources and also provide long-run incentives for firms to search for cheaper ways of reducing emissions.

To date developing countries have been following in the early footsteps of the developed economies; that is, they have relied primarily on command-and-control policies. There are some exceptions. Emission charge plans have been instituted in Colombia, China, Malaysia, and the Philippines. A tradeable permit system has been initiated by authorities in Chile to address air pollution in Santiago.[11] Singapore has instituted a program to charge drivers for using urban roads during heavily congested peak-use times of the day. The primary element of the program is the requirement that drivers using the central city at peak hours purchase daily or monthly licenses. Substantial improvements in air quality have resulted.[12]

Nevertheless, command and control is still the dominant trend in environmental policy in most developing countries. This may be the result of relatively weak policy institutions. It is a common observation that the capacities and performance of public regulatory agencies are relatively weak in many third-world countries. This problem, of course, is not unique to them; administrative deficiencies in developed countries account for part of the large gap between the laws and their enforcement. But most observers agree that this is a particularly thorny problem for developing countries. It is not solely a matter of professionalism and lack of political clout. It is also very generally true in the developed world that public concern and activist political participation by private environmental interest groups are often weak.

[11]For information on these programs, see David B. Wheeler, *Greening Industry: New Roles for Communities, Markets, and Governments,* Oxford University Press for the World Bank, New York, 2000.
[12]Theodore Panayotou, "Economic Incentives in Environmental Management and Their Relevance to Developing Countries," in Denizhan Erôcal (ed.), *Environmental Management in Developing Countries,* Organization for Economic Cooperation and Development, Paris, 1991, pp. 83–132.

For some observers, this institutional and political weakness implies that developing countries ought to move away from command-and-control measures toward economic incentive policies. For others, who perhaps are impressed that developed countries themselves are only beginning to place greater reliance on incentive measures, these institutional shortcomings imply that environmental regulations in developing countries are best kept relatively simple and direct; in other words, simple command-and-control strategies through uniform standards. The Brundtland Commission itself concluded that in developing countries, "regulations imposing uniform performance standards are essential to ensure that industry makes the investments necessary to reduce pollution."[13]

Perhaps a partial resolution of this question rests on recognizing that the category "developing countries" actually includes a wide range of experience. At one end of the spectrum are countries that are still almost totally agricultural, substantially uniform technologically, and with only the beginnings of a modern economic sector. At the other end of the spectrum are countries that have developed relatively large industrial, financial, and transportation sectors; important economic links to the rest of the world; and, most importantly, comparatively sophisticated political institutions. In the former countries, simple command-and-control approaches are likely to be best: a prohibition on a certain pesticide, for example, or limits on a certain irrigation practice. These may be enforced without sophisticated monitoring, and technical uniformity among producers means that these steps will be reasonably cost-effective. But in more advanced developing countries, incentive-based policies have much more to recommend them. Here the necessary political institutions may have been put in place, technological complexity makes it much more difficult to achieve acceptable levels of cost-effectiveness with command-and-control approaches, and strong long-run incentives for continued technical innovation in pollution control are of paramount importance. Example 19-1 discusses the attempts by China to institute emission charges.

THE ROLE OF THE DEVELOPED COUNTRIES

Developing countries are struggling with a wide array of economic, political, and social problems that stand in the way of lasting economic modernization. To graft environmental concerns onto the process puts an added burden on everyone in these countries, whatever their position. The developed countries have an important role to play in helping the third world to make this transition, not just for humanitarian reasons but also because many environmental problems are becoming increasingly international in scope. As these countries catch up to the developed economies, their technical choices and emission-control efforts will have a direct bearing on important global problems, such as CO_2 emissions and the global greenhouse effect, toxic chemical releases, nuclear radiation emissions, and so on.

---

[13]World Commission on Environment and Development, *Our Common Future,* Oxford University Press, New York, 1987, p. 220.

EXAMPLE 19-1

INCENTIVE-BASED POLICIES IN DEVELOPING ECONOMICS

CHINA CHARGES FOR POLLUTION

By Michel Potier

As is Chinese custom, reforms are usually given field trials in provinces or cities before being applied to the whole country. In 1992, for example, China began testing a sulphur tax in nine towns and two provinces.

The environment-protection bureau of the city of Chongquig (Sichuan province) has begun levying a charge on sulphur dioxide emissions, to try to improve the serious problems of air pollution generated by acid rain falling over the municipality. Because of the difficulty of measuring and monitoring these emissions, the charge is based not on the quantity of SO_2 released into the atmosphere but on the amount and sulphur content of the coal burned by each factory. The rate charged is 0.20 yuan per kilo of sulphur. The purpose of the charge is to induce industry to save energy and use higher grade coal. The reform was accompanied by other measures aimed at restricting the burning of coal in certain areas and providing incentives for firms willing to delocate away from the industrialized centre of the town.

The environment-protection bureau of the city of Yichang (Hubel province) introduced its own charge on SO_2 in 1992. In view of the lack of national standards for SO_2 pollution and of local by-laws, it was no easy task obtaining the support of the local authorities. After three years of negotiating, the decision was nonetheless taken to levy a charge designed to curb emissions from the 26 factories and industrial plants accountable for 80% of the coal consumption in the city (population 440,000). Along with the charge were introduced discharge permits—an idea already experimented with in China since 1987 for effluent discharges in water and since 1991 for atmospheric emissions—to take account of the assimilation capacity of different environments.

The SO_2 charge was applied wherever discharge permits were exceeded. The success of a system obviously depends on its enforcement in practice. During the introductory phase, the industries required to communicate their pollution data to the environment protection bureau grossly underreported their emissions and paid only a portion of the charges they should have done. The checks carried out by inspectors from the bureau, using resource tallies and consumption figures for water and coal, showed that the firms had concealed three-quarters of their emissions. Charge rates were raised accordingly. The reforms now appear to be working satisfactorily, since atmospheric concentrations of SO_2 have fallen by 30% and the frequency of acid rain precipitations has declined by 17%.

Source: OECD Observer, No. 192, February/March 1995.

Technology Transfer

By "technology transfer" we refer to the transfer, from developed to developing countries, of technologies and skills that can provide the impetus for economic development with lower environmental impacts than could be attained without the transfer. The focus is on the transfer of knowledge that citizens of developing countries themselves can adapt to their own needs and styles of operation. **Technology transfer** is an important concept in economic development. But it has taken on new urgency in light of the growing awareness of the scale of environmental problems faced by developing countries. Technology transfer means making technology available to countries so that their pace of economic development can be increased; this will have a positive impact on the demand for improved environmental quality, as discussed above. Transfer of environmental technology has the objective of reducing the environmental impacts of economic development, below what would occur otherwise, and perhaps below what has occurred historically in the developed world. It has become evident that if the rest of the world goes through the same high-pollution course of development as the developed countries have done, the drain on world resources will be enormous and the impact on the global environment potentially disastrous.

Concrete provisions for the transfer of technology have been written into some **international environmental treaties.** The 1989 Basel Convention on Hazardous Waste obligates the signatories to provide technical assistance to developing countries in the implementation of the treaty. The 1990 amendments to the Montreal Protocol on protection of the ozone layer has a requirement that developed countries make available to developing countries, on reasonable terms, new reduced-CFC technology; it also establishes a fund to help developing countries meet the requirements for reduced emissions.[14] In 1990, the five Nordic countries formed the Nordic Environment Finance Corporation to provide help for environmentally sound investment in Eastern and Central Europe. The Global Environment Fund Management Corporation (GEFMC) is an effort to raise money from institutional investors in the United States with the backing of the Overseas Private Investment Corporation, a U.S. government agency. The objectives of the GEFMC include investing in such activities as wastewater treatment facilities, renewable energy projects, and efficient industrial process programs.

Technology transfer has two important parts. The first is the initial development of new technologies and procedures. These are a product of innovation in industries searching for ways of reducing emissions and in the pollution-control industry itself. Thus, one element in technology transfer is the provision of incentives for a brisk level of innovation in the originating countries. This implies pollution-control policies that provide these incentives, about which we have said a lot in earlier chapters. In particular, we have discussed the positive incentives for innovation provided by economic-incentive types of policies and the negative effects provided by technology-based standards.

The second element of environmental technology transfer is getting the ideas, technical means, and necessary training effectively into the receiving countries. The word "effectively" is important because history is full of cases in which transferred techniques have failed to work as anticipated. It is much

---

[14]Chapter 21 contains a discussion of international environmental treaties in general, and Chapter 20 discusses the specific provisions of the Montreal Protocol.

more than just moving a machine from one location to another; a tremendous array of problems must be worked out to bridge the informational, cultural, commercial, and political gaps that separate people in different countries. At the end of the process, which normally will involve many different business, trade, political, and environmental groups, the objective is to transfer technology that is compatible with local skills and labor availabilities.

Most environmental technologies in the developed world have been developed by firms in the private sector. In the United States the **envirotech sector** consists of thousands of large and small firms in all phases of environmental activity. Getting technology and practices transferred and adopted in the developing world, therefore, involves creating effective connections between these firms and the responsible public and private agencies of the developing world. Exhibit 19-2 discusses a specific example of technology transfer, in this case in the area of water quality technology moving from the United States to India. It illustrates several things: the way in which the technological need was specifically framed, the practices involved (water quality officials in India, public officials and private sector people in the United States), and the necessity of adapting the U.S. technology to the Indian situation.

Technology transfer must be looked at in the light of recent concerns about **globalization.** This concept has come to mean a lot of different things, one of which is the quality of the commercial contacts between multinational firms (and firms of the developed world) and people in the developing world. At issue is whether envirotech firms with potential technology treat this as an opportunity simply for short-run profit maximization; or whether they make sure that technology is adapted to the long-run needs and capabilities of people in developing nations. We will have more to say about globalization issues in the last chapter of the book.

Debt-for-Nature Swaps

Suppose you and I are neighbors and I owe you $100 on a past loan. Suppose further that I keep a very untidy yard, never mowing the grass and keeping several junk cars next to my garage. You offer to wipe out the $100 debt if I will agree to clean up my yard. That is a debt-for-nature swap. Many developing countries owe large sums to lenders in developed countries, particularly commercial banks. These loans have been made for a variety of purposes, primarily to support investment and consumption in the developing countries. In many cases the debtor nations have found it difficult to pay back the loans. Debt-for-nature swaps are where environmental groups in the developed world buy portions of this debt and retire it in return for environmental preservation efforts by the developing country that owes the debt.

The first debt-for-nature swap was in 1987. Conservation International, a private group, bought $650,000 of Bolivia's commercial debt from the Citicorp Investment Bank for $100,000. In return for retiring this debt, the government of Bolivia agreed to place a four-million acre piece of tropical rain forest in protected status and create a fund for the management of the area. Debt-for-nature

---

EXHIBIT 19-2

SEARCHING FOR TECHNOLOGY TRANSFER

BERKELEY, Calif.—Top West Bengal government officials and experts met with scientists from a cutting-edge research firm based here to explore the possibility of importing technology to treat water in vast areas of West Bengal where the groundwater is contaminated by arsenic.

"About six million people live in nine districts in West Bengal where the groundwater is contaminated by arsenic," said R. K. Tripathy, who is leading the five-member delegation from West Bengal. "We have to give tube wells for every 150 people."

Tripathy is principal secretary of the state's Public Health Engineering Department, and supervises the implementation of water supply programs in the state.

He said his team was in the U.S. "to explore the possibilities of finding the companies which are manufacturing arsenic removal plants, which can be fitted to the tube wells and the bigger diameter wells in the arsenic-affected areas of West Bengal."

In the beginning session, seminar participants briefly presented their views about the crisis of arsenic contamination. CalEPA scientist Rash Ghosh, from GRA, made an impassioned plea for multilateral organizations and the Western world to help out West Bengal and Bangladesh in this looming crisis. "Destruction of water is the beginning of the destruction of civilization," he said.

Later, Robert Clarke and Samaresh Mohanta from EDA made a presentation of the prototype they have developed for treating arsenic contaminated water.

Describing the device developed by scientists at EDA, Clarke and Mohanta pointed out its key benefits: It is extremely low cost compared to other devices, is easy to maintain, and has the inestimable advantage of screening out arsenic very selectively, so that the resulting screened material is of very low quantity.

Tripathy said he liked what he heard.

"To be very frank, we are really impressed," he told India West. "This is one company which has done very well in finding out [a device] which is easy to regenerate and the disposal is not a problem. If they can bring out a prototype which can be fitted to the village tube wells I think we will welcome it."

The Indian team, in addition to Tripathy, included Prasanta Kumar Mitra, chief engineer of the state Public Health Engineering Department; Arunava Jajumder, a professor at the All India Institute of Hygiene and Public Health; S. P. Sinha Ray, with the Central Ground Water Authority; and Kamal Mazumdar, with the Rajiv Gandhi Drinking Water Mission.

The trip was sponsored by US-AEP, which was started a few years ago by USAID "to solve environmental problems in that region of the world utilizing expertise and technologies from the U.S.," Patico told India-West. "The United States–Asia Environmental Partnership is so called because it is set up in a very cooperative, collaborative sort of mode," he said. "It involves not only USAID, but also in a large way the U.S. Department of Commerce through its foreign commercial service."

Source: India West Business Magazine, February 4, 2000, reprinted on web page of USAEP (United States–Asia Environmental Partnership), **www.usaep.org/articles/article50.htm.**

---

swaps have since been concluded with numerous other countries, including Ecuador, Costa Rica, the Philippines, Madagascar, and the Dominican Republic.[15]

How effective debt-for-nature swaps can be is a difficult question. As a debt-retiring device, the approach can have little impact because of the vast amount of debt outstanding. As an environmental tool, it can be more effective, even

---

[15]Catherine A. O'Neill and Cass R. Sunstein, "Economics and the Environment: Trading Debt and Technology for Nature," *Columbia Journal of Environmental Law,* Vol. 17, Winter 1992, pp. 93–151.

though the scope of the overall problem is huge in comparison to the means. Perhaps their primary use will be to target very specific instances where critical environmental links are threatened or where they can be used to get a larger program started. Even in these cases, however, significant problems remain. One of the most difficult is something we have talked about throughout this book: enforcement. Once a private group has bought and retired a certain amount of debt, it may be hard to ensure that the country with which they have made the agreement will continue to abide by the deal.

Environmental Values in International Aid Institutions

Some of the most egregious cases of environmental damage in developing countries actually have stemmed from projects initiated and funded by international aid organizations, whose objectives are primarily to help these countries develop economically. A well-publicized example is the project funded partly by the World Bank to build roads and encourage colonization in the northwestern part of Brazil. The building of the roads attracted many more migrants into the area than was anticipated, "making already underfunded public agencies even less capable of controlling large-scale deforestation."[16] Many international donors have leaned toward the big project: dams, power stations, infrastructure, and so on. These often have been pursued in ways that were not sensitive to environmental impacts because the donors, together with governments in recipient countries, have been so focused on spurring economic growth.

What this problem calls for is a more complete adoption of the general benefit–cost approach, interpreted broadly to mean the accounting for, and comparison of, all benefits and costs, whether or not they can be monetized in a formal framework. In particular, more attention must be given to working out the environmental impacts of these development projects. In recent years many international lending organizations have begun to take the environmental issues of developing countries more seriously. For example, the World Bank created a new Environmental Department and changed its procedures so that the environmental implications of proposed projects will be taken into account in making lending decisions. Bank policy now requires complete environmental assessments for all projects that have significant impacts on the environment.

SUMMARY

Environmental problems in developing countries have become increasingly critical in the last few decades. While the appearance of global issues has helped people to see that all countries are inextricably linked in the global environment, more attention also has been directed at traditional air and water pollution problems of developing countries. The issue of long-run sustainability of the natural resource and environmental assets of these countries has become a policy focus point.

[16]World Bank, *World Development Report 1992, Development and Environment,* Oxford University Press, New York, 1992, p. 80.

Analysis of past trends shows that development tends to make some environmental problems worse and others better. Some phenomena, such as SO_2 pollution, seem to get worse as countries initially begin to develop rapidly and then improve as development leads to higher per-capita incomes. There is some evidence, although it is not particularly strong, that "dirty" industries in developed countries have been migrating to developing ones, but the reasons for this are still not clear. The "pollution-haven" hypothesis does not receive strong support in the data.

Policy institutions in developing countries historically have been relatively weak, but this is changing. Most environmental policy in these countries has followed the lead of the developed world, in terms of being based on command-and-control principles. Some have suggested that developing countries should emphasize incentive-based policies so as to achieve higher levels of cost-effectiveness. Population control has frequently been recommended as a means of lessening environmental impacts. Although lower rates of population growth may facilitate environmental improvements, they are not sufficient for attaining improvements in environmental quality.

Finally, the developed world can play a substantial role in helping third-world countries develop without large-scale environmental destruction. The primary mechanism for this is through technology transfer, understood broadly to include the transfer of skills and technological capabilities that are culturally sound and not solely the transfer of Western capital goods.

QUESTIONS FOR FURTHER DISCUSSION

1 What is the relationship between economic growth, population growth, and environmental quality in developing countries?

2 Environmental pollution is, for the most part, reversible, in the sense that it can be decreased if the appropriate steps are taken. What are the pros and cons, therefore, of using sustainability as a criterion for evaluating environmental policies?

3 When a multinational business firm from the developed world opens operations in a developing nation, should it be held to the environmental standards of its country of origin or to those of the country in which it is operating?

4 Suppose we introduce a new criterion, "administrative feasibility," for evaluating environmental policies in developing countries. How might this affect choices among different types of policies?

WEBSITES

The World Bank, **www.worldbank.org/environment/,** has a great deal of information on economic development and environmental protection; a second major site in this area is the World Resources Institute; **www.wri.org;** see also the sites listed in the web page associated with this book, **www.mhhe.com/economics/field3.**

SELECTED READINGS

Azzoni, Carlos R., and Joao Y. Isai: "Estimating the Costs of Environmental Protection in Brazil," *Ecological Economics*, Vol. 11, 1994, pp. 127–133.

Baker, Doug S., and Daniel B. Tunstall (eds.): *1990 Directory of Country Environmental Studies: An Annotated Bibliography of Environmental and Natural Resource Profiles and Assessments*, World Resources Institute, Washington, DC, 1990.

Binswanger, Hans P.: "Brazilian Policies That Encourage Deforestation in the Amazon," *World Development*, 19(7), July 1991, pp. 821–829.

Bojo, Jan, Karl-Goran Maler, and Lena Unemo (eds.): *Environment and Development: An Economic Approach*, Kluwer Academic Publishers, Boston, 1992.

Eröcal, Denizhan (ed.): *Environmental Management in Developing Countries*, Organization for Economic Cooperation and Development, Paris, August 1991.

Eskeland, Gunnar, and Emmanuel Jimenez: "Choosing among Policy Instruments in Pollution Control: A Review," Country Economics Department, World Bank, Washington, DC, June 20, 1990.

Eskeland, Gunnar S., and Emmanuel Jimenez: "Curbing Pollution in Developing Countries," *Finance and Development*, 28(1), March 1991, pp. 15–18.

Hettige, M., M. Huq, S. Pargal, and D. Wheeler: "Determinants of Pollution Abatement in Developing Countries, Evidence from South and Southeast Asia," World Development, December 1996.

Lyon, Randolph M.: "Transferable Discharge Permit Systems and Environmental Management in Developing Countries," *World Development*, 17(8), August 1989, pp. 1299–1312.

May, P. and R. S. I. Motta (eds.): *Pricing the Planet, Economic Analysis for Sustainable Development*, Columbia University Press, New York, 1996.

Pargal, S., and D. Wheeler: "Informal Regulation in Developing Countries, Evidence from Indonesia," *Journal of Political Economy*, December 1996.

Pearce, David, Edward Barbier, Anil Markandya, Scott Barrett, R. Kerry Turner, and Timothy Swanson: *Blueprint 2: Greening the World Economy*, Earthscan Publications, London, 1991.

Rao, P. K.: *Sustainable Development: Economics and Policy*, Blackwell Publishers, Malden, MA, 2000.

Russell, Clifford S., and Philip T. Powell: "Choosing Environmental Policy Tools, Theatrical Cautions and Practical Considerations," Interamerican Development Bank, No. ENV-102, Washington, DC, June 1996.

Wheeler, David B.: *Greening Industry: New Roles for Communities, Markets, and Governments*, Oxford University Press for the World Bank, New York, 2000.

CHAPTER 20

THE GLOBAL
ENVIRONMENT

People all around the world are struggling to come to grips with local environmental problems and improve their immediate surroundings. But over the last few decades people also have had to broaden their outlooks to recognize that there is a **global environment** that is critical to human welfare. Moreover, the scale of human activities has become so widespread and intense that it has begun to have an impact on this global environment in significant ways.

For all of history, one of the ways humans have reacted to local environmental destruction is migration. But at the planetary level this option is not available. There is no escape if we inadvertently make the planet less habitable.

Complementing the daunting physical facts are the sobering political/economic facts that have made it very difficult for the world's nations to act collectively. There is a race on between the accumulating scientific data that scientists, still with great uncertainty, are straining to interpret, and the growing efforts to develop international institutions and perspectives that will make concerted action possible.

In this chapter we look at several of these global environmental problems. The primary focus is on problems of the global atmosphere and its degradation, specifically stratospheric ozone depletion and the global greenhouse effect. We then look at the issue of diminishing biological diversity, which, although it is occurring at different rates in various parts of the world, has truly global significance. Each of these issues is very complicated scientifically and politically, so the chapter can touch on only their most important aspects.

OZONE DEPLETION

The Physical Problem

At sea level ozone is a pollutant produced when emissions of hydrocarbons and nitrogen oxides interact in the presence of sunlight. A variety of health problems and agricultural crop damages have been traced to elevated levels of surface ozone. But most of the ozone in the earth's atmosphere is located in the stratosphere, a zone extending from about 10 km to about 50 km in altitude. This stratospheric ozone is critical in maintaining the earth's radiation balance. The atmosphere surrounding the earth essentially acts as a filter for incoming electromagnetic radiation. The atmospheric gas responsible for this is ozone, which blocks a large percentage of incoming low-wavelength, or ultraviolet, radiation.

Several decades ago scientific evidence began to appear that the ozone content of the atmosphere was showing signs of diminishing. In the late 1970s a large hole appeared in the ozone layer over Antarctica. More recently, significant ozone reduction has been found throughout the entire stratosphere, including those areas over the more populated parts of the world. In the 1970s scientists discovered the cause of this phenomenon. It had been known for some time that the chemical content of the atmosphere has been changing at a rapid rate and on a global scale. Ozone disappearance was linked to the accumulation of chlorine in the stratosphere. Chlorine was found to insert itself into what was normally a balanced process of ozone production and destruction, vastly increasing the rate of destruction. And the source of the chlorine turned out to be a variety of manufactured chemicals, which, released at ground level, slowly migrated up to higher altitudes. The culprits are substances called **halocarbons,** chemicals composed of carbon atoms in combination with atoms of chlorine, fluorine, iodine, and bromine. The primary halocarbons are called **chlorofluorocarbons** (CFCs), which have molecules consisting of combinations of carbon, fluorine, and chlorine atoms. Another subgroup is the halons, composed of these elements plus bromine atoms; bromine, in fact, acts similarly to chlorine in breaking down ozone molecules. Carbon tetrachloride and methyl chloroform also are implicated in ozone destruction.

CFCs were developed in the 1930s as a replacement for the refrigerants in use at the time. Unlike those they replaced, CFCs are extremely stable, nontoxic, and inert relative to the electrical and mechanical machinery in which they are used. Thus, their use spread quickly as refrigerants and also as propellants for aerosols (hair sprays, deodorants, insecticides), industrial agents for making polyurethane and polystyrene foams, and industrial cleaning agents and solvents. Halons are widely used as fire suppressors. When these substances were introduced, attention was exclusively on their benefits; there was no evidence that they could have long-run impacts on the atmosphere. But the very stable nature of these gases allows them to migrate very slowly in the atmosphere. After surface release, they drift up through the troposphere into the stratosphere, where they begin a long process of ozone destruction.

Damages from Ultraviolet Radiation

Several years ago it was thought that ozone depletion might confine itself to small parts of the stratosphere, in which case damages from the increasing surface flux of ultraviolet radiation would be limited. But recently strong evidence has appeared that significant ozone depletion is occurring over large portions of the world's highly populated regions. Thus, damages are likely to be much more widespread.

Current research indicates that there are two main sources of damage to humans: **health impacts** and **agricultural crop losses.** Health damages are related to the increased incidence of skin cancers and eye disease. The dose–response relationships developed by the EPA indicate that for each 1 percent increase in UV_B radiation, basal-cell and squamous-cell cancer cases would increase by 1 percent and 2 percent, respectively, while melanoma skin cancers would increase by less than 1 percent and cataracts by about 0.2 percent.[1] Increased UV_B radiation also can be expected to increase food production costs because of the physical damages it produces in growing plants. Damages also are expected in other parts of the earth's physical ecosystem.

Policy Responses

The potential seriousness of the ozone-depletion problem has concentrated people's minds and led to some relatively vigorous policy responses. Initially several countries took **unilateral actions.** In 1978 the United States and several other countries (Canada, Sweden, Norway, Denmark) banned CFCs in aerosol cans, but not as a refrigerant. In the 1980s the continued scientific evidence of ozone depletion led to international action. Under the auspices of the United Nations, 24 nations signed in 1987 the *Montreal Protocol on Substances That Deplete the Ozone Layer.* It committed the high CFC-using signatories to a phasedown of CFCs and halons to 50 percent of their 1986 levels, to be achieved by 1998. Signatory countries currently using low levels of CFCs were given a 10-year grace period: Starting in 1999 they were to cut back to 1995–1997 levels, as shown in Table 20-1.

Soon after the Montreal agreement, it became clear that this reduction was not enough, partly because continuing research showed that the problem was getting worse, and partly because some large CFC-producing countries had not signed the original agreement. Thus, in 1990 the Montreal Protocol countries agreed to phase out the production of CFCs completely by the year 2000, to add carbon tetrachloride and methyl chloroform to the list, and to introduce a longer-run schedule for phasing out HCFCs. It also instituted a fund, created from contributions of developed countries, to be used to help finance CFC-reducing technological changes in developing countries. Additional countries signed the agreement in subsequent years.

The Montreal Protocol has been a success in many ways. It has found wide agreement among nations of the world. It very effectively focused attention on the burgeoning body of scientific evidence of ozone depletion, using it to motivate political agreement. And it created conditions where both developed and developing countries could find agreement. It remains to be seen whether it will provide a model for future international agreements.

What is unique in the CFC agreement is that it deals essentially with a restricted set of substances. In all producing countries, the CFC-producing industry is composed of a few large chemical companies. So international policy has been driven not only by scientific results, but also by international com-

[1]U.S. Environmental Protection Agency, *Regulatory Impact Analysis: Protection of Stratospheric Ozone,* Vol. II, Appendix E, Washington, DC, 1987, pp. E3–E4.

TABLE 20-1
SUMMARY OF THE TERMS OF THE MONTREAL PROTOCOL
FOR OZONE-DESTROYING CHEMICALS

Original 1987 Agreement

Substances controlled: CFCs-11, -12, -113, -114, -115, halons 1211, 1301, 2402.

High-CFC-using countries:
  Reduce production and consumption to 50% of 1986 levels by 1998.
  As of 1992, halon production to be held at or below 1986 levels.

Low-CFC-using countries:
  As of 1999, cut back to 50% of 1995–1997 levels over the next 10 years.

1990 Agreement

Regulates 10 additional substances, including CCl_4.

High-using countries (consumption greater than 0.3 kg/person):
  20% reduction in production and consumption from 1986 levels by 1993.
  50% reduction in production and consumption from 1986 levels by 1997.
  100% reduction in production and consumption from 1986 levels by 2000.

Halons frozen at 1986 levels by 1992, then phased out by 2000, except for certain "essential" uses.

CH_4 to be phased out by 2005.

Low-CFC-using countries: 10-year grace period on phaseout schedules, no export of CFCs.

Multilateral fund to aid developing countries with phaseout problems and to foster technology transfer.

No imports or exports of controlled substances with nonparties after 1990.

Subsequent Agreements (London, 1990; Copenhagen, 1992; Vienna, 1995*; Montreal, 1997*; Beijing, 1999*)

Accelerated phaseout schedules for CFCs, HCFCs, halons, CH_4, and methyl chloroform; extended control to methyl bromide, hydrobromofluorocarbons; developed a system of licensing to control imports and exports; replenished the multilateral fund.

*Not yet ratified by the U.S. Senate.
Sources: U.S. Office of Technology Assessment, *Changing by Degrees: Steps to Reduce Greenhouse Gases*, Washington, D.C., 1991, pp. 67–68, Larry Parker, "Stratospheric Ozone Depletion: Implementation Issues," Congressional Research Service Issue Brief IB97003, Washington, DC, 2000.

petition in this industry. U.S. firms have been leaders in developing substitutes for CFCs, and they, therefore, have led the charge for a CFC phaseout. Other international environmental agreements in the future may not have the same kind of economic realities behind them.

The Montreal Protocol appears to have been reasonably successful so far. "The total combined abundance of ozone-depleting compounds in the lower atmosphere peaked in 1994 and is now slowly declining. Total chlorine is declining, but total bromine is increasing."[2] This result is probably related to the effectiveness of the Montreal Protocol. But more remains to be done. As of

[2]World Meteorological Association, "Scientific Assessment of Atmospheric Ozone," 1998.

this time (spring 2001), atmospheric ozone still was showing diminishment, presumably related to emissions of many years ago. Continued progress toward stopping this diminishment and healing the ozone layer will require continued action to tighten and enforce the terms of the agreement.

The Economics of CFC Controls

In economic terms the problem here is similar to the phasing out of leaded gasoline. The objective is reasonably clear and widely shared; the basic problem is how to bring it about in different countries. In advanced economies the main focus has been put on developing **substitute chemicals** that will perform the same tasks as CFCs—as refrigerants, cleaning agents, and so on—but have little or no ozone-depleting impact. Table 20-2 shows the major CFCs and some of the substances chemists are looking at as substitutes. CFC-11, -12, and -113 are the most common substances in use, but these have very long atmos-

TABLE 20-2
MAJOR OZONE-DEPLETING CHEMICALS

		Atmospheric lifetime (years)	Estimated ozone-depletion potential*
Chlorofluorocarbons			
CFC-11	CCl_3F	40–80	1.0
CFC-12	CCl_2F_2	80–150	1.0
CFC-113	$C_2F_3Cl_3$	100	0.8
CFC-114	$C_2F_4Cl_2$	270	1.0
CFC-115	C_2F_5Cl	600	0.6
Halons			
H-1211	CF_2BrCl	15	3.0
H-1301	CF_3Br	110	10.0
H-2402	$C_2F_4Br_2$		6.0
Carbon tetrachloride	CCl_4	60	1.06
Methyl chloroform	$C_2H_3Cl_3$	6	0.1
Hydrochlorofluorocarbons			
HCFC-22	$CHClF_2$	20	0.05
HCFC-123	CF_3CHCl_2	2	0.02
HCFC-124	$CHClFCF_3$	4	0.02
HCFC-141b	CCl_2FCH_3	10	0.1
HCFC-142b	CH_3CClF_2	22	0.06
Hydrofluorocarbons			
HFC-125	CHF_2CF_3	15	0.0
HFC-134a	CH_2FCF_3	5	0.0
HFC-143a	CH_3CF_3	40	0.0
HFC-152a	CH_3CHF_2	2	0.0

*The ozone-depletion potential (ODP) of a compound is defined as the estimated ozone depletion of a unit mass of the compound divided by the ozone depletion of a unit mass of CFC-11.
Source: U.S. Congress, House Committee on Energy and Commerce, Subcommittee on Oversight and Investigations, *Ozone Layer Depletion*, Hearings, 101st Congress, 1st Session, May 15, 1989.

pheric lifetimes and rather high ozone depletion potentials (ODPs). The halons have even higher ODPs. Research has emphasized the development of a variety of substances that have both shorter atmospheric lifetimes and much lower, or zero, ODPs. So what is essentially driving the rate of CFC phaseout in advanced economies is the **cost of developing these substitutes,** together with the costs of changeover from the old to the new chemicals. Some substances may be simply "drop-in" substitutes, whereas others will require getting rid of old capital equipment (refrigerators, air conditioners, etc.) and installing new equipment.

To meet the phaseout timetables agreed upon under the Montreal Protocol, each country adopted some explicit control policy on production, imports, and exports of the targeted substances. The policy enacted in the United States was to create declining production quotas for each of the firms producing CFCs, quotas that would eventually reach zero in 1998. This was later changed to 1995. To reap the benefits of differential costs of reducing CFC output, these production quotas were made transferrable, similar to the transferrable quota program that was used in the phasing out of leaded gasoline.

A major problem with setting production ceilings in this way is that it can lead to unwarranted increases in profits for current manufacturers of CFCs. In effect it gives firms in the industry, who may have been operating as rivals, a way of acting like monopolists. Figure 20-1 illustrates this with a simple

FIGURE 20-1
Government-Imposed Production Limitations Lead to Monopoly Profits.

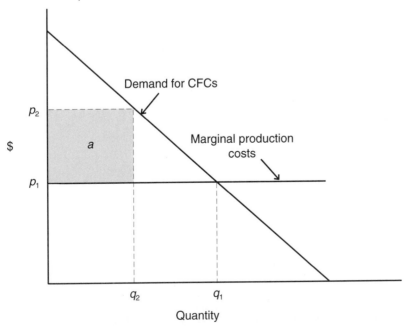

market model. It shows a typical downward sloping demand curve for CFCs, together with a flat marginal cost curve. Left to itself, competitive forces would lead to a production level of q_1 and a price that equals marginal production costs. But if public authorities limit production to q_2, the price will increase to p_2, which is substantially above production costs. Thus, an amount equal to area a becomes potential **excess profits** earned in the industry because of the output restrictions.

When tighter CFC controls and faster phaseouts of CFCs were being discussed by the U.S. Congress in the late 1980s, there was widespread feeling that at least some of these excess profits should accrue to the public. Several means were discussed. One was to **auction** off CFC production rights to the various chemical-producing companies. The bidding process, if it worked well, would transfer some portion of the excess profits to the public. The other approach, which was finally adopted, was to tax the production of CFCs. In theory, a tax equal to $(p_2 - p_1)$ would transfer all of the excess profits to the public. It then could be used for any number of purposes, perhaps put into general revenues or used specifically to help the CFC conversion process.

The system that was adopted established a base tax rate, then set different taxes on the various ozone-depleting chemicals according to the formula

Tax rate = Base rate × Ozone-depleting potential.

The base rate was originally set at $1.37 per pound but has since been increased. The current (2000) rate is $7.60 per pound.

The 1990 Clean Air Act Amendments contained a number of other parts on ozone depletion. It established a phaseout program for HCFCs, with production to be eliminated by 2030. It established a national recycling program for CFCs used in refrigerators and air conditioners, and it introduced prohibitions on the venting of CFCs from equipment currently containing these substances.

In an earlier chapter we talked about how lead trading was used to reduce the overall cost of switching to no-lead gas. The Montreal Protocol contains the same type of approach for switching out of the production plus consumption[3] of substances controlled by the agreement. This is the trading of **emission reduction credits** among countries. Thus, if a country fails to meet its required production cutback because of the needs of "industrial rationalization," it is supposed to offset the excess emissions by getting comparable reductions in other countries.

Although phasing out the production of some material might sound like a simple task, this is not really true. CFCs are produced throughout the world, so enforcement runs into important international complications. Reducing the production of virgin CFCs also has been made more difficult by the need to capture and recycle the existing stock of CFCs in use. On problems of enforcement, see Exhibit 20-1.

---

[3]"Production plus consumption" is defined as production plus imports minus exports.

EXHIBIT 20-1

CFC PRODUCTION: ENFORCING A BAN ON A POPULAR CHEMICAL

To meet the conditions of the Montreal Protocol, countries have had to find ways of stopping people from using a chemical that has become widely used throughout the economy. The huge, modern air conditioning industry, among others, has been built on CFCs, the wonder chemical that was developed in the 1930s. While passing laws limiting its use is one thing, implementing the laws through regulations and enforcement is quite another. Paradoxically, taking steps to reduce CFC use, if successful, will lead to a rise in the price of this material, which will actually create stronger incentives to find ways of circumventing the laws that are trying to phase it out.

The first big problem is smuggling. It is estimated that up to 20 percent of current CFC use may be of smuggled material. This is because CFC production is still legal in many developing countries, even as the developed world attempts to stop using it. Thus, CFC production is surging in some developing countries, which means big profits for anybody who can smuggle it into the U.S. or Europe. It appears that CFCs have become, in some parts of entry, second only to drugs in terms of illegal shipments. One possibility for smugglers is to take advantage of the loophole that allows importation of recycled CFC. Virgin CFC can be altered with a few squirts of oil to make it appear like recycled product.

Other schemes have been tried. A Texas man was arrested for smuggling 75,000 pounds of CFC-12 into the U.S. from Venezuela. The technique they used was to build special industrial refrigerators that could hold very large amounts of the banned refrigerant. They then sent these to Venezuela, had them filled, and returned to the U.S. where the material was pumped into smaller cylinders for resale. The smuggled material had a street value of about $600,000. Two men in Texas were convicted of illegally importing CFCs worth $720,000; shipping documents indicated they were bound to Mexico, but instead they were shipped to Long Island.

A California man was fined for selling recycled CFCs that did not meet the level of purity required by federal law. A Colorado man was given a fine and jail term for smuggling CFCs; he had imported one ton of R-12 refrigerant without the required import allowances.

More elaborate machinery has been necessary to enforce the many detailed regulations that the EPA has put in place to avoid the venting of CFCs into the atmosphere.

In Texas, a person was fined for producing false CFC technician certificates. Regulations require that people handling refrigerator equipment must properly handle CFC-based refrigerants. To enforce this, these people are supposed to be trained and pass a certification exam; they then receive an operating certificate. In this case, an individual produced and distributed a large number of counterfeit operator certificates.

In Illinois, a company in the scrap business was fined for following procedures that led to the release of CFCs from scrapped air conditioners. The company had to put in place revised handling procedures and send periodic compliance reports to the EPA.

The city of New York was fined for crushing discarded household appliances, some of which contained CFCs. The U.S. Treasury was cited by the EPA for servicing air conditioners and water coolers without using required CFC recovery and recycling equipment, as well as for suing an uncertified technician to do the work. A number of people have also been cited with replacing CFCs with unapproved substitutes. The 1990 Clean Air Act requires that auto technicians use only EPA-approved refrigerants in cars and trucks.

Source: Compiled from enforcement information on EPA's Ozone Depletion website: www.epa.gov/ozone/index.html.

GLOBAL WARMING

The Physical Problem

Another major global problem is the threat of a long-run increase in the surface temperature of the earth. This goes under the name of "global warming," or sometimes the "greenhouse effect." The principle of a greenhouse is that the enclosing glass or plastic allows the passage of incoming sunlight, but traps a portion of the reflected infrared radiation, which warms the interior of the greenhouse above the outside temperature. Greenhouse gases in the earth's atmosphere play a similar role; they serve to raise the temperature of the earth's surface and make it habitable. With no greenhouse gases at all, the surface of the earth would be about 30°C cooler than it is today, making human life impossible.

Under "normal" (i.e., preindustrial) conditions, trace amounts of greenhouse gases were in global balance. They were given off by decaying plant and animal materials and absorbed by forests and oceans. Into this rough balance came human beings and one of their greatest cultural accomplishments: the industrial revolution. That event was basically a revolution in energy use, involving a vast increase in the extraction of energy from fossil fuels—first coal and later petroleum and natural gas. Combustion of fossil fuels, together with deforestation and a few other activities, has led to an increase in the CO_2 content of the atmosphere by about 20 percent from the beginning of the industrial revolution. In the last three decades alone it has increased 8 percent, and many scientists predict an approximate doubling by the middle of the next century. While CO_2 is the most important **greenhouse gas** (GHG), it is not the only one. Others are methane, nitrous oxide, and carbon monoxide. The main greenhouse gases, their approximate proportionate contribution to global warming, and their major sources are shown in Table 20-3.

Accompanying this buildup of GHGs has been a rise in mean surface temperatures around the globe. Study of temperature records, the composition of long-lived glaciers, and other sources shows that the earth has warmed about 0.5°C (1°F) over the past 100 years. Some scientific models predict that over the next century temperatures could rise 1.5 to 4.5°C. The rate of heating is put at about 0.3°C per decade. This may not sound like a very rapid change, but historical studies have shown that in past episodes of warming and cooling, dur-

TABLE 20-3
MAJOR GREENHOUSE GASES AND THEIR PRIMARY SOURCES

Gas	Proportionate effect (%)	Major source
CO_2	49	Fossil fuel combustion, deforestation, cement production
CH_4 (methane)	18	Landfills, agriculture, termites
N_2O (nitrous oxide)	6	Fertilizers, land clearing, biomass burning, fossil fuel combustion
Other (CO, NO_x, ...)	13	Various

ing which agricultural societies of the time suffered major dislocations, climate change occurred at a rate of only about 0.05°C per decade. Today's rate of change, in other words, is expected to be very much faster than those faced by humans in the past.

Global warming is expected to bring about a general rise in sea level because of the expansion of sea water, the melting of glaciers, and perhaps eventually the breaking up of polar ice sheets. Although this will be a general rise, it will have different local impacts on tidal and current patterns. Changes in meteorological patterns also will vary widely among regions. In the northern hemisphere, polar regions will warm faster than equatorial zones; on the continental landmasses the centers will become drier than the peripheries, and so on. Our ability to predict these changes will improve as the global climate models of atmospheric scientists are better developed.

Human and Ecosystem Impacts

Although this is a problem of the global environment, its impacts on humans and the ecosystem will vary greatly from one country and region to another. A sea-level rise would have devastating impacts in certain societies, such as those of the Pacific islands or those concentrated in low river deltas. Impacts will be relatively less in countries where development may be redirected toward interior regions. The drowning of coastal wetlands throughout the world could have important impacts on fisheries and, thus, on societies that rely heavily on marine resources. There will be very substantial impacts on ecosystems and individual species of plants and animals, not just because of the amount of change but also because the rate of change will be fast by evolutionary standards. In ice ages of the past, weather changes have happened slowly enough to allow species of plants and animals to migrate and survive. The rapid pace of change expected in the greenhouse phenomenon may be too quick for many organisms to adjust to changing habitats. It also will put a severe strain on species that occupy narrow ecological niches because relatively small changes in weather patterns can destroy the habitats on which they depend.

Perhaps the biggest impacts on humans will be through the effects of changed climate patterns on **agriculture and forestry.** Here the story gets very complicated, not only because weather patterns will be differently affected throughout the world, but also because crops, and the systems of cultivation adopted by farmers, vary a lot in terms of their ability to withstand changes in temperature and water availability. A study commissioned by the EPA concludes that the agricultural impacts of atmospheric warming will hit developing nations harder than developed countries. It is expected that African nations will bear the greatest impact. Some studies had tended to conclude that agriculture could be adapted to future climate changes through crop development and technical changes. But others cast some doubt on the ability of many developing countries to do this because many of their crops are already closer to the limits of tolerance for warmer temperatures. Research on the impacts of the greenhouse effect will challenge scientists for many years to come.

Scientific Uncertainties and Human Choice

The primary weight of scientific opinion is that human-produced global warming is a real phenomenon. Although there is still scientific uncertainty about its exact dimensions, people are becoming increasingly convinced that steps ought to be initiated to do something about it. Exhibit 20-2 illustrates some of the steps people and organizations are beginning to take.

In a sense there are two fundamental choices for this problem: **mitigation** and/or **adaptation.** Mitigation refers to taking steps today to reduce greenhouse gas emissions so as to delay or reduce global temperature increases. Adaptation refers to the efforts of future generations to adjust in ways that will substantially reduce the negative impacts of these temperature increases.

Some have argued that the scientific uncertainties about the extent of global warming make it unwise to undertake costly mitigation steps. This is especially so, they argue, in developing countries where attempts to reduce CO_2 emissions could vastly increase the costs of achieving economic development.

The counter argument is that this strategy would put all the reliance on future adaptation. This could be devastating for countries that cannot easily adapt; therefore, from an equity standpoint it argues for doing something today to mitigate emissions. But even without the equity issue, action is still needed.

In Chapter 6 we introduced a few concepts to help in analyzing situations involving risk, in particular the concept of risk aversion in cases involving small probabilities of very large losses. There is scientific uncertainty about the extent of global warming in the future, but the potential negative consequences are so great that it behooves us to be risk averse. In plain terms: better to be safe than sorry. All of which suggests strongly that significant steps be undertaken today to reduce the probability of serious global warming in the future. It needs to be recognized, however, that there are many things that could be done to mitigate CO_2 emissions, and that these come at different costs. It is very important, therefore, to keep the concept of **cost-effectiveness** closely in mind when developing contemporary mitigation steps.

Technical Responses to the Greenhouse Effect

The greenhouse effect results from an increase in the production of greenhouse gases relative to the ability of the earth's ecosystems to absorb them. So the primary means of reducing the warming lies in reducing the output of greenhouse gases and/or augmenting the GHG-absorbing capacity of the natural world. Because CO_2 is the main greenhouse gas, we focus on the issue of reducing global CO_2 emissions.

To get an overall view of the current world production rate of CO_2 and how it may be altered, consider the following equation:

$$\text{Total } CO_2 \text{ production} = \text{Population} \times \frac{GDP^4}{\text{person}} \times \frac{\text{Energy}}{GDP} \times \frac{CO_2}{\text{energy}}$$

[4]Gross domestic product.

EXHIBIT 20-2

GLOBAL WARMING MOVES FROM IMPASSIONED WORDS TO MODEST DEEDS

By Kirk Johnson

Forget the diplomats dithering over protocols and the scientists agonizing over equations. The next wave of the global warming debate is about nuts and bolts. In the New York metropolitan area and in other cities and states, ordinary people in corporations and government—engineers, teachers and bureaucrats—are quietly beginning to plan for a future in which climate and geography may be decidedly different.

Many steps are tiny and incremental and uncertain. Many are also self-contained, in some cases the result of a single individual in a city or state agency who has taken up the issue. But environmentalists and politicians say that early steps, in a field where the time horizon stretches into decades, are often the most crucial because they set the patterns and precedents that future generations in the region are likely to have to build upon if the full potential of global warming becomes real.

"There's still scientific uncertainty, without a doubt, about what climate change will bring," said William D. Solecki, a professor in the earth and environmental studies department at Montclair State University in New Jersey and a director of a recent federal study on the effects of planetary warming on the New York metropolitan region. "But there's a growing recognition that the future will be different from today."

On Long Island, the Army Corps of Engineers is looking at how to help communities protect themselves from rising sea levels that could bring storm surges miles inland. On Wall Street, El Niño seminars and weather-risk financing have become hallmarks of the newly climate-conscious. In some New York City public schools, complex fluid-dynamic equations of global warming are used to teach math and environmental consciousness.

In New Jersey, which environmentalists say is one of the most active states in coordinating climate-change policies, the state government has begun an aggressive program of buying out property owners whose homes or businesses are in vulnerable flood plains. State economic development officials have been enlisted to promote the idea that global warming defenses can even encourage economic growth, through an energy-efficiency program that helps businesses reduce emissions of greenhouse gases and save money on utility bills.

"It's a balance—you have to look out in 50- and 100-year increments, but you also have to grapple up front, what your preventative measures can result in now," said New Jersey commissioner of environmental protection, Robert C. Shinn Jr.

Some experts say the new activity is a product of the region's reservoir of intellectual and financial capital, some of which is finding an outlet in climate-change work and tapping specialties as diverse as energy, oceanography and risk management.

The United Nations, for instance, has become a leading research center on global climate issues. Columbia University's Earth Institute has taken the lead in examining local climate consequences, and the financial district is expected to become a global player in the climate-change economics that are involved in such systems as international trade in greenhouse gas emissions credits. How such a trading system should work is a main agenda item at the international global warming conference now under way in The Hague.

"The metro area is a powerhouse of global warming stuff," said Michael Glantz, a senior scientist at the environmental and societal impact group within the National Center for Atmospheric Research in Boulder, Colorado. "There's a lot of innovation, awareness, intellect and knowledge." What's missing, he said, are coordination and communication. "People are still working in their own worlds and not crossing lines," he said.

Source: New York Times, November 19, 2000. Copyright © 2000 by the New York Times. Reprinted by permission.

Area	Rates of change				
Global	1.7	1.7	1.0	−0.6	−0.4
India	4.5	2.0	1.2	1.2	0.1
United States	3.7	0.9	3.8	−1.0	0.0

The quantity of CO_2 emissions depends on the interaction of four factors. The first is **population.** Other things remaining equal, larger populations will use more energy and therefore emit larger amounts of CO_2. The second term is **GDP per capita,** a measure of the domestic output of goods and services per capita. We normally associate increases in this factor with economic growth.

Neither population nor per capita GDP can be considered likely candidates for reducing CO_2 emissions in the short run. Deliberate population control measures are unlikely to be effective, and no country is likely to be willing to reduce its rate of economic development. In the long run, however, the interaction of these two factors will be important, as history seems to show that lower population growth rates can be achieved by substantial improvements in economic welfare.

This means that significant near-term CO2 reductions will have to come from the last two terms in the expression. The third factor is what we mean by **"energy efficiency,"** the amount of energy used per dollar (or per franc or rupee or cedi) of output. The key here is to move toward technologies of production, distribution, and consumption that require relatively smaller quantities of energy. The last term is **CO_2 produced per unit of energy used.** Because different energy forms have markedly different CO_2 outputs per unit, reductions in CO_2 can be achieved by switching to less CO_2-intensive fuels.

The table under the equation shows how these four factors have been changing in recent years. The first row shows the annual growth rate in global CO_2 output, which is the sum of the global growth rates of the factors comprising the formula. Note that, worldwide, although energy efficiency and CO_2 intensity are declining, these are being more than offset by high growth rates in population and GDP per capita. But growth rates in the underlying factors differ a great deal among countries. The table shows data for India and the United States for illustrative purposes. In India, increases in all factors, especially population, have contributed to a very rapid rate of growth in CO_2 emissions. In the United States, lower population growth rates, together with increases in energy efficiency (decreases in energy per GDP) have moderated the growth rate of CO_2 emissions. It is differences among countries in these contributing factors that complicate the adoption of effective worldwide agreements to limit CO_2 emissions.

The Kyoto Protocol

The focal point for international reductions in GHG emissions is the **Kyoto Protocol,** an agreement negotiated under the auspices of the United Nations in 1997.[5] It covers six greenhouse gases and establishes emission reduction targets

[5]The Kyoto Protocol is a furtherance of the United Nations Framework Convention on Climate Change, which was completed in 1992.

EXHIBIT 20-3

THE KYOTO PROTOCOL FOR LIMITING GREENHOUSE GAS EMISSIONS

At a conference held in December 1997 in Kyoto, Japan, the parties to the United Nations Framework Convention on Climate Change agreed to an historic protocol to reduce emissions of greenhouse gases into the Earth's atmosphere toward the objective of forestalling the phenomenon of global warming.

Key aspects of the Protocol include emission reduction targets for the industrialized countries, and timetables for reaching them. The specific limits vary from country to country, as indicated. For most key industrial countries the reductions are about 8 percent (7 percent for the United States).

The framework for these targets includes the following:

- Emissions targets are to be reached over a five-year budget period rather than by a single year. Allowing emissions to be averaged across a budget period increases flexibility by helping to smooth out short-term fluctuations in economic performance or weather, either of which could spike emissions in a particular year.
- The first budget period will be 2008–2012. The parties rejected budget periods beginning as early as 2003, as neither realistic nor achievable. Having a full decade before the start of the binding period will allow more time for companies to make the transition to greater energy efficiency and/or lower carbon technologies.
- The emissions targets include all six major greenhouse gases: carbon dioxide, methane, ntirous oxide, and three synthetic substitutes for ozone-depleting CFCs that are highly potent and long-lasting in the atmosphere.
- Activities that absorb carbon, such as planting trees, will be used as offsets against emissions targets. "Sinks" were also included in the interest of encouraging activities like afforestation and reforestation. Accounting for the role of forests is critical to a comprehensive and environmentally responsible approach to climate change. It also provides the private sector with low-cost opportunities to reduce emissions.

	Quantity of emissions (in CO_2 equivalents) as percentage of emissions in base year
Australia	108
Austria	92
Belgium	92
Bulgaria	92
Canada	94
Croatia	95
Czech Republic	92
Denmark	92
Estonia	92
European Community	92
Finland	92
France	92
Germany	92
Greece	92
Hungary	94
Iceland	110
Ireland	92
Italy	92
Japan	94
Latvia	92
Liechtenstein	92
Lithuania	92
Luxembourg	92
Monaco	92
Netherlands	92
New Zealand	100
Norway	101
Poland	94
Portugal	92
Romania	92
Russia	100
Slovakia	92
Slovenia	92
Spain	92
Sweden	92
Switzerland	92
Ukraine	100
United Kingdom	92
United States	93

Sources: U.S. Environmental Protection Agency, "Fact Sheet on the Kyoto Protocol," EPA, Washington, DC, October 1999, p. 2; United Nations, "Framework Convention on Climate Change," New York, March 18, 1998, p. 30.

that countries are obligated to reach by the years 2008 to 2012. The targets are in terms of aggregate anthropogenic CO_2-equivalent emissions, expressed as a percentage of 1990 emissions in the various countries. The agreements contain commitments from 39 countries and one country group, the European Union. These are primarily European countries and the former communist countries of Eastern Europe, together with the United States, Canada, Russia, and Japan. The agreed-upon reductions are shown in Exhibit 20-3.

There are a number of controversial aspects to this international agreement. One is the fact that the treaty follows the Montreal Protocol in differentiating between developed and developing countries. In particular there are no requirements on, or commitments by, any of the developing countries to reduce their GHG emissions. There are some in the developed world who believe that some degree of commitment ought to be registered by countries of the developing world, especially since their GHG emissions are expected to increase very substantially in the next few decades.

Other questions about the Kyoto agreement are being addressed in a series of meetings among the signatory countries. These include enforcement issues and the introduction and use of **flexibility mechanisms** that would presumably help countries meet their cutback targets with a lower overall cost. Flexibility approaches include **international trading programs** in GHG emission permits and **joint implementation,** in which developed countries may get partial credit for meeting their targets by financing emission reduction projects in developing countries. We will have more to say about these issues below.

Reducing Domestic GHG Emissions

Effective global action to combat global warming will require individual countries to undertake steps to reduce their GHG emissions. The question is: How should this be undertaken? In the short run, say over the next 20 years or so, the emphasis will be on getting increases in fuel conservation and efficiency, switching to low-carbon fuels, and reducing the use and emissions of chemicals with high greenhouse impacts. From a policy perspective, perhaps the first thing to note is that there is no single source we could call on to get drastic reductions in GHG production. Instead, changes could be made in hundreds of different places—transportation, industry, households, and agriculture—as Table 20-4 illustrates. These changes are both technological—for example, a switch to more fuel-efficient equipment and low-carbon fuels—and behavioral—for example, a change in driving habits and the adoption of less energy-intensive life styles.

Given the long histories of command-and-control policies in the United States and other countries, many are likely to be attracted to technology or emission standards. In some cases governments may be able effectively to dictate certain economywide technology choices; for example, the widespread adoption of nuclear power in France. Or a country might adopt performance or emission standards; for example, the corporate average-fuel economy (CAFE) standards in the United States. These require that car manufacturers meet minimum average mileage standards among all models made in a given year. But

TABLE 20-4
MEANS OF REDUCING GREENHOUSE GASES

Energy production:
  Reduce demand for electricity (see Households).
  Switch to nonfossil fuels (solar, biomass, nuclear, hydroelectric).
  Switch from high-carbon (coal) to low-carbon (gas) fossil fuels.
  Reduce energy transmission losses.
  Remove carbon from fuel and emissions.

Households:
  Reduce demand for energy (less heating, air conditioning, etc.).
  Switch to less energy-intensive products.
  Switch to more energy-efficient technologies (solar heaters, insulation, etc.).
  Switch out of CFCs in car air conditioners, and so on.

Industry:
  Increase energy efficiency of production processes.
  Switch to low- or no-carbon fuels.
  Increase energy efficiency in buildings, lighting, and so on.
  Switch out of CFCs and other greenhouse gases.

Transportation:
  Reduce miles driven and travel speeds.
  Increase fuel efficiency of vehicles.
  Switch to mass transit systems.

Agriculture and food system:
  Reduce methane production from livestock production and rice paddies.
  Improve energy efficiency in farming.
  Reduce CFC use in refrigeration.
  Reduce energy use in transportation.
  Increase land uses that lead to greater carbon storage.

Forestry:
  Reduce rates of deforestation.
  Increase rates of reforestation.

Source: From material in U.S. Office of Technology Assessment, *Changing by Degrees, Steps to Reduce Greenhouse Gases,* Washington, DC, 1991.

the enormous number and variety of different fuel-using technologies would work against using technology or performance standards as the primary policy approach to CO_2 reduction.

In addition, there are likely to be substantial differences in the costs of GHG emission reduction among the different approaches. Table 20-5 shows some cost-effectiveness results obtained in a large study by the U.S. Office of Technology Assessment (OTA). They show the estimated costs per ton of reducing CO_2 emissions in the United States by adopting different technical alternatives. The estimates are relatively short run, in the sense that the OTA was looking at things that could be accomplished during the next 25 years. Several options have negative CO_2 reduction costs. These are approaches that would pay for themselves without even considering CO_2 removal, primarily through savings in energy. Several things stand out in these numbers. Many are in the general range of \$100–\$300 per ton of CO_2 removed. Considering that the total

TABLE 20-5
COST-EFFECTIVENESS OF ALTERNATIVE MEANS OF REDUCING CO_2, UNITED STATES

Means	Costs per ton of CO_2 ($)
Co-firing boilers with natural gas	510
Early retirement of coal plants, replaced with nonfossil fuels	280
Increased energy efficiency in homes	175 to 300
Increased energy in commercial buildings	−190 to 75
Cogeneration—commercial	85 to 210
Increased fuel efficiency in cars	−220 to −110
Increased fuel efficiency in light trucks	−510 to −410
Mass transit	1,150 to 2,300
Cogeneration—industry	55 to 120
Urban tree planting	180
Afforestation with CRP*	35
Increased CO_2-absorbing capacity through management of existing forests	150 to 200

*CRP stands for Conservation Reserve Program, a program to help farmers reduce production on marginal lands. The program would emphasize tree planting on these acreages.
    Source: U.S. Office of Technology Assessment, *Changing by Degrees, Steps to Reduce Greenhouse Gases,* Washington, DC, 1991, Appendix A.

quantity of CO_2 emissions in the United States today is about 5 billion tons per year, one can get a rough idea of the costs of decreasing these emissions by a substantial fraction. These are also marginal costs; that is, they are costs of reducing CO_2 emissions starting with where we are today. If we ever succeed in moving to a much more energy-efficient economy, the costs of making further reductions in CO_2 emissions will no doubt increase, probably a lot.

Some cost figures that stand out are the low estimates for afforestation, as essentially an add-on to the current conservation reserve program, and the high costs of CO_2 removal through shifting to mass transit. Afforestation is not an emission reduction method, but an attempt to augment the CO_2-absorbing capacity of the earth's ecosystem. Afforestation looks like a good buy for CO_2 removal, but the other side of the coin is that because of the relatively small numbers of acres involved, the total amount of CO_2 that could be removed through this means in the United States is relatively modest. As far as the high cost estimates for rapid transit, these numbers show the effects of the long-run growth patterns in the economy. The trends in population dispersion and transportation technology over the last century have left us with a situation that is not amenable to mass transit to reduce transportation energy requirements. This is a strong reminder, if one is needed, of how decisions taken at one point in time can have consequences much later, when conditions have totally changed.

In situations like this, where there are substantial differences in control costs among different control types, incentive-based policies are to be recommended. For example, the situation would lend itself well to the use of carbon taxes to provide the incentive to reduce fuel consumption and to shift to lower-carbon forms of energy. These would be charges on the carbon content of fuels consumed. In a study of carbon taxes in the United States, the Congressional Budget Office estimated that charges starting at $10/ton of carbon in 1991 and rising to \$100/ton by 2000 would have resulted in reductions in CO_2 emissions of 8–16 percent in 2000 below what they would have been without the tax.[6] Naturally the coal industry and heavy energy-using industries would be the hardest hit by such a tax. In recent years many countries have considered the adoption of carbon taxes.[7]

International Efforts in Global Warming

As mentioned above, continuing efforts are underway, under the auspices of the United Nations, to develop effective **international agreements** for the reduction of greenhouse gases. The Kyoto Protocol specifies specific quantitative cutbacks by countries of the developed world. As we have discussed many times, quantitative limits such as these have built-in perverse incentives: They reward those who have been profligate in the past and penalize those who have been frugal. Countries such as the United States, where relatively little emphasis has been placed on fuel efficiency, will have an easier time meeting such standards for CO_2 reduction than coun tries such as France, where carbon output per dollar of GDP is one-half that of the United States.

Studies have shown, in fact, that the expected costs of CO_2 reduction vary substantially from one country to another. Table 20-6 summarizes some of these studies, with carbon reduction costs expressed in terms of the reduction in gross domestic product ("end year GDP as percentage of baseline"). Note that the estimates vary a lot; they range from a low of –0.2 percent to –15.0 percent. Even the estimates for the United States vary greatly among the different studies. To a large extent this is because of different research approaches—different assumptions, data, and the like. But it also reflects the inherent difficulty and uncertainty of doing studies that try to extrapolate well into the future. This is especially true when we make assumptions about rates of technological change that are likely to occur in the future, in situations with and without the constraints on CO_2 emissions.

We have talked many times in this book about the cost-ineffectiveness of proportionate cutbacks in emissions from different sources, especially when abatement costs differ substantially among the sources. The same principles are at work here, with "sources" now interpreted to mean countries. To have a CO_2 program that is *globally* cost-effective, some economists have suggested that we institute a system of **transferable discharge permits at the international level.** Countries would be allocated CO_2 emission permits equal to their permitted base-level emissions, as determined by some formula such as one of those discussed previously. These permits then would be tradable among countries. The marginal costs of CO_2 reduction could be expected to differ substantially

---

[6]U.S. Congressional Budget Office, *Carbon Charges as a Response toGlobal Warming: The Effects of Taxing Fossil Fuels,* Washington, DC, August 1990.

[7]These countries are Australia, Austria, Canada, Denmark, France, Germany, Japan, The Netherlands, New Zealand, Norway, Sweden, and the United Kingdom. See Peter M. Morrisette and Andrew J. Plantinga, "The Global Warming Issue. Viewpoints of Different Countries," *Resources,* Issue 103, Resources for the Future, Spring 1991, p. 3.

TABLE 20-6
RESULTS OF STUDIES ON THE COSTS OF CO_2 REDUCTIONS

Study	Emission reduction from baseline (end year)	End-year GDP as percentage of baseline
Mann-Richels		
United States	−20 (2030)	−3.3
Other OECD	−20 (2030)	−1.2
Russia, Eastern Europe	−20 (2030)	−4.5
China	−20 (2030)	−5.0
Rest of world	−20 (2030)	−1.0
Congressional Budget Office (U.S.)	−36 (2000)	−0.6
Jorgenson/Wilcoxen (U.S.)	−36 (2060)	−1.1
Blitzer et al. (Egypt)	−35 (2002)	−15.0
Glomered et al. (Norway)	−26 (2010)	−2.7
NEPP (Netherlands)	−25 (2010)	−4.2
Bergman (Sweden)	−51 (2000)	−5.6
Dixon et al. (Australia)	−47 (2005)	−0.2

Sources: The studies were summarized in P. Hoeller, A. Dean, and J. Nicolaisen, "A Survey of Studies of the Costs of Reducing Greenhouse Gas Emissions," Working Paper No. 89, Organization for Economic Cooperation and Development, Department of Economics and Statistics, Paris, 1990; and Joel Darmstadter, "The Economic Cost of CO2 Mitigation: A Review of Estimates for Selected World Regions," Discussion Paper ENR91-06, Resources for the Future, Washington, DC, 1991.

among countries, on the basis of such factors as wealth and economic growth rates, fossil fuel availabilities, and energy technologies. Thus, trading opportunities exist that could substantially reduce the overall global costs of reducing CO_2 emissions. Another salutary feature of global carbon TDPs is that they easily could be used to address questions of international equity. The current belief is that it will cost developing countries more, relative to their current wealth, to reduce CO_2 emissions than developed economies. Thus, the direction of transfers would go in general from less to more developed countries. On top of this, developing countries might be given proportionately larger numbers of permits in the initial distribution. In buying these extra permits, developed nations would be transferring extra amounts of wealth to the developing countries, which they could use to switch to low-carbon development paths. However, the political practicability of this approach is open to serious question.

In any system of transferable discharge permits, controversy surrounds the initial allocation of permits to the participating parties. This would be especially true in a global allocation of permits. What formula might be followed in setting these allocations? Consider the following possibilities:

- Equiproportionate reduction in emissions.
- Ability to pay. Base emission reductions/transfer payments on current per-capita income levels.
- Polluter pays principle. Base emission reductions/transfer payments on current or past contributions to the problem.
- Equal per-capita consumption. Base emission reductions on the idea that all per-capita consumption levels should be the same.

TABLE 20-7
ECONOMIC AND CARBON EMISSIONS DATA FOR SELECTED COUNTRIES, 1987

Country	Population (millions)	GDP percapita ($)	Total emissions (million tons)	Emissions per capita (tons)	Emissions per dollar GDP (grams)	Emissions (% of total)
China	1,031.9	320*	578	0.56	2,024	9.6
France	54.3	16,234	92	1.70	133	1.5
India	685.2	371	130	0.19	655	2.2
United States	226.5	18,506	1,139	5.03	276	18.9
World (average or total)			6,030	1.08	327	—

*1989
Sources: Emissions per capita and total emissions taken from John Walley, "The Interface Between Environmental and Trade Policies," *The Economic Journal*, 101(405), March 1991, p. 103. Population and income data are from United Nations, *1987 Demographic Yearbook*, New York, 1989, pp. 173–175.

These rules would have substantially different implications for different countries of the world. The data in Table 20-7 show population, income, and CO_2 emissions data for a selected group of countries. The countries were selected to illustrate the differential impacts of the rules, not because they are in any way more significant than others. If the cutback were based on total emissions, the largest reduction would be allocated to the United States, followed by China, then India, and France. But if it were based on emissions per capita, the order would be the United States, France, China, and India. If emissions reductions were based on energy efficiency, the largest cutbacks would actually be allocated to China and India because, although their emissions per capita are low, incomes are even lower, giving them relatively high numbers for emissions per dollar of GDP. Finally, if we were to allocate emission reductions on the basis of proportionate share of total CO_2 emissions, the United States would have the largest cutback, followed by China, India, and France.

Suggestions also have been made for a worldwide CO_2 emissions tax, a single tax that would apply to all sources in all countries. This would achieve cost-effectiveness at both the intercountry level and intersource level within each country, provided governments did nothing to thwart the uniform application of the tax domestically. Economic studies of this approach have been neatly summarized by Nordhaus. Figure 20-2 shows the relationship between different levels of carbon tax and the percentage of reduction in CO_2 emissions. The points shown in the graph are the results of the different studies reviewed by Nordhaus. The studies differed in terms of the countries and exact circumstances to which they applied, but they do seem to tell a reasonably consistent story. The curved line is drawn through the points, representing what the author feels is the best summary of the studies. In effect the curve shows the marginal costs of reducing CO_2 emissions. To get a worldwide reduction of 20 percent in CO_2 emissions would require a tax of about $45/ton of carbon. A 50 percent CO_2 reduction would need a $140 tax, and the curvature of the graph shows that deeper CO_2 cutbacks would require progressively larger taxes.

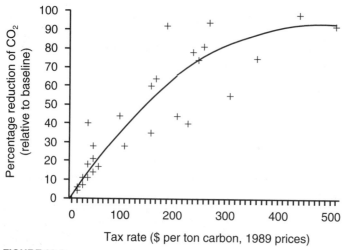

FIGURE 20-2
Estimates of the Reductions of CO_2 Emissions Produced at Different Tax
Rates. *(Source: Based on William D. Nordhaus, "A Survey of Estimates of
the Cost of Reduction of Greenhouse Gas Emissions," paper presented for
the National Academy of Science, Committee on Science, Engineering,
and Public Policy, February 1990.)*

Whether any significant international effort can be mounted to establish a
worldwide carbon tax is highly problematic. A tax high enough to produce significant CO_2 reductions would be especially burdensome in developing countries. Support might be encouraged if the proceeds of the tax could be shared
out among countries so as to reduce the overall impact on poorer nations.
Along with these equity matters, real questions exist about the difficulties of
monitoring and enforcing the tax. Self-monitoring by the individual countries
is likely to be the only practical solution to this issue because it is unlikely that
countries would willingly permit international monitoring efforts. Sanctioning
countries that exceed their TDP quotas or fail to pay taxes would be difficult.
The United Nations lacks executive power to enforce international environmental agreements. The International Court of Justice (ICJ) acts chiefly as a
place for discussing disputes and lacks mechanisms to enforce rulings. This
leaves enforcement up to a combination of moral pressure and whatever unilateral actions states might take, such as trade sanctions.

One important item these data do not include is the costs to the various
countries of doing nothing; that is, simply adapting to global warming. These
costs are likely to place limits on the extent to which any particular country will
readily accept CO_2 emission reduction requirements, since no country is likely
to want to spend more in control costs than the cost of accommodating to the
change. For cooler countries in higher latitudes, with relatively little critical
shoreline, adaptation costs may be fairly "modest." Countries in the opposite
situation will have very high costs of adapting to higher temperatures and rising sea levels. Countries differ also in terms of agricultural adaptability, the
ability to shift crops, varieties, cultivation methods, and so on, to maintain pro-

duction in the face of climate changes. So countries are likely to have very different perceptions about how they will be affected by global warming. The obstacles to an effective international agreement on CO_2 reduction are many, and the need for creative treaty diplomacy is great.

BIOLOGICAL DIVERSITY

Another problem that many people have begun to appreciate in recent years is the worldwide reduction in diversity among the elements of the biological system. This can be discussed at several levels: diversity in the stock of genetic material, species diversity, or diversity among ecosystems. But the long-run health of the whole system requires that there be diversity among its parts. Biological uniformity produces inflexibility and weakened ability to respond to new circumstances; diversity gives a system the means to adapt to change.

The human population cannot maintain itself without cultivating certain species of animals and plants. But the continued vigor of this relationship actually depends also on the stock of wild species. This dependence can manifest itself in a variety of ways. About 25 percent of the **prescription drugs** in the developed societies are derived from plants.[8] Diseases are not static; they evolve in response to efforts made to eradicate them. Thus, wild species of plants constitute a vital source of raw material needed for future medicines. Wild species are also critical for **agriculture.** Through traditional plant and animal breeding, and even more through modern methods of **biotechnology,** genetic material and the qualities they entail may be transferred from wild species into cultivated ones. In 1979 a species of wild maize resistant to an important crop virus was discovered in a remote corner of Mexico. When transferred to species of domestic corn, this characteristic substantially enhanced the agricultural value of that crop.

The stock of species at any particular time is a result of two processes: the random mutations that create new species of organisms and the forces that determine rates of extinction among existing species. Scientists currently estimate the number of extant species at between 5 and 10 million, of which about 1.4 million have been described. When a species goes extinct, we lose forever whatever valuable qualities that organism may have had. The normal, long-run rate of species extinction has been estimated at about 9 percent per million years, or 0.000009 percent per year.[9] Thus, this is the normal rate at which the information contained in the species stock vanishes. At several times in the geological past, the rate of extinctions has been very much higher. One of these times was the period, millions of years ago, during which the dinosaurs died off. Another is today. But while the earlier period was the result of natural causes, today's rapid destruction of the stock of species is due primarily to the actions of human beings.

---

[8]U.S. Office of Technology Assessment, *Technologies to Sustain Tropical Forest Resources and Biological Diversity,* Washington, DC, May 1992, p. 60.
[9]Edward O. Wilson (ed.), *Biodiversity,* National Academy Press, Washington, DC, 1986.

Some species go extinct because they are **overexploited.** But the vast majority are under pressure because of **habitat destruction.** This comes primarily
from commercial pressures to exploit other features of the land: logging off the
trees for timber or wood, converting the land to agricultural uses, clearing the
land for urban expansion, and so on. This has been a particular problem in
many third-world countries, which contain a disproportionately large share of
the world's wild species, but which are also under great pressure to pursue
modern economic development.

The information contained in the global stock of genetic capital has consis-
tently been **undervalued.** This is partly because we do not know what is there
or what portions of it may turn out to be important in the future. It is also
because, almost by definition, it is impossible to know the value of the genes in
a species that has gone extinct; we cannot miss something we never realized we
had. But primarily the undervaluation of the stock of wild germ plasm is a
function of the **institutions** governing the management of wild species.
Whereas the market values of conventional products ensure that their production will be pursued with vigor, there are normally no comparable market values for the information contained in the wild gene pool.

In the United States the Endangered Species Act (ESA) of 1973 was enacted
to help preserve individual species. When a species is listed as either "endangered" or "threatened," steps may be undertaken toward its preservation. This
includes prohibitions on the "taking" (killing or wounding) of any individual
of that species, and a requirement that actions authorized or funded by any federal agency not put in jeopardy the continued existence of the species. This **ESA
type of approach** is pursued also in a number of other federal laws (e.g., the
Bald Eagle Protection Act of 1940, the Marine Mammal Protection Act of 1972,
and the Salmon and Steelhead Conservation and Enhancement Act of 1980).
Each state also has its own endangered species laws. Although these laws have
had some success in preserving individual species, they are relatively ineffective at preserving diversity, which is not a matter of a single species but of a
relationship among a large number of species.

The effective maintenance of biodiversity depends on the **maintenance of
habitats** in amounts big enough that species may preserve themselves in complex biological equilibria. This involves first identifying valuable habitats and
then protecting them from development pressures that are incompatible with
preserving the resident species. In the United States, a large network of reserved
lands has been preserved in the public domain, national parks, wilderness areas,
wildlife refuges, and the like. The fact of the matter is, however, that the world's
primary areas of genetic and species abundance and diversity are in developing
countries in Central and South America, Africa, and Southeast Asia.[10]

Efforts have been made in some of these countries, sometimes vigorously
and sometimes not, to protect areas of high biological value by putting them
into some sort of **protected status**—sanctuaries, reserves, parks, and so on. But

---

[10]The countries especially recognized for biological diversity are Mexico, Colombia, Brazil,
Zaire, Madagascar, and Indonesia.

here the situation is usually much more complicated by high population pressures. People who are struggling to get enough resources to achieve some degree of economic security may feel that something called biological diversity is not particularly relevant. Land reservation for species preservation is essentially a zoning approach, and it suffers the same fundamental flaw of that policy: It does not reshape the **underlying incentives** that are leading to population pressure on the habitats.

One suggestion that has been made to change this is to create a more complete **system of property rights** over genetic resources. At the present time, property rights are recognized for special breeder stock, genetically engineered organisms, and newly developed medicines. This provides a strong incentive for research on new drugs and the development of improved crops. But this incentive does not extend backward to the protection of wild gene plasm, especially in developing countries. Thus, the suggestion is to clarify property rights in wild species and let countries themselves exercise these property rights in world markets for genetic information. By allowing them to sell the rights to parts of the genetic stock, countries would have a way of realizing the values inherent in these stocks and would therefore be motivated to devote more effort and resources to their protection. Countries also would have stronger incentives to inventory and describe species that are still unknown.

In fact, events may be moving in this direction already. A contract was recently signed between Merck and Company, a U.S. pharmaceutical firm, and the Instituto Nacional de Biodiversidad of Costa Rica. The contract calls for an upfront payment of $1 million, plus royalties on discoveries of commercial value, while the Costa Rican agency will undertake steps to catalogue and preserve biological resources in that country. The American Cancer Institute has negotiated contracts with Zimbabwe, Madagascar, and the Philippines for access to genetic resources in these countries. A British firm named Biotics is functioning as a broker between potential suppliers and buyers of genetic resources.[11]

Especially important is how this type of approach would filter down to affect individuals who are actually using the land. It is highly doubtful if substantial amounts of land could be put off limits to any type of development if **population pressure** continues high. So attention needs to be directed also at developing modes of commercial agriculture that are compatible with genetic and species preservation. Production based on retaining natural habitat requires two things: that cultivators have secure property rights and that there be strong markets for the types of "crops" produced in this kind of system.

SUMMARY

In recent years we have seen the rise of truly global environmental problems, especially those dealing with the disruption of the global atmosphere. In these cases it is as if all the nations of the world were homeowners living around a

---

[11]R. David Simpson and Roger A. Sedjo, "Contracts for Transferring Rights to Indigenous Genetic Resources," *Resources*, 109, Fall 1992, Resources for the Future, Washington, DC, pp. 1–5.

small lake, each one dependent on the lake for water supply, but each one also using the lake for waste disposal.

Depletion of the earth's protective ozone layer has been a result of the widespread use of chlorofluorocarbons for refrigerants, solvents, and other uses. What once were regarded as miracle chemicals now have turned out to be life threatening. The increased ultraviolet radiation this will produce at the earth's surface is expected to increase skin cancers and eye cataracts and have a substantial impact on agricultural production. In recent years chemical companies have had success in developing substitutes for CFCs. This greatly facilitated the signing of the Montreal Protocol, an international agreement among most of the nations of the world that will lead to a phaseout of the production and consumption of CFCs over the next few decades.

The global greenhouse effect will be more difficult to deal with. Burning fossil fuels has increased the CO_2 content of the atmosphere, affecting the earth's radiation balance and leading to an increase in mean global temperatures. Substantial impacts are expected on weather patterns around the globe. These are expected to disrupt agricultural operations in significant ways. A rise in the sea level will have profound impacts on coastal communities. A substantial attack on the phenomenon will require cutting back on the use of fossil fuels. Virtually all countries are dependent to a greater or lesser extent on fossil fuels to power their economies. Thus, we must emphasize cost-effective policies to improve energy efficiency and to switch to fuels that emit less CO_2. The Kyoto Protocol is the first step toward effective international efforts to reduce global CO_2 emissions.

The destruction of biological diversity is a subtler global problem, but it may be just as costly in the long run. Dealing with this problem will require greater efforts to preserve habitat and develop agriculture that is compatible with species preservation. Effective action will mean doing something about the incentives that currently lead to species destruction.

QUESTIONS FOR FURTHER DISCUSSION

1 Many countries are adopting a "wait and see" strategy on CO_2 emissions and atmospheric warming. What would a rational "wait and see" strategy look like?

2 When CFCs were first introduced 50 years ago, their benefits were obvious, and nobody appreciated the long-run impacts they might have. How do we guard ourselves against unforeseen long-run effects such as this?

3 In the absence of a worldwide agreement to reduce CO_2 through a carbon tax, how effective might it be if just one country, or a small number of countries, instituted a tax unilaterally?

4 Rather than placing a tax on fuels or the carbon content of fuels, taxes might be put on fuel-using items, such as "gas-guzzling" cars, less efficient appliances, or houses with poor insulation. Which type of tax would be more efficient?

5 Global warming is predicted to affect countries differently, which is one reason it is difficult to get all countries to agree on a global CO_2 treaty. Do you think it will be easier to get agreement *after* the results start showing up in different countries?

6 How many different formulas can you think of for allocating a reduction in global CO_2 among the nations of the world? Compare and contrast these in terms of efficiency and equity.

WEBSITES

A very good site on global warming is maintained by the Intergovernmental Panel on Climate Change, **www.ipcc.ch;** the EPA **www.epa.gov/globalwarming,** also has a major site on the issue. See also the links listed on the website of this book, **www.mhhe.com/economics/field3.**

SELECTED READINGS

Barrett, Scott: "The Political Economy of the Kyoto Protocol," *Oxford Review of Economics and Politics,* 14(4); Winter 1998, pp. 20–39.

Benedick, Richard: *Ozone Diplomacy,* Harvard University Press, Cambridge, MA, 1991.

Dudek, Daniel J., and Joseph Goffman: "Building an Effective International Greenhouse Gas Control System," Environmental Defense Fund, New York, 1997.

Hahn, Robert W.: "The Economics and Politics of Climate Change," American Enterprise Institute, Washington, DC, 1998.

International Panel on Climate Change: *Climate Change 1995: Economic and Social Dimensions of Climate Change. The Contribution of Working Group III to the Second Assessment Report of the Intergovernmental Panel on Climate Change,* edited by J. P. Bruce, H. Lee, and E. F. Haites, Cambridge University Press, Cambridge, MA, 1996.

Manne, Alan S., and Richard G. Richels: *Buying Greenhouse Insurance, The Economic Cost of CO_2 Emission Limits,* MIT Press, Cambridge, MA, 1992.

Morrisette, Peter M.: "The Evolution of Policy Responses to Stratospheric Ozone Depletion," *Natural Resources Journal,* 29(3), Summer 1989, pp. 793–820.

Nordhaus, William D.: *Managing the Global Commons,* MIT Press, Cambridge, MA, 1994.

Nordhaus, William D. (ed.): *Economic and Policy Issues in Climate Change,* Resources for the Future, Washington, DC, 1998.

Schelling, Thomas C.: *Costs and Benefits of Greenhouse Reduction,* AEI Press, Washington, DC, 1998.

Victor, David G., Kal Raustiala, and Eugene B. Skolnikoff: "Introduction and Overview," in David G. Victor, Kal Raustiala, and Eugene B. Skolnikoff (eds.), *The Implementation and Effectiveness of International Environmental Commitments,* MIT Press, Cambridge, MA, 1997.

CHAPTER 21

INTERNATIONAL ENVIRONMENTAL AGREEMENTS

In the last chapter we discussed several global environmental issues. In one of these—stratospheric ozone depletion—nations of the world have signed an international agreement to reduce emissions of the main chemicals causing the problem. The Kyoto Protocol of 1997 addresses some issues of global warming. As countries continue to grow, more and more environmental problems will spill beyond national borders—not just these global cases, but also a rising number of environmental externalities inflicted by people in one country on those of another. So while environmental policies continue to evolve within individual countries, there will be a growing need to develop **multicountry** attacks on environmental problems.[1] In the final chapter of this book, therefore, we take a look at some of the economic issues involved in the creation of **international environmental agreements.**

International environmental policy has a distinctly different character from national policies. The most salient difference is that on the international level there are **no effective enforcement** institutions. Within any country, authoritative regulatory authorities can be called upon to enforce whatever laws are passed, although this does not imply by any means that all environmental laws will be adequately enforced. But on the international level enforcement authorities do not exist. Thus, environmental policy at this level consists essentially of international agreements among sovereign states, where each country pledges

---

[1]The international scope of many environmental problems was first highlighted by the 1972 United Nations Conference on the Human Environment (the "Stockholm Conference" or first "earth summit"), which led to the United Nations Environment Program (UNEP) and the 1992 global environmental conference in Brazil.

to follow certain specified courses of action as regards emissions reductions or other steps for environmental protection. Enforcement then has to be carried out either through voluntary means like moral suasion, or else through retaliation by whatever pressure a country or group of countries may be able to exert on recalcitrant countries.

In this chapter we review some of the main features of international environmental agreements, focusing especially on the incentive situations facing countries that are considering an agreement. The discussion begins with a brief descriptive section that shows the great variety of international environmental agreements that have been concluded to date. It then moves to cases that involve just two countries, followed by the case of multiple-country agreements. The chapter ends with a discussion of an issue that will become increasingly important as national economies continue to grow: the environmental quality implications of **international trade.**

GENERAL ISSUES

The history of international agreements on natural resource matters goes back many centuries, to the time when countries sought to agree on navigation rules to cover ocean passages. In the 20th century international treaties proliferated as a result of the rapidly expanding list of environmental problems involving multiple countries. Table 21-1 shows a partial list of **current multilateral agreements** pertaining to natural and environmental resources. The number of countries involved varies from 3 to 161.

Numerous treaties have been concluded on marine pollution, beginning with oil-pollution agreements and later extending to more general pollution-control measures. Although much attention has been given recently to the issue of protecting the resources of biological diversity, the first international treaties on flora and fauna were actually made decades ago. By now there are many such treaties, including the important 1973 convention on international trade in endangered species.[2]

A standard international agreement will contain provisions specifying the actions to be undertaken by each signatory country, as well as numerous institutional and logistical matters, such as what kind of governing agency is to be established, how its work is to be funded, what information is to be shared, and so on.

Many of the multilateral treaties are actually regional in scope. This includes, for example, the water and air pollution–control treaties among the countries of Europe. The United Nations has sponsored a number of regional agreements involving countries bordering particular seas (Mediterranean Sea, Red Sea, southeastern Pacific Ocean, western African coastal waters, Caribbean Sea, etc.).

---

[2]A "treaty" is an agreement in which all the details have presumably been worked out and expressed in the document to which each signing country agrees. A "convention" is an agreement in which parties agree on a general framework that is expected to be supplemented in the future by one or more "protocols" that work out the details.

TABLE 21-1

SELECTED INTERNATIONAL ENVIRONMENTAL AGREEMENTS

Name of agreement	Date of adoption	Date of entry into force	Number of signatories
Marine Pollution			
International Convention for the Prevention of Pollution of the Sea by Oil (as amended 11/4/62 and 10/21/69)	1954	1958	71*
Agreement for Cooperation in Dealing with Pollution of the North Sea by Oil	1969	1969	8
International Convention on Civil Liability for Oil Pollution Damage (as amended)	1969	1975	63
International Convention Relating to Intervention on the High Seas in Cases of Oil Pollution Casualties	1969	1975	54
Convention on the Prevention of Marine Pollution by Dumping of Wastes and Other Matter ("London Dumping")	1972	1975	—
International Convention for the Prevention of Pollution from Ships, 1973	1973	—	19
Convention on the Prevention of Marine Pollution from Land-Based Sources	1974	1978	13
Convention for the Protection of the Mediterranean Sea Against Pollution	1976	1978	18
International Rivers			
Protocol Concerning the Constitution of an International Commission for the Protection of the Moselle Against Pollution	1961	1962	3
Agreement Concerning the International Commission for the Protection of the Rhine Against Pollution	1963	1965	6
Convention on the Protection of the Rhine Against Chemical Pollution	1976	1979	6
Convention Creating the Niger Basin Authority and Protocol Relating to the Development Fund of the Niger Basin	1980	1982	8
Flora and Fauna			
European Treaty on the Conservation of Birds Useful to Agriculture	1902	1902	11
Convention Relative to the Preservation of Fauna and Flora in Their Natural State	1933	1936	54
Convention of Nature Protection and Wildlife Preservation in the Western Hemisphere	1940	1942	19

*Four countries have renounced the Convention.
(Continued on next page)

TABLE 21-1
SELECTED INTERNATIONAL ENVIRONMENTAL AGREEMENTS (CONTINUED)

Name of agreement	Date of adoption	Date of entry into force	Number of signatories
Flora and Fauna			
International Convention for the Regulation of Whaling (as amended)	1946	1948	43[†]
International Convention for the Protection of Birds	1950	1963	10
International Plant Protection Convention	1951	1952	92
International Convention for the High Seas Fisheries of the North Pacific Ocean (as amended)	1952	1953	3
Convention on Fishing and Conservation of the Living Resources of the High Seas	1958	1966	35
International Convention for the Protection of New Varieties of Plants (as amended)	1961	1968	17
Convention on the African Migratory Locust	1962	1963	16
African Convention on the Conservation of Nature and Natural Resources	1968	1969	29
European Convention for the Protection of Animals During International Transport	1968	1971	20
Benelux Convention on the Hunting and Protection of Birds (as amended)	1970	1972	3
Convention on Wetlands of International Importance Especially as Waterfowl Habitat	1971	1975	50
Convention for Conservation of Antarctic Seals	1972	1978	12
Convention on International Trade in Endangered Species of Wild Fauna and Flora	1973	1975	96
Agreement on Conservation of Polar Bears	1973	1976	5
Convention on Conservation of Nature in the South Pacific	1976	—	3
Convention on Migratory Species	1979	1983	70
Convention on Biological Diversity	1992	1993	168
Nuclear			
Convention on Third Party Liability in the Field of Nuclear Energy (as amended)	1960	1968	14
Vienna Convention of Civil Liability for Nuclear Damage	1963	1977	10
Treaty Banning Nuclear Weapon Tests in the Atmosphere, in Outer Space and Under Water	1963	1963	117
Treaty on the Prohibition of the Emplacement of Nuclear Weapons and Other Weapons of Mass Destruction on the Sea-Bed and the Ocean Floor and in the Subsoil Thereof	1971	1972	79
Convention on Early Notification of a Nuclear Accident	1986	1986	31

[†]Three withdrawals
(Continued on next page)

TABLE 21-1
SELECTED INTERNATIONAL ENVIRONMENTAL AGREEMENTS (CONTINUED)

Name of agreement	Date of adoption	Date of entry into force	Number of signatories
Air Pollution			
#TB:Convention on Long-Range Transboundary Air Pollution	1979	1983	30
Protocol to the 1979 Convention on Long-Range Transboundary Air Pollution on			
Long-Term Financing of the Co-operative Programme for Monitoring and Evaluation of the Long-Range Transmission of Air Pollutants in Europe (EMEP)	1984	1988	27
Protocol to the 1979 Convention on Long-Range Transboundary Air Pollution on the			
Reduction of Sulphur Emissions or Their Transboundary Fluxes by at Least 30 Percent	1985	1987	18
Protocol to the 1979 Convention on Long-Range Transboundary Air Pollution Concerning the Control of Emissions of Nitrogen Oxides or Their Transboundary Fluxes	1988	—	24
Vienna Convention for the Protection of the Ozone Layer	1985	1988	36
Montreal Protocol on Substances that Deplete the Ozone Layer	1987	1989	43
Kyoto Protocol to the United Nations Framework Convention on Climate Change	1999	—	—

(Continued on next page)

Besides the multilateral treaties there are hundreds of bilateral treaties, addressing the environmental problems of just two countries. The United States and Canada have concluded a number of bilateral agreements, including agreements dealing with acid rain and with the management of the Great Lakes. The United States and Mexico also have worked out several environmental agreements dealing with hazardous waste shipments, the use of the Colorado and Rio Grande rivers, and other matters.

THE ECONOMICS OF INTERNATIONAL AGREEMENTS

When international agreements are being negotiated, the focus is usually on political issues. This is natural, since what is going on are complex negotiations among sovereign states. But underlying the political interactions—national sovereignty, political assertiveness, creative diplomacy, and so on—lie many bedrock economic factors that affect the **perceived benefits and costs** accruing to the different participants and the incentives they have for entering into environmental agreements. In the next few sections we discuss some of these issues.

TABLE 21-1
SELECTED INTERNATIONAL ENVIRONMENTAL AGREEMENTS (CONTINUED)

Name of agreement	Date of adoption	Date of entry into force	Number of signatories
Miscellaneous			
The Antarctic Treaty	1959	1961	32
European Convention on the Protection of the Archaeological Heritage	1969	1970	17
Ramsar Convention on Wetlands	1971	1975	123
Convention on the Prohibition of the Development, Production and Stockpiling or Bacteriological (Biological) and Toxin Weapons, and on Their Destruction	1972	1975	101
Convention Concerning the Protection of the World Cultural and Natural Heritage	1972	1975	98
Treaty for Amazonian Co-operation	1978	1980	8
Convention on the Conservation of Antarctic Marine Living Resources	1980	1982	21
Convention Concerning Occupational Safety and Health and the Working Environment	1981	1983	9
United Nations Convention on the Law of the Sea	1982	—	161
Convention on the Regulation of Antarctic Mineral Resource Activities	1988	—	6
Basel Convention on the Control of the Transboundary Movements of Hazardous Wastes and Their Disposal	1989	—	116

Source: Scott Barrett, "Economic Analysis of International Environmental Agreements: Lessons for a Global-Warming Treaty," in Organization for Economic Cooperation and Development (ed.), *Responding to Climate Change, Selected Economic Issues,* Paris, 1991.

Bilateral Agreements

First consider the case of just two countries—call them Country A and Country B. B is downwind from A, so SO_2 emissions from A contribute to acid rain both at home and in B. In B, SO_2 emissions contribute to acid rain only in that country; because of prevailing wind patterns, there is no reciprocal acid rain externality inflicted by B upon A. This situation is pictured in Figure 21-1. It shows the marginal abatement costs in A (MAC) and the marginal damage functions associated with the emissions of that country. Marginal damages arising in A itself are shown as MD_A, whereas MD_T are aggregate marginal damages for both A and B. The marginal damages in B from A's emissions, in other words, are $(MD_T - MD_A)$. If A were managing its emissions without regard to the externalities produced in B, it would regard point e_1 as the efficient level of emissions.

But for emissions in A to be internationally efficient, it is necessary to take into account the effects on B. The **"globally efficient"** level of emissions is e_2.

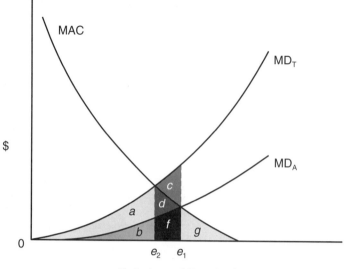

FIGURE 21-1
Bilateral Transboundary Pollution and the Economics of Reaching an Agreement.

The added attainment costs in A to achieve this further reduction in emissions is an amount equal to the area $(d + f)$. But this is more than offset by a reduction in damages totaling $(c + d + f)$, of which f represents damage reduction in A, whereas $(d + c)$ is damage reduction in B.

We saw in Chapter 10 that negotiations between polluters and those damaged can result in efficient emission levels, given that property rights are clearly defined and that transactions costs are minimal. On the international level, direct negotiations between private parties involved are essentially ruled out, because under international law private citizens of one country do not have the right to sue private citizens in another country. Instead, negotiations must be carried out among political authorities of the two countries. This is where diplomacy comes in because, in the example given previously, the reduction in A's emissions from e_1 to e_2 involves negative net benefits *in that country*—added costs of $(d + f)$ and reduced damages of only f. So, in effect, authorities would be asking people in Country A to make a sacrifice to benefit people in another country. This kind of thing happens all the time within individual countries. But across countries the institutions of policy are weaker, depending essentially on diplomatic skills and whatever international sanctioning can be carried out through moral, economic, or political means.

According to the precedents in international law, cases like this are supposed to be covered by a **polluter pays principle** (PPP). The *Trail Smelter* case of 1935 is an important source of that precedent. Trail Smelter was a metal refinery in British Columbia whose SO_2 discharges damaged farm crops across the border in the United States. The tribunal finding in favor of the farmers stated that under the principles of international law "no State has the right to use or permit the use of its territory in such a manner as to cause injury by fumes in or to the territory of another."[3] This declaration was embodied in the Declaration of the 1972 United Nations Conference on the Human Environment (the first "earth summit"), which covered all types of transboundary pollution. Most international agreements seek to incorporate the polluter pays principle.

But because international agreements are voluntary, it may be supposed that individual countries will never sign any agreement that makes them worse off. In other words, each prospective signatory must regard the agreement as leaving them at least as well off as they would be without it. In our example, this means that the two countries may have to shift partially to a **"victim pays principle"** (VPP). The net loss to A in going from e_1 to e_2 would have to be compensated by Country B. Country A has added abatement costs of $(d + f)$ in going from e_1 to e_2, but it also experiences added benefits (reduced damages) of f, so its extra costs are equal to d. Since B's damage reduction totals $(c + d)$, it could compensate A for these costs and still be ahead by an amount equal to c.

There are many issues that come up in international bargaining about environmental externalities of this type. Bargaining depends critically on the **perceptions** by each country of its own marginal damages and marginal abatement costs, as well as on how convincing it can be in expressing these views to other countries. In the case of Figure 21-1, for example, A has an interest in convincing B that the added abatement costs of going from e_1 to e_2 are very high, whereas its own domestic benefits from this move are quite low. B, however, has an interest in convincing A that it would experience real reductions in damages from a reduction in emissions, but not so high that it could afford very large compensation payments. For a discussion of some of the complexities of these types of problems, see Exhibit 21-1.

Countries engaged in negotiations of this type will usually be involved at the same time in negotiations on other problems, as well as with negotiations with other countries. Thus, they will be concerned with the net outcome of all these negotiations, and this could dictate a position on this one issue quite different from what one would expect solely on the basis of the merits of this particular case. John Krutilla's study of the agreement between the United States and Canada over use of the Columbia River, for example, indicates that the distribution of costs in the treaty was primarily related to the desire of the United States to stimulate economic development in Canada.[4]

Multilateral Agreements

Consider now a situation where a number of countries all contribute to an environmental problem that affects all of them. Examples are acid rain pollution stemming from SO_2 emissions, pollution of a regional sea by riparian countries,

---

[3]Quoted in William A. Nitze, "Acid-Rain: A United States Perspective," in Daniel Barstow Magraw (ed.), *International Law and Pollution*, University of Pennsylvania Press, Philadelphia, 1991, p. 346.
[4]John V. Krutilla, *The Columbia River Treaty: A Study of the Economics of International River Basin Development*, Johns Hopkins Press, Baltimore, MD, 1968.

EXHIBIT 21-1

TWO NATIONS IN ONE NEIGHBORHOOD CLEAN UP THEIR AIR

El Paso, Texas, and Jaurez, Mexico, Cooperate to Curb Pollution from Vehicle Emission and Industry

By Scott Pendleton, staff writer of the Christian Science Monitor, El Paso, Texas

On horseback or in pale green Suburban trucks, the United States Border Patrol has clamped down on illegal immigration in this desert metropolis of 700,000.

Authorities are powerless, though, to stop another un-wanted flow: air pollution from the sputtering cars, dirt roads, and home-grown industries of Juarez. That Mexican city of 1.5 million and El Paso, Texas, interlock like puzzle pieces, separated only by the Rio Grande.

Citizens of this essentially single, bi-national community have not waited for Washington and Mexico City to solve the air-quality problem. Instead, they have initiated action. "The regulatory community wasn't going to clean up our air," says Danny Vickers, an El Paso businessman who chairs the Paso del Norte Air Quality Task Force. "The community has got to stand up and say, 'We're behind you.' It's a matter of survival."

Mr. Vickers's bi-national task force is composed of businessmen, educators, environmentalists, local officials, and local representatives of state and federal regulatory agencies. Formed in 1993, it has launched pollution-reduction projects to scrub the smog-filled skies that now rest on the cities' shared airshed like a dingy sombrero.

Excessive amounts of carbon monoxide, fine dust particles, and ground-level ozone put El Paso on the U.S. Environmental Protection Agency's (EPA) list of cities not in compliance with the Clean Air Act Amendments of 1990.

"The air quality here is awful," says Matthew Witosky, the EPA's new border liaison in El Paso.

One reason is that Juarez residents and those in El Paso own older cars that lack modern pollution-control equipment. "We're the dumping ground for used vehicles in the Southwest," says Jesus Reynoso, supervisor of the El Paso City-County air-quality program. Vehicle ages average four years in the U.S., seven in El Paso, and 13 in Juarez.

In recent years, however, air quality has shown improvement. El Paso has had no violations for particulates or fine dust in two years and for carbon monoxide in a year. Heat causes ground-level ozone, or smog, to form, but last summer when temperatures topped 100 degrees F. for 24 days in a row, the city exceeded ozone limits on just five days.

Officials attribute the progress to wintertime sales of cleaner-burning oxygenated gasoline in El Paso, and to road-paving projects and vehicle-inspection programs in both cities. Changing the spark plugs and points in a Juarez vehicle, Reynoso says, can cut its emissions 99 percent.

After cars, the second-leading source of air pollution is the Juarez brickmaking indus-

---

stratospheric ozone depletion through emissions of CFCs, and the greenhouse effect stemming from CO_2 emissions. In these cases the damages suffered by each country are related to the level of total emissions, present and probably past, of all the countries. From an economic standpoint there are both **efficiency** and **equity** issues in these types of international agreements. There is the basic efficiency question of balancing overall benefits and costs. For most international agreements, especially the truly global ones, there are enormous difficulties in estimating total global benefits with any accuracy. The impacts are too massive, and there are extraordinarily difficult problems of trying to compare

---

EXHIBIT 21-1 (CONTINUED)

TWO NATIONS IN ONE NEIGHBORHOOD CLEAN UP THEIR AIR

El Paso, Texas, and Jaurez, Mexico, Cooperate to Curb Pollution from Vehicle Emission and Industry

By Scott Pendleton, staff writer of the Christian Science Monitor, El Paso, Texas

try. Scattered throughout the city are 266 primitive brick kilns fueled by sawdust and sometimes old tires or motor oil.

A Juarez-based nonprofit organization called FEMAP has established a school to teach brickmakers more efficient and environmentally friendly methods, such as using natural gas for fuel. Another goal, assisted by the task force, is to relocate the brickmakers to a common area with modern facilities. One advantage for brickmakers would be more bargaining power with customers and suppliers. Higher earnings would help make less-polluting practices more affordable.

The most ambitious aim of the task force is to nudge the U.S. and Mexico toward creating the world's first "international air quality management district." This entity would have the jurisdiction to set aside national and state laws and to impose and enforce a single set of environmental regulations.

"Only a cooperative joint strategy guarantees the lowest-cost solution," says Environmental Defense Fund senior scientist Peter Emerson, who helped found the task force to agitate for management district status. He says negotiations between the two countries could begin this spring. The optimum outcome would be an "Annex Six" to their 1983 La Paz agreement, which authorized joint efforts to solve border environmental problems.

Meanwhile, Texas will be working to fulfill its Clean Air Act obligations, for El Paso by developing an airshed-wide cleanup strategy by 1998, then seek to enlist Mexican support.

"That process is not going to solve the problem" even by 2098, Dr. Emerson warns. "We have to face that. Mexico doesn't have a real interest in this until you get them involved."

A big advantage of an air quality management district would be local decision-making authority, free of the centralized bureaucracy of Mexico City. The district would also end embarrassing disparities in regulation, justified or not.

"The worst setback is the fact that the attitude in El Paso for environmental controls has gone out the window," Reynoso says, referring to the political efforts to end the city's vehicle-inspection program.

"That is being felt in Juarez," he adds. "People there say if El Paso is relaxing environmental laws, why are the laws getting stronger in Juarez?"

---

benefits across countries that are in very different economic circumstances. So on the benefit side we usually settle for an enumeration of the physical impacts of various environmental changes and some idea of how these impacts might be distributed among countries. This means that most of the emphasis is likely to be placed on abatement costs and their distribution.

There are two major issues related to cost: (1) what methods to adopt in various countries to meet the performance required by the agreements and (2) how to share the overall costs among the participating countries. Of course, the questions are related because cost-effective measures undertaken by signatory countries can substantially reduce the costs of the overall program that must be shared. The importance of cost distribution arises because these global emission control agreements supply **global public goods**. The benefits accruing to any particular country from, say, a 20 percent cut in CO_2 will be the same no matter where, and by whom, the CO_2 is reduced.[5] Thus, each country has some incentive to get other countries to bear as much of the total global abatement costs as they can. The incentive difficulties are very similar to those we discussed when introducing the concept of **public goods** in Chapter 4. They can be illustrated with a simple numerical example.

Suppose a country (call it "country A") is trying to decide whether to invest $10 billion in reducing CO_2 emissions. These emissions contribute to a global problem of temperature increases. Suppose that the proposed action is part of a multilateral effort by countries all around the world to reduce global emissions by getting each country to reduce its emissions. There are three interesting situations that might occur. The following tabulation shows the benefits and costs to country A in each of these cases:

Situation	Costs	Benefits	Net benefits
1. All countries agree to reduce emissions.	10	20	10
2. No agreement is reached.	0	–5	–5
3. All other countries agree to reduce emissions, but country A does not.	0	19	19

If all countries follow the agreement, country A devotes $10 billion to control costs and then experiences, for example, $20 billion in benefits. The net benefits to country A in this case are $10 billion.

If there is no agreement, however, country A has no control costs. But it now experiences negative benefits, in the form of environmental costs, of $5 billion. Its net benefits in this case are therefore –$5 billion. It would seem rational for country A to be part of the global agreement.

But there is a third possible situation. Country A may try to take advantage of an agreement entered into by all the other countries. It could do so by staying out of the agreement and experiencing zero control costs. Its benefits would then appear to be $19 billion (a billion less than if it were to join the agreement because it won't be cutting back its own emissions), so its net benefit would be $19 billion. It can gain with an agreement, but it could gain even more by staying out of the agreement put together by the other countries. In this case it is **free riding** on the control efforts of the others.

The problem is, if one country perceives that it could better its circumstances by trying to free ride, other countries can have the same perception. But in that case there would be no agreement.

---

[5]This does not mean that the benefits will be the same for all countries—we know this is not true because of the way the global meteorological system works—only that the effects on any particular country are invariant to the source of the reduction.

The Distribution of Costs

The control costs that a country experiences can be affected in three ways:

1 In the choices it makes about reducing its own emissions; for example, through strict command-and-control measures or through greater reliance on incentive-based policies. This factor is important whether or not a country is part of a large multilateral agreement.

2 Through the choice of the rules chosen in an international agreement as to how overall emission reductions will be distributed among countries.

3 By payments made by some countries to others as part of an international agreement to help offset costs in the recipient countries. These are transfer payments, sometimes called, in the jargon of economics, **side payments.**

Side payments can take many forms. In the Montreal Protocol dealing with global CFC reductions, the advanced economies agreed to help the developing countries through **technology transfer,** a process whereby the recipient countries are aided financially and technically to adapt and adopt technologies produced in the developed countries for reducing CFC use.

International Agreements in Practice

Numerical examples such as that used in the last section are useful to depict the incentives facing individual countries that might be considering an international environmental agreement. But it's impossible to use them to predict the results of such agreements because international negotiations on environmental treaties are only one dimension of the full set of international interactions among countries. How an individual country behaves in bargaining over, for example, a treaty reducing CO_2 emissions depends not only on the merits of that particular problem but on the whole gamut of international relationships in which it is involved. If it is involved simultaneously in negotiations on other matters, it may be more concerned with the total outcome and be willing to compromise in some areas in return for concessions in others. In addition, when countries are involved in many negotiations, they may be concerned particularly with shoring up their reputations as **hard bargainers,** which may lead them to behave in certain cases in ways that look to be inconsistent with their self-interest. The outcomes of treaty negotiations depend on context and the **strategic possibilities** that the times have made available, which is another reason we use the simple examples of the previous section for depicting the underlying economic logic of international agreements and not for actually predicting events.

Cost-Effectiveness in Multinational Agreements

The previous discussion was couched in terms of an international agreement to secure certain emission reductions from each of the participating countries. This is the way most international agreements are shaped; there is a strong bias toward treating each country in the same way by applying the same reduction goals to each. Only in the recent treaty for the reduction of CFCs and other ozone-depleting substances has there been a differentiation among countries, and here it was a simple distinction between developed countries as a group and developing ones as another group. Within each broad group the CFC-reducing targets are the same for each country.

We have discussed the efficiency aspects of this approach many times. The main problem is that it does not take advantage of differences in marginal abatement costs among sources, meaning countries in this case. To accomplish this would require larger cutbacks from nations with relatively low marginal abatement costs and less reduction from those with higher costs. But these nonuniform reductions appear to run counter to the principle of treating everybody alike. Suppose each of two countries would benefit the same amount from cutbacks in emissions, but have different marginal abatement cost functions. These are pictured in Figure 21-2. The marginal abatement costs of Country A rise much more steeply than those of Country B. Current emissions are 100 from Country A and 80 from Country B. An agreement requiring a uniform 50 percent reduction would put A at 40 and B at 50. But the costs of achieving this would be much higher for A ($a + b + c$) than for B ($d + e$). Country A might very well fail to agree with uniform reductions when there would be such a large discrepancy in total abatement costs. If it were desired nonetheless to specify a treaty in terms of specific cutbacks from each, they could perhaps be set so that the total abatement costs of each country were the same (assuming each country had reliable information about the other country's abatement costs), but this would violate the uniform emission reduction principle, and it would not be cost-effective.

When abatement costs differ among countries, in other words, it will be difficult to achieve cost-effectiveness if there is strong allegiance to the same type of equiproportionate rule. One possible way of doing this might be to institute a global **transferable discharge permit** (TDP) system, whereby the number of permits given out in the initial distribution met some equiproportionate reduction principle, with trading then moving the distribution of permits toward one

FIGURE 21-2
Cost-Effectiveness in International Agreements.

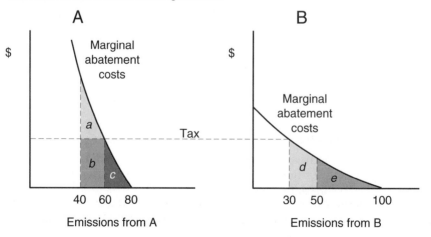

that more nearly satisfied the equimarginal rule. Whether this is even remotely feasible in today's international political climate is highly doubtful.

INTERNATIONAL TRADE AND THE ENVIRONMENT

Profound changes are occurring in the world economy and in the economic interactions among the 200 or so countries that make it up. It once appeared simple: Industrialized countries produced manufactured goods, some of which they traded among themselves, and some of which they exported to developing countries in return for primary products. But at the beginning of the 21st century things are changing dramatically through the rise of the multinational company, owing allegiance to customers and suppliers, not to particular countries; the development of a truly global, integrated financial market; the appearance of briskly expanding industrial countries from among the previously less developed group; the development of huge new regional trading blocs of southeast Asia, North America, and the European Community; and the massive change in the old socialist bloc and its reintegration into the world economy. These changes collectively have come to be called **globalization.**

The full range of environmental implications of globalization will be hard to sort out. One major feature of globalization is substantially increased levels of trade among the countries of the world. The connections between increased trade and environmental factors can be summarized as follows:

- The reciprocal interaction of trade flows and environmental protection: How will increased trade affect environmental damages in trading countries, and how will national efforts to protect the environment have an impact on international trade? These issues can be looked at from the standpoint of just two trading countries or from that of more comprehensive trading networks.
- The question of whether, and under what conditions, an individual country may legitimately put restrictions on its trade, by restricting either imports or exports, in the name of preserving environmental quality.
- The circumstances under which the world community as a whole can effectively improve the world environment by placing restrictions on international trade.

Free Trade vs. Environmental Trade Restrictions

Over the last four decades or so, the countries of the world have made special efforts to foster free and unhindered trade. This has been done in the name of improved economic welfare. **Free trade** allows countries to prosper by giving them expanded markets for things on which they have a comparative advantage in production and gives them greater opportunities to procure goods for which they have a comparative disadvantage. The prosperity of many countries, both developed and developing, depends critically on international trade. The problem is whether the emphasis on moving toward free trade may make it more difficult for countries to protect the environmental resources that they value.

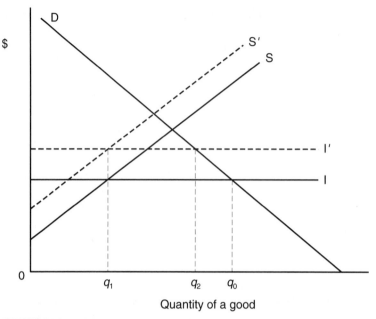

FIGURE 21-3
Effects of Environmental Regulations on Domestic Production and Imports.

The main international institution governing trade is the World Trade Organization (WTO).[6] Its purpose is to set out a list of rules and procedures to be followed by nations in their international trade relationships. It is especially aimed at reducing the barriers to trade, to get nations to refrain from putting tariffs and quotas on imports or subsidies on exports, and in general to move toward conditions of free trade among the world's nations, almost all of whom are members of the WTO. One section of the WTO agreement also outlaws what are called nontariff barriers such as excessive inspection requirements, excessive product specifications, and the like. But there is a very broad list of conditions that are exceptions to WTO rules; one is that governments are allowed to set restrictions in order to achieve the "protection of human, animal or plant life or health," and the "conserving of natural resources."

Consider the analysis of Figure 21-3. It shows the behavior of producers and consumers of a product in a particular country that also relies upon imports for a large part of its supply. The demand curve (D) is domestic demand for the product, whereas S is the domestic supply curve; that is, the supply curve of domestic producers. Without imports, price and quantity would settle at the intersection of these two curves. But let us introduce an import supply curve, labeled I. This supply curve is actually horizontal because we assume that a relatively large amount of this item is produced in the world, so this importing

[6]WTO is the successor to the General Agreement on Tariffs and Trade (GATT), which came into being in the 1940s as an international effort to foster an increase in world trade.

country could import larger or smaller quantities without affecting the world price. With the addition of imports, this country now ends up with a total consumption at q_0. Domestic production, meanwhile, is q_1. The difference, $(q_0 - q_1)$, is imported. With imports, the domestic price is also equal to the world price.

WTO rules allow governments to set import restrictions on products that have direct health implications, as long as it is done in a nondiscriminatory way. Suppose the good in question is automobiles, the use of which causes air pollution. Setting tight emission standards increases the production costs for automobiles and therefore their prices. The importing country may require imported cars to meet strict emission standards, which would have the effect of lifting the import supply curve to I'. This is nondiscriminatory as long as domestic producers are held to the same standards, in effect shifting the domestic supply curve up to S'. The result of this is first to lower the total quantity of cars purchased by people in this country, from q_0 to q_2. Second, assuming that the emission standards increase the costs of domestic supply as much as they do imports, the pollution control applied to both domestically produced cars and imports will leave domestic production unchanged but reduce imports, from $(q_0 - q_1)$ to $(q_2 - q_1)$.

In this case the purpose of the strict emission standards was to protect human health. When it is not a matter of human health but, say, one of environmental aesthetics, the case may be less clear. In recent years Denmark placed a ban on the use of nonrefillable drink containers. This was presumably done in the name of reducing litter. It also proceeded to ban the importation of nonrefillable containers from neighboring European countries. These countries objected, saying that the ban was really just a way of protecting Danish drink producers from competition. But in this case the European court ruled in favor of Denmark.

Things become decidedly less clear when it is not the consumption of a good that causes pollution but its production. Suppose that a country produces a product and in the process also causes a certain amount of air pollution. Suppose further that it adopts an air pollution program to curb emissions from this industry. Suppose even further that the item is produced in other countries and imported, but that the countries from which it is imported do not undertake any type of pollution-control efforts. The producers of the importing country are now at somewhat of a cost disadvantage because they have to operate under environmental constraints and their competitors don't. Can this country legally (i.e., within the WTO rules) put a tariff on the importation of this item to equalize the cost burden? One might argue that this would tend to protect people in other producing countries who are exposed to air pollution from the firms making this item, but WTO rules presumably allow countries to take action only to protect their own citizens, not those in other countries. And a tariff against the good may have no impact on lessening air pollution in other countries; the only way that could be done would be through explicit pollution-control programs in those countries, and there is certainly no way for the first country to enforce such programs.

The interrelationship of environmental issues and trade problems has recently raised the possibility that environmental standards will be co-opted by those whose interest is primarily to protect themselves against international competition. It is a familiar sight to see representatives of some industry that feel threatened by producers in other countries appealing to political authorities for a tariff or some other barrier against imports. Environmental factors now may give them added ammunition. If they can plausibly argue that the foreign competitors are causing damage to environmental resources, they may be better able to justify the trade barrier. The key is whether the environmental impacts of foreign producers are legitimately a concern of the importing country. In a recent case, the United States barred imports of tuna from Mexico that had been caught using methods that cause excessive mortality among dolphins. The question that needs to be sorted out is whether Americans really do have a substantial willingness to pay for protecting dolphins, wherever they may be, or whether this was just being used as an excuse by U.S. tuna companies to shield themselves from foreign competition.

Trade Restrictions to Advance International Environmental Goals

In some cases international environmental agreements involve trade agreements.

Montreal Protocol   As part of the international effort to reduce ozone-depleting chemicals, the Montreal Protocol prohibits exports of controlled substances (basically CFCs) from any signatory nation to any state not a party to the Protocol. Furthermore, signatory countries may not import any controlled substance from any nonsignatory state. The purpose of these trade regulations is to ensure that production of CFCs and other ozone-depleting chemicals does not simply migrate to nonsigning countries.

London Guidelines on Chemicals   As we have discussed many times throughout this book, one major obstacle to controlling environmental pollutants is lack of information—information on pollutant emissions, damages, control costs, and so on. On the international level the problem is even more severe than it is domestically because of the different ways countries have approached pollution-control problems and the vastly different information requirements and availabilities among them. In 1989, 74 countries agreed to adopt the "London Guidelines for the Exchange of Information on Chemicals in International Trade," under the auspices of the United Nations Environment Program (UNEP). The guidelines require that any country banning or severely restricting a particular chemical notify all other countries of its actions, so that the latter can assess the risks and take whatever action they deem appropriate. The guidelines also encourage "technology transfer," stating that states with more advanced chemical testing and management technology should share their experience with countries in need of approved systems.

Basel Convention on Transboundary Movements of Hazardous Wastes
This 1989 agreement is aimed at the issue of international trade in hazardous

wastes. It does not prohibit this trade but does put requirements on it, especially information requirements. It puts an obligation on countries to prohibit any export of hazardous wastes unless appropriate authorities in the receiving country have consented in writing to the import and unless it has assurances that the waste will be properly disposed of. It also has provisions on notification, cooperation on liability matters, transmission of essential information, and so on.

Convention on International Trade in Endangered Species of Wild Fauna and Flora (CITES)   There is currently a large international trade in flora and fauna, dead and alive: roughly 500,000 live parrots, 10 million reptile skins, 10 million cactus plants, 350 million ornamental fish, 50 million furs, and so on, each year.[7] CITES came into force in 1975. Under it, each country is supposed to establish its own permit system to control the movement of wildlife exports and imports. It is also supposed to designate a management body to handle the permit system and a scientific body to determine whether trade is likely to be detrimental to the survival of the species. Species are separated into three classes: I—species threatened with extinction, in which commercial trade is banned and noncommercial trade regulated; II—species that may become threatened if trade is not held to levels consistent with biological processes, for which commercial trade is allowed with conditions; and III—species that are not currently threatened but for which international cooperation is appropriate, for which trade requires permits.

The endangered species trade is considered by many to be a qualified success, although much more remains to be done, especially in improving national permit processes. There are some simple lessons to be derived from considering this type of trade restriction, which we will pursue by looking at an international supply-and-demand model of an endangered species. The same conclusions can apply to other cases; for example, export restrictions on logs to protect rain forests. Consider the market model of Figure 21-4. This shows the world, or aggregate, supply and export-demand conditions for a species of wildlife. The supply function is based on the costs of hunting, transporting, processing, recordkeeping, and so on necessary to bring the wildlife to the point of export. It is an aggregate supply function made up of the supply function of the various countries in which that species grows. The demand function shows the quantities that the export market will take at alternative prices. The intersection of the two functions shows the market price and quantity of this type of wildlife that will be traded in a year's time.

Two types of trade constraints could be used to reduce the quantity of this species moving in international trade: export controls and import controls. Each will reduce the quantity traded, but they will have very different impacts on price. Export controls work by essentially making exporting more costly, which has the

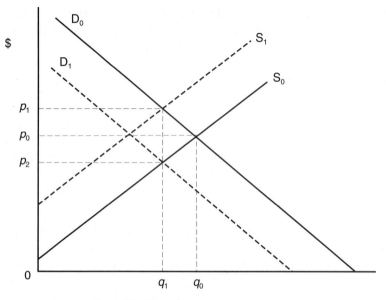

Quantity of trade in an endangered species

FIGURE 21-4
Effects of Trade Policy on the International Market in an Endangered Species.

effect in Figure 21-4 of shifting the supply function upward from supply curve S_0 to supply curve S_1. The result of this is a reduction in quantity traded, in this case to q_1. The amount that quantity falls depends on the extent to which the supply curve shifts up and also on the slope of the demand function; the steeper this slope the less will quantity contract. But this approach to trade reduction also leads to an increase in price, from the original price p_0 to p_1. This price increase could have several impacts, depending essentially on property rights. Imagine a case where the endangered species is subject to private ownership, either by individuals or by small, well-defined groups. Perhaps the habitat of the species is under private ownership, for example. The higher price for the species now becomes a signal for its owners to be more concerned about its safety and welfare because, in this circumstance, efforts at conservation will have a direct market payoff.

The added price will have the opposite effect, however, when property rights in the endangered species are ill-defined or completely absent, which is the usual case. Most of the habitats for the world's endangered species are common property, in the sense that either everybody has the right to enter and harvest the animal or plant, or that, as in public parks, authorities are unable to keep people from taking the species "illegally." We saw, in Chapter 4, the problem to which common-property resources are prone: Because other users cannot be kept out, nobody has an incentive to conserve the resource. It's either use it or lose it to some other harvester. The increased price for the endangered species in this case will work against conservation. It will encourage higher rates of extraction, higher rates of poaching on common-property habitats, and thus higher pressure on the endangered species.

Controlling imports, however, drives the price downward. Import controls have the effect of reducing the demand for the imported species. In Figure 21-4 this leads to a backward shift in demand, from D_0 to D_1. This has been drawn so as to give the same quantity reduction as before. But in this case the price drops to p_2. The effect of this price decrease is to decrease the incentives discussed in the previous paragraphs. In particular, where endangered species are subject to common-property exploitation, the lower price would lead to reduced pressure to harvest and less rapid population decline. Something of this sort has happened recently as a result of an international ban on ivory imports. The ban has led to a substantial drop in the world price of ivory, which has reduced the pressure of poachers on the elephant in many parts of Africa.

SUMMARY

With environmental issues becoming more international in scope and significance, there will be increasing interest among countries to address these issues with international agreements. International agreements are much more problematic than domestic policies because enforcement is much weaker on the international level. International externalities are essentially of two types. In the first, one country's pollution causes damage in another country. Here the problem of who pays (polluter or victim) when agreements are negotiated is of primary relevance. In the second, each country's emissions affect all countries, including itself. Here the basic problem is how to get individual countries to forgo attempts to free ride on the control efforts of others. The strength of the incentive to free ride depends on a country's perceived benefits and costs of an international agreement, together with whatever "side payments," money subsidies, technology transfers, and so on are part of the agreement.

In recent years serious issues have arisen over the relationship of environmental damage and international trade. Some people see free international trade as being environmentally destructive and are in favor of placing restrictions on trade in the name of environmental values. In these cases there is a problem in sorting out legitimate and justified concern for elements of the environment, especially in another country, from purely commercial interests that are seeking shelter from international competition.

QUESTIONS FOR FURTHER DISCUSSION

1 Below are illustrative numbers indicating benefits and costs to Country A of taking specific actions on an international treaty to reduce CO_2 emissions. The choice is either to adhere to the CO_2 emissions cutbacks called for by the treaty or to disregard the treaty.

	Costs	Benefits	Net benefits
All countries adhere to treaty	10	20	10
No countries adhere to treaty	0	–5	–5
Other countries adhere to treaty, Country A does not	0	19	19

What is the incentive for Country A to free ride on the abatement efforts of other countries? If all countries become free riders, what is the result?

2 We talked about "side payments" in the form of technology transfers, given to developing countries to lower the costs to them of joining international environmental agreements. What other types of side payments might be effective in this regard?

3 Suppose Country A imports a product from Country B, and that Country B lacks environmental laws governing the production of the item. Under what conditions might Country A be justified in putting a tariff on the imported item?

4 If all countries adopted the same emission standards in similar industries, would this tend to equalize production costs and put each country on the same footing with respect to environmental matters?

5 "International environmental agreements are very much shaped by the fact that enforcement on the international level is difficult, if not impossible." Discuss.

6 In the early 1990s, the United States attempted to put restrictions on the importation of tuna from Mexico because Mexican fishers used methods that destroyed relatively large numbers of dolphin when catching the tuna. These fishing methods are illegal for U.S. tuna fishers. Is this trade restriction efficient? Is it equitable?

WEBSITES

Many of the international treaties mentioned in the text have their own web pages, for example the Basel Convention, **www.basel.int,** and the Convention on International Trade in Endangered Species of Wild Fauna and Flora, **www.cites.org;** see also the links listed on the website of this book, **www.mhhe.com/economics/field3.**

SELECTED READINGS

Anderson, Kyn, and Blackhurst, Richard (eds.): *The Greening of World Trade Issues,* Harvester Wheatsheaf, Hemel Hempstead, England, 1992.

Ausubel, J. H., and David G. Victor: "Verification of International Environmental Agreements," *Annual Review of Energy and the Environment,* Vol. 17, 1992, pp. 1–43.

Barrett, Scott: "Economic Analysis of International Environmental Agreements: Lessons for a Global Warming Treaty," in Organization for Economic Cooperation and Development, *Responding to Climate Change: Selected Economic Issues,* Paris, 1991, Chapter 3.

Batabyal, Amitrajeet A. (ed.): *The Economics of International Environmental Agreements,* Ashgate, Burlington, VT, 2000.

Esty, D. C.: *Greening the GATT,* Institute for International Economics, Washington, DC, 1994.

Heal, Geoffrey: "Formation of International Environmental Agreements," in C. Carraro (ed.), *Trade, Innovation, Environment,* Kluwer Academic, Dordrecht, 1994.

Low, Patrick (ed.): *International Trade and the Environment,* Discussion Paper No. 159, World Bank, Washington, DC, 1992.

U.N. Environment Program: *Environment and Trade, A Handbook,* International Center for Sustainable Development, Winnipeg, Canada, 2000

Victor, David G., Kal Raustiala, and Eugene B. Skolnikoff: *The Implementation and Effectiveness of International Environmental Agreements,* MIT Press, Cambridge, MA, 1997.

ABBREVIATIONS AND ACRONYMS USED IN THE BOOK

AQCR	Air quality control region
ATU	Allotment trading unit
BACT	Best available control technology
BAT	Best available technology
BMP	Best management practice
BOD	Biochemical oxygen demand
BPT	Best practicable technology
Btu	British thermal unit
CAA	Clean Air Act
CAC	Command and control
CEQ	Council on Environmental Quality
CERCLA	Comprehensive Environmental Response, Compensation and Liability Act
CES	Country environmental study
CFC	Chlorofluorocarbon
CITES	Convention on International Trade in Endangered Species of Wild Fauna and Flora
CO	Carbon monoxide
COD	Chemical oxygen demand
CPSA	Consumer Products Safety Act
CV	Contingent valuation
CWA	Clean Water Act
DO	Dissolved oxygen
DOE	Department of Energy
DOI	Department of the Interior
DOT	Department of Transportation
EBDC	Ethylene bisdithiocarbamate
EIA	Environmental impact analysis
EPA	Environmental Protection Agency
ERC	Emission reduction credit
ESA	Endangered Species Act
EV	Electric vehicle
FC	Fecal coliform
FDCA	Food, Drug and Cosmetic Act
FIFRA	Federal Insecticide, Fungicide and Rodenticide Act
GATT	General Agreement on Tariffs and Trade
GDP	Gross domestic product
GEFMS	Global Environmental Fund Management System
GEMS	Global Environmental Monitoring System (of the U.N.)
GHG	Greenhouse gas
HCFC	Hydrochlorofluorocarbons
HLW	High-level wastes
I&M	Inspection and maintenance
ICJ	International Court of Justice
IPCC	Intergovernmental Panel on Climate Change
IPM	Integrated pest management
LAER	Lowest achievable emission rate
LEG	Liquified energy gas

LLW	Low-level wastes
MAC	Marginal abatement cost
MACT	Maximum available (or achievable) control technology
MC	Marginal cost
MCL	Maximum containment level
MD	Marginal damages
MSW	Municipal solid waste
NAAQS	National ambient air–quality standards
NCP	National contingency plan
NEPA	National Environmental Policy Act
NO$_x$	Nitrogen oxides
NPL	National priorities list
NPS	Nonpoint source
NSPS	New-source performance standards
NSR	New-source review
OECD	Organization for Economic Cooperation and Development
OEM	Office of Environmental Management
OSHA	Occupational Safety and Health Act
OTA	Office of Technology Assessment
PEL	Permissible exposure level
PM$_{2.5}$	Particulate matter smaller than 2.5 micrometers in diameter
PM$_{10}$	Particulate matter smaller than 10 micrometers in diameter
PPC	Production possibility curve
PPP	Polluter pays principle
PRP	Potentially responsible party
PSD	Prevention of significant deterioration
PVC	Polyvinyl chloride
R&D	Research and development
RACT	Reasonably available control technology
RCRA	Resource Conservation and Recovery Act
RECLAIM	Regional Clean Air Incentive Market (of Southern California)
SIP	State implementation plan
SMSA	Standard metropolitan statistical area
SO$_2$	Sulfur dioxide
SRF	State revolving fund
TBES	Technology-based effluent standard
TDP	Transferable discharge permit
TMDL	Total maximum daily load
TOC	Total organic carbon
TRI	Toxic release inventory
TSCA	Toxic Substances Control Act
TSDF	Treatment, storage, or disposal facility
TSP	Total suspended particulates
TSS	Total suspended solids
UNEP	United Nations Environment Program
USAID	U.S. Agency for International Development
VC	Vinyl chloride
VMT	Vehicle miles traveled
VOCs	Volatile organic compounds
VOM	Volatile organic material
WHO	World Health Organization
WPCA	Water Pollution Control Act
WTO	World Trade Organization
WTP	Willingness to pay
ZEV	Zero-emission vehicle

NAME INDEX

SUBJECT INDEX

Abatement cost functions, 93
 see also Marginal abatement cost functions
 actual marginal costs, 97
 for Boston Harbor cleanup, 94–95
 lowest possible marginal costs, 97–98
Abatement costs, 93, 108–109
 see also Marginal abatement costs
 aggregate marginal, 98–100
 of emissions charges, 235–236, 238, 239
 equimarginal principle and, 100
 total, standards and, 212–213
 upper limits, 97
Abatement subsidies, 252–254
 deposit-refund systems as, 254, 349, 360, 403
 as opportunity cost, 252
Ability to pay, wealth and, 46
Acid rain, 36, 38, 266
Agricultural chemicals, 39, 250, 276, 278
 see also Pesticides
Agriculture
 benefits from reduced production costs, 140–142
 best management practices, 280, 292
 biological diversity and, 457
 external benefits, 79
 global warming impacts, 445, 460
 subsidies for, 162, 423
 ultraviolet radiation damages, 438
Air pollutants, 304
 see also Criteria pollutants
 emissions trends, 305
 sources in the U.S., 305
 toxic, 308

Air pollution, 303–304
 see also National ambient air-quality standards; Technology-based emission standards (air quality)
 in developing countries, 414
 dose-response relationship, 142–143
 health damages from, 138, 139
 as a land-use issue, 380–381
 materials damage from, 142
 smog, 36, 309, 367
Air pollution control
 see also Motor vehicles; Pollution control
 CAC vs. least-cost programs, 313–315
 laws, 306–309, 346–347
  listed, 307–308
 Mexico-U.S. bilateral agreement, 470–471
 for mobile sources, 321–322
 State Implementation Plans, 366
 for stationary sources, 311–316
Air Pollution Control Act of 1955, 307
Air Quality Act of 1967, 306
Air Quality Control Regions, 311–312
Ambient air-quality standards; *see* National ambient air-quality standards (NAAQS)
Ambient quality, 34–37, 77
 damages and, 34–37
 defined, 33
 emissions and, 34–37
 levels, 36
Analysis, scientific, defined, 43
Aral Sea, degradation, 405, 406